# Personal financial planning

# PERSONAL FINANCIAL PLANNING

## SECOND EDITION

### HAROLD A. WOLF
University of Texas at Austin

GINN PRESS

*Dedicated to the memory of my parents*

The first three editions of this book were authored by Maurice A. Unger and Harold A. Wolf. The first seven editions were published under the title *Personal Finance*.

Printed in the United States of America
10  9  8  7  6  5  4  3  2

BA    9349
ISBN  0-536-58237-8

 **GINN PRESS**

160 Gould Street/Needham Heights, MA  02194
Simon & Schuster Higher Education Publishing Group

# Contents

v

# Preface

This book was specifically designed for students beginning their studies to become CFP™ licensees (Certified Financial Planner™). Much of its contents has been distilled and refined from my earlier books, *Personal Finance* and *Personal Financial Planning*, which have been used as college textbooks.

In recent years, financial planning has become much more sophisticated, and increasingly important to more and more people. With that growth in demand, there has been a parallel growth in the financial planning profession.

Financial planning is a very complex and rapidly changing field. It is complex and rapidly changing because the underlying disciplines which make it up are complex and rapidly changing.

Financial planning encompasses the mainstream of a number of disciplines. It is a blend of finance, accounting, law, economics, actuarial science, and political science or government, to name only the most obvious. Financial planning also encompasses the various specialities within these disciplines. Under finance it includes insurance and risk management, real estate, thrift and financial institutions, securities, credit and interest rates. Within the discipline of accounting, financial statements, budgeting, depreciation and taxes are involved. Law includes the specialities of taxes, government, consumer protection, retirement planning, wills, gifts, trusts and estates. Economics covers the broad field of income, savings, investment, inflation, and the political, financial and economic environment within which planning must take place.

Actuarial science deals with the logic and mathematics of interest rates and retirement planning. Political science (or government) deals with the political and social environment within which business, the

---

™CFP and Certified Financial Planner are certification marks of the International Board of Standards and Practices for Certified Financial Planners (IBCFP).

consumer and the investor must function. Since there is an overlap among these various disciplines, financial planning is a blend of them all.

The book is organized in five parts. Part I consists of three chapters. Chapter one spells out the importance of financial planning and how it can help a person achieve his or her goals. Chapter two deals with record keeping and the personal budget, two important aspects of planning. Chapter three introduces two important tools of financial planning—the balance sheet and the cash flow statement.

Part II (Chapters 4 through 8) deals with managing income and assets. These chapters cover first the various depository institutions, consumer credit, and consumer protection laws to enable the planner's client to obtain more for his or her money. Personal income tax planning, to legally minimize taxes, and home ownership, the largest single asset for many people, are discussed at some length.

Part III, which includes four chapters, covers all types of insurance. Chapter 9 covers risk management, the principles of insurance and sets the stage for what is to come. Then there is a separate chapter on life insurance, health care and health insurance, followed by property and liability insurance.

Part IV introduces the various investment outlets. Chapter 13 covers investing in the various depository institutions which, generally speaking, are the safest investment, and are where the client's emergency funds are frequently put to work. Then direct investments in securities are analyzed in the next three chapters. Chapter 17, the last chapter in this section, deals with investing in securities indirectly, that is, through mutual funds. Next other outlets for surplus funds are examined, such as mortgages, rental real estate, commodities and collectibles. While many of these may not be appropriate for most of us, they may be for some investors.

Part V has a chapter on retirement planning and one on estate planning. Retirement planning is necessary to enable a person to enjoy "the good life" when the working years are over. Nearly everyone has Social Security to build on, and building on it is a necessity. The various methods of doing so are discussed. The last chapter, Estate Planning, is designed to minimize the government's take of the deceased's assets; estate taxes are involved in this connection. It also considers final distribution of assets according to the individual's wishes. A glossary is included at the end of the book.

# Acknowledgments

In the preparation of any project of this nature there are many who need to be thanked for having so graciously given of their time and encouragement.

Particular credit must be given to the hundreds of students and faculty members throughout the United States and Canada who have used my earlier college textbooks over the years, and who have provided much valuable feedback. Credit is also due to the editors and production people at Ginn Press and Allyn & Bacon. Specifically I wish to express my gratitude to Andrea Shaw, Don Kilburn, and John Gilman. Credit is also due members of the academic staff of the College for Financial Planning.

In addition, I wish to acknowledge Professor H. Wayne Snider and Mary Wold of the Temple University insurance department faculty. Virginia Affleck of the Utah State Retirement System was most helpful in the area of retirement planning, especially that part dealing with colleges and universities, and certain other nonprofit organizations. I also wish to thank James G. Branscome, Senior Vice President of the Standard and Poor's Corporation, for the information and the artwork he made available for the chapters on security investments. Fred C. Cohn, editor and publisher of Johnson's Charts, Inc., also deserves recognition for providing artwork found in the chapters dealing with securities and retirement planning.

Last, but not least, I must express my gratitude to my manuscript typist Mary Wingo, who did—as always—a beautiful job in preparing the material for the editors.

For any errors or shortcomings which may remain, the author will have to assume full responsibility.

Harold A. Wolf
The University of Texas at Austin

# Introduction to financial planning

Part I consists of just three chapters. Chapter one, The Importance of Personal Financial Planning and Some Fundamentals, spells out what financial planning is about, how it can help a person achieve certain goals, and how to enjoy more benefits in life. It also examines the current economic and financial environment within which planning must take place. In addition, Chapter one introduces inflation and the consumer price index.

Chapter two, Record Keeping and Budgeting, deals with two of the first requirements of financial planning, and the title indicates what they are. Records are essential in the financial planning process, because they are needed to set goals, determine present financial position, and plan intelligently. They are needed at the beginning of the financial planning process.

The budget is another important financial planning tool. It is like a blueprint or a road map and serves as a guide in the planning process. Without a budget the individual is like a traveler without a map—lost. A good budget helps the individual achieve financial goals by setting consumption limits and savings targets.

Chapter three examines two other items which are at the heart of financial planning: the financial statements, including the balance sheet and the cash flow statement (sometimes called the income statement). They are important because they will indicate where the individual has been financially and where he or she is now, and will help plan where he or she is going.

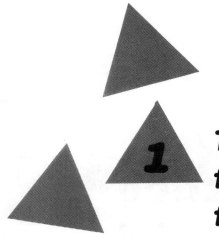

# The importance of personal financial planning and some fundamentals

**HIGHLIGHTS**

In this chapter we will examine the importance and purpose of personal financial planning. In doing so we will examine the following:

1   The goals of personal finance
2   The various expenditures: consumers, business investments, and government spending
3   Specifically what financial planning consists of
4   The current economic environment in which personal finance must operate
5   Inflation and how it affects the consumer
6   How inflation is measured
7   What the rest of this book is about

## INTRODUCTION

Individuals constantly make choices when disposing of their income. Even when these choices are not well thought out, it is nonetheless true that they require at least some degree of planning. Financial planning, money management, and personal financial management are all terms that are used interchangeably. In an economy such as ours, money is used to both purchase the goods and services we desire and reward us for the goods and services we provide to others. Consequently, everyone who has money at his or her disposal must necessarily do some money management. In its most basic form, financial planning has to do with the allocation of scarce resources (money income) among many alternative and competing ends. Human wants are virtually unlimited, while money income—the means to satisfy these wants—is usually quite limited. A dollar spent on clothing cannot be spent on food. Thus, choices must be made and priorities established.

Financial planning can help accomplish several things: increase income, improve the "mileage" from each dollar of expenditures, protect assets already owned, and achieve financial goals. Some individuals will plan their own finances; others will turn to professional financial planners for assistance.

## THE GOALS OF FINANCIAL PLANNING

The objective of financial planning is to achieve certain goals. There are certain common goals shared by all; then there may be others which will vary from person to person, and from time to time during an individual's life cycle. They will vary as income changes, as marital status changes, and as the size and demographic factors of the person's family change.

### Goals

The overall general goal is to manage all financial affairs more intelligently. A number of benefits will stem from this; income will stretch further and a person may also be able to increase his or her income. A general goal might therefore be to increase the standard of living. Planning can help a person achieve "the good life"—or at least a better one.

On the other hand, the goal might be to increase net wealth—financial planners call this "net worth"—and increasing it is frequently related to saving and investing. An increase in savings helps increase a person's net worth and, especially in the long run, a person's standard of living.

In the short run savings may require a temporary reduction in the standard of living; but since it will bear fruit over a period of time, it may serve to increase the standard of living later. It cannot be emphasized too much that virtually every budget should include an item for savings.

From time to time a person will engage in activities such as borrowing money, using credit cards, investing savings, paying taxes, buying insurance, automobiles and homes. A general goal of financial planning then is to do all of these things more intelligently.

Financial planning involves looking ahead in order to develop a strategy that will enable a person to be where he or she wants to be,

4

financially speaking, in five, ten, and twenty years. This should include a plan for retirement; a person should not wait until he or she is 60 or 65 years of age to do this.

Other goals or objectives of financial planning may include the following items:

**(1)** Acquisition and protection of property, which will be discussed In this book under investments (acquisition) and insurance (protection).

**(2)** Protection against financial losses relating to premature death, illness and injury, and liability. All of these can affect the income stream and assets. Use of insurance is one means of protecting against financial losses associated with these risks.

**(3)** Minimizing taxes both on the income stream during the earning years and on the person's estate upon death. Related to this is a plan for the transfer of assets to heirs. Tax planning, wills, gifts, and trusts are useful tools in this area.

In addition, there may be certain specific goals that are unique to an individual. Examples include: acquiring assets to fund a college education (this should be done as soon as possible after a child is born), starting a business, purchasing a home or a car, or planning a vacation trip around the world. The specific goals must, of course, be integrated with the general goals.

*Specific goals*

The steps In financial planning may be summarized as including the following:

**THE STEPS IN FINANCIAL PLANNING**

1. Setting goals. These goals must be set realistically with respect to the client's income, age, temperament, and any other pertinent factors.
2. Collecting all relevant data, as will be explained in the next chapter.
3. Identifying any barriers in achieving goals.
4. Setting a time frame within which to achieve goals.
5. Developing methods and procedures to help achieve those goals.
6. Developing a personal budget where appropriate, to aid the client in achieving his or her goals.
7. Periodically re-examining goals and monitoring the progress made in achieving them.
8. Periodically modifying goals and methods of achieving them as conditions change. For example, as the client's income, marital status, family structure, etc., change, the goal will often change.

Financial planning, then, is not a one-shot affair. Rather, it is an ongoing process. This does not mean a person must become a slave to a plan. A great deal of time is not needed; a few hours per month is frequently sufficient. Financial planning, moreover, may begin at any age; an individual is never too young or old. Moreover, he or she need not be rich to benefit from planning. Everyone will be better off with a financial plan than without one. However, the sooner in life that planning begins, the more it will help the individual to achieve his or her goals.

## THE CURRENT ECONOMIC AND FINANCIAL ENVIRONMENT

The trinity of groups that make up most of the U.S. economy consists of businesses, consumer-producers and governments.[1] Each of these three groups makes decisions in attempting to achieve certain goals they have set for themselves. Each group, moreover, influences the other two, as well as the financial environment. We will briefly examine each group and the relationships among them.

### Businesses

Most of the goods and services produced in the United States today are produced by the business sector. There are hundreds of thousands of business firms, some large like General Electric, some small like many one- or two-owner corner grocery stores. Business firms employ the majority of the labor force and are the means through which most of the income of the American people is earned. Business entities are probably the most important single factor in the economic environment. They must operate within the legal framework spelled out by the various levels of government. The business community is, however, largely a system of free enterprise and private property.

A free enterprise system is one where anyone may go into business for him- or herself. He or she need only obey the various laws that spell out the framework within which the various businesses must operate. For example, restaurants must meet minimum health and sanitation standards; no business may develop a monopoly and arbitrarily fix prices; and, of course, there are a number of consumer protection laws that businesses must adhere to. These consumer protection laws will be discussed in a later chapter.

A business system of "private property" means simply what it says. The means of production—manufacturing plants, machinery, and so on—is owned by individuals, not by the government. Most of the goods and services (output) produced in the U.S., and most of the income

---

1. There are others: for example, there are churches, various nonprofit institutions, farmers, self-employed professionals, and labor unions. However, farmers and self-employed professionals are really businesses, and the members of labor unions are also part of the consumer-producers. Churches and certain nonprofit organizations, while important, account for only a small part of the total output of goods and services. There are also some people who are consumers but not producers—for example, children, the retired, and people who have been institutionalized.

earned, is produced and earned in the private business sector. It is a very important part of the economic and financial environment.

Everyone is a consumer, and every consumer who is in the labor force is also a producer. Many consumers thus serve in a dual capacity in our economy; they buy goods and services and sell their labor services. Consumers are demanders of output and suppliers of labor to produce it. To enjoy the good life one must earn an income. In the short run individuals have to operate within a given economic environment. But as a group (for example, through unions, consumer groups, and the ballot box) individuals can also affect, to some extent, the economic environment.

*Consumer-producers*

    The economic environment, then, consists of a relationship between the governments, businesses, and consumer-producers. This is illustrated in Figure 1–1, which shows consumer-producers providing labor services to business firms in exchange for money incomes. These money incomes are then used to make money payments to business firms in exchange for goods and services, which are purchased. These are consumption expenditures. The diagram shows the circular flow of money (represented by the outside arrows), which finances the flow of real goods and services (depicted by the arrows on the inside). The diagram also shows the payments of taxes by businesses and consumer-producers

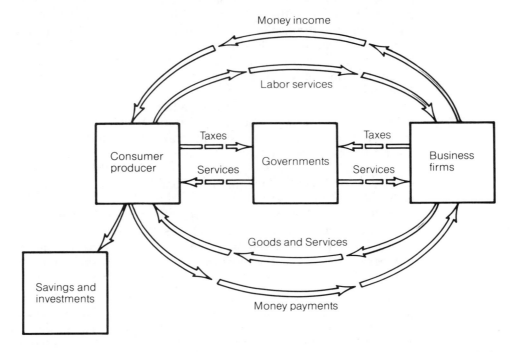

*The economic environment.*

Figure 1–1

(individuals) to governments in return for the services supplied by various levels of government. Also shown is a withdrawal in the form of savings from this income stream. These savings will flow back into the system when one buys bonds or stock or deposits money in a savings account. In doing this, one is making an investment expenditure or accumulating wealth in the form of earnings assets. Money, then, is the oil in the system, which is necessary for the relationships and permits the production and exchange of real goods and services.

## Government

The three levels of government—federal, state, and local—each have specific functions to perform. Each level of government imposes taxes and provides a variety of services. The federal government's major source of revenue is the personal income tax; for the states it is sales taxes and income taxes; and for local governments it is the property tax, although some local governments also have a sales and an income tax.

At one time it was believed that the government's main role was that of umpire. It was to see that the law was carried out, and it enforced contracts between individuals. In addition, it provided for the national defense. To carry out its function, the government levied taxes and made certain expenditures.

Today the role of the government has been expanded to include regulation of businesses and even individuals. More restrictions are imposed than formerly to protect the public and the environment. The philosophy is that the government is to do those things that citizens cannot do for themselves, or cannot do as well. The government has more of a welfare function now. This is sometimes called the safety net. While social security is not, strictly speaking, welfare, it is part of the safety net and is important enough that it will be discussed separately in a later chapter.

The government's actual production of services (technically referred to as "the government sector") is equal to the total wages and salaries of all government employees (federal, state, and local) including the armed forces. This is because there is no market mechanism and prices to allocate these services. We pay for them through taxes and then receive the services, for the most part, without making an additional payment via the price mechanism.

The total number of government employees (at all levels including the armed forces) at year end 1991 was 19.9 million people. They earned approximately $627.2 billion during 1991. This 627.2 billion dollars is the best measure of the government's (federal, state and local) contribution to gross domestic product (GDP), or our well being.[2]

---

2. Prior to 1991 the term gross national product (GNP) was used. Gross domestic product (GDP) is now used because it more accurately reflects the economic activity that takes place in the U.S. To move from GNP to GDP the Department of Commerce subtracts

# TOTAL OUTPUT, INCOME, AND SPENDING
## GROSS NATIONAL PRODUCT

In the second quarter of 1990, according to revised estimates, current-dollar gross national product (GNP) rose 5.1 percent (annual rate) or $67.9 billion. Real GNP (GNP adjusted for price changes) rose 0.4 percent and the implicit price deflator rose 4.7 percent.

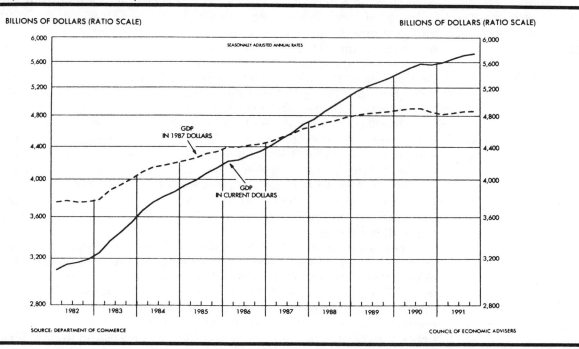

(Source: Economic Indicators, January 1991, *Council of Economic Advisors, U.S.* Figure 1–2 *Department of Commerce, Bureau of Economic Analysis, p. 1).*

Gross domestic product can be defined as the total economic pie produced in the United States per year. A more precise definition states "it is the total of all final *goods* and *services* produced in the U.S. per year." All goods and services are valued at their market price.

Gross domestic product in 1991 was about $5,671.8 billion (about 5.7 trillion dollars). The government contribution to this gross domestic product was about 11.0 percent and, as noted above, that is the best measure of the government's direct contribution to the economy.

The business sector, on the other hand, contributed approximately $4,802.9 billion (4.8 trillion dollars) to GDP by paying producer-

---

from GNP income earned abroad by U.S. citizens either because they live and work abroad or because they own property abroad. For the same reason the Department adds to GNP (to get GDP) all income generated in the U.S. but received by foreigners.

consumers that much in wages and salaries to produce that many goods and services. This amounted to 84.7 percent of GDP.[3] Figure 1–2 illustrates the growth in GNP since 1982.

*The integration of the government and business sectors*

While the government produces only services, it does consume (buy) many goods and services from the business sector. When, for example, the government builds a post office (it's built by a private contractor; the government merely pays for it), buys an F-16, a computer, or just some paper clips, these products are typically purchased from businesses. Virtually all of the goods, and many of the services, which the government buys are bought from various businesses, and hence are included in production of the business sector noted above.

The fact that the government contributes only about 11 percent to the production of GDP, as noted above, does not mean that the government's impact on the economy is small. On the contrary, the government's impact is huge; but its impact is felt mainly through the business sector. Government expenditures may contribute to inflation or to higher interest rates, and in this way to reductions in business investments. However, they may also contribute to greater sales and hence business profits.

Government taxes may also contribute to declines in business investments by reducing profits. In addition, taxes may contribute to declines in consumption on the part of producer-consumers. They may also reduce the public's saving and in this way contribute to further increases in interest rates and hence business investments. Consequently, the government has a huge impact upon the economy (and hence on GDP) but, as noted, it is felt largely through the business sector.

The government, of course, also has a major impact on the private sector of the economy through the various regulatory powers noted above. The government, therefore, has a big impact on the economic and financial environment in which financial planning must take place.

*Inflation*

**Inflation** is also an important part of the economic environment. Inflation can affect the individual's standard of living because it affects how much his or her income can purchase. In this sense, inflation can be defined in two ways: a rise in the general level of prices throughout the entire economy or a decline in the value of the dollar. The amount of the decline in the dollar's value is equal to the reciprocal of the rate of inflation. On the other hand, **deflation** is an appreciation in the value of

---

3. The other approximately 43 percent was produced by nonsalaried (self-employed) individuals or nonprofit institutions.

the dollar, and it comes about through a **decrease** in the overall price level. Deflation happens less frequently than inflation. During periods of inflation, those having fixed incomes find themselves with less and less buying power, while those whose incomes rise more rapidly than prices are better off.

Adjusting money, or **nominal,** income to take into account the effects of inflation provides what is known as **real income.** Real annual income is simply money income less the effects of inflation. If prices are rising by 5 percent per year, an individual must obtain a 5 percent annual increase in income just to stay even. Conversely, if the person's income is fixed, he or she is about 5 percent worse off every year. In 1985, the average per capita money income in the United States was about $11,861; by yearend 1991 this had grown to about $18,691. However, much of this increase was due to inflation. In real terms, average income had increased only to about $14,880.

*Nominal and real income*

After-tax money income is nominal income less taxes—federal, state and local. Taxes will, of course, vary widely from individual to individual, but even this tax adjustment will only give us after-tax nominal income. The best measure is income adjusted for both inflation and taxes; that is, after-tax real income. To obtain after-tax real income, nominal income must first be adjusted for taxes, and then further adjusted for inflation.

*Taxes and after-tax real income*

*Future prices*

Table 1–1

*Likely future prices on common items under inflation*

| | | Price in 5 years | | Price in 10 years | |
| --- | --- | --- | --- | --- | --- |
| | Current price | Inflation 5 percent | Inflation 10 percent | Inflation 5 percent | Inflation 10 percent |
| 1 lb. cheese | $ 2.29 | $ 2.92 | $ 3.69 | $ 3.73 | $ 5.94 |
| Loaf of bread | 1.09 | 1.39 | 1.76 | 1.78 | 2.83 |
| Ribeye steak (per lb.) | 6.99 | 8.92 | 11.26 | 11.39 | 18.13 |
| 1 gal. milk | 1.99 | 2.54 | 3.20 | 3.24 | 5.16 |
| 1 lb. hamburger meat | 1.84 | 2.35 | 2.96 | 3.00 | 4.77 |
| Dozen eggs | 0.95 | 1.21 | 1.53 | 1.55 | 2.46 |
| Men's suit | 300.00 | 382.88 | 483.15 | 488.67 | 778.12 |
| Ladies' dress | 150.00 | 191.44 | 241.58 | 244.33 | 389.06 |
| Automobile | 17,850.00 | 22,781.63 | 28,747.60 | 29,075.77 | 46,298.30 |
| Shoes | 70.00 | 89.34 | 112.74 | 114.02 | 181.56 |

Prices may vary somewhat regionally, as well as with special sales, and some perhaps seasonally.

*Other problems
with inflation*

In addition to changing people's incomes in real terms, inflation erodes savings held in the form of fixed assets. The dollars held in bank accounts, bonds, and insurance policies will buy less and less as prices rise. Even interest earned by these investments must be adjusted for inflation. For example, if savings accounts can earn 10 percent interest but prices rise at an annual rate of 7 percent, then the real interest rate is only 3 percent per year. In some years the rate of inflation has been higher than the money interest rate, making the real return on fixed investments negative.

Inflation also changes the debtor-creditor relationship. For example, suppose that an individual buys a home today by assuming a $100,000 mortgage. If the interest rate at the time of purchase was 10 percent, this borrower would be obligated to repay about $10,000 per year over the next thirty years. However, notice that this amount owed to the lender will always be paid in nominal dollars. Even if inflation causes prices to double over the next ten years, the homeowner is still obligated to pay only the amount originally agreed on, despite the fact that each dollar has only half the purchasing power it had in the beginning. In this case, the borrower has benefited from inflation at the expense of the creditor by being able to repay the mortgage in "cheaper" dollars.

Since inflation is part of the economic and financial environment, it is necessary to consider it when engaging in financial planning. That is, minimizing the effects of inflation is an important consideration in investment and financial planning. Therefore, it is necessary to understand how changes in the purchasing power of money, and hence income, can affect the planning process.

*Fringe benefits
and psychic
income*

Statistics on money income often exclude fringe benefits, even though their monetary value can be calculated in many cases. Such things as free, or reduced cost, health insurance, sick leave, paid vacation, and retirement benefits often vary from job to job. Employers view these costs as legitimate costs of obtaining labor, and employees should also include them in their total income.

If a client has very generous fringe benefits, both the personal budget (Chapter two) and the financial plan may reflect this. The dollar amount of savings as well as where these savings are to be invested may be affected by fringe benefits.

Psychic income, while it may be important to some people, is difficult to quantify. Some jobs are more pleasant than others, and the degree of pleasure or unpleasantness provided by any given job varies. Thus there is often an element of nonpecuniary (or psychic) income involved. Some people are willing to accept a lower money income for the prestige attached to a job. Other people may prefer to live in sunny Florida and attach some return to being able to do so. If a person wants to live in the crisp, cool air of Colorado and be within a few miles of the fine skiing slopes, he or she may have to sacrifice some money income.

And, of course, money income is a main factor which must be taken into account in financial planning.

Since inflation is intended to describe changes in the overall level of prices, a decision has to be made as to which of the thousands of prices for available goods and services will be used in the calculation. The method most commonly used to measure inflation is a statistical device known as an *index number.*

The Department of Labor computes and publishes what it calls the *consumer price index (CPI),* which serves as an estimate for the level of inflation. As just discussed, if a person's income does not keep up with the rise in this index, the individual is falling behind in what his or her income will purchase. For this reason, the CPI is also commonly called the *cost of living index* and is issued monthly by the Department of Labor's Bureau of Labor Statistics. To construct this index the prices of some four hundred goods and services are gathered in fifty-six cities. According to the Bureau of Labor Statistics, the index covers prices of everything people buy for living—food, clothing, automobiles, homes, house furnishings, household supplies, fuel, drugs, and recreational goods: fees to doctors, lawyers, beauty shops; rent, repair costs, transportation fares, public utility rates, etc. It deals with prices actually charged to consumers, including sales and excise taxes. It also includes real estate taxes on owned homes, but does not include income or social security taxes.[4]

The prices are weighted and averaged and then used to calculate an index number. The prices over the years 1982-1984 were combined and then used as the index base and set to equal 100. Inflation is then measured from that base of 100. Since the index has risen to 137.9 by December 1991, prices have risen by 37.9 percent since the base period, or as the newspapers would say, the cost of living has risen 37.9 percent since that time.

Figure 1–3 shows how the cost of living has risen over the past few years. The cost of living is classified into several broad categories such as food items, nonfood items, and services such as medical services, and a composite is made up of all of these items.

*Measuring prices and inflation; the consumer price index*

The material in this book is organized into five parts. The sequence in which they appear was chosen after a great deal of planning, experimentation, and pedagogical research. Since the book was first published over 25 years ago, hundreds of students, financial planners, college

**WHAT THE REST OF THIS BOOK IS ABOUT**

---

4. U.S. Department of Labor, Bureau of Labor Statistics, *Supplement to Economic Indicators* (Rev. January 1967), Washington: U.S. Government Printing Office, 1967, p. 94.

## CONSUMER PRICES—ALL URBAN CONSUMERS

In August, the consumer price index for all urban consumers rose 0.8 percent, seasonally adjusted (0.9 percent not seasonally adjusted). The index was 5.6 percent above its year-earlier level.

Figure 1–3

(Source: *Economic Indicators*, January 1992, *Council of Economic Advisors*, *U.S. Department of Labor*, *Bureau of Labor Statistics*, p. 23).

professors, and others have given us feedback, which has proven invaluable in reorganizing the material in this major revision.

The five units are:

1. Introduction to Financial Planning
2. Managing Income
3. Managing Insurance Programs
4. Managing Investments
5. Retirement and Estate Planning

Part I, "Introduction to Financial Planning," consists of three chapters designed to set the tone of things to come. The personal budget, balance sheet, and cash flow (or income) statement are presented in this part.

Part II, "Managing Income," is designed to give more mileage per dollar of expenditure, including when a person should use credit or borrow money. Part II includes a chapter on taxes; legally minimizing taxes is an important goal of financial planning. Careful planning can reduce taxes, and doing so is another way of increasing spendable income. Also included here is a chapter on housing, the largest single expenditure for many people.

Part III deals with the various types of insurance frequently used by consumers—homeowner's, car, life, and health. Property insurance protects assets in that if they are damaged or destroyed, they may be replaced or repaired. Health insurance helps meet expenses in the event of illness or replaces income in the event of disability. Liability insurance protects the insured from the loss of assets or income that may result if he or she is found liable for injury or death of another person or destruction of property.

Part IV deals with the investment of assets. Commonly held investment vehicles will be explored.

Part V covers retirement and estate planning. Ensuring adequate retirement income is an important goal for most people, and requires careful planning. Estate planning enables appropriate distribution of assets upon an individual's death, while reducing estate taxation and settlement expenses.

## SUGGESTED READINGS

Brown, James and Clayton, Gary E., *Economics: Principles and Practices*. Columbus, Ohio: Charles E. Merrill, 1983.

"Consumer Views." New York: CitiBank. Monthly newsletter.

"Credit Guide." Chicago: Federal Reserve Bank of Chicago.

*Economic Indicators*. Washington, D. C.: Council of Economic Advisers for the Joint Economic Committee. Monthly publication.

*Economic Outlook U.S.A.* Ann Arbor, Mich.: University of Michigan Survey Research Center. Quarterly publication.

*Finance Facts Yearbook*. Washington, D.C.: National Consumer Finance Association. Annual publication.

"Measuring Price Changes." Richmond, Va.: The Federal Reserve Bank of Richmond.

*Personal Financial Planner*. New York: Financial World Partners. Monthly publication

"Primer on Inflation." New York: The Federal Reserve Bank of New York.

Samuelson, Paul A. *Economics: An Introductory Analysis,* 12th ed. New York: McGraw-Hill, 1985

"The Story of Inflation." New York: The Federal Reserve Bank of New York.

*U.S. Census, Income of Families and Individuals in the U.S. in Current Population Reports; Consumer Income*. Series P-60. Get latest series of this quarterly publication.

"Your Inflation Guide, Dollars and Sense." New York: The Advertising Council.

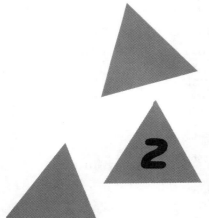

# 2 Record keeping and budgeting

**HIGHLIGHTS**
In order to plan properly, records and a budget are necessary. In this chapter we will examine the following:

1 The importance of keeping good records
2 Permanent records
3 More temporary records
4 Where records should be stored
5 Objectives and benefits of budgeting
6 Budgetary preliminaries
7 Financial goals and priorities
8 General rules of budgeting
9 The actual budgetary process
10 Suggestions for successful budgeting
11 Method of estimating income and expenditures
12 Techniques for controlling expenditures
13 Techniques for successful budgeting
14 How a computer may be used as a budgeting tool
15 How failure to budget may result in personal bankruptcy

## INTRODUCTION

Most people have to live within their incomes. While this is not completely true in any one year (for example, a person may borrow to finance a large item such as a car), it is true for most people most of the time. A person who consumes more than his or her income in one year will probably be forced to consume less during the next year while repaying what was borrowed. Over a lifetime if one consumes more than one's income, one can only get out from under debts through court action—that is, through bankruptcy.

While persons have command over their money income, they have only two main alternatives as to what to do with it: consume it or save it. Most people divide their income, and while they consume most of it, they save some. Once they have committed a part of their income to consumption, they must make further decisions regarding what type of items to buy. Once a person has decided to save, say, 20 percent of his or her income, a second decision regarding where and how to invest it must be made. In this consuming and investing process, a person must constantly choose between alternatives. A limited income can never stretch over all the alternatives, so priorities must be assigned and choices made. This is more effectively carried out through financial planning. An important part of planning is organizing financial records, taking a financial inventory, and developing a budget to achieve goals. In the first part of this chapter we will discuss the records an individual should keep, how long they should be kept and when certain ones should be discarded. Then the budget will be examined. In order to do an effective job of managing money and financial affairs, it is frequently necessary to budget. As we will see, the budgeting process involves planning. A budget is really a projection of a cash flow statement. Technically speaking, a cash flow statement is a look backward at what has happened. A budget, on the other hand, is a look forward; it allocates expected future income among alternative uses. A cash flow statement (also referred to as an income statement) will indicate how an individual allocated income in the past and will help him or her budget for the future. By necessity a budget must often be an estimate of future receipts and expenditures. A ***budget***, then, is a plan in the form of a projected cash flow statement that uses current and future operations to achieve certain goals that might otherwise be beyond one's reach.

## RECORD KEEPING

In order to develop an appropriate financial plan for the client, the planner must be provided with adequate financial data. As the financial plan is implemented, it is important that the client maintain adequate financial records so that progress may be monitored and new strategies implemented as needed.

While the client needs to keep a lot of things, he or she need not keep everything. Moreover, some items may be discarded after a few years; others should be kept indefinitely.

1. Birth certificates.
2. A copy of financial statements, which will be introduced in a later chapter.
3. Insurance policies. These should be easily accessible in the event of a claim. Not only life insurance policies, but health, property, and liability, on both the home and the car, should be easily available. These may be kept in a filing cabinet in the home. Property and liability policies are generally renewed every year; and if a claim does not exist, the expired policies may be discarded. Some cautious people, however, keep these policies an extra year. Photos of household contents, especially scheduled property, should be kept also.
4. A file of the person's Social Security and any pension and other retirement benefits which have built up should be maintained permanently.
5. The title to the automobile and the deed to the home, together with other mortgage papers, should be neatly filed. In the case of the home, detailed records should be kept of every item. Canceled checks of mortgage payments should be kept. Also all records of improvements made on the home should be kept. If the client rents, the lease or rental agreement should be on file.
6. Marriage and divorce records are important and should be kept permanently.
7. Passports.
8. A record of all credit cards and their numbers, so that in the event of loss their use can be blocked more easily.
9. The legal documents from any court settlement in which the client was involved.
10. Securities and other investments. Corporate stocks and bonds, jewelry, gold coins, and other very valuable items should probably be held in a fireproof strong box (called a safety deposit box) rather than in the home. These may be rented at commercial banks and other depository institutions.
11. Wills. Most people keep their will in a safety deposit box in a bank, although a copy should be kept in the home for immediate access. Copies might also be retained by the attorney who drafted the will and by the executor.

Some records need be kept only a few years and some even less.

Installment sales contracts should be kept until the item purchased is paid for. After that, the copy that the merchant or lending institution has is obtained and both copies may be destroyed. The same is true of any loans the individual may make. The paper that is signed (called a promissory note) when he or she lends someone money must be filed until the debt is paid.

*Warranties.* When an individual buys a refrigerator, television set, automobile, and so on, usually the manufacturer provides a warranty. After a few years when the warranties expire, these are of no value and may be discarded. Any service contracts should be treated the same as warranties.

Records of credit card purchases should be treated like checks. They should be held a few years and then destroyed.

Bank statements, canceled checks, and tax records should be kept for some time. Canceled checks and receipts for items that are tax deductible should be filed separately so they will be easily accessible at tax time. After the taxes have been paid, these receipts and checks as well as other checks for large amounts should be kept for at least three years, because that is the time the statute of limitations runs out. (The planner should note that there are some exceptions to this; in certain cases, tax returns may be audited beyond three years from the filing date.) Less important checks can be destroyed once a year. If items are charged on a credit card, and one check pays for many purchases, separate the charge receipts and treat them just like the checks. Records of tax-deductible items should be maintained carefully. Many people, fearful of the Internal Revenue Service, have consistently overpaid their taxes. If a person keeps adequate records, legal deductions may be taken without fear.

Keeping records, paying bills, and reconciling the monthly bank statement are things in which both members of a married couple should be involved. The same is true regarding all major financial decisions. Then in the event one of the partners is left alone in the future, he or she will not be inexperienced in these matters.

*Where records should be stored*

There are two possibilities for storing records: a filing cabinet in the home, and a fireproof strong box, which may be rented at a bank or other depository institution. Really valuable items such as securities, jewelry, gold coins, and the like should be stored in the strong box. Some people also store their will and life insurance policy in their safety deposit box. Others do not because in some states a court order is required to open the box of a deceased person. This takes some time, and because the insurance policy and the will may be needed almost immediately, some people keep a second copy in their home. In the case of a husband and wife, however, the safety deposit box should be rented jointly and then the above problem is solved. If the insurance policy is kept in the home, a record of the policy number should be kept in the safety deposit box.

When all important papers are stored systematically, an easily accessible retrieval system exists for any item needed.

**THE PERSONAL BUDGET**

Since a budget is a financial guide to spending, establishing a budget will enable one to run one's personal financial affairs better than can those persons who fail to keep a budget. By using it, one can make a real attempt to live within one's income.

A budget will also enable an individual to estimate more effectively his or her income than can a person who does not use a budget. It will force the individual into a more acute consciousness of the sums that must be set aside to meet future expenses. The individual will learn to allocate available funds among specific expenses and to estimate what may be left over for savings. Sometimes, through good habits, savings are voluntarily set aside; sometimes they are forced, as when one purchases a home or life insurance. In either case a budget makes the situation clear. Furthermore, a budget may help one identify alternative ways of spending that can lead to additional savings.

A budget will help the individual to achieve his or her financial goals. It will prevent individuals from "getting in over their head" when they borrow money and assume fixed repayment obligations. This is especially true in the case of credit cards. A budget will pinpoint credit card abuse.

It may even save an individual from filing for bankruptcy. In doing all these things, a budget will enable the planner to help increase net worth and provide more financial security.

*The benefits and objectives of a personal budget*

Before a planner actually begins work on the budget there are some preliminary steps that should be taken in order to generate the required data, develop a set of goals and priorities, and develop a team approach to budgeting, if necessary. In many cases a client will need help in budgeting. While the client will usually be required to generate the necessary data, the professional planner will be in a position to help the client to organize it, and to set goals and priorities.

*Budgetary preliminaries*

After a preliminary family planning session, there should be an analysis of past expenditure patterns. If a past cash flow statement is available, this is a good place to begin. Look at current expenditures; find out where most of the money is going. To do this all family members should keep daily records of all expenditures for a few weeks. (This will give individuals a feel for their spending habits.) Total the daily expenditures each week to see how much is spent on the various categories.

After several weeks of expenditures have been generated, it is time for the second family planning session. The group can now decide which, if any, expenditures seem out of line. The individual is now ready to take the next step in budgeting—setting goals and priorities.

Gathering the data

Both short- and long-run goals should be established. One goal might be to increase savings; this may necessitate either cutting expenditures or increasing income. The decision might be made to establish a college

Setting goals

"Yes, I think I can get along on this budget for food. But how are you going to eat?" (Source: Permission Cartoon Features Syndicate; from The Wall Street Journal.)

fund for the children or to accumulate a down payment to buy a home. Plans may be made to generate a vacation fund or make the down payment on a new car. If a larger emergency liquid savings fund is needed, this could become a goal.

Longer-run goals might be to increase a person's net worth by so much over the next five or ten years, or to set up a special retirement fund. While it is difficult to convince most young people that they should start planning for retirement that early, the longer this decision is postponed, the less the dollar amount that can be accumulated for that purpose. There also may be higher-priority items for a young person than retirement planning—such as acquiring a house, emergency funds, and so on. Nevertheless, everyone including young people should be aware that they will need to plan for retirement some day.

Both long- and short-run goals should be monitored and periodically reevaluated. This will indicate what progress is being made and whether goals should be changed. For example, as income rises, one might consider raising his or her sights and setting new, higher goals.

**Establishing priorities**    After the goals have been set, they should be ranked in accordance with the priority assigned to each one. Priorities will vary from family to family, or individual to individual. A younger person will assign a lower priority to retirement planning than will an older person. A person with a large number of dependents will assign a higher priority to life insurance than otherwise. Priorities will also vary with tastes. Some people will assign a higher value to a beautiful automobile; others view a car more functionally and merely want good transportation. Moreover, as some goals are achieved (e.g., home ownership), other goals can move up on the list.

No budget will be the same for any two families or individuals, even if they both have the same income. In addition to the goals and priorities discussed above, there are some rules of thumb which are helpful.

Some rules on budgeting

1. The budget should be developed with reasonable goals in mind. For example, while a budget may permit the individual to stretch his or her income, it will not permit the person to live beyond it. If savings must be increased to provide funds for a child's education, other items must be trimmed, or income must be increased. Variations in preferences, incomes, ages, and sizes of families will result in different goals for different families.
2. The fixed items of expenditure must be provided for first; such items as rent or mortgage payments, life insurance premiums, and installment loan repayments are first priority "must" items.
3. Savings should also be a high priority. Budgeting should not be done in a manner so that savings emerge as a residual, because then they may not emerge at all. Savings must be a planned outflow in the budget to ensure meeting future goals.
4. Certain variable expenditures that are also high-necessity items—such as food, clothing, and transportation—are next.
5. Big-expense items paid less frequently than the budget period may have to be spread so that each income period bears a share of these expenses. For example, property taxes not included in monthly mortgage payments might need to be set aside monthly. The same is true of life and auto insurance where premiums are usually paid only once a year. Some people have a special "set-aside" budget in which one-twelfth of each large annual payment is allocated monthly. This set-aside budget is then incorporated into the regular budget. Table 2–1 shows a set-aside budget.
6. A major expense cannot necessarily be cut just because it is large. For example, food may take a sizeable part of the budget, and that item may appear easy to cut-on paper.
7. A budget should help to develop a set of priorities on general items of expenditure, but it need not consist of a detailed set of accounts indicating where every penny is spent. While there are some rules of thumb on major items, there are also value judgments involved in choosing among different items. One person or family, because of different preferences, will spend more on clothes and less on housing than another similar family.
8. Adequate records should be kept indicating how much has been spent on each major category.

Table 2-1   Set-aside budget

|  | Annual | Monthly |
|---|---|---|
| Life insurance | $ 480 | $ 40 |
| Auto insurance | 420 | 35 |
| Vacation fund | 2,700 | 225 |
| Total | 3,600 | 300 |

| | Jan. | Feb. | March | April | May | June | July | Aug. | Sept. | Oct. | Nov. | Dec. | Annual |
|---|---|---|---|---|---|---|---|---|---|---|---|---|---|
| Monthly set-aside | $300 | $300 | $300 | $300 | $300 | $300 | $300 | $300 | $300 | $300 | $300 | $300 | $3,600 |

After the person has done some preliminary planning, reviewed recent past and present expenditure patterns, set some goals, and established priorities, the actual budgeting process may begin. The budget has three parts or stages which need to be completed. The three stages are (1) estimating income, (2) estimating expenditures, and (3) finalizing income and expenditures to make sure savings materialize. Do not expect savings to emerge as a residual; they must be viewed as a planned expense. This does not mean savings must appear every month, but there should be some savings in virtually all cases on an annual basis.

*The budgetary process*

The form of the budget is not critical and almost any type can be used. Table 2–2 might serve as a budget. Many financial institutions have budget variations of similar forms and will be delighted to furnish a copy.

There is also a filled-in budget shown for a young married couple both of whom have earned income. Table 2–3 shows the estimate of income, and Table 2–4 combines income and expenditures.

The form of the budget

*A budget plan*

Table 2–2

| Item | Amount |
|------|--------|
| Money income after taxes | $_____ |
| Savings: | |
|     Future goals and emergencies | $_____ |
|     Seasonal and large irregular expenses | _____ |
| Regular monthly expenses: | |
|     Rent or mortgage payment  $_____ | |
|     Utilities  _____ | |
|     Installment payments  _____ | |
|       Other  _____ | |
|       Total | _____ |
| Day-to-day expenses: | |
|     Food and beverages  $_____ | |
|     Household operation and maintenance  _____ | |
|     House furnishings and equipment  _____ | |
|     Clothing  _____ | |
|     Transportation  _____ | |
|     Medical care  _____ | |
|     Education and reading  _____ | |
|     Recreation  _____ | |
|     Personal and miscellaneous  _____ | |
|     Gifts and contributions  _____ | |
|       Total | _____ |
|       Total | $_____ |

Table 2–3   Cash budget, estimate of income

| | Jan. | Feb. | March | Apr. | May | June | July | Aug. | Sept. | Oct. | Nov. | Dec. | Annual |
|---|---|---|---|---|---|---|---|---|---|---|---|---|---|
| Salary (take home): | | | | | | | | | | | | | |
| Rudy | $1,525 | $1,525 | $1,525 | $1,525 | $1,525 | $1,525 | $1,525 | $1,525 | $1,525 | $1,525 | $1,525 | $1,525 | $18,300 |
| Sharon | 1,400 | 1,400 | 1,400 | 1,400 | 1,400 | 1,400 | 1,400 | 1,400 | 1,400 | 1,400 | 1,400 | 1,400 | 16,800 |
| Year-end bonus | | | | | | | | | | | | 1,500 | 1,500 |
| Interest | | | 50 | | | 50 | | | 50 | | | 50 | 200 |
| Dividend | | | 25 | | | 25 | | | 25 | | | 25 | 100 |
| Rent | | | | | | | | | | | | | |
| Other | | | | | | | | | | | | | |
| Total income | $2,925 | $2,925 | $3,000 | $2,925 | $2,925 | $3,000 | $2,925 | $2,925 | $3,000 | $2,925 | $2,925 | $4,500 | $36,900 |

Table 2–4  Monthly cash budget

| | Jan. | Feb. | Mar. | Apr. | May | June | July | Aug. | Sept. | Oct. | Nov. | Dec. | Annual |
|---|---|---|---|---|---|---|---|---|---|---|---|---|---|
| **Income:** (from Table 3–3) | $2,925 | $2,925 | $3,000 | $2,925 | $2,925 | $3,000 | $2,925 | $2,925 | $3,000 | $2,925 | $2,925 | $4,500 | $36,900 |
| **Expenditures:** | | | | | | | | | | | | | |
| Rent | 710 | 710 | 710 | 710 | 710 | 710 | 710 | 710 | 710 | 710 | 710 | 710 | 8,520 |
| Utilities | 250 | 280 | 230 | 200 | 175 | 150 | 200 | 220 | 200 | 210 | 220 | 250 | 2,585 |
| Food | 400 | 400 | 400 | 400 | 400 | 400 | 400 | 400 | 400 | 400 | 400 | 400 | 4,800 |
| Clothing | 250 | 250 | 250 | 250 | 500 | 250 | 250 | 250 | 800 | 250 | 250 | 250 | 3,800 |
| Transportation | 250 | 250 | 250 | 250 | 600 | 250 | 250 | 400 | 250 | 250 | 250 | 250 | 3,500 |
| Insurance (set-aside): | | | | | | | | | | | | | |
| Life | | | | | | | | | | | 480* | | |
| Car | | | | | | | 2,700* | | | | | 420* | |
| Vacation (set-aside) | | | | | | | | | | | | | |
| Medical | 75 | 75 | 75 | 75 | 75 | 75 | 75 | 75 | 75 | 75 | 75 | 75 | 900 |
| Recreation and entertainment | 200 | 200 | 200 | 200 | 200 | 200 | 300 | 300 | 200 | 200 | 200 | 200 | 2,600 |
| Gifts and charities | 50 | 100 | 50 | 50 | 50 | 50 | 50 | 50 | 100 | 50 | 50 | 800 | 1,450 |
| Taxes | 75 | 75 | 75 | 75 | 75 | 75 | 75 | 75 | 75 | 75 | 75 | 75 | 900 |
| Savings | 150 | 150 | 225 | 150 | 150 | 225 | 150 | 150 | 225 | 150 | 150 | 1,225 | 3,100 |
| Household supplies | 20 | 20 | 20 | 20 | 20 | 20 | 20 | 20 | 20 | 20 | 20 | 20 | 240 |
| Set-aside budget: (insurance and vacation fund) | 300 | 300 | 300 | 300 | 300 | 300 | 300 | 300 | 300 | 300 | 300 | 300 | 3,600 |
| Other (miscellaneous) | 75 | 75 | 75 | 75 | 75 | 75 | 75 | 75 | 75 | 75 | 75 | 75 | 900 |
| Total | $2,805 | $2,885 | $2,860 | $2,755 | $3,330 | $2,780 | $2,855 | $3,025 | $3,430 | $2,765 | $2,775 | $4,630 | $36,895 |
| Surplus/(deficit) | $ 120 | 40 | 140 | 170 | (405) | 220 | 70 | (100) | (430) | 160 | 150 | (130) | 5 |
| Cumulative surplus/(deficit) | $ 120 | 160 | 300 | 470 | 65 | 285 | 355 | 255 | (175) | ( 15) | 135 | 5 | |

*These items do not result in an additional cash payment because the funds needed are generated in the set aside budget lower down on the chart.

**Explanatory notes to Sharon and Rudy's budget:**

Some expenditures vary from month to month. For example, utility bills vary usually, and expenditures on gifts are higher on birthdays and during Christmas. Expenditures on clothing and transportation too are unlikely to be uniform throughout the year.

Sharon and Rudy have a health insurance plan with their employers, but it does not provide complete coverage; consequently, they have provided for this in their budget. They have also budgeted for federal income taxes so that in the event that their withholdings are inadequate, they will have the funds with which to pay.

Savings are $1,225 in December because they have decided to save $1,000 of their bonus. They have also saved all of their interest and dividend income throughout the year, and even a bit more. Their high savings in December make their expenditures $4,630 that month. Savings are, of course, invested (spent on acquiring earning assets).

The table shows the deficit or surplus each month and the cumulative deficit or surplus. Their budget contains a $5 surplus for the entire year.

A person can plan a budget on a weekly, monthly, or annual basis. Some experts feel it is best to plan a budget period equal to the period between income receipts—a weekly budget if one is paid weekly, and a monthly budget if one is paid monthly. Others feel this can lead to problems if the pay period (and hence the budget) is less than one month because some monthly expenses are greater than the weekly take-home pay. A person in this situation might want to budget monthly and also break the budget down by the week in order to set aside some money each week to meet large expenditures on a monthly basis. Some people, however, have a yearly and a monthly budget as well as the pay-period budget; for those whose income does not come in uniform amounts at regular intervals, the monthly or yearly budget is probably best. People who have a fluctuating income will find a budget particularly useful, since they may have a problem estimating their income accurately over whatever time period they select.

**Estimating income**

If the only source of income is in the form of salary or wages earned by the head of the family, there is no problem except to make a realistic estimate of the income available. Just because the head of the family is employed at $30,000 per year does not necessarily mean that income can be listed as $30,000. Instead, it might be wise to list take-home income after all deductions have been made, such as withholding taxes, Social Security, health insurance premiums that are withheld at the source, and the like. On the other hand, if an individual is self-employed, he or she might want to take the gross income and budget the taxes and Social Security payments.

If income derives from a business or profession, a more difficult problem arises. Frequently the breadwinner's annual or weekly income can be estimated, based on the volume of business the previous week, month, or year. However, some types of business might be called "feast or famine." In some months or even certain years, income is exceedingly high, and in other months or years, very low. If this is so, it is probably best to make a low estimate and have the family attempt to live within that amount.

**Estimating expenditures**

The reverse side of the budget coin is the expenditures. There are certain "must" items over which the individual has little control, such as rent or mortgage payments. In the long run a person can move to a cheaper apartment or sell a home and reduce these payments; in the short run these expenditures are fixed.

A person should give some immediate thought to taxes. Taxes, after all, are an expenditure, and by means of tax planning (which is part of financial planning) they can in many cases be reduced. Certain other expenditures such as food and clothing outlays can be controlled more readily. While it is difficult to reduce the food item in a budget, some reductions can be made by wiser shopping and by buying less expensive grades of food. It is also true that different families will spend different amounts for the same items. Family size differs, as noted above.

Another problem arising in budgeting concerns large annual or semiannual expenditures. If all expenditures were neatly broken down into monthly bills and if all paychecks were received monthly, one problem of budgeting would be eliminated. Unfortunately, necessary payments are frequently not so easily broken down. One might have to pay an insurance premium of $500 every September. Semiannual or annual insurance premiums are less costly than payment on a monthly basis, and consequently one might decide to take advantage of this saving. Some individuals authorize their bank to deduct one-twelfth of their annual insurance premium from their checking account and automatically put it into a special savings account. Then at the end of the year, the premium dollars are available and in the meantime a few dollars of interest will have been earned.

Inflation presents another problem in estimating expenditures. If prices are rising by, say, 5 or 6 percent per year, this must be taken into account and more money may have to be spent on food and other necessities. Inflation is a constant, ongoing process and most people receive a salary adjustment only once every year or two. Hence for a time at least, higher food prices may require lower expenditures on other items. With luck, after a lag, the breadwinners will receive an increase in income and recoup.

**Savings**

In addition to consumption expenditures, a budget should contain an item to assure that in most cases the individual (or family) will have some savings. Not all income should be consumed. In the absence of a carefully planned savings program, all too often savings will not materialize. Many people erroneously feel they can budget their expenditures and generate savings as a residual. But conscious effort is usually required to generate savings.

Many financial planners recommend saving 5–10 percent of income annually. Developing a cash flow statement will show the individual whether savings are too low. If they are and if one finds it difficult to save, arrangements can be made with the bank to have a specific amount transferred automatically from the checking to the savings account each month.

**Finalizing the budget**

If at first expenditures (including planned savings) exceed income, then, unless the individual had planned to dip into past savings that year, he or she should go back and reanalyze expenditures. The budget should at least balance. Often on the first go around a person may be a bit extravagant. On the second analysis, items that may be cut often emerge until the budget is balanced. On the other hand, some individuals tend to underestimate consumption. Be aware of this; for the budget to work, estimates must be realistic.

**Sample budgets**

Table 2–5 shows some sample budgets developed by the Bureau of Labor Statistics for a four-person family; there is a budget for a lower, intermediate, and higher income family. Each budget applies to the

Table 2—5   *Annual budget expenditures for a four-person family at three levels of living in the urban United States*

|  | *Lower budget* | *Intermediate budget* | *Higher budget* |
|---|---|---|---|
| Total budget | $15,323 | $25,407 | $38,060 |
|   Total consumption | 12,069 | 18,240 | 25,008 |
|     Total food | 4,545 | 5,843 | 7,366 |
|       At home | 3,894 | 4,866 | 5,788 |
|       Away from home | 651 | 977 | 1,578 |
|     Total housing | 2,817 | 5,546 | 8,423 |
|       Shelter | 2,114 | 4,348 | 5,851 |
|       House furnishings and operations | 703 | 1,199 | 2,266 |
|     Transportation | 1,311 | 2,372 | 3,075 |
|     Clothing | 937 | 1,333 | 1,947 |
|     Personal care | 379 | 508 | 719 |
|     Medical care | 1,436 | 1,443 | 1,505 |
|     Other family consumption | 644 | 1,196 | 1,972 |
|     Other items | 621 | 1,021 | 1,718 |
|   Social Security payments | 1,036 | 1,703 | 1,993 |
|   Personal income taxes | 1,596 | 4,443 | 9,340 |

*Source:* Bureau of Labor Statistics. *News,* U.S. Department of Labor, "Urban Family Budgets," 1980, Latest Figures Available (Adjusted to 1987 values by applying CPI)

urban United States as a whole. Table 2–6 gives some budget figures developed for different cities that have different costs of living. Anchorage, Alaska, is the most expensive of all U.S. cities, according to the Bureau's figures. It should be noted that these budgets reflect a certain level of well-being, but this should not be taken as a minimum level set by the government as desirable. Note that the budgets contain only consumption items and Social Security and personal income taxes. The individual should allow for savings as an additional item in the personal budget.

### Keys to successful budgeting

Successful budgeting involves first and foremost controlling expenditures and living within the budget. However, a budget also needs to be flexible and reasonably drawn in light of the individual's income. It may need to be adjusted modestly from time to time. In the long run a budget is even more dynamic and will vary over the years as circumstances change, even if income were relatively constant. In controlling expenditures it is helpful to use an expenditures log such as shown in Table 2–7, which provides an easy method of analyzing the individual accounts as well as the total budget.

### Surplus and deficit budgets

The individual need not be a slave to a budget. As noted above, it is permissible to exceed budgeted expenditures in a given category in any

*Annual budget for four-person family at three levels of living in various cities*     Table 2—6

|  | *Lower* | *Intermediate* | *Higher* |
|---|---|---|---|
| Boston | $15,402 | $29,213 | $44,821 |
| New York | 15,705 | 29,540 | 47,230 |
| Philadelphia | 15,116 | 26,567 | 39,560 |
| Chicago | 15,587 | 25,358 | 37,368 |
| Cleveland | 15,176 | 25,598 | 37,487 |
| Detroit | 15,107 | 25,208 | 37,721 |
| St. Louis | 15,112 | 24,498 | 35,965 |
| Atlanta | 14,419 | 23,273 | 34,623 |
| Baltimore | 15,315 | 25,114 | 38,090 |
| Dallas | 14,392 | 22,678 | 33,769 |
| Washington, D.C. | 16,702 | 27,352 | 41,137 |
| Denver | 15,093 | 24,820 | 36,979 |
| Los Angeles | 16,618 | 25,025 | 38,516 |
| Seattle | 17,124 | 25,881 | 37,396 |
| Honolulu | 20,319 | 31,893 | 50,317 |
| Anchorage | 22,939 | 31,840 | 45,119 |
| U.S. | 15,323 | 25,407 | 38,060 |

*Source:* Bureau of Labor Statistics, *News*, U.S. Department of Labor, "Urban Family Budgets," 1980, Latest Figures Available (Adjusted to 1987 values by applying CPI)

one month if there is a legitimate reason. For example, if the individual has a freezer, he or she might buy a side of beef and lay in a supply of vegetables during the growing season. In future months this should reduce the expenditures on food. Or a family may exceed its clothing expenditures in, say, September, if there are children to equip for school. To some extent these overbudgeting expenditures may be offset by reductions in other categories during the same month, but it is also possible that they will throw the entire budget into a deficit. There should, then, be some monthly budgetary surpluses later to offset them. After all, in the case of sales the individual will exceed the budgeted sums to save money in the longer run. One word of caution is in order, however. The individual should not let too many items show a deficit for too long a period of time. In addition, the total budgetary deficit for any one month should not be allowed to become too large. If a person falls into either of these traps, there is a danger that he or she will not be able to generate the necessary offsetting surplus. Over a number of months, the personal budget should be balanced with an allowance for some savings.

It was noted previously that expenditures vary somewhat from family to family because of differences in family sizes, tastes, priorities, and preferences. Expenditures also vary substantially for any given family as the years pass. To some extent, income, too, varies for any given family

Budgetary variations over the life cycle

TABLE 2–7 Expenditures log

| | January | | | February | | | March | | |
|---|---|---|---|---|---|---|---|---|---|
| | Budgeted for | Spent | Surplus (+) or Deficit (−) | Budgeted for | Spent | Surplus (+) or Deficit (−) | Budgeted for | Spent | Surplus (+) or Deficit (−) |
| Utilities | $250 | $240 | $ +10 | $280 | $290 | $ −10 | $230 | $225 | $ + 5 |
| Food | 400 | 405 | − 5 | 400 | 450 | −50 | 400 | 375 | +25 |
| Clothing | 250 | 260 | −10 | 250 | 150 | +100 | 250 | 300 | −50 |
| Transportation | 250 | 240 | +10 | 250 | 265 | −15 | 250 | 225 | +25 |
| Recreation | 200 | 220 | −20 | 200 | 250 | −50 | 200 | 200 | — |
| Gifts | 50 | 55 | − 5 | 100 | 110 | −10 | 50 | 60 | − 10 |
| Savings | 150 | 140 | +10 | 150 | 150 | — | 225 | 210 | +15 |
| Other | 75 | 75 | — | 75 | 70 | + 5 | 75 | 70 | + 5 |

While such a log does not lend itself well to controlling fixed items such as rent and insurance, it is useful in analyzing variable expenditures over which one has more control.

over the years. These variations over the years are referred to as "life cycle variations."

When persons reach their peak earning period, income will vary with the job or profession. A person employed as an unskilled or semiskilled worker will reach the maximum within a year or two of initial employment. Unskilled or semiskilled laborers who go to work at age eighteen or twenty will have achieved their maximum income by their early twenties. This maximum (or ceiling) will rise a little bit each year as the union wins cost-of-living wage increases, as well as increases based upon additional productivity (better tools and machinery will permit workers to produce more), and workers will remain at their rising ceiling until they retire.

Skilled laborers like carpenters or electricians will reach their maximum income somewhat later in life. They have long apprenticeships to serve at a relatively low income. They will achieve their maximum income in from four to six years, sometimes even longer. (Again, this maximum ceiling rises as the years pass.) For example, pilots who bring super tankers into Houston harbor have to serve an apprenticeship of fourteen years.

Professional people like doctors, lawyers, and corporate executives generally have the longest training period of all. Doctors and lawyers are usually about thirty years old before they can practice, and then it takes additional years before they develop a clientele. Doctors and lawyers generally achieve their maximum income during their fifties. This is also generally true of corporate executives. These professional people's income often declines a bit during the last few years before they retire, especially if self-employed.

People's expenditures also follow a life cycle pattern. Young, single adults generally have no real responsibilities and usually save little. While they consume most of their income, it tends to be relatively low. Later, as they marry and start to raise families, they will begin to save as they build up an equity in houses and life insurance. However, the years between the late twenties and about forty or forty-five are also years of heavy consumption, because the family is growing up and needs to acquire durable consumer goods to fill the house it is buying. By this time incomes usually have risen substantially. After about age forty-five, consumption (certainly as a percentage of income, and perhaps absolutely) may begin to decline and savings rise. By now the children are on their own and the house is nearly paid for and is stocked with paid-for furniture and appliances. The years of heavy forced consumption are over. Individuals at this stage may begin to consume more services like travel, but they also can save more, and they will have an incentive to do so because of the approaching retirement years.

During the retirement stage of the life cycle, both income and expenditures usually decline. The standard of living does not necessarily decline. Often retired couples move to a less expensive section of the country. Also, certain payments need no longer be made. The house should be fully paid for, and life insurance no longer needed. Older people also receive an additional standard deduction amount. On the other hand, people over sixty-five usually have higher medical expenses than younger people. Not only is their budget lower, but it also contains different items. However, if they budgeted properly and were able to make substantial savings during the heavy savings years (age forty-five to sixty-five) of the life cycle, their retirement years can be pleasant.

**The personal computer as a budgetary—and other—tool**

More and more people are getting a personal computer, and while computer owners are still a minority they are a growing group. Using a personal computer to help manage personal financial affairs will not only enable a person to perform this task more efficiently, but will save a great deal of time. For example, the budget may be kept on a computer or a bank statement reconciled on a computer. Income from all sources is punched in as well as major categories of expenditures such as food, clothing, housing, transportation, and the others, and the computer will do the rest. As the expenditures of the various items are punched in, the computer can give a running total on each one, and tell a person whether he or she is running behind or ahead of the budget, and which items are out of line and by how much.

The computer can do an almost unlimited number of things. It can assist in balancing and reconciling bank accounts, and can analyze and monitor security investments. The computer can also become the filing cabinet; by keeping a record of expenditures classified according to the various tax-deductible items it can speed the preparation of the tax returns, and in so doing, can make sure all legal deductions are taken. A computer can aid in tax planning. Some clients may wish to use personal computers to assist them in simplifying financial matters.

**The budget and personal bankruptcies**

A budget may also help to avoid bankruptcies. Most personal bankruptcies come about because people are careless in their financial planning. Often they over extend themselves by the careless use of credit. There has been a growing trend to bankruptcies over the past ten years. If an individual should ever be so unfortunate as to have to declare bankruptcy, there is a regular procedure to follow.

Bankruptcies can be classified into business and personal bankruptcies. Each in turn can be broken down into voluntary and involuntary bankruptcies; involuntary ones are forced on a person by creditors. Bankruptcy proceedings are conducted under federal law, but this law does allow for some variations from state to state. Nevertheless, a good deal of uniformity exists. The first step in filing for bankruptcy is to buy a bankruptcy kit, available for a few dollars at any store handling legal papers. This kit contains forms on which must be listed all assets, liabilities, and creditors; the forms are then filed in federal district court. A $50 per-person fee must be paid to the court upon filing. If the case appears to be complex, an attorney should be retained. After the filing, all the creditors are notified and a hearing is held before a bankruptcy referee who is acting under the jurisdiction of the federal court. While the creditors can contest the bankruptcy, it is virtually impossible to prevent a personal bankruptcy from being made effective.

A person may file for personal bankruptcy under Chapter 7 or Chapter 13 of the federal bankruptcy laws. Under Chapter 7, the person gets out from under debts by letting the creditors have those assets which they may legally seize. Under Chapter 13, the person works out a new repayment schedule over several years. Even under Chapter 13, however, debts are usually scaled down, and creditors do not receive full payment. Therefore, many people who have substantial assets choose Chapter 13.

After the bankruptcy is granted, a trustee usually is appointed to take over what assets remain and pay off those debts that can be paid. The debts are classified into an order of priorities; the administrative costs of handling the bankruptcy have first priority. They are followed by wage claims, up to a point, and then taxes. These debts are paid first and then if any assets are left, general claims receive a prorated payment.

In 1986, a new federal bankruptcy law went into effect. It significantly changed the relationship between the creditor and the debtor filing for bankruptcy. It did this by making the federal law more sympathetic toward the debtor. There are now certain assets that federal law protects from seizure to satisfy creditors' claims. The federal law also provides that if the state law is more lenient in the state where the bankruptcy is filed than is the federal law in protecting assets from seizure, the person filing bankruptcy may choose the state exemptions if he or she wishes to do so. The federally protected assets become the starting point and establish a minimum on the assets that are protected. Federally exempt assets include up to $7,500 equity in homestead property ($15,000 if one files jointly with a spouse), $1,200 in a motor vehicle, and $300 each in furniture, clothing, and other household goods. Exempt assets vary from state to state, but generally they include the homestead, a car (in some states two cars) regardless of its value, and the "tools of a trade." A house or car, however, is not protected if it has been pledged to pay off a specific debt. Therefore, a house can be seized to pay off a mortgage or a car to pay off the loan that financed the car.

There was formerly a stigma attached to personal bankruptcies, but this is less true today. Bankruptcy relieves the person of debts, and the logic behind this is that a person who has too many debts becomes economically unproductive. Relieving the individual makes him or her productive again, and hence benefits society as well as the individual. While many lenders no doubt would not lend to anyone who has ever declared bankruptcy, the person is not as bad a credit risk as one might imagine. The bankrupt person is debt-free, and the law does not permit bankruptcy to be filed again for six years. While some people have, no doubt, deliberately run up large debts and then taken the easy way out, most bankruptcies appear to be due to poor planning and poor budgeting.

## SUGGESTED READINGS

*A Guide to Budgeting for the Family.* Home and Garden Bulletin. Washington, D.C.: U. S. Government Printing Office.

Anthony, Robert, and Welsch, Glen. *Fundamentals of Financial Accounting.* Homewood, Ill: Richard Irwin, 1986.

"*Bankruptcy and Alternatives.*" Chicago: The American Bar Association Information Services.

"Financial Pathfinder Service." New York: Merrill Lynch, Pierce, Fenner, and Smith.

Golonka, Nancy. *How to Protect What's Yours.* Washington. D. C.: Acropolis Books, 1985.

"How to Read a Financial Report." New York: Merrill Lynch, Pierce, Fenner, and Smith.

"How to Understand Financial Statements." New York: New York Stock Exchange.

*Money Management* A series of pamphlets published by the Household Finance Corporation. Topics include (1) your food dollar, (2) your clothing dollar, (3) your housing dollar, (4) your home furnishing dollar, (5) your equipment dollar, (6) your shopping dollar, (7) your automobile dollar, (8) your recreation dollar, and (9) your savings and investment dollar. Contact your local Household Finance Company office for more information on these booklets.

National Consumer Finance Association. *Finance Facts Yearbook.* Washington. D.C. Annual publication.

U. S. Department of Agriculture. *Family Economics Review.* Washington. D. C.: Consumer and Food Economic Research Division, U. S. Department of Agriculture. Quarterly publication.

*U.S. Bureau of the Census. Income of Families and Individuals in the U.S. in Current Population Reports; Consumer Income.* Series P-60. Get latest series of this quarterly publication.

U. S. Department of Labor, Bureau of Labor Statistics. *News.* An annual publication on budgeting.

U. S. Department of Labor. Bureau of Labor Statistics. *The Occupational Outlook Handbook,* 1989-1990 ed.

"Your Guide to Consumer Credit and Bankruptcy." Chicago: The American Bar Association.

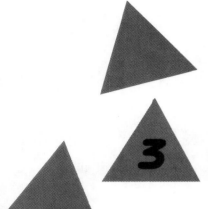

# Financial statements; the tools of financial planning

**HIGHLIGHTS**   In order to plan properly, financial statements are necessary. In this chapter we will examine the following:

1   The personal balance sheet
2   The classification of assets
3   The various liabilities
4   Net worth
5   The personal cash flow (or income) statement
6   Cash inflows and outflows
7   An analysis of the balance sheet
8   The importance of net worth
9   An analysis of financial statements

| **INTRODUCTION;** | After having collected all pertinent data, the next step in taking a financial |
| **TAKING A** | |
| **FINANCIAL** | |
| **INVENTORY** | |

**INTRODUCTION; TAKING A FINANCIAL INVENTORY**

After having collected all pertinent data, the next step in taking a financial inventory is to develop the personal financial statements. These will show the client's current position. These financial statements are the **balance sheet** and the **cash flow statement**, which is also sometimes called the income statement. The balance sheet shows where the client is with respect to the wealth he or she has accumulated. The cash flow statement shows a historical record of cash inflows and outflows for a given period of time.

**THE PERSONAL BALANCE SHEET; STATEMENT OF FINANCIAL POSITION**

A **balance sheet** is a financial statement that depicts the individual's financial position at a particular moment in time; in this respect it is like a photograph. It shows wealth as of a given point in time. Its three main components are assets, liabilities, and the difference between the two, called "net worth." The balance sheet is summarized by the following accounting equation:

$$\text{assets} - \text{liabilities} = \text{net worth.}$$

Or transposed,

$$\text{assets} = \text{liabilities} + \text{net worth.}$$

**Assets**

The terms "wealth" and "assets" mean the same thing; anything of value is wealth and can also be looked upon as an asset. **Assets**, then, are the tangible and intangible property an individual owns.

The things a person is buying but has not yet completely paid for are nevertheless included fully among assets at their total dollar value. The amount of money still owed is included on the other side of the balance sheet under liabilities, as we shall see below. The total value of a home, then, is an asset and the unpaid mortgage is a liability. Or in the case of a $10,000 car on which an individual still owes $6,000, the entire $10,000 is included among the assets, and the $6,000 is among the liabilities.

In order to obtain a total dollar figure for the assets, they should all be listed at their market value—that is, the price at which they could be sold (or purchased).

**Classification of assets**

Assets may be divided into (1) cash and cash equivalents, (2) investment assets, and (3) use (or personal assets). Assets may also be broken down into earning and nonearning assets and financial and nonfinancial assets.

1.   Cash and cash equivalents include such assets as checking accounts, savings accounts, money market funds and accounts, and the cash surrender value of life insurance policies. Some of these assets should be earmarked for the client's emergency fund.

2. Investment assets include bonds, mutual funds, stocks, gold, gems and precious metals, collectibles, investment real estate, fine art, ownership interest in closely-held businesses, vested pension benefits, and similar assets.

3. The third category, use assets (sometimes also called personal assets), includes the client's residence, automobiles, boats, recreational real estate, and personal effects such as furnishings, clothes, jewelry, and similar assets.

4. Earning assets are similar to, and in part a combination of, cash and cash equivalents and investment assets described above. They are assets that yield a return. Stocks, bonds, savings accounts, and real estate that can be rented are earning assets in that they yield a return in the form of interest, dividends, or rental income. Earning assets also include the cash value of life insurance, a pension, and other retirement benefits.

5. Nonearning assets (or assets which are sometimes also referred to as personal assets) consist of personal automobiles, clothing, jewelry, household furniture, and the like. They yield no money return but they are valuable and are wealth or assets, because they provide a service to the owner. Owner-occupied homes are also considered nonearning assets; rental property, on the other hand, is included as an earning asset.

6. Financial assets include such things as stocks, bonds, bank accounts, and cash or currency.

7. Nonfinancial assets include clothes, real estate, automobiles, household furniture and appliances, and so on.

There is some overlap between certain asset classifications. For example, all financial assets except some checking accounts and idle currency are also earning assets. Most nonearning assets are also nonfinancial assets, but there are exceptions. For example, a cattle ranch or a wheat farm is an earning asset, but it is not a financial asset. It is an earning asset because the wheat or the cattle produced are valuable and may be sold; hence there is a return. However, the piece of paper (the mortgage on it) can be considered a financial asset to the lender. This is because the mortgage is a debt instrument which yields an interest income. Any piece of paper which is a legal claim to something of value is a financial asset. Therefore, a bond (a certificate of indebtedness), a stock (a certificate of ownership), or a mortgage (a specialty type of a certificate of indebtedness on real estate) are all financial assets. The largest single asset for most families is their home, and the largest single liability is the mortgage on it.

When the personal balance sheet is constructed, assets are listed on the left with a dollar value attached to them that reflects their fair market value.

Table 3–1 shows some of the major assets most commonly held by individuals. With the exception of cash-on-hand and possibly the check-

Table 3–1    *Assets*

| | |
|---|---|
| 1. Cash-on-hand | 8. Home |
| 2. Checking account | 9. Automobile |
| 3. Savings deposits | 10. Boat |
|    a. At bank | 11. Motorcycle |
|    b. At credit union | 12. Personal property |
| 4. U.S. government savings bonds |    a. Household furniture |
| 5. Corporate stocks |    b. Appliances |
| 6. Corporate bonds |    c. Clothing |
| 7. Life insurance (cash value) |    d. Jewelry |
| |    e. Home computer |

ing account, the assets through number 7 are earning assets. (Some checking accounts earn interest and some do not, as will be shown in Chapter 4). Assets 8 through 12 are nonearning assets; or use assets. The first seven assets are also financial assets, while numbers 8 through 12 are nonfinancial assets.

*Liabilities*

**Liabilities** are the debts the individual owes to others. The amount he or she still owes on a car and the sum run up on the gasoline credit card and other charge accounts are examples. The unpaid balance (mortgage) on the family home is another example. Generally speaking, interest must be paid on the debts owed.

1.  Liabilities may be broken down into debt that must be paid relatively soon and debt that is paid over a longer period of time. Very short-term debt is called "bills outstanding" and includes credit card charges, dental bills, utilities, rent, and so on. Many of these, especially credit card charges, are incurred for convenience; i.e., many bills can be paid with one monthly check.
2.  Intermediate-term debt, such as an automobile installment loan, is incurred to enable a person to acquire a car earlier than otherwise would be possible. Other installment loans would include those to finance household furniture or appliances.
3.  Long-term debt is most often acquired to buy a home; the home yields a service over a long period of time, and the debt is repaid over a long period of time. However, some long-term debt may be incurred in order to buy earning assets such as a rental house or a business. Long-term debt may also be incurred to finance a college education. When developing a personal balance sheet, only the outstanding loan balance should be shown for installment, mortgage, and other long-term loans.

SPECIAL CHECKING

DEPOSITS WITHDRAWALS

BORROWING FROM PETER TO PAY PAUL

*Source: Drawing by Mort Gerberg © 1979 The New Yorker Magazine, Inc.*

Table 3–2 shows the typical set of liabilities most people will encounter during a lifetime.

*Net worth*

**Net worth** is the actual wealth of a person or family for whom the balance sheet was developed at a given point in time. It is assets minus liabilities and is usually shown by the accounting equation of

Total Assets – Total Liabilities = Net Worth.

*Liabilities*                                                                  Table 3—2

---

1.  Bills outstanding
    a.  Department store charge account
    b.  Bank credit card charges
    c.  Gasoline credit card charges
    d.  Rent due
    e.  Repair bills
2.  Installment loans
    a.  Automobile loan (balance due)
    b.  Refrigerator (balance due)
    c.  College loan
3.  Mortgage loans
    a.  Owner-occupied
    b.  Rental
4.  Other loans

---

As such, it is the truest reflection of what the person is actually worth. If a person were to sell all of his or her assets and pay off all debts, that is what would remain. Assets are nearly always greater than liabilities, but in those relatively rare cases where they are not, the person is, technically speaking, bankrupt. Bankruptcy was examined in Chapter 2.

In order to calculate net worth it is necessary to calculate the dollar value of both liabilities and assets. The dollar amount of liabilities is easier to obtain than of assets because they are already stated in dollar terms. Assets, however, may not be. Moreover, assets may appreciate or depreciate over time. Therefore, in calculating the value of assets, their market value should be used and not what was paid for them. If an organized market exists, assets can be evaluated easily. If not, estimates need to be made. In the case of securities, their market price may be published in the financial pages of the daily newspaper. In the case of a home, it is more difficult, but any realtor is able to give an accurate estimate. Similar houses that are advertised for sale may also be considered in assessing the value. The value of a car may be estimated by looking at newspaper ads of similar cars for sale. In addition, the car's

Table 3–3   *Example of a balance sheet*

| Assets | | Liabilities and net worth | |
|---|---|---|---|
| Cash | | Unpaid bills | |
| Currency | $ 50 | Bank credit card | $ 150 |
| Checking account | 500 | | |
| Cash value of life | | Other charge cards | 75 |
| insurance | 1,200 | Repair bill on car | 125 |
| Savings deposit | 1,000 | Telephone bill outstanding | 12 |
| Investments | | Installment loan | 800 |
| Government bonds | 1,200 | | |
| Corporate bonds | 1,000 | Mortgage loan | |
| Corporate stocks | 1,500 | Owner-occupied | 50,000 |
| Mutual funds | 1,200 | Other rental | 35,000 |
| Real estate | | Total liabilities | 86,162 |
| Owner-occupied | 70,000 | | |
| Rental property | 50,000 | | |
| Personal property | | | |
| Automobile | 5,000 | Net worth | $ 52,688 |
| Household furniture | 4,000 | | |
| Clothes | 1,500 | | |
| Jewelry | 200 | | |
| Other assets | 500 | | |
| Total assets | $138,850 | | |

blue book value will provide a second approximation. The cash value of a life insurance policy may be obtained by calling the insurance agent who sold the policy or by reviewing the annual statement.

Personal property such as household furniture, appliances, jewelry, rare coins, and clothing is more difficult to evaluate. Jewelry and rare coins may need to be appraised in order to get an accurate value. In the case of other personal property, probably the best one can do is to take its original price and adjust it downward somewhat based on its age.

Table 3–3 shows a balance sheet for a typical family. The financial assets are listed first; they go through mutual funds. The other items are nonfinancial assets. Remember in the construction of any balance sheet, the assets are always to the left. The liabilities are always to the right. Below the liabilities is shown the net worth, which, together with the liabilities, is equal to total assets.

The **cash flow statement** is another important financial tool useful in planning the client's personal financial affairs. The balance sheet depicts the financial condition at a given point in time; the cash flow statement shows what has happened to the financial position over a period of time, say a year. It is an historical statement in that it indicates what has happened in the past. Nevertheless, it is a flow concept. It can be compared to a stream of water that is measured in terms of flow: so many gallons of water per minute. The personal cash flow statement measures salaries and other income as inflows and various expenditures as outflows. The statement does not consider only consumption expenditures as outflows, however. This is because each statement should have a category of savings outflows. Savings must be positively planned for and the savings that are achieved flow out and become investments, as we shall see below. Therefore the cash flow statement has three main parts: income, consumption expenditures, and savings expenditures.

## THE PERSONAL CASH FLOW STATEMENT

Wages and salaries are the major source of income for most people. However, some people have interest income that they receive on savings deposits and government and corporate bonds, as well as dividends on corporate stock. Some individuals also have rental property and receive rental income. People who own small businesses receive income from those sources. Also, any of the following should be considered as income: tips; bonuses; tax rebates; gifts; inheritances; social security and other retirement benefits; and money received from the sale of securities, an automobile, or any other asset. While many people feel that money received from the sale of assets is not really income, it is part of the cash inflow; and it is the total cash inflow for the period (usually one year) that the cash flow statement is presenting and that must be taken into account.

*Cash inflows: Income and other cash inflows*

Table 3—4    *Yearly income flow*

| | Jan. | Feb. | March | April | May | June | July | Aug. | Sept. | Oct. | Nov. | Dec.* | Annual |
|---|---|---|---|---|---|---|---|---|---|---|---|---|---|
| After-tax wages or salary of breadwinner | $2,000 | $2,000 | $2,000 | $2,000 | $2,000 | $2,000 | $2,000 | $2,000 | $2,000 | $2,000 | $2,000 | $2,500 | $24,500 |
| Dividend | 25 | | | 25 | | | 25 | | | 25 | | | 100 |
| Interest income | 50 | | | 50 | | | 50 | | | 50 | | | 200 |
| Other possible income | | | | | | | | | | | | | |
| Total | $2,075 | $2,000 | $2,000 | $2,075 | $2,000 | $2,000 | $2,075 | $2,000 | $2,000 | $2,075 | $2,000 | $2,500 | $24,800 |

*Includes Christmas bonus.

Expenditures consist of all the items on which the client spends money. *Cash outflows*
There should be a category for food, clothing, transportation, housing,
medical care, recreation, and the like. Some of these can then be further
broken down into subcomponents.

Only money actually disbursed should be counted as expenditures.
Bills coming due in the future are to be counted in the future. For
example, automobiles purchased on the installment plan and paid for
over several years appear on the cash flow statement for several years
with the dollar amount each year equal to the payments each year.

Finally, the cash flow statement should have an item for savings. This *Savings*
item is listed as a separate category of expenditure to emphasize the
importance of saving and investing. Some financial planners list savings
before other expenditures to emphasize that savings and investing is a
planned outflow, not simply a residual of income less other expenses.

To be sure, savings are not held in the form of idle cash but are
invested to become an earning asset; hence, they flow out on the cash
flow statement. Nevertheless, they are different from other outflows,
which are mostly consumption items. A sample of monthly income flow
is shown in Table 3–4 and a sample annual cash flow statement is shown
in Table 3–5.

*Cash flow statement*    Table 3–5

|  | Annual | Monthly |
| --- | --- | --- |
| Income |  |  |
| Wages and salaries | $24,000 | $2,000.00 |
| Interest | 200 | 16.66 |
| Dividends | 100 | 8.33 |
| Christmas bonus | 500 | 41.67 |
| Other | — | — |
| Total | $24,800 | $2,066.66 |
| Expenditures |  |  |
| Food | $ 5,600 | $ 466.66 |
| Clothing | 1,258 | 104.83 |
| Transportation | 2,100 | 175.00 |
| Housing | 5,200 | 433.33 |
| Medical care | 1,300 | 108.33 |
| Recreation | 1,000 | 83.33 |
| Other | 1,400 | 166.66 |
| Taxes |  |  |
| Social security | 1,642 | 136.83 |
| Personal income tax | 4,100 | 341.66 |
| Property taxes |  |  |
| Savings and investments | 1,200 | 100.00 |

**FINANCIAL STATEMENT ANALYSIS**

Both the balance sheet and the cash flow statement are analytical devices that can help in achieving the client's financial goals. Comparing these statements from year to year will show what progress is being made. As the years pass, income generally rises, as does the net worth portion of the balance sheet. Financial statements can also be used to plan ahead, especially in the purchase of big items such as automobiles, homes, and life insurance. They also can provide clues as to whether more life insurance is needed or a larger home is within the family's financial means or if it would be desirable to increase savings.

*Balance sheet analysis*

The assets, liabilities, and the net worth are the crucial parts of the balance sheet.

Assets

Examine assets. What are they earning? Could their yield be increased by investing them differently? Is too much money in any one asset? Should the portfolio be diversified more? Is life insurance adequate for the client? Is there too much (or too little) in highly liquid, low-earning cash or passbook savings accounts? These are the client's emergency funds, and an amount equal to about three to six months' income is considered adequate by most experts.

Liabilities

Examine liabilities. Is the client overextended in the use of credit? If he or she has a difficult time meeting savings objectives, this is sometimes the reason. What is the interest cost on debts? If it is relatively high and excess liquid assets are earning much less, the client should consider paying off some debts.

Net worth

It is important to look at net worth to see how it is changing from year to year. Let us return now for a moment to the accounting equation introduced earlier: Assets – Liabilities = Net Worth. If assets increase, either liabilities or net worth increase, or some combination of the two. If assets decrease, either liabilities, net worth, or both decrease. If assets increase faster than liabilities, net worth increases. If the reverse happens, net worth declines. If liabilities exceed assets, net worth becomes negative. If this happens, the individual is technically insolvent—that is, bankrupt; great care should be taken not to allow this to happen. Bankruptcy, discussed in Chapter 2, is nearly always the result of poor financial planning.

A major goal of many people is to increase net worth. If assets and liabilities are both increased by the same dollar amount, the net worth is unchanged. This could happen if someone borrows money and buys something with it. Normally, however, when an asset is purchased with borrowed funds, the buyer must make a down payment. For example, if the buyer borrows $15,000, takes $2,850 out of his or her savings account, and buys a new car for $17,850, net worth stays the same. His or her liabilities increase by $15,000 (installment debt) and so do assets;

he or she has a new $17,850 car, but cash is down $2,850 and net worth is unchanged. The following changes would be reflected on his or her balance sheet. Only the changes are shown (a plus means an increase and a minus a decrease).

| Assets | | Liabilities and net worth | |
| --- | --- | --- | --- |
| New car | +$17,850 | Installment loan | +$15,000 |
| Cash | 2,850 | Net worth | no change |

But if a person increased assets without having increased liabilities, net worth increases. The key to doing that is through savings. This brings us to the cash flow statement. If the cash flow statement has savings of $1,000 and liabilities remain unchanged, net worth will increase. The following changes are reflected on the balance sheet. As before, we show only the changes, depicted here by plusses.

| Assets | | Liabilities and net worth | |
| --- | --- | --- | --- |
| Savings account | +$1,000 | Liabilities | no change |
| | | Net worth | +$1,000 |

On the other hand, if a person was required to spend savings to meet expenses, both assets and net worth decline. The changes reflected on the balance sheet for this appear below:

| Assets | | Liabilities and net worth | |
| --- | --- | --- | --- |
| Savings account | – $1,000 | Liabilities | no change |
| | | Net worth | – $1,000 |

Paying off debt reduces liabilities, and, if the individual's assets are not affected, it increases net worth. If each monthly payment reduces the $15,000 automobile loan by $400, the following changes would be reflected on the balance sheet:

| Assets | | Liabilities and net worth | |
| --- | --- | --- | --- |
| no change | | Installment loan | – $400 |
| | | Net worth | +$400 |

Thus, consumption and savings choices will affect the balance sheet. Savings will increase net worth, and liquidating savings and investments to meet expenses will reduce net worth. It should be noted that net worth is a good indicator of financial strength, and that a growing net worth indicates that the person is financially becoming stronger. Comparing balance sheets from year to year—assets, liabilities, and net worth—will show what progress the client is making.

*The cash flow statement analysis*     The cash flow statement should be examined to see if the client is accomplishing his or her goals. The savings portion of the cash flow statement is the key to that document. Many financial planners recommend annual savings of 5–10 percent of income; of course the achievement of specific goals may require a greater (or smaller) amount of savings. A budget may be helpful in assisting clients in achieving savings goals, because it aids the client in making choices. The personal and family budget was discussed in Chapter 2.

Expenditures should also be examined to determine if any are out of line relative to income.

## SUGGESTED READINGS

Anthony, Robert, and Welsch, Glen. *Fundamentals of Financial Accounting.* Homewood, Ill: Richard Irwin, 1986.

"Financial Pathfinder Service." New York: Merrill Lynch, Pierce, Fenner, and Smith.

Golonka, Nancy. *How to Protect What's Yours.* Washington, D. C.: Acropolis Books, 1985.

"How to Read a Financial Report." New York: Merrill Lynch, Pierce, Fenner, and Smith.

"How to Understand Financial Statements." New York: New York Stock Exchange.

National Consumer Finance Association. *Finance Facts Yearbook.* Washington, D. C. Annual publication.

*U.S. Bureau of the Census. Income of Families and Individuals in the U.S. in Current Population Reports; Consumer Income. Series P-60.* Get latest series of this quarterly publication.

# Managing income and assets

Chapters 4 through 8 deal with the expenditure of an individual's income.

Chapter 4 covers liquid assets, income, and the means of making payments. Chapter 5 discusses financing "big ticket" items, and Chapter 6 outlines the federal consumer protection laws that are there to protect consumers from unscrupulous merchants and lenders.

In Chapter 7 we examine Caesar's tribute—taxes. The tax bite is severe, and this chapter is designed to minimize the severity of that bite.

Chapter 8 discusses the largest single expenditure most people will ever make, purchasing a home. Buying a home requires planning and some knowledge of a specialized nature. It is our hope that the chapter will aid the reader in acquiring that knowledge.

# Depository institutions and the services they provide

**HIGHLIGHTS**    In order to provide an understanding of the various depository institutions and the services they provide, this chapter examines the following:

1   Checking accounts—both interest-bearing and non-interest-bearing —and how they work
2   The various depository institutions
3   How checks are cleared
4   The monthly bank statement
5   Certified and cashier's checks
6   The latest automation in depository institutions' services
7   Money orders and travelers' checks
8   Safety of deposited funds
9   Savings deposits and the various other services of depository institutions

## INTRODUCTION

Financial planners are in a position to evaluate clients' expenses as well as the means of holding assets. Therefore planners should be familiar with the types of accounts and services available through depository institutions. Until recently checking accounts did not pay interest, but now a number of different kinds of checking accounts have evolved, some of which do. Four types of payment media (coins and currency, checking accounts, credit cards, and debit cards) are currently what we use to pay for day-to-day transactions. Credit and debit cards will be discussed in Chapter 5—credit cards because they involve the use of credit or borrowed money since payment is delayed, and debit cards because they are similar to credit cards but payment is immediate. Coins, currency, and checking accounts will be discussed in this chapter as will be the various depository institutions that issue checking accounts.

## CASH BALANCES, LIQUIDITY AND CHECKS

Liquidity is a relative concept indicating how close something is to money.[1] Money is the most liquid thing in the world, and an old pair of shoes that still has value is perhaps one of the least liquid things. Cash balances—or money—consist of currency, coin, and checking accounts.

### The traditional checking account

A check is a written order, drawn on a depository institution by a depositor, ordering the bank to pay on demand and unconditionally a definite amount of money to the bearer or to the order of a specific person or business firm named on the check. Funds in traditional checking accounts are called **demand deposits**, and they earn no interest. Checks are always payable on demand, and must be demanded within a reasonable length of time. The Uniform Commercial Code states that a check is not to be paid after six months have elapsed since it was written. For this reason checks are dated.

There are three parties to a check. The person drawing the instrument is called the **drawer**; the party requested to pay the stated amount is known as the **drawee**; and the person to whom the instrument is made payable is known as the **payee**.

There are also specialized checks referred to as **drafts**. Drafts are specialized checks written by one bank on its account in another bank. They are usually sold to a person who wishes to pay someone in a different section of the country. For example, a person in Denver might buy a draft written on a New York bank from a Denver bank and use it to pay for purchases in New York. A bank draft can be a **sight draft** (payable on demand) or a **time draft** (payable at some predetermined future time).

---

1. Some financial experts have defined liquidity as being how quickly and easily an asset can be converted to money without making a price concession.

Interest-bearing checking accounts, or **NOW Accounts** (Negotiated Order of Withdrawal), may be viewed as specialized checking accounts that bear interest or specialized savings accounts on which checks may be written. The NOW Account was originally authorized in 1972 but only for certain institutions in Massachusetts and New Hampshire. In March 1980, a federal law was passed that makes these accounts legal for all depository institutions throughout the United States. This specialized account is not restricted to commercial banks, but may also be issued by credit unions, mutual savings banks, and savings and loan associations. While these accounts are all NOW accounts, they are referred to by a variety of names—share drafts, save-or-spend, net worth checking, investor checking, check action, paymaster, and many others. They pay a relatively low rate of interest, and often there are substantial monthly service charges unless a minimum balance is maintained.

*Interest-bearing checking accounts*

Five institutions provide checking accounts as well as certain other services.[2] They are commercial banks, savings and loan associations, credit unions, mutual savings banks, and industrial banks.

**DEPOSITORY INSTITUTIONS AND DEPOSITS —CHECKING ACCOUNTS**
*Banks*

The financial institutions we call banks are technically defined as commercial banks. Commercial banks have been called "the department stores of financial institutions" because under one roof they can do almost everything. Banks make loans to businesses, farmers and ranchers, individuals, and all levels of government. Banks perform the role of trustee, make available strongboxes for safekeeping valuables, and administer the nationwide credit card system that some of them have developed. Some banks also offer discount brokerage services. But the most important role of banks for the general public is to establish and service checking accounts, including clearing checks, which in turn permits our complex society to function.

Savings and loan (S & L) associations (also called building and loan associations in some states) are evolving rapidly and are becoming more like commercial banks. At one time savings and loans performed, for the most part, only two functions, accepting savings deposits and making mortgage loans. Now S & L's make consumer loans and commercial loans, provide trustee services, provide credit cards, and provide checking accounts. They clear checks and are now full-fledged depository institutions just like commercial banks.

*Savings and loan associations*

---

2. Some money market mutual funds do permit check-writing privileges, but do not provide all the other services the depository institutions provide. Money market funds are discussed in a later chapter.

*Mutual savings banks*

Mutual savings banks (MSB) are much like savings and loan associations. MSBs, however, are all true "mutuals." They have no stockholders, and in theory the depositors are the owners. At one time, they, too, limited their activities to accepting savings deposits and making mortgage loans, but have now expanded into other areas, and accept interest-bearing checking accounts.

*Credit unions*

Credit unions are voluntary cooperative associations. Members have a common bond—usually this consists of the employees of some enterprise. They still specialize in making consumer loans to their members, using these same members' savings deposits to finance the loan. In addition, credit unions may offer first and second mortgages. Credit unions do not deal with outsiders. A person must be eligible and then voluntarily join; one may not just walk in off the street and do business with a credit union. However, credit unions do offer a wide variety of deposits including the interest-bearing checking account. They clear checks and provide all the necessary checking account services for their members.

*Industrial banks*

Industrial banks, or "Morris Plan banks," are another type of thrift institution, and are found in about twenty states. They accept both passbook savings and certificates of deposit (CDs). In some states they are also permitted to accept the interest-bearing account, the NOW account. There are not many statistics about industrial banks so most comments are only generalizations. Industrial banks are typically regulated by state banking commissions, and to a degree the regulations vary from state to state. They are specifically forbidden to act as trustees. Frequently they are required to establish reserve accounts, often as high as 15 percent of their savings deposits. In some states the law prohibits borrowing by any of the bank's officers or stockholders, and usually the state banking commissioner conducts periodic examinations of the bank. Industrial banks do not exist in many states. Most industrial banks do not provide insured deposits; they also sometimes make riskier loans. Because of this they generally pay higher interest rates than other depository institutions. Nevertheless, there are some good, well-managed industrial banks.

*Service charges*

Most institutions have service charges, which vary not only from institution to institution but also with the type of deposit. Service charges should be considered when selecting a checking account to minimize the cost.

Service charges are generally higher on the NOW account than on others. However, the participant earns interest on deposits, which tends to offset the service charges. If the minimum monthly balance is fairly high, the consumer will usually come out ahead with a NOW account; if it is small, a traditional account may be more appropriate.

Many institutions require a minimum monthly balance of as high as $2,000 before they waive monthly service charges on a NOW account.

Credit unions, however, as a rule require much less, as do some other institutions. If service charges are assessed, they generally run from $5 to $10 per month. Some institutions also charge 10¢ or 15¢ per check.

With a regular checking account, usually no service charges are assessed if the minimum monthly balance does not fall below a certain level (usually $300, but sometimes $500). If the account falls below the minimum, a service charge is levied, usually a flat fee of $3, $4, or $5 per month. In some cases, if the minimum balance falls even lower, say below $200, this flat fee may rise a dollar or two; and if the balance falls below $100, the service charge may rise another dollar. Some institutions also add a 10¢ or 15¢ fee per check to their flat fee service charge if the balance falls below a specified minimum.

Some banks also have special noninterest-bearing (traditional) checking accounts. In such a case, usually no minimum balance is required. Rather, there is a monthly service charge of 50¢ or $1.00 and a further charge of 15¢ or 20¢ per check. Special accounts are not very popular, but they appeal to certain groups such as students who write few checks and whose balance either is low all the time or fluctuates a great deal.

It is often desirable for a married couple to open a joint account. To do this both individuals must endorse the signature card. A specimen of this type of card is shown in Figure 4–1. Once the account is opened, both persons may write checks or, more precisely, draw against the account.

*Joint accounts*

There are a number of advantages in opening a joint account. The bank regards it as one account; therefore, the service charges are less than they would be if the husband and wife had separate accounts. The most important advantage, however, arises in the event of the death of one of the parties. If the husband has an individual account and the wife has an individual account and the husband dies, then, until the estate of the deceased is probated, the bank will refuse to honor any checks drawn against the husband's account by the man's wife. However, when the husband and wife have a joint account, because of the nature of a joint tenancy with the right of survivorship, title to the fund usually passes immediately upon death to the survivor. The practical effect is that the wife can draw checks on the joint account after having obtained a release from the tax commission in those states having state inheritance taxes. The lease can be arranged by a bank for the survivor within a few days. The major disadvantage to a joint account is that sometimes neither party knows what checks the other has drawn, and the account might be overdrawn.

Account No._____

Account Name _____

No. of Signatures

Required _____

# TEXAS STATE BANK
### AUSTIN, TEXAS

All the conditions on the reverse side of this card pertaining to this agreement have been read and agreed to by the undersigned. The Texas State Bank is authorized to recognize the following signatures in the payment of funds and all other transactions dealing with this account.

1. _____   Soc. Sec. No. _____

2. _____   Soc. Sec. No. _____

3. _____   Soc. Sec. No. _____

4. _____   Soc. Sec. No. _____

Res.                                               Res.
Address _____   Phone _____

City _____   State _____   Zip Code _____

Employer _____

Bus.                                               Bus.
Address _____   Phone _____

Perm.
Address _____   City _____

Prev.
Bank _____   City _____

Identification _____

New A/C                                            Initial
Clerk _____   Date _____   Deposit _____

Type Account      ☐ Comm      ☐ Reg      ☐ Tex    ☐ 2 + Ck
                  ☐ Reg Sav   ☐ S/I Sav          ☐ 2 + Sav

Corresponding 2 + No. _____

Checks Ordered _____   Passbook Issued _____

Comments: _____

**JOINT ACCOUNT BECOMING PROPERTY OF SURVIVOR UPON DEATH OF OTHER PARTY**

We agree and declare that all funds now, or hereafter, deposited in this account are, and shall be, our joint property and owned by us as joint depositors with right of survivorship, and not as tenants in common; and upon the death of either of us any balance in said account shall become the absolute property of the survivor. The entire account or any part thereof may be withdrawn by, or upon the order of, either of us or the survivor and the bank shall have the right to pay the entire balance to said survivor and upon such payment shall be discharged of all liability.

**NOTICE:** This agreement is not effective between a husband and wife as to community funds.

_____      _____

**NOTICE: Read Additional Terms and Conditions on Reverse Side**

Figure 4–1   *Example of signature card.* (Source: *Texas Bank of Austin.*)

*Clearing checks*

Virtually all checks in the United States are now cleared by computer, using "magnetic ink character recognition" (MICR). This is possible because each customer has an account number on his or her checks. It is printed with special ink and characters so that a computer can read it. When the customer writes a check, the bank deducts that amount from the account, and the person receiving the check has that sum added to his or her account. If two different banks are involved, then one bank has a claim on the other. Since hundreds of checks are presented for payment each day, all banks have funds flowing both in and out. Hence, in net terms, a bank will lose (or gain) very little on any given day. The clearing of checks is usually carried out by a clearinghouse association or by the Federal Reserve System. It nets the checks and then debits and credits the accounts of the proper bank.

*Monthly statement*

Most institutions send monthly statements to their depositors indicating the balance at that time. These statements show all deposits and withdrawals during the month, the balance at the beginning and at the end of the month, and the service charges, if any. The canceled checks are returned at the same time. Although such statements are usually sent toward the end of the month, some banks send them out over several days or even weeks to spread the work of preparing them. These monthly statements can be used by the depositors to reconcile their balances. Figure 4–2 shows an example of a monthly bank statement.

*Truncation*

Truncation is a system where canceled checks are not returned to the drawer with the monthly bank statement. Rather the statement consists of a computer printout that lists each check, its number, the dollar amount, and to whom paid. This statement would serve as proof of payment. The checks would be retained by the bank for a time and later microfilmed and the checks destroyed. Approximately 40,000 checks can be stored on a cassette tape four inches in diameter. It is estimated that stopping this avalanche of paper would save financial institutions several billion dollars per year.

Initially, some opponents of the truncation system claimed that people would resist the concept of not being able to retain their canceled checks. To address this worry, many depository establishments that have adopted the truncation method also offer their customers a ***duplicate draft*** system. Duplicate drafts are nothing more than carbon copies made of each check at the time it is written. They are nonnegotiable; they simply provide the customer with a record of exactly what was written on the actual drafts. In this way the customer can feel more secure about his or her check-writing activities, while the bank, S & L, or credit union can avoid the expense of returning canceled checks through the mail. With well over fifty billion checks processed annually, the duplicate draft system should allow the public to avoid greatly increased service charges in the future.

# Texas Bank
### REPUBLIC
### OF TEXAS

John Doe
2205 5th Street
Austin, TX 78767

AREA CODE 512   PHONE: 476-6711
P.O. BOX 1328   •   AUSTIN, TEXAS 78767

# Statement

| ACCOUNT NUMBER |
| --- |
| 000-000-0 |

| 2 | 10 | 81 | DATE |
| --- | --- | --- | --- |

| BEGINNING BALANCE | NO. OF CHECKS | TOTAL AMOUNT OF CHECKS PAID | NO. OF DEPOSITS | TOTAL AMOUNT OF DEPOSITS | OUT OF TOWN CHECKS DEP | BALANCE FOR SERVICE CHARGE | SERVICE CHARGE |
| --- | --- | --- | --- | --- | --- | --- | --- |
| 891.09 | 36 | 1,531.39 | 2 | 918.22 | | 70 | 5.00 |

| DATE | CHECK | CHECK | DEPOSIT | BALANCE |
| --- | --- | --- | --- | --- |
| 7-23 | | BALANCE FORWARD | | 891.09 |
| 7-24 | 20.00 | 40.00 | | |
| 7-24 | 171.58 | | | 659.51 |
| 7-25 | 40.00 | 160.00 | | 459.51 |
| 7-28 | 8.66 | 21.00 | | |
| 7-28 | 73.73 | | | 356.12 |
| 7-29 | 40.00 | | | 316.12 |
| 7-31 | 20.00 | | | 296.12 |
| 8-1 | 20.00 | | | 276.12 |
| 8-4 | 10.11 | 20.00 | | |
| 8-4 | 33.00 | | | 213.01 |
| 8-5 | 20.00 | 40.00 | | 153.01 |
| 8-6 | 40.00 | | | 113.01 |
| 8-7 | 40.00 | | | 73.01 |
| 8-8 | | | 469.77 | 542.78 |
| 8-11 | 58.70 | | | 484.08 |
| 8-12 | 6.70 | 25.00 | | |
| 8-12 | 40.00 | 44.25 | | 368.13 |
| 8-14 | 40.00 | | | 328.13 |
| 8-18 | 8.15 | 13.51 | | |
| 8-18 | 50.00 | | | 256.47 |
| 8-19 | 4.00 | 20.00 | | 232.47 |
| 8-20 | 110.00 | | | 122.47 |
| 8-21 | 20.00 | | 448.45 | 550.92 |
| 8-25 | 6.30 | 8.00 | | |
| 8-25 | 40.00 | 58.70 | | |
| 8-25 | 160.00 | 5.00 SC | | 272.92 |

| AT | AUTOMATIC PAYMENT | DM | DEBIT MEMO | LP | LOAN PAYMENT | PR | PAYMENT REVERSAL |
| --- | --- | --- | --- | --- | --- | --- | --- |
| BC | BANK CLUB | EC | ERROR CORRECTION | MD | MAIL DEPOSIT | RT | RETURNED CHECK |
| CR | DEPOSIT OR CREDIT | FC | FINANCE CHARGE | MP | MANUAL PAYMENT | SC | SERVICE CHARGE |
| DC | DEPOSIT CORRECTION | GA | GENERATED ADVANCE | OD | OVERDRAWN | TR | TRANSFER |
| DD | DIRECT DEPOSIT | | | | | | |

Figure 4-2   *A monthly bank statement. (Source: Texas Bank of Austin.)*

Contracts frequently call for payment by certified check. A ***certified check*** is one signed by the drawer and made payable to the payee in the same way any other check is drawn; however, the drawer takes the check to his or her bank and asks to have it "certified." The cashier or some other employee of the bank takes the check to the bank's bookkeeping department, and the amount of the check is subtracted from the balance of the drawer's account. The bank employee then stamps the check "certified." The bank is substituting its credit for that of the drawer, so that even if the drawer attempts subsequently to withdraw the amount from the account, he or she cannot. Furthermore, the payee of an uncertified check may have the check certified by requesting that the bank do so. Certified checks are a means of assuring the payee that the check is good in those cases where he or she lacks confidence in the drawer.

*Certified checks*

A cashier's check is drawn by a bank on its own order to a designated payee or to his or her order. If differs from the certified check in that it is a liability of the bank, not of an individual. A person wishing to buy a cashier's check goes to the bank and pays the face value of the check which the bank will write on itself. There is a small fee for this service. The cashier's check serves the same purpose as the certified check. It gives the payee absolute assurance that the check can be converted into cash.

*Cashier's check*

However, a cashier's check can be bought from a bank by a non-depositor, whereas certified checks can be obtained only by a depositor. Some banks will sell only cashier's checks and not certified checks. Figure 4–3 shows a sample of a cashier's check.

In recent years, banks and other depository institutions have installed a fully automated twenty-four-hour-a-day teller; a machine that will accept

*Automated teller machines (ATM)*

A cashier's check. (Source: *Texas Bank of Austin.*)      Figure 4–3

deposits or allow withdrawals. A special card is issued that has a magnetic strip on the back on which the customer's bank account number has been placed. The machine is activated by placing the card in a slot and punching in a code on the keyboard. The automated teller then carries out the desired transaction. These automated teller machines are placed outside the building of the institution issuing the card and are accessible at all times. In recent years they have also been placed in shopping centers, office buildings, and other places.

*Automatic funds transfer (AFT): The sweep accounts*

In recent years many institutions have established automatic funds transfer accounts, which permit the transfer from a higher-interest-paying savings account to a lower-paying checking account, and vice versa. This permits a person to hold the bulk of his or her money in a higher-paying savings account and minimize the amount of money in a lower-paying checking account. Then as checks are written and come into the bank for clearing, the needed funds are transferred into the checking account by computer.

An agreement is made that the checking account is not to fall below a certain minimum, a minimum that will vary according to the desires and needs of the customer. When checks come in which reduce the checking account below the minimum, funds are transferred. Some institutions will also provide two-way transfers. That is, if the checking account climbs above the minimum, the computer transfers funds from it to the savings account. How often the computer sweeps the account varies from institution to institution as well as with the size of the deposits. Some are swept daily, others weekly. The various institutions charge varying fees for these services. The AFT system, then, provides overdraft protection, and is also a means of keeping most of the customer's deposits in higher interest-bearing accounts.

*Automatic (computer-assisted) payment of bills*

In those cases where the customer has a regular monthly bill of a uniform size (like a mortgage or rent payment) he or she may authorize the payee to write a draft on the checking account on a certain day.

More recently some banks and savings and loan associations have gone one step further and have developed computer-assisted check writing and bill payment systems. Sometimes these are also tied in with the automatic funds transfer system discussed above, and hence most of the individual's funds can be kept in an interest-bearing savings account until the bills are due. The customer has access to the institution's computer by telephone, and checks are generated by the computer and mailed to the desired recipient upon punching the correct sequence of numbers on the telephone.

*Electronic debit*

Similar to the automatic payment of bills is the electronic debit. Under this system a computer pays the customer's bills automatically at the time of a purchase, usually through the use of a debit card. A debit card, unlike a credit card, transfers funds immediately and automatically, and no check need ever be written. The debit card is discussed in greater detail in the next chapter.

What would happen to a depositor's money if an institution should fail? *Deposit safety* In nearly all cases depositors are protected against such possibilities. The Federal Deposit Insurance Corporation (FDIC), a federal agency, insures deposits up to $100,000 against such loss. Virtually all banks in the United States are insured by the FDIC. Savings and loan associations, credit unions, and mutual savings banks have the same insurance, either with the FDIC or with a similar U.S. government agency. Only a few institutions have chosen not to have this deposit insurance. All insured institutions have metal signs indicating that they have insurance in prominent places or near the tellers' counters. If an insured bank should fail depositors would be reimbursed by an agency of the U.S. government. Even if an institution is robbed or burns down, depositors do not lose their money because depository institutions carry private insurance against losses from such risks.

A married couple may have insurance covering a total of $500,000 per institution—$100,000 deposited in the wife's name, $100,000 in the husband's name, $100,000 held jointly, and $100,000 in a qualified revocable trust in the wife's name with the husband the beneficiary and another such trust in the husband's name with the wife the beneficiary.[3] Table 4–1 shows the insuring agencies for the various depository institutions.

There are a number of other services provided by depository institutions,[4] including: (1) accepting savings accounts, (2) selling travelers' checks, (3) providing safety deposit boxes, and (4) providing trustee services (discussed in greater detail in a later chapter). **OTHER SERVICES PROVIDED BY DEPOSITORY INSTITUTIONS**

While savings deposits are discussed in greater detail in Chapter 13 on *Savings accounts* thrift institutions, a few words about them are in order here. Savings accounts are not as liquid as checking accounts and consist, in general, of funds that can be invested by the banks for the long run.[5] For this

---

3. The same type of arrangement may be set up by both the husband and wife with each of their children. Hence it is possible for a single family's insured deposits to exceed one million dollars in a single institution. Moreover, they can make such an arrangement with each of the thousands of institutions in the U.S.

4. Loans are not included in this discussion. These institutions make all kinds of loans, and they are discussed in a later chapter.

5. Liquidity is a relative term, but it refers to how close something is to money, i.e.,

Table 4–1    *Deposit insurance*

| Institution | Government insuring agency | Dollar amount* |
|---|---|---|
| Commercial bank | Federal Deposit Insurance Corporation (FDIC) | $100,000 |
| Credit union | Nation Credit Union Administration (NCUA) | $100,000 |
| Mutual savings bank | Federal Deposit Insurance Corporation (FDIC) | $100,000 |
| Savings and loan association | Federal Deposit Insurance Corporation (FDIC)** | $100,000 |

*The maximum dollar amount of insurance is per depositor per institution. Since there are thousands of insured institutions in the U.S., no one needs to keep deposits in any uninsured institution. See the footnote on the previous page which explains how the insurance applies to each deposit and not to each depositor and how a married couple may have several insured accounts.

**In 1990 the law was changed and the FDIC now insures all S & L deposits using a newly-established special fund (the Savings Association Insurance Fund—SAIF), which replaced the former Federal Savings and Loan Insurance Fund (FSLIC) as the insuring agency.

reason institutions pay higher interest on savings than on checking deposits and do not assess service fees, as is often the case on checking accounts.

There are a number of different savings deposits with which you should be familiar. First, there is the passbook savings account, which up until a few years ago was the major savings deposit. While withdrawals may be made from it at any time—hence, it is highly liquid—it is not as liquid as a checking account because checks may not be written on it. In order to make a withdrawal from a passbook savings account, it is sometimes necessary to make a trip to the institution; although most institutions provide for withdrawals by mail and telephone.

In addition there are various savings certificates of deposit (CDs). In some cases CDs run over several years before they mature and may not be withdrawn before that time without a penalty. For this reason they are considered less liquid than passbook or checking accounts, and for this reason they also receive a higher rate of interest. They are discussed in greater detail in Chapter 13.

---

how easily and quickly it can be converted to money. While anything of value can be sold and converted into money, some things can be converted more quickly and easily than others: hence, they are more liquid. Money is the most liquid commodity of all.

There are also several other specialized savings accounts not yet discussed, and checks may be written on some of them. They may also pay a higher rate of interest than the passbook account. They too will be discussed in detail in Chapter 13 which deals with saving and investing through savings institutions.

*Money orders and travelers' checks*

Although in terms of dollar volume these instruments rank low compared with checks, money orders and travelers' checks should be mentioned briefly because some disbursements are made in this way. Money orders are a means of transmitting funds and serve much the same function as checks. There are three parties to the money order: the **payer**, who buys the money order; the **payee**, who receives it; and the **drawee**, which is the institution ordered to make the payment. One such institution is the U. S. Post Office. Postal money orders, which are purchased for a small fee from any United States Post Office, permit only one endorsement and are collected by presentation at either a post office or a commercial bank. Although postal money orders are very safe, they are not as convenient to use in paying bills as checks because they require a trip to the post office. In recent years, other institutions—such as banks, savings and loan associations, and even some convenience stores and major food chains—have begun to sell money orders.

The money orders sold by these institutions are not considered quite as safe as those issued by the post office and hence are not as convenient a means of payment. The money orders issued by the post office are an obligation of the U.S. government. As such they are universally acceptable. The money orders issued by other institutions are usually accepted but sometimes not until they have cleared through a bank.

Travelers' checks were at one time issued only by the American Express Company and by Thomas Cook Company, both private corporations. They are issued in much the same manner as money orders; the basic difference between the two is that the express money order can pass from hand to hand by continuous endorsement. Traveler's checks are sold by many depository institutions, most travel agencies, and at the offices of the American Express Company, which can be found in any large city. They come in denominations of $10, $20, $50, $100, and $500. The fee charged is $1 per $100 of checks purchased. They are often used by people who travel, since they are universally known and accepted almost everywhere just like money itself. They are very safe because they must be endorsed before they can be exchanged. If they are lost or stolen, the original issuer will replace them. The checks are numbered, and the buyer should make a separate copy of these numbers since they will be needed if a lost or stolen claim is to be filed. The American Express Company has offices in most foreign countries, and their checks are widely accepted abroad.

In recent years a number of competitors (mostly large city banks) have entered this field. The Bank of America now has its own negotiable and nearly universally accepted travelers' checks. The First National City Bank of New York and a number of other large city banks now also provide this service. These travelers' checks are sold to the public nationally by banks and travel agencies having ties to the issuing banks. The purchase and use conditions of the American Express travelers' checks also apply to these competitors' checks.

*Safety deposit box*   Safety deposit boxes are heavy steel boxes inside a special walk-in vault. The vault door is locked when the bank is closed. Inside the walk-in vault are individual boxes, each with its own separate lock, that may be rented by the bank's customers. These boxes come in several sizes, and rental fees vary with size and range from about five dollars to about sixty dollars per year. Each customer has a key to the box he or she rents and the bank has a second key; both are needed to open the box. Safety deposit boxes are protected by alarms and heavy metal, and are fire proof insofar as possible. All valuables that could be lost by fire or burglary and that are compact should be kept in a safety deposit box. This includes such things as stock certificates, bonds, wills, insurance policies, and savings account passbooks. Safety deposit boxes are normally sealed upon the death of an owner; therefore, it is sometimes appropriate that a married couple hold the box in a joint name. Thus, the box is accessible to the survivor upon the death of a spouse.

*Trustee services*   Commercial banks are authorized by law to perform the role of a trustee. This involves managing the assets of someone else. Sometimes a will of a deceased person will set up an estate for the heirs. The trust department of a bank can manage the estate. The bank will also look after the financial affairs of a minor. Large banks have well-established trust departments that invest billions of dollars of other people's money. The trustee service is discussed in greater detail in a later chapter. Recently, savings and loan associations have also been authorized to provide trustee services.

## SUGGESTED READINGS

*Bankers Magazine.* Boston: Warren, Gorham and Lamont. Published every other month.

Dalgaard, Bruce R. *Money, Financial Institutions and Economic Activity.* Glenview, Ill: Scott Foresman and Company, 1987.

*The Electronic Fund Transfer Commission and Finance Companies: Report of the NCFA Task Force.* Washington, D.C.: National Consumer Finance Association.

*Electronic Fund Transfers: Current Legal Developments,* New York: Practicing Law Institute.

*Finance Facts Yearbook.* Washington, D.C.: Research Services Division, National Consumer Finance Association. Annual publication.

Garcia, F. L. *How to Analyze a Bank Statement.* Boston: Bankers Publishing. 1985.

Hutchinson, Harry D. *Money, Banking, and the U.S. Economy.* Englewood Cliffs, N.J.: Prentice Hall 1988.

*Journal of Bank Research.* Published quarterly by the Bank Administration Institute, 303 South Northwest Highway, Park Ridge, Ill.

*Money and Credit Management Education: A Descriptive Catalogue of Educational Materials for the Classroom Teacher or Counselor.* Washington, D. C.: National Consumer Finance Association.

"Money, Master or Servant." New York: The Federal Reserve Bank of New York.

Money and Your Marriage. Washington, D.C.: Educational Services Division, National Consumer Finance Association.

"Monitor, A Summary of Current Research in Consumer and Mortgage Credit," West Lafayette, Ind.: Credit Research Center, Krannert School of Management, Purdue University. Semimonthly report.

# 5 Consumer credit

**HIGHLIGHTS**　　　In order to provide a fundamental understanding of consumer credit and how it is used, this chapter discusses the following:

1　The various types of consumer credit
2　How credit is established
3　Why consumers borrow
4　The benefits and disadvantages of consumer credit
5　How to calculate the dollar amount and the interest rate on consumer credit
6　Where consumer credit may be obtained
7　Credit cards
8　A number of other things a person should know about consumer credit
9　The financial documents that accompany consumer loans

## INTRODUCTION

Financial planners evaluate the income and debt of clients in considering barriers to and opportunities for achieving client goals, and therefore should be familiar with consumer credit issues. For most of the things that can be purchased by consumers, there are a number of choices as to the best method of payment. In the case of such items as food, clothing, and monthly bills, payments are generally made using the checking account discussed in the previous chapter. However, for larger items, such as automobiles, consumer credit may be used to buy them on the installment plan. In this chapter we will examine the relevant issues associated with using credit to finance consumer transactions.

## THE FUNDAMENTALS OF CONSUMER CREDIT

Why do people buy on the installment plan? It would be cheaper to pay cash for all items because interest and service charges would be eliminated. Interest costs are also incurred when you borrow money at a bank in order to buy an item. Why do most people not save enough money through a budget to pay cash for large items like cars or household furniture? They are impatient. The money for a car would probably take several years to save. Some people, even if they had a budget, would never be able to save enough to pay cash for a car. So they go into debt, buy the car, and then engage in a negative form of savings when liquidating the debt.

To be sure, some people's incomes are so high that they can easily pay cash for any purchase and this group borrows little money. At the other extreme are the very low-income groups who are unable to borrow much money because their credit ratings are such that lenders are hesitant to lend to them. The great bulk of consumer credit, as it is called, is extended to the middle class, those whose incomes are high enough to give them a good credit rating and enable them to borrow, but too low to allow them to pay cash.

### The classification of consumer credit

Consumer credit is credit extended to individuals for the purchase of final consumer items. Consumer credit is sometimes classified into sales credit and loan credit. **Sales credit** is extended by a merchant, and the person gets goods and promises to pay later. **Loan credit** is extended by a financial institution, and the person gets money (credit) with which to buy something and must then repay the loan. A second classification is perhaps superior; it is used by the Federal Reserve Board and consists of (1) installment credit and (2) noninstallment credit. Most of the credit extended by merchants is installment credit. Financial institutions make both installment loans and what is referred to as noninstallment single repayment loans.

In addition, consumer credit is extended through the use of credit cards. Credit card credit is classified as installment credit, even though many people liquidate their bill every month when due.

Installment credit consists of all credit extended to individuals that is to be repaid in two or more installments. It can be broken down into the type of product that it finances, such as:

**1.** Automobile loans
**2.** Revolving charge accounts (credit cards)
**3.** Mobile homes
**4.** Other

Credit extended for the purchase of autos is the largest single category. Most automobiles sold in the United States are financed through the use of installment credit. Revolving consumer credit is that which is extended through the use of credit cards. The balance due on most credit cards need never be fully liquidated; only a certain proportion of the principal and the interest need be paid each month when billed. Credit cards finance a wide variety of goods such as gasoline, clothing, and some household items.

Credit extended for the purchase of mobile homes is self-explanatory. Most of this credit is extended by commercial banks and finance companies, but in some states savings and loan associations also make it available.

Other consumer credit finances all other durable goods such as television sets, household appliances, home improvements, and other items. It also includes personal loans which may be made to individuals to purchase other goods and services, even a vacation. Table 5–1 shows these classifications, the dollar amounts, and the institutions that extended the credit, over the past few years. Figure 5–1 shows the relative shares of the major consumer lenders, and Figure 5–2 shows the types of installment debt by major types.

Noninstallment credit consists primarily of single payment loans and service credit. It also, however, consists of those few charge accounts in which the entire sum charged is due and payable at the end of each month.

Substantial interest savings may be available to a consumer who borrows if he or she agrees to repay the loan, together with interest, in one lump sum at a specific future time. The major reason why a person can obtain a much lower rate on a noninstallment-type consumer loan is because the lender incurs fewer bookkeeping, record keeping, and collection costs. If one borrows from an insurance company on a noninstallment basis, the annual percentage rate may be about 8 percent. If the individual then sets aside a sum every week or month in a passbook savings account, he or she will earn about 5 percent for a net cost of about 3 percent. A single repayment loan from a bank, savings and loan association, mutual savings bank, or credit union will cost about 13 to

Table 5–1   *Source: Federal Reserve Bulletin, Feb. 1991, Board of Governors of the Federal Reserve System, p. A39.*

**CONSUMER INSTALLMENT CREDIT Total Outstanding and Net Change[1]**

Millions of dollars, amounts outstanding, end of period

| Holder and type of credit | 1989 | 1990 | 1991 | | | | | | | | | |
| --- | --- | --- | --- | --- | --- | --- | --- | --- | --- | --- | --- | --- |
| | | | Feb. | Mar. | Apr. | May | June | July | Aug. | Sept.r | Oct. | |
| | | | Seasonally adjusted | | | | | | | | | |
| 1 Total | 718,863 | 735,102 | 732,762 | 732,442 | 733,621 | 732,289 | 730,591 | 729,962 | 729,108 | 729,151 | 729,953 | |
| 2 Automobile | 290,676 | 284,585 | 282,626 | 280,689 | 279,746 | 276,494 | 274,496 | 273,565 | 271,906 | 270,223 | 270,051 | |
| 3 Revolving | 199,082 | 220,110 | 221,556 | 224,817 | 225,994 | 227,301 | 227,737 | 228,199 | 229,453 | 232,070 | 233,412 | |
| 4 Mobile home | 22,471 | 20,919 | 20,200 | 20,123 | 20,098 | 19,796 | 19,907 | 19,615 | 19,495 | 18,892 | 18,764 | |
| 5 Other | 206,633 | 209,487 | 208,379 | 206,813 | 207,782 | 208,697 | 208,451 | 208,582 | 208,253 | 207,966 | 207,725 | |
| | | | Not seasonally adjusted | | | | | | | | | |
| 6 Total | 730,901 | 748,300 | 729,264 | 725,462 | 727,907 | 727,717 | 728,023 | 727,754 | 731,531 | 732,183 | 730,359 | |
| *By major holder* | | | | | | | | | | | | |
| 7 Commercial banks | 342,770 | 347,466 | 339,282 | 335,754 | 336,425 | 334,746 | 333,442 | 334,273 | 335,662 | 335,509 | 335,403 | |
| 8 Finance companies | 140,832 | 137,450 | 133,021 | 131,552 | 133,462 | 134,045 | 133,903 | 134,120 | 135,509 | 132,471 | 131,778 | |
| 9 Credit unions | 93,114 | 92,911 | 91,131 | 90,772 | 91,413 | 91,549 | 91,924 | 92,017 | 92,843 | 93,305 | 93,388 | |
| 10 Retailers | 44,154 | 43,552 | 38,864 | 38,497 | 37,817 | 36,782 | 36,702 | 36,392 | 37,296 | 37,281 | 37,359 | |
| 11 Savings institutions | 57,253 | 45,616 | 43,875 | 42,491 | 41,707 | 40,764 | 39,827 | 39,012 | 37,893 | 37,036 | 35,774 | |
| 12 Gasoline companies | 3,935 | 4,822 | 4,404 | 4,296 | 4,357 | 4,507 | 4,591 | 4,712 | 4,857 | 4,753 | 4,529 | |
| 13 Pools of securitized assets[2] | 48,843 | 76,483 | 78,687 | 82,100 | 82,726 | 85,324 | 87,634 | 87,228 | 87,471 | 91,828 | 92,128 | |
| *By major type of credit[3]* | | | | | | | | | | | | |
| 14 Automobile | 290,705 | 284,813 | 279,913 | 277,798 | 277,508 | 275,582 | 275,018 | 274,222 | 274,190 | 273,358 | 272,130 | |
| 15 Commercial banks | 126,288 | 126,259 | 124,745 | 123,411 | 122,710 | 121,631 | 121,605 | 121,319 | 120,577 | 119,730 | 119,276 | |
| 16 Finance companies | 82,721 | 74,396 | 70,287 | 69,233 | 70,500 | 69,689 | 70,304 | 70,444 | 71,571 | 69,853 | 69,364 | |
| 17 Pools of securitized assets[2] | 18,235 | 24,537 | 26,872 | 27,755 | 26,875 | 27,085 | 26,039 | 25,609 | 25,071 | 26,812 | 26,803 | |
| 18 Revolving | 210,310 | 232,370 | 220,714 | 221,400 | 222,627 | 224,301 | 225,596 | 226,145 | 229,224 | 231,281 | 231,615 | |
| 19 Commercial banks | 130,811 | 132,433 | 125,673 | 124,619 | 126,009 | 126,047 | 124,106 | 124,645 | 125,787 | 125,524 | 126,235 | |
| 20 Retailers | 39,583 | 39,029 | 34,509 | 34,179 | 33,513 | 32,458 | 32,381 | 32,076 | 32,962 | 32,964 | 33,055 | |
| 21 Gasoline companies | 3,935 | 4,822 | 4,404 | 4,296 | 4,357 | 4,507 | 4,591 | 4,712 | 4,857 | 4,753 | 4,529 | |
| 22 Pools of securitized assets[2] | 23,477 | 44,335 | 44,451 | 46,722 | 47,116 | 49,667 | 52,897 | 53,094 | 54,017 | 56,438 | 56,290 | |
| 23 Mobile home | 22,240 | 20,666 | 20,362 | 20,030 | 20,052 | 19,721 | 19,875 | 19,639 | 19,468 | 18,996 | 18,847 | |
| 24 Commercial banks | 9,112 | 9,763 | 9,730 | 9,632 | 9,565 | 9,386 | 9,652 | 9,552 | 9,534 | 9,614 | 9,600 | |
| 25 Finance companies | 4,716 | 5,252 | 5,330 | 5,328 | 5,573 | 5,595 | 5,652 | 5,669 | 5,700 | 5,300 | 5,358 | |
| 26 Other | 207,646 | 210,451 | 208,275 | 206,234 | 207,720 | 208,113 | 207,534 | 207,748 | 208,649 | 208,548 | 207,767 | |
| 27 Commercial banks | 76,559 | 79,011 | 79,134 | 78,092 | 78,141 | 77,682 | 78,079 | 78,757 | 79,764 | 80,641 | 80,292 | |
| 28 Finance companies | 53,395 | 57,801 | 57,404 | 56,991 | 57,388 | 58,761 | 57,947 | 58,007 | 58,238 | 57,318 | 57,056 | |
| 29 Retailers | 4,571 | 4,523 | 4,355 | 4,318 | 4,304 | 4,324 | 4,321 | 4,316 | 4,334 | 4,317 | 4,304 | |
| 30 Pools of securitized assets[2] | 7,131 | 7,611 | 7,364 | 7,603 | 8,735 | 8,572 | 8,698 | 8,525 | 8,383 | 8,578 | 9,035 | |

1. The Board's series on amounts of credit covers most short- and intermediate-term credit extended to individuals that is scheduled to be repaid (or has the option of repayment) in two or more installments.
Data in this table also appear in the Board's G.19 (421) monthly statistical release. For ordering address, see inside front cover.

2. Outstanding balances of pools upon which securities have been issued: these balances are no longer carried on the balance sheets of the loan originator.
3. Totals include estimates for certain holders for which only consumer credit totals are available.

15 percent depending upon the size of the loan and the borrower's credit rating and current interest rate. This amounts to a net cost of about 8 to 10 percent if a passbook savings account is used to budget the repayment. It should be noted that in order to borrow from many lenders on a noninstallment basis, the borrower's credit rating must be better than that of many installment borrowers.

## Service credit

Service credit is that which is extended by professional practitioners and some establishments such as hospitals. Because of the growing use of medical insurance this type of credit is not as important as formerly, but

## CONSUMER INSTALLMENT CREDIT
### MAJOR HOLDERS
SEASONALLY ADJUSTED, END OF QUARTER

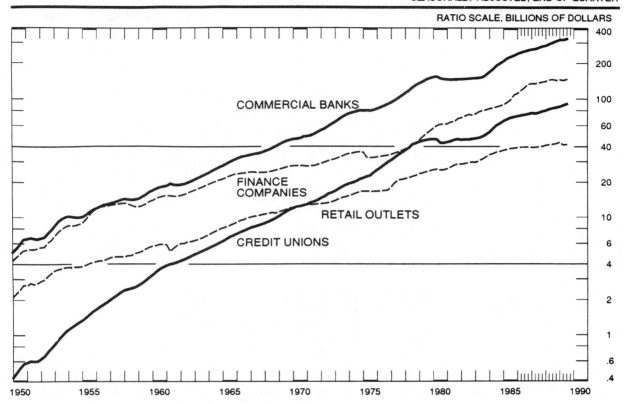

Relative shares of the major consumer lenders. (Source: 1989 Historical Chart Book, Board of Governors of the Federal Reserve System, p. 67.)    Figure 5–1

it includes unpaid medical and dental bills and moneys owed to hospitals or to the accountant who prepared the individual's tax returns. The amounts owed to utilities after deducting deposits are also part of the statistics of service credit. Figure 5–3 shows how total consumer install-ment debt has risen over the last few years.

**Secured and unsecured loans**

Loans to consumers may be secured or unsecured. If the loan is secured, usually that which is financed is pledged as collateral, such as an automobile or household furniture. This is accomplished by having the borrower give a security agreement to the lender. (See the end of the chapter for an example of a security agreement.) An unsecured loan is called a signature loan; no collateral is pledged, and the borrower has

CONSUMER INSTALLMENT CREDIT
MAJOR TYPES
SEASONALLY ADJUSTED, END OF QUARTER

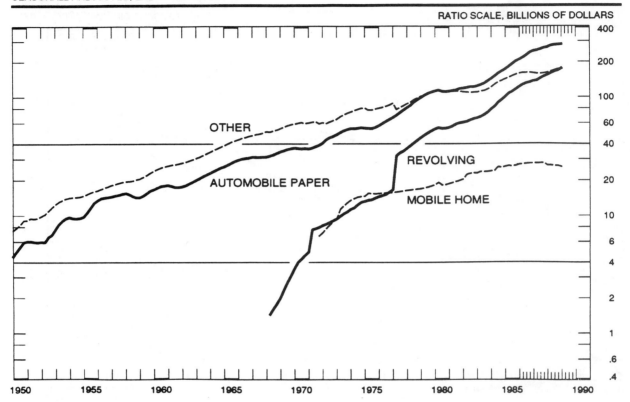

Figure 5–2   Consumer installment credit: Major types. Seasonally adjusted, end of quarter. (Source: 1989 Historical Chart Book, Board of Governors of the Federal Reserve System, p. 66.)

a good enough credit rating to obtain the loan by merely signing a promissory note to repay it.

Sometimes a borrower will pledge other assets as security such as marketable bonds or stock. In such a case the risk to the lender is reduced substantially because if the lender defaults on the loan, the securities may be sold and the proceeds used to liquidate the loan. Therefore, the interest rate charged is lower. Or if an individual borrows from a financial institution in which he or she has a savings account, pledging it as security may lower the interest rate.

*Establishing credit*     Lenders' willingness to extend credit is based on their appraisal of the potential borrower's credit-worthiness; that is, how much of a credit risk is he or she? This in turn is based on their appraisal of the ability to

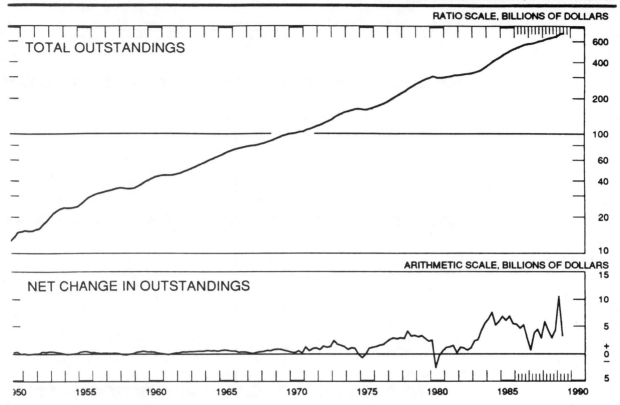

# CONSUMER INSTALLMENT CREDIT
## TOTAL
### SEASONALLY ADJUSTED, END OF QUARTER

RATIO SCALE, BILLIONS OF DOLLARS

TOTAL OUTSTANDINGS

600
400
200
100
60
40
20
10

ARITHMETIC SCALE, BILLIONS OF DOLLARS

NET CHANGE IN OUTSTANDINGS

15
10
5
+
0
−
5

1950  1955  1960  1965  1970  1975  1980  1985  1990

*Consumer installment credit: Total. Seasonally adjusted, quarterly averages. (Source: 1989 Historical Chart Book, Board of Governors of the Federal Reserve System, p. 65.)*   Figure 5–3

repay; and the past credit repayment is one of the factors lenders take into account. However, the following other factors are considered as well: income, savings, other debts if any, and net worth of the borrower.

Whether one is going to open a charge account or apply for any other type of installment loan, one must make an application for credit. The credit application is a request for information concerning place of employment, address, size of income, bank account, assets and liabilities, and whether or not one has ever had credit (see Figure 5–4). From this information, the credit investigation is made.

*The credit (or loan) application*

After one has applied for credit, the information is generally forwarded to a local credit bureau for verification. Every credit bureau maintains

*The credit bureau's report*

# UNIVERSITY FEDERAL CREDIT UNION

P.O. Box 4069
4611 Guadalupe
Austin, Texas 78765
(512) 467-8080

Medical Branch
428 Postoffice Street
Galveston, Texas 77550
(409) 765-9999

**NOTICE:** Married applicants may apply for a separate account. Check the box indicating the type of credit you are applying for:
☐ **Individual Credit:** 1) Complete applicant section if you are relying only on your own income and assets to establish credit. 2) Complete other applicant section providing information about your spouse or former spouse if you reside in a community property state (AZ, CA, ID, LA, NM, TX, WA, WI) or if you are relying on alimony, child support or separate maintenance payments to establish credit.
☐ **Joint Credit:** 1) Complete applicant and co-applicant section providing information about you and the other party.

| Amount Requested $ | Purpose and Collateral |
|---|---|

| Applicant | ■ Co-Applicant   ■ Spouse   ■ Guarantor |
|---|---|

| Name | Name |
|---|---|

| Account Number | Drivers License Number | Social Security Number | Account Number | Drivers License Number | Social Security Number |
|---|---|---|---|---|---|

| Birth Date | Home Phone ( ) | Business Phone ( ) | Birth Date | Home Phone ( ) | Business Phone ( ) |
|---|---|---|---|---|---|

| Present Address (Street, City, State, Zip) | Years at this address ☐ Own ☐ Rent | Present Address (Street, City, State, Zip) | Years at this address ☐ Own ☐ Rent |
|---|---|---|---|

| Previous address (Street, City, State, Zip) (if at present address less than 5 years) | Years at this address ☐ Own ☐ Rent | Previous address (Street, City, State, Zip) (if at present address less than 5 years) | Years at this address ☐ Own ☐ Rent |
|---|---|---|---|

Complete for joint credit, secured credit or if you live in a community property state:
☐ Married   ☐ Separated   ☐ Unmarried (Single, Divorced, Widowed)

Complete for joint credit, secured credit or if you live in a community property state:
☐ Married   ☐ Separated   ☐ Unmarried (Single, Divorced, Widowed)

| Number of Dependents other than listed by Co-Applicant (exclude self) | Ages | Number of Dependents other than listed by Applicant (exclude self) | Ages |
|---|---|---|---|

| Employment and Income Information | Employment and Income Information |
|---|---|

| Name and address of employer | Name and address of employer |
|---|---|

| Position | Supervisor | Position | Supervisor |
|---|---|---|---|

| Starting Date | Self Employed ☐ Yes ☐No | Type of Business | Starting Date | Self Employed ☐ Yes ☐No | Type of Business |
|---|---|---|---|---|---|

| Military: Is duty station transfer expected during next year? ☐ Yes ☐ No | Where | Military: Is duty station transfer expected during next year? ☐ Yes ☐ No | Where |
|---|---|---|---|

NOTICE: Alimony, child support, or separate maintenance income need not be revealed if you do not choose to have it considered.

NOTICE: Alimony, child support, or separate maintenance income need not be revealed if you do not choose to have it considered.

| Employment income ☐ Gross ☐ Net $ per | Other income $ per | Source | Employment income ☐ Gross ☐ Net $ per | Other income $ per | Source |
|---|---|---|---|---|---|

If employed in current position less than five years, complete the following:

If employed in current position less than five years, complete the following:

| Previous employer name & address | Starting date | Previous employer name & address | Starting date |
|---|---|---|---|
| | Ending date | | Ending date |

| Position | Supervisor | Position | Supervisor |
|---|---|---|---|

| These Questions Apply to Both Applicant & Co-Applicant | | | | | | | | | |
|---|---|---|---|---|---|---|---|---|---|

| If a "Yes" answer is given to a question, explain on an attached sheet | Applicant Yes | No | Co-Applicant Yes | No | If a "Yes" answer is given to a question, explain on an Attached Sheet | Applicant Yes | No | Co-Applicant Yes | No |
|---|---|---|---|---|---|---|---|---|---|
| Have you any outstanding judgments? | | | | | Is your income likely to reduce in the next two years? | | | | |
| In the last 10 years, have you been declared bankrupt or filed a petition for Chapter 13? | | | | | Are you a co-maker or co-signer on any loan? | | | | |
| Have you had property foreclosed upon or given title or deed in lieu thereof, in the last 7 years? | | | | | For whom (name of others obligated on loan): | | | | |
| Are you a party in a law suit? | | | | | To whom (name of creditor): | | | | |
| Are you other than a U.S. Citizen or Permanent Resident alien? | | | | | | | | | |

| References | | References | |
|---|---|---|---|

| Name & address of nearest relative not living with you | Relationship | Name & address of nearest relative not living with you | Relationship |
|---|---|---|---|
| | Home phone | | Home phone |
| Name & address of personal friend—not a relative | Home phone | Name & address of personal friend—not a relative | Home phone |

**Continued on Reverse Side**

Figure 5–4    *Loan application*

records containing information on many individuals, much of it obtained from the office of the clerk of the county in which one lives. For example, the fact that any judgments have been recorded against one is entered in the record. In addition, home ownership and all existing mortgages and recorded bills of sale are included.

# Consumer credit  77

**Assets**

| A-Applicant / C-Co-Applicant | Name of Depository | Address | Balance |
|---|---|---|---|
| Checking Account(s) | | | |
| Savings Account(s) | | | |
| Certificate(s) of Deposit | | | |
| IRA | | | |
| Annuities | | | |
| Stocks/Bonds | | | |
| Life Insurance | | | |
| Other | | | |
| Other | | | |
| Other | | | |
| Other | | | |

| Auto(s) Owned | Make | Model | Year |
|---|---|---|---|

**Outstanding Debts**
(List everything-attach other sheets if necessary.)

| A-Applicant / C-Co-Applicant | Creditor Name & Address | Account Number | Present Balance | Monthly Payment | Number of Months Past Due |
|---|---|---|---|---|---|
| Rent | | | | | |
| Home Mortgage (Market Value $) | | | | | |
| Second Mortgage | | | | | |
| Real Estate Other Than Home | | | | | |
| Auto Loan (Make, Year) | | | | | |
| Auto Loan (Make, Year) | | | | | |
| UFCU | | | | | |
| Other Credit Union | | | | | |
| Finance Company | | | | | |
| Credit Card | | | | | |
| Credit Card | | | | | |
| Credit Card | | | | | |
| Credit Card | | | | | |
| Alimony | | | | | |
| Other | | | | | |
| Other | | | | | |
| Other | | | | | |
| Other | | | | | |

List any names under which credit has previously been received          **Totals**

I (we) certify that all information contained in this application is correct to the best of my (our) knowledge and I (we) have disclosed all outstanding obligations currently owed. I (we) agree to give the Credit Union authorization to check on my (our) credit; employment history; obtain a credit report; and to answer questions about our credit experience with you. I (we) understand that it may be a federal crime punishable by fine or imprisonment (or both) to knowingly make any false statements concerning any of the above facts as applicable under the provisions of the United States Criminal Code.

| Applicant's Signature | Date | Co-Applicant's Signature | Date |
|---|---|---|---|
| X | Seal | X | Seal |

**Do Not Write Below—For Credit Union Use Only**
**Credit Committee/Loan Officer Action**

**Loan Officer:**  Date

☐ I approve the advance as submitted.
☐ Advance referred to CC.
☐ Advance rejected (where permissible.)
☐ Counter-offer will be made, if accepted advance approved.

| Secured $ | Unsecured $ | Line of Credit $ | Overdraft Protection $ |
|---|---|---|---|
| Reason loan referred to Credit Committee | | Loan Officer Signature | |

**Credit Committee:**  Date    Describe Counter-Offer ►

☐ We approve the advance as submitted.
☐ We reject the advance as submitted.
☐ Counter-offer will be made, if accepted advance approved.

Specific reason(s) for rejection

| Outside information considered | ☐ Yes ☐ No | Describe |
|---|---|---|

| Signature | Date | Signature | Date | Signature | Date |
|---|---|---|---|---|---|

☐ ECOA Notice and Reason for Rejection set or delivered on   | Date | Signature

Credit bureaus also keep records of all previous credit extended, going back generally seven years. Credit bureaus are the "middle men;" they receive information from all merchants and institutions that extend credit, store it, and then sell it to any legitimate third party. A legitimate third party is anyone entering into a business transaction involving credit with the person on whom a credit report is requested. If the person requesting credit has established credit elsewhere locally, generally a phone call to the credit bureau is all that is necessary. The bureau will give the merchant the necessary information over the phone, and the fee for this service is only a few dollars. If the person requesting credit is newly arrived in town, it may be necessary for the credit bureau to telephone a bureau in some other town. In such cases, the cost of a credit report can grow quickly.

When a credit bureau receives a request from a merchant or lending institution, it will pass on what information it has gathered; but the bureau usually will not assign a credit rating such as poor, fair, good, or excellent. Generally, the information the credit bureau will pass on includes the following:

1. The person's place of employment
2. Length of time with employer
3. Position with the firm
4. Income
5. Husband or wife's income, if any
6. All credit extended over the past seven years and the date it was extended
7. The dollar amount of the extension
8. How the loan was paid off (whether in accordance with the agreement)
9. What kind of security, if any, was required on past loans
10. Whether the person rents or owns his or her own home
11. Judgments, if any, recorded against the person
12. Bankruptcies, if any, that the person has filed

In the case of a young person requesting credit for the first time, no record exists and the credit bureau cannot help as much. The merchant must make a decision based on the person's place of employment, position, income, bank accounts, and any other information the merchant can obtain. Generally, if the person has a responsible position and is not asking for more credit than his or her income warrants, it will be granted. Then a person begins to build a "track record;" if he or she repays credit in accordance with the agreement, these regular payments will be reported by the merchant and recorded by the credit bureau.

Generally, a credit investigation is made only the first time one applies for credit. Once one has used credit, one will have established what is known as a "line of credit." The lending institution and merchants keep their own records and will extend credit up to a maximum amount almost routinely. In such cases, one may still have to fill out an application form but will not have to wait for a credit investigation.

*Why consumers borrow*

Consumers borrow or use consumer credit for different reasons, just as savers save for different reasons. One individual may save to pay her son's tuition, while another may have to borrow to pay the tuition. Some people pay cash while on vacation; others use credit cards.

1.  *High cost of durables.* A main reason for the use of consumer credit is the high unit cost of durable consumer goods. A **consumer durable** is a good having a relatively long life, such as a television set, a household appliance, or an automobile. Of the $700 billion consumer debt in 1990, over one-third resulted from the extension of automobile credit. The cheapest and possibly the best way to buy this type of durable good would, of course, be to save and pay cash. But to save, one must abstain from present consumption. Many consumers find this to be difficult. Suppose, for example, we planned to save to buy an auto priced at $14,000; we would have to defer the use of the car and put aside, say, $2,800 per year for five years before we would be able to buy the car. For most people, saving $2,800 per year for five years for the purpose of buying a car is a formidable task. So when it comes to high unit cost durable goods, most people buy on time. The product may be used immediately instead of being deferred until a future date and perhaps not being obtained at all. For this current use, many people are willing to pay interest.

2.  *Financial emergencies.* Unfortunately, many people frequently are forced to borrow because of unforeseen emergencies. Unusually high medical and dental bills not completely covered by insurance are examples. Noninsured flood damage to a home is another. There are dozens of types of emergencies and other reasons for which consumer loans may be necessary.

3.  *Financing vacations.* Many people finance their vacations with consumer credit. Not only do they make extensive use of credit cards while on their trips, but often they borrow money at a financial institution to spend at their destination and to finance their transportation costs.

There are some benefits but also some possible dangers stemming from the use of consumer credit.

*Benefits and dangers of consumer credit*

1.  *Obtaining goods more quickly.* As noted above, consumer credit will enable the borrowers to consume certain items more quickly than otherwise would be possible. If a person goes into debt to buy an automobile, he or she is then forced to save out of future income to repay the loan. Without consumer credit the person may end up with neither savings nor the car. With consumer credit he or she at least has the car.

2.  *Benefits to society.* Society as a whole may benefit from consumer credit provided that those granting it do not overdo it. Credit extension may lead to increased demand and hence increased

production of goods and services, and help to maintain full employment. The extension of consumer credit can lead to a lower unit cost of goods. For example, as a result of increased effective demand created by the extension of credit, certain firms are led to large-scale production. Up to a point, large-scale production brings about certain efficiencies that result in lower costs; and in a competitive economy these savings are frequently passed on to the consumer.

3.  *Higher cost.* One argument against extension of consumer credit is that the resultant interest costs actually reduce the amount of consumer goods persons might have purchased had they saved the money in the first place. As has been previously pointed out, however, it may be that the cost of borrowing is offset because credit extension increases sales and consequently has a tendency to lower unit costs as a result of mass production. This depends to some extent on the amount of competition involving a particular product, and on whether any cost savings are actually passed on to the consumer in the form of lower prices.

4.  *Getting in over one's head.* When an individual borrows money, he or she takes on an obligation of making a fixed payment on a time schedule. This payment is interest and repayment of the principal. Such a fixed payment comes off the top of the budget before the remainder of the individual's income is allocated among alternative wants. How large a fixed payment an individual can accept is determined largely by his or her income. But if credit is easy to obtain and a person lacks discipline, it is possible that he or she will have so many debts that it becomes impossible to meet the fixed monthly payments because they take too large a portion of income. Those who miss a payment or two may have their car or furniture repossessed. Worse still, they may be forced into bankruptcy. This is not really a danger of consumer credit, but rather a danger that comes from abusing consumer credit. It is the unwise and excessive use of consumer credit that gets people in over their heads. Frequently, this may be just as much the lender's fault as the borrower's. Consumer credit should not be feared, but it should be used only when needed, after careful planning, and when one can take on the additional fixed payment required.

5.  *Convenience.* Rather than writing many checks, a consumer can use his/her credit card and write one check to pay off the credit card. In addition, credit cards may help in timing of expenses versus timing of inflows. For example, a person is paid semi-monthly, but has a big outflow, such as a mortgage payment following receipt of his or her first pay check; this limits cash available for other needs. However, use of the credit card for these needs "floats" cash until payment of the card, which takes place after the receipt of a second check.

It is often less costly for consumers to purchase those items of merchandise they need for cash; however, for most people, installment purchases or cash borrowing are often the alternatives. The financial planner should be aware of the costs associated with borrowing to help clients minimize expenses consistent with their goals.

*INTEREST RATES*

One of the fundamental problems of borrowing is to determine just how much interest is being charged. The borrower should be able to answer the question: What is the effective rate of interest that I must pay? What is the real cost of interest charged as a percentage of the loan?

*Interest rate calculations*

Although the mathematics of obtaining a precise answer to "How much interest am I paying?" is complex, there is a formula that will provide the approximate answer. The formula is:

$$R = \frac{2 \times m \times I}{P(n+1)} \text{ or, transposed, } I = \frac{R \times P(n+1)}{2 \times m}$$

In the above formula:

$R$ = annual interest rate in decimal form
$I$ = dollar cost of the credit
$m$ = the number of payment periods in a year
    (twelve if paying monthly and fifty-two if weekly)
$n$ = the number of payments scheduled in total
$P$ = the net amount of credit or principal advanced

At this point it is useful to distinguish between simple interest, discounted interest, add-on interest, and annual percentage rate.

In the case of **simple interest**, interest is charged only on the actual loan balance outstanding. If a person borrows $1,000 for one year at 12 percent to be paid back in one lump sum, the interest would be $120. The interest rate is:

Simple interest

$$\frac{\$120}{\$1000} = 12 \text{ percent.}$$

**Discounted interest** is paid in advance; it is deducted from the principal amount borrowed. For example, if a person borrowed $1,000 for one year discounted at 12 percent to be paid back in one lump sum, he or she would receive $880 of borrowed funds. One year later, the individual would repay $1,000; of this $120 would be interest. Hence the true rate is:

Discounted interest

$$\frac{\$120}{\$880} = 13.6 \text{ percent.}$$

*"Getting back to those interest rates, could you be a little more specific than 'it's going to cost a pretty penny?"* (Source: Permission Cartoon Features Syndicate; *from* The Wall Street Journal.)

Discounting results in a higher interest rate than does simple interest.

**Add-on interest**

Add-on interest is applied to the original balance owed even though on an installment loan the balance owed declines as the months pass and payments are made. For example, if a $1,000 loan at 12 percent is to be repaid in twelve equal monthly installments over a year, it is referred to as a 12 percent add-on loan. The so-called add-on interest must be converted to simple interest, a better measure of the true interest burden. The above-mentioned formula will approximate this conversion.

**Annual percentage rate (APR)**

The annual percentage rate (APR), which is the true actuarial interest rate, is the best (and real) measure of the interest rate. The above rate formula will convert the discounted interest rate and the add-on rate to the simple interest rate, which is, however, only an approximation of the annual percentage rate. The formula will do this whether the loan is discounted or not and whether it is an installment loan or a single repayment loan.

The formula to calculate the annual percentage rate of interest precisely is very complex. However, there are tables that will permit you to convert the add-on rate to the APR as we shall see below.

**Some examples**

Suppose that Ms. Stein borrows $1,000 at 12 percent, and must pay back $1,120 in twelve equal monthly installments of $93.33. The total cost is $120, but what is the interest rate? Substituting the figures into the formulas above:

$$
\begin{aligned}
I &= \$120 \\
m &= 12 \\
n &= 12 \\
P &= \$1,000
\end{aligned}
$$

$$R = \frac{2 \times 12 \times \$120}{\$1000 \ (12 + 1)} = \frac{2880}{13,000} = 22.15 \text{ percent}$$

As noted above, the formula only approximates the true annual percentage rate (APR).

A loan can be both discounted and repaid in installments; but the above formulas will still approximate the APR If you use the net amount of the principal advanced. If the above $1,000 installment loan had also been discounted at 12 percent, the formula would use:

$$
\begin{aligned}
I &= \$120 \\
m &= 12 \\
n &= 12 \\
P &= \$880
\end{aligned}
$$

and the result is:

$$R = \frac{2 \times m \times I}{P(n+1)} = \frac{2 \times 12 \times 120}{880 \times (12+1)} = \frac{2880}{11440} = 25.17 \text{ percent}$$

The reason why the true interest rate (APR) is so much higher than the add-on rate is because when repaying a loan on an installment basis, the add-on interest applies to (and must be paid) on the original balance throughout the entire period of the loan. When loans are repaid on the installment basis, the amount of money actually owed declines with each repayment. To calculate the true interest rate, one must take into account this declining balance; otherwise the borrower is paying interest on money even after he or she has already repaid it. The formulas discussed above do this, but to understand the logic of how interest rates work a person must think in terms of the declining balance. An illustration will make this clear.

When an individual borrows money that is repaid on an installment basis, there are three balances: an original balance, a declining balance, and an average balance. We can illustrate this system with another method of calculating the true interest rate. Remember, however, that this second method of calculating the interest rate is somewhat cruder and hence a little less accurate than the formula explained above.

Let us assume that the individual borrows $1,200 from a bank to purchase a used automobile and agrees to repay it in twelve equal monthly installments of $110. A total of $1,320 will be paid back: $120 of that total is interest (the i in the formula above). This at first glance appears to be 10 percent, and insofar as add-on interest is concerned, it is. However, while the original balance owed is $1,200, after one month the first payment is made and the loan balance now due (the declining balance) is $1,100; a month later another $100 is paid on the principal and the balance now owed is $1,000; and so on. The balance owed declines each month, as shown in Table 5–2.

Table 5—2    *Estimating interest costs*

| Original balance: The amount originally borrowed | Month | Balance | Average balance: The amount of money you actually have on the average for the full year |
|---|---|---|---|
| $1200 | 1 | $1,200 | |
| | 2 | 1,100 | |
| | 3 | 1,000 | |
| | 4 | 900 | |
| | 5 | 800 | $650 |
| | 6 | 700 | |
| | 7 | 600 | |
| | 8 | 500 | |
| | 9 | 400 | |
| | 10 | 300 | |
| | 11 | 200 | |
| | 12 | 100 | |

At the end of six months, $600 has been repaid and only $600 is now owed; the borrower is still paying 10 percent interest on the full $1,200. To calculate and pay interest monthly, take 10 percent of the declining balance and divide it by twelve to get the true interest cost at 10 percent. But to approximate the rate actually being paid, average the balance over the year (the first and last month's balance divided by two, or $650) and calculate the interest rate on it. Since interest charges are $120 and the average amount really borrowed is only $650, the interest rate is 18.46 percent.

Let us take another case, in which $1,800 is borrowed at 10 percent add-on, to be repaid in eighteen equal monthly installments. Ten percent of $1,800 is $180 per year, but since the loan is for a year and a half, an additional interest payment of $90 is called for. The total interest cost, dollar-wise, is $270. An average balance could be calculated for the first year and again for the next six months to get the true interest rate, but the formula introduced above provides us with an easier way.

$$I = \$270$$
$$m = 12$$
$$n = 18$$
$$P = \$1800$$

Thus:

$$\frac{24 \times 270}{1800 \times 19} = \frac{6480}{34200} = 18.95 \text{ percent}$$

In the past, lenders and merchants offering installment contracts found all kinds of devious ways of disguising the true interest rates. Often they would merely say, "so much down and so much per month," and the true interest cost (the i in the formula) or the net amount of credit advanced (the P in the formula) could not always be ascertained. If asked what the interest rate amounted to, lenders would often become evasive and sometimes even tell outright lies. In many cases, the borrower paid 12, 30, or 42 percent or even more without knowing it. All of this changed with the passage of the federal truth-in-lending law in 1968 (the Consumer Credit Protection Act). This law does not limit the rate that may be charged; it merely requires that the lender tell the borrowers what they are paying, both dollar wise and as a percentage of the loan. (A number of different agencies enforce truth in lending. See Chapter 6 for a complete list.) Lenders and merchants who extend credit do not work through the formulas presented above to determine the interest rates they charge. Rather they use tables that have been worked out in advance to tell the buyer the dollar amount of the finance charge and the annual percentage rate (APR) of these charges. Table 5–3 is such a table that can be used to obtain the true (APR) interest cost of any add-on rate. The various add-on rates are shown in the first column; to the right are shown the true rates for the various installment loans repaid monthly. For example, a 10 percent add-on rate is really 14.94 percent if paid back in three installments; 17.97 percent if paid back in twelve; and 17.92 percent if repaid in thirty-six.

*Interest rates on consumer loans and credit cards*

State laws set the maximum rate that may be charged on consumer credit transactions. Hence there is variation from state to state.

Some states have a number of different laws covering specific lending institutions, while others have just one or two to regulate all consumer lending. The laws also allow for different rates on different items. For example, rates on auto loans generally run from 12 to 18 percent, depending on whether a new or used car is being financed. Conversely, on very small loans for short periods of time, some states allow rates in excess of 100 percent on an annual basis. To illustrate this, consider borrowing $100 for thirty days with a fixed minimum interest charge of $10. This represents a monthly charge of 10 percent, which annualizes to 120 percent.

Credit card charges also vary somewhat depending on the issuing institution and the applicable state usury laws (which set the maximum allowable rate). Generally, interest rates on bank credit cards, such as Visa and MasterCard, run up to 1.5 percent per month.

The interest charge is assessed on any unpaid balance in the customer's account. For instance, if a credit card was used to pay for a $600 stereo but the borrower was able to pay only $200 when the bill came, a charge of $6 (i.e., [$600 – $200 × .015]) would be added to the next monthly statement. However, the interest cost could be higher than it is in the above example. Although some merchants still charge only on the unpaid balance at the end of the month, more and more of them are assessing interest on the average daily balance from billing date to

Table 5—3    *Actuarial equivalents of add-on rates. The annual add-on rate is shown as the left hand index. If this rate is applied to the original amount for the full term and the loan is repaid monthly, then the body of the table shows the actuarial rate of return on the money actually outstanding.*

| Add-on rate per year | Term months | | | | | | | |
|---|---|---|---|---|---|---|---|---|
| | 3 mo. | 6 mo. | 9 mo. | 12 mo. | 15 mo. | 18 mo. | 24 mo. | 30 mo. |
| 1.00 | 1.50 | 1.71 | 1.80 | 1.84 | 1.87 | 1.89 | 1.91 | 1.92 |
| 2.00 | 3.00 | 3.42 | 3.59 | 3.67 | 3.72 | 3.76 | 3.79 | 3.81 |
| 3.00 | 4.49 | 5.12 | 5.37 | 5.49 | 5.56 | 5.61 | 5.66 | 5.68 |
| 3.50 | 5.24 | 5.98 | 6.26 | 6.40 | 6.48 | 6.53 | 6.58 | 6.60 |
| 4.00 | 5.99 | 6.82 | 7.14 | 7.30 | 7.39 | 7.45 | 7.50 | 7.52 |
| 4.25 | 6.36 | 7.25 | 7.59 | 7.75 | 7.85 | 7.91 | 7.96 | 7.97 |
| 4.50 | 6.74 | 7.67 | 8.03 | 8.21 | 8.30 | 8.36 | 8.41 | 8.42 |
| 4.75 | 7.11 | 8.10 | 8.47 | 8.66 | 8.76 | 8.82 | 8.87 | 8.88 |
| 5.00 | 7.48 | 8.52 | 8.91 | 9.10 | 9.21 | 9.27 | 9.32 | 9.33 |
| 5.25 | 7.86 | 8.94 | 9.36 | 9.55 | 9.66 | 9.73 | 9.78 | 9.78 |
| 5.50 | 8.23 | 9.37 | 9.79 | 10.00 | 10.11 | 10.18 | 10.23 | 10.23 |
| 5.75 | 8.60 | 9.79 | 10.23 | 10.45 | 10.57 | 10.63 | 10.68 | 10.67 |
| 6.00 | 8.98 | 10.21 | 10.67 | 10.90 | 11.02 | 11.08 | 11.13 | 11.12 |
| 6.25 | 9.35 | 10.64 | 11.11 | 11.34 | 11.45 | 11.53 | 11.57 | 11.56 |
| 6.50 | 9.72 | 11.06 | 11.55 | 11.79 | 11.91 | 11.98 | 12.02 | 12.00 |
| 6.75 | 10.10 | 11.48 | 11.99 | 12.23 | 12.36 | 12.43 | 12.47 | 12.44 |
| 7.00 | 10.47 | 11.90 | 12.43 | 12.68 | 12.81 | 12.87 | 12.91 | 12.88 |
| 7.25 | 10.84 | 12.32 | 12.87 | 13.12 | 13.25 | 13.32 | 13.35 | 13.32 |
| 7.50 | 11.22 | 12.74 | 13.30 | 13.57 | 13.70 | 13.77 | 13.80 | 13.76 |
| 7.75 | 11.59 | 13.17 | 13.74 | 14.01 | 14.14 | 14.21 | 14.24 | 14.19 |
| 8.00 | 11.96 | 13.59 | 14.18 | 14.45 | 14.59 | 14.65 | 14.68 | 14.63 |
| 8.25 | 12.33 | 14.01 | 14.61 | 14.89 | 15.03 | 15.10 | 15.12 | 15.06 |
| 8.50 | 12.71 | 14.43 | 15.05 | 15.34 | 15.48 | 15.54 | 15.55 | 15.49 |
| 8.75 | 13.08 | 14.85 | 15.49 | 15.78 | 15.92 | 15.98 | 15.99 | 15.92 |
| 9.00 | 13.45 | 15.27 | 15.92 | 16.22 | 16.36 | 16.42 | 16.43 | 16.35 |
| 9.25 | 13.82 | 15.69 | 16.35 | 16.66 | 16.80 | 16.86 | 16.86 | 16.78 |
| 9.50 | 14.19 | 16.11 | 16.79 | 17.10 | 17.24 | 17.30 | 17.29 | 17.21 |
| 9.75 | 14.57 | 16.53 | 17.22 | 17.53 | 17.68 | 17.74 | 17.73 | 17.63 |
| →10.00 | 14.94 | 16.94 | 17.66 | 17.97 | 18.12 | 18.17 | 18.16 | 18.06 |
| 10.25 | 15.31 | 17.36 | 18.09 | 18.41 | 18.56 | 18.61 | 18.59 | 18.48 |
| 10.50 | 15.68 | 17.78 | 18.52 | 18.85 | 18.99 | 19.05 | 19.02 | 18.90 |
| 10.75 | 16.05 | 18.20 | 18.95 | 19.28 | 19.43 | 19.48 | 19.44 | 19.32 |
| 11.00 | 16.43 | 18.62 | 19.39 | 19.72 | 19.36 | 19.91 | 19.87 | 19.74 |
| 11.25 | 16.80 | 19.04 | 19.82 | 20.15 | 20.30 | 20.35 | 20.30 | 20.16 |
| 11.50 | 17.17 | 19.45 | 20.25 | 20.59 | 20.73 | 20.78 | 20.72 | 20.57 |
| 11.75 | 17.54 | 19.87 | 20.68 | 21.02 | 21.17 | 21.21 | 21.15 | 20.99 |
| 12.00 | 17.91 | 20.29 | 21.11 | 21.46 | 21.60 | 21.64 | 21.57 | 21.41 |
| 12.25 | 18.28 | 20.70 | 21.54 | 21.89 | 22.03 | 22.07 | 21.99 | 21.82 |
| 12.50 | 18.65 | 21.12 | 21.97 | 22.32 | 22.47 | 22.50 | 22.42 | 22.23 |
| 12.75 | 19.03 | 21.54 | 22.40 | 22.76 | 22.90 | 22.93 | 22.84 | 22.64 |
| 13.00 | 19.40 | 21.95 | 22.83 | 23.19 | 23.33 | 23.36 | 23.26 | 23.05 |
| 13.50 | 20.14 | 22.79 | 23.68 | 24.05 | 24.19 | 24.21 | 24.09 | 23.87 |
| 14.00 | 20.88 | 23.62 | 24.54 | 24.91 | 25.04 | 25.06 | 24.92 | 24.68 |
| 14.50 | 21.62 | 24.45 | 25.39 | 25.77 | 25.90 | 25.91 | 25.75 | 25.49 |
| 15.00 | 22.36 | 25.28 | 26.24 | 26.62 | 26.75 | 26.75 | 26.58 | 26.30 |
| 15.50 | 23.10 | 26.10 | 27.09 | 27.48 | 27.60 | 27.60 | 27.40 | 27.10 |
| 16.00 | 23.84 | 26.93 | 27.94 | 28.33 | 28.45 | 28.43 | 28.22 | 27.89 |
| 16.50 | 24.58 | 27.76 | 28.79 | 29.18 | 29.29 | 29.27 | 29.03 | 28.69 |
| 17.00 | 25.32 | 28.58 | 29.64 | 30.03 | 30.14 | 30.10 | 29.85 | 29.48 |
| 18.00 | 26.80 | 30.23 | 31.32 | 31.72 | 31.81 | 31.76 | 31.46 | 31.04 |
| 19.00 | 28.28 | 31.88 | 33.01 | 33.40 | 33.48 | 33.41 | 33.06 | 32.60 |
| 20.00 | 29.76 | 33.52 | 34.68 | 35.07 | 35.14 | 35.05 | 34.65 | 34.14 |

*Term-months*

| 36 mo. | 42 mo. | 48 mo. | 54 mo. | 60 mo. | 72 mo. | 84 mo. | 96 mo. | 108 mo. | 120 mo. |
|---|---|---|---|---|---|---|---|---|---|
| 1.93 | 1.93 | 1.93 | 1.94 | 1.94 | 1.94 | 1.93 | 1.93 | 1.93 | 1.92 |
| 3.82 | 3.82 | 3.82 | 3.82 | 3.82 | 3.80 | 3.79 | 3.77 | 3.75 | 3.74 |
| 5.68 | 5.68 | 5.67 | 5.66 | 5.64 | 5.61 | 5.57 | 5.54 | 5.50 | 5.46 |
| 6.60 | 6.59 | 6.58 | 6.56 | 6.54 | 6.49 | 6.44 | 6.39 | 6.34 | 6.29 |
| 7.51 | 7.50 | 7.47 | 7.45 | 7.42 | 7.36 | 7.30 | 7.23 | 7.17 | 7.11 |
| 7.96 | 7.94 | 7.92 | 7.89 | 7.86 | 7.79 | 7.72 | 7.65 | 7.58 | 7.51 |
| 8.41 | 8.39 | 8.36 | 8.33 | 8.29 | 8.22 | 8.14 | 8.06 | 7.98 | 7.91 |
| 8.86 | 8.84 | 8.80 | 8.77 | 8.72 | 8.64 | 8.55 | 8.47 | 8.38 | 8.30 |
| 9.31 | 9.28 | 9.24 | 9.20 | 9.15 | 9.06 | 8.97 | 8.87 | 8.78 | 8.69 |
| 9.76 | 9.72 | 9.68 | 9.63 | 9.58 | 9.48 | 9.37 | 9.27 | 9.17 | 9.08 |
| 10.20 | 10.16 | 10.11 | 10.06 | 10.01 | 9.89 | 9.78 | 9.67 | 9.56 | 9.46 |
| 10.64 | 10.60 | 10.54 | 10.49 | 10.43 | 10.31 | 10.18 | 10.06 | 9.95 | 9.84 |
| 11.08 | 11.03 | 10.97 | 10.91 | 10.85 | 10.72 | 10.58 | 10.46 | 10.33 | 10.21 |
| 11.52 | 11.47 | 11.40 | 11.34 | 11.27 | 11.12 | 10.98 | 10.85 | 10.71 | 10.59 |
| 11.96 | 11.90 | 11.83 | 11.76 | 11.68 | 11.53 | 11.38 | 11.23 | 11.09 | 10.96 |
| 12.39 | 12.33 | 12.25 | 12.17 | 12.09 | 11.93 | 11.77 | 11.61 | 11.47 | 11.32 |
| 12.83 | 12.76 | 12.68 | 12.59 | 12.50 | 12.33 | 12.16 | 11.99 | 11.84 | 11.69 |
| 13.26 | 13.18 | 13.10 | 13.01 | 12.91 | 12.73 | 12.55 | 12.37 | 12.21 | 12.05 |
| 13.69 | 13.61 | 13.51 | 13.42 | 13.32 | 13.12 | 12.93 | 12.75 | 12.57 | 12.41 |
| 14.12 | 14.03 | 13.93 | 13.83 | 13.72 | 13.52 | 13.31 | 13.12 | 12.94 | 12.76 |
| 14.55 | 14.45 | 14.35 | 14.24 | 14.13 | 13.91 | 13.69 | 13.49 | 13.30 | 13.12 |
| 14.97 | 14.87 | 14.76 | 14.64 | 14.53 | 14.29 | 14.07 | 13.86 | 13.66 | 13.47 |
| 15.40 | 15.29 | 15.17 | 15.05 | 14.92 | 14.68 | 14.45 | 14.23 | 14.02 | 13.82 |
| 15.82 | 15.70 | 15.58 | 15.45 | 15.32 | 15.07 | 14.82 | 14.59 | 14.37 | 14.16 |
| 16.24 | 16.12 | 15.99 | 15.85 | 15.71 | 15.45 | 15.19 | 14.95 | 14.72 | 14.51 |
| 16.66 | 16.53 | 16.39 | 16.25 | 16.11 | 15.83 | 15.56 | 15.31 | 15.07 | 14.85 |
| 17.08 | 16.94 | 16.80 | 16.65 | 16.50 | 16.21 | 15.93 | 15.67 | 15.42 | 15.19 |
| 17.50 | 17.35 | 17.20 | 17.04 | 16.89 | 16.58 | 16.29 | 16.02 | 15.77 | 15.53 |
| 17.92 | 17.76 | 17.60 | 17.44 | 17.27 | 16.96 | 16.66 | 16.38 | 16.11 | 15.86 |
| 18.33 | 18.17 | 18.00 | 17.83 | 17.66 | 17.33 | 17.02 | 16.73 | 16.45 | 16.20 |
| 18.75 | 18.58 | 18.40 | 18.22 | 18.04 | 17.70 | 17.38 | 17.08 | 16.79 | 16.53 |
| 19.16 | 18.98 | 18.79 | 18.61 | 18.42 | 18.07 | 17.74 | 17.42 | 17.13 | 16.86 |
| 19.57 | 19.38 | 19.19 | 19.00 | 18.80 | 18.44 | 18.09 | 17.77 | 17.47 | 17.19 |
| 19.98 | 19.78 | 19.58 | 19.38 | 19.18 | 18.80 | 18.45 | 18.11 | 17.80 | 17.52 |
| 20.39 | 20.18 | 19.97 | 19.77 | 19.56 | 19.17 | 18.80 | 18.46 | 18.14 | 17.84 |
| 20.79 | 20.58 | 20.36 | 20.15 | 19.94 | 19.53 | 19.15 | 18.80 | 18.47 | 18.17 |
| 21.20 | 20.98 | 20.75 | 20.53 | 20.31 | 19.89 | 19.50 | 19.13 | 18.80 | 18.49 |
| 21.60 | 21.37 | 21.14 | 20.91 | 20.68 | 20.25 | 19.85 | 19.47 | 19.13 | 18.81 |
| 22.01 | 21.77 | 21.53 | 21.29 | 21.05 | 20.61 | 20.19 | 19.81 | 19.45 | 19.13 |
| 22.41 | 22.16 | 21.91 | 21.66 | 21.42 | 20.96 | 20.54 | 20.14 | 19.78 | 19.44 |
| 22.81 | 22.55 | 22.30 | 22.04 | 21.79 | 21.32 | 20.88 | 20.47 | 20.10 | 19.76 |
| 23.61 | 23.33 | 23.06 | 22.79 | 22.52 | 22.02 | 21.56 | 21.14 | 20.75 | 20.39 |
| 24.40 | 24.11 | 23.82 | 23.53 | 23.25 | 22.72 | 22.24 | 21.79 | 21.38 | 21.01 |
| 25.19 | 24.88 | 24.57 | 24.26 | 23.97 | 23.41 | 22.91 | 22.44 | 22.02 | 21.63 |
| 25.98 | 25.64 | 25.32 | 24.99 | 24.68 | 24.10 | 23.57 | 23.09 | 22.64 | 22.24 |
| 26.76 | 26.41 | 26.06 | 25.72 | 25.39 | 24.79 | 24.23 | 23.73 | 23.27 | 22.85 |
| 27.53 | 27.16 | 26.80 | 26.44 | 26.10 | 25.46 | 24.88 | 24.36 | 23.88 | 23.45 |
| 28.30 | 27.91 | 27.53 | 27.16 | 26.80 | 26.14 | 25.54 | 24.99 | 24.50 | 24.05 |
| 29.07 | 28.66 | 28.26 | 27.87 | 27.50 | 26.81 | 26.18 | 25.62 | 25.11 | 24.65 |
| 30.59 | 30.14 | 29.70 | 29.28 | 28.88 | 28.13 | 27.46 | 26.86 | 26.31 | 25.82 |
| 32.10 | 31.61 | 31.13 | 30.67 | 30.24 | 29.44 | 28.72 | 28.08 | 27.51 | 26.99 |
| 33.60 | 33.06 | 32.54 | 32.05 | 31.58 | 30.73 | 29.97 | 29.29 | 28.69 | 28.14 |

billing date. For example, suppose an individual is billed $200 on his or her credit card but forgets to pay for twenty days. If he or she then makes another $100 credit purchase on the same day that the last month's statement is finally paid, then the unpaid balance at the end of the current month would be $100. However, to calculate the average daily balance, the bank would multiply $100 by ten days and $200 by twenty days. These figures are added together ($5,000) and divided by thirty, which gives us the average daily balance of $166.67, on which interest is calculated. Many credit cards are now calculating their interest rates on some version of this average daily balance method. Credit cards are discussed more fully below, under "Sources of Consumer Credit."

Interest rates on all consumer loans are usually higher than on business or mortgage loans. One reason for this is that consumer loans are smaller and the cost of making them is higher per dollar lent. The second reason for higher rates on consumer loans is that most individuals represent riskier customers than established corporations or merchants.

## SOURCES OF CONSUMER CREDIT

Consumer credit is made available by a number of financial institutions either directly or indirectly—directly when the borrower goes to an institution and borrows money and indirectly when he or she goes to a merchant and buys something on the installment plan.

### Merchants

If an individual goes to a merchant and buys a car or some household furniture, all he or she need do is sign the papers. The merchant arranges the financing because he or she has an agreement with some financial institution. Sometimes the latter happens without the consumer's knowledge until after it takes place. For example, the consumer signs papers promising to pay so much per month for so many months. Then, the merchant takes this paper to a financial institution, turns it over to the institution, and gets his or her money. This is called "selling the paper" or, more properly, discounting it. The institution gets the interest as the monthly payments are made, and the borrower is told to make the monthly payments to the institution.

Financial institutions may also be extending credit indirectly when a consumer uses his or her credit card. This is because some banks issue credit cards, and also because merchants who have issued credit cards (e.g. Sears or a gasoline company) must borrow more money at a bank to carry the user until he or she pays the bills on the card.

### Financial institutions

There are a number of financial institutions that deal with consumer credit in the form of cash. The major ones are:

1. Commercial banks
2. Savings and loan associations
3. Mutual savings banks
4. Credit unions
5. Life insurance companies
6. Small loan companies
7. Pawnshops

Commercial banks, savings and loan associations, and mutual savings banks are similar in their consumer lending activities. They all make installment and single repayment loans. Rates will vary depending on the borrower's credit rating, the prevailing interest rate, the amount borrowed, whether the loan is secured, and whether it is on an installment or single-payment basis. The interest rates charged by these institutions are a bit lower than those charged by some other lenders because they screen the borrower more carefully and make loans to people with better credit ratings. Rates generally run from 12 to 15 percent.

Credit unions are voluntary associations whose members have a common bond, usually that of a common employer. They will accept deposits and make consumer loans only to their members. Traditionally, credit unions paid a bit more on deposits and charged a bit less on loans than even banks and savings and loan associations (S & Ls). To some extent this is still true, but not to the extent that it was a few years ago. Their rates, however, are competitive with banks and S & Ls.

Life insurance companies make loans to their policyholders if the policy has a cash surrender value (see Chapter 10). Life insurance policy loans need never be repaid. If the policy owner were to die, the loan would be deducted from the face value, which would then be paid to the beneficiaries. Interest rates charged by life insurance companies are usually the lowest available anywhere—generally from 5 to 8 percent, although some insurance companies do charge variable rates based on current money market rates.

The small loan company, also known as the consumer finance company or personal finance company, is a firm specializing in loans to consumers. Interest rates charged by finance companies are generally a bit higher than those charged by banks and S & Ls because their loans are often smaller, and they lend to poorer credit risks. These companies make loans for almost any conceivable purpose, but personal loans and automobile loans constitute the bulk of their business. Pawnshop operators accept personal property that is pledged as collateral for the loan. The loans are never for more than 40 to 50 percent of the value of the property. The borrower receives a pawn ticket and has a certain period of time in which to repay the loan and redeem his property. If he or she doesn't do so, the pawnbroker may sell the article. The interest rate charged generally runs from 25 to 42 percent per year. Table 5–4 shows the major sources of consumer credit.

Table 5–4    *Sources of consumer credit*

|  | *Type of loan* | *Cost and lending policies* |
|---|---|---|
| Commercial banks | Single payment<br>Installment<br>Secured<br>Signature<br>Passbook<br>Home improvement | Lower interest than some<br>Make lower risk loans<br>Make larger loans |
| Savings and loan associations | Same as commercial banks | Same as commercial banks |
| Mutual savings banks | Same as commercial banks | Same as commercial banks |
| Credit unions | Single payment<br>Installment<br>Share draft secured<br>Home improvement | Lower interest than most others<br>Lend only to members<br>Make lower risk loans |
| Life insurance companies | Single payment | Lend policyholders their own money<br>Assume no risk |
| Finance companies | Installment<br>Second mortgages<br>Home improvement | Higher interest than some<br>Assume more risk<br>Make smaller loans |

*Credit cards*

No discussion of consumer credit is complete without comments about credit cards. Traditionally, the credit card permitted consumers to obtain merchandise without paying and at the end of the month one bill was sent for all purchases. Credit was extended for a few weeks at most. Now, however, most credit cards are using what is referred to as a rotating or revolving charge account, where the buyer is still permitted to liquidate the bill monthly but need not do this. Those who choose not to do so move into an automatic monthly payment plan. While these plans vary somewhat, they all are similar. They require a minimum monthly payment (usually $10 or 10 percent of the total amount due). They also have a maximum amount (usually $500 to $3,000) beyond which credit will not be extended unless special arrangements are made. Under these rotating charge accounts consumers need never liquidate their total bill. The only requirement is that they make the minimum monthly payment and do not exceed the maximum. In the case of gasoline credit cards, however, most companies exclude gasoline from the credit that need not be liquidated monthly. They permit only items such as tires, batteries, and so forth to be financed on a rotating basis.

Some merchants still charge interest only on the unpaid balance. This has the effect that if you liquidate your charge in full every month when due, you never have any finance charges. But more and more of them are charging interest on the average daily balance from billing date to billing date; this results in charging interest on future purchases. For example, suppose an individual is billed $200 on his or her credit card and pays $100. If he or she makes no further purchases for, say, 10 days, the average daily balance for those 10 days is $100. If the individual now charges another $100, the average daily balance for the next 20 days is $200. To calculate the average daily balance, the bank would multiply $100 by 10 days and $200 by 20 days. These figures are added together ($5,000) and divided by 30, which gives us the average daily balance of $166.67, on which interest is calculated. Many credit cards are calculating their interest rates on some version of this average daily balance method. The rates they charge vary from state to state because of state usury laws. But rates from 14 to 21 percent are typical.

There are two major credit cards that have been developed by banks: Visa issued by the Bank of America and MasterCard by CitiBank of New York. Many financial institutions throughout the country have entered into an agreement with these two banks and provide these cards. Until recently most of these institutions charged only interest, and not an annual fee. More recently, however, more and more have added an annual fee as well. Most of the institutions providing Visa or MasterCard calculate their interest charges on the average daily balance or some version of it. Interest rates typically run up to 21 percent. In some states, however, usury ceilings prevent charges this high, and consequently some of the financial institutions issuing these cards have moved their credit card operations to Delaware or South Dakota, which have no interest ceilings.

With certain national credit cards such as American Express, the credit card holder pays an annual fee of about $45. The cardholder is billed monthly and must liquidate the bill monthly except for bills for airline tickets, where a twelve-month payoff is permitted. If a twelve-month payoff is chosen, an additional 1 percent per month interest on the declining balance is added. If the bill is paid every month, American Express does not assess interest.

The national credit card firms usually receive about 5 or 6 percent of the amount collected from the merchant for whom they collect it. This is their service charge and should be looked upon as a cost of credit. This fee is included in the price of the final goods and services, and, to a slight extent, those who do not have these credit cards subsidize those of us who do.

At one time credit cards were sent to people on an unsolicited basis, but this is no longer so. Now persons who want a credit card not only must apply, but most qualify. The criterion used to determine whether a person qualifies is primarily income; however, nearly anyone who has an annual income of $12,000 or more can obtain a national credit card upon application, if he or she has a good credit record.

*The selection of a credit card*

All credit cards are not the same. Some charge higher interest rates than others, and in addition some have annual fees (and those fees vary) and some do not. However, some cards with no annual fees charge a higher interest rate; hence, give that some consideration. Some cards have a longer grace period (often up to 30 days) than others; if the bill is paid in full by then, interest is not charged.

Not all credit card companies calculate the balance to which the interest rate is applied the same way. Some use the average daily balance from billing date to billing date, some the previous unpaid balance, some the ending balance (balance at the billing date), and some have an interest-free grace period if bills are paid promptly.

State usury laws set the maximum interest rate that credit card companies may charge, and these charges vary. Consumers may save money by obtaining an out-of-state card. However, even within a state some cards have a lower rate than others.

There are still some cards around that have no annual fees, low interest rates (but 14 to 18 percent is about as low as one can expect), and have a grace period in which bills that are paid on time have no interest charges whatsoever. There are fewer and fewer of these, however. But if the consumer shops around, he or she can minimize credit card expenses; indeed these expenses can be zero in some cases. It is important that the financial planner be aware of this in order to minimize his or her client's credit card expenses.

*The checkless society: the debit card*

Now that banks have developed national credit cards and they have been widely accepted, the next step will be to use the electronic computers of these banks to pay bills automatically. The result will be to do away with checks almost completely. This involves the use of what is known as the ***debit card***.

With a debit card, when an individual makes a purchase, the card is put into a machine that is tied to the computers of the individual's bank and the merchant's bank. The computer will automatically transfer the amount out of the individual's bank account and into the merchant's bank account. The computer can do this immediately at the time of the purchase or at the end of the month in accordance with whatever arrangement is made. The computer, through the merchant's machine, will give the individual a receipt and a bank statement. He or she will get a bank statement each time a purchase is made rather than monthly. If the transfer of accounts is made at the end of the month rather than when purchases are made, the individual still gets a monthly statement rather than a statement with each purchase.

Automatic loans will be granted by the computer as needed, in accordance with predetermined maximums. The need for checks will virtually be over.

The debit card, however, is not popular as yet. While some people use debit cards, there is some concern over how a consumer could do the equivalent of stopping the payment of a check if purchased goods were defective. Other critics are concerned about electronic fraud. Someone might be able to manipulate the computer and steal almost limitless funds.

Electronic debit is similar to the debit card, but with certain differences. With this method the bank automatically pays the customer's regular fixed monthly bills such as the mortgage, rent, or car loan payment. In order to do this, an authorization form must be completed and the computer does the rest. The customer's weekly or monthly paycheck may also be automatically deposited in the individual's bank by the employer.

*Electronic debit*

The preceding discussion has concentrated on the availability and direct costs of using consumer credit. However, there are several other related matters of which a consumer should be aware. The most important of these matters are considered below.

**OTHER THINGS A PERSON SHOULD KNOW ABOUT CONSUMER CREDIT**

Sometimes the lender will insist that the installment buyer purchase life insurance in an amount equal to the debt. The lender is the beneficiary; and in the event of the death of the buyer, the balance of the debt is paid off by the insurance company. The cost of this life insurance is passed on to the installment buyer. In the case of lending institutions, this cost often shows up in the form of an extra 0.5 percent interest per month. In arrangements made with merchants, it either shows up as an added service charge or is included in the price of the item. In some cases, the lender actually keeps a portion of the insurance premiums; only part of them is necessary to buy insurance. This is another illustration of a price pack to enhance the return of the lender or dealer.

*Credit life insurance*

Not all lenders and dealers will insist that the buyer take the credit life insurance. In some states, it is against the law to require that the installment buyer buy credit life insurance. However, the buyer seldom knows this, and the law is very difficult to enforce. The lender can simply let it be known that the credit life insurance will have to be purchased as a condition to granting the loan.

It is possible to buy credit card insurance. This protects the consumer from fraudulent use of the card in case it is lost or stolen. However, this is not as necessary as it once was because now, by federal law, a card-holder's liability is limited to $50 per card even if it is not reported right away. Nevertheless, this insurance appeals to some people who have numerous cards. Once a card has been reported as lost or stolen, the consumer may not be held responsible for any fraudulent use. All

*Credit card insurance*

credit card numbers should be recorded in a safe place, and loss of cards should be reported promptly.

*Credit card abuse*

Many financial planners believe that credit cards are most appropriately used as a convenience. Misuse or overuse of credit cards can lead to significant financial problems. In general, credit card balances should be paid in full each month. This is particularly true since consumer interest is no longer tax deductible after 1990.

*Why interest rates vary*

Why do interest rates on consumer loans vary from one institution to another? Aside from reasons involving legislative permissions enabling the various institutions to charge different rates for small loans, there are other considerations. Management expenses tend to vary greatly among the lending institutions. For a small loan company management expenses are fairly high, because many of their loans are small, and it costs just as much to manage a $200 or $300 loan as it does for a $2,000 or $3,000 loan. In addition, small loan companies make loans to people who are poorer credit risks. Because of this risk, they charge higher interest rates.

Interest rates charged by credit unions are among the lowest. They are voluntary cooperatives, and as such they have eliminated the middleman. Members lend to members. Their philosophy is to give the depositor a fair return and charge the borrower a fair rate. Their record of losses is very low, and they are given a tax advantage over other lending institutions.

The insurance company suffers no risk of loss when making a policy loan, and its cost of collection is very low because these loans are similar to single-payment loans that will eventually be repaid.

Commercial banks generally make loans only to the better credit risks. Because of this circumstance, their loss record is low, a fact that their interest charges reflect. Savings and loan associations also accept only the better risks. Hence their rates are usually below those of finance companies and are comparable to those of commercial banks.

The maximum interest rate permitted on small loans (consumer loans) is higher than the rate permitted under the general usury laws. There are three reasons for this difference in interest rates:

1. Usually the cost of the credit investigation is higher per dollar lent. It takes just as much time to run a credit check and determine the credit-worthiness of a person borrowing $100 or $1,000 as it does of a person borrowing $10,000 or $20,000.
2. The bookkeeping and record-keeping costs are higher on a small loan than on a larger loan per dollar loaned.
3. There is often more risk to the lender because of the credit rating of many of the people borrowing from small loan companies.

Because of the higher risk of default, the lender insists upon a higher rate of interest as compensation for assuming the greater risk.

Suppose that sometime soon after assuming some consumer debt, a consumer experiences good fortune and discovers that he or she is able to repay it far in advance of the installment schedule. The question is, if the debt is paid off in advance, is an interest rebate given? The answer is yes, in most cases. Generally the method used to calculate this rebate is referred to as the **rule of 78**, but this figure is misleading. It could just as well be called the rule of 21 or the rule of 171. A few examples will make this clear.

*Early repayments: the rule of 78*

> Suppose that Mr. Wilson borrowed $1,200 to be paid off in twelve equal monthly installments at 6 percent add-on interest. This makes his true interest rate just under 11 percent over the entire twelve months and his monthly payments $106. Then, when the third monthly payment is due he decides to liquidate the entire debt. How is the interest recalculated?

First, take the sum of all numbers from 1 to 12; they equal 78. If the loan is repaid in full after one month, the lenders receive 12/78 of the interest that they would have received had the loan been outstanding the entire year; if it is liquidated after two months, the lenders receive 12 + 11 or 23/78; if after three months, 12 + 11 + 10 or 33/78 and so on. Only if the loan is outstanding the full twelve months does the lender receive the full 78/78 of the agreed-upon interest. Calculating the interest for early repayments by this method results in the lender getting somewhat more than a strictly pro rata distribution of interest.

For example, after three months on a pro rata basis, the lender would get only one-fourth of the total interest, which would be 19.5/78 in the example used above. This would be a true interest rate of about 6.6 percent for these three months. It is less than the annual 11 percent that would have applied if the loan had been amortized normally because the declining balance (and hence the average balance) is relatively high during the early months of the loan. But because of the sum-of-the-digits method, the lender gets 33/78, which in our example is 33/78 of $72 or a total interest payment of $30.45. This is about 11 percent per year simple interest over these three months. What the sum of the digits does is to increase the interest rate on installment loans to put it back up where it would have been had the loan been amortized normally.

Suppose that in another case $900 is borrowed to be paid back in six monthly installments of $150, but after two months the entire loan is liquidated. This could be called the rule of 21 (the sum of the digits from 1 to 6 = 21). The lenders would receive 11/21 of the total interest if the loan is repaid after two months. The sum of the digits is the rule, and it can be used to calculate the interest on an early repayment for a loan of any length. All that is needed is to know the total number of payments and the total interest, in dollars, that would be paid if the loan were not liquidated early.

Assume, for example, that an eighteen-month installment loan is repaid in full after six months. The sum of the digits here gives us 171 (18 + 17 + 16 + 15, etc.). Since six months have elapsed, the lender receives 93/171 (18 + 17 + 16 + 15 + 14 + 13 =93) of the interest that would have been received had the loan been outstanding the entire eighteen months.

To be sure, lenders do not calculate these rebates in this manner because tables have been prepared and the lender merely looks up the rebate from the tables. These tables have been prepared, however, by using the sum-of-the-digits method described above.

*Credit counselors*

As a financial planning practitioner, you may encounter individuals with substantial financial difficulties arising from abuse of credit. It may be wise to refer these people to credit advisors or credit counselors. Credit advisors are not a source of credit and they do not lend any money. They provide two useful services.

First, they help a person to manage his or her personal affairs; they may set up a budget and persuade the client to live within it. For example, if a person has monthly payments in excess of his or her ability to pay, the credit counselor will attempt to stretch out the debt over a longer time period and in this way reduce the monthly payments. Second, after having worked out a new payment plan that the individual can meet, the credit advisor will act as the middleman and attempt to persuade the lender to accept the new reduced monthly payments. As a disinterested third party, he or she can often do this more easily than can the person involved.

Some cities provide free counseling services under their consumer protection division. In some cases they will have the counselee send them one weekly or monthly check as soon as they receive their wage or salary. The counselor will then disburse it to the various creditors. Many lenders too will act as credit counselors and in many cases will stretch out payments to keep the borrower afloat.

*A typical installment contract*

When a consumer buys something or borrows money on the installment plan, he or she must sign some papers. The financial planner must be acquainted with the client's liabilities to make an accurate assessment of his or her financial situation. This requires a familiarity with contracts used to establish credit. Figures 5–5, 5–6, 5–7, and 5–8 show several such agreements. The first is a combined promissory note, disclosure statement, and security agreement. It is used to finance the purchase of automobiles. The security agreement part of it is on the backside and is shown separately as Figure 5–6. The security agreement permits the lending institution to repossess the car in the event the buyer misses

**COMBINED PROMISSORY NOTE, DISCLOSURE STATEMENT AND
SECURITY AGREEMENT (Closed End)**

University Federal _____ Credit Union, ___ September 1 ___, 19 87 ___

Borrower(s): _ John J. Member _____ Account No: 000-00-0000 ___ Note No: -00 ___

Address: _ Some Where _____ Austin _____ Texas ____ 78701 _____
_____ (City) _____ (State) _____ (Zip Code)

Items preceded by a box ☐ applicable only if checked.

| ANNUAL PERCENTAGE RATE — The cost of your credit as a yearly rate. | FINANCE CHARGE — The dollar amount the credit will cost you. | Amount Financed — The amount of credit provided to you or on your behalf. | Total of Payments — The amount you will have paid after you have made all payments as scheduled. |
|---|---|---|---|
| 9.9 % | $1,792.53 | $11,200.00 | $12,992.53 |

You have the right to receive at this time an itemization of the Amount Financed.  ☐ I want an itemization
☐ I do not want an itemization.

Your payment schedule will be:

| Number of Payments | Amount of Payments | When Payments are Due |
|---|---|---|
| 35 | $360.91 | Starting Oct 1, 1987  every 1st thereafter |
| 1 | $360.68 | Final |

**Security:** You are giving a security interest in: your shares and/or deposits.
☐ the goods or property being purchased.
☒ other _____
_____ 1987 Toyota Tercel 4dr.  VIN:JTM10435H5201BM56 _____
Collateral securing other loans with us may also secure this loan.
☒ Filing fees $ _ N/A __          ☐ Non-Filing Insurance $ _ N/A __
☒ **Late Charge:** If a payment is late, you may be charged  25% of the interest due if more than 7 days late
_____ $10.00 minimum and $25.00 maximum
**Prepayment:** If you pay off early, you will not have to pay a penalty.

**See** the rest of this credit document for any additional information about nonpayment, default, any required repayment in full before the scheduled date, and prepayment refunds and penalties.

_____
e means an estimate

**PROMISE TO PAY:** By signing this document and receiving the money advanced and/or the benefits received, you promise to pay to the credit union or its order, the sum of $ _ 11,200.00 _____ Dollars plus interest on the unpaid balance until it is paid in full at _____ 9.9 ____ % per year in the amounts and on the dates disclosed above. When received, your payment will be applied in this order: Collection costs, late charges, interest due, and unpaid principal balance. Any unpaid interest will be paid by later payments and will not be added to your unpaid principal balance. If any payment is made late, you may be charged a late charge as disclosed above. In the event that applicable law is interpreted so that the interest or other charges collected or to be collected in connection with this loan would exceed permitted limits, any such charge shall be reduced by the amount necessary to reduce the total charge to the permitted limit and any sums already collected which exceeded permitted limits shall be credited to the principal amount of your loan or refunded at the discretion of the credit union.

**SECURITY:** You are giving the credit union a security interest in all present and future shares and/or deposits in any account in the credit union in which you have an interest. You authorize the credit union to take that money and apply it to what you owe if you are in default. The credit union may, but does not have to, allow you to withdraw a portion of your shares or deposits without affecting its security interest.

No withdrawal will be permitted if it will reduce the amount of your total shares and/or deposits in the credit union below $ _ 50.00 _____ or the amount you owe the credit union at the time of the withdrawal, whichever is less. You are not giving a security interest in any shares or deposits in an IRA, SEP, KEOGH, or any other account which, if pledged, would result in the loss of special tax treatment under the Internal Revenue Code.
☐ As additional security you are giving the credit union a security interest in the following goods or property _____
_____ N/A _____

In signing the security agreement on the reverse side of this document, you agree to all its terms and conditions.

**PROPERTY INSURANCE:** You may obtain property insurance from anyone you want that is acceptable to the credit union.
☐ If you get the insurance through the credit union you will pay $ _____ N/A _____ for a term of ___ N/A ___ .

**CREDIT INSURANCE:** If available, credit life insurance and credit disability insurance are not required to obtain credit and will not be provided unless you sign and agree to pay the additional cost. You may select any insurance company of your choice.

| Type | Premium | Signature |
|---|---|---|
| Credit Life | | I want credit life insurance ☐ Yes ☒ No          Signature: |
| Credit Disability | | I want credit disability insurance ☐ Yes ☒ No          Signature: |
| Credit Life and Disability | | I want credit life and disability insurance ☐ Yes ☒ No  Signature: |

**DEFAULT:** You will be in default if you break any promise made in this document, if you fail to make a payment when due, if anyone tries by any legal means to take any money you have which is in the possession of the credit union, if you are the subject of an order for relief under the Federal Bankruptcy Code, or if anything happens which the credit union reasonably believes endangers the collateral or your ability to repay what you owe. If you are in default, the credit union can require immediate payment of all you owe. That means you will have to pay your entire unpaid principal balance plus any interest earned as well as unpaid late charges and collection costs. The credit union has the right to file suit to collect what you owe. This document and applicable law authorize the credit union to take this action, and the credit union may rely on any or all of those sources. If the credit union incurs any expenses in taking these actions, you promise to reimburse the credit union and pay for all reasonable attorney's fees, court costs and disbursements. You waive any right to advance notice before the credit union takes any action resulting from your default unless the waiver is expressly prohibited by law.

**CREDIT UNION RIGHTS:** The credit union may delay taking any action to protect its rights as many times as it wants and as long as it wants without losing them. If the credit union agrees to change any of the terms of this loan, you agree that any security interest will continue to protect the credit union. Use of the term "you" includes any person who signs this document. By signing, any such person agrees to all the terms and conditions and promises to perform all the obligations, requirements and duties contained in this document.

**ACKNOWLEDGEMENT:** I(we) acknowledge receipt of a copy of the credit document completely filled in.

_____          _____
Borrower                          Comaker/Guarantor

_____          _____
Date Signed                      Date Signed
C.E.—2 (TX 1-82)

*Combined promissory note, disclosure statement and security agreement (closed end)*   Figure 5–5

**SECURITY AGREEMENT**

**SECURITY INTEREST:** By signing this document and receiving the benefits of your loan described on the reverse side, you are giving the Credit Union a security interest in the property described on the reverse side. This security interest covers not only that property but all proceeds, substitutions or replacements, accessions, improvements, all proceeds from insurance and all refunds of unearned premiums. Any time this agreement refers to collateral, it means any or all of the property described above. You are giving this interest to secure repayment of your loan as well as any other amounts you now owe or will owe the Credit Union. The collateral also secures your performance of all other obligations under your loan, this security agreement and any other agreement you have with the Credit Union.

**OWNERSHIP OF COLLATERAL:** You promise that you will use the proceeds of the loan advance to buy the collateral or that you own the collateral and that no one else has any interest in it or claim against it. You agree not to sell, lease it, or give it as collateral to anyone else until you have repaid what you owe the Credit Union or the Credit Union gives its written permission.

**USE OF COLLATERAL:** Until what you owe the Credit Union is fully repaid, you promise: To defend the collateral from third-party claims and protect it from forced sale by such persons; to protect the collateral and keep it in good repair; not to use the collateral for any unlawful purpose; to obtain written permission from the Credit Union before making major alterations or improvements; to notify the Credit Union in writing before changing your mailing address or the location of the collateral; and to help the Credit Union to protect the rights you have given it.

**PROPERTY INSURANCE AND TAXES:** You are required to fully insure the collateral against loss and damage. You may obtain this insurance through any insurance company of your choice, unless the Credit Union, for good cause, refuses to accept it. If you obtain insurance through the Credit Union, the cost and the term is disclosed on the reverse side of this document. If you fail to obtain or maintain insurance, the Credit Union may buy any type of insurance it feels is necessary to protect its interest in the collateral. This could result in less protection for you and at a higher cost. The credit union will add the premium for this insurance to the applicable loan account and charge you a **FINANCE CHARGE** at the applicable rate. You promise to have any insurance policy payable to the Credit Union, and, if asked, to deliver it to the Credit Union. You also promise to pay all taxes due on the collateral. If you fail to do so, the Credit Union may, but does not have to, pay the taxes and add the amount to the unpaid principal balance of the loan and charge you a **FINANCE CHARGE** at the same rate as your loan.

**DEFAULT AND REPOSSESSION:** You will be in default if you break any promise made under this agreement, if you are in default on your loan, if you fail to obtain or maintain the required insurance, or if anything happens which the Credit Union reasonably believes endangers the collateral or your ability to repay what you owe.

If you are in default, the Credit Union may require that you deliver the collateral to it at a time and place of its choosing. You agree that the Credit Union can take possession of the collateral without judicial process and without giving you advance notice unless waiver of the notice is otherwise expressly prohibited by law. This agreement, the Texas Business and Commerce Code, and other applicable law, authorize the Credit Union to take various actions, and the Credit Union may rely on any or all of those sources.

The Credit Union may also file suit to recover the collateral and/or collect what you owe. If the Credit Union incurs any expenses in taking these actions, or in protecting its rights to the collateral, you promise to reimburse it and pay for all reasonable attorneys' fees, court costs and disbursements. If the Credit Union repossesses the collateral, you promise to also pay for actual and reasonable out-of-pocket expenses incurred by the Credit Union in connection with repossession or foreclosure, including costs of storing, reconditioning, and reselling the collateral. Any disposition of the collateral will be in accordance with the standards of good faith and commercial reasonableness as well as the procedures set by the Texas Business and Commerce Code, as amended.

**OTHER RIGHTS:** The Credit Union may delay taking any action to protect its rights as many times as it wants and as long as it wants without losing them. If the Credit Union changes any of the terms of this agreement or the loan, you agree that the security interest will continue to protect the Credit Union. Use of the term "you" includes any person who signs this document. By signing, any such person agrees to all the terms and conditions and promises to perform all the obligations, requirements and duties contained in this agreement.

_____    _____
Date                          Borrower

_____    _____
Date                          Borrower

Figure 5–6    *Security agreement*

payments. It provides that the borrower pay all court and attorney's fees if they are necessary to collect payments.

The promissory note lists the car. It is a Toyota. It had a list price of $14,000, but after a 20 percent down payment, $11,200 was financed. The note shows the terms of the loan as required by law. The interest rate is 9.9 percent; the 36 monthly payments are $360.91, except for the last one, which is a few pennies less. It also stipulates the penalty for late payments. The total dollar interest cost is $1,792.53.

This is a **closed-end note**, which means it has a specific period of time (thirty-six months) to maturity. The note is drawn up in accordance with the Uniform Commercial Code and also conforms to the federal truth-in-lending law. Consequently, with slight variations, contracts similar to it are used for new cars throughout the United States. This type of contract is also employed to finance other durable goods. However, sometimes an **open-end note** is used to finance less expensive items. Figure 5–7 shows such a note (open-end loan advance request voucher and security agreement). It finances $5,000 worth of furniture. It is a signature loan, which means there is no collateral behind the note. However, the furniture could be used as collateral in which case the security agreement on the back of the note would be used. The note

# OPEN-END LOAN ADVANCE
## REQUEST VOUCHER AND SECURITY AGREEMENT

**UNIVERSITY FEDERAL CREDIT UNION**

(COMPLETE SHADED PORTION ONLY)

MAIN OFFICE
1611 GUADALUPE
P.O. Box 4069
AUSTIN, TX 78765
(512) 467-8080

MEDICAL BRANCH
428 Postoffice St.
GALVESTON, TX 77550
(409) 765-9999

### INFORMATION CONCERNING CREDIT INSURANCE

Group Credit Insurance is available on loans made to Credit Union members. Insurance is voluntary and not required to obtain credit. If you would like your loan protected by Group Credit Insurance check below.

☐ SINGLE CREDIT LIFE INSURANCE ☐ JOINT CREDIT LIFE INSURANCE ☐ CREDIT DISABILITY INSURANCE

The Credit Union will disclose the cost of this voluntary insurance to you if checked above. A separate insurance election disclosing the term and conditions of the credit insurance must be signed for the coverage to become effective.

MEMBERS NAME (Please Print)     ACCOUNT NO. (Soc. Sec. No.)

STREET ADDRESS    CITY    STATE    ZIP

HOME PHONE    MARITAL STATUS — Do not complete unless you reside or are relying on property located in a community property state (AZ, CA, ID, LA, NM, NV, TX, WA) ☐ MARRIED ☐ UNMARRIED ☐ SEPARATED

HAVE YOU CHANGED EMPLOYERS SINCE YOUR LAST LOAN? ☐ YES ☐ NO    EMPLOYER AND ADDRESS    EMPLOYMENT PHONE NO.

Your monthly income (net) $    Income from Alimony, Child Support or maintenance payments need not be revealed if you choose not to disclose or list this income in this application.    Source of other income:    Amount of other income

SUBJECT TO THE TERMS AND CONDITIONS OF YOUR OPEN-END CREDIT PLAN AGREEMENT, YOU HEREBY REQUEST A LOAN IN THE AMOUNT OF: $ *5000.00*    YOU MAY REQUEST A PAYMENT OF: $

PURPOSE OF THIS ADVANCE IS: *Buy Furniture*    SECURITY (IF ANY)

I WOULD LIKE THE FUNDS FROM THIS ADVANCE AS:
☐ CASH ($1,000 maximum)
☐ CREDIT TO MY UFCU SHARE DRAFT ACCT.
☐ CREDIT TO MY REGULAR SHARES
☐ CHECK
☐ DEALER DRAFT (Auto purchases only)
☐ CREDIT TO ACCT. NO. _____

I WOULD LIKE TO MAKE PAYMENTS BY:
☐ CASH (Counter or Mail Payments)
☐ DEDUCTED FROM UT CHECK (Net pay only)
☐ TRANSFER FROM REGULAR SHARES
☐ TRANSFER FROM SHARE DRAFT
☐ BANK DRAFT ON MY BANK ACCOUNT
☐ TRANSFER FROM ACCOUNT NO. _____
☐ PAYROLL DEDUCTION (Medical Branch only)

### —SECURITY—

| Item | MAKE | MODEL | YEAR | I.D. NUMBER | LOAN VALUE OR PURCHASE PRICE |
|---|---|---|---|---|---|
| 1. | | | | | |
| 2. | | | | | |
| 3. Other (Describe): *Signature* | | | | | |

By accepting this advance you agree to pay the Credit Union according to the terms of your Open End Credit Plan Agreement and this Advance Voucher. You are giving the Credit Union a security interest in the collateral described above. The terms and conditions of the security agreement are shown on the reverse side of this voucher and incorporated in your Open End Credit Plan Agreement.

| TLR. I.D. | SEQUENCE NUMBER | CURRENT DATE | EFFECTIVE DATE | ANNUAL PERCENTAGE RATE | To obtain this advance, you agree to maintain a minimum regular share balance of: | Total filing fees deducted from proceeds are: |
|---|---|---|---|---|---|---|
| | | *09/01/87* | *09/01/87* | *14* % | $ *50.00* | $ *0* |

| SUB-ACCOUNT TYPE | | | | | | | |
|---|---|---|---|---|---|---|---|
| TRANS. CODE | PAYMENT AMOUNT | FIRST PAYMENT DATE | PREVIOUS LOAN BALANCE | NEW MONEY | INTEREST ADJUSTMENT | NEW LOAN BALANCE | |
| | *240.10* | *10/1/87* | *0* | *5000.00* | | *5000.00* | ☐ OPEN END ADV. ☑ INSTALLMENT LN. |

| SUB-ACCOUNT TYPE | | | | | | |
|---|---|---|---|---|---|---|
| TRANS CODE | PREVIOUS SHARE BALANCE | SHARE AMOUNT | NEW SHARE BALANCE | FEE | LOAN OFFICER APPROVAL | DATE APPROVED |
| | | | | | DISAPPROVED BY CR. COMMITTEE APPROVED | DATE DISAPPROVED APPROVED |
| | | | | | CREDIT COMMITTEE | |

SIGNATURE OF BORROWER    DATE    CREDIT COMMITTEE

SIGNATURE OF SPOUSE, JOINT APPLICANT OR OTHER PARTY    DATE

**SEE REVERSE SIDE FOR TERMS AND CONDITIONS OF THE SECURITY AGREEMENT.**

*Open-end loan advance: Request voucher and security agreement*     Figure 5–7

**OPEN-END CREDIT PLAN SECURITY AGREEMENT**

SECURITY INTEREST: By signing this document and receiving the benefits of your open-end advance described on the reverse side, you are giving the Credit Union a security interest in the property described on the reverse side. This security interest covers not only that property but all proceeds, substitutions or replacements, accessions, improvements, all proceeds from insurance and all refunds of unearned premiums. Any time this agreement refers to collateral, it means any or all of the property described above. You are giving this interest to secure repayment of your Open End Advance Loan, as well as any other amounts you now owe or will owe the Credit Union. The collateral also secures your performance of all other obligations under the Open End Credit Plan Agreement, this security agreement and any other agreement you have with the Credit Union. If the collateral is household goods as defined in the Federal Trade Commission Fair Credit Practices Rule, it only secures obligations for the purchase money for that collateral or a refinancing or consolidation of such obligations.

OWNERSHIP OF COLLATERAL: You promise that you will use the proceeds of the loan advance to buy the collateral or that you own the collateral and that no one else has any interest in it or claim against it. You agree not to sell, lease it, or give it as collateral to anyone else until you have repaid what you owe the Credit Union or the Credit Union gives its written permission.

USE OF COLLATERAL: Until what you owe the Credit Union is fully repaid, you promise: To defend the collateral from third-party claims and protect it from forced sale by such persons; to protect the collateral and keep it in good repair; not to use the collateral for any unlawful purpose; to obtain written permission from the Credit Union before making major alterations or improvements; to notify the Credit Union in writing before changing your mailing address or the location of the collateral; and to help the Credit Union to protect the rights you have given it.

PROPERTY INSURANCE AND TAXES: You are required to fully insure the collateral against loss and damage. You may obtain this insurance through any insurance company of your choice, unless the Credit Union, for good cause, refuses to accept it. If you obtain insurance through the Credit Union, the cost and the term will be disclosed to you at that time. If you fail to obtain or maintain the insurance, the Credit Union may buy any type of insurance it feels is necessary to protect its interest in the collateral. This could result in less protection for you and at a higher cost. The Credit Union will add the premium for this insurance to the applicable loan account and charge you a **FINANCE CHARGE** at the applicable rate. You promise to have any insurance policy payable to the Credit Union, and, if asked, to deliver it to the Credit Union. You also promise to pay all taxes due on the collateral. If you fail to do so, the Credit Union may consider this failure as a request for a loan advance under your Open-End Credit Plan Agreement. In that event, the Credit Union may, but does not have to, pay the taxes and add the amount to the appropriate loan account and charge you a **FINANCE CHARGE** at the applicable rate.

DEFAULT AND REPOSSESSION: You will be in default if you break any promise made under this Agreement or if you are in default under the Open-End Credit Plan Agreement.

If you are in default, the Credit Union may require that you deliver the collateral to it at a time and place of its choosing. You agree that the Credit Union can take possession of the collateral without judicial process and you authorize a right of entry for that purpose and said repossession may occur without giving you advance notice unless waiver of the notice is otherwise prohibited by law. This agreement, The Texas Business and Commerce Code, and other applicable law, authorize the Credit Union to take various actions, and the Credit Union may rely on any or all of those sources.

The Credit Union may also file suit to recover the collateral and/or collect what you owe. If the Credit Union incurs any expenses in taking these actions, or in protecting its rights to the collateral, you promise to reimburse it and pay for all reasonable attorneys' fees, court costs and disbursements. If the Credit Union repossesses the collateral, you promise to also pay for actual and reasonable out-of-pocket expenses incurred by the Credit Union in connection with respossession or foreclosure, including costs of storing, reconditioning, and reselling the collateral. Any disposition of the collateral will be in accordance with the standards of good faith and commercial reasonableness as well as the procedures set by the Texas Business and Commerce Code, as amended.

OTHER RIGHTS: The Credit Union may delay taking any action to protect its rights as many times as it wants and as long as it wants without losing them. If the Credit Union changes any of the terms of this Agreement or the Open-End Credit Plan Agreement, you agree that the security interest will continue to protect the Credit Union. Use of the term "you" includes any person who signs this document. By signing, any such person agrees to all the terms and conditions and promises to perform all the obligations, requirements and duties contained in this Agreement.

| | |
|---|---|
| Date | Borrower |
| Date | Borrower |

shows the monthly payment ($240.10) and the interest rate (14 percent). There are twenty-four monthly payments, which make the interest rate dollar-wise $762.40. The number of monthly payments and the total dollar interest cost, however, are generally not shown on an open-end note. This is because additional items may be added and financed with the same note. For example, if after a year, with twelve payments ($2,881.20) remaining, the buyer wanted to buy a $500 refrigerator, the monthly payments could be increased to include that. This could go on forever in theory; hence the term "open-end." When using an open-end note, the law requires that an additional form (Figure 5–8, open-end credit plan disclosure for fixed rate loans) be used. This spells out the exact dollar cost of the note, as well as the annual percentage rate.

---

**ATTACHMENT "A" — OPEN-END CREDIT PLAN DISCLOSURES FOR FIXED RATE LOANS**

### University Federal Credit Union

P.O. Box 4069
4611 Guadalupe
Austin, Texas 78765
(512) 467-8080

Medical Branch
428 Post Office Street
Galveston, Texas 77550
(409) 765-9999

Your minimum periodic payment is calculated after each advance as described below:
UNSECURED OPEN-END/LINE OF CREDIT LOANS — $3.50 per $100, or fraction of $100, of your balance.
ALL OTHER LOANS — Payment based on available terms, and your loan officer.

FIXED RATE SUB-ACCOUNT LOANS

| LOAN SUB-ACCOUNT DESCRIPTION | ESTIMATED TERM | BASIC MONTHLY PAYMENT | % ABOVE INDEX | DAILY PERIODIC RATE | ANNUAL PERCENTAGE RATE |
|---|---|---|---|---|---|
| NEW VEHICLES | | | | | |
| 20% Down Payment | 12 months | | | .0189041% | 6.9% |
| 20% Down Payment | 18 months | | | .0216438% | 7.9% |
| 20% Down Payment | 24 months | | | .0243836% | 8.9% |
| 20% Down Payment | 36 months | | | .0271233% | 9.9% |
| 20% Down Payment | 42 months | Minimum payment due | | .0284932% | 10.4% |
| 20% Down Payment | 48 months | will always be at least | | .0298630% | 10.9% |
| 20% Down Payment | 60 months | $30.00. | | .0326027% | 11.9% |
| 20% Down Payment | 84 months | | | .0353425% | 12.9% |
| USED VEHICLES | | | | | |
| 20% Down Payment | | | | | |
| Current, Plus 6 years | 42 months | | | .0315068% | 11.5% |
| 7 years and older | 30 months | | | .0383561% | 14.0% |
| Share/Certificate Loans | | | 3% | _____% | _____% |
| All other secured loans | | | | .0434658% | 15.50% |
| Unsecured Loans | | | | | |
| ($0 - $2,500) | 60 months max. | | | .0452055% | 16.5% |
| ($2,501 - $4000) | 60 months max. | | | .0424658% | 15.5% |
| ($4,001 - OVER) | 60 months max. | | | .0383561% | 14.0% |
| Real estate (all) | 180 months max. per policy limits | | | .0369863% | 13.5% |
| COMPUTERS | | | | | |
| 20% Down Payment | 36 months max | | | .0369863% | 13.5% |
| Home Improvement $5,000 - $25,000 | 180 months max. | | | .0369863% | 13.5% |
| 80% of Equity or $25,000 - OVER | 180 months max. | | | .0315068% | 11.5% |
| 80% Market Value $0 - $5,000 | 60 months max. | | | .0369863% | 13.5% |

For Certificate Secured advances the **ANNUAL PERCENTAGE RATE** will be the dividend rate being paid on the certificate on the date of the advance (Index) plus the percentage shown in the "% Above Index" column above. The certificate offered as security must be renewed until the advance is completely paid. When the certificate is renewed the **ANNUAL PERCENTAGE RATE** on existing balances will be 3% above the rate being paid on the new certificate. Failure to renew the certificate will result in default under the plan. The **ANNUAL PERCENTAGE RATE** will never exceed the rate permitted under the Federal Credit Union Act or a minimum of 10.8%. Any increase in the **ANNUAL PERCENTAGE RATE** will take the form of more payments of the same amount.

Borrower's Signature _____

FIXED RATE LOANS:   When the Annual Percentage Rate I select is a Fixed Rate, this is the rate I will pay for the life of my loan, subject to the terms previously agreed to in the Open-End Credit Plan Agreement.

*Open-end plan disclosures for fixed interest rate loans*       Figure 5–8

## SUGGESTED READINGS

*Banking Journal of the American Bankers Association.* New York: American Bankers Association. Monthly publication.

*"Borrowers, Lenders and Interest Rates."* Richmond, VA.: The Federal Reserve Bank of Richmond.

Cole, Robert H. *Consumer and Commercial Credit Management, 4th ed.* Homewood, III: Irwin, 1980.

"Consumer Credit Counseling." Silver Springs, Md.: The National Foundation for Consumer Credit.

"Consumer Credit Terminology Handbook." New York: The Federal Reserve Bank of New York.

*Consumer Credit and You.* Greenfield, Mass: Channing I. Bete Company.

*Consumer Finance News.* Washington, D.C.: National Consumer Finance Association. Monthly publication.

*Consumer Finance Rate and Regulation Chart* Washington, D.C.: National Consumer Finance Association. Revised annually.

*Consumer Loan and Sales Finance Rate and Regulation Chart* Washington, D.C.: National Consumer Finance Association Revised annually.

*Consumer Reports.* Mt. Vernon, N.Y.: Consumer's Union of the United States. Monthly publication.

*Cost of Personal Borrowing in the United States.* Boston: Financial Publishing Company. Annual publication.

*Credit.* Washington, D.C.: *National Consumer Finance Association.* Bimonthly publication.

"Credit Research Center Working Papers." West Lafayette, Ind.: Credit Research Center, Purdue University. A series of research studies on topics significant to consumer credit.

*Family Budget Guide.* Washington, D.C.: National Consumer Finance Association.

*Finance Facts Yearbook.* Washington, D.C.: National Consumer Finance Association. Annual publication.

"Getting a Hold on Credit." Silver Springs, MD.: The National Foundation for Consumer Credit.

"How Much Are You Really Worth?" Silver Springs, MD.: The National Foundation for Consumer Credit.

"How Much Credit Can You Afford?" Silver Springs, MD.: The National Foundation for Consumer Credit.

"How to Establish and Use Credit." Philadelphia: The Federal Reserve Bank of Philadelphia.

*International Credit Union Yearbook, 1981.* Madison, Wis.: CUNA International, Inc. Annual publication.

"Monitor: A Summary of Current Research in Consumer and Mortgage Credit." West Lafayette, Ind.: Credit Research Center of the Krannert Graduate School of Management, Purdue University. Bimonthly publication.

*NCFA Research Report on Finance Companies.* Washington, D.C.: Research Services Division, National Consumer Finance Association. Annual publication.

"The Rule of 78's or What May Happen When You Pay Off a Loan Early." Philadelphia: The Federal Reserve Bank of Philadelphia.

"The Story of Consumer Credit." New York: The Federal Reserve Bank of New York.

Taylor, John. *Consumer Lending.* Reston, VA.: Reston Publishing Company, 1982.

U.S. Department of Agriculture, *Consumers All, The Yearbook on Agriculture.* Washington, D.C.: U.S. Department of Agriculture. Annual publication.

Wood, Oliver G., Jr., and Barksdale, William. *How to Borrow Money.* New York: Van Nostrand Reinhold, 1981.

"Your Credit Rating." Philadelphia: The Federal Reserve Bank of Philadelphia.

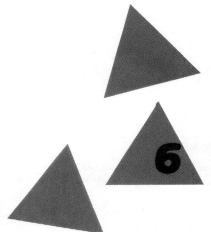

# 6 Consumer protection

**HIGHLIGHTS**          In order to provide an understanding of protection available to the consumer, we will examine the following:

1    The various federal consumer protection laws and what they do
2    Private, voluntary consumer organizations that sometimes help, especially in giving advice
3    The holder-in-due-course doctrine
4    The federal and state agency to which the consumer should go if a federal law has been violated

## INTRODUCTION

In recent years legislation has been passed to protect the consumer. There is, however, no uniformity among various states' laws. Many states have usury laws that have been on the books for years. In some states these usury laws apply to consumer credit, and in some they do not; and special laws have been passed that set the upper limits on consumer credit interest rates. Regular usury laws do, however, usually apply to mortgage loans made to individuals and to business loans.

In most states there is a consumer credit commission or a similar office that regulates consumer credit lenders and enforces state laws that cover, among other things, the maximum interest rate that may be charged. In a few states this office may listen to consumer complaints and even take action if the complaint is legitimate. But an official state agency to help the consumer is the exception rather than the rule, and generally an individual must initiate legal action unless a federal or state statute has been violated. Private voluntary consumer organizations also exist in some areas. Some groups may aid an individual and bring strength of numbers to bear, or they may provide financial and legal aid in the event of a lawsuit. These groups may also lobby for stronger consumer protection laws. But unless a law has been violated there is often little that can be done, even if one has been treated shabbily. Consequently, the consumer should read carefully any installment contract before signing it.

## FEDERAL CONSUMER PROTECTION LAWS

When a consumer borrows money or buys something on the installment plan, there are certain federal laws that protect him or her. As a financial planner, you should be familiar with this protection and know where consumers can go if a law has been broken. Currently, federal legislation covers the following general areas:

Truth in lending
Fair credit reporting
Equal credit opportunity
Fair credit billing
Consumer leasing
Fair debt collection practices

### Truth in lending

Officially known as the Consumer Credit Protection Act, the federal truth-in-lending law was passed in 1968 and has been amended several times since then. "Truth in Lending" does what its title suggests: it requires that certain facts be disclosed when consumer loans are made.

### Interest costs

The lender must inform the borrower of the "true" or actuarially correct percentage interest rate that he or she is paying. As pointed out in a previous chapter, this is called the annual percentage rate (APR) and must be distinguished from the so-called add-on interest rate. The add-on rate is misleading because it is calculated on the original balance, which is actually declining if paid off in installments. The borrower must also be told the total dollar amount of interest together with any service charges, extra loading fees, and points. If a product is being financed (rather than money being borrowed at a bank), the cash price as well as credit price must be spelled out.

The cost of any credit life insurance must be explained; the same is true of accident, health, or disability insurance written in connection with any credit transaction. While the lender may require that the borrower accept credit life insurance, if he or she does, its premium is included in the cost of the loan (APR), which is subject to the various states' usury laws.

Credit life

The truth-in-lending law also requires that the "right of rescission" clause be inserted into every contract in which the borrower's home is used as collateral (including mobile homes). This gives the borrower three business days in which to nullify any such contract. The borrower's home is frequently used as collateral when a major repair or remodeling job is being done. In such a case, work may not begin until the three days have passed unless the borrower, in writing, waives the right of rescission. If the borrower cancels during the three days, this must also be done in writing.

Right of rescission

This law also protects the borrower in the event a credit card is lost or stolen. Once the missing card has been reported, the cardholder is not liable for bills stemming from its unauthorized use. It is up to the issuer to block its illegal use. Even if the missing card is not reported, the maximum liability is $50 per card. Consequently, any missing cards should be reported immediately, first by telephone and then by certified or registered letter.

Lost or stolen credit or debit cards

In 1980, Congress passed the Electronic Funds Transfer Act which covered lost or stolen debit cards. However, there are some differences. On a debit card the consumer's loss is limited to $50, only if it is reported within two business days after learning of the loss. If the customer does not inform the card issuer within two days after learning of the loss, his or her liability could be as much as $500. It cannot be proven when one learned of the loss; hence it is assumed the customer learned of it at the latest when he or she received the bank statement. If unreported within two days after that, the loss is now limited to $500. For an individual who is out of the country and doesn't report the loss within sixty days after receiving the bank statement, the loss is unlimited.

In 1970 an amendment to the truth-in-lending law spelled out the maximum amount of a person's income that may be garnished to meet unpaid debts. This maximum is now either 25 percent of a person's weekly take-home pay or the amount by which his or her weekly take-home pay exceeds 30 times the minimum hourly wage, whichever is smaller.

Garnishment of wages

The federal law then sets the maximum penalty with respect to garnisheeing wages. Moreover, it provides that in those states that have a garnisheeing law more lenient to the debtor than the federal law, the state law shall prevail. The law also prohibits an employer from firing an employee whose wages were garnisheed to satisfy any one debt. Formerly, firing was frequent because garnisheeing wages meant extra bookwork for the employer.

*Fair credit reporting act*

The Fair Credit Reporting Act guarantees certain consumer rights in reporting credit information about consumers to credit granters. For example, it gives the consumer the right to see his or her credit file. All cities of any size have professional credit bureaus that collect and store pertinent financial data on virtually all individuals in the community. They then sell these data (known as "inspection reports") to institutions and individuals who extend credit. They also sell reports to prospective employers and life insurance companies that are considering an individual for life insurance. The credit file includes personal data as well as data on where the individual works, his or her position, how long the individual has held that position, annual income, spouse's income, assets, whether he or she rents or owns a home, previous job and address, number of dependents, credit history and experience, and any judgments that may have been recorded against the individual.

Checking the file

If an individual merely wishes to check his or her credit file routinely, he or she will have to pay the regular fees a lender pays—a few dollars. If credit has been denied because of a credit report, the lender or merchant must disclose this. In such a case the individual has thirty days during which he or she may see the credit report free of charge; all data in it must be revealed and its source disclosed. Any errors found must be corrected, and any falsehoods deleted. If the file contains information subject to two or more interpretations, the individual's interpretation must be added and included in all future reports. The corrected version must also be sent to all possible creditors who have received a report on the individual during the last six months, and all prospective employers who have received a report during the past two years, at no cost to the individual.

Adverse information limitation

The limits to how long adverse information in the credit file may be made available in a credit report are as follows:

Information on bankruptcies—10 years
Suits and judgments against the consumer—7 years or until the statute of limitations has expired, whichever is the longer
Paid tax liens, collection accounts, accounts charged to bad debts, arrests, indictments, convictions, and other damaging information—7 years

However, none of these limitations applies if the credit reports are to be used in connection with a credit or life insurance transaction involving $50,000 or more, or employment involving an annual salary of $20,000 or more.

Although the consumer may see his or her credit file, it is strictly confidential to almost all others. Those who have a legitimate need may see a credit report as may those whom the consumer authorizes. Those who may receive a report without consumer authorization because they have a legitimate need are: prospective creditors, creditors or their agents trying to collect past debts, prospective employers, and employees of life insurance companies considering the individual for life insurance. For anyone else a court order is needed. Even the government cannot see one's file or receive a report unless it is considering employing the individual, granting a license of some kind, considering him or her for security clearance, or thinks back taxes are owed. For the IRS to receive a report, it must have a legitimate case.

*Who may see the file*

The Equal Credit Opportunity Act (ECOA) became effective in October, 1975, and it banned discrimination in the granting of credit on the basis of sex or marital status. In 1976 this act was amended so that it now also prohibits discrimination on the basis of race, color, religion, and age. The act also bans discrimination against welfare or other public assistance recipients and borrowers who exercise their rights under consumer protection laws. Moreover, it provides that if people are denied credit, they must be told why in writing.

*Equal credit opportunity act*

Prior to the passage of ECOA, women had more difficulty getting credit than men. A married woman often had to rely on her husband's credit. In addition, single and divorced people often had a more difficult time getting credit than married couples. Now this discrimination as well as other types is unlawful.

*Women and credit*

Women should establish credit in their own names if they have an income, even if they are married. If a woman relies upon her husband's credit, then upon death or divorce she may be without it temporarily. To be sure, ECOA will permit her to establish credit in her own name in such a case, but this takes time.

Prior to the passage of ECOA, it was alleged that lenders sometimes refused to grant credit to older people. This act prevents the arbitrary denial of credit to the elderly, who for the purpose of the provision in this act are defined as persons 62 and older. Credit may still be denied on the basis of inadequate income, excessive debts, a person's credit record, and the like, but the reason for refusing credit must be spelled out in writing.

*Age and credit*

*Fair credit billing act*

The Fair Credit Billing Act (FCBA) does three things: It permits merchants who so desire to grant cash discounts, it permits the consumer to withhold payments for defective merchandise purchased with credit cards, and it provides some safeguards in the case of billing errors.

Cash discounts

Twenty or thirty years ago cash discounts were often granted by merchants to people who paid cash. This practice had all but ceased until very recently when there has been a reemergence of the cash discount. Because of this, some major credit card companies included a provision in their contract with retail merchants prohibiting cash discounts. The FCBA prohibits such "no cash discounts" provisions. The act does not require cash discounts; it merely says that merchants may grant them if they wish. Obviously, expenses are minimized if the individual uses cash in instances where a cash discount is available. This discount is limited to 5 percent because otherwise it would be in violation of the truth-in-lending law.[1]

Merchants granting cash discounts must have signs so stating in clear sight, such as near cash registers or on doors at entrances. Moreover, merchants granting cash discounts must grant them to all buyers, not just to credit card holders.

Withholding payments

The FCBA permits consumers to stop making payments for defective merchandise or service purchased with credit cards. If the merchant who sold the merchandise is also the issuer of the credit card, all the consumer need first do is make a good faith effort to return the merchandise or resolve the problem by having the merchant replace or repair the item. In the event that a third party issued the credit card (for example, Visa or MasterCard), the consumer may still withhold payment, but now there are two additional restrictions. First, the purchase must have exceeded $50, and, second, it must have taken place in his or her state or within 100 miles of his or her current address.

By withholding payments the consumer can generate pressure to have the grievance resolved. If a third party's credit card is involved, the consumer can, by withholding payment, enlist that party as an ally in bringing pressure on the retailer.

Billing errors

In some cases the consumer may be billed incorrectly because of accounting errors, goods that were delivered to the wrong address, goods returned or not accepted, or other reasons. The FCBA makes it easier to settle such disputes. The consumer has sixty days after receiving such a bill to report an error. This must be done in writing and the nature of the dispute explained. The creditor has thirty days in which to send a written reply. While the dispute is being settled, the creditor may

---

1. Discounts in excess of 5 percent would constitute a finance charge under the truth-in-lending law and hence would necessitate further regulations and red tape.

"It says, 'This is your final notice. If you do not pay immediately, we will destroy your credit and have you thrown in jail. Have a happy day.' " (Source: Permission Cartoon Features Syndicate; from The Wall Street Journal.

not collect any disputed amount, nor add interest charges. During this time the creditor may not close the account nor give the consumer a bad credit rating because of the claim.

What these provisions of the FCBA have done is to make the creditor more cooperative in settling disputes; complaints must now be investigated. Even though legally complaints must be in writing, in many cases disputes can be settled on the telephone. National credit card companies have established regional offices throughout the country with full-time people who handle only complaints. Often the address and phone numbers for complaints are listed on the monthly bills, and the numbers are often toll-free.

**Consumer leasing act**

While fewer consumers are involved in leasing than in purchasing, there is some legal protection for those who do lease automobiles, furniture, and other items.

There are two types of leases and both are covered by the Federal Consumer Leasing Act. Under a **closed-end lease** the consumer pays so much per month, and when the lease is over he or she may return the car or furniture and the lease is terminated. As a result of this simplicity, closed-end leases usually have a higher monthly payment than open-end leases.

An **open-end lease** is a bit more complicated. The consumer has the option of buying the car or other item when the lease expires. The car must be depreciated according to a schedule calculated in advance, and its estimated value at the expiration of the lease must be stated in advance. If the car is worth more than that, the consumer may keep it, sell it, and pocket the difference. If the car is worth less than that, the consumer needs to make up the difference. However, this difference cannot be more than three times the monthly payment. There is a penalty, then, if the individual has been overly hard on a car.

The leasing law covers personal property leased by an individual for more than four months for personal family or household use. The law does not cover the following:

- Daily, weekly, or monthly car rentals
- Houses or apartments, or furniture that comes with these residential units
- Property leased to companies or individuals for business use

*Fair debt collection practices act*

The Fair Debt Collection Practices Act (FDCPA) spells out the maximum amount of harassment that may be used to collect bills. It limits the number of phone calls that may be made and the time of day during which they may be made. Phone calls must be made at convenient times, which generally are defined as between 8:00 A.M. and 9:00 P.M. The debtor, however, cannot be contacted at his or her place of employment, if it is known that the employer prohibits or discourages this. The total amount of contacts of any sort is fixed, and of course threats, overt or implied, are prohibited. This act, however, has one loophole. It does not apply to the lenders directly, but only to third parties collecting for them. A creditor can call a debtor anytime but a collection agency cannot.

*Holder-in-due-course doctrine*

The Federal Trade Commission (FTC), which enforces many of the federal consumer protection laws, has by means of regulations weakened (but not completely eliminated) the holder-in-due-course doctrine. Holder-in-due-course is the legal concept that, if a merchant entered into a credit relationship with a consumer to finance, say, a refrigerator and then sold the installment contract to a third party (say, a finance company), a legally binding contract existed between the consumer and the finance company. The payments were then made to the finance company which bought the paper in good faith and was not a party to the agreement. In short, under the old holder-in-due-course doctrine you had to pay for the refrigerator even if it was defective. Normally you can generate great pressure to have a defective item repaired or replaced by withholding payments; this was not possible formerly if a third party was involved.

FTC regulations now permit the consumer to stop making payments to third parties (even if a credit card is not involved) for defective merchandise or services. Both the seller and the third party may now be held partly liable. This permits the consumer to generate greater pressure. If it comes to legal court action, he or she can go after both the seller and the financial institution, since both are equally liable. The person now has the same rights against the third party as against the seller.

The FCBA strengthens the hand of the consumer somewhat by permitting payments to be withheld. However, if it comes to a legal battle, sellers and creditors are often not liable. This is because often the warranty is granted by the manufacturer, not the seller. While the lender and the retailer share any warranty granted at that level, neither is liable if it is granted by the manufacturer. This is especially true if a disclaimer clause is inserted into a contract. The retailer and creditor are then freed of liability for defective products if there is a court case. Nevertheless, the new law is a plus for the consumer because he or she can now withhold payments, generate some additional pressure on the retailer and creditor, and enlist them as allies against the manufacturer.

The FTC's regulations now also prohibit the waiver of defense clauses in installment contracts. These were formerly used by some retailers and protected them against action on the part of the consumer.

The Federal Consumer Credit Laws offer these major protections:

*Summary of consumer credit laws*

1.  The *Truth in Lending Act* requires disclosure of the "finance charge" laws and the "annual percentage rate"—and certain other costs and terms of credit—so that prices of credit from different sources can be compared. It also limits liability on lost or stolen credit cards.
2.  The *Equal Credit Opportunity Act* prohibits discrimination against an applicant for credit because of age, sex, marital status, race, color, religion, national origin, or receipt of public assistance. It also prohibits discrimination because a consumer has made a good faith exercise any of his or her rights under the federal consumer credit laws. If the consumer has been denied credit, the law requires that he or she be notified in writing and that he or she have the right to request the reason for the denial.
3.  The *Fair Credit Billing Act* sets up a procedure for the prompt correction of errors on a credit account and prevents damage to the consumer's credit rating while he or she is settling a dispute.
4.  The *Fair Credit Reporting Act* sets up a procedure for correcting mistakes on the credit record and requires that the record be kept confidential.
5.  The *Consumer Leasing Act* requires disclosure of information that helps the consumer compare the cost and terms of one lease with another and with the cost and terms of buying on credit or with cash.
6.  The *Fair Debt Collection Practices Act* spells out the amount of pressure collection agencies may use to collect past due bills.
7.  The *Real Estate Settlement Procedures Act* requires that the consumer be given information about the services and costs involved at settlement, when real property transfers from seller to buyer.
8.  The *Home Mortgage Disclosure Act* requires most lending institutions in metropolitan areas to let the public know where they make their mortgage and home improvement loans.

Pamphlets describing some of these laws in more detail are available from the Federal Reserve Bank in your district.

## ENFORCING AGENCIES AND OTHER COURSES OF ACTION

When a consumer has a grievance with a merchant or financial institution, there are several courses of action available, including legal action. First, he or she should attempt to settle the dispute himself or herself. Legal action should be seen as a last resort, and then only if a substantial amount of money is involved.

### Voluntary consumer organizations

If the consumer does not receive satisfaction from working directly with the company, another course of action is working through voluntary organizations. While voluntary organizations are not enforcing agencies because they have no power, they can sometimes bring pressure to bear because of the power of numbers. In many states and communities, voluntary groups of consumers have developed various programs to help themselves and advance their version of the consumers' cause. These groups generally have been assisted in their growth and activities by the Consumer Federation of America (CFA), a Washington, D.C. based coalition of over two hundred national, state, and local organizations. CFA's affiliates have their own memberships of more than thirty million persons in consumer, farmer, cooperative, labor, and other endeavors. Ralph Nader has founded a number of specialized consumer organizations, and others have arisen in recent years to deal with problems in individual industries such as food, electric utilities, broadcasting, and housing.

Consumer groups developed rapidly following the activities of homemakers a few years ago in a well-publicized eruption of sentiment, pickets, and boycotts of supermarkets over rising prices. The activities of the groups that emerged reflect particular interests and special conditions of the urban, suburban, or rural areas in which they flourish.

Some groups make frequent statewide and local area comparisons of store prices for drugs, household items, and food. Others demand financial settlement for members who have received poor treatment. Voluntary consumer organizations generally do three things: (1) they engage in lobbying at all levels of government to obtain stronger consumer protection laws; (2) they engage in consumer education by sponsoring seminars and lectures on many topics of interest to consumers; (3) they provide consumer counseling.

### Federal agencies

There are a number of federal and state enforcing agencies. If the consumer has a complaint and the law has been violated, the correct agency to handle the complaint depends on the creditor involved. Figure 6–1 illustrates where a consumer may go for help. The following list summarizes agencies responsible for enforcing federal laws:

| Creditor | Federal agency |
|---|---|
| National commercial banks | The Comptroller of the Currency<br>United States Treasury Department<br>Washington, D. C.<br>The Comptroller has regional offices in a number of major cities. Check the telephone directory. |
| State banks that are members of the Federal Reserve System | The Federal Reserve Bank serving the area in which the bank is located.<br>The Federal Reserve has 12 regional offices |
| State nonmember banks that are insured by the Federal Deposit Insurance Corporation | The Federal Deposit Insurance Corporation<br>Washington, D. C.<br>The FDIC has regional offices in a number of major cities. Look in the telephone directory. |
| State nonmember noninsured banks | Division of Consumer Credit<br>The Federal Trade Commission<br>Washington, D. C.<br>The Federal Trade Commission has regional offices in a number of major cities. There are very few such noninsured banks, however. |
| Federal savings and loan associations | The Federal Home Loan Bank Board<br>Washington, D. C.<br>The FHLBB has regional offices in a number of major cities. |
| State savings and loans associations insured by the Federal Deposit Insurance Corporation (FDIC) | The Federal Deposit Insurance Corporation (FDIC)<br>Washington, D. C.<br>The FDIC has regional offices in a number of major cities. |
| State savings and loan associations that are not insured | Division of Consumer Credit<br>The Federal Trade Commission<br>Washington, D. C.<br>The FTC has regional offices in a number of major cities. Look in the telephone directory. There are very few such noninsured savings associations. |
| Mutual savings banks | The Federal Deposit Insurance Corporation<br>Washington, D. C.<br>The FDIC has regional offices in a number of major cities. Virtually all mutual savings banks are insured by the FDIC and hence regulated by them. |

| Creditor | Federal agency |
|---|---|
| Federally chartered credit unions and insured state-chartered credit unions | The National Credit Union Administration Washington, D.C. The NCUA has regional offices in a number of major cities. |
| State-chartered noninsured credit unions | Division of Consumer Credit The Federal Trade Commission Washington, D.C. The FTC has a number of regional offices. There are very few noninsured credit unions. |
| Retail merchants, including department stores, finance companies, nonbank credit card issuers, and most others | Division of Consumer Credit The Federal Trade Commission Washington, D.C. The FTC has a number of regional offices. |
| Airlines and other creditors subject to Civil Aeronautics Board | Director, Bureau of Enforcement Civil Aeronautics Board |
| Meat packers, poultry processors, and other creditors subject to Packers and Stockyards Act | Nearest Packers and Stockyards Administration area supervisor. |
| Creditors subject to Interstate Commerce Commission | Office of Proceedings Interstate Commerce Commission Washington, D.C. |

The Federal Reserve System and the Comptroller of the Currency have established an Office of Consumer Affairs at all of their regional offices, as have many of the other federal agencies, where complaints can be taken by mail. The Office of Consumer Affairs at the Regional Federal Reserve Bank of your district of the Federal Reserve System will send the consumer a complaint form that can be filled out and returned to them. A sample of such a complaint form is shown in Figure 6–2.

The Department of Health, Education and Welfare (HEW) established an Office of Consumer Affairs some time ago. Although this office has no power of enforcement, it listens to complaints from consumer organizations. It plays the role of advocate and will report any violations of federal law to the proper enforcement agencies.

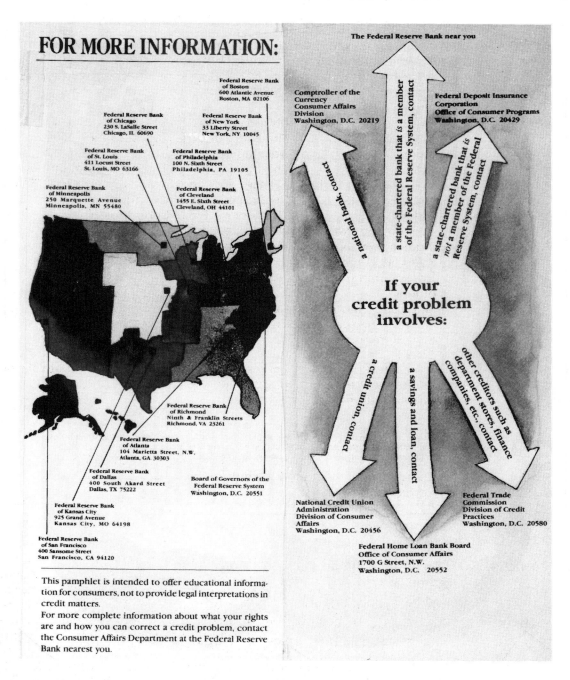

*Where to go for help. (Source: Board of Governors of the Federal Reserve System.)*    Figure 6–1

---

**COMPLAINT FORM**                                    **Federal Reserve System**

Name _____      Name of Bank _____

Address _____      Address _____
　　　　　　　Street　　　　　　　　　　　　　　　　　　　　　　City　　　　State　　Zip

_____
　City　　　　　State　　　　Zip

Daytime telephone _____      Account number (if applicable)_____
　　　　　　　(include area code)

The complaint involves the following service: Checking Account ☐      Savings Account ☐      Loan ☐

　Other: Please specify _____

I have attempted to resolve this complaint directly with the bank: No ☐      Yes ☐

　　If "No", an attempt should be made to contact the bank and resolve the complaint.

　　If "Yes", name of person or department contacted is _____
　　　　　　　　　　　　　　　　　　　　　　　　　　　　　　　　　　　　　　Date

MY COMPLAINT IS AS FOLLOWS (Briefly describe the events in the order in which they happened, including specific dates and the bank's actions to which you object. Enclose copies of any pertinent information or correspondence that may be helpful. Do not send us your only copy of any document.):

_____
_____
_____
_____
_____
_____
_____
_____
_____
_____
_____

This information is solicited under the Federal Trade Commission Improvement Act. Providing the information is voluntary; complete information is necessary to expedite investigation of your complaint. Routine use of the information may include disclosing it to bank(s) or others involved or to other governmental agencies as deemed appropriate.

Date _____      Signatures _____

_____

**Figure 6–2**   *Complaint form. (Source: Board of Governors of the Federal Reserve System.)*

**State agencies**

There are state agencies to enforce state laws. All states have banking commissioners by that or some other name. Some have credit union commissioners, savings and loan commissioners, and consumer credit commissioners. Some have a similar state agency to enforce all state laws dealing with consumer credit including the maximum interest rates that may be charged. Some states also have deceptive trade legislation on the books, and some have established offices of consumer protection or consumer affairs, either within the Attorney General's office or elsewhere.

**Small claims court: legal action**

Legal action should probably be used as a measure of the last resort. In most cases where small dollar amounts are involved, such action should be taken through a small claims court, which is often able to handle claims effectively, quickly, and at a much lower cost than regular legal action. However, the amount of damages for which a person may sue is limited in a small claims court, in most states to under $1,000. If the consumer has suffered damages (and would like to collect) in excess of that amount, he or she will probably have to hire an attorney and go to a regular court. The effectiveness of a small claims court depends on particular state laws and on the availability of the courts in particular locations. In most states hiring a lawyer is not required. Procedures are usually handled in an informal manner and the legal rules of evidence and procedure are often waived. The consumer simply tells the magistrate what happened in his or her own words.

In some states the small claims courts are under the jurisdiction of the justice of the peace (JP), and in others under the alderman. Both of these are elected officials at the lowest (precinct) political subdivision.

The cost of filing a claim in a small claims court is only a few dollars. Actual court costs are also modest. More information about the small claims court in your area may be obtained by calling your county clerk, the justice of the peace or alderman for your precinct.

## SUGGESTED READINGS

*Alice in Debitland; Consumer Protection and the Electronic Fund Transfer Act.* Washington, D.C.: Board of Governors of the Federal Reserve System.

"The American Lawyer: How to Choose and Use." Chicago: The American Bar Association.

*Annual Buying Guide, Consumer Reports.* Published in December of each year by Consumer's Union of the United States.

*Changing Times.* The Kiplinger Magazine. A weekly publication with a good deal of material of interest to the consumer.

*Charting Mortgages.* Department of Consumer Affairs, Federal Reserve Bank of Philadelphia.

*Consumers, Credit Bureaus, and the Fair Credit Reporting Act.* Associated Credit Bureaus. Check with your local credit bureaus; they may have similar publications by credit bureaus near you.

*Consumer Handbook to Credit Protection Laws.* Washington, D.C.: Board of Governors of the Federal Reserve System.

*Consumer Information Catalog.* Pueblo, Col.: Consumer Information Center. Quarterly publication.

*Consumer News.* Washington, D.C.: Office of Consumer Affairs.

*Consumer Reports.* Mt. Vernon, N.Y.: Consumer's Union of the United States. Monthly publication.

*Credit Guide.* Federal Reserve Bank of Chicago.

*Equal Credit Opportunity Act . . . and Age.* Washington, D.C.: Board of Governors of the Federal Reserve System.

*Equal Credit Opportunity Act and . . . Credit Rights in Housing.* Washington, D.C.: Board of Governors of the Federal Reserve System.

*Equal Credit Opportunity Act and . . . Doctors, Lawyers, Small Retailers, and Others Who May Provide incidental Credit.* Washington, D.C.: Board of Governors of the Federal Reserve System.

*Equal Credit Opportunity Act and . . . Women.* Washington, D.C.: Board of Governors of the Federal Reserve System.

*Fair Credit Billing.* Washington, D.C.: Board of Governors of the Federal Reserve System.

*Fair Debt Collection Practices Act.* Department of Consumer Affairs, Federal Reserve Bank of Philadelphia.

*How to File a Consumer Credit Complaint.* Washington, D.C.: Board of Governors of the Federal Reserve System.

*If You Borrow to Buy Stock.* Washington, D.C.:

Board of Governors of the Federal Reserve System.

*If You Use a Credit Card.* Washington, D.C.: Board of Governors of the Federal Reserve System.

Myerson, Bess. *Consumer Guidelines to Shopping by Mail.* New York: Direct Mail Marketing Association.

Richardson, Lee. *Consumer Newsletter.* Columbia, Md.

Rosenbloom, Joseph. *Consumer Complaint Guide.* New York: Macmillan, 1984.

*Truth in Leasing.* Prepared jointly by the Federal Trade Commission and the Board of Governors of the Federal Reserve System.

U.S. Office of Consumer Affairs. *A Consumer's Shopping List of Inflation-Fighting Ideas.* Pueblo, Col.: Consumer Information Center.

*What Truth in Lending Means to You.* Revised ed. Washington, D.C.: Board of Governors of the Federal Reserve System.

*"When You Move—Do's and Don'ts."* Pueblo, Col.: Consumer Information Center.

*Your Credit Rating.* Department of Consumer Affairs, Federal Reserve Bank of Philadelphia.

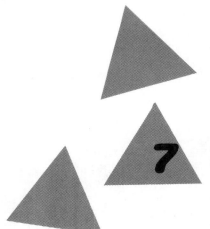

# 7 Taxes and tax planning

**HIGHLIGHTS**

In order to help the reader understand the tax regulations, this chapter examines the following:

1. State and local taxes
2. The federal income tax and how it works
3. Who must file a return and pay a tax
4. The standard deduction
5. The personal exemptions
6. The tax forms
7. Income that is and is not taxable
8. Adjusted gross income and the deductions allowed to arrive at adjusted gross income
9. Allowable itemized deductions
10. Certain tax credits that can reduce taxes
11. The alternative minimum tax
12. The course of action to follow in the event of an audit

## INTRODUCTION

Individuals cannot avoid paying taxes, but with proper planning they can lessen the amount they would otherwise pay. There are state, local, and federal taxes, and each one of them can take a significant part of a person's income. There are also Social Security taxes, but they will be discussed in Chapter 18. In this chapter we will discuss taxes of all the three above-mentioned levels of taxing entities; but we will concentrate on federal income taxes because they are the most complex, and for many of us they take away the largest dollar amount of our income. After a brief analysis of state and local taxes, we will work through the current federal personal income tax law, with an emphasis on legally minimizing taxes. Many people overpay income taxes because of lack of knowledge or carelessness.

There is a difference between evading and avoiding taxes. Evading taxes is deliberately cheating and not paying taxes that are due. It is illegal and a person guilty of this is subject to penalties, fines, and even confinement in a federal penitentiary. Avoiding taxes is legal; it consists of using a knowledge of the law to minimize taxes. Chief Justice Oliver Wendell Holmes said that "every man has a right to so arrange his affairs as to minimize his taxes."

"Your return was neat and accurate and indicated that you understood the forms completely . . . what we want to know is how?" (Source: Permission Cartoon Features Syndicate; from The Wall Street Journal.)

Government expenditures at all levels have risen sharply in recent years. Federal expenditures (or outlays as they are officially called) were $96.5 billion in 1965. In 1991 they exceeded one trillion dollars. In 1992 they are expected to be about $1.5 trillion. Among the reasons are growth in population and the increase in the demand for more government services. Along with greater government expenditures came an increase in taxes.

Comparing taxes and expenditures with national income and gross national product is one indicator of the cost (or burden) of government, since taxes are paid out of income. Table 7–1 shows federal taxes and expenditures, together with national income figures. The figures in Table 7–1 are aggregates.

At the personal level a person can compare his or her total taxes

**TAXES, EXPENDITURES, AND NATIONAL INCOME**

*U.S. taxes, expenditures, and national income (in billions)*

Table 7–1

| Year | Receipts | Outlays[1] | National income | Receipts as a % of National income | Outlays as a % of National income |
|------|----------|----------|----------|----------|----------|
| 1971 | $ 188.4 | 211.4 | 858.1 | 22.0% | 24.6% |
| 1972 | 208.6 | 232.0 | 951.9 | 21.9 | 24.4 |
| 1973 | 232.2 | 247.1 | 1,064.6 | 21.8 | 23.2 |
| 1974 | 264.9 | 269.6 | 1,136.0 | 23.3 | 23.7 |
| 1975 | 281.0 | 326.2 | 1,215.0 | 23.1 | 26.9 |
| 1976 | 300.0 | 366.4 | 1,359.8 | 22.1 | 27.0 |
| 1977 | 357.8 | 402.7 | 1,525.8 | 23.5 | 26.4 |
| 1978 | 402.0 | 450.8 | 1,724.3 | 23.3 | 26.1 |
| 1979 | 465.9 | 493.6 | 1,924.8 | 24.2 | 25.6 |
| 1980 | 532.2 | 572.7 | 2,117.1 | 25.1 | 27.1 |
| 1981 | 599.3 | 657.2 | 2,352.5 | 25.4 | 27.9 |
| 1982 | 617.8 | 728.4 | 2,436.6 | 25.3 | 29.8 |
| 1983 | 600.6 | 808.5 | 2,718.3 | 22.9 | 29.7 |
| 1984 | 66.5 | 851.1 | 3,039.3 | 21.9 | 28.0 |
| 1985 | 734.0 | 945.9 | 3,104.4 | 23.6 | 30.5 |
| 1986 | 769.1 | 989.8 | 3,386.4 | 22.7 | 29.2 |
| 1987 | 854.1 | 1,004.6 | 3,635.3 | 23.5 | 27.6 |
| 1988 | 909.2 | 1,055.9 | 3,849.8 | 23.6 | 27.4 |
| 1989 | 990.7 | 1,142.6 | 4,223.3 | 23.5 | 27.1 |
| 1990 | 1,031.3 | 1,251.7 | 4,459.6 | 23.1 | 28.1 |
| 1991 | 1,091.4 | 1,409.6 | 4,559.8 | 23.9 | 31.0 |
| 1992* | 1,165.0 | 1,445.9 | — | — | — |
| 1993* | 1,252.7 | 1,454.2 | — | — | — |

1. It should be noted that receipts are not quite the same as taxes. Receipts are slightly larger because they include fines and judgements levied, certain loans that were repaid, and certain other revenue such as admissions charged to national parks.

*Estimates

Source: *Economic Indicators*, Council of Economic Advisors, Feb. 1992, p 32.

paid with his or her income. The percent of one's income paid to the government in the form of taxes is called the effective tax rate, and it can be considered as the person's personal tax burden—or cost of government. The figures in Table 7–1 include only federal tax. In order to get the total cost of all governments, the taxpayer must make the same analysis of state and local taxes. This calculation can be made quite accurately for state and city income taxes and for property taxes. In the case of sales taxes, however, the taxpayer will probably have to rely on an estimate as to total sales-tax dollars.

*State and local taxes*

While some states and even some cities impose income taxes, the bulk of state and local tax revenues are from sales and property taxes. The largest single portion of the property tax goes to support the schools, but city and county governments also derive some revenue from it. Many cities today also have a sales tax. The bulk of sales tax receipts, however, flow into state treasuries. Other major sources of revenue for states in addition to income taxes are excise taxes, such as gasoline, liquor, and cigarette taxes.

*Sales taxes*

Sales taxes are imposed at the retail level. In some states, there are certain exempted or nontaxed items, and in others there are none. The most commonly exempted items are food consumed in the home and services such as doctors' fees, haircuts, laundry bills, and the like. Generally, rates vary from 4 to 7 percent for the states' share, and some cities add a bit more to this, usually 1 or 2 percent. The retail merchant must collect this tax and usually can keep a small part of it (this varies from state to state but generally is 1 percent of the taxes due) to cover collection costs.

The sales tax is considered to be regressive because it takes away a larger portion of a low income than a high one. It is a tax on consumption, and low-income persons consume a higher percentage (save less) of their income than do high-income persons. For example, let us assume that Mr. A has $20,000 after withholding tax take-home income per year, and let us say he saves $500 and consumes $19,500 and lives in an area that levies a 7 percent sales tax. Depending on whether or not food and services are taxed, he will pay about $1,365 in sales taxes per year. This is 6.82 percent of his take-home pay. Let us assume Ms. B is earning $50,000 take-home pay per year and lives in the same town. But she consumes $45,000 and saves $5,000 of it; hence, she pays about $3,150 in sales taxes, which is 6.3 percent of her income.[2] As incomes

---

2. A sales tax of 7 percent may result in taxes of more than 7 percent of total consumption, because most purchases are in small amounts and fractional dollars are taxed at a higher rate. There are breaking points on the tables that merchants use to calculate the tax and often the seven cents per dollar tax is reached at seventy cents.

rise further, the percentage taken away under the sales tax generally declines further. Even though sales taxes are taxes on consumption, many citizens seem to prefer this kind of tax to a state or local income tax. This may be because it is paid in small amounts and seems more painless. The sales tax has the virtues of being broad-based and raising a lot of revenue; the administrative and collection cost is low relative to the revenue it raises.

*Property taxes*

While some state and local governments impose a personal property tax (on automobiles, boats, and the like) and some even on intangible personal property (on bank accounts and securities), these taxes do not raise much revenue. The biggest single property tax for most individuals is on real estate—that is, on the person's home. The real property tax is an ancient device. It is not considered the best tax, but it will no doubt remain with us because it raises a good deal of revenue. Some states have abandoned the property tax levying, leaving it as a source of revenue for the local taxing units.

Paying the tax

The property tax is generally shared by the city government, the county government, and in some cases the state government, and the school system, with the latter getting the largest share. Sometimes, however, a portion of the tax is also earmarked for specific items such as a sewer or water district. In some areas, the tax is paid to one of the above governments (usually the city or the county) and is then disbursed to the other units in accordance with the predetermined percentage share each is to get. In other areas, various local governments cannot get together and the home owner must write two (or more) checks and pay the county's share and the city's share separately. In most cases, if a client is paying off a mortgage loan on a home, the lending institution will add one-twelfth (1/12) of the estimated annual tax to the monthly payment and then pay this tax for the home owner when due.

Computation of the property tax

The computation of the property tax is roughly the same everywhere. The only variables are the appraised (or assessed) value and the tax rate or millage rate. The assessed value generally varies from about 20 percent to 75 percent of the market value of the property.

The tax rate applied to assessed value to obtain the actual tax liability is stated either as a percentage (so much dollarwise per $100 of assessed valuation) or in mills (a mill is one-tenth of one cent). A house with a $100,000 assessed value could be taxed at 6 percent of its assessed valuation or 60 mills per the assessed valuation. In both cases the tax on it is $6,000. Generally speaking, real estate is reappraised every few years to take into account appreciation in the market value. Periodically, too, the tax rate is raised.

*State and local income taxes*

A growing number of states and a few cities have an income tax. A few years ago most of the states having income taxes had laws that did not take advantage of the federal income tax. Therefore, after filing federal taxes, one had to go file again at the state level. Recently, more states have tied their income taxes into the federal government's. Consequently, after filing the federal form, a copy of it could be sent to the state authorities as verification of earned income and deductions and only a relatively simple additional state form would be needed.

*Other state and local taxes*

A number of other taxes are levied by state and local governments. The most important of these are gasoline and tobacco taxes, taxes on liquor and hotel rooms, the personal property tax, personal intangible property tax, license and fees on a car, estate and inheritance taxes, and corporate income taxes. These are the major ones in use today.

## FEDERAL PERSONAL INCOME TAXES

Although there are other federal taxes (for example, on corporations), the federal personal income tax is the largest revenue producer and the tax that has the biggest impact on the average citizen. In fiscal 1991 the federal government collected about $468.0 billion through personal income taxes.[3] This was about 44.4 percent of total tax receipts. (The second largest source of revenue is the Social Security tax and the third largest, the corporate income tax.) Figure 7–1 provides estimates of where the federal dollar comes from and where it goes for the years 1992 and 1993.

In 1986, Congress passed and the president signed The Tax Reform Act of 1986. It contained massive changes in the tax code. It was intended to be revenue neutral in that it was not to increase aggregate tax receipts. In order to do this, it was inevitable that it would change the burden of who pays how much tax. Minor changes are usually made each year, with a major change made every 4–5 years.

*Who must file a return?*

Generally speaking, any individual must file an income tax return in 1991 if he or she had a gross income of $5,550 or more, if single. If married and filing jointly, the figure is $10,000, and for a head of household it is $7,150.[4] If married and filing separately, the magic figure is $5,000. This is because of the standard deduction and the personal exemption. These deductions and exemptions are indexed annually to offset inflation.

---

3. The fiscal year differs from the calendar year. The fiscal year runs from October 1 through September 30. The fiscal year 1992, then, covers October 1, 1991, through September 30, 1992.

4. See section on head of household in this chapter.

# THE FEDERAL GOVERNMENT DOLLAR
## FISCAL YEAR 1992 ESTIMATE

**Where It Comes From...**

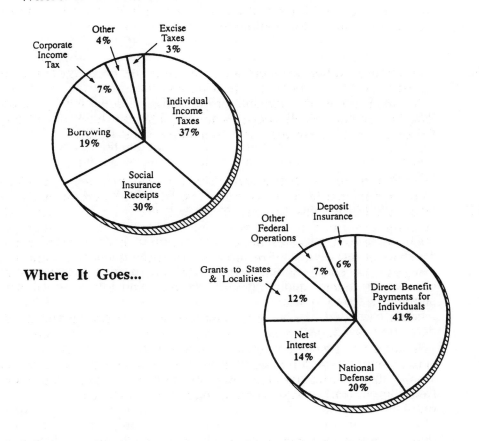

**Where It Goes...**

| RECEIPTS, OUTLAYS, DEFICIT/SURPLUS UNDER THE PRESIDENT'S PROPOSED POLICY | | | | | | | |
|---|---|---|---|---|---|---|---|
| (In billions of dollars) | | | | | | | |
| | 1990 | 1991 | 1992 | 1993 | 1994 | 1995 | 1996 |
| Receipts | 1,031.3 | 1,091.4 | 1,165.0 | 1,252.7 | 1,365.3 | 1,467.3 | 1,560.7 |
| Outlays | 1,251.7 | 1,409.6 | 1,445.9 | 1,454.2 | 1,427.1 | 1,470.3 | 1,540.8 |
| Surplus or Deficit (+/−) | −220.4 | −318.1 | −280.9 | −201.5 | −61.8 | −2.9 | +19.9 |

*The budget dollar, fiscal year 1991 and estimates for 1992 and 1993. (Source: The United States Budget, Fiscal Year 1991, 1992, and 1993, Office of Management and the Budget, Washington, D.C.)*    Figure 7–1

**The standard deduction**

There is a standard deduction for taxpayers who do not itemize their deductions. The following table shows the standard deduction for 1991 and 1992.

|                           | Standard Deductions | |
| ------------------------- | ------- | ------- |
|                           | *1991*  | *1992*  |
| Married filing jointly    | $5,700  | $6,000  |
| Unmarried                 | 3,400   | 3,600   |
| Heads of household        | 5,000   | 5,250   |
| Married filing separately | 2,850   | 3,000   |

These standard deductions are adjusted annually for inflation. Taxpayers age sixty-five and over and those who are blind are allowed an additional deduction of $900 if single and $700 if married for 1992. If the taxpayer is both blind and over 65, the above figures become $1,700 and $1,300.[5] These additional deductions are also adjusted annually for inflation.

Taxpayers may elect to itemize deductions if this will give them a larger dollar amount. This is discussed below.

**The personal exemption**

Each taxpayer also has a personal exemption of $2,000 for tax years after 1988 (adjusted annually for inflation) for every qualifying dependent. In 1991 the personal exemption is $2,150. A married taxpayer with two children (four total qualifying exemptions), filing jointly, and taking the standard deduction would not pay any taxes in 1991 until his or her income exceeded $14,300 (the exemptions of $8,600 plus the standard deduction of $5,700).

A person receives an exemption for himself or herself, his or her spouse, and for each person qualifying as a dependent for tax purposes. To qualify as a dependent, the person must meet the requirements of five different tests, one of which is that he or she must receive more than one-half of his or her support from the taxpayer. Married taxpayers may file jointly and claim two personal exemptions (assuming no other dependents), or separately and each claim only himself or herself. Table 7–2 illustrates who must file a tax return and possibly pay a federal income tax.

If a person does not owe a tax but has had taxes withheld and is entitled to a refund, he or she must, of course, file a return to obtain the refund.

---

5. The additional allowance for the elderly and the blind was converted from an additional exemption to an additional deduction by the 1986 tax change. This means that the taxpayers who itemize deductions do not receive it as an additional benefit.

*Deductions and exemptions, 1991*                                    Table 7–2

| Category | Standard deduction* | Exemptions* | Income not taxed* |
|---|---|---|---|
| Single | $3,400 | $ 2,150 | $ 5,550 |
| Single over 65 | 4,250 | 2,150 | 6,400 |
| Married joint return | 5,700 | 4,300 | 10,000 |
| Married joint return— one spouse over 65 | 6,350 | 4,300 | 10,650 |
| Married filing separately** | 2,850 | 2,150 | 5,000 |
| Married joint return—3 children | 5,700 | 10,750 | 16,450 |
| Unmarried head of household | 5,000 | — | 7,150 |

*These figures will be adjusted annually for inflation.
**Each spouse receives that amount.

For 1991 and beyond, the deduction for personal exemptions is reduced by 2% for each $2,500 (or portion thereof) of which the AGI exceeds a threshold amount. The threshold amounts for 1992 are as follows:

*The personal exemption phase-out*

$157,900 for joint returns
$131,550 for heads of household
$105,250 for singles
$ 78,950 for married filing separately (the $2,500 is replaced by $1,250 for separate filers)

Example: John and Kathy are joint filers with two dependent children. Their AGI for 1992 is $195,300. Without a phase-out, they would be entitled to a $9,200 exemption deduction. However, because their AGI exceeds the threshold amount of $157,900 they are required to reduce the $9,200 by 2% for each $2,500 (*or portion thereof*) by which their AGI exceeds the threshold amount. Since the $37,400 excess AGI includes 14.92 multiples of $2,500, we will reduce the $9,200 by 15 multiples of 2%, or 30%. Thus John and Kathy would be allowed a deduction of $6,440 ($9,200 less 30%).

There are three basic forms from which certain individuals may choose when filing their taxes. These are (1) 1040EZ, which is very short; (2) the 1040A, which is also quite short; and (3) the 1040, which is longer and is required for more complex returns.

*The tax forms*

The 1040EZ form may be used only if the taxpayer:

■    is single and claims *only* his or her own personal exemption.

- has income *only* from wages, salaries and tips, taxable scholarships and fellowships, and interest of $400 or less.
- has taxable income of less than $50,000.
- does not itemize deductions or claim any adjustments to income or tax credits.
- is not liable for any special taxes.
- is neither blind nor age 65 or older.
- did not receive any advance earned income credit payments.
- is not a nonresident alien.

Form 1040A may be used if the taxpayer:

- had income *only* from wages, salaries, tips, taxable scholarships and fellowships, taxable IRA distributions, taxable pensions and annuities, taxable social security benefits, unemployment compensation, interest, or dividends.
- has taxable income of less than $50,000.
- does not itemize deductions.
- claims as an adjustment to income only the deduction for an IRA contribution.
- claims only the child and dependent care credit, the credit for the elderly or the disabled, or the earned income credit.
- is not liable for any special taxes.
- is not a nonresident alien.

Another difference between Form 1040A and 1040EZ is that married taxpayers may use 1040A, but not 1040EZ. The 1040A is a two-page form and is easy to fill out.

All others must use Form 1040. The 1040 is a two-page form and may be used without any attachments by many taxpayers. If a person has income solely from wages, salaries, tips, interest and dividends, or certain miscellaneous income and does not itemize deductions, the basic two-page form is all that need be completed. If the taxpayer has income from other sources, wishes to itemize deductions, or wishes to claim certain credits, supplementary schedules must be filled out and attached to the 1040. After having calculated his or her taxable income, the taxpayer must use the appropriate tax table to obtain the tax liability if his or her taxable income is less than $50,000. These tables are found in the "Tax Forms and Instructions" booklet made available by the IRS. This booklet, incidentally, is a very valuable source of information when filing taxes, because it contains the answers to many questions the taxpayer may have. (A number of tax booklets and guides to assist the taxpayer may be obtained free of charge from the IRS.)

If the taxpayer has a taxable income of more than $50,000, he or she cannot use the tax tables, but must use the appropriate Tax Rate Schedule (either Schedule X, Y-1, Y-2, or Z) furnished by the IRS and included in the 1040 "Tax Forms and Instructions" booklet.

If deductions are itemized, the individual should compare them with the standard deduction, and take whichever is the larger. The itemized deduction (or standard deduction) is subtracted from adjusted gross income (AGI); then the personal exemptions are subtracted from that; this brings the taxpayer to taxable income on which taxes are calculated.

An example of one page of the tax tables is shown in Table 7–3. Shown, too, are the tax forms 1040EZ, 1040A, 1040, and the Tax Rate Schedules X, Y-1, Y-2, and Z (for single taxpayers, married taxpayers, and qualifying heads of household). These sample forms follow as Tables 7–4 through 7–6.[9]

The IRS requires that certain other forms be attached to the 1040 return in some cases. For example, Schedule A, which shows itemized deductions, must be attached if the taxpayer itemizes. This form, too, is shown as Table 7–6. If the taxpayer has farm income, sole proprietorship business income, capital gains, or certain other income or tax credits, additional schedules and forms would need to be submitted. These additional forms are explained in the IRS "Forms and Instructions" booklet.

At one time it was possible for a child to be counted as a double exemption, especially if he or she were a student. This is no longer possible. Either the child or the parent gets the exemption, but not both. If the child is eligible to be claimed as a dependent on the parent's return, then he or she cannot use an exemption on his or her return.

*When a taxpayer loses a child as an exemption*

If the child has income, then, even though a dependent and not allowed to take the personal exemption, he or she may take the standard deduction in some cases, as will be explained below.

A child with earned income is allowed to use his or her standard deduction, and the income is taxed at the child's presumably lower rate. However, if a child under the age of fourteen has unearned income (i.e., investment income) in excess of $1,200 (in 1992), the amount over $1,200 is taxed at the parent's higher rate.[6] The child, while he or she may not have the personal exemption, does have a special $600 standard deduction. This special $600 deduction applies to the unearned income of a child under 14. The first $600, then, is not taxed. The next $600 of unearned income is taxed at the child's rate and the remainder at the parents' rate. The following table illustrates this.

*A child with unearned income*

---

6. The IRS defines unearned income as that income from investments such as interest and dividends, and earned income as that from wages and salaries.

Table 7–3

*1991 tax table*

---

**1991 Tax Table—Continued**

| If line 37 (taxable income) is— | | And you are— | | | |
|---|---|---|---|---|---|
| At least | But less than | Single | Married filing jointly * | Married filing separately | Head of a household |
| | | Your tax is— | | | |

### 41,000

| At least | But less than | Single | Married filing jointly | Married filing separately | Head of a household |
|---|---|---|---|---|---|
| 41,000 | 41,050 | 8,842 | 7,067 | 9,277 | 7,938 |
| 41,050 | 41,100 | 8,856 | 7,081 | 9,291 | 7,952 |
| 41,100 | 41,150 | 8,870 | 7,095 | 9,307 | 7,966 |
| 41,150 | 41,200 | 8,884 | 7,109 | 9,322 | 7,980 |
| 41,200 | 41,250 | 8,898 | 7,123 | 9,338 | 7,994 |
| 41,250 | 41,300 | 8,912 | 7,137 | 9,353 | 8,008 |
| 41,300 | 41,350 | 8,926 | 7,151 | 9,369 | 8,022 |
| 41,350 | 41,400 | 8,940 | 7,165 | 9,384 | 8,036 |
| 41,400 | 41,450 | 8,954 | 7,179 | 9,400 | 8,050 |
| 41,450 | 41,500 | 8,968 | 7,193 | 9,415 | 8,064 |
| 41,500 | 41,550 | 8,982 | 7,207 | 9,431 | 8,078 |
| 41,550 | 41,600 | 8,996 | 7,221 | 9,446 | 8,092 |
| 41,600 | 41,650 | 9,010 | 7,235 | 9,462 | 8,106 |
| 41,650 | 41,700 | 9,024 | 7,249 | 9,477 | 8,120 |
| 41,700 | 41,750 | 9,038 | 7,263 | 9,493 | 8,134 |
| 41,750 | 41,800 | 9,052 | 7,277 | 9,508 | 8,148 |
| 41,800 | 41,850 | 9,066 | 7,291 | 9,524 | 8,162 |
| 41,850 | 41,900 | 9,080 | 7,305 | 9,539 | 8,176 |
| 41,900 | 41,950 | 9,094 | 7,319 | 9,555 | 8,190 |
| 41,950 | 42,000 | 9,108 | 7,333 | 9,570 | 8,204 |

### 42,000

| At least | But less than | Single | Married filing jointly | Married filing separately | Head of a household |
|---|---|---|---|---|---|
| 42,000 | 42,050 | 9,122 | 7,347 | 9,586 | 8,218 |
| 42,050 | 42,100 | 9,136 | 7,361 | 9,601 | 8,232 |
| 42,100 | 42,150 | 9,150 | 7,375 | 9,617 | 8,246 |
| 42,150 | 42,200 | 9,164 | 7,389 | 9,632 | 8,260 |
| 42,200 | 42,250 | 9,178 | 7,403 | 9,648 | 8,274 |
| 42,250 | 42,300 | 9,192 | 7,417 | 9,663 | 8,288 |
| 42,300 | 42,350 | 9,206 | 7,431 | 9,679 | 8,302 |
| 42,350 | 42,400 | 9,220 | 7,445 | 9,694 | 8,316 |
| 42,400 | 42,450 | 9,234 | 7,459 | 9,710 | 8,330 |
| 42,450 | 42,500 | 9,248 | 7,473 | 9,725 | 8,344 |
| 42,500 | 42,550 | 9,262 | 7,487 | 9,741 | 8,358 |
| 42,550 | 42,600 | 9,276 | 7,501 | 9,756 | 8,372 |
| 42,600 | 42,650 | 9,290 | 7,515 | 9,772 | 8,386 |
| 42,650 | 42,700 | 9,304 | 7,529 | 9,787 | 8,400 |
| 42,700 | 42,750 | 9,318 | 7,543 | 9,803 | 8,414 |
| 42,750 | 42,800 | 9,332 | 7,557 | 9,818 | 8,428 |
| 42,800 | 42,850 | 9,346 | 7,571 | 9,834 | 8,442 |
| 42,850 | 42,900 | 9,360 | 7,585 | 9,849 | 8,456 |
| 42,900 | 42,950 | 9,374 | 7,599 | 9,865 | 8,470 |
| 42,950 | 43,000 | 9,388 | 7,613 | 9,880 | 8,484 |

### 43,000

| At least | But less than | Single | Married filing jointly | Married filing separately | Head of a household |
|---|---|---|---|---|---|
| 43,000 | 43,050 | 9,402 | 7,627 | 9,896 | 8,498 |
| 43,050 | 43,100 | 9,416 | 7,641 | 9,911 | 8,512 |
| 43,100 | 43,150 | 9,430 | 7,655 | 9,927 | 8,526 |
| 43,150 | 43,200 | 9,444 | 7,669 | 9,942 | 8,540 |
| 43,200 | 43,250 | 9,458 | 7,683 | 9,958 | 8,554 |
| 43,250 | 43,300 | 9,472 | 7,697 | 9,973 | 8,568 |
| 43,300 | 43,350 | 9,486 | 7,711 | 9,989 | 8,582 |
| 43,350 | 43,400 | 9,500 | 7,725 | 10,004 | 8,596 |
| 43,400 | 43,450 | 9,514 | 7,739 | 10,020 | 8,610 |
| 43,450 | 43,500 | 9,528 | 7,753 | 10,035 | 8,624 |
| 43,500 | 43,550 | 9,542 | 7,767 | 10,051 | 8,638 |
| 43,550 | 43,600 | 9,556 | 7,781 | 10,066 | 8,652 |
| 43,600 | 43,650 | 9,570 | 7,795 | 10,082 | 8,666 |
| 43,650 | 43,700 | 9,584 | 7,809 | 10,097 | 8,680 |
| 43,700 | 43,750 | 9,598 | 7,823 | 10,113 | 8,694 |
| 43,750 | 43,800 | 9,612 | 7,837 | 10,128 | 8,708 |
| 43,800 | 43,850 | 9,626 | 7,851 | 10,144 | 8,722 |
| 43,850 | 43,900 | 9,640 | 7,865 | 10,159 | 8,736 |
| 43,900 | 43,950 | 9,654 | 7,879 | 10,175 | 8,750 |
| 43,950 | 44,000 | 9,668 | 7,893 | 10,190 | 8,764 |

### 44,000

| At least | But less than | Single | Married filing jointly | Married filing separately | Head of a household |
|---|---|---|---|---|---|
| 44,000 | 44,050 | 9,682 | 7,907 | 10,206 | 8,778 |
| 44,050 | 44,100 | 9,696 | 7,921 | 10,221 | 8,792 |
| 44,100 | 44,150 | 9,710 | 7,935 | 10,237 | 8,806 |
| 44,150 | 44,200 | 9,724 | 7,949 | 10,252 | 8,820 |
| 44,200 | 44,250 | 9,738 | 7,963 | 10,268 | 8,834 |
| 44,250 | 44,300 | 9,752 | 7,977 | 10,283 | 8,848 |
| 44,300 | 44,350 | 9,766 | 7,991 | 10,299 | 8,862 |
| 44,350 | 44,400 | 9,780 | 8,005 | 10,314 | 8,876 |
| 44,400 | 44,450 | 9,794 | 8,019 | 10,330 | 8,890 |
| 44,450 | 44,500 | 9,808 | 8,033 | 10,345 | 8,904 |
| 44,500 | 44,550 | 9,822 | 8,047 | 10,361 | 8,918 |
| 44,550 | 44,600 | 9,836 | 8,061 | 10,376 | 8,932 |
| 44,600 | 44,650 | 9,850 | 8,075 | 10,392 | 8,946 |
| 44,650 | 44,700 | 9,864 | 8,089 | 10,407 | 8,960 |
| 44,700 | 44,750 | 9,878 | 8,103 | 10,423 | 8,974 |
| 44,750 | 44,800 | 9,892 | 8,117 | 10,438 | 8,988 |
| 44,800 | 44,850 | 9,906 | 8,131 | 10,454 | 9,002 |
| 44,850 | 44,900 | 9,920 | 8,145 | 10,469 | 9,016 |
| 44,900 | 44,950 | 9,934 | 8,159 | 10,485 | 9,030 |
| 44,950 | 45,000 | 9,948 | 8,173 | 10,500 | 9,044 |

### 45,000

| At least | But less than | Single | Married filing jointly | Married filing separately | Head of a household |
|---|---|---|---|---|---|
| 45,000 | 45,050 | 9,962 | 8,187 | 10,516 | 9,058 |
| 45,050 | 45,100 | 9,976 | 8,201 | 10,531 | 9,072 |
| 45,100 | 45,150 | 9,990 | 8,215 | 10,547 | 9,086 |
| 45,150 | 45,200 | 10,004 | 8,229 | 10,562 | 9,100 |
| 45,200 | 45,250 | 10,018 | 8,243 | 10,578 | 9,114 |
| 45,250 | 45,300 | 10,032 | 8,257 | 10,593 | 9,128 |
| 45,300 | 45,350 | 10,046 | 8,271 | 10,609 | 9,142 |
| 45,350 | 45,400 | 10,060 | 8,285 | 10,624 | 9,156 |
| 45,400 | 45,450 | 10,074 | 8,299 | 10,640 | 9,170 |
| 45,450 | 45,500 | 10,088 | 8,313 | 10,655 | 9,184 |
| 45,500 | 45,550 | 10,102 | 8,327 | 10,671 | 9,198 |
| 45,550 | 45,600 | 10,116 | 8,341 | 10,686 | 9,212 |
| 45,600 | 45,650 | 10,130 | 8,355 | 10,702 | 9,226 |
| 45,650 | 45,700 | 10,144 | 8,369 | 10,717 | 9,240 |
| 45,700 | 45,750 | 10,158 | 8,383 | 10,733 | 9,254 |
| 45,750 | 45,800 | 10,172 | 8,397 | 10,748 | 9,268 |
| 45,800 | 45,850 | 10,186 | 8,411 | 10,764 | 9,282 |
| 45,850 | 45,900 | 10,200 | 8,425 | 10,779 | 9,296 |
| 45,900 | 45,950 | 10,214 | 8,439 | 10,795 | 9,310 |
| 45,950 | 46,000 | 10,228 | 8,453 | 10,810 | 9,324 |

### 46,000

| At least | But less than | Single | Married filing jointly | Married filing separately | Head of a household |
|---|---|---|---|---|---|
| 46,000 | 46,050 | 10,242 | 8,467 | 10,826 | 9,338 |
| 46,050 | 46,100 | 10,256 | 8,481 | 10,841 | 9,352 |
| 46,100 | 46,150 | 10,270 | 8,495 | 10,857 | 9,366 |
| 46,150 | 46,200 | 10,284 | 8,509 | 10,872 | 9,380 |
| 46,200 | 46,250 | 10,298 | 8,523 | 10,888 | 9,394 |
| 46,250 | 46,300 | 10,312 | 8,537 | 10,903 | 9,408 |
| 46,300 | 46,350 | 10,326 | 8,551 | 10,919 | 9,422 |
| 46,350 | 46,400 | 10,340 | 8,565 | 10,934 | 9,436 |
| 46,400 | 46,450 | 10,354 | 8,579 | 10,950 | 9,450 |
| 46,450 | 46,500 | 10,368 | 8,593 | 10,965 | 9,464 |
| 46,500 | 46,550 | 10,382 | 8,607 | 10,981 | 9,478 |
| 46,550 | 46,600 | 10,396 | 8,621 | 10,996 | 9,492 |
| 46,600 | 46,650 | 10,410 | 8,635 | 11,012 | 9,506 |
| 46,650 | 46,700 | 10,424 | 8,649 | 11,027 | 9,520 |
| 46,700 | 46,750 | 10,438 | 8,663 | 11,043 | 9,534 |
| 46,750 | 46,800 | 10,452 | 8,677 | 11,058 | 9,548 |
| 46,800 | 46,850 | 10,466 | 8,691 | 11,074 | 9,562 |
| 46,850 | 46,900 | 10,480 | 8,705 | 11,089 | 9,576 |
| 46,900 | 46,950 | 10,494 | 8,719 | 11,105 | 9,590 |
| 46,950 | 47,000 | 10,508 | 8,733 | 11,120 | 9,604 |

### 47,000

| At least | But less than | Single | Married filing jointly | Married filing separately | Head of a household |
|---|---|---|---|---|---|
| 47,000 | 47,050 | 10,522 | 8,747 | 11,136 | 9,618 |
| 47,050 | 47,100 | 10,536 | 8,761 | 11,151 | 9,632 |
| 47,100 | 47,150 | 10,550 | 8,775 | 11,167 | 9,646 |
| 47,150 | 47,200 | 10,564 | 8,789 | 11,182 | 9,660 |
| 47,200 | 47,250 | 10,578 | 8,803 | 11,198 | 9,674 |
| 47,250 | 47,300 | 10,592 | 8,817 | 11,213 | 9,688 |
| 47,300 | 47,350 | 10,606 | 8,831 | 11,229 | 9,702 |
| 47,350 | 47,400 | 10,620 | 8,845 | 11,244 | 9,716 |
| 47,400 | 47,450 | 10,634 | 8,859 | 11,260 | 9,730 |
| 47,450 | 47,500 | 10,648 | 8,873 | 11,275 | 9,744 |
| 47,500 | 47,550 | 10,662 | 8,887 | 11,291 | 9,758 |
| 47,550 | 47,600 | 10,676 | 8,901 | 11,306 | 9,772 |
| 47,600 | 47,650 | 10,690 | 8,915 | 11,322 | 9,786 |
| 47,650 | 47,700 | 10,704 | 8,929 | 11,337 | 9,800 |
| 47,700 | 47,750 | 10,718 | 8,943 | 11,353 | 9,814 |
| 47,750 | 47,800 | 10,732 | 8,957 | 11,368 | 9,828 |
| 47,800 | 47,850 | 10,746 | 8,971 | 11,384 | 9,842 |
| 47,850 | 47,900 | 10,760 | 8,985 | 11,399 | 9,856 |
| 47,900 | 47,950 | 10,774 | 8,999 | 11,415 | 9,870 |
| 47,950 | 48,000 | 10,788 | 9,013 | 11,430 | 9,884 |

### 48,000

| At least | But less than | Single | Married filing jointly | Married filing separately | Head of a household |
|---|---|---|---|---|---|
| 48,000 | 48,050 | 10,802 | 9,027 | 11,446 | 9,898 |
| 48,050 | 48,100 | 10,816 | 9,041 | 11,461 | 9,912 |
| 48,100 | 48,150 | 10,830 | 9,055 | 11,477 | 9,926 |
| 48,150 | 48,200 | 10,844 | 9,069 | 11,492 | 9,940 |
| 48,200 | 48,250 | 10,858 | 9,083 | 11,508 | 9,954 |
| 48,250 | 48,300 | 10,872 | 9,097 | 11,523 | 9,968 |
| 48,300 | 48,350 | 10,886 | 9,111 | 11,539 | 9,982 |
| 48,350 | 48,400 | 10,900 | 9,125 | 11,554 | 9,996 |
| 48,400 | 48,450 | 10,914 | 9,139 | 11,570 | 10,010 |
| 48,450 | 48,500 | 10,928 | 9,153 | 11,585 | 10,024 |
| 48,500 | 48,550 | 10,942 | 9,167 | 11,601 | 10,038 |
| 48,550 | 48,600 | 10,956 | 9,181 | 11,616 | 10,052 |
| 48,600 | 48,650 | 10,970 | 9,195 | 11,632 | 10,066 |
| 48,650 | 48,700 | 10,984 | 9,209 | 11,647 | 10,080 |
| 48,700 | 48,750 | 10,998 | 9,223 | 11,663 | 10,094 |
| 48,750 | 48,800 | 11,012 | 9,237 | 11,678 | 10,108 |
| 48,800 | 48,850 | 11,026 | 9,251 | 11,694 | 10,122 |
| 48,850 | 48,900 | 11,040 | 9,265 | 11,709 | 10,136 |
| 48,900 | 48,950 | 11,054 | 9,279 | 11,725 | 10,150 |
| 48,950 | 49,000 | 11,068 | 9,293 | 11,740 | 10,164 |

### 49,000

| At least | But less than | Single | Married filing jointly | Married filing separately | Head of a household |
|---|---|---|---|---|---|
| 49,000 | 49,050 | 11,082 | 9,307 | 11,756 | 10,178 |
| 49,050 | 49,100 | 11,096 | 9,321 | 11,771 | 10,192 |
| 49,100 | 49,150 | 11,110 | 9,335 | 11,787 | 10,206 |
| 49,150 | 49,200 | 11,124 | 9,349 | 11,802 | 10,220 |
| 49,200 | 49,250 | 11,138 | 9,363 | 11,818 | 10,234 |
| 49,250 | 49,300 | 11,152 | 9,377 | 11,833 | 10,248 |
| 49,300 | 49,350 | 11,166 | 9,391 | 11,849 | 10,262 |
| 49,350 | 49,400 | 11,182 | 9,405 | 11,864 | 10,276 |
| 49,400 | 49,450 | 11,199 | 9,419 | 11,880 | 10,290 |
| 49,450 | 49,500 | 11,213 | 9,433 | 11,895 | 10,304 |
| 49,500 | 49,550 | 11,228 | 9,447 | 11,911 | 10,318 |
| 49,550 | 49,600 | 11,244 | 9,461 | 11,926 | 10,332 |
| 49,600 | 49,650 | 11,259 | 9,475 | 11,942 | 10,346 |
| 49,650 | 49,700 | 11,275 | 9,489 | 11,957 | 10,360 |
| 49,700 | 49,750 | 11,290 | 9,503 | 11,973 | 10,374 |
| 49,750 | 49,800 | 11,306 | 9,517 | 11,988 | 10,388 |
| 49,800 | 49,850 | 11,321 | 9,531 | 12,004 | 10,402 |
| 49,850 | 49,900 | 11,337 | 9,545 | 12,019 | 10,416 |
| 49,900 | 49,950 | 11,352 | 9,559 | 12,035 | 10,430 |
| 49,950 | 50,000 | 11,368 | 9,573 | 12,050 | 10,444 |

* This column must also be used by a qualifying widow(er).

50,000 or over — use tax rate schedules

*1040 EZ sample*                                              Table 7–4

Department of the Treasury—Internal Revenue Service

Form **1040EZ**
**Income Tax Return for**
**Single Filers With No Dependents** (0)    **1991**    OMB No. 1545-0675

**Name & address**    Use the IRS label (see page 10). If you don't have one, please print.

Please print your numbers like this:

$$9\ 8\ 7\ 6\ 5\ 4\ 3\ 2\ 1\ 0$$

L A B E L    Print your name (first, initial, last)

H E R E    Home address (number and street). (If you have a P.O. box, see page 11.)    Apt. no.

City, town or post office, state, and ZIP code. (If you have a foreign address, see page 11.)

Your social security number

**Please see instructions on the back. Also, see the Form 1040EZ booklet.**

**Presidential Election Campaign** (see page 11)    Note: *Checking "Yes" will not change your tax or reduce your refund.* ▶
Do you want $1 to go to this fund?

Yes  No

Dollars    Cents

**Report your income**

**Attach Copy B of Form(s) W-2 here.** Attach tax payment on top of Form(s) W-2.

1  Total wages, salaries, and tips. This should be shown in Box 10 of your W-2 form(s). (Attach your W-2 form(s).)    1

2  Taxable interest income of $400 or less. If the total is more than $400, you cannot use Form 1040EZ.    2

3  Add line 1 and line 2. This is your **adjusted gross income.**    3

4  Can your parents (or someone else) claim you on their return?
☐ **Yes.** Do worksheet on back; enter amount from line E here.
☐ **No.** Enter 5,550.00. This is the total of your standard deduction and personal exemption.    4

**Note:** *You must check Yes or No.*

5  Subtract line 4 from line 3. If line 4 is larger than line 3, enter 0. This is your **taxable income.**    5

**Figure your tax**

6  Enter your Federal income tax withheld from Box 9 of your W-2 form(s).    6

7  **Tax.** Use the amount on **line 5** to find your tax in the tax table on pages 16-18 of the booklet. Enter the tax from the table on this line.    7

**Refund or amount you owe**

8  If line 6 is larger than line 7, subtract line 7 from line 6. This is your **refund.**    8

9  If line 7 is larger than line 6, subtract line 6 from line 7. This is the **amount you owe.** Attach your payment for full amount payable to the "Internal Revenue Service." Write your name, address, social security number, daytime phone number, and "1991 Form 1040EZ" on it.    9

**Sign your return**

Keep a copy of this form for your records.

I have read this return. Under penalties of perjury, I declare that to the best of my knowledge and belief, the return is true, correct, and complete.

Your signature    Date

X    Your occupation

For IRS Use Only—Please do not write in boxes below.

For Privacy Act and Paperwork Reduction Act Notice, see page 4 in the booklet.    Cat. No. 11329W    Form **1040EZ** (1991)

**Use this form if**

- Your filing status is single.
- You do not claim any dependents.
- You had **only** wages, salaries, tips, and taxable scholarship or fellowship grants, and your taxable interest income was $400 or less. **Caution:** *If you earned tips (including allocated tips) that are not included in Box 13 and Box 14 of your W-2, you may not be able to use Form 1040EZ. See page 12 in the booklet.*
- You did not receive any advance earned income credit payments.

- You were under 65 and not blind at the end of 1991.
- Your taxable income (line 5) is less than $50,000.

If you are not sure about your filing status, see page 6 in the booklet. If you have questions about dependents, see Tele-Tax (topic no. 155) on page 25 in the booklet.

If you can't use this form, see Tele-Tax (topic no. 152) on page 25 in the booklet.

**Completing your return**

Please print your numbers inside the boxes. Do not type your numbers. Do not use dollar signs.

Most people can fill out the form by following the instructions on the front. But you will have to use the booklet if you received a scholarship or fellowship grant or tax-exempt interest income (such as on municipal bonds). Also use the booklet if you received a 1099-INT showing income tax withheld (backup withholding) or if you had two or more employers and your total wages were more than $53,400.

**Remember,** you must report your wages, salaries, and tips even if you don't get a W-2 form from your employer. You must also report all your taxable interest income, including interest from savings accounts at banks, savings and loans, credit unions, etc., even if you don't get a Form 1099-INT.

If you paid someone to prepare your return, that person must also sign it and show other information. See page 15 in the booklet.

**Standard deduction worksheet for dependents who checked "Yes" on line 4**

Fill in this worksheet to figure the amount to enter on line 4 if someone can claim you as a dependent (even if that person chooses not to claim you).

| | |
|---|---|
| **A.** Enter the amount from line 1 on front. | **A.** _____ |
| **B.** Minimum amount. | **B.** _____ 550.00 |
| **C. Compare** the amounts on lines A and B above. Enter the LARGER of the two amounts here. | **C.** _____ |
| **D.** Maximum amount. | **D.** _____ 3,400.00 |
| **E. Compare** the amounts on lines C and D above. Enter the SMALLER of the two amounts here and on line 4 on front. | **E.** _____ |

**If you checked "No"** because no one can claim you as a dependent, enter 5,550.00 on line 4. This is the total of your standard deduction (3,400.00) and personal exemption (2,150.00).

**Avoid common mistakes**

This checklist is to help you make sure that your form is filled out correctly.

1. Are your name, address, and social security number on the label correct? If not, did you correct the label?
2. If you didn't get a label, did you enter your name, address (including ZIP code), and social security number in the spaces provided on page 1 of Form 1040EZ?
3. Did you check the "Yes" box on line 4 if your parents (or someone else) can claim you as a dependent on their 1991 return (even if they choose not to claim you)? If no one can claim you as a dependent, did you check the "No" box?
4. Did you enter an amount on line 4? If you checked the "Yes" box on line 4, did you fill out the worksheet above to figure the amount to enter? If you checked the "No" box, did you enter 5,550.00?
5. Did you check your computations (additions, subtractions, etc.) especially when figuring your taxable income, Federal income tax withheld, and your refund or amount you owe?
6. Did you use the amount from **line 5** to find your tax in the tax table? Did you enter the correct tax on line 7?
7. Did you attach your W-2 form(s) to the left margin of your return? And, did you sign and date Form 1040EZ and enter your occupation?

**Mailing your return**

Mail your return by **April 15, 1992.** Use the envelope that came with your booklet. If you don't have that envelope, see page 19 in the booklet for the address to use.

*Table 7—5     1040A sample*

| | |
|---|---|
| Form<br>**1040A** | Department of the Treasury—Internal Revenue Service<br>**U.S. Individual Income**<br>**Tax Return** (0)           **1991**           OMB No. 1545-0085 |

**Step 1**
**Label**

(See page 16.)

Use the IRS label. Otherwise, please print or type.

| L A B E L  H E R E | Your first name and initial        Last name | Your social security no. |
|---|---|---|
| | If a joint return, spouse's first name and initial        Last name | Spouse's social security no. |
| | Home address (number and street). (If you have a P.O. box, see page 16.)        Apt. no. | **For Privacy Act and Paperwork Reduction Act Notice, see page 3.** |
| | City, town or post office, state, and ZIP code. (If you have a foreign address, see page 16.) | |

**Presidential Election Campaign Fund** (see page 17)

Do you want $1 to go to this fund? . . . . . . .     ☐ Yes ☐ No
If joint return, does your spouse want $1 to go to this fund?     ☐ Yes ☐ No

**Note:** *Checking "Yes" will not change your tax or reduce your refund.*

**Step 2**
**Check your filing status**
(Check only one.)

1 ☐ Single
2 ☐ Married filing joint return (even if only one had income)
3 ☐ Married filing separate return. Enter spouse's social security number above and spouse's full name here ▶
4 ☐ Head of household (with qualifying person). (See page 18.) If the qualifying person is a child but not your dependent, enter this child's name here ▶ _____
5 ☐ Qualifying widow(er) with dependent child (year spouse died ▶ 19 ____ ). (See page 19.)

**Step 3**
**Figure your exemptions**
(See page 20.)

If more than seven dependents, see page 23.

6a ☐ **Yourself.** If your parent (or someone else) can claim you as a dependent on his or her tax return, do not check box 6a. But be sure to check the box on line 18b on page 2.

b ☐ **Spouse**

c **Dependents:**

| (1) Name (first, initial, and last name) | (2) Check if under age 1 | (3) If age 1 or older, dependent's social security number | (4) Dependent's relationship to you | (5) No. of months lived in your home in 1991 |
|---|---|---|---|---|
| _____ | | | | |
| _____ | | | | |
| _____ | | | | |
| _____ | | | | |
| _____ | | | | |

**No. of boxes checked on 6a and 6b** ____

**No. of your children on 6c who:**
• lived with you ____
• didn't live with you due to divorce or separation (see page 23) ____

**No. of other dependents listed on 6c** ____

d If your child didn't live with you but is claimed as your dependent under a pre-1985 agreement, check here . . . ▶ ☐
e Total number of exemptions claimed.

**Add numbers entered on lines above** ☐

**Step 4**
**Figure your total income**

Attach Copy B of your Forms W-2 and 1099-R here.

Attach check or money order on top of any Forms W-2 or 1099-R.

| | |
|---|---|
| 7 Wages, salaries, tips, etc. This should be shown in Box 10 of your W-2 form(s). (Attach Form(s) W-2.) | 7 |
| 8a **Taxable** interest income (see page 26). (If over $400, also complete and attach Schedule 1, Part I.) | 8a |
| b **Tax-exempt** interest. (DO NOT include on line 8a.)   8b | |
| 9 Dividends. (If over $400, also complete and attach Schedule 1, Part II.) | 9 |
| 10a Total IRA distributions.   10a    |   **10b** Taxable amount (see page 27). | 10b |
| 11a Total pensions and annuities.   11a    |   **11b** Taxable amount (see page 27). | 11b |
| 12 Unemployment compensation (insurance) from Form(s) 1099-G. | 12 |
| 13a Social security benefits.   13a    |   **13b** Taxable amount (see page 31). | 13b |
| 14 Add lines 7 through 13b (far right column). This is your **total income.** ▶ | 14 |

**Step 5**
**Figure your adjusted gross income**

| | |
|---|---|
| 15a Your IRA deduction from applicable worksheet.   15a | |
| b Spouse's IRA deduction from applicable worksheet. **Note:** *Rules for IRAs begin on page 33.*   15b | |
| c Add lines 15a and 15b. These are your **total adjustments.** | 15c |
| 16 Subtract line 15c from line 14. This is your **adjusted gross income.** (If less than $21,250, see "Earned income credit" on page 41.) ▶ | 16 |

Cat. No. 11327A

**1991     Form 1040A**                                                                                   Page 2

| | | |
|---|---|---|
| **Step 6** | **17**  Enter the amount from line 16. | 17 |

**18a** Check ⎧ ☐ **You** were 65 or older   ☐ Blind ⎫ **Enter number of**
       if:  ⎩ ☐ **Spouse** was 65 or older ☐ Blind ⎭ **boxes checked ▶**  18a ☐

   **b** If your parent (or someone else) can claim you as a dependent,
        check here . . . . . . . . . . . . . . . . . . ▶ 18b  ☐

   **c** If you are married filing separately and your spouse files Form
        1040 and itemizes deductions, see page 37 and check here . ▶ 18c  ☐

**Figure your standard deduction,**

**19** Enter the **standard deduction** shown below for your filing status.
**But if you checked any box on line 18a or b,** go to page 37 to
find your standard deduction. **If you checked box 18c,** enter -0-.

- Single—$3,400   • Head of household—$5,000
- Married filing jointly or Qualifying widow(er)—$5,700
- Married filing separately—$2,850                                    19

**20** Subtract line 19 from line 17. (If line 19 is more than line 17, enter -0-.)  20

**exemption amount, and**

**21** Multiply $2,150 by the total number of exemptions claimed on line 6e.  21

**taxable income**

**22** Subtract line 21 from line 20. (If line 21 is more than line 20, enter -0-.)
This is your **taxable income.**  ▶  22

**Step 7**

**Figure your tax, credits, and payments**

If you want the IRS to figure your tax, see the instructions for line 22 on page 38.

**23** Find the tax on the amount on line 22. Check if from:
☐ Tax Table (pages 44–49) or ☐ Form 8615 (see page 39)   23

**24a** Credit for child and dependent care expenses.
Complete and attach Schedule 2.   24a

   **b** Credit for the elderly or the disabled.
        Complete and attach Schedule 3.   24b

   **c** Add lines 24a and 24b. These are your **total credits.**   24c

**25** Subtract line 24c from line 23. (If line 24c is more than line 23, enter -0-.)  25

**26** Advance earned income credit payments from Form W-2.   26

**27** Add lines 25 and 26. This is your **total tax.**  ▶  27

**28a** Total Federal income tax withheld. (If any
tax is from Form(s) 1099, check here ▶ ☐ .)   28a

   **b** 1991 estimated tax payments and amount
        applied from 1990 return.   28b

   **c** **Earned income credit.** Complete and
        attach Schedule EIC.   28c

   **d** Add lines 28a, 28b, and 28c. These are your **total payments.**  ▶ 28d

**Step 8**

**Figure your refund or amount you owe**

Attach check or money order on top of Form(s) W-2, etc., on page 1.

**29** If line 28d is more than line 27, subtract line 27 from line 28d.
This is the amount you **overpaid.**   29

**30** Amount of line 29 you want **refunded to you.**   30

**31** Amount of line 29 you want **applied to your
1992 estimated tax.**   31

**32** If line 27 is more than line 28d, subtract line 28d from line 27. This is the
**amount you owe.** Attach check or money order for full amount payable to
the "Internal Revenue Service." Write your name, address, social security
number, daytime phone number, and "1991 Form 1040A" on it.   32

**33** Estimated tax penalty (see page 43).   33

**Step 9**

**Sign your return**

Keep a copy of this return for your records.

Under penalties of perjury, I declare that I have examined this return and accompanying schedules and statements, and to the best of my knowledge and belief, they are true, correct, and complete. Declaration of preparer (other than the taxpayer) is based on all information of which the preparer has any knowledge.

| Your signature | Date | Your occupation |
|---|---|---|
| Spouse's signature if joint return, BOTH must sign | Date | Spouse's occupation |

**Paid preparer's use only**

| Preparer's signature ▶ | Date | Check if self-employed ☐ | Preparer's social security no. |
|---|---|---|---|
| Firm's name (or yours if self-employed) and address ▶ | | E.I. No. | |
| | | ZIP code | |

*U.S. Government Printing Office: 1991 — 285-154

Table 7–6  Form 1040 sample

**Form 1040** — Department of the Treasury—Internal Revenue Service
**U.S. Individual Income Tax Return 1991** (O)

For the year Jan.–Dec. 31, 1991, or other tax year beginning _____ , 1991, ending _____ , 19 ___ | OMB No. 1545-0074

**Label** (See instructions on page 11.) Use the IRS label. Otherwise, please print or type.

L A B E L   H E R E

Your first name and initial | Last name | Your social security number

If a joint return, spouse's first name and initial | Last name | Spouse's social security number

Home address (number and street). (If you have a P.O. box, see page 11.) | Apt. no.

City, town or post office, state, and ZIP code. (If you have a foreign address, see page 11.)

**For Privacy Act and Paperwork Reduction Act Notice, see instructions.**

**Presidential Election Campaign** (See page 11.)
Do you want $1 to go to this fund? . . . . . . . . . | Yes | No
If joint return, does your spouse want $1 to go to this fund? . | Yes | No
**Note:** Checking "Yes" will not change your tax or reduce your refund.

**Filing Status**
Check only one box.

1 ☐ Single
2 ☐ Married filing joint return (even if only one had income)
3 ☐ Married filing separate return. Enter spouse's social security no. above and full name here. ▶ _____
4 ☐ Head of household (with qualifying person). (See page 12.) If the qualifying person is a child but not your dependent, enter this child's name here. ▶ _____
5 ☐ Qualifying widow(er) with dependent child (year spouse died ▶ 19 ___ ). (See page 12.)

**Exemptions** (See page 12.)

6a ☐ **Yourself.** If your parent (or someone else) can claim you as a dependent on his or her tax return, do not check box 6a. But be sure to check the box on line 33b on page 2.
b ☐ **Spouse** . . . . . . . . . . . .

| c **Dependents:** (1) Name (first, initial, and last name) | (2) Check if under age 1 | (3) If age 1 or older, dependent's social security number | (4) Dependent's relationship to you | (5) No. of months lived in your home in 1991 |
|---|---|---|---|---|
| | | | | |
| | | | | |
| | | | | |
| | | | | |
| | | | | |
| | | | | |

**No. of boxes checked on 6a and 6b** ___
**No. of your children on 6c who:**
• lived with you ___
• didn't live with you due to divorce or separation (see page 14) ___
**No. of other dependents on 6c** ___

If more than six dependents, see page 13.

d If your child didn't live with you but is claimed as your dependent under a pre-1985 agreement, check here ▶ ☐
e Total number of exemptions claimed
**Add numbers entered on lines above** ▶ ___

**Income**

Attach Copy B of your Forms W-2, W-2G, and 1099-R here.

If you did not get a W-2, see page 10.

Attach check or money order on top of any Forms W-2, W-2G, or 1099-R.

| | | |
|---|---|---|
| 7 | Wages, salaries, tips, etc. (attach Form(s) W-2) . . . . . . . . | 7 |
| 8a | Taxable interest income (also attach Schedule B if over $400) . . | 8a |
| b | Tax-exempt interest income (see page 16). DON'T include on line 8a | 8b |
| 9 | Dividend income (also attach Schedule B if over $400) . . . . . | 9 |
| 10 | Taxable refunds of state and local income taxes, if any, from worksheet on page 16 . . . | 10 |
| 11 | Alimony received . . . . . . . . . . . . . . . . . | 11 |
| 12 | Business income or (loss) (attach Schedule C) . . . . . . . | 12 |
| 13 | Capital gain or (loss) (attach Schedule D) . . . . . . . . | 13 |
| 14 | Capital gain distributions not reported on line 13 (see page 17) . | 14 |
| 15 | Other gains or (losses) (attach Form 4797) . . . . . . . | 15 |
| 16a | Total IRA distributions . 16a ___ 16b Taxable amount (see page 17) | 16b |
| 17a | Total pensions and annuities 17a ___ 17b Taxable amount (see page 17) | 17b |
| 18 | Rents, royalties, partnerships, estates, trusts, etc. (attach Schedule E) | 18 |
| 19 | Farm income or (loss) (attach Schedule F) . . . . . . . | 19 |
| 20 | Unemployment compensation (insurance) (see page 18) . . . . | 20 |
| 21a | Social security benefits. 21a ___ 21b Taxable amount (see page 18) | 21b |
| 22 | Other income (list type and amount—see page 19) . . . . . | 22 |
| 23 | Add the amounts shown in the far right column for lines 7 through 22. This is your **total income** ▶ | 23 |

**Adjustments to Income** (See page 19.)

| | | |
|---|---|---|
| 24a | Your IRA deduction, from applicable worksheet on page 20 or 21 | 24a |
| b | Spouse's IRA deduction, from applicable worksheet on page 20 or 21 | 24b |
| 25 | One-half of self-employment tax (see page 21) . . . | 25 |
| 26 | Self-employed health insurance deduction, from worksheet on page 22 | 26 |
| 27 | Keogh retirement plan and self-employed SEP deduction | 27 |
| 28 | Penalty on early withdrawal of savings . . . | 28 |
| 29 | Alimony paid. Recipient's SSN ▶ _____ | 29 |
| 30 | Add lines 24a through 29. These are your **total adjustments** . . . . . . ▶ | 30 |

**Adjusted Gross Income**

31 Subtract line 30 from line 23. This is your **adjusted gross income.** If this amount is less than $21,250 and a child lived with you, see page 45 to find out if you can claim the "Earned Income Credit" on line 56. . . . . . . . . . . . . . . . . . . ▶ | 31

Cat. No. 11320B

Form 1040 (1991)                                                                                                          Page **2**

**Tax Compu-tation**

If you want the IRS to figure your tax, see page 24.

| 32 | Amount from line 31 (adjusted gross income) . . . . . . . . . . . . . . . | **32** | |
|---|---|---|---|

**33a** Check if: ☐ **You** were 65 or older, ☐ Blind; ☐ **Spouse** was 65 or older, ☐ Blind.
Add the number of boxes checked above and enter the total here · · · ► **33a**

**b** If your parent (or someone else) can claim you as a dependent, check here ► **33b** ☐

**c** If you are married filing a separate return and your spouse itemizes deductions, or you are a dual-status alien, see page 23 and check here · · · · · ► **33c** ☐

**34** Enter the larger of your:
{ **Itemized deductions** (from Schedule A, line 26), **OR**
**Standard deduction** (shown below for your filing status). **Caution:** If you checked **any** box on line 33a or b, go to page 23 to find your standard deduction. If you checked box 33c, your standard deduction is zero.
• Single—$3,400       • Head of household—$5,000
• Married filing jointly or Qualifying widow(er)—$5,700
• Married filing separately—$2,850 }

| **34** | |
|---|---|

| 35 | Subtract line 34 from line 32 . . . . . . . . . . . . . . . . . . . | **35** | |
|---|---|---|---|
| 36 | If line 32 is $75,000 or less, multiply $2,150 by the total number of exemptions claimed on line 6e. If line 32 is over $75,000, see page 24 for the amount to enter . . . . | **36** | |
| 37 | **Taxable income.** Subtract line 36 from line 35. (If line 36 is more than line 35, enter -0-.) . | **37** | |
| 38 | Enter tax. Check if from **a** ☐ Tax Table, **b** ☐ Tax Rate Schedules, **c** ☐ Schedule D, or **d** ☐ Form 8615 (see page 24). (Amount, if any, from Form(s) 8814 ► **e** ___ .) | **38** | |
| 39 | Additional taxes (see page 24). Check if from **a** ☐ Form 4970 **b** ☐ Form 4972 . . . | **39** | |
| 40 | Add lines 38 and 39 . . . . . . . . . . . . . . . . . . . . . ► | **40** | |

**Credits**

(See page 25.)

| 41 | Credit for child and dependent care expenses (attach Form 2441) | **41** | |
|---|---|---|---|
| 42 | Credit for the elderly or the disabled (attach Schedule R) . . | **42** | |
| 43 | Foreign tax credit (attach Form 1116) . . . . . . . | **43** | |
| 44 | Other credits (see page 25). Check if from **a** ☐ Form 3800 **b** ☐ Form 8396 **c** ☐ Form 8801 **d** ☐ Form (specify) ___ | **44** | |
| 45 | Add lines 41 through 44 . . . . . . . . . . . . . . . . . | | **45** | |
| 46 | Subtract line 45 from line 40. (If line 45 is more than line 40, enter -0-.) . . . . . ► | | **46** | |

**Other Taxes**

| 47 | Self-employment tax (attach Schedule SE) . . . . . . . . . . . . . . | **47** | |
|---|---|---|---|
| 48 | Alternative minimum tax (attach Form 6251) . . . . . . . . . . . . . | **48** | |
| 49 | Recapture taxes (see page 26). Check if from **a** ☐ Form 4255 **b** ☐ Form 8611 **c** ☐ Form 8828 . | **49** | |
| 50 | Social security and Medicare tax on tip income not reported to employer (attach Form 4137) . | **50** | |
| 51 | Tax on an IRA or a qualified retirement plan (attach Form 5329) . . . . . . . . | **51** | |
| 52 | Advance earned income credit payments from Form W-2 . . . . . . . . . . | **52** | |
| 53 | Add lines 46 through 52. This is your **total tax** . . . . . . . . . . . . ► | **53** | |

**Payments**

Attach Forms W-2, W-2G, and 1099-R to front.

| 54 | Federal income tax withheld (if any is from Form(s) 1099, check ► ☐) | **54** | |
|---|---|---|---|
| 55 | 1991 estimated tax payments and amount applied from 1990 return . | **55** | |
| 56 | **Earned income credit** (attach Schedule EIC) . . . . . | **56** | |
| 57 | Amount paid with Form 4868 (extension request) . . . . | **57** | |
| 58 | Excess social security, Medicare, and RRTA tax withheld (see page 27) . | **58** | |
| 59 | Other payments (see page 27). Check if from **a** ☐ Form 2439 **b** ☐ Form 4136 | **59** | |
| 60 | Add lines 54 through 59. These are your **total payments** · · · · · · · · ► | **60** | |

**Refund or Amount You Owe**

| 61 | If line 60 is more than line 53, subtract line 53 from line 60. This is the amount you **OVERPAID** · ► | **61** | |
|---|---|---|---|
| 62 | Amount of line 61 to be **REFUNDED TO YOU** . . . . . . . . . . . . ► | **62** | |
| 63 | Amount of line 61 to be **APPLIED TO YOUR 1992 ESTIMATED TAX** ► | **63** | |
| 64 | If line 53 is more than line 60, subtract line 60 from line 53. This is the **AMOUNT YOU OWE.** Attach check or money order for full amount payable to "Internal Revenue Service." Write your name, address, social security number, daytime phone number, and "1991 Form 1040" on it. | **64** | |
| 65 | Estimated tax penalty (see page 28). Also include on line 64. | **65** | |

**Sign Here**

Keep a copy of this return for your records.

Under penalties of perjury, I declare that I have examined this return and accompanying schedules and statements, and to the best of my knowledge and belief, they are true, correct, and complete. Declaration of preparer (other than taxpayer) is based on all information of which preparer has any knowledge.

| ► Your signature | Date | Your occupation |
|---|---|---|
| ► Spouse's signature (if joint return, BOTH must sign) | Date | Spouse's occupation |

**Paid Preparer's Use Only**

| Preparer's signature ► | Date | Check if self-employed ☐ | Preparer's social security no. |
|---|---|---|---|
| Firm's name (or yours if self-employed) and address ► | | E.I. No. | |
| | | ZIP code | |

*U.S. Government Printing Office: 1991 — 285-148

*Schedule A*   Table 7–6 (continued)

| SCHEDULES A&B<br>(Form 1040)<br><br>Department of the Treasury<br>Internal Revenue Service  (0) | **Schedule A—Itemized Deductions**<br>(Schedule B is on back)<br>▶ Attach to Form 1040. ▶ See Instructions for Schedules A and B (Form 1040). | OMB No. 1545-0074<br>**1991**<br>Attachment<br>Sequence No. **07** |
|---|---|---|
| Name(s) shown on Form 1040 | | Your social security number |

| | | | |
|---|---|---|---|
| **Medical<br>and<br>Dental<br>Expenses** | | Caution: *Do not include expenses reimbursed or paid by others.* | |
| | 1 | Medical and dental expenses. (See page 38.) . . . . | 1 |
| | 2 | Enter amount from Form 1040, line 32 ⌐ 2 ¬ | |
| | 3 | Multiply line 2 above by 7.5% (.075) . . . . . . . | 3 |
| | 4 | Subtract line 3 from line 1. Enter the result. If less than zero, enter -0- . . . ▶ | 4 |
| **Taxes You<br>Paid**<br><br>(See<br>page 38.) | 5 | State and local income taxes . . . . . . . . | 5 |
| | 6 | Real estate taxes . . . . . . . . . . . | 6 |
| | 7 | Other taxes. (List—include personal property taxes.) ▶ | 7 |
| | 8 | Add lines 5 through 7. Enter the total . . . . . . . . . . . ▶ | 8 |
| **Interest<br>You Paid**<br><br>(See<br>page 39.)<br><br>**Note:**<br>Personal<br>interest is<br>no longer<br>deductible. | 9a | Home mortgage interest and points reported to you on Form 1098 | 9a |
| | b | Home mortgage interest not reported to you on Form 1098. (If<br>paid to an individual, show that person's name and address.) ▶<br>------------------------------------------------<br>------------------------------------------------ | 9b |
| | 10 | Points not reported to you on Form 1098. (See<br>instructions for special rules.) . . . . . . . | 10 |
| | 11 | Investment interest (attach Form 4952 if required). (See<br>page 40.) . . . . . . . . . . . . . . | 11 |
| | 12 | Add lines 9a through 11. Enter the total . . . . . . . ▶ | 12 |
| **Gifts to<br>Charity**<br><br>(See<br>page 40.) | | Caution: *If you made a charitable contribution and<br>received a benefit in return, see page 40.* | |
| | 13 | Contributions by cash or check . . . . . . . | 13 |
| | 14 | Other than cash or check. (You **MUST** attach Form 8283<br>if over $500.). . . . . . . . . . . . | 14 |
| | 15 | Carryover from prior year. . . . . . . . . | 15 |
| | 16 | Add lines 13 through 15. Enter the total . . . . . . . . . . ▶ | 16 |
| **Casualty and<br>Theft Losses** | 17 | Casualty or theft loss(es) (attach Form 4684). (See page 40.) . . . . . . ▶ | 17 |
| **Moving<br>Expenses** | 18 | Moving expenses (attach Form 3903 or 3903F). (See page 41.) . . . . . . ▶ | 18 |
| **Job Expenses<br>and Most Other<br>Miscellaneous<br>Deductions**<br><br>(See<br>page 41 for<br>expenses to<br>deduct here.) | 19 | Unreimbursed employee expenses—job travel, union<br>dues, job education, etc. (You **MUST** attach Form 2106<br>if required. See instructions.) ▶ ......................... | 19 |
| | 20 | Other expenses (investment, tax preparation, safe<br>deposit box, etc.). List type and amount ▶...............<br>------------------------------------------------ | 20 |
| | 21 | Add lines 19 and 20 . . . . . . . . . . . | 21 |
| | 22 | Enter amount from Form 1040, line 32. ⌐ 22 ¬ | |
| | 23 | Multiply line 22 above by 2% (.02). . . . . . . | 23 |
| | 24 | Subtract line 23 from line 21. Enter the result. If less than zero, enter -0- . . ▶ | 24 |
| **Other<br>Miscellaneous<br>Deductions** | 25 | Other (from list on page 41 of instructions). List type and amount ▶ ...............<br>------------------------------------------------ ▶ | 25 |
| **Total<br>Itemized<br>Deductions** | 26 | ● If the amount on Form 1040, line 32, is $100,000 or less ($50,000 or<br>less if married filing separately), add lines 4, 8, 12, 16, 17, 18, 24, and<br>25. Enter the total here.<br>● If the amount on Form 1040, line 32, is more than $100,000 (more than<br>$50,000 if married filing separately), see page 42 for the amount to enter. | 26 |
| | | Caution: *Be sure to enter on Form 1040, line 34, the* **LARGER** *of the<br>amount on line 26 above or your standard deduction.* | |

For Paperwork Reduction Act Notice, see Form 1040 instructions.     Cat. No. 11330X     **Schedule A (Form 1040) 1991**

Table 7–6 (continued)    *Tax Rate Schedules*

Schedules A&B (Form 1040) 1991    OMB No. 1545-0074    Page **2**

Name(s) shown on Form 1040. (Do not enter name and social security number if shown on other side.)    Your social security number

## Schedule B—Interest and Dividend Income
Attachment Sequence No. **08**

**Part I Interest Income**

(See pages 15 and 43.)

If you received more than $400 in taxable interest income, or you are claiming the exclusion of interest from series EE U.S. savings bonds issued after 1989 (see page 43), you must complete Part I. List ALL interest received in Part I. If you received more than $400 in taxable interest income, you must also complete Part III. If you received, as a nominee, interest that actually belongs to another person, or you received or paid accrued interest on securities transferred between interest payment dates, see page 43.

| Interest Income | Amount |
|---|---|
| 1  Interest income. (List name of payer—if any interest income is from seller-financed mortgages, see instructions and list this interest first.) ▶ | 1 |

**Note:** If you received a Form 1099-INT, Form 1099-OID, or substitute statement, from a brokerage firm, list the firm's name as the payer and enter the total interest shown on that form.

| | |
|---|---|
| 2  Add the amounts on line 1 | 2 |
| 3  Enter the excludable savings bond interest, if any, from Form 8815, line 14. Attach Form 8815 to Form 1040 | 3 |
| 4  Subtract line 3 from line 2. Enter the result here and on Form 1040, line 8a ▶ | 4 |

**Part II Dividend Income**

(See pages 16 and 43.)

If you received more than $400 in gross dividends and/or other distributions on stock, you must complete Parts II and III. If you received, as a nominee, dividends that actually belong to another person, see page 43.

| Dividend Income | Amount |
|---|---|
| 5  Dividend income. (List name of payer—include on this line capital gain distributions, nontaxable distributions, etc.) ▶ | 5 |

**Note:** If you received a Form 1099-DIV, or substitute statement, from a brokerage firm, list the firm's name as the payer and enter the total dividends shown on that form.

| | |
|---|---|
| 6  Add the amounts on line 5 | 6 |
| 7  Capital gain distributions. Enter here and on Schedule D* . 7 | |
| 8  Nontaxable distributions. (See the inst. for Form 1040, line 9.). 8 | |
| 9  Add lines 7 and 8 | 9 |
| 10  Subtract line 9 from line 6. Enter the result here and on Form 1040, line 9 ▶ | 10 |

*If you received capital gain distributions but do not need Schedule D to report any other gains or losses, see the instructions for Form 1040, lines 13 and 14.

**Part III Foreign Accounts and Foreign Trusts**

(See page 43.)

If you received more than $400 of interest or dividends, OR if you had a foreign account or were a grantor of, or a transferor to, a foreign trust, you must answer both questions in Part III.

| | Yes | No |
|---|---|---|
| 11a  At any time during 1991, did you have an interest in or a signature or other authority over a financial account in a foreign country (such as a bank account, securities account, or other financial account)? (See page 43 for exceptions and filing requirements for Form TD F 90-22.1.) | | |
| b  If "Yes," enter the name of the foreign country ▶ | | |
| 12  Were you the grantor of, or transferor to, a foreign trust that existed during 1991, whether or not you have any beneficial interest in it? If "Yes," you may have to file Form 3520, 3520-A, or 926 . | | |

For Paperwork Reduction Act Notice, see Form 1040 instructions.    Schedule B (Form 1040) 1991

*U.S. Government Printing Office: 1991 — 285-170

| | |
|---|---|
| Unearned income | $1,200 |
| Standard deduction | 600 |
| Net unearned income | $ 600 |
| Taxed at child's rate | × 15% |
| Tax | $ 90.00 |

Congress did this to prevent people from transferring substantial earning assets to their children and saving taxes for the family. However, modest amounts of tax savings are still possible. This is important if a parent wishes to establish a college trust fund for his or her children, and it is explained in greater detail in Chapter 19.

If a child is fourteen or over, then the child's entire unearned income (as well as earned income) is taxed at his or her rate rather than at the parents' rate. In addition, the child may apply the full standard deduction to earned income at the age of 14 or older.

A child with earned income who is taken as a dependent by his or her parents cannot, of course, claim his or her own personal exemption on his or her tax return. However, he or she may still qualify for the standard (or itemized) deduction, but it may be less than the regular standard deduction. Rather, the child must take a special standard deduction which is equal to $600 or earned income, whichever is the greater up to the maximum of $3,600 in 1992.

*A child with both earned and unearned income*

All income, unless specifically excluded by law, is subject to tax. This includes wages, salaries, bonuses, tips, commissions, royalties, farm and business income, gambling winnings, interest, rental income, dividends, the value of prizes won, and alimony received—in other words, nearly everything.

*Income subject to tax*

Moreover, in most cases the taxpayer must report the income when he or she earned it and could have received it. For example, interest on a savings account must be reported in the year in which it was earned and credited to his or her account, not when actually withdrawn. On the other hand, interest on U.S. Government savings bonds (called series EE bonds and discussed in Chapter 13) need not be reported and is not taxed until received some years later.

Unemployment benefits are fully taxable. So too are prizes and awards. Nobel Prizes were formerly not taxed; now they are. So too are college scholarships and fellowships—but only to the extent that the money is not spent on tuition, course-related equipment or expenses such as travel, research, and clerical help and equipment by degree candidates.

In the case of farm, business, and certain other professional income, there are certain expense items that the person may first deduct before reporting the income. These will be discussed below.

Income from a pension (including Social Security) receives special treatment, but in many cases is taxed, as will be explained in Chapter 18.

*Nontaxable income*

The major item not taxable today is the interest income on many state and local bonds. Even here not all state and local bonds are tax exempt. All such bonds issued before August 7, 1986, are exempt in all cases. Municipal bonds issued since August 7, 1986, have been classified, for tax purposes, as public activity bonds and private activity bonds. The interest on public activity bonds is tax exempt; the interest on some private activity bonds is tax exempt. On others it is not. The investor should verify this if purchases are contemplated. The income on private activity nontaxable bonds is considered a tax preference item by the IRS and as such may be subject to the alternative minimum tax (AMT), which is discussed below.

Certain other items, too, need not be included as income. Most government payments made to veterans and their families, worker's compensation payments, casualty insurance payments received, gifts, life insurance proceeds received by the beneficiary, disability and death payments awarded by the courts, and inheritances are not subject to the income tax. Rebates for the overpayment of federal income taxes are not taxable but the interest paid on them is. On the other hand, refunds of state and local income taxes may be subject to the federal tax if deducted as an itemized deduction in a prior year. There are separate gift and inheritance taxes at both the state and federal levels, but at the federal level there are high exemptions. Moreover, strategies exist by which inheritance and gift taxes can be avoided legally. Gift and inheritance taxes are explained in Chapter 19. Table 7-7 illustrates various sources of income not subject to the federal income tax.

*The tax rates*

For most people, there are just three tax rates in 1991—15, 28, and 31 percent. (See Table 7–8 for a chart of various tax rates in 1991.) For a single taxpayer the 31 percent tax rate would apply to all income in excess of $49,300 in 1991. The marginal tax rate is defined as that tax rate which is applicable to the last dollar of taxable income. This is also called the marginal tax bracket, and it, of course, applies to the last dollar in that bracket. For example, in the case of a single taxpayer with a taxable income of $50,000 he or she would pay the following taxes for 1991.

*Checklist of nontaxable income (in most cases)* Table 7–7

---

*Accident insurance proceeds*
*Bequests*
*Board furnished for convenience of employer*
*Child support received*
*Clergymen—rental value of parsonage furnished as part of compensation*
*Damages awarded by a court due to a physical injury*
*Dividends on life insurance policies*
*Gifts*
*Inheritances*
*Interest on bonds of a state, city, or other political subdivision\**
*Insurance benefit payments\**
*Legacies*
*Marriage settlement, lump-sum payment received*
*Old age benefits under Railroad Retirement Act*
*Political campaign contributions received by candidates*
*Scholarships\* (if spent by degree candidates on tuition or course-related expenses*
*Sick pay (taxable in most cases)*
*Social Security benefits\*\**
*Worker's compensation benefits*

---

\*In most cases.
\*\*Social Security benefits are partially taxable in some cases, and not taxable in others.

*The following table shows the various tax rates* Table 7–8

| Married | Taxable income | Tax rate |
|---|---|---|
| Filing jointly | Up to $34,000 | 15% |
| | $34,000–$82,150 | 28% |
| | Over $82,150 | 31% |
| Filing separately | Up to $17,000 | 15% |
| | $17,000–$41,075 | 28% |
| | Over $41,075 | 31% |
| Single | Up to $20,350 | 15% |
| | $20,350–$49,300 | 28% |
| | Over $49,300 | 31% |
| Head of household | Up to $27,300 | 15% |
| | $27,300–$70,450 | 28% |
| | Over $70,450 | 31% |

| | | | | |
|---|---|---|---|---|
| $20,350 taxed at 15 percent | | = | | $ 3,052.50 |
| $28,950 taxed at 28 percent | | = | | $ 8,106.00 |
| $ 700 taxed at 31 percent | | = | | $ 217.00 |
| TOTAL TAX | | | | $11,375.50* |

|  | | Percent rate |
|---|---|---|
| Marginal Tax $217 ÷ $700 | = | 31.00% |
| Average Tax $11,375.50 ÷ $50,000 | = | 22.75% |

There is also a concept called the effective tax rate which would be the total tax divided by taxable income. In the example above, the effective tax rate would be 23% (11,375.50 ÷ 50,000).

*Tax withholdings*

Employers are required to withhold a portion of their employees' wages for income tax purposes. This is referred to as collection at the source, or pay-as-you-go. Its purpose is both to assure the government that the taxes will be paid and to make it easier for the taxpayer. Before the enactment of the withholding tax law, many taxpayers had to borrow to pay their income taxes on time.

When persons begin work with an organization, they file with the employer a withholding tax exemption certificate (the W-4 form), which contains a statement of the number of exemptions to which they are entitled. The employer will then withhold a percentage of wages based on the number of exemptions and the level of the wage or salary. The greater the number of exemptions, the lower the amount withheld. The taxpayer should attempt to withhold as close to what the actual tax liability will be as possible. Substantial under-withholding could result in the taxpayer having to pay a penalty and interest. On the other hand, over-withholding results in the IRS holding funds that could be earning interest for the taxpayer elsewhere. Over-withholding is really an interest-free loan to the IRS. A W-4 withholding allowance certificate is shown in Figure 7-2.

At the end of the year the employer gives the employee two or three copies of a W-2 form, showing the amount paid in wages, the amount of income tax withheld, and the amount of Social Security tax withheld, if any. The W-2 form is the basis for the tax returns of those persons working for wages and salaries. The original copy of the W-2 form is submitted by the employer to the Social Security Administration which provides the information on it to the IRS. The information submitted by the Social Security Administration is used by the IRS to check the accuracy of the figures submitted by the taxpayer. The taxpayer's first

*The reader should note that this calculation is shown for purposes of illustration only. The actual calculation would be made using the tax schedule (Table 7–6). However, the resulting tax payable would remain the same.

*Figure 7—2*   *W-4 Withholding allowance certificate.*

# 19**92** Form W-4

**Department of the Treasury**
**Internal Revenue Service**

**Purpose.** Complete Form W-4 so that your employer can withhold the correct amount of Federal income tax from your pay.

**Exemption From Withholding.** Read line 7 of the certificate below to see if you can claim exempt status. *If exempt, complete line 7; but do not complete lines 5 and 6.* No Federal income tax will be withheld from your pay. Your exemption is good for one year only. It expires February 15, 1993.

**Basic Instructions.** Employees who are not exempt should complete the Personal Allowances Worksheet. Additional worksheets are provided on page 2 for employees to adjust their withholding allowances based on itemized deductions, adjustments to income, or two-earner/two-job situations. Complete all worksheets that apply to your situation. The worksheets will help you figure

the number of withholding allowances you are entitled to claim. However, you may claim fewer allowances than this.

**Head of Household.** Generally, you may claim head of household filing status on your tax return only if you are unmarried and pay more than 50% of the costs of keeping up a home for yourself and your dependent(s) or other qualifying individuals.

**Nonwage Income.** If you have a large amount of nonwage income, such as interest or dividends, you should consider making estimated tax payments using Form 1040-ES. Otherwise, you may find that you owe additional tax at the end of the year.

**Two-Earner/Two-Jobs.** If you have a working spouse or more than one job, figure the total number of allowances you are entitled to claim on all jobs using worksheets from only one Form

W-4. This total should be divided among all jobs. Your withholding will usually be most accurate when all allowances are claimed on the W-4 filed for the highest paying job and zero allowances are claimed for the others.

**Advance Earned Income Credit.** If you are eligible for this credit, you can receive it added to your paycheck throughout the year. For details, get Form W-5 from your employer.

**Check Your Withholding.** After your W-4 takes effect, you can use Pub. **919**, Is My Withholding Correct for 1992?, to see how the dollar amount you are having withheld compares to your estimated total annual tax. Call 1-800-829-3676 to order this publication. Check your local telephone directory for the IRS assistance number if you need further help.

**Personal Allowances Worksheet**

For 1992, the value of your personal exemption(s) is reduced if your income is over $105,250 ($157,900 if married filing jointly, $131,550 if head of household, or $78,950 if married filing separately). Get Pub. 919 for details.

| | | |
|---|---|---|
| **A** | Enter "1" for **yourself** if no one else can claim you as a dependent . . . . . . . . . . . . . | **A** _____ |
| **B** | Enter "1" if: { • You are single and have only one job; or<br>• You are married, have only one job, and your spouse does not work; or<br>• Your wages from a second job or your spouse's wages (or the total of both) are $1,000 or less. } . . | **B** _____ |
| **C** | Enter "1" for your **spouse.** But, you may choose to enter -0- if you are married and have either a working spouse or more than one job (this may help you avoid having too little tax withheld) . . . . . . . . . | **C** _____ |
| **D** | Enter number of **dependents** (other than your spouse or yourself) whom you will claim on your tax return . . . . . | **D** _____ |
| **E** | Enter "1" if you will file as **head of household** on your tax return (see conditions under "Head of Household," above) . | **E** _____ |
| **F** | Enter "1" if you have at least $1,500 of **child or dependent care expenses** for which you plan to claim a credit . . | **F** _____ |
| **G** | Add lines A through F and enter total here. **Note:** *This amount may be different from the number of exemptions you claim on your return* ▶ | **G** _____ |

For accuracy, do all worksheets that apply.
- If you plan to **itemize or claim adjustments to income** and want to reduce your withholding, see the Deductions and Adjustments Worksheet on page 2.
- If you are **single** and have **more than one job** and your combined earnings from all jobs exceed $29,000 **OR** if you are **married** and have a **working spouse or more than one job,** and the combined earnings from all jobs exceed $50,000, see the Two-Earner/Two-Job Worksheet on page 2 if you want to avoid having too little tax withheld.
- If **neither** of the above situations applies, **stop here** and enter the number from line G on line 5 of Form W-4 below.

------------------ **Cut here and give the certificate to your employer. Keep the top portion for your records.** ------------------

Form **W-4**
Department of the Treasury
Internal Revenue Service

**Employee's Withholding Allowance Certificate**

▶ **For Privacy Act and Paperwork Reduction Act Notice, see reverse.**

OMB No. 1545-0010

19**92**

| | | |
|---|---|---|
| **1** Type or print your first name and middle initial | Last name | **2** Your social security number |
| Home address (number and street or rural route) | **3** ☐ Single ☐ Married ☐ Married, but withhold at higher Single rate.<br>**Note:** *If married, but legally separated, or spouse is a nonresident alien, check the Single box.* | |
| City or town, state, and ZIP code | **4** If your last name differs from that on your social security card, check here and call 1-800-772-1213 for more information . ▶ ☐ | |

**5** Total number of allowances you are claiming (from line G above or from the Worksheets on back if they apply) . . . . . | **5** _____

**6** Additional amount, if any, you want deducted from each paycheck . . . . . . . . . . . . | **6** $ _____

**7** I claim exemption from withholding and I certify that I meet **ALL** of the following conditions for exemption:
- Last year I had a right to a refund of **ALL** Federal income tax withheld because I had **NO** tax liability; **AND**
- This year I expect a refund of **ALL** Federal income tax withheld because I expect to have **NO** tax liability; **AND**
- This year if my income exceeds $600 and includes nonwage income, another person cannot claim me as a dependent.

If you meet all of the above conditions, enter the year effective and "EXEMPT" here . . . ▶ | **7** 19

**8** Are you a full-time student? (**Note:** *Full-time students are not automatically exempt.*) . . . . . . . . . | **8** ☐ Yes ☐ No

Under penalties of perjury, I certify that I am entitled to the number of withholding allowances claimed on this certificate or entitled to claim exempt status.

Employee's signature ▶                                    Date ▶                        , 19

**9** Employer's name and address (Employer: Complete 9 and 11 only if sending to the IRS) | **10** Office code (optional) | **11** Employer identification number

Cat. No. 10220Q

Form W-4 (1992)                                                                                                   Page **2**

## Deductions and Adjustments Worksheet

**Note:** *Use this worksheet only if you plan to itemize deductions or claim adjustments to income on your 1992 tax return.*

| | | | |
|---|---|---|---|
| 1 | Enter an estimate of your 1992 itemized deductions. These include: qualifying home mortgage interest, charitable contributions, state and local taxes (but not sales taxes), medical expenses in excess of 7.5% of your income, and miscellaneous deductions. (For 1992, you may have to reduce your itemized deductions if your income is over $105,250 ($52,625 if married filing separately). Get Pub. 919 for details.) | 1 | $_____ |
| 2 | Enter: { $6,000 if married filing jointly or qualifying widow(er) / $5,250 if head of household / $3,600 if single / $3,000 if married filing separately } | 2 | $_____ |
| 3 | **Subtract** line 2 from line 1. If line 2 is greater than line 1, enter -0- | 3 | $_____ |
| 4 | Enter an estimate of your 1992 adjustments to income. These include alimony paid and deductible IRA contributions | 4 | $_____ |
| 5 | **Add** lines 3 and 4 and enter the total | 5 | $_____ |
| 6 | Enter an estimate of your 1992 nonwage income (such as dividends or interest income) | 6 | $_____ |
| 7 | **Subtract** line 6 from line 5. Enter the result, but not less than -0- | 7 | $_____ |
| 8 | **Divide** the amount on line 7 by $2,500 and enter the result here. Drop any fraction | 8 | _____ |
| 9 | Enter the number from Personal Allowances Worksheet, line G, on page 1 | 9 | _____ |
| 10 | **Add** lines 8 and 9 and enter the total here. If you plan to use the Two-Earner/Two-Job Worksheet, also enter the total on line 1, below. Otherwise, **stop here** and enter this total on Form W-4, line 5, on page 1 | 10 | _____ |

## Two-Earner/Two-Job Worksheet

**Note:** *Use this worksheet only if the instructions for line G on page 1 direct you here.*

| | | | |
|---|---|---|---|
| 1 | Enter the number from line G on page 1 (or from line 10 above if you used the Deductions and Adjustments Worksheet) | 1 | _____ |
| 2 | Find the number in **Table 1** below that applies to the **LOWEST** paying job and enter it here | 2 | _____ |
| 3 | If line 1 is **GREATER THAN OR EQUAL TO** line 2, subtract line 2 from line 1. Enter the result here (if zero, enter -0-) and on Form W-4, line 5, on page 1. **DO NOT** use the rest of this worksheet | 3 | _____ |
| **Note:** | *If line 1 is **LESS THAN** line 2, enter -0- on Form W-4, line 5, on page 1. Complete lines 4–9 to calculate the additional dollar withholding necessary to avoid a year-end tax bill.* | | |
| 4 | Enter the number from line 2 of this worksheet | 4 | _____ |
| 5 | Enter the number from line 1 of this worksheet | 5 | _____ |
| 6 | **Subtract** line 5 from line 4 | 6 | _____ |
| 7 | Find the amount in **Table 2** below that applies to the **HIGHEST** paying job and enter it here | 7 | $_____ |
| 8 | **Multiply** line 7 by line 6 and enter the result here. This is the additional annual withholding amount needed | 8 | $_____ |
| 9 | Divide line 8 by the number of pay periods remaining in 1992. (For example, divide by 26 if you are paid every other week and you complete this form in December of 1991.) Enter the result here and on Form W-4, line 6, page 1. This is the additional amount to be withheld from each paycheck | 9 | $_____ |

### Table 1: Two-Earner/Two-Job Worksheet

| Married Filing Jointly | | All Others | |
|---|---|---|---|
| If wages from **LOWEST** paying job are— | Enter on line 2 above | If wages from **LOWEST** paying job are— | Enter on line 2 above |
| 0 - $4,000 | 0 | 0 - $6,000 | 0 |
| 4,001 - 8,000 | 1 | 6,001 - 10,000 | 1 |
| 8,001 - 13,000 | 2 | 10,001 - 14,000 | 2 |
| 13,001 - 18,000 | 3 | 14,001 - 18,000 | 3 |
| 18,001 - 22,000 | 4 | 18,001 - 22,000 | 4 |
| 22,001 - 26,000 | 5 | 22,001 - 45,000 | 5 |
| 26,001 - 30,000 | 6 | 45,001 and over | 6 |
| 30,001 - 35,000 | 7 | | |
| 35,001 - 40,000 | 8 | | |
| 40,001 - 60,000 | 9 | | |
| 60,001 - 80,000 | 10 | | |
| 80,001 and over | 11 | | |

### Table 2: Two-Earner/Two-Job Worksheet

| Married Filing Jointly | | All Others | |
|---|---|---|---|
| If wages from **HIGHEST** paying job are— | Enter on line 7 above | If wages from **HIGHEST** paying job are— | Enter on line 7 above |
| 0 - $50,000 | $340 | 0 - $27,000 | $340 |
| 50,001 - 100,000 | 640 | 27,001 - 58,000 | 640 |
| 100,001 and over | 710 | 58,001 and over | 710 |

copy is submitted with the tax return and a duplicate copy is retained for the taxpayer's files.

If the taxpayer has income not subject to withholding, he or she may have to file a declaration of estimated income (a 1040-ES) and pay a tax on it quarterly. People who are self-employed and those with substantial interest, dividend, or other so-called nonwage income have to do this. If there is only a small amount of income not subject to withholding, the taxpayer may avoid filing this form quarterly by increasing the amount withheld from his or her salary over what it normally would be. The general rule is that if the withholdings and estimated payments are 90 percent or more of the total tax liability for the current year or 100% of the total tax liability for the prior taxable year, there is no penalty for underpayment of estimated taxes. Generally, the underpayment penalty is approximately 10 percent of underpayment times the period of underpayment.

*Payment of estimated tax*

    If a late payment penalty is assessed, it is quite severe. It is currently one-half (1/2) of one percent *per month* up to a maximum of 25 percent on the unpaid amount. In addition to a late payment penalty, there is also an interest charge on any tax payment that is late. It was 10 percent at year end 1991, but it may be adjusted up or down quarterly as the market interest rates vary.

In most cases, married couples have an option of filing separately or jointly. Ordinarily when a married couple files a joint return, as opposed to filing separately, they save substantially in taxes. Whether a couple is married for tax purposes is determined by their status on December 31 of the year in question. There is one exception to this rule: if one of the members of a marriage dies, the survivor may elect to file a joint return that year. If a widow (widower) with a dependent child does not remarry, he or she may continue to file a joint return for the two subsequent years following the spouse's death.

*Joint or separate returns*

    Occasionally it may be advantageous for each member to file a separate return. If there is any doubt, a married couple should calculate their taxes both jointly and separately to determine which is the most beneficial. Filing jointly will usually save taxes but there are exceptions. For example, sometimes filing separately will lower the AGI to the point where the itemized deductions will exceed the standard deduction. In most cases however, if one spouse itemizes deductions, the other spouse must itemize also.

    Married couples living in community property states must apply special rules when filing separately. Anyone who is in this category should study the IRS guide very carefully or consult a tax specialist when considering filing separately. (The community property states are Arizona, California, Idaho, Louisiana, Nevada, New Mexico, Texas, and Washington.)

*Head of a household*

Persons qualifying as heads of household are granted approximately 50 percent of the benefits given to married couples filing a joint return.

To qualify as head of household, an individual must be unmarried or qualify as an abandoned spouse at the end of the tax year. Further, he or she must have maintained a household in which lives any closely related or non-related person for whom the taxpayer would ordinarily be entitled to a dependency deduction. The taxpayer must contribute over half the cost of maintaining the home, which has been interpreted to include property taxes, maintenance costs, mortgage payments or rent, and the like, plus the cost of food consumed on the premises.

## ADJUSTMENTS TO INCOME: ADJUSTED GROSS INCOME

A number of items may be deducted from gross income to arrive at adjusted gross income (AGI); for example, a deductible IRA or a Keogh contribution, one-half of any self-employment tax paid, penalty on early withdrawal of savings, 25% of self-employed health insurance premiums (subject to several restrictions), and alimony paid. These are taken on page one of the 1040 form.[7] Many people do not have many page one deductions. Later, certain other expense deductions may be taken in order to reduce AGI to move toward taxable income; these are the personal exemptions, and either the itemized deductions or the standard deduction. These will be examined below; but first we will examine those items that can be taken in moving from gross income to adjusted gross income shown on the bottom of page one of form 1040 under "Adjustments to Income."

*Payments to a Keogh and an Individual Retirement Account (IRA)*

The Keogh plan and the Individual Retirement Account (IRA) are discussed in greater detail in Chapter 18. They are a means whereby an eligible taxpayer may set aside and earmark funds for retirement. A portion or all of the contributions made may be deducted from gross income to arrive at adjusted gross income. In addition the income they earn is tax deferred until withdrawn upon retirement. In some cases, however, IRA contributions may not be deductible; this is discussed further in Chapter 18. A Keogh plan is only for the self-employed and eligible employees. In some cases a person may have both a deductible IRA and a Keogh plan; in others not.

*Penalty on early withdrawal of savings*

There is a penalty assessed in some but not all cases when a person withdraws savings early from banks and savings and loan associations. The penalty is assessed in the form of reduced interest on early withdrawals, before maturity (see Chapter 13). The penalty is tax deductible

---

7. The deduction for 25% of self employed health insurance premiums was scheduled to expire on Dec. 31, 1991. However, the Tax Extension Act of 1991 extended this 25% deduction to cover premiums paid before July 1, 1992.

and taken on page one of the 1040 form to obtain adjusted gross income.

Periodic alimony payments or separate maintenance payments made under a court order may be deducted. Payments made under a written separation agreement may also be deducted. The taxpayer may not deduct lump-sum cash or property settlements, voluntary payments, or amounts specified as child support.

*Alimony paid*

Taxable income is the sum upon which taxes are calculated. Taxable income is calculated on page two of the form 1040 under the section titled "Tax Computation." Certain deductions may be taken by the taxpayer who qualifies in moving from **adjusted gross income** to **taxable income**. These are the itemized deductions. Some people do not need to itemize because their legitimate deductions do not exceed the standard deduction. The standard deduction was $5,700 in 1991 for marrieds and $3,400 for singles. This will be adjusted for inflation annually.

ITEMIZED DEDUCTIONS: "SCHEDULE A" (AND OTHER) DEDUCTIONS

    The itemized deductions that can be taken only on Schedule A are of no value unless they exceed the standard deduction. If the taxpayer has a few large items, however, such as interest on a home mortgage and property taxes, these alone will often give a deduction in excess of the standard amount. If this is the case, it is worthwhile to keep records so that all the various smaller items can be added. Table 7–6 shows Schedule A with the various itemized deductions.

The taxpayer adds all such expenditures on Schedule A to arrive at total itemized deductions. For 1991 and beyond, a taxpayer's otherwise allowable itemized deductions are reduced by the *lesser* of (a) 3% of the excess of AGI over a specified amount, or (b) 80% of the otherwise allowable itemized deductions for the year. The specified amount for 1992 is $105,250 ($52,625 in the case of a married individual filing a separate return). The reduction (phase-out) of the itemized deductions does *not* apply to medical expenses, investment interest, casualty and theft losses, and gambling losses.

*The itemized deduction phase-out*

*Example 1:* Mary, a single taxpayer, has AGI of $225,000. She has $30,000 of itemized deductions, consisting of $2,125 of deductible medical expenses (after the 7.5% floor), $8,000 of home mortgage interest, $11,000 of taxes, $4,000 of charitable contributions, and $4,875 of investment interest.

    Mary's itemized deductions are reduced by $3,592.50 (3% of $119,750) to $26,407.50.

*Example 2:* Assume the same facts as in Example 1 except that Mary has $950,000 of AGI. In this situation, 3% of $844,750 is $25,342.50. However, the reduction can not exceed 80% of the deductions other than medical expenses and investment interest. Thus the maximum reduction is 80% of $23,000, (the sum of the home mortgage interest, taxes, and charitable contributions) or $18,400. As a result of the $18,400 reduction, Mary may deduct $11,600 ($30,000 – $18,400).

Total itemized deductions are then subtracted from adjusted gross income, if they exceed the standard deduction amount. Alternatively, the standard deduction amount will be used to reduce adjusted gross income if it exceeds total itemized deductions.

*Taxes*

Certain state and local taxes paid by the taxpayer during the taxable year are deductible. The major taxes involved are state and local income taxes and real estate taxes. Sales taxes are no longer allowed as a deduction.

Real estate taxes are probably the most important single tax for the average person. If an individual has an adjusted gross income of $50,000 per year and his or her real property tax is $4,000, that alone will reduce the taxable income to $46,000.

*Interest*

Interest is another big deduction for many taxpayers, especially if they are paying off a mortgage. Interest payments have been broken down into two varieties: mortgage interest and investment interest.

1. *Mortgage interest.* All mortgage interest is usually fully deductible if the home is the principal residence of the taxpayer. If a person has a second home, the mortgage interest on it too is usually fully deductible. During the first few years when the individual is making payments on a mortgage, much of the money is for the payment of interest and will constitute a major deduction.

   On a $100,000 mortgage amortized over 30 years at 10 percent interest, the monthly payment (including only interest and reduction of principal and not insurance and taxes) is $877.57 per month. Of this, $833.33 is interest the first month. The interest portion then declines a bit each month, but over the first twelve months it amounts to $7,974.97. The interest portion then declines a bit each year in the future, but is still substantial and constitutes a major deduction.

   In the case of very expensive homes, there is a limit to the mortgage interest which may be deducted. It is tied to the total debt. The interest deductible limit is the interest on all debt up to $1,000,000. This $1,000,000 debt limitation applies to the combined debt on both the principal residence and the second home.[8]

---

8. There is a grandfather clause in the law regarding this. All pre 10-13-1987 mortgage interest is fully deductible regardless of the application of the proceeds or size of the total debt or the interest. Even if a pre 10-13-1987 mortgage debt is refinanced after

At one time consumer interest (interest on a car loan or credit card) could be deducted. However, Congress eliminated it as a deductible item beginning in 1991. There is, however, a way to get around that interest exclusion if a person is a home owner. An individual may use his or her home as collateral and borrow on it (this is referred to as a home equity mortgage and is discussed in the next chapter). He or she may then use these funds to buy a car. Then instead of car payments, the person has home equity (second mortgage) payments to make and the interest is fully deductible.[9] There is a limit to how much a person may borrow to take advantage of this deduction, and therefore there is a limit to the interest which is deductible. The debt limit is equal to the taxpayer's equity in the home or $100,000, whichever is less.

**2.** *Investment interest.* Interest paid on loans to finance investments, except to purchase securities which yield tax-free interest such as municipal bonds, is deductible. It is deductible, however, only by an amount equal to the taxpayer's investment income. Investment income here includes dividends, interest, and capital gains. If a taxpayer has interest expense greater than investment income, the law allows it to be carried forward indefinitely.

*Charitable deductions*

Charitable deductions may be itemized and deducted on Schedule A. Contributions to approved institutions operated for religious, charitable, literary, scientific, educational, or eleemosynary purposes may be deducted, although such deductions generally may not exceed 50 percent of the taxpayer's adjusted gross income. However, there are different limits in some cases if the gifts were assets that had appreciated since purchased by the donor.

Charitable contributions may include cash as well as assets or personal property (called "other than cash"). Noncash property contributions valued at more than $5,000 require a certification of value by an independent appraiser. In addition, transportation expenses on behalf of charitable organizations may be deducted at 12 cents per mile.

*Medical expenses*

Medical expenses may be deducted only to the extent that they exceed 7.5 percent of adjusted gross income (AGI). Medical expenses include, but are not limited to, dental, doctors, hospitals, prescription drugs, and the cost of eyeglasses and hearing aids. Also included is the cost of

---

that date, the interest is still grandfathered as long as the refinanced amount is not in excess of the remaining amount on the original mortgage.

9. In Texas and a few other states the law does not allow second (or home equity) mortgages on owner-occupied homes, except for home improvement loans.

medical insurance premiums paid by the taxpayer. However, all medical expenses should be reduced by insurance reimbursement before calculating the allowable deduction. Since 1991, expenses related to most cosmetic surgery have not been deductible as a medical expense.

An often-overlooked medical deduction is transportation costs for medical purposes. Mileage to and from doctor's offices, etc., may be deducted at 9 cents per mile. Other medically-required transportation/travel expenses may be deducted, but there are strict limitations set by the IRS. If an individual has medical travel away from home, he or she should consult with the Federal Tax Guide for the requirements of this deduction.

The following table shows how the medical deduction works. Because of the 7.5-percent-of-AGI reduction, only fairly substantial medical expenses may be deducted.

| | |
|---|---:|
| Adjusted Gross Income (AGI) | $ 30,000 |
| Medical insurance premium | $   875 |
| Medical bills not covered by insurance | 1,500 |
| Prescription drugs | 350 |
| Dental bills | 200 |
| Total | $  2,925 |
| 7.5 percent of AGI | 2,250 |
| Medical deduction | $   675 |

*Casualty and theft losses*

A casualty is the destruction of property resulting from an identifiable event of a sudden, unexpected, or unusual nature. It must be due to an external cause and not a defect in the product itself.

Casualty and theft losses are tax deductible to some extent. The loss of personal (non-business) property as the result of accident, fire, theft, vandalism, hurricane, tornado, flood, or other casualty loss not reimbursed by insurance is sometimes deductible. The amount of the casualty loss is the *lesser* of: the property's basis for determining loss on sale of property or the property's decline in fair market value as a result of the casualty. This rule applies whether the property is totally destroyed or merely damaged. The amount of the casualty is then reduced by a $100 "floor," as it is called. The $100 floor is normally a reduction of each casualty established by the IRS. It is normally applicable to each separate casualty or theft loss of personal-use property that occurs during the tax year. The amount is further reduced by ten percent of AGI, to arrive at the deductible portion.

If casualty and theft losses are to be used on Schedule A, the taxpayer must fill out Form 4684 to determine the steps involved in the calculation.

Capital gains and losses (e.g. appreciation or depreciation of security values) are now treated like most other income except that there is a cap which limits the tax on gains to 28 percent.

*Capital gains and losses*

First both short term gains and losses are netted as are long term gains and losses. Then the short and long term positions are netted and the final figure is taken on schedule D which provides for the 28 percent maximum tax cap.

If the net position is a loss, only $3,000 per year of it may be offset against other income, but it may be carried forward indefinitely against other income at the $3,000.00 per year rate. The loss carry forward, however, is unlimited dollarwise against any future capital gains.

Moving expenses for job-related moves may be deducted in many cases.

*Moving expenses*

If an individual moves to a new job location, he or she may be able to deduct some or all of the moving expenses. To obtain the deduction, however, two tests must be met: (1) the new job must be at least 35 miles farther from the old residence than was the old job, and (2) the individual must be employed full time at the new job for at least 39 weeks during the 12 months immediately following the move. Temporary moves do not count. If the person is self-employed, he or she must work full-time for at least 39 weeks during the first 12 months and 78 weeks during the 24 months right after the move. For first time employees (or returnees after having been out of the labor force for some time) to obtain the deduction, the place of work must be at least 35 miles from the former home—note the very slight difference in wording. One is 35 miles from old home to first job; the other, 35 miles from the old job to the new job.

If a person qualifies under these tests, most of the direct moving costs may be deducted on Schedule A, including the cost of moving household and personal goods and reasonable travel costs for the entire family, including lodging and 80% of meals. Auto expenses for driving to the new location may also be taken, either by keeping actual receipts or by using a 9 cents per mile transportation deduction.

Certain indirect moving costs may also be deducted, such as househunting trips and temporary quarters. After an individual has moved, the reasonable cost of lodging in temporary quarters up to 30 days and 80% of meals may be deducted as indirect moving costs. Costs of selling, buying, or leasing a home, including brokers' and attorneys' fees and the like are other examples of indirect moving costs which may be taken. There is, however, an overall limit on indirect moving cost deductions of $3,000, of which no more than $1,500 may be for house-hunting and temporary living expenses.

The deductions for moving expenses must be calculated on Form 3903 before transferring the deduction to Schedule A.

*Job expenses and other miscellaneous deductions*

A number of other miscellaneous deductions may be included on Schedule A. These miscellaneous itemized deductions usually encompass expenses necessary for the production of income or the protection and enhancement of the taxpayer's wealth. These include such things as unreimbursed employee expenses, investment expenses, job-seeking expenses, tax preparation expenses, hobby expenses, gambling losses, etc. The total of most, but not all, of the miscellaneous itemized deductions are subject to a reduction of two percent of AGI before being summed on Schedule A.

Let's look at an example of a miscellaneous itemized deduction which is NOT subject to the 2-percent-of-AGI reduction. Gambling losses to the extent of winnings are not subject to the reduction of 2 percent of AGI. All gambling winnings are taxable income on page one of Form 1040. The gambling losses associated with these winnings may be deducted on Schedule A, but only up to a limit of the amount of these winnings.

The miscellaneous itemized deductions discussed in the remainder of this section are, after totalled, subject to a reduction of 2 percent of AGI.

Unreimbursed employee expenses

Unreimbursed ordinary and necessary employment expenses such as job travel, union dues and job education may be deducted on Schedule A under certain circumstances. Form 2106 is used to report many employee expenses, and must be completed if ANY of a person's employment-related expenses are reimbursed by the employer, or if claiming a deduction for any meal, entertainment, travel, or transportation expenses. For unreimbursed employment-related expenses, other than those listed above, Form 2106 is not necessary.

Employee business expenses

If a taxpayer's job requires travel, these travel costs may be deducted (including an allowance for car expenses, discussed below), meals and lodging, and necessary entertainment of clients. The employee may take portions of these expenses subject to IRS limitations (such as 80% of meals and entertainment) only to the extent that the employer does not provide reimbursements. The costs must be necessary business travel costs, and may not include commuting to and from work. These expenses are included on Form 2106. They are subject to the 2-percent-of-AGI reduction. (Only that portion in excess of 2 percent of AGI may be deducted).

Other types of employee business expenses include parking fees and tolls which are not reimbursed by the employer.

Transportation (auto) expenses

Transportation expenses to produce self-employment income are deducted from that income (on Schedule C). Transportation expenses to take care of rental property are deducted from rental income (on Schedule E). In some cases, transportation (auto) expenses of employees are deductible on Schedule A as part of miscellaneous itemized deductions subject to the 2-percent-of-AGI reduction.

If a car is used for business purposes, the expense of running it can be deducted. If the taxpayer's car is used for both business and pleasure, the expense must be prorated in accordance with the rules on Form 2106. The cost (or mileage) of driving to and from work (commuting) is not considered a business expense and hence is not deductible. If expenses are prorated, good records must be kept. Expenses for the vehicle such as oil and gas, repairs, taxes, insurance, etc., including an allowance for depreciation (explained in detail below) may be used. Accurate records must be kept of miles driven for both business and pleasure. All calculations must be made on Form 2106 for this auto deduction.

An alternative method of calculating auto expenses is to take the standard mileage rate per mile of business mileage driven. The business mileage rate is 27.5 cents per mile used for business for 1991 and is scheduled to be 28 cents per mile in 1992.

**Travel expenses**

Travel expenses away from home (or job site) are deductible only if they directly relate to a trade, business or employment, and only to the extent not reimbursed by the employer. Travel as a form of education is no longer allowed. Travel expenses to a luxury resort or on a cruise ship, even if directly related to a trade, business or employment, are limited.

**Depreciation**

Although most people have only one source of income, many have income other than that from wages and salaries and consequently may become involved with depreciation. A person who owns rental property may depreciate the home or apartment building and take the depreciation as a deduction on Schedule E. An accountant, lawyer, physician, or other professional or self-employed person may recover the cost of books and certain equipment through depreciation on Schedule C.

Depreciation is defined as wear and tear on property used in a trade or business as well as obsolescence. To take depreciation as a deduction on the income tax return, the taxpayer must have certain kinds of property; one cannot claim depreciation on land, stocks, bonds, or securities. The taxpayer must also know the date the property was acquired or placed in service for business purposes, because its life is figured from that date. The cost or other basis of the property must also be known by the taxpayer.

Depreciation is generally computed on the cost of the property as of the date purchased or placed in service. The useful life of the asset generally is determined by IRS guidelines, and may be depreciated for tax purposes over this period of time, which varies from asset category to asset category. For example, furniture has a depreciable life of seven years; computers and computer peripherals, 5 years. In the case of automobiles the amount of depreciation deduction is determined by IRS tables or percentages, as defined by IRS regulations. In the case of an automobile (or any other asset as well) if it is used only partly for business, the depreciation must be prorated on the same basis.

**Home office deduction**

Office-in-home expenses of self-employed individuals are deducted on Schedule C but form 8829 must first be filled out to verify the office use. Certain office-in-home expenses of other employees are deductible only if deductions are itemized on Schedule A. Office-in-home expenses are very limited and must meet restrictive guidelines by the IRS. The office must be used exclusively and regularly as the principal place of the taxpayer's business or place to meet customers, patients, or clients.

If an employee must maintain an office in part of his home, as a requirement of the job and not as a convenience of the employee, he or she may deduct expenses for an office in the home on Schedule A, if itemizing deductions. If a person qualifies under the rules set by the IRS, he or she may deduct depreciation (explained above), insurance, and utility bills; or if a person rents instead of owning a home, a portion of the rent may be used instead of depreciation. However, these items must be prorated by one of two methods—by number of rooms in the home or by square footage of the home. If the office comprises one-ninth of the home, then one-ninth of the expenses may be deducted on Schedule C if self-employed, or on Schedule A under Miscellaneous Deductions if itemizing. The Schedule A deduction is subject to the 2-percent-of-AGI reduction.

**Other miscellaneous deductions**

If a person is a member of a union or professional society, union and professional society dues may be deducted on Schedule A, as well as subscriptions to professional journals connected with one's job. The taxpayer may also deduct any fee paid to have his or her tax return prepared the previous year. A safe deposit box rental may be deducted if the box contains income-producing documents, such as stocks, bonds, or securities. Job-seeking fees are deductible, as are special uniforms required by the place of employment and not suitable for regular wear, including the cost of cleaning and repairing them. Investment expenses such as management fees of mutual funds are another example of a miscellaneous deduction. All of these miscellaneous items are subject to the 2-percent-of-AGI reduction.

**TAX CREDITS**

Itemized deductions, or the standard deduction, are used to reduce adjusted gross income (AGI). Allowable personal exemptions are also subtracted from the adjusted gross income to arrive at taxable income. At this point, the tax liability is calculated. Then there *may* be **tax credits**, which reduce the actual tax itself. That is, after the actual tax liability has been calculated, each dollar of tax credit available will reduce taxes dollar for dollar.

Expenditures incurred in rehabilitating buildings built before 1936 will qualify for a 10 percent credit. If a person buys such an old building for $50,000 and spends $20,000 rebuilding, he or she may take a $2,000 credit and reduce taxes by that amount.

*Rehabilitation and low-income housing credits*

Buildings that have been certified by the IRS as being historical structures will earn a 20 percent credit. If the building in the above case were in this category, final taxes would be reduced by $4,000.

The low-income housing credit is designed for owners of residential rental projects providing low-income housing, and is available for property placed in service after December 31, 1986.

Child care expense is another tax credit to which some taxpayers are entitled. The same is true of expenses for other dependents, including a spouse, if they are disabled. The child care or care of other dependents must be incurred in order to enable the taxpayer to be gainfully employed. The person being cared for must be under thirteen years old or disabled. The credit may be taken by a couple even if only one works full-time, if the other works part-time, or is a full-time student. The credit also includes the cost of services received outside the taxpayer's home such as in a day care center. It is allowed even if the care is provided by a relative or member of the household if such person is not a dependent of the taxpayer.

*Child and other dependent care credit*

There are, however, limits to how large a child care credit may be taken. First, the credit may not exceed 30 percent of the total cost of the care, up to $2,400 for one individual and $4,800 for two or more. This makes the maximum credit $720 and $1,440 respectively. The above amounts, however, apply only if adjusted gross income (AGI) is $10,000 or less. The 30 percent is adjusted downward by 1 percent for each $2,000 (or fraction thereof) of income in excess of $10,000. The maximum downward adjustment, however, will not go below 20 percent, which it becomes when the taxpayer's AGI exceeds $28,000. A person who uses this credit must calculate the credit on (and submit) Form 2441.

The earned income credit is available for low-income people who have a dependent child. It could be a single person, a married couple, a surviving spouse with a child, or the head of a household with a qualified child living with him or her. Eligible taxpayers can claim the earned income credit if earned income (no investment income counts) and AGI were both less than IRS stated maximum levels, which in 1991 was $21,250. These figures are adjusted periodically for inflation. The IRS publishes EARNED INCOME TAX TABLES from which the credit must be calculated.

*Earned income tax credit*

## INCOME (LOSSES) FROM PASSIVE INVESTMENTS

The 1986 change in the tax law defined passive income (and losses) for the first time. Congress has defined the income (and losses) from such limited partnerships as "passive." ***Passive income (and loss)*** has been defined as any income (or loss) received from activity in which the taxpayer does not materially participate in the management of the enterprise. Passive income is, of course, fully taxable like any income. Passive losses, however, are not fully tax deductible. Passive losses may be deducted from passive income, but these losses may not be fully offset against other (say, salary) income as they once were. Congress's intent was to eliminate this form of tax shelter because too many people were using it, and the 1986 tax law did accomplish Congress's intent.

After 1990, current passive losses may no longer be used to reduce active or portfolio income for tax purposes. However, once an asset producing passive income is sold, all prior disallowed passive losses may be taken and used to offset any current year income.

One way in which passive factors arise is if a person invests in a limited partnership. A limited partnership is a means whereby an investor and many other small investors put in dollars (usually the minimum is $5,000); the large sum generated this way is pooled and invested by the managing (or general) partner. The limited partners assume no risk over and above their own individual investment. The large sum of money generated this way is invested in shopping centers, apartment houses, office buildings, warehouses, computer parts, and the like. Some limited partnerships are designed as income partnerships—rent and lease income—and some are designed as tax shelters; some have both income and tax sheltering as their goal. The income comes about in the form of rental income. The tax-shelter aspect works primarily through depreciation (as discussed above) with respect to rental property.

## ALTERNATIVE MINIMUM TAX (AMT)

If an individual is a high-income taxpayer, he or she may also have to pay an alternative minimum tax. It was imposed because Congress felt everyone should pay some taxes. A few high-income people had so arranged their affairs that they paid little or no taxes. Congress had provided certain beneficial provisions in the tax laws. Many of these were eliminated by the 1986 tax law changes, but some still remain. If a person takes excessive advantage of these, the tax law attempts to recapture part of the gain. The alternative minimum tax, then, generally affects people who have a lot of tax-sheltered income, through what are called ***tax preference or other adjustment items***. Tax preference items include:

1.  The appreciation in the market value of charitable gifts. For example, if a taxpayer donates $20,000 of stock, which was purchased for $10,000 five years ago, to the Ogalla School for Wayward Boys,

the $10,000 capital gain is a tax preference item. It is taxed under the AMT but not under the regular income tax. (This item is not applicable for 1991 or through June 30, 1992; it is applicable for contributions made after June 30, 1992.) The appreciation on use related, tangible personal property, i.e., a painting to an art museum, ONLY is not a preference item through June 30, 1992. A donation of stock (intangible) would be a preference item.

**2.** The tax exempt interest on certain private activity municipal bonds.

**3.** The bargain element of incentive stock options. This is the difference between the exercise price and the stock's trading price when the options are exercised.

**4.** The accelerated portion of depreciation on real and personal property. Personal property—such as a car used for business—may still be depreciated in excess of straight line, as may rental houses purchased before August 1986. You must add in here the difference between accelerated and straight-line depreciation.

**5.** Personal exemptions allowed.

**6.** Standard deductions. Also, there are increased limits on some itemized deductions.

In addition to the tax preferences, certain other items, too, have an impact on the AMT. For example, state and local income taxes are not deductible in computing the AMT. Taxpayers living in high state-income tax states may be pushed into an AMT status by that fact alone.

The AMT rate is a flat 24 percent in 1991 (up from 21 percent in 1990), which is well below the top rate under the regular tax rules. Nevertheless, AMT will increase some taxpayer's tax liability because it (the tax base) applies to a greater amount of their income. The preference items and other adjustments are things that taxpayers can deduct or do not have to report on their regular returns.

In order to calculate the alternative minimum tax, the person must first calculate the alternative minimum tax income (AMTI). The taxpayer must begin by taking his or her regular taxable income and adding back the items noted above. There is, however, an AMT exemption which may be deducted.

*Alternative minimum tax exemption*

There is an AMT exemption, which is $40,000 for couples filing jointly, $20,000 each if filing separately, and $30,000 for singles. However, the exemption is phased out for taxpayers with income above certain levels. The exemption is subtracted from the AMTI to obtain the AMT taxable income. In 1991 the AMT is a flat 24 percent (up from 21 percent in 1990) of the alternative taxable income. The alternative minimum tax is compared with the regular income tax, and the higher of the two is paid.

The calculation of AMT is complex. If a taxpayer believes he or she is subject to it, probably professional help should be sought.

**OTHER THINGS THE TAXPAYER SHOULD KNOW ABOUT TAXES**

In 1990, national income was $4,651.5 billion and total personal income tax receipts were about $508.4 billion. This means that if the entire income had been subject to taxes, an average rate of only about 10.92 percent would have provided the same revenue. But the entire income is not subject to taxes.

*The taxation of annuities, Social Security, and pensions*

The income from these sources is taxed differently than income currently being earned. Years ago Social Security was not taxed at all but now it is if it together with other income exceeds a certain level. There are several types of pensions, and the taxation of their benefits varies with the type. Life insurance annuities are also special and are taxed differently. The taxation of all these will be discussed in Chapter 18, Retirement Planning. We will note here, however, that never more than one-half of all social security benefits will be taxed, and in many cases much less.

*Legal tax avoidance*

Deductions for interest on mortgages, local property taxes, and income splitting apply to many individuals. Other ways of reducing taxes are to invest in certain state and local bonds on which the interest is not taxable, or in corporate pension plans, Keogh plans, and an IRA (see Chapter 18). Many of these tax shelters that permit legal tax avoidance (as opposed to illegal evasion) are complex. Any person to whom they apply should check with a competent tax accountant. After all, everyone should so arrange his or her affairs so as to minimize taxes.

*Capital gains on owner-occupied homes*

Many assets, such as homes, appreciate in value as the years pass, and when sold the owner has a nice capital gain. Capital gains used to receive more preferable tax treatment; now they are generally taxed like other income, with 28% being the highest rate at which they are taxed. In addition, capital gains on the sale of owner-occupied houses, if reinvested in another house within twenty-four months, are not taxed. However, if the former house sells for more than the cost of the new one, then the differential is taxable as income.

Congress also provided a once-in-a-lifetime exclusion in some cases. Any taxpayer, age fifty-five or over, may take a once-in-a-lifetime tax exclusion of $125,000 on the sale of a house that has been his or her principal residence for at least three years during the last five years ending on the date of sale of the house. This provision applies to homes sold after July 26, 1978.

*IRS audits*

If a taxpayer has filled out the tax return correctly, the chances of being audited are remote. There are three kinds of audits. First is the correspondent audit, where a few items might be questioned; this does not usually take much time. The IRS will write the taxpayer a letter. Usually such an audit can be handled by writing letters or making a telephone call. If the items are in a gray area, there may be some bargaining. The IRS may compromise and allow some deductions but not others. Second, there is an office audit, in which the taxpayer appears at the IRS office to discuss the items in question. Third, there is the field audit, in which the IRS comes to the taxpayer's home or office.

Returns selected for audit are based upon the IRS's discriminant functions system (DIF) program which is developed through Taxpayer Compliance Measurement Program (TCMP) audits. TCMP audits are an item-by-item examination of the taxpayer's entire return. People picked for the TCMP are chosen at random. The purpose of the TCMP is to give the IRS a feeling for the various legitimate expenses of various income groups in order to update their computer, which scans millions of tax forms to spot irregularities. Statistics obtained this way are fed into the IRS's discriminant functions system (DIF) program to determine norms. These statistics are then used to select returns for audit based upon variances from established norms.

*How to avoid an audit*

The chances of being audited are small. Only about 1 percent of all returns are selected for an audit. If the taxpayer's income is above $100,000, the chances are about four percent.

Generally speaking, if there are high itemized deductions on a return, the chances of being audited are greater. The IRS has average dollar amounts of deductions for various levels of income. The greater a person's deductions are above the averages, the greater the likelihood of an audit. If some deductions are unusually high in a given year, the taxpayer might attach a note explaining why. For example, if there are unusually large dental bills because of orthodontic work, this may be explained in an attached note. This may be done for any high deductible item that is legitimate.

Substantial declines in income, if the person is self-employed, too, may trigger an audit.

## SUGGESTED READINGS

Commerce Clearing House. *Federal Tax Return Manual,* Chicago: Commerce Clearing House. Annual publication.

"Federal Tax Course." Chicago: Commerce Clearing House. Annual publication.

"Federal Tax Courses." Englewood Cliffs, N.J.: Prentice Hall. Annual publication.

"Highlights of the Tax Reform Act of 1986." Chicago: Arthur Andersen & Co.

Internal Revenue Service. "Employer's Tax Guide, Circular E." Washington, D.C.: Internal Revenue Service. Annual publication.

"Instructions for Preparing Form 1040." An annual IRS publication which can be obtained at any post office during tax time and at any regional IRS office at other times.

"Instructions for Preparing Form 1040A." An annual IRS publication which can be obtained at any post office during tax return time and at any regional IRS office at other times.

"Master Tax Guide." Chicago: Commerce Clearing House. An annual publication.

"The National Debt." Philadelphia: The Federal Reserve Bank of Philadelphia.

"Price Waterhouse Guide to the New Tax Law." New York: Bantam Books, 1987.

"Price Waterhouse Retirement Planning Adviser" 1990–1991 Edition. New York: Pocket Books, a division of Simon & Schuster, Inc. 1990.

Sommerfeld, Ray M., Anderson, Hershel M., and Brock, Horace R. *An Introduction to Taxation,* 4th ed. New York: Harcourt, Brace & World, 1988.

*Tax Guide for Small Business.* Washington, D.C.; U.S. Government Printing Office. Annual publication.

"Tax Reform 1988." Chicago: Arthur Andersen & Co.

"22 Ways to Save Money on Income Taxes." Dean Witter Reynolds, Inc. You may obtain this from your Dean Witter broker.

*United States Budget.* Washington, D.C.: U. S. Government Printing Office. Annual publication.

"Year-End Tax Strategy for Individuals; Planning for 1986 and Beyond." Chicago: Arthur Andersen & Co.

*Your Federal Income Tax.* An annual IRS publication which gives a far more detailed explanation than the "Instructions for Preparing Form 1040." It can be obtained at any IRS regional office.

# 8 Housing

The buy-down mortgage
Equity build-up mortgage (EBM) and
    shared appreciation mortgage
    (SAM)
Some dangers of innovative mortgages
OTHER THINGS TO KNOW ABOUT HOME
    OWNERSHIP

Points
Making an offer on a house; earnest
    money
Closing costs
SUGGESTED READINGS

**HIGHLIGHTS**  In order to present the basic information needed for home ownership,
this chapter examines the following:

1  The advantages and disadvantages of home ownership
2  Renting versus owning
3  How homes are financed, and the cost of financing them
4  How home mortgages are paid off or amortized
5  Refinancing a home
6  Large versus small down payments
7  The new innovative mortgages
8  The closing costs of buying a home

## INTRODUCTION

Home ownership is important in a budget. Most people who own homes must meet a monthly mortgage payment that is a substantial proportion of the budget, a fixed payment that must be paid for many years. In addition, many people consider part of this monthly payment to be forced saving because with each monthly payment the individual's equity or ownership in the home increases. Others relate home ownership to the family budget because the interest paid as well as the real property taxes constitute large tax-deductible items.

The popularity of home ownership is shown by the fact that currently about 64 percent of United States families own their own homes. The rate of increase, however, has slowed in the last few years, generally because of the greater availability of rental units and increases in construction costs.

## FACTORS TO CONSIDER

Some people attach great importance to the peace of mind, pride, security, greater privacy, and convenience that owning a home provides. Some also feel that homes are often located in less congested areas than apartments, and provide a better environment in which to raise children.

### Advantages of home ownership
Tax advantages

There are several advantages to owning a home. Some of these are enumerated in the following discussion.

There is a considerable tax advantage to home ownership. A home owner pays interest on the mortgage and local property taxes on the home, while a person who rents an apartment pays rent. The latter, however, includes a sum to enable the landlord to pay the interest and tax; hence the renter pays these costs indirectly. Because of this hidden cost for the renter, home owners have a tax advantage over renters. If their income, exemptions, and other deductions are the same as the renter's, they will usually pay lower taxes. This is because home owners may deduct from their incomes, when calculating their taxes, interest on their mortgage and property taxes. Rent, of course, cannot be deducted. This can best be illustrated by an example. Consider two childless couples whose circumstances are identical except that one rents and one owns a house. Both have adjusted gross incomes of $30,000, and total deductions because of medical expenses, contributions to charity, and so forth, amount to $2,000. The couple owning a home, however, has additional deductions of $6,900 due to interest and property taxes ($75 per month taxes and about $500 per month interest is not unreasonable for even a modest home). The couple owning a home will take a total deduction of $8,900, while the one renting can take only the $5,700 standard deduction that married couples may take if filing jointly.[1] The home owner's taxable income is $3,200 lower. The nature of our tax laws

---

1. The standard deduction for married couples filing jointly for 1991 was $5,700. This standard deduction is adjusted for inflation based on the Consumer Price Index.

enables the home owner to pass part of the interest and property taxes on to Uncle Sam, if they have enough total deductions to itemize deductions on their tax return.

In some states, laws have been enacted making it possible for persons to declare their home to be their homestead. This prevents the home from being seized to satisfy certain private debts. In some states, there is a dollar limit to the amount of real estate protected against seizure. The homestead act does not prevent the mortgage lender from foreclosing if mortgage payments are not made. Also, the government is not prevented from seizing the property if it has a valid claim against the owner. But with these two exceptions, the property is protected. In some areas, property taxes are also reduced by a modest amount if a homestead claim is filed.

Homestead

A home is often thought of as a good inflationary hedge. Generally, a home will appreciate as much as inflation, and sometimes more than overall prices during times of inflation, because when prices rise, so do building materials and labor costs. Consequently, during inflation, the cost of building new houses rises; this generally brings up the price of older houses as well.

A home as an inflationary hedge

During the decade of the 1970s the price of houses rose much more rapidly than the overall rate of inflation. However, by the middle 1980s this rapid home price escalation slowed; indeed in some depressed areas of the country, prices have actually declined. In most areas, however, the price of homes has still kept up with inflation and in many cases has exceeded it. In addition, the past few years is likely to prove an ephemeral phenomenon. If history is any guide, the future price of homes will more than keep up with inflation in the long run. Table 8–1 shows the sale of one-family homes and median prices since 1970.

Some people consider maintenance as a disadvantage of home ownership. The house must be painted every few years, and from time to time the roof will need repairs. Occasionally, a plumber will have to be called, and certain built-in appliances like the hot water heater, furnace, and air conditioner wear out and must be repaired or replaced. These things can be avoided by the apartment dweller, as well as work like raking leaves, cutting the lawn, and shoveling snow. Since most people do these chores themselves, little monetary cost is involved, but the home owner's time is committed.

*Disadvantages of home ownership*

It has been estimated that maintenance costs will be about 1½ percent of the cost of the house per year. This is the average cost, and in some years the cost will be considerably higher. Some people consider the big investment required to be a home owner a disadvantage. The fact

Table 8—1     *New and existing one-family homes sold*

| | Number (thousands) | | | Dollar volume (billions) | | | Median price | |
|---|---|---|---|---|---|---|---|---|
| Year | New homes | Existing homes | Total homes | New homes** | Existing homes | Total homes | New homes | Existing homes |
| 1970 | 485 | 1,612 | 2,097 | $12.9 | $ 41.4 | $ 54.3 | $23,4000 | $23,000 |
| 1971 | 656 | 2,018 | 2,674 | 18.6 | 56.5 | 75.1 | 25,200 | 24,800 |
| 1972 | 718 | 2,252 | 2,970 | 21.9 | 67.8 | 89.7 | 27,600 | 26,700 |
| 1973 | 634 | 2,334 | 2,968 | 22.5 | 76.8 | 99.3 | 32,500 | 28,900 |
| 1974 | 519 | 2,272 | 2,791 | 20.2 | 81.3 | 101.5 | 35,900 | 32,000 |
| 1975 | 549 | 2,476 | 3,025 | 23.4 | 96.6 | 120.0 | 39,300 | 35,300 |
| 1976 | 646 | 3,064 | 3,710 | 31.0 | 129.3 | 160.3 | 44,200 | 38,100 |
| 1977 | 819 | 3,650 | 4,469 | 44.4 | 174.8 | 219.2 | 48,800 | 42,900 |
| 1978 | 817 | 3,986 | 4,803 | 51.1 | 221.2 | 272.3 | 55,700 | 48,700 |
| 1979 | 709 | 3,827 | 4,536 | 50.9 | 245.7 | 296.6 | 62,900 | 55,700 |
| 1980 | 545 | 2,973 | 3,518 | 41.6 | 216.4 | 258.0 | 64,600 | 62,200 |
| 1981 | 436 | 2,419 | 2,855 | 36.2 | 189.4 | 225.6 | 68,900 | 66,400 |
| 1982 | 412 | 1,990 | 2,402 | 34.6 | 160.2 | 194.8 | 69,300 | 67,800 |
| 1983 | 623 | 2,719 | 3,342 | 55.9 | 225.9 | 281.8 | 75,300 | 70,300 |
| 1984 | 639 | 2,868 | 3,507 | 62.4 | 246.6 | 309.0 | 79,900 | 72,400 |
| 1985 | 688 | 3,214 | 3,902 | 69.4 | 291.9 | 361.3 | 84,300 | 75,500 |
| 1986 | 749 | 3,565 | 4,314 | 83.7 | 351.5 | 435.2 | 91,700 | 80,300 |
| 1987 | 671 | 3,526 | 4,197 | 85.4 | 374.8 | 460.2 | 104,500 | 85,600 |
| 1988* | 677 | 3,594 | 4,271 | 93.6 | 405.4 | 499.0 | 112,500 | 89,300 |

*Preliminary.

**Computed from number of homes sold and average sales price.

Sources: Bureau of the Census; National Association of Realtors; Savings Institutions Sourcebook, 1989, p. 42.

that a home is not very liquid and requires time to sell reinforces this disadvantage.

*To rent or own a home*

When comparing renting and buying, many people compare renting an apartment with buying a house. This is not completely valid because two different things are being compared. Usually (but not always), a house is larger than an apartment. In addition, the home owner has more privacy than a tenant in an apartment and a backyard, which the tenant lacks. Also, home owners are building up an equity in their houses. Consequently, you cannot compare the monthly mortgage payment on a house with the monthly rental payment and reach a decision. You must also give some weight to all the things discussed above under advantages and disadvantages of home ownership.

To be sure, houses can also be rented. If you were to compare the monthly rent on a house with the mortgage payment on a similar house, you would have a more meaningful comparison.

The two options must be compared in the long run and the short run. A home owner does not build up much equity during the first few years of home ownership, because most of the monthly payments go for interest. Also, the first year will necessitate additional closing costs and possibly expenditures for putting in a lawn and other landscaping.

When buying a house as opposed to renting, an individual is almost certainly better off financially to buy, except possibly in the short run. That has been the case in the past, and it is likely to be so in the future. However, if a person is only going to live in a community a year or two, he or she might want to rent for the somewhat greater convenience and possibly less expense: for example, no maintenance cost, no landscaping (needed on new homes only), no closing costs, no possible realtor's fee when selling, and the like. In the long run, especially if the monthly mortgage payment is lower than the monthly rent, probably an individual should buy.

If it does not matter to the individual whether he or she lives in an apartment or buys a house, and the decision between buying or renting is made strictly on a financial basis, then the task is more complex. The following will need to be considered:

1.  The monthly rent and the monthly mortgage payment
2.  The dollar amount of property taxes and interest, as well as the individual's tax bracket, since these two items are tax deductible
3.  How much the house is likely to appreciate in price per year
4.  How long the individual is likely to be living in the community before moving
5.  The cost of insurance and maintenance

Whether a person should buy or rent is a question that must be analyzed individually. It will vary from time to time and place to place and person to person. An individual might be living in an area that is over built with apartments; hence, rents might be relatively low. If that is the case at a time when interest rates are very high and few homes are being built and hence are very costly, he or she could be better off to rent at least for a time. If, later, apartments are no longer over built and rents rise and at the same time interest rates decline, this might be the time to investigate home ownership.

When an individual decides whether to rent or buy, the material on the personal budget and on housing expenditures in Chapter 2 should be reviewed. Housing expenses from renting and from buying should be compared. Table 8–2 is a place to begin in making the analysis.

In it we are assuming a $90,000 home with an $80,000 thirty-year mortgage at 12 percent. This will make the monthly mortgage payment about $823. The annual rent for a comparable home is $8,400. However, it and some of the other items may differ according to the geographical area.

In the case shown in Table 8–2, the cost of owning a home at the 15 percent tax bracket exceeds the cost of renting by $2,230 even after taking taxes into account. However, this $2,230 shrinks to $868 at the 28 percent tax bracket. If we also consider appreciation to be 4 percent

Table 8–2     *Expenses of renting versus buying a home*

| | | |
|---|---:|---|
| COST OF RENTING: $700/month × 12 | $8,400 | per year |
| COST OF BUYING A HOME: | | |
|   Mortgage payment $823/month × 12 | $9,876 | per year |
|   Maintenance $50/month × 12 | 600 | |
|   Interest foregone on $10,000 down payment | | |
|     ($10,000 × 9%)              $900 | | |
|   Less taxes at 15%           – 135 | | |
| | 765 | |
|   Property taxes $75/month × 12 | 900 | |
|   Insurance on house $30/month × 12 | 360 | |
| Total Cost | $12,501 | |
| Less tax benefits from deducting interest and | | |
|     property taxes: | | |
|       Interest   $9,576 | | |
|       Taxes       900 | | |
|              $10,476 × 15% tax rate | $1,571 | |
| Less equity build-up $25/month × 12 | – 300 | |
| Net cost; $12,501 – $1,871 | $10,630 | |

Adjust further by price appreciation of house. To be sure, the value of homes does not always appreciate. However, generally homes have appreciated enough to keep up with inflation in the long run, and in many cases by more.

| | |
|---|---:|
| Net cost at the | |
|   28% tax bracket:   $12,501 – $3,233 | $9,268 |

per year, then even the person in the 15 percent tax bracket might be better off by buying, because he or she has an inflationary hedge. In addition, the longer an individual owns a home, the better off he or she will be relative to the renter; because as the years pass, the total dollar cost of interest declines and the equity build-up increases. It should also be noted that as the years pass, rent is more likely to rise as a result of inflation; whereas house payments (on a fixed mortgage) will remain constant (although some portions may rise such as taxes and insurance).

*How much house can an individual afford?*

There used to be, and to some extent still are, five rules of thumb used by mortgage lenders to indicate how much of a house a prospective home owner could afford. They are:

**1.**    The price of the home (including the lot) should be no more than two and one-half times the purchaser's annual gross (before tax) income.

2.   The amount borrowed to purchase a home should be no more than two times the purchaser's gross annual income.
3.   The monthly mortgage payments of a home owner (which include reduction of principal, interest, taxes, and insurance—PITI) should be no more than 25 percent of the home owner's gross income. This assumes a 10 percent down payment. If you pay down more than 10 percent, this 25 percent figure may be scaled up to as much as 28 percent.
4.   Total monthly housing costs should not exceed one week's net take-home pay.
5.   Total monthly payment on all debts (including consumer installment debt) should not exceed 36 percent of gross monthly income. To be sure, the aforementioned percentage figures will vary some from state to state and between lenders.

The first three rules all work out about the same. Under the first rule, a person making $25,000 per year could buy a house worth $62,500. He or she could also finance about $50,000 of it under the second rule and hence would need a down payment of about $12,500. This is the often standard 20 percent.

Under the third rule, the person could pay $520 per month ($25,000 ÷ 12 = $2,083 × 25% = $520). Moreover, historically about 1 percent of the mortgage would cover the monthly payment needed for the reduction of principal, interest, taxes, and insurance. In the $50,000 mortgage noted above, this amounts to $500.

Rule four has more often been applied to renters, but sometimes to homeowners. Under it, the person would not quite qualify. One week's gross pay is $480 ($25,000 ÷ 52). The net after taxes would be even less.

Under rule five the person making $25,000 per year could assume debts requiring monthly payments of up to $750.

In recent years all of the rules have been stretched a bit, especially for two-income families. Obviously the higher a down payment you are able to make, the more house you can afford. But the rules have been modified in other ways. The 2 times rule is now sometimes the 3 times rule and the 25 percent has been modified to 28 percent in some cases. In such a case, the person making $25,000 could afford a monthly payment of $583. This has been done because interest costs and construction costs, and hence housing costs, have risen faster than income. In addition, many people have been willing to make a greater sacrifice to acquire a home because home ownership has proven to be a good investment. The individual who does this must do so with care, and budget wisely.

*Condominium or house?*

Some people prefer a condominium to a house. A condominium provides some of the benefits of owning a house and some of the benefits of apartment living. Condominiums are apartmentlike structures, but residents receive *title* to their units. They must make a down payment and arrange their mortgage, if financed, just as for a house. Moreover, they can sell at any time. Condominium owners have the same tax benefits as home owners and build up equity like a home owner. They have all the building maintenance problems to take care of in their unit.

A condominium owner is more like an apartment dweller in that there is no yard work to perform. There may be a common yard that can be enjoyed with other condominium owners in the building. Sometimes this includes a common swimming pool, tennis court, and putting green. Instead of maintaining these facilities, the individual is assessed a fee each month, and a maintenance crew is hired.

When buying a condominium, the owner joins the condominium association, and all members have one vote in deciding matters in accordance with the provisions as set forth in the condominium agreement that all members must agree to abide by. Generally speaking, condominium owners may sell their unit to anyone they choose.

Choosing between a house and a condominium is a personal matter. Those who want some of the benefits of home ownership but not all of the problems might choose this compromise, although they give up some backyard privacy.

## Co-ops

In some cities, there are co-op apartments and even co-op homes. These co-ops are nonprofit corporations, and the residents of a co-op housing unit, technically speaking, do not own their unit. The corporation owns it, and each resident owns some stock (certificates of ownership) of the corporation. Often the number of apartments in a co-op is large, and home co-ops may cover an entire city block. Generally, the homes are connected and are built facing the street on all four sides of the block. The center then becomes a courtyard and serves as a common backyard.

Since the apartments (or homes) in a co-op are of varying sizes (and values), the amount of stock a co-op has is prorated accordingly. The price residents have to pay for the stock is then similar to the down payment on a house. The co-oper makes a monthly payment (which varies in accordance with the value of the individual unit) to the co-op; this includes interest, taxes, insurance, and reduction of principal, and the coop makes one mortgage payment to the mortgage holder. There is one common mortgage on twenty or, thirty different rental units rather than each one being financed separately. As the years pass and the mortgage is reduced, the theoretical value of the co-op shares rises.

Since co-op housing is a relatively new development, few of them have been around long enough to have their mortgage paid off. However, when the common mortgage is paid, there is usually some arrangement for the co-op to be dissolved and all co-opers to obtain title to their units. Each co-oper may be expected to help in doing yard work, or there may be a monthly fee to have this done.

A co-op is similar to a condominium, but legally different. In a condominium, each unit has a separate mortgage and each resident has title to his or her property. In a co-op, there is one mortgage and the resident owns shares in the co-op. However, co-op owners may sell their shares to qualifying buyers.

That portion of the co-oper's monthly payment for the payment of interest or property taxes is fully deductible for tax purposes, just as in the case of the home or condominium owner. The co-op may offer one advantage over the individual residential unit, since on a mortgage often for hundreds of thousands of dollars (or even millions) the interest rate may be a little lower.

One question may have occurred to you. Since a co-op is a nonprofit corporation, who would have an incentive to establish one? The answer is realtors, builders, and land developers, who would stand to make a profit due to realtors' fees or in the construction of the building. One possible disadvantage to owning a co-op is that since there is one mortgage and since the value of the co-op shares rises as equity is built up, the new prospective buyer would need a large down payment to buy a coop unit. In the case of an individual mortgage, it can be refinanced, but with a common mortgage this is not possible. This problem can be solved in some states where banks and savings and loan associations can make long-term loans using co-op stock as security.

Recently more and more people have been buying mobile homes. At one time these units appealed primarily to people whose jobs required that they move a good deal, such as construction workers. Today, however, primarily because they are so much cheaper than a conventional home, many young couples as well as older retired people are buying them.

*Mobile homes*

There are two varieties of mobile homes. There is the true mobile home, which is on wheels and is moved from place to place. Many retired people have these trailers and go south during the winter. Then there is the so-called **mobile home**, which is on blocks and may have elaborate extensions built onto it. It can never again be moved and will remain permanently in a trailer or mobile home park.

In the past a mobile home was always a trailer with or without wheels. Recently, **motor homes** have been developed: self-propelled units generally built on a truck frame. Many of these units have become the second homes discussed below.

Mobile homes were financed like cars until a few years ago. Loans for them were considered consumer loans, the interest rates were similar to rates on cars, and they had to be amortized over several years like auto loans. Some lenders still feel this way; if mobile homes have wheels, they can be moved, and thus loans for them are similar to an auto loan. However, in the last few years, a number of changes have been made. Mobile home loans are now made for up to fifteen years. One reason is that the cost of a mobile home may now be as much as $50,000 and sometimes even more. Interest rates on mobile home loans are generally 2 to 3 points above regular home loans. In general at least a 15 percent down payment is required to obtain a mobile home loan.

*Prefabricated houses*

Until recently, the use of prefabricated homes was greatly restricted by zoning laws. While still true in many areas this is slowly changing. Often prefabricated homes are found in the low-income areas of the community or are used as vacation homes. Until recently lenders did not finance them over more than ten years. This too is slowly changing. Prefabricated homes, while still cheaper than others, now sell for up to $75,000 and are a much better product than a decade ago. An advantage of buying a prefabricated home is that it takes much less time to assemble it than to construct a conventional home. The major disadvantage is that the buyer will have less choice and flexibility as to style and design.

*Second or vacation homes*

Some of the more affluent members of society have summer or vacation homes. These are, if not mobile, usually located on a lake, at the beach, in the mountains, or at some other resort area. In some cases these homes are also an investment property. Arrangements can be made to rent them when they are not used by the owner. Most large resort areas have a service that makes the rental arrangements. People have purchased single-family units, condominiums, motor homes, prefabs, and trailers for their second homes. Of these single-family units, condominiums are the easiest to rent, since a service usually exists to do this for the property owner.

**HOME FINANCING**

About nine out of ten Americans who purchase or build a residence do so with the help of mortgage financing, the security for the debt. The borrower is called the mortgagor and the lender the mortgagee. The borrower gives the mortgage and the lender is said to take the mortgage. Most mortgage loans are made by financial institutions and a few by individuals. The institutions involved are savings and loan associations, mutual savings banks, life insurance companies, mortgage banks, and some commercial banks. In addition, the trust departments of some commercial banks may finance a few mortgages, and recently credit unions were authorized to do so. However, up to now very few credit unions have been active in mortgage financing.

Historically there were three types of mortgages; *conventional*, *FHA-Insured*, and *VA-guaranteed*. These were all fixed mortgages. This means the interest rate was fixed the entire twenty or thirty years over which the mortgage runs. Recently, however, a number of innovative mortgages have been developed which will be discussed below.

In some states *deeds of trust* are used. This is a special kind of mortgage. The regular mortgage involves only two parties, the borrower (mortgagor) and the lender (mortgagee). In the deed of trust, the borrower conveys the realty not to the lender but to a third party, in trust, for the benefit of the lender, but for all practical purposes a deed of trust and a mortgage are the same.

A conventional fixed-payment mortgage is an arrangement solely between the lending institution and the buyer of the home. The institution lends its money and, until a few years ago, assumed the entire risk of loss, but now there is insurance that pays any losses suffered by the lender due to a default. Conventional mortgage loans may be made for as long as thirty years, but many of them last much less than this.

*The conventional mortgage*

   In most states, savings and loan associations are now able to make loans up to 90 percent of the value of the home. At one time, 80 percent was the maximum amount in most states because there was no mortgage insurance available on conventional mortgages. However, with the coming of **private mortgage insurance** (PMI), lenders are willing to make larger loans and the law allows it in most states. PMI works just like any insurance plan. A premium is assessed against the home owner, and this goes into a fund used to pay any losses the lender might suffer if there is a default. To be sure, the interest charged on a 95 percent mortgage loan is usually a little higher than on a 90 percent loan, which in turn is higher than on an 80 percent one. While lenders may lend up to 95 percent of the value of the home, how much they actually advance varies. When money is scarce, they require a larger down payment than when money is plentiful.

   The interest rate on mortgages varies from time to time and place to place. It varies from state to state because the demand for loans relative to the supply of mortgage money varies geographically. Generally speaking, all geographical areas have relative shortages of money at times and relatively plentiful supplies at others (but as noted above the relative degree varies regionally). Occasionally mortgage money is so scarce that it is difficult and sometimes even impossible to obtain at any interest rate.

The FHA mortgage is a loan secured by a mortgage and given by an approved lending institution, but the loan is insured by the Federal Housing Administration. The government does not do the lending but merely acts as an insurance company. The borrower pays a fee of about 3.8 percent (the fee varies a bit from time to time) of the loan for this insurance. However, the borrower need not pay this in one lump sum; rather it is added to the mortgage, and financed over thirty years. In the event of default in the payment of the loan by the buyer, the lending institution is paid for certain losses.

*The FHA mortgage*

There is an upper limit to the insurance provided by the FHA, but this upper limit is scaled upward periodically as the prices of homes rise. Check with a realtor to find the current maximum.

For a prospective home buyer to qualify for an FHA-insured loan, he or she must meet certain credit and income requirements. In addition, the home must meet minimum appraisal standards as established by the FHA, providing the buyer with some protection. This necessitates FHA inspection of the home. This and other FHA "red tape" result in more time being required for an FHA loan to be approved than for a conventional loan. Although the maximum length of FHA loans changes from time to time, the current maximum maturity is thirty years. The minimum down payment required on an FHA mortgage varies as FHA regulations change and with the value of the house. Currently the minimum is between 5 and 10 percent depending on the value of the home. Because these loan-to-value ratios are frequently changed by the FHA commissioner, it is necessary to obtain the current figures by asking a real estate broker or lending institution.

The maximum interest rate on an FHA-insured loan is set by the federal housing commissioner, subject to statutory limitations, and it is changed from time to time.

*The VA-guaranteed mortgage*

A VA-guaranteed mortgage is a loan on which the Veterans Administration guarantees payment to the lending institution or to an individual lender in the event of default by the veteran-buyer under the terms of the Servicemen's Readjustment Act of 1944 as amended. There are limits, however, to the dollar amount the VA will guarantee ($144,000 in 1990). These limits change from time to time; see a realtor for current figures. A VA loan does not require a down payment; consequently the entire price of the house may be financed, if it is within the upper limit. For homes above $144,000, a down payment is required.

To be eligible for a VA loan the person must be an honorably discharged veteran of the United States Armed Forces. The law also permits veterans who have had one VA loan and who sold the house which it financed, to obtain a second VA loan in certain cases.

The present legal ceiling on VA-guaranteed mortgages is 10 percent, but this changes periodically. The maximum maturity period is now thirty years. The VA borrower pays a small fee for this mortgage guarantee which varies a bit with the down payment but currently is about one percent.

Billions of dollars of investors' money are tied up in various types of mortgages. Figure 8–1 and Table 8–3 illustrate total residential mortgages outstanding over the years, as well as mortgages outstanding by type of lender.

*Second mortgages*

Sometimes second mortgages are needed to finance a home. Second mortgages come into existence when the purchaser does not have

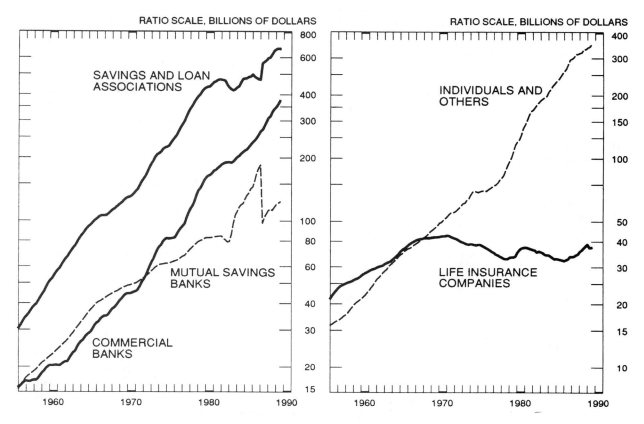

*Residential mortgage debt: type of lender. Amount outstanding, end of quarter* (Source:   Figure 8—1
1989 Historical Chart Book, *Board of Governors of the Federal Reserve System, p. 75.)*

sufficient funds to make the necessary down payment to pay the owner his or her equity in an existing (not a new) home. The purchaser pays off what proportion of the equity he can and assumes a second mortgage for the remainder.

Second mortgages are riskier than first mortgages. In the event of a foreclosure and sale of a house on which the mortgagor (borrower) has defaulted, the second mortgage is not paid off until after the first mortgage has been completely repaid. An illustration will make the second mortgage clear. Assume that a buyer wishes to buy a home for $100,000 and the home has a $60,000 mortgage on it. If the buyer could pay the seller $40,000 in cash, he could assume the old outstanding $60,000 mortgage. However, if he has only $30,000 for a down payment, he could pay that and give the seller a $10,000 second mortgage. Second mortgages are for smaller dollar amounts and run over fewer years than first ones. Generally they are for four, five, or perhaps up to ten years. The new home owner now has two monthly payments to make. Interest rates are higher on second mortgages than on first because they are riskier.

Table 8—3    *Mortgage loans outstanding, by type of property and lender, year-end 1988\**
             *(billions of dollars)*

| Lender | Residential properties | | | Commer-cial properties | Farm proper-ties | Total mortgage loans |
| | One- to four-family | Multi-family | Total | | | |
|---|---|---|---|---|---|---|
| Savings associations | $ 552.1 | $ 87.5 | $ 639.6 | $119.5 | $  0.0 | $ 759.1 |
| Savings banks | 104.9 | 19.3 | 124.2 | 29.4 | 0.0 | 153.6 |
| Thrift institutions | $ 657.0 | $106.8 | $ 763.8 | $148.9 | $  0.0 | $ 912.7 |
| Commercial banks | 311.8 | 36.8 | 348.6 | 301.3 | 15.6 | 665.5 |
| Life insurance companies | 15.3 | 23.6 | 38.9 | 185.6 | 9.2 | 233.8 |
| All others | 1,143.7 | 126.0 | 1,269.7 | 77.7 | 62.0 | 1,409.0 |
| Total | $2,127.8 | $293.2 | $2,421.0 | $713.5 | $ 86.8 | $3,221.3 |

*Note:* components may not add to totals due to rounding.

\*Preliminary.

*Source:* Federal Reserve Board; *Savings Institutions Sourcebook,* 1989.

Recently mortgages referred to as **home equity loans** have been developed. This is simply a fancy name for a second mortgage. However, these mortgages are not used to finance the purchase of a home like the traditional second mortgage described above. Rather they are used when a home owner has paid off a substantial part of his or her mortgage and also has a large price appreciation, and hence has a big equity in his or her home. The home owner borrows on his or her equity to finance vacations, luxury cars, trips abroad, home improvements, college education for the kids, and perhaps new investments.[2]

*Amortizing a home loan*

A mortgage loan is paid off or amortized by having the home owner make monthly payments, which pays off the mortgage loan in installments. A fixed monthly payment includes interest, reduction of principal, and perhaps taxes and insurance. A $50,000, 30-year mortgage at 12 percent would require a monthly payment of $514.31 to be amortized in 30 years, exclusive of taxes and insurance. Since the interest is calculated each month on the unpaid balance, that balance and the interest paid declines a bit each month. Inasmuch as the $514.31 payment is constant, the savings in interest are applied to reduce the principal more each month. These calculations have been made and printed in table

[2] As noted above in Chapter 7 such loans are illegal in Texas and a few other states except in the case of home improvement loans.

form, and such an amortization table may be obtained from most banks or savings and loan associations.

The first $514.31 monthly payment mentioned above includes interest of $500 the first month and $14.31 for the reduction of the principal. If we add $75 for taxes and $25 for insurance, the total monthly payment becomes $614.31. The second monthly payment would include less interest and a little more reduction of principal: for example, $499.86 and $14.45 respectively. The insurance and tax payments would presumably remain constant in the short run although every few years they are adjusted upward. These four monthly payments and the way they appear over time can be depicted graphically, as in Figure 8–2. Time is measured on the horizontal axis and the monthly payments on the vertical axis. This same relationship can be shown in a different manner, as illustrated by Table 8–4. You will note that after the last payment (the 360th payment) is made a principal of $53.38 remains. This is because a mortgage payment this long cannot always be made to come out exactly even.

*Assumption versus refinancing*

The prospective buyer who has the necessary down payment to buy the equity in a house can often take over or assume an older existing mortgage. He or she then assumes all the obligations of paying it off. This is often advantageous because by taking over an older existing mortgage the buyer may obtain funds at the interest rate prevailing several years before, which might have been lower. On the other hand, if rates were higher several years ago, the buyer might want to consider refinancing that is, taking out a new mortgage that pays off the old one.

Sometimes lending institutions will not let a buyer assume an

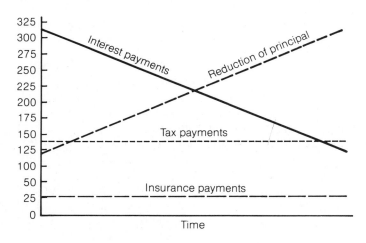

*Relationships among the four payments included in single monthly loan payments. The graph is not geometrically accurate; it is only intended to illustrate the principle of amortization of mortgages. The tax and insurance payments may be adjusted upward periodically as taxes and premiums are raised.*        Figure 8–2

Table 8–4    *Relationship between interest and principal*

| Payment number | Interest | Principal | Balance |
|---|---|---|---|
| 1 | $500.00 | $ 14.31 | $49,985.69 |
| 2 | 499.86 | 14.45 | 49,971.24 |
| 3 | 499.71 | 14.60 | 49,956.64 |
| 4 | 499.57 | 14.74 | 49,941.90 |
| 5 | 499.42 | 14.89 | 49,927.01 |
| 6 | 499.27 | 15.04 | 49,911.97 |
| 7 | 499.12 | 15.19 | 49,896.78 |
| 8 | 498.97 | 15.34 | 49,881.44 |
| 9 | 498.81 | 15.50 | 49,856.94 |
| 10 | 498.66 | 15.65 | 49,850.29 |
| 351 | 49.20 | 465.11 | 4,454.40 |
| 352 | 44.54 | 469.77 | 3,984.63 |
| 353 | 39.85 | 474.46 | 3,510.17 |
| 354 | 35.10 | 479.21 | 3,030.96 |
| 355 | 30.31 | 484.00 | 2,546.96 |
| 356 | 25.47 | 488.84 | 2,058.12 |
| 357 | 20.58 | 493.73 | 1,564.39 |
| 358 | 15.64 | 498.67 | 1,065.72 |
| 359 | 10.66 | 503.65 | 562.07 |
| 360 | 5.62 | 508.69 | 53.38 |

| | | | |
|---|---|---|---|
| Final payment | $53.38 | Total no. payments | 360 |
| Total payment | $185,151.60 | Total principal | $49,946.62 |
| | | Total interest | $135,204.98 |

existing mortgage at the old interest rate. They will insist on refinancing at today's presumably higher rate, or in some cases they will permit the assumption but will escalate the interest rate to the current level. Whether or not lenders are able to force refinancing or escalate the interest rate is determined by the wording in the mortgage (deed of trust). Many (probably most) of the mortgages written during the last few years have a due-on-sale clause that permits the lender to require refinancing. Some of the older ones do not.

If an individual has to refinance, not only must he or she pay today's (possibly high) interest rates, but there is also the necessity of paying all the added closing costs, which are considerable and which are avoided if a person is able to obtain an assumption. Closing costs are discussed below.

It should be noted that the escalation of interest rates and forced refinancing are not permitted on FHA and VA mortgages.

Since, in giving a mortgage loan, the lender has made an investment of a substantial amount of money at, say 10 percent for a long period of time, the lender wants to receive the interest income year by year. Over the years, interest on a mortgage may amount to thousands of dollars. Home owners, on the other hand, might like to save this interest cost; if in the future their incomes should rise, they might want to make extra mortgage payments. Or if they should inherit a large sum of money, they might want to pay off the mortgage—perhaps even before the ink is dry. Other extra or windfall income might be used to greatly reduce or pay off a mortgage early.

*Penalties*

To prevent or discourage the buyer from repaying the mortgage more quickly than agreed, the lender often insists on a penalty clause. Lending institutions defend these penalties on the basis that administrative and investment costs are involved in reinvesting early repayments, and that they partially compensate for lost income from interest.

In some cases, a penalty clause merely states that a fee, usually I or 2 percent, is charged for mortgage payments made in advance of the schedule. For example, if a person paid off in one payment a $20,000 mortgage, the penalty would be $200 or $400. Often, then, the penalty is small enough not to discourage greatly early repayment.

In other cases the penalty clause applies only to extra payments in excess of a given amount per year, say $1,000 or $2,000. In still other cases, penalties are calculated by applying the interest rate on the mortgage against the advance payment for so many months. There are three and six-month penalty clauses. If a 10 percent $60,000 mortgage carried a six-month interest penalty and some was paid in advance, the penalty would be six months' interest on the amount paid off at 10 percent. If all of the $60,000 was paid off, the penalty would be $3,000. In some cases the penalty clause drops out completely and automatically after a given period of time. The home owner should, however, try to get a mortgage that does not contain a penalty clause. Usually the conditions in the money market will determine whether penalties are inserted into the mortgage. If funds are hard to obtain, not only will interest rates be higher but penalty clauses will more likely be inserted. If funds are plentiful, the home owner will receive a lower rate of interest and can more easily avoid a penalty clause.

If one succeeds in avoiding a penalty clause, and in some cases even if one does not, it may sometimes pay to refinance. If, for example, a person obtains a mortgage at a time when competitive conditions indicate a 15 or even 16 percent interest rate and a few years later rates are only 12 or 13 percent, it may pay to refinance. Remember that in doing this the individual has most of the closing costs to meet again, as well as the penalty; but if interest rates have declined enough, the saving may more than offset these two items. For example, if an individual had a 15 percent thirty-year, $75,000 mortgage, the principal and interest

*When does it pay to refinance?*

would come to $948.34 per month. If the mortgage could be refinanced at 12 percent, the comparable monthly payment would be $771.46, a savings of $176.88 per month. Over just ten years, this would amount to a savings of $21,226. Whether it would pay to refinance would depend on the size of the mortgage, the amount of decline in interest rates, and the dollar amount of closing costs. A sharp pencil would have to be put to each individual case to figure it out. The general rule of thumb, however, is if interest rates have come down 3 percent or more, it nearly always pays to refinance. In some cases refinancing is worthwhile even if rates have come down by less than 3 percent.

*Early payoff options*

Recently some mortgage lenders have offered home owners the option of paying off their mortgages early at rather attractive terms. These lenders offer substantial discounts to encourage early repayment to remove older, lower-yielding mortgages from their books. At first glance, both the lending institution and the home owner would benefit from this. A mortgage made twenty years ago and running over thirty years would yield about 7 or 8 percent as opposed to today's much higher rate. If the lender offered the home owner a 12 percent discount on a $20,000 mortgage, the home owner could pay it off completely for $17,860. He or she would have his or her home debt free and save $2,140 and all future interest. The lending institution, while it would be out $2,140, would have $17,860 to invest at today's market rate.

*Large down payment versus small down payment*

The size of the down payment individuals make is most often determined by the amount of cash available at the time they purchase the home. Assuming that one has a choice, however, the question is whether one should make a large or a small down payment. The buyer should consider the following factors:

1.  *The cost.* With a large down payment an individual may be able to reduce the time the loan will run before maturity, resulting in considerable interest savings. In addition, even if an individual places a large down payment on a property and the time to maturity remains the same, he or she will still save money on interest. For instance, a home buyer who borrows $50,000 at 12 percent interest for a twenty-five-year period will pay $107,986 in interest during the life of the mortgage. On the other hand, if the same borrower needed only a $40,000 mortgage for the same number of years at the same interest rate, interest payments would drop to $86,387— the person would save $21,599. In other words, the $50,000 mortgage will cost the borrower about 25 percent more than the smaller $40,000 loan. In addition, if a larger down payment is made, often the interest rate is reduced somewhat.

2. *Possibility of moving.* Each year nearly one out of every five American families moves to a new location. If there is a possibility that a person is going to move, it is advisable to put as small a down payment on a home as possible when purchasing it. Many people consider that the competition between the sale of an older home and a new home to a large degree rests with the size of the down payment, for it is easier to sell a home requiring a $5,000 down payment than it is to sell a home requiring a $20,000 down payment. Therefore, if one has a small equity in a home, it may be easier to sell if one has to move.

Both FHA-insured and VA-guaranteed loans have maximum rates of interest set by law. Sometimes the rates an individual has to pay are at this maximum level, and sometimes they are below it. The interest rate on conventional loans fluctuates from time to time and also varies from one part of the nation to another, depending on the supply of money available for mortgage loans. Interest rates may also vary slightly with the amount of the down payment. If there is a substantial down payment, interest rates may be reduced from one-quarter to one-half of 1 percent from what the rate would have been with a lower down payment. Over the years, a quarter or a half of 1 percent difference can amount to a good deal of money, especially on a big mortgage. One-half of 1 percent on $50,000, for example, is $250 per year. The total amount of interest paid over the years at different interest is truly amazing. This is shown in Table 8–5.

*Interest on mortgages*

For any given home, then, the size of the down payment will affect the size of the monthly payment as well as the total interest paid over the years. Table 8–6 shows a $60,000 home financed over twenty-five

*Monthly payments and total dollar interest costs at various interest rates on a 25-year, $50,000 mortgage*

Table 8—5

| Interest rate percent | Monthly payment | Total payments | Total interest |
|---|---|---|---|
| 10 | $454.36 | $136,308 | $ 86,308 |
| 11 | $490.06 | $147,018 | $ 97,018 |
| 12 | $526.62 | $157,986 | $107,986 |
| 12.5 | $545.18 | $163,554 | $113,554 |
| 13 | $563.92 | $169,176 | $119,176 |
| 13.5 | $582.83 | $174,849 | $124,849 |
| 14. | $601.89 | $180,567 | $130,567 |
| 14.5 | $621.09 | $185,327 | $135,327 |
| 15 | $640.42 | $192,126 | $142,126 |

Table 8–6    *Amortization of a $60,000 house with varying down payments over a twenty-five-year period at 12 percent interest*

|  | *A* | *B* | *C* |
|---|---|---|---|
| House | $ 60,000.00 | $ 60,000.00 | $60,000.00 |
| Down payment | 10,000.00 | 20,000.00 | 30,000.00 |
| Mortgage | 50,000.00 | 40,000.00 | 30,000.00 |
| Monthly payment (interest & principal only) | 526.62 | 421.29 | 315.97 |
| Total dollars paid | 157,986.00 | 126,387.00 | 94,791.00 |
| Total interest over the 25 years | 107,986.00 | 86,387.00 | 64,791.00 |

years at 12 percent with a large, a medium, and relatively small down payment. The difference in total interest over the years is substantial.

*Monthly payments*

The monthly payment varies not only with the amount of the mortgage but also with the length of the mortgage, the interest rate, and usually with the level of taxes and insurance premiums. A higher interest rate, all else being equal, tends to increase the monthly payments. The longer the number of years for which the mortgage runs, the lower the monthly payments with any given interest rate and dollar amount of the loan. However, if one reduces the monthly payments by increasing the length of the mortgage, one pays more total dollars in interest over the years.

When buying a house, the down payment is now always subject to variation; usually a person must have the $2,000 or $10,000 in cash, or whatever the figure is. The exception has been discussed previously. Buyers have some control over the length of the mortgage and, to a slight extent, over the interest rate if they shop around. If the house buyer wishes to save total interest costs, the person should select the amortization time period that makes the monthly payments as large as he or she can easily bear. On a $40,000, twenty-year, 12 percent mortgage, the monthly payment (not including insurance and property taxes) would be $440.44. Total payments over the twenty years would be $105,705.60 and interest over the years would amount to $65,705.60. The same mortgage financed over twenty-five years would have monthly payments of $421.29 and total payments of $126,387, of which $86,387 would be for interest. By reducing monthly payments by $19.15, the buyer pays an additional $20,682 in interest over the years. This is not to say that mortgages should never be stretched out to reduce monthly payments. Sometimes such a step is necessary; one of the benefits of a thirty-year mortgage is that it reduces monthly payments to the point where people can buy homes who otherwise could not do so. One should make the decision with eyes open and not lengthen the mortgage just to reduce monthly payments. Table 8–7 shows the monthly payments necessary to amortize a given loan at 12 percent interest over a given number of years. It includes interest and reduction of principal only; taxes and insurance are omitted.

Monthly payments can include four items: interest, reduction of principal, insurance premiums, and local property taxes (this is referred to as PITI). Nearly all lenders will insist that insurance to protect the house against loss due to fire or other physical damage be obtained. Even if the lending institution did not demand it, no property owner should be without fire insurance. In addition to fire insurance, sometimes a life insurance policy is bought on the mortgage so that if the borrower dies before paying off the mortgage, the insurance company will pay it.

Although property taxes vary from community to community, they must be paid annually or semiannually in most cases. Since they usually run to several hundred dollars or more, a person who does not budget for them may have difficulty paying them. Many lending institutions include one-twelfth of the annual tax liability and add it to the monthly payments. These funds then go into a special account called the escrow account, which is used by the institution to pay the taxes when due. It may do the same with insurance premiums (both mortgage credit life insurance and hazard insurance premiums).

Some people object to these monthly payments for insurance and property taxes on the ground that they are paying in advance, and the financial institution has the use of their money for a time before it pays the bills. This is the same as an interest-free loan to the bank. However, the lending institution is providing a real service. It is doing the individual's budgeting, and it also takes care of the paperwork involved in keeping the records and paying the taxes and insurance premiums. If a person objects to this advance payment, he or she should bargain with the lending institution and try to keep it out of the monthly payments. If the down payment is fairly large, a person can probably keep the life insurance and the tax payments out, but it is more difficult to avoid including fire insurance premiums, which are, however, relatively small.

If an individual succeeds in keeping some of the above items out of the monthly payments, budgeting should be done to set aside one-twelfth of the sum each month. Then not only would the person be sure of having the funds when they are due, but they can be put into a savings account (to accumulate until needed) and receive interest, perhaps from the very bank that has the mortgage.

*The biweekly (semimonthly) mortgage*

Normally mortgage payments are due the first of each month, although in most cases a grace period of from ten to fifteen days is granted the mortgagor by the lending institution.

Recently, however, a mortgage has been developed that requires payment every other week. Instead of a $500 payment each month, the home owner would pay $250 every two weeks. More people are paid

Table 8—7    *Monthly payment necessary to amortize a loan at 12 percent*

| Term amount | 15 years | 16 years | 17 years | 18 years | 19 years | 20 years | 21 years | 22 years | 23 years |
|---|---|---|---|---|---|---|---|---|---|
| $ 22500 | 270.04 | 264.09 | 259.03 | 254.69 | 250.97 | 247.75 | 244.96 | 242.54 | 240.43 |
| 23000 | 276.04 | 269.96 | 264.78 | 260.35 | 256.54 | 253.25 | 250.41 | 247.93 | 245.77 |
| 23500 | 282.04 | 275.83 | 270.54 | 266.01 | 262.12 | 258.76 | 255.85 | 253.32 | 251.12 |
| 24000 | 288.05 | 281.70 | 276.30 | 271.67 | 267.70 | 264.27 | 261.29 | 258.71 | 256.46 |
| 24500 | 294.05 | 287.57 | 282.05 | 277.33 | 273.27 | 269.77 | 266.74 | 264.10 | 261.80 |
| 25000 | 300.05 | 293.44 | 287.81 | 282.99 | 278.85 | 275.28 | 272.18 | 269.49 | 267.15 |
| 25500 | 306.05 | 299.30 | 293.56 | 288.65 | 284.43 | 280.78 | 277.62 | 274.88 | 272.49 |
| 26000 | 312.05 | 305.17 | 299.32 | 294.31 | 290.01 | 286.29 | 283.07 | 280.27 | 277.83 |
| 26500 | 318.05 | 311.04 | 305.08 | 299.97 | 295.58 | 291.79 | 288.51 | 285.66 | 283.17 |
| 27000 | 324.05 | 316.91 | 310.83 | 305.63 | 301.16 | 297.30 | 293.95 | 291.05 | 288.52 |
| 27500 | 330.05 | 322.78 | 316.59 | 311.29 | 306.74 | 302.80 | 299.40 | 296.44 | 293.86 |
| 28000 | 336.05 | 328.65 | 322.35 | 316.95 | 312.31 | 308.31 | 304.84 | 301.83 | 299.20 |
| 28500 | 342.05 | 344.52 | 328.10 | 322.61 | 317.89 | 313.81 | 310.28 | 307.22 | 304.55 |
| 29000 | 348.05 | 340.39 | 333.86 | 328.27 | 323.47 | 319.32 | 315.73 | 312.61 | 309.89 |
| 29500 | 354.05 | 346.25 | 339.61 | 333.93 | 329.04 | 324.83 | 321.17 | 318.00 | 315.23 |
| 30000 | 360.06 | 352.12 | 345.37 | 339.59 | 334.62 | 330.33 | 326.61 | 323.39 | 320.57 |
| 30500 | 366.06 | 357.99 | 351.13 | 345.25 | 340.20 | 335.84 | 332.06 | 328.78 | 325.92 |
| 31000 | 372.06 | 363.86 | 356.88 | 350.91 | 345.77 | 341.34 | 337.50 | 334.17 | 331.26 |
| 31500 | 378.06 | 369.73 | 362.64 | 356.57 | 351.35 | 346.85 | 342.95 | 339.56 | 336.60 |
| 32000 | 384.06 | 375.60 | 368.39 | 362.23 | 356.93 | 352.35 | 348.39 | 344.95 | 341.95 |
| 32500 | 390.06 | 381.47 | 374.15 | 367.89 | 362.51 | 357.86 | 353.83 | 350.33 | 347.29 |
| 33000 | 396.06 | 387.33 | 379.91 | 373.55 | 368.08 | 363.36 | 359.28 | 355.72 | 352.63 |
| 33500 | 402.06 | 393.20 | 385.66 | 379.21 | 373.66 | 368.87 | 364.72 | 361.11 | 357.97 |
| 34000 | 408.06 | 399.07 | 391.42 | 384.87 | 379.24 | 374.37 | 370.16 | 366.50 | 363.32 |
| 34500 | 414.06 | 404.94 | 397.17 | 390.53 | 384.81 | 379.88 | 375.61 | 371.89 | 368.66 |
| 35000 | 420.06 | 410.81 | 402.93 | 396.19 | 390.39 | 385.39 | 381.05 | 377.28 | 374.00 |
| 36000 | 432.07 | 422.55 | 414.44 | 407.51 | 401.54 | 396.40 | 391.94 | 388.06 | 384.69 |
| 37000 | 444.07 | 434.28 | 425.95 | 418.83 | 412.70 | 407.41 | 402.82 | 398.84 | 395.37 |
| 38000 | 456.07 | 446.02 | 437.47 | 430.15 | 423.85 | 418.42 | 413.71 | 409.62 | 406.06 |
| 39000 | 468.07 | 457.76 | 448.98 | 441.47 | 435.01 | 429.43 | 424.60 | 420.40 | 416.75 |
| 40000 | 480.07 | 469.50 | 460.49 | 452.79 | 446.16 | 440.44 | 435.48 | 431.18 | 427.43 |
| 41000 | 492.07 | 481.23 | 472.00 | 464.10 | 457.31 | 451.45 | 446.37 | 441.96 | 438.12 |
| 42000 | 504.08 | 492.97 | 483.52 | 475.42 | 468.47 | 462.46 | 457.26 | 452.74 | 448.80 |
| 43000 | 516.08 | 504.71 | 495.03 | 486.74 | 479.62 | 473.47 | 468.15 | 463.52 | 459.49 |
| 44000 | 528.08 | 516.44 | 506.54 | 498.06 | 490.77 | 484.48 | 479.03 | 474.30 | 470.17 |
| 45000 | 540.08 | 528.18 | 518.05 | 509.38 | 501.93 | 495.49 | 489.92 | 485.08 | 480.86 |
| 46000 | 552.08 | 539.92 | 529.56 | 520.70 | 513.08 | 506.50 | 500.81 | 495.86 | 491.54 |
| 47000 | 564.08 | 551.66 | 541.08 | 532.02 | 524.24 | 517.52 | 511.69 | 506.64 | 502.23 |
| 48000 | 576.09 | 563.39 | 552.59 | 543.34 | 535.39 | 528.53 | 522.58 | 517.42 | 512.92 |
| 49000 | 588.09 | 575.13 | 564.10 | 554.66 | 546.54 | 539.54 | 533.47 | 528.19 | 523.60 |
| 50000 | 600.09 | 586.87 | 575.61 | 565.98 | 557.70 | 550.55 | 544.35 | 538.97 | 534.29 |
| 51000 | 612.09 | 598.60 | 587.12 | 577.30 | 568.85 | 561.56 | 555.24 | 549.75 | 544.97 |
| 52000 | 624.09 | 610.34 | 598.64 | 588.62 | 580.01 | 572.57 | 566.13 | 560.53 | 555.66 |
| 53000 | 636.09 | 622.08 | 610.15 | 599.94 | 591.16 | 583.58 | 577.02 | 571.31 | 566.34 |
| 54000 | 648.10 | 633.82 | 621.66 | 611.26 | 602.31 | 594.59 | 587.90 | 582.09 | 577.03 |
| 55000 | 660.10 | 645.55 | 633.17 | 622.58 | 613.47 | 605.60 | 598.79 | 592.87 | 587.72 |
| 56000 | 672.10 | 657.29 | 644.69 | 633.90 | 624.62 | 616.61 | 609.68 | 603.65 | 598.40 |
| 57000 | 684.10 | 669.03 | 656.20 | 645.22 | 635.77 | 627.62 | 620.56 | 614.43 | 609.09 |
| 58000 | 696.10 | 680.77 | 667.71 | 656.54 | 646.93 | 638.63 | 631.45 | 625.21 | 619.77 |
| 59000 | 708.10 | 692.50 | 679.22 | 667.86 | 658.08 | 649.65 | 642.34 | 635.99 | 630.46 |
| 60000 | 720.11 | 704.24 | 690.73 | 679.18 | 669.24 | 660.66 | 653.22 | 646.77 | 641.14 |
| 61000 | 732.11 | 715.98 | 702.25 | 690.49 | 680.39 | 671.67 | 664.11 | 657.55 | 651.83 |
| 62000 | 744.11 | 727.71 | 713.76 | 701.81 | 691.54 | 682.68 | 675.00 | 668.33 | 662.52 |
| 63000 | 756.11 | 739.45 | 725.27 | 713.13 | 702.70 | 693.69 | 685.89 | 679.11 | 673.20 |
| 64000 | 768.11 | 751.19 | 736.78 | 724.45 | 713.85 | 704.70 | 696.77 | 689.89 | 683.89 |
| 65000 | 780.11 | 762.93 | 748.30 | 735.77 | 725.01 | 715.71 | 707.66 | 700.66 | 694.57 |
| 67500 | 810.12 | 792.27 | 777.08 | 764.07 | 752.89 | 743.24 | 734.88 | 727.61 | 721.29 |
| 70000 | 840.12 | 821.61 | 805.86 | 792.37 | 780.77 | 770.77 | 762.09 | 754.56 | 748.00 |
| 72500 | 870.13 | 850.96 | 834.64 | 820.67 | 808.66 | 798.29 | 789.31 | 781.51 | 774.71 |
| 75000 | 900.13 | 880.30 | 863.42 | 848.97 | 836.54 | 825.82 | 816.53 | 808.46 | 801.43 |
| 80000 | 960.14 | 938.99 | 920.98 | 905.57 | 892.31 | 880.87 | 870.96 | 862.36 | 854.86 |
| 85000 | 1020.15 | 997.67 | 978.54 | 962.16 | 948.08 | 935.93 | 925.40 | 916.25 | 908.29 |
| 90000 | 1080.16 | 1056.36 | 1036.10 | 1018.76 | 1003.85 | 990.98 | 979.83 | 970.15 | 961.71 |
| 95000 | 1140.16 | 1115.04 | 1093.66 | 1075.36 | 1059.62 | 1046.04 | 1034.27 | 1024.05 | 1015.14 |
| 100000 | 1200.17 | 1173.73 | 1151.22 | 1131.96 | 1115.39 | 1101.09 | 1088.70 | 1077.94 | 1068.57 |

continued

Table 8—7

| 24 years | 25 years | 26 years | 27 years | 28 years | 29 years | 30 years | 35 years | 40 years |
|---|---|---|---|---|---|---|---|---|
| 238.59 | 236.98 | 235.57 | 234.33 | 233.24 | 232.29 | 231.44 | 228.50 | 226.92 |
| 243.89 | 242.25 | 240.80 | 239.54 | 238.43 | 237.45 | 236.59 | 233.58 | 231.96 |
| 249.19 | 247.51 | 246.04 | 244.75 | 243.61 | 242.61 | 241.73 | 238.66 | 237.00 |
| 254.50 | 252.78 | 251.27 | 249.95 | 248.79 | 247.77 | 246.87 | 243.74 | 242.04 |
| 259.80 | 258.04 | 256.51 | 255.16 | 253.98 | 252.93 | 252.02 | 248.81 | 247.09 |
| 265.10 | 263.31 | 261.74 | 260.37 | 259.16 | 258.09 | 257.16 | 253.89 | 252.13 |
| 270.40 | 268.58 | 266.98 | 265.57 | 264.34 | 263.26 | 262.30 | 258.97 | 257.17 |
| 275.70 | 273.84 | 272.21 | 270.78 | 269.52 | 268.42 | 267.44 | 264.05 | 262.21 |
| 281.01 | 279.11 | 277.45 | 275.99 | 274.71 | 273.58 | 272.59 | 269.13 | 267.26 |
| 286.31 | 284.38 | 282.68 | 281.20 | 279.89 | 278.74 | 277.73 | 274.20 | 272.30 |
| 291.61 | 289.64 | 287.92 | 286.40 | 285.07 | 283.90 | 282.87 | 279.28 | 277.34 |
| 296.91 | 294.91 | 293.15 | 291.61 | 290.26 | 289.07 | 288.02 | 284.36 | 282.38 |
| 302.21 | 300.17 | 298.39 | 296.82 | 295.44 | 294.23 | 293.16 | 289.44 | 287.43 |
| 307.52 | 305.44 | 303.62 | 302.03 | 300.62 | 299.39 | 298.30 | 294.51 | 292.47 |
| 312.82 | 310.71 | 308.86 | 307.23 | 305.81 | 304.55 | 303.45 | 299.59 | 297.51 |
| 318.12 | 315.97 | 314.09 | 312.44 | 310.99 | 309.71 | 308.59 | 304.67 | 302.55 |
| 323.42 | 321.24 | 319.33 | 317.65 | 316.17 | 314.87 | 313.73 | 309.75 | 307.60 |
| 328.72 | 326.50 | 324.56 | 322.85 | 321.36 | 320.04 | 318.87 | 314.83 | 312.64 |
| 334.03 | 331.77 | 329.80 | 328.06 | 326.54 | 325.20 | 324.02 | 319.90 | 317.68 |
| 339.33 | 337.04 | 335.03 | 333.27 | 331.72 | 330.36 | 329.16 | 324.98 | 322.72 |
| 344.63 | 342.30 | 340.26 | 338.48 | 336.90 | 335.52 | 334.30 | 330.06 | 327.77 |
| 349.93 | 347.57 | 345.50 | 343.68 | 342.09 | 340.68 | 339.45 | 335.14 | 332.81 |
| 355.23 | 352.84 | 350.73 | 348.89 | 347.27 | 345.85 | 344.59 | 340.21 | 337.85 |
| 360.53 | 358.10 | 355.97 | 354.10 | 352.45 | 351.01 | 349.73 | 345.29 | 342.89 |
| 365.84 | 363.37 | 361.20 | 359.30 | 357.64 | 356.17 | 354.88 | 350.37 | 347.94 |
| 371.14 | 368.63 | 366.44 | 364.51 | 362.82 | 361.33 | 360.02 | 355.45 | 352.98 |
| 381.74 | 379.17 | 376.91 | 374.93 | 373.19 | 371.65 | 370.31 | 365.60 | 363.06 |
| 392.35 | 389.70 | 387.38 | 385.34 | 383.55 | 381.98 | 380.59 | 375.76 | 373.15 |
| 402.95 | 400.23 | 397.85 | 395.76 | 393.92 | 392.30 | 390.88 | 385.91 | 383.23 |
| 413.55 | 410.76 | 408.32 | 406.17 | 404.28 | 402.62 | 401.16 | 396.07 | 393.32 |
| 424.16 | 421.29 | 418.79 | 416.58 | 414.65 | 412.95 | 411.45 | 406.22 | 403.40 |
| 434.76 | 431.83 | 429.26 | 427.00 | 425.02 | 423.27 | 421.74 | 416.38 | 413.49 |
| 445.37 | 442.36 | 439.73 | 437.41 | 435.38 | 433.60 | 432.02 | 426.54 | 423.57 |
| 455.97 | 452.89 | 450.19 | 447.83 | 445.75 | 443.92 | 442.31 | 436.69 | 433.66 |
| 466.57 | 463.42 | 460.66 | 458.24 | 456.11 | 454.24 | 452.59 | 446.85 | 443.74 |
| 477.18 | 473.96 | 471.13 | 468.66 | 466.48 | 464.57 | 462.88 | 457.00 | 453.83 |
| 487.78 | 484.49 | 481.60 | 479.07 | 476.85 | 474.89 | 473.17 | 467.16 | 463.91 |
| 498.38 | 495.02 | 492.07 | 489.49 | 487.21 | 485.21 | 483.45 | 477.31 | 474.00 |
| 508.99 | 505.55 | 502.54 | 499.90 | 497.58 | 495.54 | 493.74 | 487.47 | 484.08 |
| 519.59 | 516.08 | 513.01 | 510.31 | 507.95 | 505.86 | 504.03 | 497.62 | 494.17 |
| 530.20 | 526.62 | 523.48 | 520.73 | 518.31 | 516.18 | 514.31 | 507.78 | 504.25 |
| 540.80 | 537.15 | 533.95 | 531.14 | 528.68 | 526.51 | 524.60 | 517.94 | 514.34 |
| 551.40 | 547.68 | 544.42 | 541.56 | 539.04 | 536.83 | 534.88 | 528.09 | 524.42 |
| 562.01 | 558.21 | 554.89 | 551.97 | 549.41 | 547.16 | 545.17 | 538.25 | 534.51 |
| 572.61 | 568.75 | 565.36 | 562.39 | 559.78 | 557.48 | 555.46 | 548.40 | 544.59 |
| 583.22 | 579.28 | 575.83 | 572.80 | 570.14 | 567.80 | 565.74 | 558.56 | 554.68 |
| 593.82 | 589.81 | 586.30 | 583.22 | 580.51 | 578.13 | 576.03 | 568.71 | 564.78 |
| 604.42 | 600.34 | 596.77 | 593.63 | 590.87 | 588.45 | 586.31 | 578.87 | 574.85 |
| 615.03 | 610.88 | 607.24 | 604.05 | 601.24 | 598.77 | 596.60 | 589.02 | 584.93 |
| 625.63 | 621.41 | 617.71 | 614.46 | 611.61 | 609.10 | 606.89 | 599.18 | 595.02 |
| 636.23 | 631.94 | 628.18 | 624.87 | 621.97 | 619.42 | 617.17 | 609.33 | 605.10 |
| 646.84 | 642.47 | 638.65 | 635.29 | 632.34 | 629.74 | 627.46 | 619.49 | 615.19 |
| 657.44 | 653.00 | 649.12 | 645.70 | 642.71 | 640.07 | 637.74 | 629.65 | 625.27 |
| 668.05 | 663.54 | 659.59 | 656.12 | 653.07 | 650.39 | 648.03 | 639.80 | 635.36 |
| 678.65 | 674.07 | 670.05 | 666.53 | 663.44 | 660.71 | 658.32 | 649.96 | 645.44 |
| 689.25 | 684.60 | 680.52 | 676.95 | 673.80 | 671.04 | 688.60 | 660.11 | 655.53 |
| 715.76 | 710.93 | 706.70 | 702.98 | 699.72 | 696.85 | 694.32 | 685.50 | 680.74 |
| 742.27 | 737.26 | 732.87 | 729.02 | 725.63 | 722.66 | 720.03 | 710.89 | 705.95 |
| 768.78 | 763.59 | 759.05 | 755.06 | 751.55 | 748.47 | 745.75 | 736.28 | 731.17 |
| 795.29 | 789.92 | 785.22 | 781.09 | 777.46 | 774.27 | 771.46 | 761.67 | 756.38 |
| 848.31 | 842.58 | 837.57 | 833.16 | 829.30 | 825.89 | 822.90 | 812.44 | 806.80 |
| 901.33 | 895.25 | 889.91 | 885.24 | 881.13 | 877.51 | 874.33 | 863.22 | 857.23 |
| 954.35 | 947.91 | 942.26 | 937.31 | 932.96 | 929.13 | 925.76 | 914.00 | 907.65 |
| 1007.37 | 1000.57 | 994.61 | 989.38 | 984.79 | 980.75 | 977.19 | 964.78 | 958.08 |
| 1060.39 | 1053.23 | 1046.96 | 1041.45 | 1036.62 | 1032.36 | 1028.62 | 1015.55 | 1008.50 |

weekly or biweekly than monthly; hence, a biweekly mortgage is often easier to budget.

If a given traditional 30-year monthly mortgage were, instead, financed as a biweekly mortgage, it would be paid off in 20.29 years and would result in substantial interest savings. The mortgage is paid off more quickly because the principal is reduced a bit every two weeks rather than every month. This earlier reduction of principal lowers interest more quickly, making it possible to apply more of the biweekly payment to the principal in future payments. In addition, a biweekly mortgage would result in twenty-six payments per year, each of which would be one-half the size of twelve regular monthly payments. This, of course, amounts to the same as one extra monthly payment per year, again reducing principal more quickly and saving interest.

Table 8–8 shows the differences in payments and total interest paid between some conventional 30-year and biweekly mortgages, which are amortized over 20.29 years.

### The fifteen-year mortgage

Traditionally mortgages were financed over 30 years, although some were over 25 or even 20. Recently, however, the 15-year mortgage has become somewhat popular. While this increases the monthly payment, it saves on interest. The monthly payment on a $75,000 mortgage at 12 percent interest amortized over 30 years is $771.46; if amortized over 15 years this same mortgage would require a $900.13 monthly payment. The additional $128.67 per month would result in $115,702.20 in interest savings. That is why these shorter mortgages have become somewhat popular, especially with two-income couples. Table 8–9 illustrates the savings achieved with shorter mortgages.

It should be noted, however, that the savings are not as great as the table suggests. This is because the differences in the payments could be invested and earn interest if a longer mortgage were chosen. Also taxes must be taken into account, because mortgage interest paid, as well as interest earned, is tax deductible (or taxable, as the case may be).

Nevertheless, a shorter mortgage will save a great deal of interest cost. This is especially true if the after-tax mortgage interest rate is greater than the after-tax rate on investments.

### The graduated equity mortgage

The graduated equity mortgage starts out as a straight, conventional, 30-year mortgage with a proviso that monthly payments will be escalated by a predetermined amount each month. This increased payment is applied entirely to the reduction of principal. The entire 30-year mortgage is then paid off over 13, 14, or 15 years rather than 30, saving a great deal of interest. This type of mortgage is fine for someone whose income is rising and who can afford the escalating monthly payments. This mortgage is no different than the traditional old-fashioned fixed

*Differences between biweekly and conventional mortgages*  Table 8—8

### $75,000 mortgage based on 10.50% interest rate

|  | Conventional mortgage | Biweekly mortgage | Percent savings |
|---|---|---|---|
| Payments | $686.05 every month | $343.03 every 2 weeks |  |
| Paid in full | 30 years | 20.29 years |  |
| Total interest paid | $171,898.38 | $106,352.98 |  |
| Interest saved |  | $65,636.40 | 38 |

### $100,000 mortgage based on 10.50% interest rate

|  | Conventional mortgage | Biweekly mortgage | Percent savings |
|---|---|---|---|
| Payments | $914.74 every month | $457.37 every 2 weeks |  |
| Paid in full | 30 years | 20.29 years |  |
| Total interest paid | $229,304.00 | $141.800.18 |  |
| Interest saved |  | $87,503.82 | 38 |

### $150,000 mortgage based on 10.50% interest rate

|  | Conventional mortgage | Biweekly mortgage | Percent savings |
|---|---|---|---|
| Payments | $1,372.11 every month | $686.06 every 2 weeks |  |
| Paid in full | 30 years | 20.29 years |  |
| Total interest paid | $343,956.62 | $212.700.18 |  |
| Interest saved |  | $131,256.44 | 38 |

*Source:* Commercial National Mortgage Corporation, Shreveport, La.

*$75,000 mortgage at 12 percent*  Table 8—9

|  | 15-year mortgage | 20-year mortgage | 25-year mortgage | 30-year mortgage |
|---|---|---|---|---|
| Monthly payment | $ 900.13 | $ 825.82 | $ 789.92 | $ 771.46 |
| Total payment | $162,023.40 | $198,196.80 | $236,976.00 | $277,725.60 |
| Total interest | $ 87,023.40 | $123,196.80 | $161,976.00 | $202,725.60 |

30-year mortgage which permits early repayments, except that a prede-termined schedule of early repayment is worked out.

*Seller-financed mortgages*

Seller-financed mortgage loans are extended by the seller to the buyer, usually at lower than the going market rate, in order to expedite the sale of the home. These are sometimes called **purchase money loans**. Often these are second mortgages for five or ten years. Moreover, if they are for five years, they may have a final balloon payment. If this is the case, be certain that there is also a provision which will obligate the lender to refinance the balloon.

*Reverse mortgages*

Older people whose mortgage is paid off and who wish to retire may sign a reverse mortgage whereby they sell their home back to a lending institution. Instead of making a monthly payment, they receive one. As time passes they own a smaller and smaller portion of their home; a larger and larger mortgage debt is built up on it again, as their equity in it declines. Usually only a portion of the value of the house (about 50 to 75 percent) can be reverse-mortgaged this way. While this can provide retirement income for a time, it is risky because after a number of years if the retirees are still living, they will have to sell their home to pay off the debt. Or they can try to refinance it and pay off another regular mortgage once again. Another option for individuals considering reverse mortgages might be to sell the home outright and move into a smaller home or apartment while investing the remaining proceeds of the sale in order to receive income.

## INNOVATIVE MORTGAGES

In addition to the traditional fixed rate mortgage discussed above, a number of new innovative mortgages have been developed. These were popular during the 1970s and early 1980s because interest rates were very high and mortgage money was in short supply. They made it possible for people who otherwise might not qualify to qualify and afford a home. Recently some of these new mortgages have become less popular because rates have come down, and mortgage money is more plentiful again. However, two of them are still widely used. They are the Adjustable Rate Mortgage (ARM) and the Renegotiable Mortgage.

*The adjustable (variable) rate mortgage*

The **variable rate mortgage** (VRM) is also referred to as the "adjustable rate mortgage" (ARM). With variable interest mortgages, the rate can be adjusted every six months or so, but only if certain other rates such as marketable U.S. government (or corporate) bond rates change. Some-times the lending institution will tie the adjustment to the average rate they pay on deposits. (The variable mortgage rate is usually one to three percentage points above the index to which it is tied.) Generally rates will only go up by a fraction of 1 percent every time they are adjusted. Normally there is also a limit (usually 3 to 5 percent) on the overall upward or downward movement during the life of the mortgage. There are three methods of adjusting the variable interest rate: The first is to change the monthly payment with the maturity remaining constant. The second is to change the length of the maturity with the monthly payment remaining constant. The third is a combination of the first two.

The difficulty in using a variable rate is that when rates are high the borrower may be willing to sign a variable contract and hope that rates come down, but the lending institution is reluctant to do so. During times when rates are low, the reverse is the case: the lender favors variable rates, the borrower does not. Another problem with the VRM is that in some states there is no limit to how high rates may go. In addition, if the rates are adjusted to the extent that the life of the mortgage is lengthened, the individual really has a negatively amortizing mortgage which would in theory never be paid off. Sometimes the VRM is written so that when interest rates are escalated, the monthly payment stays the same and the principal is reduced, but only for, say, three or five years. After this time, the original amortization schedule returns. When this is so, it may require a large increase in the monthly payment.

Usually, but not always, when the borrower has the choice between a fixed and variable mortgage, the variable one is a bit lower. Figure 8–3 illustrates a checklist to evaluate an adjustable rate mortgage.

*Renegotiable mortgages*

A modification of the variable interest rate mortgage is the **renegotiable mortgage**, sometimes called the rollover mortgage. Under it, interest rates are fixed but renegotiated every three, four, or five years as the case may be. There would be a negotiated rate change as the market changed, but it would not be an automatic adjustment tied to some money market indicator. Under this mortgage the lender is obliged to renegotiate and renew the mortgage; he cannot cancel it. The borrower, on the other hand, may pull out at renewal time and get a new mortgage elsewhere.

*The rollover mortgage*

The rollover mortgage is a variation of the renegotiable mortgage. It is generally written for five years, and it differs from the renegotiable in that when it comes due, the lender is not obliged to renew it. These are also sometimes referred to as "balloon" mortgages, because monthly payments are made for, say, five years, after which time the unpaid remainder is due in one large payment.

*Other less common innovative mortgages*

There are variations of the aforementioned mortgages which are less commonly used. Some examples include the wrap-around mortgage, the blended mortgage, the buy-down mortgage, the equity build-up mortgage and the shared appreciation mortgage.

An adjustable rate mortgage should be looked at very carefully before finalization. If a person signs one, he or she is assuming the risk that the market interest rate will change up or down. It is most important that the individual makes certain it has an overall cap for the life of the mortgage.

| | | |
|---|---|---|
| Original interest rate | | _____% |
| Original monthly payment | | $_____ |
| Frequency of adjustment: | Yes | No |
|     Every 6 months | ____ | ____ |
|     Every year | ____ | ____ |
|     Every 2 years | ____ | ____ |
| Maximum adjustment (cap): | | |
|     Per adjustment | | _____% |
|     Per year | | _____% |
|     Over the life of the mortgage | | _____% |
| | Yes | No |
| Can the rate go down as well as up? | ____ | ____ |
| Is there a downward floor? | ____ | ____ |
| If the interest rate rises: | | |
|     Will the monthly payment rise? | ____ | ____ |
|     Will the amount of the mortgage rise (negative amortization)? | ____ | ____ |
|     Will a combination of the two occur? | ____ | ____ |
| What is the ARM tied to (index)? | | |
|     U.S. treasury securities? | ____ | ____ |
|     Overall cost of deposits? | ____ | ____ |
|     Other? | ____ | ____ |
|     How much above the index is the rate? | | _____% |

Figure 8—3    *Checklist to evaluate an adjustable rate mortgage*

**The wrap-around mortgage**

One way of financing a home if the buyer does not have enough funds to assume an existing mortgage is to use the wrap-around mortgage, often done if the seller is willing and able to finance the sale and assume the wrap-around mortgage; the new mortgage figuratively wraps around the old mortgage. This technique works particularly well if the existing mortgage is small. For example, suppose a seller has an older home for sale for $100,000 with only a $20,000 mortgage left on it. If the buyer has $40,000, he could pay that as a down payment, and the seller could take a $60,000 mortgage which includes (wraps around) the $20,000 due on the original. The seller would then continue to pay off the original $20,000 mortgage, and the buyer would need to worry about only the new $60,000 one.

Wrap-arounds may also be illegal in some cases. Only if the mortgage is assumable or if the institution holding the original mortgages gives its permission is a wrap-around possible. Older mortgages often are assumable; but in the last seven or eight years, more and more institutions have placed due-on-sale clauses in their loan contracts, and in such a case wrap-arounds are not possible.

If a wrap-around is not possible, an individual might be able to negotiate a blended mortgage. In the above wrap-around case, for example, if it had not been legal the home might not have sold if the entire mortgage of $80,000 had to be financed at a higher rate. To get the old 8 percent loan off the books, many institutions will negotiate a new one at a favorable rate. The above $80,000 new mortgage could be an average of the $40,000 at 8 percent and $40,000 at a bit above the current market rate. This would make the blend somewhat below the market rate.

*The blended mortgage*

The buy-down mortgage is a misnomer, but it is a means of reducing the interest rate from, say, 13 percent to 10 percent. In reality, the buyer pays a lump sum (usually at closing) in return for which the lender will reduce the interest rate. This amounts to prepaying some of the interest and, upon closer examination, may not be the best arrangement for the buyer. For example, a $50,000 mortgage at 13 percent over 30 years requires a $553.10 per month amortization payment. However, if the buyer pays an additional $4,115.16 at closing, the interest rate is reduced to 10 percent and the monthly amortization payment drops to $438.79. The buy-down was calculated by taking the difference between the two monthly payments ($553.10 – $438.79 = $114.31) and multiplying it by 36. The buy-down rate is therefore effective for three years, after which time the rate escalates to 13 percent or is renegotiated at the then market rate. The result may be that a buyer who did not qualify for a loan previously now does. Psychologically it may also be beneficial for the buyer to obtain 10 percent financing. In reality, however, it might have been better for the buyer to make a larger down payment and finance a smaller principal sum at a higher rate. If the buyer does not have the required buy-down charges, the seller may provide it by means of a second mortgage. Some builders do this.

*The buy-down mortgage*

At one time the equity build-up and sharing mortgages were used. These are also called shared appreciation mortgages (SAM) and shared equity mortgages (SEM). With these, when the home owner sells his or her home, a shared appreciation portion (say, 20 to 25 percent) of the capital gain attributable to inflation is remitted to the mortgagee (lender). For this, the buyer receives a more favorable interest rate.

*Equity build-up mortgage (EBM) and shared appreciation mortgage (SAM)*

The major danger of innovative mortgages is that interest rates may escalate wildly. In the case of a fixed mortgage at least the individual knows what the cost is—and will remain. To be sure, ceilings may be placed on the amount of interest escalation, but this is not always done. In the case of a variable rate mortgage, there is also the problem of what the rate should be tied to, i.e., what determines when rates are to rise. Probably the best indicator is the long-term U.S. government bond rate. The variable mortgage rate could be 1.5 or 2 points above the government rate.

*Some dangers of innovative mortgages*

If a mortgage has a balloon on it and no guaranteed refinancing provision, the person may be in serious difficulty when it comes due. This is not to say that individuals should never use innovative mortgages, but only that they should go into such an arrangement with their eyes open, and be careful. A home owner should not expect a continued rise in home prices to bail him or her out if there is financial difficulty.

## OTHER THINGS TO KNOW ABOUT HOME OWNERSHIP

When buying something as expensive as a home there may be certain hidden costs that might occur. Then there are the mechanics of making an offer on a home. The financial planner needs to be aware of the costs of purchasing a home and the home offer procedure in order to evaluate all options.

### Points

Sometimes points are used when a loan is made. Generally, points are added during periods of tight money, and the tighter the money supply the greater the number of points added. A point is one percentage point of the mortgage loan and normally is paid by the buyer of the home. On a $60,000 mortgage loan on which two points are assessed, this amounts to $1,200 and is added to the closing costs if the buyer pays them (see below). However, sometimes points are paid, at least in part, by the seller. It depends on the market. If the market is tight and a shortage of homes exists in the area, the buyer will probably pay the points. If, on the other hand, there is a surplus of homes, the seller will almost invariably pay at least part of the points in order to make the sale. In short, points are negotiable.

The lending institution receives these "points," and it is a means of increasing interest rates the first year. If the seller pays these points, and an institution makes a $40,000 loan on a $50,000 house in which the seller has a $10,000 equity and assesses two points, then the institution advances the seller only $9,200. The buyer assumes a $40,000 mortgage at 10 percent, but the lender really receives 12 percent return the first year. In some cases these points are deductible for federal income tax purposes by the buyer if properly handled.

### Making an offer on a house; earnest money

When a seller offers a house, he or she or the real estate agent draws up a sales contract. This piece of paper spells out the terms of the sale. It will describe the house, list the asking price and note the present mortgage. By signing this contract a prospective purchaser agrees to buy the house. However, usually the prospective buyer will make a counter-offer by changing the terms somewhat, perhaps lowering the price.

To ascertain whether or not the offering price is reasonably close to the true market value, ask a realtor, who can give a fairly good answer.

Also check the selling price (not the offered price) of other comparable homes that have been sold recently. Many sellers will price their house above the realistic market value in the hope that they will find a naive person who will pay it. In addition, some home owners have an inflated opinion of the value of the house. Often sellers will come down from their offering price. A buyer can negotiate with the seller but only indirectly through the realtor. It is also best to find out from the realtor whether selling prices generally have been close to asking prices.

When a buyer finally decides what he or she is willing to pay, a counteroffer is then made. This counteroffer is signed by the prospective buyer and conveyed to the seller by the realtor with a down payment (usually $500 to $1,000, depending on the price of the house) called **earnest money**. There may be several counteroffers between the buyer and seller; this is the negotiation over the price. The buyer must sign any counteroffer he or she makes and present earnest money with it. If the seller signs the buyer's counteroffer, it is a binding deal.

In some states this earnest money goes to the seller immediately and in others it goes into an escrow account until the transaction is closed. In any event, when both buyer and seller have signed the contract, it is binding and either can force the other to comply. However, in practice the seller can nearly always back out by returning the earnest money, because it would require a lawsuit to force compliance. A buyer who wanted to back out, however, would generally lose the earnest money. That is why the offer (sales contract) must carefully spell out all the conditions desired by both parties. For example, the buy offer will always be a conditional offer and effective only if satisfactory financing can be arranged. An earnest money contract is shown in Figure 8–4. Note that under the heading "special conditions," a number of provisions have been written into the contract. This is more often done on older homes than on new homes.

*Closing costs*

When the buyer and seller of a house have reached an agreement, they and the realtors involved get together to close the deal and sign the necessary papers. A representative of the lending institution also attends the closing which indeed may be held at the office of the lending institution. Up until recently, it was often at the closing that the surprised buyer first became aware that closing costs were involved. Now, however, the lending institution must disclose closing costs in advance. If the institution is not certain what they will amount to, a good-faith estimate must be made. Closing costs (not counting points) generally run from 2 to 3 percent of the mortgage.

The question is, what do these costs consist of? The totals generally vary with the section of the country in which the loan is being made. In addition to the points discussed above, closing costs generally include the following:

02-08-85

## ONE TO FOUR FAMILY RESIDENTIAL EARNEST MONEY CONTRACT (RESALE)
## ALL CASH, ASSUMPTION, THIRD PARTY CONVENTIONAL OR OWNER FINANCED

### PROMULGATED BY TEXAS REAL ESTATE COMMISSION

NOTICE: Not For Use For Condominium Transactions

1. PARTIES: Samuel D. Seller and wife, Selina Ann Seller _____ (Seller) agrees to sell and convey to Peter D. Purchaser and wife, Penelope L. Purchaser _____ (Buyer) and Buyer agrees to buy from Seller the property described below.

2. PROPERTY: Lot 22 , Block G  Brushy Creek North, Section 4 Addition, City of Austin , Travis , County, Texas, known as 10056 Forever Drive, Austin, Texas (Address); or as described on attached exhibit, together with the following items, if any: curtains and rods, draperies and rods, valances, blinds, window shades, screens, shutters, awnings, wall-to-wall carpeting, mirrors fixed in place, ceiling fans, attic fans, mail boxes, television antennas, permanently installed heating and air conditioning units and equipment, built-in security and fire detection equipment, lighting and plumbing fixtures, water softener, trash compactor, garage door openers with controls, shrubbery and all other property owned by Seller and attached to the above described real property. All property sold by this contract is called the "Property".

3. CONTRACT SALES PRICE:
   A. Cash payable at closing .................................................. $ 25,000.00
   B. Sum of all financing described in Paragraph 4 below ......................... $ 125,000.00
   C. Sales Price (Sum of A and B) ............................................ $ 150,000.00

4. FINANCING: (Check applicable boxes below)
   ☐ A. ALL CASH: This is an all cash sale; no financing is involved.
   ☐ B. ASSUMPTION:
      (1) Buyer's assumption of the unpaid principal balance of a first lien promissory note payable to _____ in present monthly installments of $_____, including principal, interest and any reserve deposits, with Buyer's first installment payment being payable on the first installment payment date after closing, the assumed principal balance of which at closing will be $_____.
      (2) Buyer's assumption of the unpaid principal balance of a second lien promissory note payable to _____ in present monthly installments of $_____, including principal, interest and any reserve deposits, with Buyer's first installment payment being payable on the first installment payment date after closing, the assumed principal balance of which at closing will be $_____.
   Buyer's assumption of an existing note includes all obligations imposed by the deed of trust securing the note.

   If the total principal balance of all assumed loans varies in an amount greater than $350.00 at closing either party may terminate this contract and the Earnest Money shall be refunded to Buyer. If the noteholder on assumption (a) requires Buyer to pay an assumption fee in excess of $_____ in B(1) above or $_____ in B(2) above and Seller declines to pay such excess or (b) raises the existing interest rate above _____% in B(1) above or _____% in B(2) above, Buyer may terminate this contract and the Earnest Money shall be refunded to Buyer. The cash payable at closing shall be adjusted by the amount of any variance in the loan balance(s) shown above.
   NOTICE TO BUYER: Monthly payments, interest rates or other terms of some loans may be adjusted after closing. Before signing the contract, examine the notes and deeds of trust to determine the possibility of future adjustments.

   ☒ C. THIRD PARTY FINANCED:
      ☐ 1. A third party first lien note of $ 125,000.00 , due in full in 30 year(s), payable in initial monthly payments of principal and interest not exceeding $ 1,096.98 for the first 30 year(s) of the loan.
      ☐ 2. A third party second lien note of $_____, due in full in _____ year(s), payable in initial monthly payments of principal and interest not exceeding $_____ for the first _____ year(s) of the loan.
   NOTICE TO PARTIES: Before signing this contract Buyer is advised to determine the financing options from lenders. Certain loans have variable rates of interest, some have monthly payments which may not be sufficient to pay the accruing interest, and some have interest rate "buydowns" which reduce the rate of interest for part or all of the loan term at the expense of one or more of the parties to the contract.

   ☐ D. TEXAS VETERANS' HOUSING ASSISTANCE PROGRAM LOAN:
      This contract is also subject to approval for Buyer of a Texas Veterans' Housing Assistance Program Loan (the Program Loan) in an amount of $_____ for a period of at least _____ years at the interest rate established by the Texas Veterans' Land Board at the time of closing.

   ☐ E. SELLER FINANCED: A promissory note from Buyer to Seller in the amount of $_____, bearing _____% interest per annum, and payable:
      ☐ 1. In one payment due _____ after the date of the note with interest payable _____.
      ☐ 2. In installments of $_____ [ ] including interest [ ] plus interest beginning _____ after the date of the note and continuing at _____ intervals thereafter for _____ year(s) when the entire balance of the note shall be due and payable.
      ☐ 3. Interest only in _____ installments for the first _____ year(s) and thereafter in installments of $_____ [ ] including interest [ ] plus interest beginning _____ after the date of the note and continuing at _____ intervals thereafter for _____ year(s) when the entire balance of the note is due and payable.
      ☐ 4. This contract is subject to Buyer furnishing Seller evidence of good credit within _____ days from the effective date of this contract. If notice of disapproval of Buyer's credit is not given within five (5) days thereafter, Seller shall be deemed to have approved Buyer's credit. Buyer hereby authorizes Buyer's credit report to be furnished to Seller.
   Any Seller financed note may be prepaid in whole or in part at any time without penalty. The lien securing payment of such note will be inferior to any lien securing any loan assumed or given in connection with third party financing. If an Owner's Policy of Title Insurance is furnished, Buyer shall furnish Seller with a Mortgagee's Title Policy.

   Buyer shall apply for all third party financing or noteholder's approval of Buyer for assumption and waiver of the right to accelerate the note within 7 days from the effective date of this contract and shall make every reasonable effort to obtain the same. Such financing or assumption shall have been approved when Buyer has satisfied all of lender's financial conditions, e.g., sale of other property, requirement of co-signer or financial verifications. If such financing or noteholder's approval and waiver is not obtained within 45 days from the effective date hereof, this contract shall terminate and the Earnest Money shall be refunded to Buyer.

5. EARNEST MONEY: $ 5,000.00 is herewith tendered by Buyer and is to be deposited as Earnest Money with Gracy Title Company , at 220 West 7th at Lavaca, Austin (Address), as Escrow Agent, upon execution of the contract by both parties. ☐ Additional Earnest Money of $ n/a shall be deposited by Buyer with

**101**

TREC NO. 20-0

Figure 8—4 *One to four family residential earnest money contract (resale) all cash, assumption, third party conventional or owner-financed*

One To Four Family Residential Earnest Money Contract — Page Two                                    02-08-85

the Escrow Agent on or before _____ n/a _____, 19__.

6.  TITLE: Seller shall furnish to Buyer at Seller's expense either:

☒ A.  Owner's Policy of Title Insurance (the Title Policy) issued by _Gracy Title Company_
in the amount of the Sales Price and dated at or after closing; OR

☐ B.  Abstracts of Title certified by an abstract company (1) from the sovereignty to the effective date of this contract (Complete Abstract) and (2) supplemented to the Closing Date (Supplemental Abstract).

NOTICE TO SELLER AND BUYER: AS REQUIRED BY LAW, Broker advises Buyer that Buyer should have an Abstract covering the Property examined by an attorney of Buyer's selection, or Buyer should be furnished with or obtain a Title Policy. If a Title Policy is to be obtained, Buyer should obtain a Commitment for Title Insurance (the Commitment) which should be examined by an attorney of Buyer's choice at or prior to closing. If the Property is situated in a Utility District, Section 50.301 Texas Water Code requires the Buyer to sign and acknowledge the statutory notice from Seller relating to the tax rate and bonded indebtedness of the District.

7.  PROPERTY CONDITION: (Check A or B)

☒ A.  Buyer accepts the Property in its present condition, subject only to any lender required repairs and _repair of sprinkler_
_system_

☐ B.  Buyer requires inspections and repairs required by any lender and the Property Condition Addendum attached hereto.

On Seller's receipt of all loan approvals and inspection reports, Seller shall commence repairs and termite treatment required of Seller by the contract, any lender and the Property Condition Addendum, if any, and complete such repairs prior to closing. Seller's responsibility for the repairs, termite treatment and repairs to termite damage shall not exceed $_500.00_. If Seller fails to complete such repairs, Buyer may do so and Seller shall be liable for the amount specified and the same paid from the proceeds of the sale. If the repair costs will exceed the stated amount and Seller refuses to pay such excess, Buyer may (1) pay the additional cost or (2) accept the Property with the limited repairs unless such repairs are required by lender or (3) Buyer may terminate this contract and the Earnest Money shall be refunded to Buyer. Buyer shall make his election within three (3) days after Seller notifies Buyer of Seller's refusal to pay such excess. Failure of Buyer to make such election within the time provided shall be deemed to be Buyer's election to accept the Property with the limited repairs, and the sale shall be closed as scheduled; however, if lender required repairs prohibit Buyer's acceptance with the limited repairs, this contract shall terminate and Earnest Money shall be refunded to Buyer.

If the repair costs will exceed five (5) percent of the Sales Price of the Property and Seller agrees to pay the cost of such repairs, Buyer shall have the option of closing the sale with the completed repairs, or terminating the sale and the Earnest Money shall be refunded to Buyer. Buyer shall make this election within three (3) days after Seller notifies Buyer of Seller's willingness to pay the cost of such repairs that exceed five (5) percent of the Sales Price. Failure of Buyer to make such election within the time provided shall be deemed to be Buyer's election to close the sale with the completed repairs.

Broker(s) and sales associates have no responsibility or liability for inspections or repairs made pursuant to this contract.

8.  BROKER'S FEE: _Wehelpu Realtors_, Listing Broker, and any Co-Broker represent Seller unless otherwise specified herein. Seller agrees to pay Listing Broker the fee specified by separate agreement between Listing Broker and Seller. Escrow Agent is authorized and directed to pay Listing Broker said fee from the sale proceeds.

9.  CLOSING: The closing of the sale shall be on or before _November 30_, 19_87_, or within seven (7) days after objections to title have been cured, whichever date is later (the Closing Date); however, if financing or assumption approval has been obtained pursuant to Paragraph 4, the Closing Date shall be extended daily up to fifteen (15) days if necessary to complete loan requirements. If either party fails to close this sale by the Closing Date, the non-defaulting party shall be entitled to exercise the remedies contained in Paragraph 16 immediately and without notice.

10. POSSESSION: The possession of the Property shall be delivered to Buyer on _closing and funding_ in its present or required improved condition, ordinary wear and tear excepted. Any possession by Buyer prior to or Seller after closing that is not authorized by the Buyer's Temporary Residential Lease or Seller's Temporary Residential Lease Forms promulgated by the Texas Real Estate Commission shall establish a landlord-tenant at sufferance relationship between the parties.

11. SPECIAL PROVISIONS: (Insert factual statements and business details applicable to this sale.)

Ceiling fans to convey.

12. SALES EXPENSES TO BE PAID IN CASH AT OR PRIOR TO CLOSING:

A.  Loan appraisal fees shall be paid by _buyer_

B.  The total of the loan discount and any buydown fees shall not exceed $_3,750.00_ of which Buyer shall pay the first $_937.50_ and Seller shall pay the remainder.

C.  Seller's Expenses: Prepayment penalties on any existing loans paid at closing, plus cost of releasing such loans and recording releases; tax statements; ½ of any escrow fee; preparation of deed; preparation and recording of any deed of trust to secure assumption; any Texas Veterans' Housing Assistance Program Participation Fee; other expenses stipulated to be paid by Seller under other provisions of this contract.

D.  Buyer's Expenses: Application, origination and commitment fees; private mortgage insurance premiums and any loan assumption fee; expenses incident to new loan(s) (e.g., preparation of any note, deed of trust and other loan documents, survey, recording fees, copies of restrictions and easements, Mortgagee's Title Policies, credit reports, photos); ½ of any escrow fee; any required premiums for flood and hazard insurance; any required reserve deposits for insurance premiums, ad valorem taxes and special governmental assessments; interest on all monthly installment payment notes from date of disbursements to one (1) month prior to dates of first monthly payments; expenses stipulated to be paid by Buyer under other provisions of this contract and any customary Texas Veterans' Housing Assistance Program Loan costs for Buyer.

E.  If any sales expenses exceed the maximum amount herein stipulated to be paid by either party, either party may terminate this contract unless the other party agrees to pay such excess.

13. PRORATIONS: Taxes, flood and hazard insurance (at Buyer's option), rents, maintenance fees, interest on any assumed loan and any prepaid unearned mortgage insurance premium which has not been financed as part of any assumed loan and which is refundable in whole or in part at a later date shall be prorated through the Closing Date. If Buyer elects to continue Seller's insurance policy, it shall be transferred at closing.

14. TITLE APPROVAL:

A.  If abstract is furnished, Seller shall deliver Complete Abstract to Buyer within twenty (20) days from the effective date hereof. Buyer shall have twenty (20) days from date of receipt of Complete Abstract to deliver a copy of the examining attorney's title opinion to Seller, stating any objections to title, and only objections so stated shall be considered.

B.  If Title Policy is furnished, the Title Policy shall guarantee Buyer's title to be good and indefeasible subject only to (1) restrictive covenants affecting the Property (2) any discrepancies, conflicts or shortages in area or boundary lines, or any encroachments, or any overlapping of improvements (3) taxes for the current and subsequent years and subsequent assessments for prior years due to a change in land usage or ownership (4) existing building and zoning ordinances (5) rights of parties in possession (6) liens created or assumed as security for the sale consideration (7) utility easements common to the platted subdivision of which this Property is a part and (8) reservations or other exceptions permitted by the terms of this contract. Exceptions permitted in the Deed and zoning ordinances shall not be valid objections to title. If the Title Policy will be subject to exceptions other than those recited above in sub-paragraphs (1) through (7) inclusive, Seller shall deliver to Buyer the Commitment and legible copies of any documents creating such exceptions that are not recited in sub-paragraphs (1) through (7) above at least five (5) days prior to closing. If Buyer has objection to any such previously undisclosed exceptions, Buyer shall have five (5) days after receipt of such Commitment and copies to make written objections to Seller. If no Title Commitment is provided to Buyer at or prior to closing, it will be conclusively presumed that Seller represented at closing that the Title Policy would not be subject to exceptions other than those recited above in sub-paragraphs (1) through (7).

C.  In either instance if title objections are raised, Seller shall have fifteen (15) days from the date such objections are disclosed to cure the same, and the Closing Date shall be extended accordingly. If the objections are not satisfied by the extended closing date, this contract shall terminate and the Earnest Money shall be refunded to Buyer, unless Buyer elects to waive the unsatisfied objections and complete the purchase.

D.  Seller shall furnish tax statements showing no delinquent taxes, a Supplemental Abstract when applicable, showing no additional title exceptions and a General

**101**     TREC NO. 20-0

| | | | | |
|---|---|---|---|---|
| 1. Title insurance | $400 | | 7. Tax reserve | $500 |
| 2. Credit reports | 50 | | 8. Survey | 50 |
| 3. Attorney's fees | 100 | | 9. Recording fee | 50 |
| 4. Origination fee | 500 | | 10. Closing fee | 100 |
| 5. Appraisal fee | 150 | | 11. Points | |
| 6. Fire and other hazard insurance reserve | 40 | | | |

Title insurance costs vary depending on the amount of the loan and the company with which the policy is placed. Fire insurance rates, credit reports, and attorney's fees all vary somewhat regionally. Furthermore, the closing costs differ depending on whether the loan is a conventional mortgage, a VA-guaranteed mortgage, or an FHA-insured mortgage; in general the same items are included.

In purchasing as important and expensive an item as a home, it is worthwhile for the first-time buyer to engage the services of an attorney. The $100 or $150 cost is usually well spent. When entering into a legal agreement, it is best to have an expert explain all of the fine print. This is over and above the attorney's fees shown on the closing costs statement. The latter are for the fees of the lender's attorney who draws up the papers.

In past years it was also necessary to have a title search, to confirm the fact that the legal title of the property was vested in the seller and that he or she could legally transfer it to you. Presently most people buy title insurance rather than have their attorney conduct such a search. This insurance policy protects the buyer against any loss because of a defect in the title. While this is typically paid for by the seller, sometimes the buyer also has to buy title insurance. In this latter case it is to protect the lender; that purchased by the seller protects only the buyer.

Another item under closing costs consists of what is called the **_origination fee_** (sometimes called finder's fee) or lender's fee. This is generally 1 percent of the mortgage, and if one is buying from a builder or a real estate broker it is supposedly a fee he or she receives for making the arrangements for the loan. Even if one is dealing directly with a financial institution, the fee is often charged. It is essentially then a means to increase the return to the broker, or the financial institution. Again conditions vary from one section of the country to another, but generally the only way to avoid paying the finder's fee is for the buyer to individually make the arrangement for the loan with a financial institution.

Other typical costs are appraiser's fees, credit reports, the cost of hiring a surveyor to survey the property and ascertain its exact boundaries, and a fee for an amortization table. There may or may not be a charge for these. Sometimes hazard insurance is shown twice on a closing statement, once for the first year's premiums, which must be paid in advance, and again for a one-or two-month premium, which goes into an escrow account for next year's premiums. Property taxes must also be

Form Approved
OMB NO. 63-R1501

| A. | U.S. DEPARTMENT OF HOUSING AND URBAN DEVELOPMENT | B. TYPE OF LOAN: |
|---|---|---|

| B. TYPE OF LOAN: | | |
|---|---|---|
| 1. ☐ FHA | 2. ☐ FMHA | 3. ☐ CONV. UNINS. |
| 4. ☐ VA | 5. ☒ CONV. INS. | |
| 6. FILE NUMBER    UTGAME | | 7. LOAN NUMBER    07208777 |
| 8. MORTG. INS. CASE NO. | | |

**SETTLEMENT STATEMENT**

C. **NOTE:** This form is furnished to give you a statement of actual settlement costs. Amounts paid to and by the settlement agent are shown. Items marked "(p.o.c.)" were paid outside the closing; they are shown here for informational purposes and are not included in the totals.

| D. NAME OF BORROWER | E. NAME OF SELLER | F. NAME OF LENDER |
|---|---|---|
| PETER D. PURCHASER AND WIFE, PENELOPE L.PURCHASER | SAMUEL D. SELLER AND WIFE, SELINA ANN SELLER | LIFETIME MORTGAGE COMPANY 1227 PAYMENT BLVD. SWEET HOME, WISCONSIN |

| G. PROPERTY LOCATION | H. SETTLEMENT AGENT | I. SETTLEMENT DATE: |
|---|---|---|
| LOT 22, BLOCK G, BRUSHY CREEK NORTH, SECTION 4, TRAVIS COUNTY, TEXAS 10056 FOREVER DRIVE AUSTIN, TEXAS 78754 | GRACY TITLE COMPANY 220 W. 7TH ST., AUSTIN TX 78701 PLACE OF SETTLEMENT GRACY TITLE COMPANY 220 W. 7TH ST., AUSTIN TX 78701 | 9-09-87 Proration date: 9-10-87 |

| J.   SUMMARY OF BORROWER'S TRANSACTION | | K.   SUMMARY OF SELLER'S TRANSACTION | |
|---|---|---|---|
| 100 GROSS AMOUNT DUE FROM BORROWER: | | 400. GROSS AMOUNT DUE TO SELLER: | |
| 101. Contract sales price | 150,000.00 | 401. Contract sales price | 150,000.00 |
| 102. Personal property | | 402. Personal property | |
| 103. Settlement charges to borrower (line 1400) | 8,157.01 | 403. | |
| 104. | | 404. | |
| 105. | | 405. | |
| Adjustments for items paid by seller in advance: | | Adjustments for items paid by seller in advance: | |
| 106. City/town taxes          to | | 406. City/town taxes          to | |
| 107. County taxes          to | | 407. County taxes          to | |
| 108. Assessments          to | | 408. Assessments          to | |
| 109. Maintenance          to | | 409. Maintenance          to | |
| 110. School/Taxes          to | | 410. Commitment Fee          to | |
| 111.          to | | 411.          to | |
| 112.          to | | 412.          to | |
| 120. GROSS AMOUNT DUE FROM BORROWER: | 158,157.01 | 420. GROSS AMOUNT DUE TO SELLER: | 150,000.00 |
| 200. AMOUNTS PAID BY OR IN BEHALF OF BORROWER: | | 500. REDUCTIONS IN AMOUNT DUE TO SELLER: | |
| 201. Deposit or earnest money | 5,000.00 | 501. Excess deposit (see instructions) | |
| 202. Principal amount of new loan(s) | 125,000.00 | 502. Settlement charges to seller (line 1400) | 12,917.50 |
| 203. Existing loan(s) taken subject to | | 503. Existing loan(s) taken subject to | |
| 204. Commitment Fee | | 504. Payoff of first mortgage loan | 107,333.27 |
| 205. | | 505. Payoff of second mortgage loan | |
| 206. | | 506. | |
| 207. CREDIT FOR REPAIRS | 325.00 | 507. CREDIT FOR REPAIRS | 325.00 |
| 208. | | 508. | |
| 209. | | 509. | |
| Adjustments for items unpaid by seller: | | Adjustments for items unpaid by seller: | |
| 210. City/town taxes 1-01-87 to 9-10-87 | 383.03 | 510. City/town taxes 1-01-87 to 9-10-87 | 383.03 |
| 211. County taxes 1-01-87 to 9-10-87 | 210.71 | 511. County Taxes 1-01-87 to 9-10-87 | 210.71 |
| 212. Assessments          to | | 512. Assessments          to | |
| 213. School/Taxes 1-01-87 to 9-10-87 | 777.91 | 513. School/Taxes 1-01-87 to 9-10-87 | 777.91 |
| 214.          to | | 514. Maintenance          to | |
| 215.          to | | 515.          to | |
| 216.          to | | 516.          to | |
| 217.          to | | 517.          to | |
| 218.          to | | 518.          to | |
| 219.          to | | 519.          to | |
| 220. TOTAL PAID BY/FOR BORROWER: | 131,696.65 | 520. TOTAL REDUCTION AMOUNT DUE SELLER: | 121,947.42 |
| 300. CASH AT SETTLEMENT FROM/TO BORROWER: | | 600. CASH AT SETTLEMENT TO/FROM SELLER: | |
| 301. Gross amount due from borrower (line 120) | 158,157.01 | 601. Gross amount due to seller (line 420) | 150,000.00 |
| 302. Less amounts paid by/for borrower (line 20) | 131,696.65 | 602. Less total reductions in amount due seller (line 520) | 121,947.42 |
| 303. CASH (☐ FROM) (☐ TO) BORROWER: X | 26,460.36 | 603. CASH (☐ TO) (☐ FROM) SELLER X | 28,052.58 |

HUD-1 (Rev. 5-76)
(10M 7-84)

*Settlement statement*                                    Figure 8—5

PAGE 2 OF OMB No. 2502-0265

| L. SETTLEMENT CHARGES | GF # UTGAME | PAID FROM BORROWER'S FUNDS AT SETTLEMENT | PAID FROM SELLER'S FUNDS AT SETTLEMENT |
|---|---|---|---|
| 700. TOTAL SALES/BROKER'S COMMISSION Based on price $ 150,000.00 @ .00 %= 9,000.00 | | | |
| Division of commission (line 700) as follows: | | | |
| 701. $ 4,500.00 to WEHELPU REALTORS | | | |
| 702. $ 4,500.00 to CLEAR TITLE REALTORS | | | |
| 703. Commission paid at settlement | | | 9,000.00 |
| 704. | | | |
| **800. ITEMS PAYABLE IN CONNECTION WITH LOAN.** | | | |
| 801. Loan Origination fee 1.0000 % LIFETIME MORTGAGE COMPANY | | 1,250.00 | |
| 802. Loan Discount 3.0000 % LIFETIME MORTGAGE COMPANY | | 937.50 | 2,812.50 |
| 803. Appraisal Fee to LIFETIME MORTGAGE COMPANY | | 275.00 | |
| 804. Credit Report $40 POC/BUYER to LIFETIME MORTGAGE COMPANY | | | |
| 805. Lender's inspection fee to LIFETIME MORTGAGE COMPANY | | 30.00 | |
| 806. Mortgage Insurance application fee to | | | |
| 807. Assumption Fee | | | |
| 808. Commitment Fee | | | |
| 809. XXXXXXXX DATA PROCESS to LIFETIME MORTGAGE COMPANY | | 50.00 | |
| 810. XXXXX TAX SERVICE FEE to LIFETIME MORTGAGE COMPANY | | 131.00 | |
| 811. UNDERWRITING FEE to LIFETIME MORTGAGE COMPANY | | 100.00 | |
| **900. ITEMS REQUIRED BY LENDER TO BE PAID IN ADVANCE.** | | | |
| 901. Interest from 9-09-87 to 10-01-87 @ $ 54.250 /day | | 1,193.50 | |
| 902. Mortgage insurance premium for 12.0 mo. to TICOR | | 904.00 | |
| 903. Hazard insurance premium for 1 yrs. to STATE FARM INSURANCE CO. | | 723.00 | |
| 904. Flood Insurance yrs. to | | | |
| 905. | | | |
| **1000. RESERVES DEPOSITED WITH LENDER** | | | |
| 1001. Hazard insurance 2 mo. @ $ 60.25 per mo. | | 120.50 | |
| 1002. Mortgage insurance 2 mo. @ $ 44.23 per mo. | | 88.46 | |
| 1003. City property taxes 11 mo. @ $ 46.23 per mo. | | 508.53 | |
| 1004. County property taxes 11 mo. @ $ 25.43 per mo. | | 279.73 | |
| 1005. Annual assessments (Maint.) mo. @ $ per mo. | | | |
| 1006. School Property Taxes 11 mo. @ $ 93.89 per mo. | | 1,032.79 | |
| 1007. Water Dist. Prop. Tax mo. @ $ per mo. | | | |
| 1008. Flood Insurance mo. @ $ per mo. | | | |
| **1100. TITLE CHARGES:** | | | |
| 1101. Settlement or closing fee to | | | |
| 1102. Abstract or title search to | | | |
| 1103. Title examination to | | | |
| 1104. Title insurance binder to | | | |
| 1105. Document preparation to VENUE, PROBATE & DEED | | 150.00 | 95.00 |
| 1106. Notary fees to | | | |
| 1107. Attorney's fees to to | | | |
| (includes above items No. ) | | | |
| 1108. Title insurance to GRACY TITLE COMPANY | | 60.00 | 936.00 |
| (includes above items No. ) | | | |
| 1109. Lender's coverage $ 40.00 + $20.00 | | | |
| 1110. Owner's coverage $ 936.00 | | | |
| 1111. Escrow Fee to GRACY TITLE COMPANY | | 40.00 | 40.00 |
| 1112. Restrictions | | | |
| 1113. Messenger Service | | | |
| **1200. GOVERNMENT RECORDING AND TRANSFER CHARGES** | | | |
| 1201. Recording fees: Deed $ 7.00 Mortgage $ 11.00 Releases $ 5.00 | | 18.00 | 5.00 |
| 1202. City/county tax/stamps: Deed $ Mortgage $ | | | |
| 1203. State tax/stamps: Deed $ Mortgage $ | | | |
| 1204. Tax Certificates to GRACY TITLE COMPANY | | | 15.00 |
| 1205. | | | |
| **1300. ADDITIONAL SETTLEMENT CHARGES** | | | |
| 1301. Survey to SURV-TECH & ASSOCIATES | | 225.00 | |
| 1302. Pest inspection to KILL-A-BUG | | 40.00 | |
| 1303. COURIER FEES-PAYOFF to GRACY TITLE COMPANY | | | 14.00 |
| 1304. | | | |
| 1305. | | | |
| 1400. TOTAL SETTLEMENT CHARGES (entered on lines 103, Section J and 502, Section K) | | 8,157.01 | 12,917.50 |

CERTIFICATION: I have carefully reviewed the HUD-1 Settlement Statement and to the best of my knowledge and belief, it is a true and accurate statement of all receipts and disbursements made on my account or by me in this transaction. I further certify that I have received a copy of HUD-1 Settlement Statement.

Borrowers _____  Sellers _____

To the best of my knowledge, the HUD-1 Settlement Statement which I have prepared is a true and accurate account of funds which were received and have been or will be disbursed by the undersigned as part of the settlement of this transaction.

Settlement Agent _____  Date _____

SELLER'S AND/OR PURCHASER'S STATEMENT Seller's and Purchaser's signature hereon acknowledge his/her approval of tax prorations and signifies their understanding that prorations were based on taxes for the preceding year, or estimate for the current year, and in the event of any change for the current year, all necessary adjustments must be made between Seller and Purchaser; likewise any default in delinquent taxes will be reimbursed to Title Company by the Seller. The parties have read the above sentences, recognize that the recitations herein are material, agree to same, and recognize Title Company is relying on the same.

Purchasers/Borrowers _____  Sellers _____

WARNING: It is a crime to knowingly make false statements to the United States on this or any other similar form. Penalties upon conviction can include a fine and imprisonment. For details see Title 18: U.S. Code Section 1001 and Section 1010.

Figure 8–5  (continued)

provided for. If it is an existing house, there may be extra funds in a tax escrow account which will have to be paid for.

We discussed points above. They are assessed at closing and are usually, but not always, paid by the buyer. All other closing costs except the premium on the title insurance, also discussed above, are paid by the buyer as well. Figure 8–5 shows a disclosure settlement statement.

## SUGGESTED READINGS

Anosike, Benji O. *How to Buy or Sell Your Own Home Without a Lawyer or Broker.* New York: Do-It-Yourself Publishers, 1985.

*The Appraisal Journal.* Chicago: American Institute of Real Estate Appraisers. Quarterly publication.

*Appraisal Review Journal.* This journal is published three times per year by the National Association of Review Appraisers.

*Arenea, Journal of the American Real Estate and Urban Economics Association.* Quarterly Publication.

"Before a House Becomes a Home." Hartford, CT.: Aetna Life Insurance Co.

Boroson, Warren. *How to Buy or Sell Your Home in a Changing Market.* Oradell N.J.: Medical Economics Books, 1986.

"Buying and Selling Your Home." Chicago: American Bar Association Information Services.

Corgel, John, and Smith, Halbert C. *Real Estate.* Homewood, Ill.: R. Irwin, 1987.

*Financial Real Estate Handbook.* Boston: Financial Publishing Co. Annual publication.

Gritz, Robert D. *The Complete Home Buying Guide.* Beverly Farms, Mass.: Kay Publishing Co., 1986.

Harwood, Bruce. *Real Estate Principles.* Englewood Cliffs, N.J.: Prentice Hall, 1986.

"Homes: Construction, Maintenance, Community Development." Washington, D. C.: U. S. Government Printing Office.

Kau, James B., and Simmons, C. F. *Tax Planning for Real Estate Investors,* 3rd ed. Englewood Cliffs, N.J.: Prentice Hall, 1985.

"Landlord and Tenants—Your Guide to the Law." Chicago: American Bar Association Information Services, 750 N. Lake Shore Dr., Chicago, Ill. 60611.

"Monthly Amortization Loan Schedule." Santa Monica, Cal.: Delphi Information Sciences Corporation.

Morton, Tom. *Real Estate Finance; A Practical Approach.* Glenview, Ill.: Scott, Foresman, 1986.

*The Real Estate Appraiser and Analyst.* Chicago: Society of Real Estate Appraisers. Bimonthly publication.

"Real Estate Center Journal." College Station, TX.: Texas A & M University. Published quarterly.

*Real Estate Review.* Boston: Warren, Gorham and Lamont. Quarterly publication.

*Savings and Loan Fact Book.* Chicago: United States Savings and Loan League. Annual publication.

*Seller Services.* This is a bimonthly publication on home ownership published by the Federal National Mortgage Association.

*The Story of Modern Home Financing.* Chicago: United States League of Savings Associations, latest edition.

*What You Should Know Before You Buy a Home.* Chicago: United States League of Savings Associations. Obtain the latest edition of this annual publication.

Wiedemer, John P. *Real Estate Investments.* Reston, Va.: Reston Publishing Company, 1987.

Wofford, Larry E. *Real Estate.* New York: John Wiley and Sons, 1986.

Wurtzebach, Charles H., and Miles, Mike E. *Modern Real Estate.* New York: John Wiley and Sons, 1987.

*Your Housing Dollar.* Chicago: Money Management Institute, Household Finance Corp., 1985.

# III Planning and managing an insurance program

The four chapters in this section cover all types of insurance. Chapter 9 is an introductory chapter that covers the risks and hazards we all face in this world. The risk of loss must be managed somehow and this chapter spells out how this can be done.

Chapter 10 develops in some detail how the risk of premature death may be planned for. Chapter 11 does the same thing for the risk that there may be a loss of income and high medical expenses because of illness or an accident.

Chapter 12 discusses protecting assets by means of property and liability insurance. Property may be destroyed because of fire or accident, and your client may be held liable for destroying other people's property or injuring them. This chapter illustrates how property and liability insurance can protect your client.

# 9 Risk and risk management: introduction to insurance and some fundamentals

**HIGHLIGHTS**

In order to present the principles of risk management and insurance, Chapter 9 analyzes the following:

1   Insurable risk
2   The various risks one faces in everyday life
3   The differences between gambling and insurance
4   Methods of successfully managing risk
5   How insurance companies spread risk over large numbers

*"In this world, nothing is certain but death and taxes."*
Benjamin Franklin, 1789

**INTRODUCTION**

If, as Benjamin Franklin said, only death and taxes are certain in this world, there must be many things that are uncertain—and indeed there are. This brings us to insurance.

The insurance industry deals with uncertainties, and it sells services which help people cope—although not perfectly—with uncertainties. When we think about insurance we also think about risk and risk management, and that is what the next three chapters are about. In this chapter we will set the stage for a discussion of insurance, define some terms that are relevant to insurance so that we all speak the same language, and then introduce some fundamentals of insurance.

*Some terms and definitions*

**1.** *Risk.*

Risk is related to uncertainty. While risk may be defined in other ways in other disciplines, in the insurance industry risk is usually defined as existing because uncertainty exists. For example, it is uncertain whether or not a person will arrive home safely this evening after work; there is the risk that the person won't make it.

The opposite of risk then is certainty, or in laymen's terms, safety; and both risk and certainty are relative terms with only two absolute certainties—death and taxes—as noted above.

Risk may be broken down into *pure* risk and *speculative* risk.

**2.** *Pure* Risk.

In the case of *pure* risk, there are only two possibilities—a loss or no loss. There is no possibility of a gain. An example would be a fire. Either a person's house catches on fire or it does not. There may be a loss, but there is never a gain.

*Speculative* risk consists of a situation in which either a loss or a gain is possible. The best example would be the purchase of securities. Their price may go up or down; there may be losses or gains.

Although speculative risks are not usually insurable, most pure risks are insurable.

**3.** *Hazard.*

A hazard is a condition that may increase either the frequency or the severity of a loss. For example, an old wooden house with a lot of burnable trash in an attached garage where the tenant also stores gasoline in an open container is a hazard. The old wooden house with trash increases the frequency; the gasoline increases the severity if fire occurs.

**4.** *Peril.*

A peril is that which actually causes a loss. In the above example the fire itself is the peril. The flammable trash and gasoline in the garage is the *hazard;* it increases the likelihood of a fire or increases the severity of loss once a fire occurs, but the fire itself is the *peril;* it is the cause of loss.

**5.** *Probability and the Law of Large Numbers.*

Probability has to do with the likelihood of an event occurring. Sometimes this is referred to as chance of loss. Probability also refers to the frequency of loss, but only if large numbers are involved. For example, if a person tosses a coin there is a 50 percent probability (chance) that it will come up heads. But a coin may not come up heads every other time, or five times out of ten or every 50 times out of 100. Only if very large numbers of times are involved will heads approach the probability of coming up 50 percent of the time.

In the insurance industry, the probability of loss can be predicted with substantial accuracy in many cases because of the large numbers involved. The best example exists in the case of life insurance, where mortality tables are used to predict death claims, and hence set insurance premiums, as we shall see in the next chapter.

**6.** Summary of Terms

Table 9–1 summarizes and defines the above mentioned common insurance terms with which the reader should be familiar.

There are some risks we face that, if the event happens, will not result in serious consequences, such as having a flat tire, or oversleeping, or the furnace's pilot light going out. However, there are other risks that can cause serious consequences, and these will be considered.

*Risk, uncertainty, and losses*

These risks include:

- damage to, or loss of, personal property, automobile, and/or home
- loss of family income due to premature death
- loss of family income due to disability
- large medical expenses for catastrophic care
- liability losses
- need for long-term care

The list of risks could continue, but we have covered the main ones.[1] Risk, however, if it is insurable (pure risk) can be insured against. Table 9–2 illustrates the major types of insurable risk, the penalty for not insuring, and the insurance protection available. Figure 9–1 shows the

---

1. For an interesting and an additional point on risk having to do with liquidity timing and marginal utility of loss, see Wayne Snider, "Alternative Methods of Analyzing Risk," *Risk Management,* July 1989, p. 38.

Table 9–1   *Common insurance terms*

| | |
|---|---|
| Risk | Uncertainty of a loss |
|   Pure | Possibility of either a loss or no loss |
|   Speculative | Either a loss or a gain could occur. |
| Hazard | A condition that increases the frequency or severity of losses |
| Peril | The actual cause of loss |
| Probability, and the Law of Large Numbers | How likely it is that the event will happen and how frequently it will occur if large numbers are involved |

Table 9–2   *Major insurance risk and protection available*

| Risk | Penalty if event occurred | Protection |
|---|---|---|
| Premature death | Loss of income | Life insurance |
| Disability | Loss of income; medical bills; home care costs, etc. | Disability insurance Medical expense insurance |
| Illness or accident | Loss of income; medical bills; home care costs, etc. | Disability insurance Medical insurance |
| Destruction of assets (car, home) | Monetary loss; loss of assets | Property insurance |
| Lawsuit (injuring others) | Monetary loss; loss of assets | Liability insurance |
| Outliving income and assets | Loss of income; possible poverty | Life insurance and annuities |
| Unemployment | Loss of income | Unemployment insurance* |

* Obtainable only through governments, generally speaking.

various life insurance types of purchases in the United States in recent years.

*Gambling versus insurance*

To understand the bare fundamentals of insurable risk, it is necessary to distinguish between gambling and insurance. A horse player visits Churchill Downs in Kentucky for the purpose of betting on horses. Although the gambler is becoming involved with the risk of loss, this risk is quite different from the risk borne by the person driving an automobile or the risk assumed by every person that he or she will die tomorrow. The gambler has created his or her own risk; namely that of attempting to pick a winner. Moreover, it is speculative risk (there can be winnings

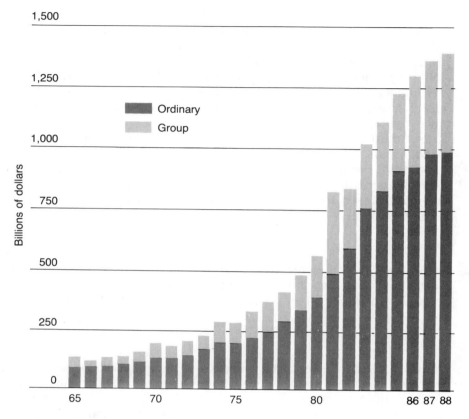

*Life insurance protection in the United States* (Source: *American Council of Life* Figure 9–1
*Insurance, Life Insurance Fact Book, 1989, p. 4)*

as well as losses) and hence it is not insurable. The driver, on the other hand, has not created the hazard being faced, and the risk he or she assumes is pure risk and hence insurable. The driver is faced with a hazard inherent in the nature of things; so is every individual because no one knows when he or she is going to die. One important distinction, then, between gambling and insurance is that gamblers create their own speculative risks, while people generally face pure risks inherent in everyday living.

A second difference between insurance and gambling is that the probability of loss in pure risk is, in many cases, predictable and hence can be transferred to an insurance company. Insurance actuaries can, if there are large numbers of drivers, predict with substantial accuracy how many of them will have accidents. They cannot predict which ones, but they can predict how many. They can also predict how many people will die each year, although they cannot tell which ones. The risk involved in gambling is not only self-created, but the possibility of winning is based on chance.

To be sure, not all insurance risk is precisely predictable. Earthquake insurance is an example. The frequency and severity of earthquakes cannot be predicted as accurately as mortality, and rates for earthquake insurance are based on judgment or what insurance experts call **subjective probability**. Even health rates cannot always be set in accordance with predictable costs. This is because, among other things, rapidly changing medical technology can cause (and has) health insurance premiums to skyrocket.

A third difference between insurance and gambling is that in gambling, losses and winnings "wash out." The winner's gains come at the expense of the loser. Hence they are socially unproductive. In insurance, *both sides of the transactions* will benefit if there are no losses, but if there are losses the insured is returned, at least in part, to his or her former position.

## LEGAL CONCEPTS OF INSURANCE

Insurance companies are regulated by state governments, and all states have laws governing how companies must operate. However, there is enough uniformity to make some general comments about insurance and the law.

### Insurable interest

There is a legal concept which applies to insurance known as **insurable interest**. For there to be an insurable interest, a relationship must exist between the insured and the event insured against so that the happening of the event will cause the injured some loss. A person insured must in some way be actually interested in the subject matter of the insurance at the time of loss. For example, let us consider a young lady who is a professional ice skater. Her professional life depends on the soundness of her limbs (oddly enough, the same is true for a race horse). If she falls and breaks a leg, she will be unable to earn any money for a long time. Therefore, she has an interest in insuring her legs: that is, an insurable interest. For someone *else* to insure the skater's legs would be in the nature of a gambling contract; such an individual ordinarily would not have an insurable interest in her legs. However, an impresario who is managing the ice show and who stands a risk of loss in the event the star's legs are broken also may be said to have an insurable interest. The individual who can suffer no loss has no insurable interest whatever. For there to be insurance, therefore, one must have an interest in the thing or in the event being insured against.

The same is true of life insurance. One cannot, generally speaking, buy a policy on a stranger. (The exception is if one lends him money. Then one has an insurable interest up to the extent of the loan. This is discussed under credit life insurance.) One can, however, buy a policy on a direct member of one's family. Most life insurance is purchased by and on the breadwinner of a family.

The **principle of indemnity** applies primarily to property insurance. The indemnity concept prevents the insured from collecting *more* than the actual loss. If it were not for the principle of indemnity, the insured could profit by buying two (or more) policies from different insurance companies. Therefore, insurance contracts contain a clause regarding other policies. Typically, such clauses provide that all policies covering the same risk will share the loss pro rata. That is, if Jones carries $60,000 of coverage with Company A and $40,000 with Company B, the two companies will share any loss on a 60-percent/40-percent basis.

*Principle of indemnity*

In this way the principle of indemnity reduces what insurance experts call **moral hazard**, which may exist in some cases. Moral hazard refers to the potential dishonesty on the part of the insured creating the increased possibility of loss. For example, if a person could make a profit from an insurance claim, he or she might purposefully burn a house or other building down.

There are two exceptions to the principle of indemnity. First, some companies will pay the entire face value of a policy, if, say, a home is completely destroyed, even though the value of the home may have fallen below the face value of the policy. The same is true of jewelry or paintings or other works of art.

Second, replacement value insurance is becoming increasingly popular. Such policies do not take into account depreciation in the value of an asset. This is particularly true of the clause that provides for hail damage to a roof. A twenty-year-old roof destroyed by hail will be replaced by the insurance company, even though its value is far below its replacement cost.

Under the **principle of subrogation** the insurance company that has indemnified a person's loss is permitted to recover that loss from any liable third party. For example, if A damages B's property, and A is at fault, B's insurance company will pay (indemnify) B and then go after A to recover the amount it paid.

*The principle of subrogation*

The principle of subrogation reinforces the principle of indemnity because it sometimes enables the insured to recover his or her losses fully. For example, the insured bears all costs up to the deductible. However, if the insurance company obtains payment from a guilty third party (A in the paragraph above), the insured could be reimbursed for the entire loss.

The principle of subrogation does not apply in the case where the insured negligently damages his or her own property. In the above case, if A carelessly and negligently drove his or her car into a tree, the insurance company would have to pay. The company could not, then, turn around and sue A to recover, because that would defeat the entire concept of insurance. However, in such a case, the insurance company may refuse to sell insurance to A in the future; or it might raise A's premiums.

Like the principle of indemnity, the principle of subrogation applies only to property insurance and not to life or health insurance.

## RISK MANAGEMENT

As noted above, some risk is insurable; some is not. Speculative risk is, generally, not insurable. Some risk is not worth insuring—for example, the risk of oversleeping. However, you can lower this risk by buying a good alarm clock.

There are five methods of managing insurable risk. They are:

> Avoiding risk
> Lessening risk; Loss control
> Retaining risk
> Self-insurance
> Transferring risk; Buying insurance

We will examine these below.

*Avoiding risk*

Some risk can be completely avoided. For example, a person may avoid the risk of his or her residence burning down by renting. There is still the risk, in this case, of the person's personal property being destroyed, but separate insurance may be purchased to cover that risk. A person may also avoid the risk of his or her car being destroyed in a collision by not owning a car. Indeed, in many cities with a well-developed public transportation system, this may be feasible, or a person might use a taxicab. In a more extreme case a person could avoid ever being involved in any traffic accident by never leaving his or her home. But this is not practical for most of us.

Generally speaking, avoiding risks has only limited possibilities.

*Lessening risk; controlling losses*

Both the frequency and the severity of loss may be lessened to some extent. For example, those individuals who neither drink nor smoke, and who exercise regularly, take vitamin supplements and watch their diet, are lessening the risk of a premature death. Those who don't drive during a blizzard are lessening the likelihood of an accident. In general, being an alert and careful driver and keeping the car in good working order will reduce the risk of an accident. Keeping a portable fire extinguisher may reduce the risk of loss due to fire in the home. Where the house is located and the type of material used in its construction have a bearing on risk. Some insurance companies charge a lower premium if the insured has reduced insurable risk.

By taking certain precautions a person may lessen the frequency of a fire or an accident (in some cases to zero), as well as the severity of any losses that do occur. For example, if a person is driving 75 or 80 miles per hour rather than 60, the likelihood of an accident is increased, and if an accident does occur the damages, both property and bodily, will usually be more severe. Sometimes taking actions such as those described above is referred to as **loss control**.

*Retaining risk*

Most people can and do retain some insurable risk themselves. For example, when an insured has a deductible on an automobile insurance policy, the insured retains some risk. Individuals who have an old car might drop collision insurance completely and assume the entire risk in this area.

It should be noted that risk retention is not quite the same as risk assumption. Risk assumption suggests a person did not have that risk before, and then took it on—dropping collision insurance on an old car, for example. But in most cases a person begins with the risk and then retains it unless he or she shifts it to an insurance company.

For health insurance, the insured virtually always retains a portion of the risk; insurance companies do not pay the entire medical bill.

How much risk to retain when one uses insurance is a question only the individual can decide; but the more risk he or she retains, the lower the premiums charged by insurance companies, other things being equal. Before deciding how much insurable risk to retain, planners can analyze their client's historical record and answer the following questions: In the case of health insurance, what have the medical expenses been in the past? What is the present condition of the client's health? For auto insurance, what kind of driver is he or she? Does he or she drive defensively? How many times has the client been involved in an accident? Has he or she ever killed or injured anyone with a car?

In the case of insurance on the home, is the home near a fire station? Is it an old wooden house or a new brick structure? In the case of life insurance, what would be the financial consequences of a premature death? How many dependents are there? What are their ages? If the spouse is not now working, could she or he become employed if necessary? All of these factors will have a bearing on how much risk to retain. Finally, the client's financial strength will have a bearing on how much risk he or she can retain. How much risk to retain and how much to transfer to an insurance company are discussed in greater detail in the next few chapters, where we will present some guidelines on how to determine the amount of the various kinds of insurance needed.

Risk retention should always be planned. That is, a conscious decision should be made to retain certain risks after an analysis of the facts. Some people retain certain risk by default, not by planning; they simply do not buy insurance which under analysis they should have, simply because of ignorance, carelessness or thoughtlessness.

Risk retention is a proper way of managing some risk, primarily those where the loss, should it occur, is not severe. Retaining some risk (e.g., a deductible on auto collision insurance) will usually save money.

*Self-insurance*

It should be noted that when the client retains some risk himself or herself, this is not self-insurance, although some people call it that. (Risk by the client is really retention, although as noted above that is a perfectly proper course of action at times—for example, when the consequence [loss] of the unfortunate event is small.) Self-insurance technically requires that the person set aside (budget) a sum regularly to establish an insurance fund to pay for damages should an event occur.

Some doctors do this on a group basis for their malpractice insurance, through medical societies or a group of doctors setting up a pool. Some large corporations also self-insure for property and liability coverage.

*Transferring risk: buying insurance*

Individuals may manage risk by transferring it to somebody else, usually an insurance company, which pools the insurable risk of many individuals and manages the aggregate risk.

Insurance is a device by which one party undertakes to assume for another party certain types of risk of loss. This occurs through a contract (called the "policy") and a consideration (called the "premium"). Insurance is social in nature since it represents cooperation for mutual protection. Through the payment of premiums by many insured persons, the risk is spread over large numbers, and the few who suffer losses are reimbursed by the insurance company with the premiums paid by the many who do not suffer losses. The individual absorbs a small but certain loss (the premium), but avoids the burden of a less likely but potentially much larger loss.

## PRINCIPLES OF INSURANCE

There are numerous types of insurance; the main kinds are life insurance, disability, health, and property and liability insurance. Life and disability insurance protect a breadwinner's income stream. Health insurance provides protection from monetary loss due to illness or accident. For most people property and liability can be broken down into insurance on the home and on the car. The property portion is to reimburse the policyholder for the physical destruction of the home or car. The liability aspect is to protect the insured against lawsuits by others in the event of damage to others—either bodily injuries or the destruction of their property.

*How life insurance companies spread risk: mortality tables*

The underlying principle of many types of insurance is the **law of large numbers**.[2] This is especially true of life insurance. In the case of life insurance there are death benefits and living benefits, as will be explained in the next chapter. Insofar as life insurance is concerned, there

---

2. As noted earlier, there are a few exceptions; for example, earthquake insurance.

is no risk of death; it is a certainty—one of only two things in the world that are. Risk comes into the picture because it is not known when death will occur. Table 9–3 and Figure 9–3 show life expectancy at various ages. The risk of a premature death can be transferred to a life insurance company, which will pay an agreed upon sum of money when death does occur.

In the case of life insurance, highly trained and specialized mathematicians called actuaries can, with an amazing degree of accuracy, determine how many young men or women thirty years of age, out of a large number of thirty-year-olds, will die within the coming year. Figure 9–2 shows how the death rate has declined in recent years. Note that emphasis has been placed on large numbers. No actuary or any other mortal can predict when any one individual of thirty years of age is going to die. But an actuary working with large numbers can predict within limitations how many young men or women out of that large number will die within the year. In short, what cannot be predicted for the individual can be predicted in the mass. This can be done because we know a good deal about deaths at every age level from past experience.

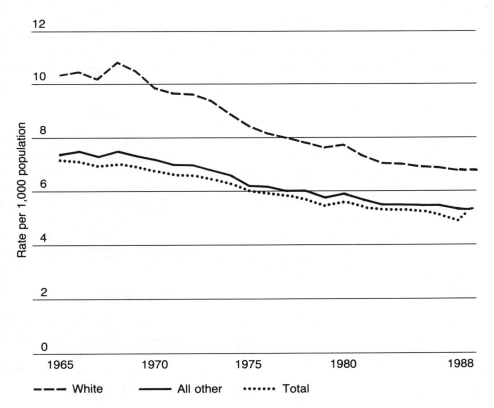

*Age-adjusted death rate in the United States* (Source: *American Council of Life*    Figure 9–2
*Insurance, Life Insurance Fact Book, 1990, p. 11)*

Table 9–3    Life expectancy in years

| Age | 1987 Male | 1987 Female | 1987 Total | 1988 Male | 1988 Female | 1988 Total | 1989 Male | 1989 Female | 1989 Total | 1990 Male | 1990 Female | 1990 Total |
|---|---|---|---|---|---|---|---|---|---|---|---|---|
| 0 | 71.5 | 78.4 | 75.0 | 71.5 | 78.3 | 74.9 | 71.8 | 78.5 | 75.2 | 71.9 | 78.7 | 75.3 |
| 15 | 57.6 | 64.3 | 61.0 | 57.6 | 64.3 | 61.0 | 57.9 | 64.5 | 61.3 | 58.0 | 64.6 | 61.3 |
| 25 | 48.4 | 54.6 | 51.6 | 48.4 | 54.6 | 51.6 | 48.7 | 54.8 | 51.8 | 48.7 | 54.9 | 51.9 |
| 35 | 39.2 | 45.0 | 42.2 | 39.3 | 45.0 | 42.2 | 39.6 | 45.2 | 42.5 | 39.6 | 45.3 | 42.5 |
| 45 | 30.3 | 35.6 | 33.0 | 30.3 | 35.5 | 33.0 | 30.7 | 35.8 | 33.3 | 30.7 | 35.9 | 33.4 |
| 55 | 21.9 | 26.7 | 24.4 | 22.0 | 26.6 | 24.4 | 22.3 | 26.9 | 24.7 | 22.3 | 26.9 | 24.7 |
| 65 | 14.8 | 18.7 | 16.9 | 14.9 | 18.6 | 16.9 | 15.2 | 18.8 | 17.2 | 15.1 | 18.8 | 17.1 |
| 75 | 9.2 | 11.8 | 10.7 | 9.1 | 11.7 | 10.7 | 9.4 | 11.9 | 10.9 | 9.3 | 11.8 | 10.8 |
| 85 | 5.2 | 6.4 | 6.1 | 5.1 | 6.3 | 6.0 | 5.3 | 6.5 | 6.2 | 5.2 | 6.5 | 6.1 |

Note: Some data are revised.

Source: National Center for Health Statistics. U.S. Department of Health and Human Services, and Metropolitan Life Insurance Company.

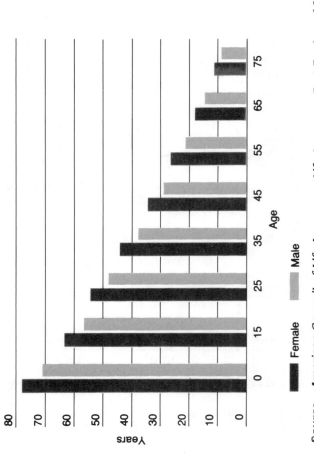

*Expectation of life at various ages in the United States, 1989*

Source: *American Council of Life Insurance, Life Insurance Fact Book. p. 108.*

Figure 9–3

Using past experience, insurance companies construct and use mortality tables to predict the loss over large numbers. In this way they are able to assess appropriate premium amounts to absorb risk. Taking our thirty-year-old men again as an example, the actuaries who have for a great many years compiled life insurance statistics will predict that out of 100,000 thirty-year-old men in good health alive at the beginning of the year, 173 will die during the forthcoming year. For women the figure is 135. Life expectancy is calculated in a similar way. Table 9–4 shows a mortality table and illustrates deaths per 100,000; as previously mentioned, Table 9–3 shows life expectancy in years.

In the simplest case (without attempting to figure in anything for the company's operating cost, profit, and the like), the premium for a thirty-year-old woman under these circumstances would be $1.35 for every $1,000 of life insurance. The way this is calculated is simply that if 100,000 thirty-year-old women buy $1,000 of life insurance policies, they would pay in a total of $135,000. In this case, then, the amount going into the company would be equal to the amount paid out to the beneficiaries of the 135 who died; and, at the end of the year, the company would have a total of zero remaining.

In real life things are not so simple. Just as in any other business, there must be additional sums included in the premium. In this case, the premiums include an amount to cover profits and operating costs.

The 100,000 thirty-year-olds referred to above must be in good physical condition. Statistics upon which the actuaries determine the probability of the number of deaths in any age group are based on the assumption that those persons insured are in good physical condition and good mental health to begin with. If it were not for the requirement of good physical and mental health, obviously anyone with a disease would immediately rush out and buy insurance, in which case the predictions of the actuaries would fall short of their mark and the companies would rapidly go out of business or premiums for all insured people would have to be raised to the point where insurance would be unaffordable.

*How insurance companies spread medical expenses*

Medical expenses cannot be predicted as accurately as death claims. Using large numbers of individuals, insurance actuaries are able to calculate the number of appendectomies or heart attacks per 100,000 individuals. However, in the case of health insurance costs, there is an additional variable. It is the cost of treatment; it is rising constantly because of inflation and technological change. Technological change increases the quality and the cost of many types of medical care. Inflation also, of course, increases the cost of medical care. Consequently, health insurance premiums rise almost yearly. Nevertheless, health insurance companies spread health care costs over large numbers of individuals and the premiums paid by all policyholders are used to pay the claims of those individuals who do have medical bills.

Table 9–4   Mortality tables

| | Commissioners 1980 standard ordinary (1970–1975) | | | | | Commissioners 1980 standard ordinary (1970–1975) | | | |
| | Male | | Female | | | Male | | Female | |
| Age | Deaths per 1,000 | Expectation of life (years) | Deaths per 1,000 | Expectation of life (years) | Age | Deaths per 1,000 | Expectation of life (years) | Deaths per 1,000 | Expectation of life (years) |
|---|---|---|---|---|---|---|---|---|---|
| 0 | 4.18 | 70.83 | 2.89 | 75.83 | 56 | 11.46 | 20.51 | 7.57 | 24.49 |
| 1 | 1.07 | 70.13 | .87 | 75.04 | 57 | 12.49 | 19.74 | 8.03 | 23.67 |
| 2 | .99 | 69.20 | .81 | 74.11 | 58 | 13.59 | 18.99 | 8.47 | 22.86 |
| 3 | .98 | 68.27 | .79 | 73.17 | 59 | 14.77 | 18.24 | 8.94 | 22.05 |
| 4 | .95 | 67.34 | .77 | 72.23 | 60 | 16.08 | 17.51 | 9.47 | 21.25 |
| 5 | .90 | 66.40 | .76 | 71.28 | 61 | 17.54 | 16.79 | 10.13 | 20.44 |
| 6 | .86 | 65.46 | .73 | 70.34 | 62 | 19.19 | 16.08 | 10.96 | 19.65 |
| 7 | .80 | 64.52 | .72 | 69.39 | 63 | 21.06 | 15.38 | 12.02 | 18.86 |
| 8 | .76 | 63.57 | .70 | 68.44 | 64 | 23.14 | 14.70 | 13.25 | 18.08 |
| 9 | .74 | 62.62 | .69 | 67.48 | 65 | 25.42 | 14.04 | 14.59 | 17.32 |
| 10 | .73 | 61.66 | .68 | 66.53 | 66 | 27.85 | 13.39 | 16.00 | 16.57 |
| 11 | .77 | 60.71 | .69 | 65.58 | 67 | 30.44 | 12.76 | 17.43 | 15.83 |
| 12 | .85 | 59.75 | .72 | 64.62 | 68 | 33.19 | 12.14 | 18.84 | 15.10 |
| 13 | .99 | 58.80 | .75 | 63.67 | 69 | 36.17 | 11.54 | 20.36 | 14.38 |
| 14 | 1.15 | 57.86 | .80 | 62.71 | 70 | 39.51 | 10.96 | 22.11 | 13.67 |
| 15 | 1.33 | 56.93 | .85 | 61.76 | 71 | 43.30 | 10.39 | 24.23 | 12.97 |
| 16 | 1.51 | 56.00 | .90 | 60.82 | 72 | 47.65 | 9.84 | 26.87 | 12.28 |
| 17 | 1.67 | 55.09 | .95 | 59.87 | 73 | 52.64 | 9.30 | 30.11 | 11.60 |
| 18 | 1.78 | 54.18 | .98 | 58.93 | 74 | 58.19 | 8.79 | 33.93 | 10.95 |
| 19 | 1.86 | 53.27 | 1.02 | 57.98 | 75 | 64.19 | 8.31 | 38.24 | 10.32 |
| 20 | 1.90 | 52.37 | 1.05 | 57.04 | 76 | 70.53 | 7.84 | 42.97 | 9.71 |
| 21 | 1.91 | 51.47 | 1.07 | 56.10 | 77 | 77.12 | 7.40 | 48.04 | 9.12 |
| 22 | 1.89 | 50.57 | 1.09 | 55.16 | 78 | 83.90 | 6.97 | 53.45 | 8.55 |
| 23 | 1.86 | 49.66 | 1.11 | 54.22 | 79 | 91.05 | 6.57 | 59.35 | 8.01 |
| 24 | 1.82 | 48.75 | 1.14 | 53.28 | 80 | 98.84 | 6.18 | 65.99 | 7.48 |
| 25 | 1.77 | 47.84 | 1.16 | 52.34 | 81 | 107.48 | 5.80 | 73.60 | 6.98 |
| 26 | 1.73 | 46.93 | 1.19 | 51.40 | 82 | 117.25 | 5.44 | 82.40 | 6.49 |
| 27 | 1.71 | 46.01 | 1.22 | 50.46 | 83 | 128.26 | 5.09 | 92.53 | 6.03 |
| 28 | 1.70 | 45.09 | 1.26 | 49.52 | 84 | 140.25 | 4.77 | 103.81 | 5.59 |
| 29 | 1.71 | 44.16 | 1.30 | 48.59 | 85 | 152.95 | 4.46 | 116.10 | 5.18 |
| 30 | 1.73 | 43.24 | 1.35 | 47.65 | 86 | 166.09 | 4.18 | 129.29 | 4.80 |
| 31 | 1.78 | 42.31 | 1.40 | 46.71 | 87 | 179.55 | 3.91 | 143.32 | 4.43 |
| 32 | 1.83 | 41.38 | 1.45 | 45.78 | 88 | 193.27 | 3.66 | 158.18 | 4.09 |
| 33 | 1.91 | 40.46 | 1.50 | 44.84 | 89 | 207.29 | 3.41 | 173.94 | 3.77 |
| 34 | 2.00 | 39.54 | 1.58 | 43.91 | 90 | 221.77 | 3.18 | 190.75 | 3.45 |
| 35 | 2.11 | 38.61 | 1.65 | 42.98 | 91 | 236.98 | 2.94 | 208.87 | 3.15 |
| 36 | 2.24 | 37.69 | 1.76 | 42.05 | 92 | 253.45 | 2.70 | 228.81 | 2.85 |
| 37 | 2.40 | 36.78 | 1.89 | 41.12 | 93 | 272.11 | 2.44 | 251.51 | 2.55 |
| 38 | 2.58 | 35.87 | 2.04 | 40.20 | 94 | 295.90 | 2.17 | 279.31 | 2.24 |
| 39 | 2.79 | 34.96 | 2.22 | 39.28 | 95 | 329.96 | 1.87 | 317.32 | 1.91 |
| 40 | 3.02 | 34.05 | 2.42 | 38.36 | 96 | 384.55 | 1.54 | 375.74 | 1.56 |
| 41 | 3.29 | 33.16 | 2.64 | 37.46 | 97 | 480.20 | 1.20 | 474.97 | 1.21 |
| 42 | 3.56 | 32.26 | 2.87 | 36.55 | 98 | 657.98 | .84 | 655.85 | .84 |
| 43 | 3.87 | 31.38 | 3.09 | 35.66 | 99 | 1,000.00 | .50 | 1,000.00 | .50 |
| 44 | 4.19 | 30.50 | 3.32 | 34.77 | 100 | | | | |
| 45 | 4.55 | 29.62 | 3.56 | 33.88 | 101 | | | | |
| 46 | 4.92 | 28.76 | 3.80 | 33.00 | 102 | | | | |
| 47 | 5.32 | 27.90 | 4.05 | 32.12 | 103 | | | | |
| 48 | 5.74 | 27.04 | 4.33 | 31.25 | 104 | | | | |
| 49 | 6.21 | 26.20 | 4.63 | 30.39 | 105 | | | | |
| 50 | 6.71 | 25.36 | 4.96 | 29.53 | 106 | | | | |
| 51 | 7.30 | 24.52 | 5.31 | 28.67 | 107 | | | | |
| 52 | 7.96 | 23.70 | 5.70 | 27.82 | 108 | | | | |
| 53 | 8.71 | 22.89 | 6.15 | 26.98 | 109 | | | | |
| 54 | 9.56 | 22.08 | 6.61 | 26.14 | 110 | | | | |
| 55 | 10.47 | 21.29 | 7.09 | 25.31 | | | | | |

Source: 1990 Life Insurance Fact Book, *American Council of Life Insurance, p. 112.*

These mortality rates are from insurance commissions which are the regulatory agencies. Many insurance companies use their own tables which are more favorable to the insured. This table then is only for illustrative purposes, and does not reflect actual mortality experience.

Like health insurance, property and liability insurance are financed over a much shorter time than is life insurance. Insurance on a house, for example, is sold for a one- or two-year period and then renewed. For an automobile, the insured period is six months or one year. The reason is that there are more variables. Inflation will cause the cost of losses to go up annually. Even without inflation, the cost of auto and home repairs could rise. Jury awards and how these awards may have risen in the recent past will also affect rates. Like other insurance companies, property and liability insurance companies make an allowance for their expenses and the interest they can earn on premium dollars when setting rates. Just as in the case of other insurance, when one transfers the risk on a car or home to an insurance company, it is spread over large numbers of people, and the premiums of all policyholders pay for the damages of the smaller number who suffer losses. The insurance companies base rates on a probability distribution for each of the various losses. Sometimes, auto insurance companies will raise rates for those drivers who have had two or more moving violation traffic tickets, on the theory that they are higher-risk drivers.

*How property and liability companies spread risk*

## SUGGESTED READINGS

Athern, James L. *Risk and Insurance,* St. Paul, Minn.: West Publishing Co. 1984.

*Best's Review, Life-Health Edition.* Oldwick, N.J.: A.M. Best Company, Inc. Monthly publication.

*Best's Review Property/Casualty Edition.* Oldwick, N.J.: A.M. Best Company, Inc. Monthly publication.

Bickelhaupt, David L. *General Insurance,* 10th ed. Homewood, Ill.: R. Irwin, 1983.

Black, Kenneth, and Skipper, Harold. *Life Insurance,* 11th ed. Englewood Cliffs, N.J.: Prentice Hall, 1987.

Cookerell, Hugh. *Lloyd's of London.* Homewood, Ill.: Dow Jones-Irwin, 1984.

Crane, Frederick G. *Insurance Principles and Practices.* New York: John Wiley and Sons, 1984.

Dorfman, Mark S. *Introduction to Insurance,* 3rd ed. Englewood Cliffs, N.J.: Prentice Hall, 1987.

Greene, Mark R., and Trieschmann, James. "Risk and Insurance." Cincinnati: South-Western, 1984.

Harris, Louis. "Risk in a Complex Society." *The Journal of Insurance,* July-August, 1980.

*Insurance Review,* New York: The Insurance Information Institute. Monthly publication.

"Journal of Insurance." New York: The Insurance Information Institute. Bimonthly publication.

*Life Insurance Fact Book.* New York: The Institute of Life Insurance. Annual publication.

Mehr, Robert I., and Cammack, Emerson. *Principles of Insurance.* Homewood, Ill.: R. Irwin, 1985.

Mehr, Robert, and Gustavson, Sandra. *Life Insurance: Theory and Practice.* Plano, Tex.: Business Publications, Inc., 1987.

*National Underwriter.* Chicago, Ill.: The National Underwriter Co. Weekly publication.

"On the Way Up; A Description of Life Insurance and Annuities." Hartford, Conn.: Aetna Life Insurance Co.

"Property/Casualty Fact Book." New York: Insurance Information Institute. Annual publication.

These tables are for the purpose of establishing liabilities, and are conservative, in some cases much higher than experience indicates. Similarly, annuity tables show lower mortality than experience indicates.

Rejda, George E. *Principles of Insurance.* Glenview, Ill.: Scott, Foresman, 1986.

Vaughan, Emmet J. *Fundamentals of Risk and Insurance,* 4th ed. New York: John Wiley and Sons, 1986.

Williams, C. Arthur, Jr., Head, George L., and Glendenning, William. *Principles of Risk Management and Insurance.* Malvern, Pa.: American Institute for Property and Liability Underwriters, 1981.

Williams, C. Arthur, Jr., and Heims, Richard M. *Risk Management and Insurance,* 4th ed. New York: McGraw-Hill, 1985.

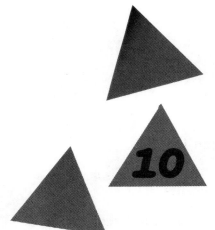

# 10 Life insurance

Reinstatement
Incontestability
Nonforfeiture value
Borrowing on a life insurance policy
Assignment
Ownership of the policy
Change of beneficiary: third party
    rights

Settlement options
Disability premium waiver
Accidental death benefits
Stock insurance companies versus
    mutual companies
Insurance dividends
Taxes and life insurance benefits
SUGGESTED READINGS

**HIGHLIGHTS**  In order to thoroughly understand insurance needs and how to satisfy
them, a financial planner should be familiar with the following:

1   Why and when to buy life insurance
2   Some guidelines to help your client decide what kind and how much
    life insurance to buy
3   The various types of ordinary life insurance
4   How some life insurance builds up a cash value
5   Group life insurance as an alternative to an individual policy
6   Some things that will help you choose a life insurance company
7   Some other things that everyone should know about life insurance

## WHY AND WHEN TO BUY LIFE INSURANCE

There are only two reasons for most people to buy life insurance: for protection and for savings. In most cases protection is primary. We discussed risk management, which is what we have in mind when we talk about protection, in Chapter 9.

### Why buy life insurance at all?

While an individual may buy life insurance with a savings feature built in, insurance is usually a poor savings vehicle. Its return is modest and will be eroded by inflation. Only if one is not disciplined and finds it impossible to save in any other way should he or she consider entering into a contract with a life insurance company in which he or she is forced to save. Some investment advisors suggest that if a client is in a high tax bracket, insurance as a savings—and investment—scheme may be advantageous because of favorable tax treatment. (See "Taxes and Life Insurance Benefits" later in this chapter for a discussion of how insurance is taxed). That may be partially true, but in many cases one may be better off buying insurance for protection alone and then investing the difference in premiums; insurance that provides only protection is cheaper than insurance that includes a savings feature.

Insurance provides protection in the event of premature death: death that occurs before the person has reached his or her full life expectancy. Insurance protects the dependents of the insured against financial hardship in the event of death of the breadwinner. The income stream is being protected. Insurance dollars are being substituted for earned dollars. That gives us a clue as to how much insurance is needed. Figure 10–1 shows the amount of life insurance purchased, in force, and life insurance benefits paid over the last few years.

### When to buy life insurance

The best time to buy life insurance is the day before death occurs, if one knows when that will be and if he or she can still buy it at that time. The person who is in ill health at an advanced age is probably uninsurable.

When should a person buy a refrigerator? Should one be bought for children when they are, say, ten years old, on the theory that the price will be lower when they are ten than when they are twenty years of age?

That's the logic some insurance salesmen will use; premiums are cheaper at age ten than age twenty. Yes, but not that much cheaper. Besides, one does not buy something that is not needed just because it's cheaper. The only valid argument for buying insurance for children is that they may become uninsurable in young adulthood. Consequently, life insurance should be purchased when it is needed and can be afforded—just like a refrigerator—that is, when the individual becomes a young adult and takes on family responsibilities.

Probably your client won't be able to buy all the insurance he or she will need or want at one time; hence, he or she should consider buying several blocks over a few years as income rises. Review the insurance program periodically because needs will change as an individual grows

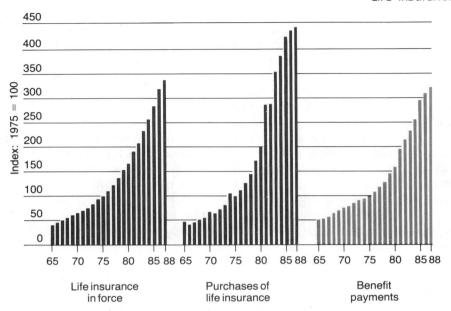

*Relative growth of life insurance in force, purchase of life insurance, and benefit payments in the United States, 1965-1985.* (Source: *American Council of Life Insurance, Life Insurance Fact Book, 1987, p. 6; 1989, p. 4*)

Figure 10–1

older. Sometimes a client will need more, and at other times the planner may recommend letting some term insurance expire, or surrendering permanent insurance for cash.

There are several ways to decide how much life insurance to buy. Some examples are the multiple income concept, the needs concept, and the human life value concept—also called the present value of the total future income stream concept.

The multiple income approach is the simplest technique for calculating the amount of insurance that should be purchased. First, take the after-tax salary and adjust it down somewhat. After-tax salary is adjusted down to take into account two factors: (1) the income earner is also an income consumer and hence less income is required for a smaller family; and (2) the higher the income the greater the downward adjustment, because a lower percentage of it is required to enable the survivors to live well. Generally the after-tax earnings are adjusted down to 75, 65, or even 60 percent. On the other hand, as income rises, the client can afford more insurance; this may tend to lessen the downward adjustment. The percentage then selected is, in reality, at least in part determined by priorities and value judgments.

Some multiple is then applied—the most common ones being 4, 5, 6, and even 10. The multiple selected is determined by age, the age and number of dependents, assets, liabilities, income from property, and

**HELPING YOUR CLIENT DECIDE HOW MUCH LIFE INSURANCE TO BUY**

priorities and value judgments. Obviously the larger the number of dependents and the younger their ages, the larger the multiplier. The age of the spouse is also taken into consideration. If the spouse is relatively young, the multiple will rise as he or she grows older, on the theory that finding employment would become far more difficult at an older age. After about age forty-five or fifty, however, the multiple declines because fewer years of dependence remain.

The larger the Social Security benefits, the lower the multiple. If the client has other employer-provided pension benefits and high investment income, the multiple is reduced. Investment income will not decline with the insured's death. An assumption is also made regarding the income that could be earned on the insurance benefits in selecting the multiple.

While this is an arbitrary way of determining insurance needs, it can be considered a rule of thumb based on experience.

*Family needs concept*

Under the family needs approach, the first step is to estimate the total family needs. Next, ascertain the resources already available to meet those needs. Such things include savings accounts, securities, any other income-earning assets, Social Security, and other insurance already owned such as group insurance with an employer. The third step is to subtract the resources already available from the needs calculated in step one. The remainder shows the insurance needs.

Under the first step list all possible family needs.

1. Funeral and other final expenses

In addition to funeral expenses, there may be final medical and hospital bills to pay. There may also be administrative expenses and attorney's fees associated with probating a will and settling an estate. These expenses will probably be a minimum of $5,000 and may be much larger, especially if the estate is fairly large.

2. Paying off the mortgage and other debts

If there is a mortgage on the house, the client may wish to pay it off as well as liquidate any other installment debt outstanding. Special mortgage and credit life insurance is available for this, or it may be included in a regular insurance policy. There is no way of estimating the dollar amount of this item; it will vary greatly from person to person. An alternative way of handling the home mortgage is not to pay it off but to include the mortgage payments in regular family living expense needs. (See below).

3. Emergency fund

The client will no doubt want an emergency fund. He or she should already have this in a savings account, but in any event it is part of an individual's needs. Many experts suggest this fund should be at least 3 to 6 times the monthly take-home pay.

4. College fund

If there are college-bound children, college expenses become part of the insurance needs. An individual need not necessarily provide for full four-year college expenses because students can earn income to help defray the cost. On the other hand, it is difficult to calculate future college costs because of rapid inflation. College costs vary greatly even among state schools, but total costs (tuition, room and board, etc.) can easily reach $12,000 per year. At private schools this figure can go as high as, or higher than, $25,000 per year!

Annual family living needs consist of the day-to-day living expenses and are related to the personal or family budget discussed in Chapter 2. The amount will vary depending on the size of the family, its age makeup, and accustomed standard of living, or the level of livelihood that the insured would like to provide. Remember, however, that this item will continue for a number of years. Moreover, this need will change (hopefully decline) as the children grow up and are on their own; this will be partly (or perhaps entirely) offset by inflation.

**5. Annual family living needs**

The amount of insurance needed for family living would also need to be adjusted (presumably downward) to take into account other earning assets, Social Security benefits, and any private corporate pension payments to be received. Social Security benefits for children continue until the children reach age eighteen. The Social Security benefits paid to a surviving spouse do not begin until she or he reaches age sixty. (The time between when the benefits for the children end and when they begin again for the surviving spouse is known as "the blackout years.")

Part of the insurance proceeds would be invested to provide income to meet living (and retirement) needs. However, arrangements must be made to take into account future inflation. Consequently, an assumption must be made regarding future inflation as well as what the capital provided by insurance will earn. It is reasonable to assume that the investment return could exceed inflation by 2, 3, or even 4 percent in the long run. This would result in the amount available for living needs rising a bit more than inflation as the years pass by. During periods of inflation, interest rates, generally speaking, also rise; hence the amount available to meet living needs rises.

**6. Capital needed to provide annual desired living needs in real terms**

The amount of insurance to meet family needs could be designed so that only the interest income is utilized; hence the capital remains intact. It will pass to the heirs eventually. The amount of insurance could also be designed so that the capital would be depleted.

Adding up the six above-mentioned points will give you the answer to the total capital needed to provide for them. Table 10-1 summarizes this. As Table 10–1 shows, the total capital needs required for its hypothetical case are $447,000. It assumes capital remains intact.

**7. Total capital needs**

However, the table also shows group insurance with the employer of $100,000 and $34,500 of other earning assets. Subtracting these from the $447,000 of capital needs shows the additional insurance needed, which is $312,500.

Table 10–1    *Insurance needs for Kimberly and Bob Jacobs*

| | | |
|---|---:|---:|
| Present income | | $ 42,000 |
| Family needs: | | |
| 1. Final expenses | | $ 10,000 |
| 2. Payment of debt | | |
| a. mortgage | $ 50,000 | |
| b. other | 5,000 | 55,000 |
| 3. Emergency fund (twice monthly income) | | $ 7,000 |
| 4. College fund | | 50,000 |
| 5. Annual living needs | | |
| a. 55% of $42,000 | $ 23,100 | |
| b. less: Social Security | – 10,100 | |
| c. net annual living needs | =13,000 | |
| 6. Capital needed to provide $13,000 annually in real terms ($325,000 at 4%) | | 325,000 |
| 7. Total capital needed | | $447,000 |
| Other resources available at 4% | | |
| 1. Savings accounts | $ 12,500 | |
| 2. Securities | 22,000 | |
| 3. Life insurance with employer (group ins.) | 100,000 | $134,500 |
| Insurance needs | | $312,500 |

In the event of death, $50,000 of the insurance proceeds would be set aside to earn interest and to be used for future college expenses. The $7,000 emergency fund would also remain intact to earn interest, and $65,000 would be used to liquidate debt and final expenses. The remainder ($190,500)—together with the group insurance of $100,000 and Bob and Kimberly's other earning assets at 4 percent, would provide the $13,000 of annual living needs. We are assuming that the $325,000 will earn 4 percent in real (after adjusted for inflation) terms. This will provide a slightly rising standard of living as the years pass.

Not all of the client's own personal entries will necessarily have a dollar figure. The individual may or may not have debts to pay off; he or she may or may not already have an emergency fund; and a college fund may or may not be needed. Remember also, however, that the item $13,000 for net family living, retirement living, or both, over and above Social Security, is an annual and recurring expense.

If the capital provided by insurance is invested and earns a return equal to or in excess of inflation, there is no problem. If the reverse is the case, the family living standard may decline as the years pass, unless they dip into the capital. While the needs concept may suggest more insurance than the client can afford, nevertheless, it is a beginning.

The human life value approach takes into account a person's entire future earnings. It is these lifetime earnings that need protecting because that is what would be cut off in the event of death. This requires an estimate of the future lifetime income, which cannot be made precisely but can be made accurately enough.

*Human life value: the future income stream*

Let us assume a thirty-five-year-old individual is making $20,000 per year after taxes. Insurance benefit payments are not subject to income tax; hence they are netted out. If the person continues at this income level until age sixty-five, he or she will earn $600,000 after taxes until retirement. However, the income will almost certainly rise above $20,000 per year, for two reasons. First, most people will probably keep up with inflation in the long run. In addition, historically salaries have on the average grown at about 2 to 3 percent in excess of inflation. Assuming inflation in the long run continues at its historical 4 to 5 percent level, it is reasonable to select 7 percent as the growth rate in the case of the $20,000 per-year income above. Compounding the $20,000 by 7 percent over the thirty-year period gives us a lifetime income stream of about $1,889,220. However, future dollars must be discounted because they are worth less than present dollars.

A present dollar will be worth more in the future because it will grow with interest ($1.00 will be worth $1.07 in a year if the interest rate is 7 percent). Using the same logic, a dollar to be received in the future is worth less than a dollar today, but it is worth something. Its value is again related to the interest rate, and at 7 percent, a dollar to be received in one year is worth about $.93 today. That is, the present value of future dollars takes interest away. Discounting $1,889,220 over thirty years at 7 percent (current interest rate) gives us $248,181. That figure is the human life value of the individual described above, making $20,000 after taxes and growing at 7 percent—it is the value of his or her lifetime income stream if received today.

That, in theory, is the upper-limit amount of insurance the individual in question should have to protect the income stream fully. Moreover, with each passing year, insurance needs decline because there is less and less future income to earn. When the person is sixty-four years old, the insurance needed to protect future income is exactly the same as the final year's earnings.

The human life approach has some shortcomings. It does not consider the other financial assets (savings accounts, securities, Social Security, and the like) that are available in the event of the breadwinner's death. The needs approach is probably the best method of determining insurance requirements.

The methods we have discussed for determining insurance needs are only benchmarks. One still has to make a decision based on what the client can afford as well as the client's value judgments and priorities.

*The final decision*

*Reevaluating insurance needs*

Insurance needs should be reevaluated at least every 5 years, if not more often. This is true regardless of which method is chosen to determine how much insurance to buy. Needs will change over the years. Single individuals need less insurance; hence, insurance needs will increase with marriage. When a child is born, insurance needs will again increase. When the children grow up and go out on their own, insurance needs may decline. In addition, as a person grows older, he or she will acquire more income-earning assets (securities and savings accounts) and will need less insurance. The heavy insurance needs are generally during the ages twenty-five to forty-five or fifty. After that the children are likely to be independent and the earning assets larger. At retirement age (or near it), insurance needs may decline further. Insurance may be needed for estate planning purposes, in some cases, however.

*Insurance for children*

Insurance for children should be a low-priority item. Children are not breadwinners as a general rule. Some people buy insurance on their children, which builds up a cash value to give them a nest egg to start out when they reach young adulthood. If the budget can afford this, such a plan is fine. But saving via insurance should be compared with the yield on alternative investment outlets. In most cases, you could find an alternative that would yield more.

*Insurance on a nonincome-earning spouse*

Although a spouse may not contribute money income to the family, the time and skills he or she provides for the family are valuable and would be costly to replace in case of death or disability.

For example, while the death of one parent may not decrease family dollar income, it may necessitate an increase in family expenditures if the household is to be properly operated and the children are to receive adequate care. To be sure, if a nonworking spouse died, there would be one less consumer in the family, and expenses would decline. The client, with your help, must decide what the net effect would be in his or her individual case.

If there are two breadwinners in the family, there may be a reason for life insurance on both. Since there is a second income to protect, the analysis above regarding how much a person is worth applies to both husband and wife. In addition, with two incomes a more generous calculation of family needs would be possible.

## TYPES OF ORDINARY LIFE INSURANCE

Most people who buy individual life insurance policies buy what is referred to as "ordinary life," and buy it from legal reserve life insurance companies. The terminology covering ordinary life is a bit confusing because not all companies use the same designations. There are only a handful of kinds of ordinary policies: *term*, *whole life*, *endowment*, combinations that include two or more of the above, and the recently developed **universal** and **variable life policies**. In addition there are two types of whole life policies, the **straight life** and the **limited pay life** policies, and they are not the same. The following classification illustrates the various ordinary policies.

Ordinary life insurance
    Term
    Whole life
        Straight life
        Limited pay life
    Endowment
    Combinations of two or more of the above
    Universal life
    Variable life

Table 10–2 shows ordinary life insurance in force in the United States by type and average size. Figure 10–2 shows the average size insurance purchased. Term life insurance is the simplest type of ordinary life insurance, and is also the cheapest; it provides the most insurance coverage per dollar of premium. Term insurance is a contract that provides protection for a specific period of time, and, when that time has expired, the policy lapses. It has no savings feature built into it, hence no living benefits, only death benefits. Consequently, most of the premiums paid into the company are also paid out in the form of death benefits. For this reason, it is cheaper than all other insurance—which is also sometimes called "permanent" insurance as opposed to term. Many term policies are **renewable.** When the term for which it is written has

*Key life insurance statistics*                                                                     Table 10–2

| | 1985 | 1986 | 1988 | Percent change 1987–86 | Percent change 1988–87 |
|---|---|---|---|---|---|
| *Life insurance in force in the United States (000,000 omitted)* | | | | | |
| Ordinary | $3,247,289 | $3,658,203 | $4,511,608 | 13.1 | 9.0 |
| Group | 2,561,595 | 2,801,049 | 3,232,080 | 8.7 | 6.2 |
| Industrial | 28,250 | 27,168 | 25,456 | – 1.8 | – 4.5 |
| Credit | 215,973 | 233,859 | 251,015 | 3.9 | 3.3 |
|   Total | $6,053,107 | $6,720,279 | $8,020,159 | 10.9 | 7.6 |
| | | | | | |
| *Average amounts of life insurance in force in the United States* | | | | | |
| Per Household | $ 63,400 | $ 69,100 | $ 87,600 | 8.9 | 5.8 |
| Per Insured Household | $ 74,600 | $ 81,200 | $ 108,200 | 9.0 | 5.9 |

*Source:* American Council of Life Insurance, 1989, page 4.

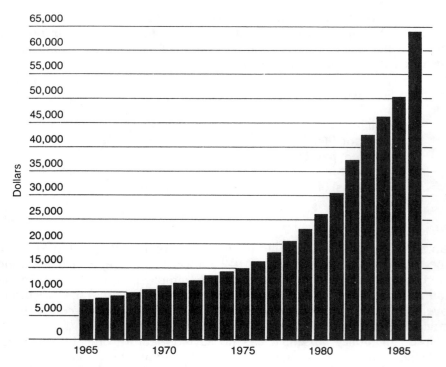

Figure 10–2    *Average size ordinary life insurance in policy purchases in the United States (Source: American Council of Life Insurance, Life Insurance Fact Book, 1989, p. 4)*

expired, it may be renewed at the option of the insured without the need for a medical examination.

A term policy may also be **convertible.** It can be converted to a permanent policy without a medical examination. There are several types of term policies, but they are basically the same in that they are financed over a specific but variable number of years.

**One-year renewable term**

A one-year renewable term policy expires after one year; it is the cheapest type to buy. At the end of the year it may be renewed for another year, and so on. Each time it is renewed, however, the insured is one year older, and a higher premium will usually need to be paid. Refer to the mortality table in the previous chapter. You will see that for a person of age twenty, deaths per 1,000 are 1.90 for males and 1.05 for females.

This indicates that for every $1,000 worth of life insurance the pure premium for a twenty-year-old female would be $1.05. If 1,000 twenty-year-olds paid that, it would raise just enough ($1,050) to pay the claims for those who died. To be sure, the premium would be more because the insurance companies add something for expenses and may even subtract a bit to take into account the interest they could earn before they had to pay it out in death claims. The mortality table referred to is a standard one, but not all companies use it. Each has developed its own, and it may be more favorable (lower premiums) because the company has had a more favorable mortality experience. Thus, individuals should shop around when buying life insurance.

The next year, the person is twenty-one years of age, and premiums would rise to $1.07 per $1,000 of insurance, and so on year after year with premiums rising. At age 40 they would still only be $2.42. Eventually premiums would get so high that they would be prohibitive. By then, however, one probably would no longer need insurance and would drop the policy. Individuals should consider dropping a policy any time they no longer need it even if the premiums are not prohibitive (e.g., if the children are grown and on their own).

*Level premium term*

Level premium term may run for five years, ten years, or even twenty years or more. Premiums are merely averaged. If a twenty year-old brought five-year level premium term, the deaths per thousand shown in the mortality table would be averaged for all ages 20 through 24. The premium ($1.87, adjusted for expenses and interest), which would be in excess of that needed in the early years, would build up a reserve to be used in later years when premiums would be deficient. Premiums can also be averaged over ten or twenty or any number of years—even over a lifetime. Figure 10–3 illustrates how a level premium policy works and how reserves are built up.

Until recently, ten- and twenty-year term policies were popular, but recently more people have switched to one-year renewable term. When a person buys level premium insurance he or she is paying some premiums in advance. Individuals can do their own budgeting and, in theory, bank the difference in premiums in the early years and develop their own reserve and earn interest, although the dollars saved in the early years by doing this may be small.

*Decreasing term insurance*

It is also possible to buy a term policy, the face value of which declines as the years or even the months pass. These are sometimes used to pay off a mortgage if the insured dies. Suppose one has a $50,000 mortgage on a home and desires to protect the family or to keep them from the necessity of paying that mortgage in the event of one's death. Under some circumstances it might be desirable for the individual to turn to the decreasing term policy for this purpose. In the amortizing type of mortgage, where part of the principal and interest is paid each month, the amount paid on the principal increases with each monthly payment. Hypothetically, let us assume that when individuals take out a $50,000 mortgage, they make a payment of $550 a month. Assume further that out of the $550 monthly payment, in the first month, $500 is paid in interest and $50 to reduce the principal. This leaves a balance due of

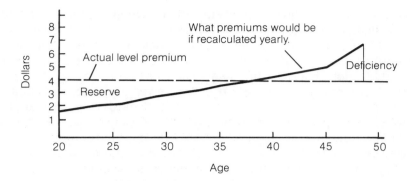

Figure 10–3    *Sample of a level premium policy, and what the premiums would be if they were recalculated on an annual basis.*

$49,950. It is obvious that for purposes of protection, by the end of the first month a $50,000 policy is no longer necessary. The mortgage could be paid off at the end of that first month if the individual or the estate had $49,950. The decreasing term policy can take care of this.

For this purpose, the companies will typically write or issue a level premium policy on a decreasing term contract for as long as the mortgage runs, and the policy will decline with the mortgage. Any payoff turned over to the beneficiary will be sufficient to pay off the mortgage. In short, the contract states in effect that as each month passes, the amount the company will pay on the policy decreases. If the insured dies when only $1,000 is due on the mortgage, this balance will be paid off; or if the insured dies at the end of the first month with a balance due of $49,950, this amount will be paid to the beneficiary. The net result is to cause the average monthly premiums to be considerably lower than they would be if a policy with a fixed amount due is purchased because, as each month passes, the amount the beneficiary will receive is reduced roughly in the same amount that the balance due on the mortgage is reduced.

**Cash value life insurance: permanent insurance**

Cash value life insurance (also called permanent insurance) has living benefits or a ***cash value***. Consequently, if a person buys permanent insurance, he or she is developing a savings and investment program via insurance. These savings earn only a modest return and are eroded by inflation. We will discuss whole life: this in turn may be broken down into straight life and limited payment life, the endowment policy, plus the recently-developed variable life and universal life.

**Straight life policy**

Straight life builds up a cash surrender value and may pay dividends. If the dividends are left with the insurance company, a straight life policy may eventually become a paid-up policy. Otherwise premiums are paid for as long as the policy is in force.[1]

As was pointed out in the discussion of the term policy, the premium rates should rise each year as the insured grows older. However, to avoid changing the rates each year, insurance companies developed the idea of averaging the first five years' cost, the second five years' cost, and so forth. Thus in the five-year renewable policy, a constant level premium is paid during the first five years the policy is in force and a new and higher rate is paid during the second five years. The rate thus changes every five years. From this idea of averaging the rates every five years there grew the concept of averaging over an entire lifetime. For example, since it is possible to determine, on the average, the remaining life of a man aged thirty, it is possible to average what the cost of protection would be over the balance of his life. This is what is done. When the thirty-year-old man buys a whole life policy, his annual premium is greater than it would be if he were to purchase the same amount of term insurance. This, in part, is because the policy never expires. All term policies eventually expire. Hence, in the averaging process a straight life policy has to take into account some very high premiums because of advanced age.

As a result of averaging premiums over a lifetime on a policy that never expires, a higher reserve is built up than in the case of a term policy that eventually does expire. Some premiums are paid in advance and are called a **reserve**, which are invested by the insurance company to earn interest income. This is the savings feature of a straight life policy and, because of it, the policy builds up a cash surrender value as the years pass. **Cash surrender value** is the amount available in cash if the owner voluntarily terminates the policy. The policy itself never expires, and premiums continue to be paid until the policyholder dies, at which time the beneficiaries are paid the face value of the policy. However, policyholders may choose to take the cash value (their living benefits) and surrender their policy. Many people do this at an advanced age because they have no one financially dependent upon them. They have had insurance protection when they needed it and they have used insurance as a vehicle to generate savings for their retirement.

The savings feature built into a straight life policy can be described as modest, not heavy, but it is precisely this modest savings feature, together with insurance protection, that has made it appealing to some people. A straight life policy may become paid up if dividends are left with the company. A **dividend** is a return of part of the premium or participating insurance to reflect the difference between the premium

---

1. A straight life policy pays dividends only if it is a participating policy. Most policies purchased from mutual companies and some purchased from stock companies are participating policies.

charged and the combination of actual mortality, expense, and investment experience.

*Limited payment life policy*

The limited payment life insurance policy is the second type of whole life policy. It carries the idea of the straight life policy a step further. If it can be determined what the annual rates or premiums should be for the straight life policy and what the average lifetime premiums will be, why not divide the lifetime premiums by twenty or thirty and get paid-up insurance? This really amounts to a limited number of installment payments of the premium on such a policy for ten, twenty, thirty years, or to age sixty-five.

This policy provides for permanent protection, but the premiums are paid only for a certain number of years though the protection afforded is for the *whole life* of the individual. The most popular forms are twenty-pay life and thirty-pay life policies. The premium calculation is the same as that for the straight life policy, but, because the payments are made over a shorter period, the yearly or monthly premiums have to be greater. The insured pays much less than the face value of the policy during the limited payment period because the company is able to invest the funds at compound interest from the time the initial payment is made until the time, on the average, when those insured will die. For example, an individual at the age of twenty might be said to have a life expectancy of an additional 51.20 years. Thus, on the average, the company will have the use of the money for many years before it has to pay it out. This also means that the cash value of the policy will continue to rise even after the period for payment of premiums has expired, until eventually, if the insured does not die first, the cash value will equal the face value, and could even rise above it. The main reason for purchasing this type of policy is that some people want to pay for their insurance during the time when their earnings are the highest.

*The endowment policy*

The endowment policy provides protection for a specified number of years, at the end of which the insured will receive the face amount of the policy. If an individual purchases a $10,000 endowment policy and dies before the end of the specified number of years, his or her beneficiaries will receive the face amount of the policy. If this person lives for the number of years specified in the policy, the policy has matured and he or she will be paid the face value of the policy. At maturity, the face value and the cash surrender value are the same. An endowment policy has a limited number of payments.

People who buy endowments usually do so because they want a specific number of dollars for a specific purpose sometime in the future. Funds to send a child to college or to provide for retirement income or a trip around the world might be financed through an endowment policy.

When the endowment plan is paid up, it is like money in the bank rather than like insurance. When endowments become paid up, they are usually surrendered and the money used for some specific purpose. However, the policy can be left with the insurance company, where the cash surrender value builds up above the face value at some specified interest rate.

The emphasis in an endowment policy is on savings. Premiums on endowment policies are even higher than on the limited payment life policy. Because these premium funds are then invested and earn interest, the amount paid by the company when the policy matures—or to the beneficiaries if the policyholder dies—is greater than the amount paid in as premiums by the individual.

In summary, one can state that in progression from term, to straight life, to limited payment life, to endowments, the premiums rise with any given age because the savings feature also rises greatly. A second reason why the limited payment life and limited payment endowment policies have higher premiums than equal amounts of a straight life policy is because premiums are, in part, paid in advance.

In recent years, two new life insurance policies have been developed: universal life and variable life policies. Both are attempts to protect both the cash value (e.g., the savings feature) and the death benefits of the policy from inflation by investing part of the premiums in high-yielding money market funds or common stock. If the investments do well and the return exceeds inflation, the cash value and the death benefits are increased. In this way, both living and death benefits, it is hoped, will be inflation proof. But it doesn't always work that way. With the premiums invested in common stock, there may be losses as well as gains, and both the cash value and the death benefit can decline. Some policies have a guarantee that the death benefit will never fall below the face value. Even if the premiums are invested primarily in high-yielding securities funds, the return may not be as high as it should be, because there may be high commissions and brokerage or loading fees. Also, money market interest rates may decline.

*Universal and variable life insurance*

Universal life is a combination of annual renewable term insurance tied to an investment program. The premiums must more than cover the cost of the term insurance for there to be a surplus to invest on the insured's behalf. Moreover, this premium rises as one grows older. Often a universal life policy is set up by making a fairly large lump sum payment, and the insurance company deducts from that deposit once a month enough money from the fund to pay the premiums for the life insurance. Periodic payments may be made into the fund at any time. The face value of term life insurance may also be increased; however term life monthly premium withdrawals will also be increased. This makes the universal policy more flexible than most others. This is an investment fund that is

*Universal life*

managed by the insurance company and from which the insurance premiums are withdrawn.

Such a fund has certain tax benefits; the interest that it earns is not taxed until withdrawn. To be sure, this is true of all insurance policy interest income.

Is universal life a good investment? That depends on how well the company manages the funds, and whether or not the company earns more than individuals could with their own investment program. Generally universal life policies are superior to other cash value insurance policies—such as straight life, limited pay life, and endowments.

*Variable life*

Variable life is similar to universal life and straight life. It differs from straight life in that premiums are invested primarily in variable assets—such as common stock—that fluctuate in price with inflation. It differs from universal life in that premiums are fixed. Variable life also was developed to protect the policyholder from inflation. Both its face value and its cash value will rise (or fall) if the insurance company is successful in investing in assets that appreciate pricewise with inflation.

*What kind of insurance—cash value or term?*

What type of life insurance should be bought depends on the individual.

Is it being bought primarily for protection or for a savings program? Persons who need protection primarily should weight their insurance program toward term, which gives the maximum amount of insurance for the money. It often appeals to young people who have small children and need a good deal of insurance but have a limited income. However, term insurance eventually expires.

It has been stated that one who can save on one's own should buy term insurance and then bank the differential in premiums between term and straight life. Would a person who did this be better off in twenty years? Whether this is true would depend upon how much interest one could earn. Probably in most cases one could earn a little more in a savings and loan association than in an insurance company, but this is not always true. Also, in some cases there is a tax advantage in saving through life insurance, because any interest earned in a savings and loan association is fully taxable as income, while interest earned via a life insurance policy may not be.[2]

*Cash value buildup and net risk to the insurance company*

We have seen why and how insurance policies, with the exception of term, build up cash surrender values. The cash surrender value should be looked on as savings by the policyholder; it is like money in the bank because the policyholder may surrender his or her policy, take the cash

---

2. How life insurance is taxed will be discussed later in the chapter.

surrender value (the living benefits), and "call it quits" at any time. This cash surrender value and the risk the insurance company assumes are illustrated in Figure 10-4. The bottom two curves are for a straight life policy, the middle two are for a twenty-pay life, and the top two are for a twenty-year endowment. The cash surrender value was calculated for a $25,000 face value policy on a twenty-year-old person in each case. The annual premiums are $322.25, $539.75, and $1,047.25, respectively. Each policy has two possible buildups: one (the lower curve) if the annual dividends are taken in cash, and one (the upper curve) if they are left to accumulate more interest. The cash surrender value builds up over the years, as depicted by the curves, and the savings are represented by the surface under the curve. The risk assumed by the insurance company is depicted by the area above the curve, and this risk declines as the years pass.

If the dividends are left with the company, the cash surrender value will build up more quickly and will equal the face value more quickly. (If

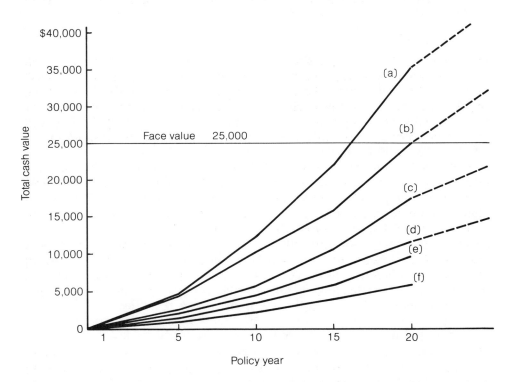

The relationships between cash surrender value and face value for each of three insurance policies for a female aged twenty: (a) twenty-year endowment, dividends accumulated; (b) twenty-year endowment, dividends withdrawn; (c) twenty-pay life, dividends accumulated; (d) twenty-pay life, dividends withdrawn; (e) straight life, dividends accumulated; (f) straight life, dividends withdrawn. Dividends accumulated at interest are based on a recent dividend scale and are not guaranteed. This figure was furnished by a large eastern mutual life insurance company.

Figure 10—4

there is a death claim, the companies pay the face value or the cash value, whichever is the larger.) The amount of insurance a person has then declines as the years pass and the cash surrender value builds up.

At the end of twenty years the limited pay life (LPL) and the endowment policy are paid up and premiums are no longer paid. The cash surrender value if not taken by the policyholder will now build up more slowly because only interest return adds to cash value. This is depicted by the dotted line in Figure 10–4. In the case of a whole life policy, the cash surrender value continues at a more uniform rate because in theory this type of policy is never paid up. There are two exceptions to this statement, however. First, if the policyholder outlives the mortality tables—which happens when one reaches the age of one hundred—the policy is paid up. At age one hundred one is actuarially dead, and insurance companies will pay off the policy. One has not won without dying, however, because cash surrender value is equal to face value. The other exception is when dividends are left with the company. In such a case, a straight life policy may become paid up before a person dies even though the person is not one hundred years of age. Whether it does depends on the age of the person when the policy was bought and upon the interest rate the insurance company is able to earn. Any policy will build up more quickly if dividends are left with the company.

## OTHER TYPES OF LIFE INSURANCE
*Group life insurance*

The major difference between life insurance sold to an individual and that sold to a group is one of administration. Insurance is often sold by the life insurance company to a business firm, and the business firm provides each insured employee with an insurance certificate. The premiums may be withheld from the employees' salaries, they may be paid entirely by the employer, or they may be shared. A second difference between group life insurance and insurance sold to an individual is that group life involves neither an individual medical examination nor an individual application for insurance.

The group insurance package commonly consists of some term, which provides for benefits on the death of the policyholder, and some medical insurance (which is health, not life, insurance and is discussed in the next chapter) to pay for all or part of the medical bills of the employees covered. Usually employees automatically lose this group insurance when they leave the company, even by retirement. However, employees have the right to convert their group insurance to an individual policy after leaving the employer, without a medical examination. If they do convert, they pay the higher premiums that individual policies require.

Group insurance is nearly always cheaper than individual insurance, for several reasons. First, the employer may pay all or part of the premiums. Even if not, the administrative cost to the insurance company is less, and part of these savings are passed on to the policyholder. Since only one policy is written for many individuals, underwriting costs are

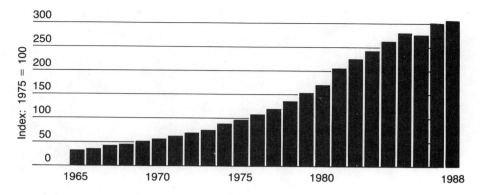

**Growth of group life insurance in the United States** (Source: *American Council* Figure 10–5
*of Life Insurance, Life Insurance Fact Book, 1989, p. 4)*

reduced. Clerical and accounting costs are less for the same reasons, and the costs of premium collection also are less because the company involved remits one check per month for all the employees. In addition, commissions to insurance salespeople are eliminated or greatly reduced, the contract being often negotiated directly by the insurance company and the business whose employees are to be covered. Finally, in some cases a person saves because the premiums are determined by the average of the employees covered. Because of this the younger members of the group subsidize the older in some cases. In other cases, the group is broken into six or eight age categories, and the premium for each category is determined by the average age therein. Most group plans are sold via a common employer; self-employed individuals should check their professional organizations, which often have a group plan. Group life insurance is the modern way to buy life insurance because it is cheaper. However, there are limits, imposed by state law, on the maximum amount of group life insurance a person may buy—usually some multiple of the person's annual income. Because of this limit, group insurance cannot be looked on as a complete insurance plan. Figure 10–5 shows the growth of group life insurance in recent years.

Another type of life insurance policy is the **credit life policy**. Many financial institutions require that anyone borrowing money on a personal note be insured for the amount of the note. Thus a bank or other lending institution will automatically sell a creditor enough insurance to cover the amount of the loan in the event the borrower dies before the debt is paid. The lender merely sells the borrower the credit insurance; the institution has an arrangement with an insurance company that actually carries the policy.

*Credit life insurance*

Credit life insurance is a specialized type of term policy. It is also

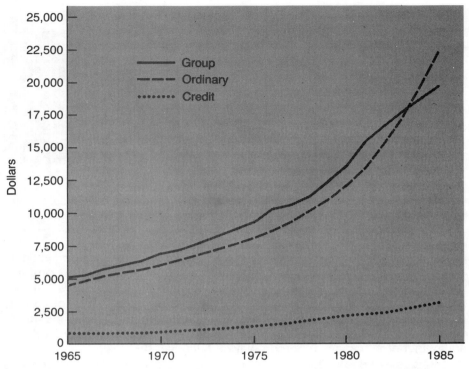

Figure 10–6     *Average size life insurance policy in force in the United States*  (Source: *American Council of Life Insurance, Life Insurance Fact Book, 1986, p. 22)*

most often sold on a group basis; the lender has an arrangement with an insurance company whereby all of its borrowing customers are covered by one plan. Figure 10-6 illustrates the average size of the various types of life insurance in effect.

*GI life insurance (government insurance)*

Military persons are eligible to buy up to $50,000 of term life insurance from the government. It is a group policy officially called Servicemen's Group Life Insurance, administered by the Veteran's Administration, with insurance provided by private insurance companies. The government acts just like an employer and buys a group plan for all service personnel. When people leave the service, they have one hundred twenty days in which to convert their insurance with a civilian insurance company without taking a medical examination. If they do not convert, the insurance lapses. The government underwrites this insurance by paying part of the premiums, but the service men and women pay $80 per month per $10,000 of insurance. This premium is fixed and does not rise with the age of the insured.

First, an insurance company must be selected. Not all companies are the same; premiums vary for a number of reasons. Life insurance benefits are taxed differently, and there are certain other benefits and options that a policyholder enjoys.

There are more than 2,100 life insurance companies in the United States, and they are not all the same. There are big and small, and stock and mutual companies. Therefore, when buying something so important, one should shop around.

*Selecting a company: why premiums vary*

Premiums of course vary with the type of policy and the age of the insured. Table 10-3 shows this variation; the premiums shown are annual premiums per $1,000 of insurance. Premiums must be set high enough to meet the expenses of running the company, expenses that are largely wages and salaries of the insurance company employees.

Premiums also vary from company to company for similar policies on individuals of the same age. The following factors help explain this variation.

1.  Some companies have a more favorable mortality experience. That is, their death claims are fewer (or come later) per ten thousand policyholders, and hence their mortality tables are more favorable than those of other companies.

*Annual premiums per $1,000 insurance*

Table 10–3

| Age | Term | Straight life | LPL | LPE |
|-----|------|------|-----|-----|
|     | 1 yr | SL | 20L | 20E |
| **Male** | | | | |
| 18 | $1.79 | $ 8.26 | $19.15 | $44.93 |
| 19 | 1.79 | 8.44 | 19.47 | 44.94 |
| 20 | 1.79 | 8.52 | 19.68 | 44.96 |
| 30 | 1.91 | 11.88 | 24.68 | 45.33 |
| 40 | 2.76 | 17.82 | 30.58 | 47.24 |
| 50 | 6.51 | 28.22 | 44.45 | 52.90 |
| **Female** | | | | |
| 18 | $1.58 | $ 7.74 | $18.63 | $44.77 |
| 19 | 1.58 | 7.91 | 18.94 | 44.77 |
| 20 | 1.58 | 8.92 | 19.13 | 44.79 |
| 30 | 1.77 | 12.95 | 23.21 | 45.09 |
| 40 | 2.24 | 15.77 | 28.53 | 46.34 |
| 50 | 5.11 | 24.40 | 36.63 | 51.06 |

Figures furnished by a large eastern mutual life insurance company.

2. Not all companies are equally efficient. Some have higher administrative and clerical costs than others.
3. Some companies earn a higher rate of return on their investments than others.

While there is an official mortality table (the Commissioners Standard Ordinary [CSO]), insurance companies are permitted to use their own mortality experience with only the proviso that it cannot be less favorable to the policyholder than the CSO. Consequently, with different mortality tables, premiums can vary somewhat from company to company.

Furthermore, not all companies are equally well managed and hence their costs are not the same. Even with companies that are equally well managed, the expense of running the insurance company, per $1,000 of life insurance in force, may vary with the size of the company and how fast it is growing. Generally newer and smaller companies have higher costs than older and larger companies, but there are exceptions. The percentage yield on the investments that a company earns will vary from company to company. A company that consistently earns more can either pay a higher dividend or charge a lower premium.

A final reason why insurance premiums vary is that two different policies from two different companies, while they appear about the same, may not be. Only one of them may have a dismemberment clause, which provides so much for the loss of an arm or a leg. A person may or may not want this coverage; but if the policy has it, he or she will pay more. Also the guaranteed cash surrender value buildup over the years may differ on two otherwise similar policies. In such a case, different amounts of savings are built into otherwise similar policies. This can, of course, be done by varying premiums or dividends.

Thus, a better bargain may be obtained by shopping around and comparing companies' policies. Some weight should also be given to the financial strength and soundness of the insurance company. While total assets of the insurer are important, they are not the only factor to consider because there are also liabilities. It is difficult to compare the financial soundness of the various insurers, but one meaningful bench mark is referred to as the policyholder's "surplus ratio." It is simple—the insurance company's net worth (assets less liabilities) divided by liabilities. It can easily be calculated from an insurance company's balance sheet.

Another suggestion is to check with an insurance agent or local library for a copy of *Best's Insurance Guide* published by A. M. Best Company, a "watchdog" of the insurance industry. Its *Guide* can give information on the company's background, financial strength, and overall rating.

Insurance companies are regulated by the states. It is the task of the regulatory agencies to make sure that the insurers are sufficiently sound. However, the rigor of these agencies (and the stringency of the laws under which they operate) varies from state to state. More confidence may be placed in an insurance company if it operates in many, and especially in all, states. Since New York state has the toughest (best from the consumer's point of view) insurance laws, some financial advisers suggest that a bit more confidence may be placed in an insurance company that operates in New York.

Comparing term policies is usually simple enough. Since often no dividend is involved and there is no cash surrender value, a simple comparison of premiums per $1,000 of face value is all that is required.

*Comparing different companies' policies*

In the case of cash value insurance, the analysis is more complex, but two or more similar policies can be analyzed to see which appears to be the better buy. This can only be approximated. First, subtract the likely dividends from the gross annual premiums. Since future dividends are unknown, they must be estimated based on past experience. This calculation will give the approximate net annual premiums. Next, multiply this by, say, 5, 10, and 20, to get the total premiums over the years. Then compare that to what the cash surrender value (which can be predicted with accuracy and which is stated in the policy) of the policy will be in 5, 10, and 20 years. If this is done with several policies, an individual will be able to spot the better buy. However, while this can give a comparison among several policies, it ignores the interest which could have been earned if the premium dollars had been invested elsewhere. It also ignores the present value of dollars payable in the future, and future dollars are likely to be worth less than present dollars.

The recently developed interest-adjusted indexes attempt to consider factors and in so doing compare the cost of different policies. In the interest-adjusted method of calculating costs, each year's premium is assumed to earn interest (at, say, 5 percent). In calculating the index we first obtain the total (say 20 years) accumulation of premiums plus interest. From this we subtract, first, all dividends plus interest on them, and, second, the cash value of the policy at the end of twenty years. The result is the total (20-year) cost of the policy. It is then divided by the number of $1,000 units of coverage to get the 20-year cost per $1,000 of insurance. This cost per $1,000 is then divided again by a factor (34.57 in our case).[3] The final result is a dollar figure that if set aside each year at 5 percent would equal the net dollar cost of the policy. This will vary from company to company, but a recent random sample of nine different companies indicated that this interest-adjusted cost figure on a straight life policy on a thirty-five-year-old man varied from a low of

---

3. This ($34.57) is the amount of money a person would have if one dollar were added per year for twenty years and these dollars were earning interest at 5 percent. In many tables this figure is 33.066, but this is because most tables accrue no interest until the end of the year, whereas in our case we earn interest continuously over the entire year.

$4.33 to a high of $6.68. While this interest-adjusted index is only an approximation, it is a useful measure of the difference in the cost of a policy.

*Grace period*

After a premium is due but not paid, there is generally a ***grace period*** of twenty-eight to thirty-one days during which the premium may be paid without penalty. In the event that a policyholder dies during the grace period, the unpaid premium is collected from the amount paid to the beneficiary.

*Reinstatement*

Most policies contain a provision for reinstatement. If a policy has lapsed, it may, within a stated period, be put into effect again provided the policyholder is insurable, and of course this implies another physical examination. If the physical is passed, the overdue premiums together with interest must then be paid.

*Incontestability*

After one or two years, a policy will ordinarily be incontestable. This means that the company is given one or two years in which to check certain information given by the policyholder when he or she made the original application for the policy. If the company discovers that a materially false statement was made, it may seek to have itself released from the policy. After the incontestable period has passed, however, the company can no longer seek such release.

*Nonforfeiture value*

What happens if one can no longer pay the premiums for some reason? Term insurance, which has no cash surrender value, will lapse after the grace period. If it is permanent life insurance and has built up a cash surrender value, one has four options. (Recall from the discussion that generally all policies except term build up a cash value after they have been in force for a few years and that this cash value increases as the years pass.) One's options are assured by the nonforfeiture values that in a sense guarantee the cash surrender value of the policy. These four options are:

1.  *Cash value.* A policy can be surrendered for its cash value. This cash surrender value can be taken in one lump sum or in a number of regular payments if it is large enough (usually $1,000 or more).
2.  *Extended term insurance.* Often a policy includes a provision that if the holder fails to pay the premiums after the grace period, the policy automatically will remain in force as a term policy for as long as the cash surrender value of the policy will permit. For example, suppose one has a $4,000 cash surrender value in a $20,000

ordinary life insurance policy and he or she has failed to pay the premium after the grace period. Under the terms of the policy, the amount of cash surrendered value ($4,000) may be enough to keep that policy in force as term insurance for nine or ten years. The $4,000 equity in the policy actually is used to pay the premium on what will now be an ***extended term policy***.

3. *Reduced paid-up insurance.* If one no longer wishes to pay premiums, one can reduce the face value of life insurance but keep it in force as paid-up permanent insurance. Then the $4,000 cash surrender value on the $20,000 policy might provide a paid-up policy with a face value of $10,000. This is now paid up and in force, and the death payment would become $10,000 but the individual no longer needs to pay premiums.

4. *Automatic premium loan* (AFL). Some insurance policies have a provision that grants the insured an automatic loan used to pay the premiums after the grace period has expired if the policy has a cash value. This is designed to prevent the policy from lapsing due to the insured accidentally forgetting to pay the premiums, which might happen if he or she is on an extended trip. Then upon the policyholder's return the loan could be repaid and the insurance continue in its original form.

*Borrowing on a life insurance policy*

A person may borrow the cash surrender value of his or her life insurance policy from the company. Most states have laws requiring these loans to be made by insurance companies. However, insurance companies may wait as long as several months before making the loan. In practice, however, they make the money available almost immediately.

Insurance companies charge about 8 percent (annual percentage rate) interest on these loans, which is as low a rate as a person can get anywhere. The insurance companies must obtain the small interest which they charge because were it not for the policy loan they would invest the money elsewhere and their investment income would be greater. Since the insurance contract is made with an assumption of certain interest income, they have to charge a rate on policy loans.

There can be a danger in borrowing from one's insurance company. First of all, these loans are single repayment rather than installment loans. Therefore, some budgeting must be done and a sum set aside every week or month in order to liquidate the loan eventually. Moreover, there is no obligation ever to repay the loan. Some people just continue to pay the interest. If there is a death claim on a policy with a loan outstanding, it is deducted before the face value is paid.

In some states the borrower is not even required to pay the loan interest. In such a case, if the amount borrowed plus the accumulating interest grow to equal the cash surrender value of the policy, it is canceled, and a person ends up with no insurance.

*Assignment*

It is frequently possible to use one's life insurance policy as collateral (and hence reduce the interest rate) when borrowing money from banks and others. Lenders may feel it desirable for them to be assigned the policy, so that if the borrower dies before repaying the obligation, the debt will be paid from the proceeds of the policy. To assign a policy, however, one must have the right to change the beneficiary; otherwise, it will be necessary to obtain the beneficiary's consent. Furthermore, the policy specifically states that no assignment will be binding on the company until the company has been notified.

*Ownership of the policy*

In a life insurance contract, there are the insured, the beneficiaries, and the owner of the policy. The meaning of *insured* and *beneficiary* is clear and needs no further elaboration, but the term *owner* requires explanation.

Usually, but not always, the insured is also the owner. The insured can turn ownership over to the beneficiary. The owner of the policy, while living, has the right to modify the policy, change the beneficiary (if he or she has reserved that right in the policy), select the settlement options, surrender or cancel the policy, receive any insurance dividends, and any other rights which may exist. On the death of the insured (who may or may not be the owner) ownership of the policy is immediately and automatically transferred to the beneficiary.

One reason why a person may want to transfer ownership to the beneficiary prior to death is to avoid estate taxes. (Estate taxes are discussed in Chapter 19.) If the beneficiary is not the owner prior to the death of the insured, then, although the beneficiary receives the insurance claim upon the death of the insured, it is subject to the deceased's estate tax (not income tax, but estate tax). If the beneficiary is the owner, this tax is avoided. To make certain that this tax savings is realized, however, the owner-beneficiary should have his or her own checking account and pay the insured's premiums with his or her own personal checks. The actual transfer of ownership to the beneficiary is also a gift, and if the cash surrender value of the policy is large, this could have gift tax implications. (See Chapter 19 for a discussion of gift taxes.)

One word of warning: if ownership of a policy is transferred to the beneficiary, the insured loses all control over it and can never change the beneficiary or the settlement options, nor will he or she receive the dividends it may pay. In addition, if the owner-beneficiary dies before the insured, the cash value of the policy becomes part of the beneficiary's estate.

*Change of beneficiary: third party rights*

There may be many reasons why one might want the beneficiary in a policy changed, such as marriage, divorce, or newborn children. To effect such a change at any time, one must have reserved the right to change the beneficiary when originally taking out the policy; most policies contain a clause giving this right. The company will furnish the proper forms. In some cases, where the insured has failed to reserve the right to change the beneficiary when taking out the policy, he or she must first obtain the consent of the present beneficiary in writing before the company will permit the change to be made.

What happens if a named beneficiary dies before the policyholder?

Normally the company pays the money directly to one's estate when the insured dies. However, one or more persons can be, and usually are, named in the policy as contingent beneficiaries. In this case, the contingent beneficiary or beneficiaries receive the proceeds of the policy should the first-named beneficiary die before the insured.

Several different settlement options may be chosen that will determine how insurance benefits are to be paid. These options may be selected by the insured or the beneficiary, depending on the circumstances. The insured has first choice, and may choose the settlement option during his or her lifetime, and he or she may change it at any time. After the insured dies, the beneficiary must live with whatever options have been chosen. If the insured dies before having chosen the options, however, then the beneficiary may choose them. *Settlement options*

There are four general options from which to choose:

1. *Lump sum.* In this case the entire sum is paid at once, and the beneficiary has the money management problem. However, when interest rates are high, this person might be able to earn more on his or her lump sum settlement than the insurance company.

2. *Interest payment only.* Under this option the insurance company retains the principal sum and pays the beneficiary the interest earned. These payments could be made for a specific period of years or for life. Eventually the principal would have to go to someone. It could go to the primary beneficiary if still alive and if the interest is paid for only a limited number of years. Otherwise the principal would go to the secondary beneficiary. If only interest is paid, the principal is never exhausted, and some provisions must be made to pay it to someone eventually. Sometimes arrangements are made whereby the beneficiary can dip into the principal within limits. This would reduce future interest payments, but would provide flexibility and an additional source of money for the beneficiary in the event of an emergency.

3. *Installment payments.* The company makes regular payments in equal amounts until the fund is exhausted. During the time that such regular payments are being made, the company will add interest to the part of the money not paid out. There are two ways this option could be set up. One would provide for a specific amount, say, $500 per month. In such a case the length of time for which the payments could be made would depend on the amount

of the payment, the dollar cash value of the policy, and the rate of interest earned by the company.

The second method is to set up the payments for a specific number of years—say, ten or fifteen. Then the amount of each payment depends on the amount of the dollar cash value, the number of years selected, and the rate of interest earned.

Thus, one can decide the payments are to be made as a stated sum per month or for a stated number of years. The installment option may also have a provision to permit the beneficiary to "commute" the remaining payments, or to stop the income payments and choose to take all the money that remains in one final payment. The policyholder may also arrange that any money left when the first beneficiary dies shall be paid in one sum or continued as income to one or more secondary beneficiaries.

4.  *Life annuity income.* One may elect to receive as a settlement a life annuity income. Briefly, a life annuity gives the beneficiary, or annuitant, a stated income for as long as he or she lives. (See Chapter 18.)

    In some annuity plans, if the annuitant dies before the payments reach a stated total amount or before the payments have been made for a stated period of time, arrangements can be made to have the payments made to a secondary beneficiary. Under the annuity option the amount of each payment depends on several factors, including the age of the annuitant when payment begins, his or her life expectancy, the rate of interest earned, the form of life annuity settlement used, and the amount of the policy's cash value. Figure 10–7 shows how life insurance benefits have grown over the last few years.

    Another variation of this option is sometimes chosen if there are two or more primary beneficiaries—the joint survivorship life income annuity. It is the same as the life annuity income just described, except that payments are made until both beneficiaries are deceased.

*Disability premium waiver*

The waiver of premium, or what is more commonly referred to as a "disability clause" in a life insurance policy, means that any premiums that fall due after the beginning of a total and permanent disability will be waived. Thus if one is disabled, the life insurance policy will continue in force because the company will make the premium payments. Disability must occur before one has reached a certain age, generally age sixty, and before the policy is paid up. In some cases, the disability must last for at least six months before premiums will be waived.

To have such a disability clause written into the policy, the insured must request it and must pay a small additional premium. The disability clause written into a policy really amounts to taking out additional insurance to insure that the premiums will continue to be paid if the policyholder is disabled. The addition to the premium is so small that its inclusion is recommended.

The clause relating to accidental death benefits is sometimes also called "double indemnity." Under the provisions of this clause, the company promises to pay twice the face value of the policy if death occurs by accidental means. If the death is to be construed as "accidental," it must occur within a certain time after one is injured. Suppose, for example, that an injury occurs that causes hospitalization for, say, one year, and after a year death can be directly attributed to the accident. In such a case, the accidental death benefit clause of the policy will probably not apply. Most policies state that death must occur within ninety days after the accident to be construed as accidental death. Furthermore, there is commonly a second limitation to the accidental death clause: the accidental death must have occurred before age sixty or sixty-five, depending on the policy.

*Accidental death benefits*

The double indemnity clause further excludes from the meaning of "accidental" death death arising from certain kinds of accidents. The reason is either that these deaths result from risks that cannot be calculated or that the cause of death is not accidental in the legal sense. For instance, if a person jumps from a moving car, his or her death is suicide, not an accident, and the double indemnity will not hold. Or if a person has a heart attack while driving a car and is killed in an accident

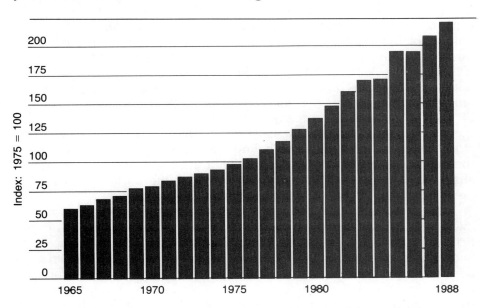

Figure 10–7   **Relative growth in average size insurance death benefit payments in the United States** (Source: *American Council of Life Insurance, Life Insurance Fact Book, 1989, p. 17*)

caused by the attack, that person is not covered even though the death is caused by the accident, not the heart attack.

It is even possible to obtain a triple indemnity clause in an insurance policy. In such a case, the company pays three times the face value in the event of accidental death as defined above. An added premium must be paid in order to obtain either a double or a triple indemnity clause.

*Stock insurance companies versus mutual companies*

There has been much discussion over the respective merits of stock insurance companies and mutual insurance companies. The **stock company** is a corporation, the ownership of which is in the hands of stockholders, and, as in any other corporation, the business affairs of the corporation are run by a board of directors. The profit, if any, is distributed to the stockholders much in the same manner as that of any corporation.

A ***mutual life insurance company***, on the other hand, is owned by the policyholders. No stock is issued. The management of the mutual company is entrusted to experts in the insurance business just as the management of the stock company is placed in the hands of experts.

*Insurance dividends*

The distinction between stock and mutual companies is important because of dividends. Historically, insurance dividends have been paid by mutual companies to their policyholders. These should not be confused with the stock dividends given as a share of the profits to the stockholders of the stock companies. In the mutual company, if the income exceeds the amount needed to pay beneficiaries and expenses, part of it is returned to the policyholders in the form of dividends. The policyholder is generally given a choice of receiving the cash, applying the amount to subsequent premiums, buying paid-up additional insurance, or leaving it with the company at interest.

To compete with dividends paid to mutual policyholders, some stock companies issue a participating type of policy, which provides that the policyholder will share in the profits of the corporation along with the shareholders. Generally the premium rates of the participating policies are higher than those of the nonparticipating policies.

Frequently, the premiums on policies issued by stock companies are lower than those issued by mutual companies. These are the nonparticipating policies. Some stock companies, then, issue both participating and nonparticipating policies. Both of these are a competitive device to offset wholly or partially the dividends paid by the mutual companies to their policyholders. Some stock companies argue that the dividends paid by the mutual companies are not all earnings being paid to the policyholders; these critics say that mutual companies charge too much in premiums in the first place and are thus merely returning the excess premiums. Mutual companies are quick to deny this charge.

When buying life insurance and trying to choose between mutual and stock companies, keep in mind both the premiums and the dividends. The problem is often difficult because dividends are not guaranteed; however, a record of past dividends is usually available.

Keep in mind, when deciding between buying a policy from a mutual or stock company, the guaranteed buildup of cash surrender value. While the guaranteed cash buildup of stock companies is often somewhat higher than that guaranteed by mutual companies, the actual achieved cash buildup of the mutuals is usually better, especially in the long run. This is because if mutual companies earn more than they guarantee, they add it to the cash value, and in recent years this has happened. In the case of stock companies, any earnings in excess of that guaranteed may go to the stockholders, not the policyholders. Hence, the actual and the guaranteed cash buildups of a policy from a stock company are more likely to be the same, or at least closer to each other.

Regardless of whether insurance dividends are a return of premiums or shared interest which the company earned with the policyholders' premiums, a policyholder receiving them must decide what to do with them.[4] There are several alternatives from which to choose.

1. Take the dividend in cash and use as any other income.
2. Apply the dividend toward the payment of future premiums. The dividend will usually grow larger as the years pass because the cash surrender value grows larger, and after a time the dividends alone may pay the entire premium.
3. Leave the dividend with the company to be compounded at the going interest rate and continue to pay the regular premiums: then the cash surrender value of the policy will build up more rapidly than if option 1 or 2 were selected. However, under option 3 the policyholder will have to declare on his or her federal income tax the *added* interest that the company earns with the dividends. The dividend itself, however, is not taxable, but the interest earned with it is; the company will send a statement indicating the amount of the interest.
4. Use the dividends to buy paid-up additional insurance. Then the face value of the policy goes up some every year, and this incremental amount is paid up. A person who needs more life insurance may want to select this fourth option because it will save commissions. However, buying paid-up additions is like buying a single-premium-payment life insurance policy. One is really paying all future premiums in advance, and while the companies make an allowance for this, it is not very high. Consequently, a single-premium paid-up policy is more expensive than buying insurance

---

4. The Internal Revenue Service has ruled that the entire dividend is a return of premiums for tax purposes. Hence, insurance policy dividends are not taxable.

**Box 10–1
The seven don'ts
for your client**

After taking out insurance policies many people handle them poorly. The following suggests that there are proper ways of handling policies.

1. *Don't let insurance go to the wrong people.* In the event of a divorce, it is necessary that the beneficiary be changed. If a person remarries and forgets to change the beneficiary, then the first spouse will receive the proceeds of the policy in the event of the insured's death. Everyone's insurance program should be periodically reviewed. Every time a situation arises that changes insurance needs, an individual should review his or her insurance program to make it conform with the changed circumstances.

2. *Don't let insurance dollars be foolishly dissipated.* The problem here is whether or not the beneficiaries should be given lump-sum payments or monthly payments. Some people cannot handle large sums properly.

3. *Don't forget to pay the premiums when they come due.* Most policies carry a thirty-one-day grace period, which means that even if one fails to pay on time, the policy will stay in force during that period. After that period, however, in order to reinstate the contract it may be necessary to take a new physical examination. In the event that an unsuspected change in one's health occurs, it may be impossible to reinstate the policy.

4. *Don't give up policies thoughtlessly.* Changing the kind of insurance one has by taking advantage of conversion privileges in one's policy is often a wise move, but not so dropping one policy and buying another. A change in policies is very likely to turn out disadvantageously. Irreplaceable guarantees may be lost. Moreover, the cost of setting up policies is substantial, and since the insurance company applies this to the policyholder in the early years, no cash surrender value is built up on a new policy for a while.

5. *Don't hide policies in out-of-the-way places.* A mislaid policy delays prompt settlement of a death claim. Make sure the family knows where policies are kept.

6. *Don't ever throw away a policy, even if the premiums become unaffordable.* Many a supposedly worthless policy has been discovered to contain valuable benefits available to an individual or his or her heirs.

7. *Don't ever overlook the borrowing power of policies.* Insurance companies will lend money against the cash value of a policy at relatively low rates of interest.

the usual way. However, one's dividends might very well add several hundred dollars of paid-up additions each year. This fourth option also results in the cash surrender value rising more rapidly than if option 1 or 2 were selected but less rapidly than if option 3 were selected. Selecting option 4 also relieves the policyholder from having to pay federal income taxes on the interest that the dividend earns as in the case of option 3, because the dividend earns no interest. It is spent on more insurance. The dividend earns no interest if option 1 or 2 is selected. Only under option 3 does the dividend earn interest. If option 4 were selected, more dividends will be earned on the insurance purchased with previous dividends.

5.  Use the annual dividend to buy one-year term. This will increase the face value of the policy by more than option 4 will for a number of years. After a time, however, option 5 may no longer be a means of providing the maximum amount of insurance because under option 4 the added insurance is permanent and the cumulative amount of it may surpass the amount of annual term which may be purchased. If this option were selected, the cash surrender value will build up at the same rate as under options 1 and 2.

Death benefits are not subject to the personal income tax but may be subject to estate taxes. Living benefits from a traditional policy are not taxable most of the time, but there are a few exceptions. There is no tax while the cash value builds up; when it is surrendered the cash value is taxable only if it is greater than the sum of the three following items:

*Taxes and life insurance benefits*

1.  The total of all of the premiums paid over the years, less any dividends taken in cash over the years.
2.  The total of all of the dividends left with the company over the years.
3.  The total of all the interest earned by dividends over the years and which was taxed along the way.

In such a case, the tax is on the excess. For example, if a policyholder surrenders his or her policy for $15,000, after having paid over the years premiums—less dividends taken in cash over the years—totaling $12,000, and having left dividends with the company of $2,000, and having earned $500 with those dividends, the tax is levied on $500.

## SUGGESTED READINGS

*American Society of Chartered Life Underwriters (CLU) Journal.* Bryn Mawr, Pa.: The American Society of Chartered Life Underwriters. Quarterly publication.

*Best's Review, Life-Health Edition.* Oldwick, N.J.: A. M. Best Company, Inc. Monthly publication.

Black, Kenneth, and Skipper, Harold. *Life Insurance,* 11th ed. Englewood Cliffs, N.J.: Prentice Hall, 1987.

Cockerell, Hugh. *Lloyd's of London.* Homewood, Ill.: Dow Jones-Irwin, 1984.

Consumer Reports Editors. *The Consumer's Union Report on Life Insurance: A Guide to Planning and Buying the Protection You Need.*

Dorfman, Mark S. *Introduction to Insurance,* 3rd ed. Englewood Cliffs, N.J.: Prentice Hall, 1987.

*Finance Facts Yearbook.* Washington, D.C.: National Consumer Finance Association. Annual publication.

Greene, Mark R., and Trieschmann, James. "Risk and Insurance." Cincinnati: South-Western, 1984.

Huebner, Solomon S., and Black, Kenneth, Jr. *Life Insurance,* 8th ed. Englewood Cliffs, N.J.: Prentice Hall, 1987.

*Insurance Review.* New York: The Insurance Information Institute. Monthly publication.

"The Journal of Insurance." New York: The Insurance Information Institute. Bimonthly publication.

Kenton, Walter S., Jr. *How Life Insurance Companies Rob You and What You Can Do About It*. New York: Random House, 1984.

*Life Insurance Fact Book*. New York: Institute of Life Insurance. Annual publication.

Mehr, Robert, and Gustavson, Sandra G. *Life Insurance; Theory and Practice*. Plano, Tex.: Business Publications, Inc., 1987.

*National Underwriter*. Chicago: The National Underwriter Co. Weekly publication.

"On the Way Up; A Description of Life Insurance and Annuities." Hartford, Conn.: Aetna Life Insurance Co.

*A Shopper's Guide to Life Insurance; A Shopper's Guide to Term Life Insurance*. Harrisburg, Pa.: Pennsylvania Insurance Dept.

*Understanding Life Insurance, A Basic Guidebook*. Milwaukee: Northwestern Mutual Life Insurance Co.

Vaughan, Emmet J. *Fundamentals of Risk and Insurance*, 5th ed. New York: John Wiley and Sons, 1988.

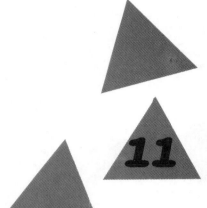

# Health care and health insurance

11

**HIGHLIGHTS**

Health care is vital; health care is also expensive. In order to help the client manage the risk of sickness and injury and learn how to finance its high cost, this chapter will examine the following:

1   The expense involved in health care
2   The various types of health insurance, both medical insurance and disability insurance, and what they are intended to do
3   Major medical insurance to cover larger costs
4   How much health insurance to buy
5   Certain other things about health insurance
6   Some nonprofit health plans
7   A checklist to enable a person to evaluate his or her health insurance

**INTRODUCTION**

There are two major risks involved insofar as health is concerned. They are:

**1.** Loss of assets (savings) due to heavy medical expenses, and
**2.** Loss of earnings when unable to work.

These risks may both be managed by buying insurance. Hospital and medical expense insurance is needed to pay for the high cost of medical care, and disability insurance to replace lost income due to accident or illness.

Physicians' fees and hospital costs have been rising rapidly in recent years and will no doubt continue to do so. It is possible, in the absence of insurance, for a major illness quickly to exhaust the savings of even upper-middle income groups and force them deeply into debt.

The cost of a hospital room can easily run in excess of $300 per day. Expensive laboratory tests and the use of other expensive equipment are extra. Doctors' and surgeons' fees can in some cases amount to thousands of dollars. The American public spent over $700 billion on health care in 1991. In recent years the cost of health care has been rising more rapidly than the overall price level because of new, expensive, sophisticated equipment, more skilled personnel, better care, and an enormous increase in the demand for medical services generated by government programs. Figure 11–1 shows national health expenditures as a percentage of gross national product over the last few years.

Table 11–1 shows how health care costs have risen relative to other items.

*Medical expense insurance*

Medical expense insurance has been developed to protect the individual from such high medical costs. **Medical insurance** covers medical expenses, including doctors' fees, cost of drugs, hospital bills, and surgical fees. In addition, there is sometimes major medical insurance to cover expenses over and above what regular medical insurance covers.

*Disability: loss of income insurance*

**Disability insurance** protects against loss of income while one is sick or disabled. Generally there is a waiting period before disability insurance pays a benefit. Short-term illnesses, then, are not covered. The length of time for which benefits are paid varies as well. All these factors will be discussed below.

*Group or individual insurance*

**Health insurance** can be purchased on a group or individual basis. To buy group insurance, however, one must be eligible, and usually group insurance is available to the employees of a firm. The premiums on group insurance are lower than on individual policies, and for this reason people who are able to take advantage of a group plan should do so.

*National Health Expenditures as a percentage of gross national product* (Source: Source Book of Health Insurance Data, 1989, *Health Insurance Association of America, Washington, D.C.)*    Figure 11–1

*Estimated expenditures for 1989 and 1990 are $597.2 billion and $647.3 billion, respectively.*

Most insurance companies have several plans to choose from, differing in various amounts of coverage and various deductible and coinsurance features. Some policies have limits to the amount they will pay for a hospital room; others do not. Some will not cover certain ailments; others will. The better the coverage, the higher the premium. Each of the various policies may be purchased to cover an individual or an entire family. There are generally as many as four different premiums quoted for any given policy—one for a single person, another for a couple with no children, a third for a couple with children, perhaps even a fourth for an employee and children.

Types of health coverage can be classified into the following categories:    **TYPES OF HEALTH INSURANCE COVERAGE**

- Medical expense
    Hospital
    Surgical
    Medical
    Major medical or comprehensive
    Other
    Dental
- Disability insurance or loss of income

Table 11-1  Consumer prices

[1982-84 = 100, except as noted; monthly data seasonally adjusted, except as noted]

| Period | All items [1] Not seasonally adjusted (NSA) | All items [1] Seasonally adjusted | Food | Housing Total [1] | Housing Shelter Total | Housing Shelter Renters' costs (Dec. 1982=100) | Housing Shelter Homeowners' costs (Dec. 1982=100) | Housing Shelter Maintenance and repairs (NSA) | Housing Fuel and other utilities | Apparel and upkeep | Transportation Total [1] | Transportation New cars | Transportation Motor fuel | Medical care | Energy [2] | All items less food and energy |
|---|---|---|---|---|---|---|---|---|---|---|---|---|---|---|---|---|
| *Rel. imp.* [3] | *100.0* | | *16.2* | *41.4* | *27.7* | *7.9* | *19.5* | *0.2* | *7.3* | *6.1* | *17.8* | *4.0* | *4.1* | *6.4* | *8.2* | *75.6* |
| 1982 | 96.5 | | 97.4 | 96.9 | 96.9 | | | 96.4 | 94.9 | 97.8 | 97.0 | 97.4 | 102.8 | 92.5 | 99.2 | 95.8 |
| 1983 | 99.6 | | 99.4 | 99.5 | 99.1 | 103.0 | 102.5 | 99.9 | 100.2 | 100.2 | 99.3 | 99.9 | 99.4 | 100.6 | 99.9 | 99.6 |
| 1984 | 103.9 | | 103.2 | 103.6 | 104.0 | 108.6 | 107.3 | 103.7 | 104.8 | 102.1 | 103.7 | 102.8 | 97.9 | 106.8 | 100.9 | 104.6 |
| 1985 | 107.6 | | 105.6 | 107.7 | 109.8 | 115.4 | 113.1 | 106.5 | 106.5 | 105.0 | 106.4 | 106.1 | 98.7 | 113.5 | 101.6 | 109.1 |
| 1986 | 109.6 | | 109.0 | 110.9 | 115.8 | 121.9 | 119.4 | 107.9 | 104.1 | 105.9 | 102.3 | 110.6 | 77.1 | 122.0 | 88.2 | 113.5 |
| 1987 | 113.6 | | 113.5 | 114.2 | 121.3 | 128.1 | 124.8 | 111.8 | 103.0 | 110.6 | 105.4 | 114.6 | 80.2 | 130.1 | 88.6 | 118.2 |
| 1988 | 118.3 | | 118.2 | 118.5 | 127.1 | 133.6 | 131.1 | 114.7 | 104.4 | 115.4 | 108.7 | 116.9 | 80.9 | 138.6 | 89.3 | 123.4 |
| 1989 | 124.0 | | 125.1 | 123.0 | 132.8 | 138.9 | 137.3 | 118.0 | 107.8 | 118.6 | 114.1 | 119.2 | 88.5 | 149.3 | 94.3 | 129.0 |
| 1990 | 130.7 | | 132.4 | 128.5 | 140.0 | 146.7 | 144.6 | 122.2 | 111.6 | 124.1 | 120.5 | 121.0 | 101.2 | 162.8 | 102.1 | 135.5 |
| 1991 | 136.2 | | 136.3 | 133.6 | 146.3 | 155.6 | 150.2 | 126.3 | 115.3 | 128.7 | 123.8 | 125.3 | 99.4 | 177.0 | 102.5 | 142.1 |
| **1990:** | | | | | | | | | | | | | | | | |
| Dec | 133.8 | 134.2 | 134.9 | 130.8 | 142.8 | 150.5 | 147.3 | 123.8 | 113.7 | 125.7 | 126.9 | 122.0 | 117.7 | 170.1 | 110.9 | 138.6 |
| **1991:** | | | | | | | | | | | | | | | | |
| Jan | 134.6 | 134.8 | 135.7 | 131.9 | 143.9 | 153.0 | 147.9 | 124.1 | 115.5 | 126.9 | 125.4 | 123.6 | 110.0 | 171.2 | 108.2 | 139.7 |
| Feb | 134.8 | 135.1 | 135.4 | 132.5 | 144.6 | 154.2 | 148.4 | 125.1 | 115.1 | 128.9 | 124.0 | 124.2 | 102.0 | 172.4 | 103.9 | 140.7 |
| Mar | 135.0 | 135.0 | 135.7 | 132.6 | 144.8 | 154.2 | 148.7 | 124.2 | 114.8 | 127.4 | 122.8 | 124.8 | 97.1 | 173.5 | 101.2 | 140.9 |
| Apr | 135.2 | 135.3 | 136.7 | 132.8 | 145.2 | 154.2 | 149.2 | 126.1 | 114.2 | 127.2 | 122.4 | 125.2 | 97.1 | 174.4 | 100.5 | 141.2 |
| May | 135.6 | 135.7 | 136.7 | 133.0 | 145.3 | 154.1 | 149.4 | 126.9 | 114.8 | 127.2 | 123.2 | 125.3 | 99.5 | 175.4 | 101.9 | 141.5 |
| June | 136.0 | 136.0 | 137.4 | 133.1 | 145.8 | 154.5 | 149.9 | 126.2 | 114.0 | 127.7 | 123.5 | 125.6 | 99.1 | 176.5 | 100.9 | 142.0 |
| July | 136.2 | 136.3 | 136.6 | 133.5 | 146.1 | 155.0 | 150.2 | 126.9 | 114.0 | 128.9 | 123.5 | 125.6 | 97.1 | 177.5 | 100.5 | 142.5 |
| Aug | 136.6 | 136.6 | 136.2 | 133.5 | 146.2 | 154.7 | 150.5 | 127.2 | 114.7 | 130.4 | 124.0 | 125.8 | 97.4 | 178.9 | 100.3 | 143.0 |
| Sept | 137.2 | 137.1 | 136.3 | 134.2 | 146.9 | 155.4 | 151.3 | 126.8 | 115.4 | 129.9 | 124.3 | 126.2 | 98.3 | 180.1 | 101.3 | 143.6 |
| Oct | 137.4 | 137.2 | 136.2 | 134.6 | 147.3 | 156.0 | 151.6 | 126.6 | 116.1 | 129.4 | 124.0 | 125.8 | 97.6 | 181.1 | 101.5 | 143.8 |
| Nov | 137.8 | 137.8 | 137.0 | 134.9 | 147.7 | 156.1 | 152.2 | 127.6 | 116.6 | 130.7 | 124.6 | 126.0 | 98.9 | 182.0 | 102.3 | 144.3 |
| Dec | 137.9 | 138.2 | 137.4 | 135.4 | 148.4 | 157.0 | 152.8 | 128.1 | 117.1 | 129.9 | 125.0 | 126.1 | 98.9 | 183.4 | 102.7 | 144.7 |

[1] Includes items not shown separately.
[2] Household fuels—gas (piped), electricity, fuel oil, etc.—and motor fuel. Motor oil, coolant, etc. also included through 1982.
[3] Relative importance, December 1990.

NOTE.—Data beginning 1983 incorporate a rental equivalence measure for homeownership costs and therefore are not strictly comparable with figures for earlier periods.
Data beginning 1987 and 1988 calculated on a revised basis.

*Source: Economic Indicators,* January, 1992, Council of Economic Advisers, p. 23.

Table 11–2 shows the number of people in the United States who are covered under some form of the more popular type of health insurance.

*Hospital expense*

Hospital expense insurance covers basic hospital costs such as room and board, nursing care, X-ray costs, drugs, anesthetists and oxygen, laboratory work such as blood tests and urinalysis, and certain other miscellaneous costs. Many hospital policies also cover other costs, for example, expenses incurred when the insured is treated in a nursing care facility. Also often covered is emergency room treatment in a hospital on an outpatient basis.

Room and board charges sometimes are limited to a stated maximum amount, and a maximum number of days per illness may be stipulated. A person could choose a $100, $150, or $200 per day hospital room allowance with premiums varying accordingly. More and more plans, however, provide for payment of a semiprivate room. Generally, most other hospital fees such as laboratory work are covered. If the patient is in intensive care, room costs are much higher. Some policies provide for a higher daily limit; others do not.

As noted above, hospital care is very expensive and is continuing to rise rapidly. For this reason hospital insurance is considered a must by most people. Figure 11–2 illustrates the average cost per day for a semiprivate hospital room by region.

*Surgical expense insurance*

Payment of surgical fees is not included in policies that cover hospital fees, and separate insurance plans have been developed to take care of

| | Northeast | | Midwest | | South | | West | |
|---|---|---|---|---|---|---|---|---|
| | Jan. 1986 | Jan. 1987 | Jan. 1986 | Jan. 1987 | Jan. 1986 | Jan. 1987 | Jan. 1986 | Jan. 1987 |
| **Dollars** | 241.00 | 260.83 | 212.16 | 242.38 | 179.60 | 195.02 | 265.54 | 293.34 |

NOTE: Northeast includes New England and Middle Atlantic states; Mideast, East North Central and West North Central states; South, South Atlantic, East South Central and West South Central states; and West, Mountain and Pacific states. Data exclude Puerto Rico.

*Average cost to patient per day for semiprivate hospital room by region* (Source: Source Book of Health Insurance Data, 1986-1987, *Health Insurance Association of America, Washington, D.C.)*

Figure 11–2

Table 11—2 *Number of persons with private health insurance protection in the United States by type of coverage (000 omitted)*

| End of year | Hospital expense | Major medical expense | Disability income | | Dental expense[†] |
|---|---|---|---|---|---|
| | | | Short-term | Long-term | |
| 1940 | 11,962 | — | N.A. | N.A. | — |
| 1945 | 32,072 | — | N.A. | N.A. | — |
| 1950 | 76,639 | — | 37,793 | * | — |
| 1955 | 101,400 | N.A. | 39,513 | * | — |
| 1960 | 122,500 | 32,590 | 42,436 | * | N.A. |
| 1961 | 125,825 | 41,974 | 43,055 | * | N.A. |
| 1962 | 129,407 | 48,393 | 45,002 | * | N.A. |
| 1963 | 133,472 | 55,382 | 44,246 | 3,029 | N.A. |
| 1964 | 136,304 | 62,112 | 45,092 | 3,363 | N.A. |
| 1965 | 138,671 | 69,666 | 46,927 | 4,514 | N.A. |
| 1966 | 142,369 | 73,843 | 49,931 | 5,068 | N.A. |
| 1967 | 146,409 | 81,550 | 51,975 | 6,778 | 4,570 |
| 1968 | 151,947 | 87,641 | 55,636 | 7,836 | 5,867 |
| 1969 | 155,025 | 95,528 | 57,770 | 9,282 | 8,858 |
| 1970 | 158,847 | 103,544 | 58,089 | 10,966 | 11,972 |
| 1971 | 161,849 | 108,813 | 59,280 | 12,284 | 15,263 |
| 1972 | 164,098 | 113,837 | 61,548 | 14,538 | 16,853 |
| 1973 | 168,455 | 124,627 | 64,168 | 17,011 | 20,418 |
| 1974 | 173,140 | 131,438 | 65,282 | 17,799 | 27,855 |
| 1975 | 178,180 | 134,092 | 62,971 | 18,396 | 30,337 |
| 1976 | 176,858 | 138,657 | 62,250 | 17,779 | 41,703 |
| 1977 | 179,853 | 139,884 | 64,627 | 19,364 | 50,737 |
| 1978 | 185,690 | 142,158 | 68,307 | 19,100 | 55,462 |
| 1979 | 185,743 | 148,805 | 65,808 | 19,920 | 61,608 |
| 1980 | 187,375 | 153,564 | 68,831 | 22,051 | 79,433 |
| 1981 | 186,193 | 153,676 | 65,301 | 22,582 | 83,245 |
| 1982 | 188,337 | 160,056 | 68,638 | 25,313 | 93,112 |
| 1983 | 186,644 | 159,612 | 64,146 | 24,655 | 100,828 |
| 1984 | 184,403 | N.A. | 59,332 | 22,944 | 102,159 |
| 1985 | 181,329 | N.A. | N.A. | 25,511 | 99,768 |
| 1986 | | | | | |
| Under 65 | 158,635 | 155,462 | N.A. | N.A. | N.A. |
| 65 and over | 21,204 | N.A. | N.A. | N.A. | N.A. |
| Total | 179,839 | N.A. | N.A. | 23,661 | 94,976 |

N.A.—Not available.

*Included in "Short-term," with the possibility of some duplication of disability income coverage for these years.

†Estimates on dental expense include fully-insured group plans, self-administered plans, plans employing third party administrators, and health maintenance organizations.

*Note:* Some data are revised from previous editions. Data for 1978 and later have been adjusted downward due to new data on average family size. For 1975 and later, data include the number of persons covered in Puerto Rico and U.S. territories and possessions. The data refer to the net total of people protected, i.e., duplication among persons protected by more than one kind of insuring organization or more than one insurance company policy providing the same type of coverage has been eliminated.

*Source: Source Book of Health Insurance Data, 1988,* Health Insurance Institute, p. 3.

them. Sometimes the company pays a given amount of dollars for certain types of operations. If the fee is above this figure, the person must pay the residual. The amount the policy will pay varies in accordance with the contract. Some policies state that reimbursable surgical fees will be based on reasonable, customary or prevailing charges for the particular procedure in that area. This makes for uncertainty, but usually a reimbursement schedule is developed based on charges normally or most frequently made by doctors in the area for a similar procedure.

Some plans require that a second medical opinion be obtained before they will pay the normal rate for a given operation. If a second opinion regarding the need for surgery is not obtained, a lesser amount is paid.

Medical expenses insurance, meant to provide for general medical expenses not covered by surgical and hospital plans, covers such items as drugs and visits to a doctor's office, as well as laboratory work. There may be provision for a maximum number of visits to a doctor per year, and there are also maximum dollar amounts—if not per illness or accident, then per year. Many of these plans have a schedule of fees indicating what they will pay for a given service. Others will pay what they consider to be the customary and reasonable charges for the services provided in that area.

*Medical expenses insurance*

Often these plans have a deductible of, say, $500 per year. The patient pays the first $500 of medical expenses per year and after that costs are usually shared, with the insurance company paying perhaps 80 percent and the patient 20 percent. This insurance will not usually cover visits to the doctor for regular checkups.

There are generally limits to the coverage provided by the basic hospital-surgical-medical plans discussed above. In such a case major medical takes over.

*Major medical expense or comprehensive insurance*

Major medical insurance covers virtually all medical expenses except dental work. It covers hospital fees, physicians' and surgeons' fees, laboratory work, drugs, and nursing care. It is in effect catastrophe insurance; if a person has very high medical bills because of a serious illness or accident, major medical coverage comes into force. Major medical insurance can be purchased on a group or individual basis, and can cover not only the individual but the entire family.

There are really two types of major medical plans. One supplements the basic hospital-surgical-medical plan discussed above. The other provides comprehensive protection, and the basic coverage and the major coverage are integrated. Indeed the term "major medical" is not even used any more in some policies.

Some major medical plans have lifetime limits on the amounts that can be collected, but these limits go up to $1 million or more.

*"Don't worry, we'll have you on your feet and out of here in no time. Your hospital insurance doesn't cover much."* (Source: *Permission Cartoon Features Syndicate;* from *The Wall Street Journal.*)

Some of the comprehensive plans even include dental coverage. More and more of the health insurance sold today is put into one comprehensive plan, reducing administrative and clerical costs and usually providing the policyholder with a better return on his or her premium dollar.

*Other (supplemental) coverage*

There are several other coverages that a few people buy. These are over and above the regular coverage just discussed, and are additional or supplemental coverage.

***Hospital confinement indemnity*** provides for the payment of a specific cash sum of so much per day, per week, or per month while the person is in the hospital. It is similar to—but should not be confused with—disability insurance discussed below. Indemnity insurance payments are short-term and often there is no waiting period before the payment is made, whereas disability insurance does have a waiting period and payments may be long-term. In addition, indemnity insurance pays a predetermined fixed amount per period, whereas the payment under disability insurance is usually a certain percentage of the person's income.

Insurance that covers only accidents may be purchased. Such a policy is not recommended because virtually all regular health policies include this.

Coverage may be obtained for one or a few specific diseases. It might cover such catastrophic and devastating diseases as cancer or heart disease.

There is also short-term coverage of a few months; this takes care of the gap between permanent coverage being arranged for and the termination of previous coverage. This gap could arise during moves from one job to another, or for graduating students who have not yet taken their first job.

Many companies are now offering dental insurance covering examinations, fillings, extractions, root canals, oral surgery, and most other dental work. There may be a limit to payments (usually $1,000) for expensive work such as orthodontics. There may also be yearly limits applied separately to each member of the family. The plans have a deductible amount; usually 80 percent of the costs above the deductible are paid by the insurance company and 20 percent by the insured. Some plans also have a proviso that they will not cover a routine examination more often than once every six months. Figure 11–3 shows dental expense protection in the United States.

*Dental insurance*

Most health insurance policies have a number of other provisions you should be aware of.

**COMMON PROVISIONS OF HEALTH INSURANCE**

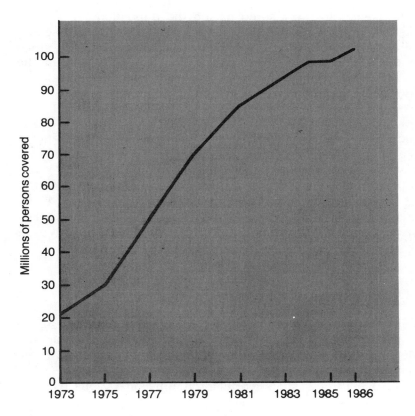

*Dental expense protection in the United States* (Source: **Source Book of Health Insurance Data, 1986-1987,** *Health Insurance Association of America, Washington, D.C.)*

Figure 11–3

*Deductible feature*

Generally health insurance policies have a **deductible** that the policyholder must pay, which may range anywhere from $100 to $500 or even higher. The higher the deductible, the lower the premium. If a policy has a $500 deductibility clause, this means the policyholder pays the first $500 of a medical bill. In most policies, the deductible feature applies on a yearly rather than on an illness basis. Therefore, once the person has paid a $500 deductible medical bill, all future medical expenses for the remainder of the year are submitted to the insurance company. Sometimes there is also a family deductible which may be less than the sum of the deductibles of the individual family members. For example, if a family of four is covered and the policy has a $500 individual deductible, every member does not need to meet the $500 before he or she is covered. Rather, once that family as a group has reached $2,000 (and sometimes even less), the deductible is considered satisfied for all family members.

*Copayments*

Most of the medical policies contain a **coinsurance** as well as a deductible feature, in accordance with which the company agrees to pay only a part of the total expense. Most companies agree to pay up to 80 percent of the cost, with the insured paying the remaining 20 percent. For example, assume a bill of $2,500 with a $500 deductible clause and an agreement on the part of the company to pay 80 percent of the total cost above the deductible; the company would pay $1,600, with the remainder to be paid by the insured ($2,500 total bill, minus $500, or $2,000 x .80 or $1,600, which is to be paid by the company).

*Copayment cap*

Some medical plans will pay 100 percent of all medical costs after a specific dollar amount has been achieved. The policy may pay 80 percent of the cost in excess of $500, and then 100 percent after the total yearly cost to the patient has reached, say, $1,000. The $1,000 then becomes the "cap" or what some call the "out-of-pocket" limit. For a person with a $500 deductible and a 20 percent copayment, this limit is reached when his or her medical bills reach $3,000. The insurance company pays

$$\$3,000 - \$500 = \$2,500 \times 80\% = \$2,000$$

and then 100 percent of any additional medical bills for the rest of the year.

This cap is very important. For example, a catastrophic illness can easily run your medical bills up to and even over several hundred thousand dollars. A 20 percent coinsurance feature without a cap could result in the insured paying tens of thousands of dollars.

Tables 11-3 and 11-4 show typical premiums on various types of policies and the possible out-of-pocket limits.

*Monthly premiums of various health plans*          Table 11—3

| | Monthly premiums | |
| --- | --- | --- |
| | Plan 1<br>$200 ded.<br>20% copayment | Plan 2<br>$500 ded.<br>20% copayment |
| Employee | $123.47 | $101.92 |
| Employee and spouse | 275.88 | 230.61 |
| Employee and children | 250.81 | 193.07 |
| Employee and family | 397.99 | 321.78 |

*Medical expense coverage*          Table 11—4

| | Plan 1 | Plan 2 |
| --- | --- | --- |
| Deductible | $200 | $  500 |
| Coinsurance limit | 500 | 500 |
| Out-of-pocket limit | 700 | 1,000 |

Most medical policies contain a maximum amount that the company will pay. Generally, this figure ranges from $50,000 to $100,000, but it may go as high as $500,000 or $1,000,000. These are usually lifetime limits. The limitation may also be written to cover any single illness or it may be written as a limitation for a year. The policy may read, for instance, that it will cover only $50,000 for any one illness, meaning that no matter how long the individual is hospitalized, the company will cease paying after the $50,000 has been used up. If the limitation applies to a policy year, then the company would make payments the following year in the event the policyholder was so unfortunate as to be hospitalized for that long.

*Limitations*

    Generally policies are written so that as the second policy year starts, the insured must first pay the deductible amount before the company becomes liable. In addition, as noted above, most policies have a lifetime limit. This lifetime limit is often several times the single illness or yearly limit, but may be much more. Figure 11–4 shows the growth of major medical insurance over the past few years.

One of the hazards we all face is the possibility that we will lose our ability to earn a livelihood temporarily or permanently due to a serious accident or illness. Some jobs themselves are dangerous; some on-the-job accidents could cripple a person for life. Certain illnesses can render

**DISABILITY INSURANCE OR LOSS OF INCOME**

Figure 11—4    *Major medical expense protection with insurance companies in the United States* (Source: Source Book of Health Insurance Data, 1986-1987, *Health Insurance Association of America, Washington, D.C.)*

a person incapable of working even after recovery. Even people in relatively safe occupations can suffer from accidents. An innocent victim might be crippled for life when some careless person runs his or her car over him. Indeed, some insurance executives believe that disability insurance is needed even more than life insurance. The probability of partial or total disability is greater than the probability of loss of life for relatively young people. Because of this likelihood, disability (often called loss of income) insurance was developed. It should be noted that most people already have some disability insurance under Social Security—this is discussed more fully in Chapter 18—but it is safe to say that Social Security disability benefits by themselves will seldom provide adequate funds.

In general, these policies are designed to cover loss of income either as the result of a temporary disability or as the result of permanent disability. The coverage will always be less than the actual earnings of the individual. If a person earns $500 per week, he or she cannot purchase a policy that would cover a loss of earnings of more than a certain percentage of that.[1]

More than a dozen varieties of limited disability insurance can be purchased to cover almost every situation imaginable. For example, an individual paying off a mortgage on a residence may purchase disability insurance to cover the mortgage payments. For a few dollars a month premium, depending on the age of the policyholder, the company will agree to make the monthly mortgage payments.

*Waiting period and length of payment*

These policies are written in different ways. Most have a waiting period before benefit payments begin, and this waiting period varies. They pay

---

1. Insurance companies will not sell a person a disability policy that pays more than about 60 or 70 percent (it varies from company to company) of his or her before-tax income, in part on the theory that if the person receives that much he or she has less (perhaps not any) incentive to overcome his or her disability.

a certain percentage (which varies) of earnings for various periods. Generally they can be grouped into those which provide short-term protection or long-term protection. The short-term policies provide benefits for various time periods up to two years; the long-term policies provide for protection for more than two years; some provide benefits for up to ten years and more. A few can provide benefits until the insured is age 65 or for a lifetime.

Premium rates vary in accordance with the above conditions; the longer the waiting period before payments begin, the lower the premiums, and the longer the period over which payments are made, the higher the premiums. The rates also vary with the occupation of the individual. Professionals and certain types of businesspeople find the premiums lower and the benefits more liberal than those for persons in more hazardous occupations.

*Dismemberment*

This type of policy also often contains a provision stating that for dismemberment the insured is to receive a lump sum equivalent to a stated number of weeks' indemnity in the case of being disabled permanently. For example, if an individual has a policy that provides for payment of $200 a week in the event of total disablement and then loses a leg in an accident, the policy may provide that the policyholder is to receive a lump-sum payment of one hundred weeks times $200, or $20,000. Where such a lump sum is received, the individual does not receive the weekly benefits provided for in the policy.

*Definition of disability*

Disability generally is defined in one of two ways. Some policies define the insured as disabled if he or she no longer has the capacity to be gainfully employed in any occupation. Other policies state that disability exists if the insured cannot perform in the previous occupation. As would be expected, with the latter definition of disability, premiums are more expensive.

*Rehabilitation*

Rehabilitation coverage may be included in a disability policy, or it may be purchased separately. This pays for the rehabilitation and retraining costs that often permit a person who otherwise might be disabled for life to become gainfully employed.

**HOW MUCH HEALTH INSURANCE TO BUY**

While life insurance is designed to protect the family economically in the event of the premature death of the breadwinner, much the same sort of economic catastrophe can result from a serious illness or accident. Indeed, a permanent disability may be more of a disaster than a death; not only is the income stream cut off, but expenses may rise. Consequently, along with life insurance, the individual needs protection against such contingencies as these.

*Medical insurance needs*

It is virtually impossible to determine precisely a person's (or family's) medical-expense insurance needs. This is because an individual cannot determine the extent of his or her potential loss due to illness or accident. Individuals cannot evaluate their health, because the cost, if they lose it, is unknown. It is strongly recommended that no breadwinner be without at least a major medical insurance policy. If one is able to obtain group insurance where one works, there is not really much choice in what kind of health insurance to buy. Usually a package is available, sometimes two or three different packages with varying benefits, so that an employee can choose from among them.

Persons who are not members of a group and hence not eligible for a group policy should consider individual policies. At the very least, everyone should have a major medical policy. The cost can be kept within reason if the person puts the deductible feature at $500. Shop around and compare the local Blue Cross-Blue Shield plan with what a private life insurance company can offer. Most insurance companies have several plans to choose from, generally referred to as Plan A, B, or C. The main differences are that the deductibles, coinsurance, and sometimes the yearly and lifetime limits vary. Naturally, the lower the deductible and the coinsurance, and the higher the limits, the higher the premiums. If one is young and healthy and on a tight budget, he or she might choose a higher deductible, but it is advised that one not skimp on annual and lifetime limitations.

*Catastrophic insurance needs*

Many major medical policies have relatively low limits. Moreover, even if a major medical policy has a $200,000 or $300,000 limit, that may not be enough. A person stricken with cancer or other deadly diseases can run up a bill of hundreds of thousands of dollars, and without coverage such a bill would devastate most families. Many experts believe catastrophic insurance is the most important protection of all. Many people overinsure for smaller, more normal costs by choosing a low deductible, and underinsure for catastrophe. It would be wise to take a higher deductible and invest the premiums saved in catastrophe insurance to provide for protection against the unlikely but catastrophic expenses should they occur.

Unless the client's major medical plan has at least a $1,000,000 limit, he or she should consider buying an "excess major medical" or catastrophic illness plan. Such plans are written with a deductible of $50,000, $100,000, or whatever the major medical plan limit may be, and take over when the other plans are exhausted. The good news is that such plans are amazingly cheap; premiums are about $100 per year for a young person. For older people, who perhaps need this type of insurance more, unfortunately rates are much higher.

*Disability insurance needs*

Disability insurance should also be high on the list of priorities. Persons who have access to a good group plan should seriously consider it. Even

*Growth of private health insurance in the United States* (Source: **Source Book of** Health Insurance Data, 1986-1987, *Health Insurance Association of America, Washington, D.C.*)

Figure 11—5

if it must be bought on an individual basis, it should still be high on the list of priorities, to assure a monthly income in the event that regular income is cut off due to a lengthy illness or serious accident. Often professional and other groups are able to obtain this sort of insurance at relatively low rates. Consequently, this is one of the most rapidly growing areas in the insurance industry. Figure 11–5 shows the growth of private health insurance in the United States.

To calculate the actual dollar amount of disability insurance needs, follow the same logic that was used when calculating life insurance needs. Since permanent disability terminates the income stream (just as does death), the amount of disability insurance could be calculated based on an individual's (or family) needs.[2]

To calculate disability insurance needs, follow these nine steps.

1. *Gross annual living expenses.* Determine gross annual living expense requirements as shown in Chapter 10 in analyzing life insurance needs. This figure could be based on the budget or income statement, discussed in Chapters 2 and 3. Or it could be the after-tax income in some cases and the after Social Security tax income in all cases.

Disability payments are taxed in some cases, not in others. See Chapter 7, section on disability income exclusion. Generally, however, disability payments are taxed if there is a group plan with the employer, who pays all or some of the premiums. They are not taxed if a person has an individual plan for which he or she pays the premiums. If the disability benefits are not taxed, subtract the tax liabilities from gross living needs. Social Security taxes too would be eliminated in the event of disability and must be netted out.

---

2. Insurance needs could, of course, be calculated based on the present value of the future income stream, or the multiple income approach could be used as in the case of life insurance. However, we concluded in Chapter 10 that the needs concept is best.

The gross living expenses would then be further reduced by the following items.

2. *Reduced living expenses stemming from disability.* Transportation costs, lunch expenses, possibly entertainment, and other costs associated with holding a job would be eliminated or reduced.

3. *Insurance premium waivers.* Life insurance premiums would be eliminated if there is a disability premium waiver clause. Mortgage payments would be eliminated if there is a policy that paid off the mortgage in the event of death or disability.

4. *Social Security.* Social Security disability benefit payments are not taxable in many cases (see Chapter 7) and should reduce living expenses further. Check with a local Social Security office to obtain an estimate of what one's Social Security benefits will be.

5. *Spouse's income.* Spouse's current income (if working), or expected future income if spouse were to go back to work in the event of a disability.

6. *Other disability benefit payments.* This would include such things as a corporate pension plan where one works.

7. *Investment income.* Investment income would continue; hence it must be accounted for.

8. *Total adjustment.* Add up all of the adjustments above that apply to the individual (items 2 through 7).

9. *Actual disability needs.* Subtract the dollar amount in item 8 from item 1. This is a realistic figure of the actual need.

All of the items (2 through 7) may not apply in every case. One may or may not have insurance premium waivers. We have also made no allowance for

1. paying off other debts,
2. a college fund,
3. an emergency fund, and
4. savings plans for retirement or other goals.

These items could be taken care of under item 1—gross annual living expenses—in which case they would remain part of the personal family budget, although conceivably they could be taken into account by insurance; then the disability insurance needs would be greater. Table

11–5 shows the disability insurance requirements of a hypothetical Mr. and Mrs. X.

A person may also wish to adjust his or her disability insurance needs to allow for future inflation. This may be done by buying a disability policy that has an annual cost-of-living adjustment (COLA) built into it. While the premiums on such a policy are higher, it will provide for an annual escalation of benefits by 4, 5, 6, or 7 percent, or whatever is agreed upon.

One may also build inflation protection into a policy himself or herself but this would entail buying more insurance than the $4,000 shown in Table 11-5. If we assume a long-run inflation rate of 5 percent and a twenty-year disability requirement, we can get the inflationary factor. It is 33.066. It indicates that if we start with one dollar, and we add one additional dollar each year, and the entire sum is growing by 5 percent per year, it will amount to $33.066 at the end of twenty years. Multiplying that by $4,000, we find that the total disability payout over twenty years will amount to $132,264. Dividing this last figure by twenty years, we obtain $6,613, which is the average disability insurance payout per year over the entire period—that is, the disability insurance needs of Mr. and Mrs. X adjusted for inflation. Currently their needs are $4,000, but this will rise to $10,612 in the twentieth year, if inflation continues at 5 percent. If they make arrangements for $6,613.00 per year, they will have a surplus during the early years ($2,613 the first year). They should put this surplus in an interest-bearing account, and then it becomes a reserve that can be used in later years when their needs rise above $6,613. Providing for disability income of $6,613 yields slightly more than $4,000 in real terms over the years, assuming 5 percent inflation, because there will be interest on the surplus during the early years. However, this provides a hedge in the event that inflation rises above 5 percent. If the time period is increased to 25 or 30 years, the disability insurance needs rise to $7,636 and $8,859 respectively. These calculations are shown in Table 11–6.

*Disability insurance needs of Mr. and Mrs. X*  Table 11—5

| | | |
|---|---:|---:|
| 1. Gross annual living expenses (adjusted as necessary for taxes) | | $24,000 |
| 2. Reduction in living expenses | $ 800 | |
| 3. Insurance premium waivers | 700 | |
| 4. Social Security benefits received | 8,000 | |
| 5. Spouse's income | 10,000 | |
| 6. Other disability benefits | — | |
| 7. Investment income | 1,000 | |
| 8. Total adjustments (deductions) | $20,500 | |
| 9. Actual annual disability needs | | $ 4,000 |

Table 11—6   *Disability insurance needs of $4,000 adjusted for inflation of 5 percent*

---

Disability insurance need                                               $4,000
  (in real terms)

Inflation: 5 percent
  Inflation factor 20 years = 33.066
  $4,000 × 33.066 = $132,264 ÷ 20 years = $6,613*

  Inflation factor 25 years = 47.727
  $4,000 × 47.727 = 190,908 ÷ 25 years = $7,636*

  Inflation factor 30 years = 66.439
  $4,000 × 66.439 = 265,756 ÷ 30 years = $8,859*

---

*Since in insurance, companies will not sell a policy that pays more than 60 to 70 percent of the person's income, the maximum amount of benefits our hypothetical person with income of $24,000 could purchase is $24,000 × 70% or $16,800. This is far more than he or she needs.

## OTHER IMPORTANT THINGS ABOUT HEALTH INSURANCE

There are a number of other important matters about health insurance that will now be discussed.

### Items not covered

Certain medical expenses are not always covered by health insurance.
  Some policies cover psychiatric care; some do not. Those that do often set a special limit on this item. Abortions may or may not be covered. The cost of regular checkups is usually not covered nor are the costs of eyeglasses and eye examinations, but treatment of eye disease or eye surgery is. Vasectomies may or may not be covered; the same is true of surgery to correct natural deformities—such as a clubfoot, or cosmetic surgery. The trend is toward broader coverage in these areas, however.

### 100 percent coverage

Since health insurance policies have a coinsurance clause that pays usually only 80 percent of the medical bills, can a person buy two policies and then receive benefits in excess of expenses? The answer is no, but one may collect more than if one had only one policy. There are, however, only a few cases where a person could get two group policies, although one could buy two individual policies; but individual policies have substantially higher premiums. Where both husband and wife work and both are eligible for group insurance, they could have two policies. Or in rare cases persons could have two group plans if they had one with their employer and another one with a professional association such as the American Accounting Association.
  How would two such policies pay off if there were a claim? One policy would be classified as the primary policy; it would pay first in

accordance with its terms, and the other policy would then pay part or all of the rest. In nearly all cases the primary policy is the one obtained with the employer. In the case of a husband-wife team, the primary policy would be the one from the employer of the person in the family making the claim.

Suppose a person has two policies, both with a $100 deductible and an 80 percent coinsurance clause: assume a claim is filed for $1,100. The primary carrier would pay 80 percent of $1,000 or $800. The secondary carrier would then pay all or part of the remaining $300, depending upon what the contract said regarding secondary claims. It could be 80 percent of the $300; 80 percent of $200 ($300 less the deductible), or 80 percent of $1,000, just as the primary carrier, with a limit of $300. In no case could a person get more than 100 percent coverage and in many cases it would be less. For this reason, it almost never pays to have two policies; a person pays double premiums and gets only marginal added protection.

*Group plans: the modern way to buy health insurance*

Any of the plans discussed above can be obtained on a group or individual basis. A group plan actually amounts to wholesaling insurance, and the features are the same as if an individual were to purchase his or her own policy. As a group member, however, one generally has the benefit of lower rates than if one were to purchase the policy on one's own.

There are a number of reasons why the rates are more favorable to the group, one being that there is a more favorable selection of risks. When it insures the group, the company usually insists that at least 75 percent of those eligible must join. Moreover, those who do join do not come with the idea that they will receive immediate benefits; and there are few cancellations. In some cases, the employee has no choice but to take the group insurance; it is a condition of employment. In other cases, it is voluntary, and it is in these cases that the insurance companies insist that the policy is not effective until 75 percent of the eligible employees have joined. Another reason for more favorable rates is that administrative costs are lower. As to collections, the employer customarily withholds the amount of the premiums from the employee's paycheck. The commission paid to the agent who sells the group policy is lower than if he or she were to sell the same number of policies individually.

Frequently group health policies are a part of the so-called fringe benefits in labor-management contracts. Often the employer pays all or a part of the premiums and agrees to handle much of the paperwork through the personnel office.

There is a growing trend toward the group method of meeting insurance needs, true not only of health insurance, but also of life insurance. The pattern today is to have one package negotiated on a group basis, which would then include some sort of a comprehensive health plan as described above together with some term insurance, all under one plan.

**Guaranteed renewable and noncancelable policies**

In some cases, the insurance company retains the right to refuse to renew the policy when it expires. Indeed, sometimes the company has the right to cancel at any time during the term of the policy. It is, however, possible to buy guaranteed renewable and noncancelable policies. A **guaranteed renewable policy** can be renewed until some predetermined age is reached, generally age sixty-five. However, each time it is renewed, premiums for a class of insureds can be increased if warranted.

A **noncancelable** policy is one that cannot be canceled during the time it was originally stated to run, and during the time, premiums cannot be raised. Therefore, if a person buys a policy that is both noncancelable and renewable, the premiums cannot be raised during the period over which the policy runs. When the period is over, the policy must be renewed if the policyholder so chooses, but premiums can be raised.

**How to apply for benefits**

It is easy to apply for benefits under most health insurance plans. Every person with a health insurance plan receives a wallet-sized card from the insurance company. A person in a group plan has a group number and a certificate number on the card. With a hospital bill often the hospital staff will fill out the form and send it in. With a doctor's bill or reimbursement for drugs, the insured must often fill out the form, but it is self-explanatory. Since in many cases the insurance company pays only part of the bill, instructions are sent indicating how much the patient is to pay above the insurance claim. Until a few years ago, companies often paid the doctor directly. Now more and more companies are paying the patient who in turn pays the doctor.

**When retired: supplemental plans**

Most insurance companies, including Blue Cross-Blue Shield, now have supplemental plans for retired individuals who are covered by Medicare because Medicare does not pay all bills. These supplemental plans are designed to pay a portion of those costs not covered by Medicare. They work very much like regular plans in that they may have deductible features and coinsurance. That is, they treat that portion of the retired person's medical bill not covered by Medicare just as they would some other person's total bill. Because they provide less coverage, their premiums are, of course, lower.

**Blue Cross-Blue Shield**

In addition to being able to buy health insurance policies from profit-making life insurance companies, one can purchase health protection from the nonprofit Blue Cross-Blue Shield organization. Blue Cross-Blue Shield plans are not health insurance, technically speaking.

The policy one might buy from an insurance company is an indemnity contract and the company pays the insured what he or she is entitled to under the contract. Blue Cross-Blue Shield is a service benefit plan whereby the hospital or physician is paid directly by Blue Cross-Blue Shield. In a sense the hospital and medical expenses are prepaid.

Blue Cross is a cooperative nonprofit organization through which members prepay hospital bills. Under Blue Cross some hospitals have agreed to provide certain services for the members who prepay a monthly fee to the organization. Blue Shield is a similar nonprofit organization designed to pay physicians' expenses. The latter is sponsored by groups of physicians, and for the most part Blue Cross handles the details of selling, billing, and collecting for Blue Shield. Blue Cross-Blue Shield also provides major medical protection, the comprehensive plan discussed above, and in some areas dental insurance and even disability insurance—in fact, most of the health coverage that other insurance companies provide.

*Blue Cross*

The payments for a Blue Cross policy depend on area; in some states, the cost of hospitalization is more expensive than in others. More important, the rates depend on the type of contract one purchases, for some contracts provide more benefits than others. In addition, rates vary depending on whether one purchases the insurance as a member of a group or singly. The period of hospitalization covered varies from plan to plan. There is also usually a limit to how much Blue Cross will pay per day for a hospital room, but generally it is the cost of a semiprivate room.

In addition, most of the plans pay all charges for operating room, recovery room, cast room, and cystoscopic room, plus all drugs in general use.

Under most Blue Cross and Blue Shield plans anyone under the age of sixty-five may enroll on an individual basis, and no physical examination is required. The policies are noncancelable except for nonpayment of dues or the fraudulent use of the membership.

When persons retire and draw Social Security, they may keep or lose their Blue Cross-Blue Shield depending on the local plan. However, more and more plans are adopting the modified Blue Cross-Blue Shield plan for retired people who wish to retain it, a policy consisting of reduced coverage (and reduced premiums), intended to complement Medicare.

*Blue Shield*

While Blue Cross is designed to cover hospitalization, Blue Shield is designed to cover physicians' fees, whether surgical, surgical-medical, or general medical. Like Blue Cross, the basic rates of Blue Shield vary from state to state and from plan to plan. Most plans agree to pay the physician according to a basic schedule. The physician might charge $600 for services, and the Blue Shield payment schedule might call for a payment of $450. In such a case the subscriber would pay the balance of $150.

How much will be paid for a given operation varies from one section of the country to another. Also there are usually two or three different packages to choose from. A purchaser who is willing to pay a higher premium can obtain a higher surgical fee schedule. More and more plans, however, do not list the dollar amounts they will pay for a given operation but they state they will pay "reasonable and customary" surgical fees. That is, in effect they pay the bill the surgeon submits, unless it is deemed unreasonable.

Most Blue Cross-Blue Shield plans have a deductible clause as well as a coinsurance clause on their plan, just like the private insurance company plans. They also have a family rate and a lower rate for only a husband and wife, and a still lower rate for a single person. As noted above, Blue Cross-Blue Shield also has a major medical plan which covers major illnesses.

*Health maintenance organizations (HMOs)*

In recent years another type of medical expense protection has developed through **health maintenance organizations.** This method provides many of the same benefits as health insurance. It consists of group pre-payment medical plans, often organized as nonprofit co-ops. These provide medical care for their members for a fixed fee per month. These groups own and operate clinics and hospitals and hire doctors, nurses, and other technicians. The professional medical personnel, including doctors, are paid an annual salary; consequently there is no set fee for each particular service. Membership may also be possible on an individual basis; but in order to join a person obviously must live in a geographical area where there is an HMO. Some of the more well-known plans are the Health Insurance Plan of Greater New York, Kaiser Foundation Health Plan, Ross-Loos Medical Group of Los Angeles, Community Health Association of Detroit, and the Group Health Cooperative of Puget Sound.

These group plans can provide most of the benefits that their members need from their own resources. If the services of a specialist are needed and none of the group's doctors qualifies, the group hires an outside specialist on a fee basis. The group cannot provide disability insurance internally, but many HMO's buy that for their members from an insurance company.

These organizations also practice preventive medicine, and have been established recently as a hopeful alternative to costly medical care. The theory behind this preventive medicine is that it is cheaper, both moneywise and in human suffering, to prevent illnesses than to cure them after they are well established. This process involves periodic medical checkups and screening programs to detect early warning signs of health breakdowns. Most of the HMOs offer more comprehensive coverage than most regular group insurance plans. Not only do they provide for regular medical checkups, but many of them have neither a deductible feature nor a coinsurance clause. That is, 100 percent of all medical expenses are taken care of.

In recent years some insurance companies have established HMOs. One of the more well known is Prucare. Some of these insurance HMOs require copayments—a small fee, usually $10 or $15 for each visit to the doctor, in addition to the fixed monthly fee. When drugs are purchased, the person may also pay up to about $10 per prescription. These copayments are much smaller than the coinsurance cost that must be paid when a person has a policy with an insurance company. All other costs, including full hospitalization and surgery, are covered, including drugs administered in the hospital.

Evidence suggests that HMOs reduce medical costs because the medical dollar goes directly to the doctor; there is no (or at least there is less) expensive bureaucracy siphoning off dollars. While the salaried doctors working for an HMO generally make less money than doctors in private practice, they seem happy because they work fewer hours and they have more regular schedules.

Another advantage of HMOs is that bothersome forms to file a claim are not needed as they are when an individual has regular health insurance.

The major disadvantage, the critics of HMOs claim, is that one does not have complete control over the choice of physician. Rather, one must be chosen from the group who works for the HMO.

*Individual practice associations (IPAs)*

IPAs are a relatively new innovation which is growing very rapidly. In essence, they are a modified HMO. However, they are slightly different, and they often provide the individual with a wider choice of physicians.

Under this plan, a group of doctors gets together and offers its services to members of the IPA. The association works very much like an HMO. The IPA members pay a fixed fee per month for all their health care needs, plus a small fee (usually about $10) for each office visit, and a small charge for drugs. The doctors, however, while paid by the IPA, are not employees of the IPA and are not on a fixed salary. Their income is dependent on the number of patients and the type of service they provide. They are self-employed, maintain their own office, staff, nurses, and so forth, and have both IPA and non-IPA patients.

In most cases there is a much larger number of doctors to choose from by belonging to an IPA.

**MEDICARE**

Probably the most far-reaching of the 1965 amendments to the Social Security Law was the Medicare provision. It provided for two kinds of health insurance for those over age sixty-five: hospital insurance and medical insurance. The hospital insurance has come to be known as Part A of Medicare and the medical insurance as Part B. Practically everyone sixty-five or older is eligible for the entire Medicare program.

Certain individuals get Part A (hospital insurance) automatically and need not pay for it. Moreover, these people get this insurance even if they are still working and hence not drawing Social Security; the test is to be over sixty-five and eligible for Social Security. The following people are all eligible for Part A of Medicare:

1.  Everyone over sixty-five and eligible for Social Security or railroad retirement benefits.
2.  Disabled people under sixty-five who have been getting Social Security disability benefits for two years or more.
3.  People insured under Social Security (but not yet getting benefits because they are under sixty-five) who need dialysis treatment or a

kidney transplant. Wives, husbands, and children of insured people under sixty-five may also be eligible if they need kidney dialysis or transplants. Moreover, these people receive all the benefits of Part A until one year after they no longer have the above-described kidney problems, e.g., a successful kidney transplant.

Those who are eligible and hence are automatically covered for Part A (hospital insurance) are not covered automatically for Part B. It is optional and may be purchased at a cost of $31.80 per month in 1992. (This cost is increased by Congress periodically. Check with the local Social Security office for the current figure.) The premiums are withheld from the retirement check of those drawing Social Security, whereas others must send them to their Social Security Field Office, on a quarterly basis.

*Hospital insurance (Part A)*

The hospital insurance provides for the following three broad classes of benefits:

All but the first $652 of hospital costs are paid by Medicare for the first sixty days of hospitalization. The $652, then, is the deductible feature. After 60 days a copayment (coinsurance) is required. This copayment rises in two steps. From the 61st to the 90th day, the patient pays $163 per day; this rises to $326 per day from the 91st to the 150th day. After that the Medicare patient is on his or her own. Consequently, while Medicare helps, a lengthy hospital stay can be expensive. Post-hospital extended care in a skilled nursing facility is available, free for 20 days, then a coinsurance payment of $81.50 per day up to a maximum of 80 days. Home health services and hospice care are also offered. The deductible feature, the coinsurance, and other pertinent facts about Medicare are changed by Congress almost yearly. Check with the local social security field office for the latest figures.

*Medical insurance (Part B)*

Medical insurance (Part B) covers treatment by physicians, as well as diagnostic tests, physical therapy, and blood transfusions. There is also a deductible, which is currently $100 per year. After that Medicare will pay 80 percent of what is referred to as the "Medicare approved" amount, which is a set amount for the various types of services. The rub is that most doctors charge more than Medicare has approved and the patient has to pay the difference.

However, there are some physicians (participating physicians) who have agreed to charge Medicare patients no more than the approved amount. Those doctors should be sought out. There is a directory of participating physicians that may be purchased from the Social Security field offices. Unfortunately, only a minority of the nation's physicians (about 20 percent currently) have agreed to participate.

Supplemental policies were discussed earlier in this chapter. Many of *Medigap policies*
these were designed specifically for Medicare patients. These should be
investigated before retirement because some are excellent, while others
are not so good.

It is also possible, if an individual is working but approaching
sixty-five, that he or she may be able to convert the employer-provided
health plan to an individual Medigap policy.

There are all kinds of health insurance plans; some are excellent, some **HOW GOOD IS A**
good, and some only fair. However, it is generally true that the quality **HEALTH**
of the policy is closely related to the premiums paid. Nevertheless, the **INSURANCE**
quality of a policy can be appraised by studying the following guidelines, **PLAN?**
and answering each question

1. What is the hospital room and board coverage?                           *Guidelines to*
   $200 to $300 per day is not too much.                                    *evaluate the*
   Full cost of semiprivate room is an important benefit.                   *quality of a health*
   Is there an extra intensive care coverage?                               *insurance plan*
2. Does it cover other hospital costs: X-ray, laboratory fees, drugs,
   anesthesia?
   Full coverage?
   Partial coverage?
3. What is the surgical coverage?
   Set fees for various procedures? What are they?
   Reasonable and customary fees with a limit?
   Reasonable and customary fees with no limit?
4. What is the basic medical coverage?
   Is there an overall dollar limit? If so, what is it?
   What is the deductible?
   What is the coinsurance?
   Does it have a coinsurance cap?
5. What is the major medical coverage?
   What is the deductible?
   What is the coinsurance?
   What is the annual limit?
   What is the per accident or per illness limit?
   What is the lifetime limit?
6. What is the limit on the catastrophic coverage? What is its deduct-
   ible?
7. What kind of disability coverage does the individual have?
   What is the waiting period before benefits are received?
   How long will benefits be paid?
   How is disability defined? A policy that defines disability as
   being unable to perform the regular duties of the person's *own*
   occupation is superior to a policy stating *any* occupation.

**8.** What are the premiums on the policies?

**9.** Is the policy noncancelable and guaranteed renewable? If so, the insurance company cannot terminate it.

**10.** Does the policy contain a waiver of premiums in the event of disability? Better policies do.

## SUGGESTED READINGS

Beam, Burton T., Jr. *Group Insurance: Basic Concepts and Alternatives*. Bryn Mawr, Pa.: The American College, 1984.

Berstein, Joan Z., and Harris, Lucy R. *Health Maintenance Organizations: Opportunities and Problems*. New York: F & S Press, 1983.

*Best's Review, Life-Health Edition*. Oldwick, N.J.: A. M. Best Company, Inc. Monthly publication.

Birenbaum, Arnold. *Health Care and Society*. Totowa, N.J.: Allanheld, Osmun and Co., 1983.

Black, Kenneth, and Skipper, Harold. *Life Insurance*, 11th ed. Englewood Cliffs, N.J.: Prentice-Hall, 1987.

*Blue Cross-Blue Shield Fact Book*. Chicago: National Association of Blue Shield Plans. Annual publication.

*Blue Cross Reports*. Chicago: Blue Cross Association. Quarterly publication.

*A Brief Explanation of Medicare*. Publication No. (SSA) 73-10043. Washington, D.C.: Department of Health, Education and Welfare.

Cockerell, Hugh. *Lloyd's of London*. Homewood, Ill.: Dow Jones-Irwin, 1984.

Davis, Karen. *National Health Insurance: Benefits, Costs, and Consequences*. Washington, D.C.: The Brookings Institution, 1985.

Dorfman, Mark S. *Introduction to Insurance*, 3rd ed. Englewood Cliffs, N.J.: Prentice Hall, 1987.

"Duplicate Coverage." Pamphlet published by Blue Cross-Blue Shield. No date.

Eusebio, Thomas C. *Guide to Health Insurance*. Indianapolis, Ind.: Rough Notes Co., 1985.

Follmann, J. F., Jr. "Dental Care Coverage." *Best's Insurance News*.

*Health Insurance for People 65 and Older*. Washington, D. C.: U. S. Department of Health, Education and Welfare. You may obtain a free copy from a Social Security field office, which can be found in any large city.

"How to Shop for Health Insurance." Pueblo, Colo.: Consumer Information Center.

*Inquiry, A Journal of Medical Care Organization, Provision and Financing*. Chicago: Blue Cross Association.

*Insurance Review*. New York: The Insurance Information Institute. Monthly publication.

"The Journal of Insurance." New York: The Insurance Information Institute. Bimonthly publication.

Mehr, Robert I., and Cammack, Emerson. *Principles of Insurance*. Homewood, Ill. Irwin, 1985.

*National Underwriter*. Chicago: The National Underwriter Co. Weekly publication.

*Source Book of Health Insurance*. New York: The Health Insurance Institute. Annual publication.

Vaughan, Emmet J. *Fundamentals of Risk and Insurance*, 5th ed. New York: John Wiley and Sons, 1988.

*Your Medicare Handbook*. Publication Number (HCFA) 79-10050. Baltimore, Md.: Department of Health and Human Services, 1986.

# 12 Property and liability risk and insurance

**HIGHLIGHTS**

In order to help plan an insurance program for the home and the automobile, this chapter will cover the following:

1 Liability and what it means
2 The general concept of insurance on the home and how it works through the homeowner's policy
3 Liability insurance on the home
4 The deductible clause, the coinsurance clause, and how they apply to the home
5 The home insurance program
6 Automobile insurance—how it works, and what it covers
7 No-fault insurance
8 Other things the reader should know about auto insurance
9 An auto insurance program

## INTRODUCTION: WHAT IS THE RISK?

Individuals who own a home (or even rent an apartment) are exposed to two risks. They are:

1. Loss of assets (property) due to various perils.
2. Loss of assets (savings) as a result of liability claims against a person.

An individual is exposed to the same two risks if he or she owns an automobile or a boat, or even if only driving one. These risks may be transferred to an insurance company by purchasing the following policies:

Home protection (both protected by a homeowner's policy)
1. To protect property
2. To protect against liability

Automobile protection (both protected by an automobile insurance policy)
1. To protect property
2. To protect against liability

Other protection (all provided by specialty insurance)
1. Boat
2. Mobile home
3. Earthquake
4. Flood
5. Malpractice

Property is subject to physical destruction from a number of hazards, such as fire, flood, theft, and others. Equally likely is the possibility that a person will destroy or damage someone else's property, as in an automobile accident. Property insurance reimburses for the value of destroyed property. A policyholder should have property insurance for both personal and real property. **Personal property** includes such things as furniture, automobiles, and clothing. **Real property** includes any buildings attached to land, such as a house or garage.

Liability insurance protects the insured against claims by others. Liability can be broken down into claims by others due to bodily injury or death, and to claims due to the destruction of the property of others.

People can be killed or injured on the insured's property, and the policyholder can be liable for these claims. Liability insurance is also necessary for those who drive automobiles, since automobile accidents often result in bodily injury as well as property damage.

Property and liability insurance premium payments should be regarded as payment for the protection of family material assets. The premiums paid on an insurance policy on a home are protection in the event of the destruction of the home by fire or some other disaster. A person who runs over someone with an auto exposes the family assets to loss by lawsuit.

Liability is related to negligence. If one can show that there was absolutely no negligence on his or her part, any lawsuit against the person would have less chance of success. However, this is often difficult to prove. Negligence is the failure to exercise reasonable and necessary care to protect others from harm or to protect their property from damage or destruction.

A person could be negligent while driving a car; a person could also be negligent for not remedying a hazard on his or her property—for example, not repairing a broken step over which someone trips. One could also be negligent if his or her dog injured someone while running down the street.

The courts are not always consistent in defining reasonable and necessary care. There is also the concept of contributory negligence, which is often used by the defendant in a lawsuit. Contributory negligence theory holds that the plaintiff contributed to the event, causing damages by also being negligent.

The principle of property and liability insurance is much like the principle behind term life insurance. The risk of loss is spread over many units, and those few who actually suffer a loss are reimbursed by the insurance company—but indirectly by those policyholders who do not suffer a loss.

## INSURANCE ON THE HOME

If a home burns down, it could be a financial disaster for the owner. There are other hazards the home owner faces that should be insured against, such as damage due to wind, flood, smoke, theft, or people running over lawns and shrubs with cars.

There is also the possibility that people will be injured on the client's property, resulting in a lawsuit and making him or her liable for damages. Or one could damage a neighbor's property, making him or her liable. An individual may be protected against all these hazards by means of the homeowner's policy.[1]

### The homeowner's policy

The homeowners policy provides five major kinds of insurance: (1) property insurance on the home, (2) personal property insurance, (3) liability insurance for bodily injury to others, (4) medical payment insurance, and (5) property liability insurance for damage to the property of others.

Most homeowner's policies have a Section I—which is the property section—and a Section II—which is the liability section.

---

1. There is also a special homeowner's policy for renters, which will be discussed below.

Section I covers:

1. Damage to the house due to fire, wind, hail, falling objects, smoke, motor vehicles, and a number of other perils, plus an allowance for living expenses in the event that the home owner has to live elsewhere for a time while the damaged home is being repaired.
2. Personal property insurance for loss of personal property due to fire, theft, mysterious disappearance, and so forth.

Section II provides:

1. Personal liability insurance to cover injuries occurring on the home owner's property.
2. Medical payment insurance to cover the medical bills of persons injured on the home owner's premises.
3. Property liability insurance to cover damage to the property of others.

Most insurance companies have several types of homeowner's policy packages to choose from, with names such as limited, basic, broad, all-inclusive, or all-risk. They are referred to as policies HO-1, HO-2, and so on. Generally the breadth of the extended coverage increases as one moves from policy 1 to policy 5; the premiums also increase.[2] The following seven HO policies are in general use:

1. Basic form (HO-1)
2. Broad form (HO-2)
3. All-risk (on home only) or special form (HO-3)
4. Contents broad form (HO-4) renters' insurance (HO-4)
5. Comprehensive form (all-risk on both home and personal property) (HO-5)
6. Condominium broad form (for condominium owners) (HO-6)
7. Modified coverage form (for older homes) (HO-8)[3]

*Breadth of coverage*

Under the homeowner's policies the breadth of the coverage will vary depending on the policy.

*1. HO-1 basic coverage.* Homeowner's policy HO-1 (basic) covers the fewest items, but it covers more than just fire. It usually includes damage due to wind, hail, vehicles, and a number of other factors. With damage

---

2. The HO-1, etc. classification is generally used; however, in Texas and a few other southern states, the HO-A, HO-B, etc. classification is used.

3. There is no HO-7 policy. No one really knows why, but when the insurance industry developed the HO-8 policy, it skipped the number HO-7. Some companies have eliminated the HO-5 policy by adding its additional protection to the HO-3 policy. Some companies are also phasing out the HO-1 policy because more and more people are choosing HO-2.

to a roof due to hail, however, the basic policy will not pay for the cost of a new roof. Rather, the damaged roof will first be depreciated, and the policy will pay for a lesser amount of damages. For example, if the roof was ten years old when it was destroyed, and it is assumed it had a useful life of twenty years, the policy will pay for one-half of the cost of a new roof.

*2. HO-2 broad coverage.* Under the broad coverage more perils are covered. In addition to the items under HO-1, damage from such things as falling objects, a collapsed roof due to the weight of snow or ice, and a number of other items is covered. Under the broad (HO-2) policy a hail-damaged roof is not first depreciated, and the policy pays for the entire cost of a new roof.

While nearly all homeowner's policies cover losses due to theft, in the case of the **broad** and **all-risk policies,** coverage is more generous. For example, they would pay for what is called mysterious disappearance, whereas the HO-1 would not; HO-1 requires proof of theft such as break-in or the like, whereas the broad or all-risk policy does not.

Some homeowner's policies also provide for living expenses if the home owner has to move into a hotel because the home has been so severely damaged that it is uninhabitable. If part of a home is rented, the fair rental value will be paid while the tenant vacates the home during repairs. There is a limit to the living expense allowance; usually it is a certain percentage of total dollar protection of the policy.

*3. HO-3 special form, all-risk coverage.* This form covers all risks except those specifically excluded, but it applies only to the house and not personal property. Generally personal property is covered under this plan only to the extent that it is in HO-2. (However, some companies sell a rider which broadens the HO-3 coverage to include personal belongings.) Generally HO-3 covers all risks except flood, earthquake, war, nuclear radiation, volcanic eruption, and any others specified in the policy. A person should check the policy for a complete list of perils excluded.

*4. HO-4 contents broad form.* This is renters' insurance. This provides no insurance on the building, which is normally the landlord's problem. It provides only personal property and liability coverage. Renters do need a personal liability policy. Even if a person is renting a house and the owner has such a personal liability policy, it generally applies only if the landlord is living in the house and it does not always protect the renter. If someone were to trip on the sidewalk and break his or her leg, the renter could be held liable.

*5. HO-5 comprehensive form, all-risk coverage.* This provides for all-risk coverage except that which is specifically excluded. It is very much like HO-3, except that it covers personal property as well as the building. HO-3, you will recall, provides all-risk coverage only to the building, and covers personal property only to the extent that HO-2 does. As noted above, some companies no longer offer the HO-5 policy.

*6. HO-6 condominium-owner broad form.*   This provides only personal property and personal liability coverage. It does not cover the building because the condominium association has separate insurance on the building. It does, however, cover built-in appliances such as ranges, dishwashers, rugs, and the like that the condominium association's insurance would not cover.

*7. HO-8 modified coverage form.*   This is similar to HO-1 in that losses are paid on the basis of actual cash value rather than replacement cost. It is designed for older homes, where the replacement cost is much higher than the market value of the home. Often neither the home owner nor the insurer would be willing to insure a home valued at $75,000 for $150,000, which might be its replacement cost. Hence Form HO-8 was developed as a compromise.

*Section I coverage: property*

This section provides against the destruction of property and the coverage varies somewhat from policy to policy. Generally, coverage is superior as one moves from HO-1, to HO-2, to HO-3, and so on.

1. *The house.*   Section I covers the dwelling for the various hazards discussed above. Most insurance requires coverage of at least 80 percent of the replacement cost of the home, but some require as much as 100 percent. See below for a more detailed discussion of this.

2. *Other structures.*   Most homeowner's policies cover "other detached structures" on the property, such as tool sheds, garages, and the like. Some policies also include fences. The coverage here is limited to a percentage of the protection on the house. Other structures are generally not covered, if they are used for business purposes or are rented to someone other than a tenant.

3. *Loss of use.*   This item concerns additional living expenses incurred by a home owner because his or her house was destroyed or otherwise made uninhabitable. It covers increased costs for housing, transportation, and other items that must be met while the home is being repaired. The limit for this item is a certain percent of the protection on the structure.

   If part of the home is rented, the fair rental value will be paid while the tenant vacates the house during repairs.

4. *Personal property coverage.*   Personal property is covered under a homeowner's policy along with real property. This covers loss of furni-

ture, clothing, cameras, rugs, drapes, furs, books, paintings, jewelry, and the like. It provides protection not only against fire but also against loss due to theft, vandalism, and in some cases mysterious disappearance. This type of policy also insures for loss of items away from the home. For example, a camera stolen from an automobile is covered by the personal property clause. This personal property coverage is written in different ways, but generally it will reimburse for losses up to 50 percent of insurance coverage carried on the home. If you have a $100,000 homeowner's policy, your personal property maximum protection would be $50,000. On certain items like jewelry, furs and collectible art, there are internal policy limits which will restrict the dollar amount recoverable for lost or damaged items.

It is wise to have a written inventory listing all personal property and its value. For expensive items such as furs, jewelry, and the like the bills of sale should be kept so that their value can be proved. Photographs are also useful. A person may buy separate **policy floaters** on very valuable items such as furs, jewelry, and works of art. Insuring these items separately may reduce the value of the other personal property to about 40 percent of the value of the house and hence it will be covered by the regular homeowner's policy. Even if the total value of the personal property is under 40 percent of the value of the home, many policies limit the coverage on furs and jewelry to $2,000 unless these items are specifically listed. If they are listed they are insured for their appraised value and often without a deductible.

Section II is the liability coverage, and it includes a number of happenings.

*Section II coverage: liability*

1. *Personal liability.* Personal liability coverage protects the insured against claims from bodily injury to other people. The insured is protected against lawsuits because of injuries to others caused by pets, boats, and bicycles. The policy would even cover an accident where the insured strikes another with a golf ball. It will cover any type of accident except automobile accidents and accidents related to business pursuits. If a guest slips on the sidewalk and breaks his or her leg, the home owner is covered. Or if a teenager runs over the neighbor's child with a bicycle and injures him or her, the insured is covered. It may even cover accidents away from home for which the insured or any member of the household is held responsible. If the client has a swimming pool, this must be noted in the policy to be certain that he or she has coverage, since a pool is legally considered an attractive nuisance in some states. Therefore, if a neighborhood child fell in the pool while the insured was not at home, he or she could be sued.

The basic amount of personal liability insurance coverage is $25,000 in most states, but larger amounts can be purchased. A personal liability

Table 12—1 *Comparison of homeowner's 76 coverages*

| Coverage | HO-1 (basic form) | HO-2 (broad form) | HO-3 (special form) |
|---|---|---|---|
| **Section I coverages** | | | |
| A. Dwelling | $15,000 min. | $15,000 min. | $20,000 min. |
| B. Other Structures | 10% of A | 10% of A | 10% of A |
| C. Personal Property | 50% of A | 50% of A | 50% of A |
| D. Loss of Use | 10% of A | 20% of A | 20% of A |
| | Fire or lightning<br>Windstorm or hail<br>Explosion<br>Riot or civil commotion<br>Aircraft<br>Vehicles<br>Smoke<br>Vandalism or malicious mischief<br>Theft<br>Breakage of glass or safety glazing material (limit of $100)<br>Volcanic eruption | Fire or lightning<br>Windstorm or hail<br>Explosion<br>Riot or civil commotion<br>Aircraft<br>Vehicles<br>Smoke<br>Vandalism or malicious mischief<br>Theft<br>Breakage of glass or safety glazing material<br>Falling objects<br>Weight of ice, snow, or sleet<br>Accidental discharge or overflow of water or steam<br>Sudden and accidental tearing apart, cracking, burning, or bulging of a steam, hot water, air conditioning, or automatic fire protective sprinkler system, or appliance for heating water<br>Freezing of a plumbing, heating, air conditioning, or automatic fire sprinkler system or from a household appliance<br>Sudden and accidental damage from artificially generated electrical current<br>Volcanic eruption | Dwelling and other structures covered against risks of direct physical loss to property except losses specifically excluded<br>Personal property covered by same perils as HO-2 plus damage by glass or safety glazing material, which is part of a building, storm door, or storm window |
| **Section II coverages** | | | |
| E. Personal Liability | $100,000 | $100,000 | $100,000 |
| F. Medical Payments to Others | $1,000 per person | $1,000 per person | $1,000 per person |

| HO-4 (Contents— broad form) | HO-6 (condominium unit— owners broad from) | HO-8 (modified coverage form) |
|---|---|---|
| **Section 1 coverages** | | |
| Not Applicable | $1,000 minimum on the unit | Same as HO-1 except losses are paid on the actual amount required to repair or replace the property using common construction materials and methods (actual cash value in some states) |
| Not Applicable | Included in Coverage A | |
| $6,000 min. | $6,000 min. | |
| 20% of C | 40% of C | |
| Same perils as HO-2 for personal property | Same perils as HO-2 for personal property | Same perils as HO-1 except theft coverage applies only to losses on the residence premises up to a maximum of $1,000; certain other coverage restrictions also apply; glass breakage is limited to $100 |
| **Section II** | | |
| $100,000 | $100,000 | $100,000 |
| $1,000 per person | $1,000 per person | $1,000 per person |

Note: Coverage E and Coverage F limits can be increased to higher limits.

*Source:* From *Principles of Insurance, 3/e* by George E. Rejda. Copyright © 1989 by Scott, Foresman and Company. Reprinted by permission of HarperCollins Publishers.

policy does not cover employees who are injured while working in the home. If a gardener, maid, or a television repairperson is injured, they are generally covered by workers' compensation, not the homeowner's policy.

2. *Coverage for damage to the property of others.* This provides coverage if the insured or a member of the family damages the neighbor's property. For example, if one is burning leaves in the backyard and the fire spreads and damages the neighbor's fence (or even her or his house), the insured is covered. Or if the lawn mower hits a stone and flings it through the windshield of a neighbor's car, the insured is covered. This property liability coverage is generally limited to $250, $300, or $1,000, however.

3. *Medical payments insurance.* Medical payments provide reasonable medical expense payments for injuries to people hurt on the premises of the insured. For example, the medical bills of a person who slips and breaks a leg on the home owner's sidewalk are paid. The coverage may apply to injuries occurring off the premises of the insured, but only if they were caused by the insured, a member of the insured's family, or their pets. Basic coverage is $500 for each person injured, but larger amounts may be purchased. Coverage is extended only to injuries of others and does not cover the home owner or members of the family.

Just as in the case of the personal liability clause in a homeowner's policy, the medical payment part does not cover employees injured while working in or around the home. In such a case, workers' compensation takes over.

*Which policy is best for the client: costs of a homeowner's policy*

Generally, in most states the HO-2 (broad) policy is the best buy. It costs only slightly more than the HO-1 and provides a good deal more protection. On the other hand, when moving from the HO-2 (broad) to the HO-3 or HO-5 (all-risks) plans, premiums rise substantially while the protection rises only modestly. However, check this carefully; it may not be true in each state.

Table 12–1 summarizes the coverage provided by the various home-owner's policies. Premiums vary with the location of the property and type of construction. Certain areas are more susceptible to damage due to certain natural phenomena. Some areas are wind areas; others are in a hail belt; others, such as Florida and the Gulf Coast, are in the hurricane belt. Consequently, little can be said regarding costs regionally. Table 12–2 shows some data for a home owner's coverage in four different areas.

Within a smaller area classified as having common hazards, rates vary primarily with the type of construction. There are generally three or four classifications and three or four rates per $1,000 of insurance.

*Regional premium variation on a homeowner's policy*

Table 12–2

| City | Premiums (annual rates) |
|---|---|
| Boston | $786 |
| Austin, Texas | 568 |
| Los Angeles | 650 |
| Ames, Iowa | 440 |

*Note:* In all cases the house is a $100,000 home exclusive of the lot. This means, of course, that there is much more house in Iowa and Texas than in Boston or Los Angeles. The premiums also include coverage on personal property, liability, and medical payments. In all cases there is an 80 percent coinsurance clause, and the deductibility is the same in all cases. The construction in all cases is the same: brick veneer. The houses are, then, the same in all respect except for size. Rates furnished by a large, well-known national company. Rates are subject to change due to rising construction costs and other factors over which the insurance industry has no control.

A number of other important things about home ownership and homeowner's insurance with which a person should be familiar will be discussed next.

Some homeowner's policies have a deductible feature, but generally it applies only to the dwelling and the personal property, not to the liability part of the policy.

The minimum deductible is $100, but many policies have more. A person may buy a $250 or a $500 deductible. The deductible may also be a percentage (usually .5 or 1 percent) of the insurance on the dwelling—and in the case of personal property, a certain percentage of that coverage. The higher the deductible, the lower the premium. For example, an insured would save about $120 per year in premiums if he or she raised the deductible from $100 to 1 percent on a $100,000 homeowner's policy.

## OTHER THINGS TO KNOW ABOUT HOME INSURANCE

*Deductible clause*

*Actual cash value versus replacement cost*

Actual cash value and replacement cost are not always the same. Actual cash value is defined as replacement cost less depreciation. (Depreciation takes into account that the property is partially worn out.) In the case of personal property (furniture), most policies will reimburse for covered losses on the basis of actual cash value at the time of the loss but not to exceed the amount needed to repair or replace the property. In many cases the replacement cost is the higher, and hence the insured would have to bear some loss of his or her personal property. (A few companies offer replacement cost coverage for personal property, but at a considerably higher premium).

On the dwelling, most policies will pay losses on the basis of replacement cost with no allowance for depreciation for partially damaged homes. However, the face value is the maximum a company will pay if a house is totally destroyed, even though the replacement cost may be the higher.

*Coinsurance*

Most policies also have a coinsurance clause to discourage the home owner from having too little insurance on the home. This is a statement that the company shall be liable, in the event of loss, only in the proportion that the actual amount of insurance bears to the insurance theoretically required. The required or proper amount of insurance is not 100 percent of the value of the house but usually about 80 percent, although some companies may require 90 or even 100 percent. This 80 or 90 percent figure, which has been set after years of experience, reflects the fact that relatively few houses are completely destroyed by fire. The purpose of the coinsurance clause is to adjust rates equitably among the various policyholders. In the absence of a coinsurance clause, it might happen that an individual would be able to collect the full amount of the loss without paying much premium. Suppose a house is valued at $100,000 and a policy is placed on it for only $60,000. A loss occurs of $20,000, and in the absence of the coinsurance clause, the full $20,000 would be collectible. This award would be unfair to other people who had insured their property for the proper amount and who had therefore been paying higher premiums.

In an 80 percent coinsurance clause, it states, "This company shall not be liable for a greater proportion of any loss or damage to the property described herein than the sum hereby bears to 80 percent of the actual cash value of said property at the time the loss shall happen, nor for more than the proportion which this policy bears to the total insurance thereon." In other words, if the insured does not carry insurance amounting to 80 percent of the cash value of the property and if a partial loss occurs, he or she must share that loss with the company. The individual may recover only that proportion of the loss that the amount of insurance he or she actually has bears to the amount of insurance he or she should have under the coinsurance clause. This principle has long since been converted into the following formula:

$$\frac{\text{Amount carried}}{\text{Amount should carry}} \times \text{Actual loss} = \text{Recovery}$$

Suppose that the actual cash value of a home is $100,000 and that there is an 80 percent coinsurance clause in the policy. A person has insurance of only $60,000, and there is a loss of $10,000. How much of the $10,000 loss can one collect? Substituting in the formula above:

$$\frac{\text{Amount carried (\$60,000)}}{\text{Amount should carry (\$100,000} \times \text{.80 or \$80,000)}} \times \text{Actual loss (\$10,000)}$$
$$= \text{Recovery of (\$7,500)}$$

On the other hand, assuming the same set of facts and assuming further that the proper amount of $80,000 of insurance was carried, then:

$$\frac{\$80,000}{\$80,000} \times \$10,000 = \$10,000 = \text{(Recovery)}$$

It should be emphasized that if a house is totally destroyed by fire, the insurance company will not necessarily pay for the entire value of the house. The company will generally pay a sum equal to the face value of the policy. Therefore, if a home owner has a house with an actual cash value or replacement cost of $100,000 and because an 80 percent coinsurance clause only carries $80,000 of insurance, that is the maximum the company will pay. If the house is lost in a fire, the home owner loses $20,000. The coinsurance clause, then, protects the company against people who buy less fire insurance than they need but who still are fully protected against a fire that does not totally or almost destroy the house. For the home owner to be fully covered in case a fire totally destroys the house, he or she needs 100 percent coverage. Indeed, many mortgage lenders require the home owner to buy 100 percent coverage as a condition of making the loan.

*If a home is totally destroyed: 100 percent coverage*

It is wise for the home owner to reappraise the value of the house occasionally and change the insurance accordingly. The value of houses may have risen substantially because of inflation. In addition, a house may rise in value for other reasons. For example, population growth will tend to make a house rise in value in those areas of rapid growth. Also, if building costs rise (say, by more than inflation) new homes, and sometimes older homes as well, will appreciate pricewise by more than the current rate of inflation.

*Keeping a policy current with inflation*

Most insurance companies provide for an automatic increase yearly. However, most companies base their annual adjustment on the increase in the consumer price index (the CPI measures inflation; see Chapter 1) or on some average of the increase in overall U.S. construction costs. If the value of homes in the area is rising more rapidly than inflation, or even the national average home increase, the automatic adjustment may be inadequate. Therefore, the increased insurance needed in the area should be determined, with the aid of an insurance agent and perhaps a realtor.

## OTHER INSURANCE FOR THE HOME OWNER

There are three other types of insurance that might be appropriate for the home owner. They are flood insurance, earthquake insurance, and mobile home insurance.

### Flood insurance

If a person buys a homeowner's policy, he or she is covered for virtually all hazards, but an individual may need one for which he or she is not covered—flood insurance. Insurance companies will not sell flood insurance because they cannot actuarially spread the risk over large numbers —the reason being that only people living in a flood plain would buy flood insurance. Flood insurance can be purchased through an agency of the federal government, the U. S. Department of Health and Urban Development (HUD). The maximum amount of insurance which may be bought is $185,000 on a single-family home and $60,000 on its contents. Premiums will vary depending upon the area of residence. A homeowner's insurance agent can help if one needs coverage.

### Earthquake insurance

Earthquake insurance, like flood insurance, is not included in the homeowner's policy. However, it may be purchased separately from many companies. If one lives in an earthquake belt like the west coast, he or she might consider it. Generally speaking, earthquake insurance has a deductible of 5 to 6 percent of total coverage provided, which means that damages caused by minor quakes would be assumed by the home owner in most cases.

### Mobile home insurance

Special mobile home insurance is available from many companies and is similar to the homeowner's policies discussed above. It covers a variety of perils—fire, wind, theft, and so on. This insurance covers the mobile home, the personal property in it, and some liability coverage, just as in the case of a homeowner's policy. In some states a separate policy is required, and in others the coverage can be obtained through either a homeowner's policy or an auto policy. Generally if a "mobile home" is not truly mobile (is on blocks in a mobile-home park), a separate policy is needed, but if it is a trailer and moves about, coverage may be obtained through an auto policy by paying an extra premium.

## A HOME INSURANCE PROGRAM

As noted above, either an HO-2 or an HO-3 should be purchased. Which one would depend on the budget, where one lives, and one's priorities.

Renters should consider the homeowner's policy for renters, HO-4. This would protect personal property and provide liability protection.

As noted above, there are special policies for condominium owners and owners of older homes (the HO-6 and HO-8). The pertinent one of these should be purchased.

Landlords who own a rental house might want an old-fashioned fire insurance policy with an extended coverage endorsement. Personal property coverage would not be needed if it is an unfurnished house, nor would medical payments coverage be needed. But a landlord would need liability coverage for the rental house. Both the tenant and the landlord need this since most policies cover only one or the other, and the provisions are not transferable. Someone who slipped and broke his or her neck on the sidewalk in front of the rental house could sue both the tenant and the owner. Each would need a separate policy; the policy of one would not cover the other. The landlord can buy this as a supplement to the same personal liability protection already provided by his or her homeowner's policy.

California residents should consider earthquake insurance because it is relatively inexpensive. The same can be said of flood insurance, for those who live in a flood plain.

There remains the question of how much insurance to buy. This is largely determined by the value of the house. Since most companies have an 80 or 90 percent coinsurance clause, this sets the floor on the amount of insurance. For full protection, however, a person would need to buy a policy with a face value equal to 100 percent of the value of the house. One's own priorities will dictate whether to select 80, 90, or 100 percent coverage. The amount of liability insurance needed to be incorporated into a homeowner's policy will also vary with the home owner's priorities.

**AUTOMOBILE INSURANCE**

Automobile insurance is an absolute must. Anyone who owns an automobile, or even one who only drives a friend's auto, is exposed to the risk of loss. These risks include:

1. Loss of assets due to the damage or destruction of property
2. Loss of assets due to death or bodily injury
3. Loss of assets due to medical bills
4. Loss of income due to injuries that prevent a person from working

Loss of income was discussed in Chapter 11 under disability insurance. The other three risks and how to manage them will be discussed here.

The above risks can be minimized by being a careful driver, and by assuming a small portion of the risk oneself—by means of a deductible—as we shall see. However, the bulk of the risk must be transferred to an insurance company by purchasing property and liability insurance. The premiums then go into a pool and the funds are used to pay the claims of those who have accidents.

*Declarations page*    This page spells out the coverage and the premiums charged; it actually consists of four separate insurance contracts as follows:

**A.**  Liability coverage, which protects the insured if he or she kills or injures someone or destroys his or her property

**B.**  Medical payment coverage (sometimes called *personal injury protection*—*see* Table 12–3), which will pay the medical expenses of all passengers injured while in the insured's car

**C.**  Uninsured and underinsured motorist coverage, which provides protection if one is hit by a motorist who has no insurance, inadequate insurance, or is a hit-and-run driver

**D.**  Coverage for damage to the auto of the insured

Table 12–3    *Declarations page*

ITEM 1:
NAMED INSURED        JOHN JONES
AND MAILING          1610 MAIN ST.
ADDRESS              AUSTIN, TX.
ITEM 2: POLICY PERIOD: 12 MONTHS FROM DECEMBER 4, 1987 TO DECEMBER 4, 1988*

ITEM 3:    DESCRIPTION OF AUTO(S) OR TRAILER(S)

| AUTO | MODEL YEAR | TRADE NAME | IDENTIFICATION NUMBER | TERR | CLASS | SYMBOL/FOB PRICE |
|------|------|------|------|------|------|------|
| 1 | 84 | HONDA | JHMAD5425EC081941 | 2323 | 1B/00 | 08 |
| 2 | 84 | CHEVR | 1G1AN69H4EX127634 | 2323 | 1A/00 | 07 |

ITEM 4:    Coverage is provided where a premium and a limit of liability are shown for the coverage.

"NA" means that a coverage is not afforded. When it appears in a premium column for a car, that coverage is not afforded for that car.

| COVERAGES | LIMITS OF LIABILITY | PREMIUMS AUTO 1 | AUTO 2 |
|------|------|------|------|
| A.  Liability Coverage | | | |
| Bodily Injury Liability | $250,000 each person | | |
| | $500,000 each accident | 118 | 110 |
| Property Damage Liability | $50,000 each accident | 112 | 104 |
| B2.  Personal Injury Protection Coverage | $2,500 each person | 29 | 23 |
| C.  Uninsured/Underinsured Motorist Coverage | | | |
| Bodily Injury Liability | $20,000 each person | | |
| | $40,000 each accident | 9 | 8 |
| Property Damage Liability | $15,000 each accident | | |
| $250 Deductible Applicable to PD Liability | | 7 | 7 |
| D.  Coverage for Damage to the Auto | | | |
| Other Than Collision | actual cash value | 93 | 76 |
| | Less  $100 deductible | | |
| Collision | actual cash value | 157 | 113 |
| | Less  $500 deductible | | |
| | Subtotal Premium | $525 | $441 |

Everyone definitely should have liability insurance. The case for medical payment coverage and uninsured motorist coverage is weaker, but it should be strongly considered because the premiums are relatively low.

If a car is old and of little value, one may wish to forgo coverage for damage to the car and bear this risk oneself. Even if a car is quite valuable the insured may wish to bear some of this risk by choosing a fairly high deductible. This is explained in greater detail below. An example of a declarations page is shown in Table 12–3.

Policies have a section that spells out the general conditions of the insurance, such as:

*Insuring agreement and general provisions*

1. *Who is covered.* Generally speaking, everyone named in a policy is covered by the automobile policy. Even if they are not mentioned, all members of the insured's family may be covered, but this varies from company to company. Check the policy to make certain on this point. If an insured lends a car to a friend, he or she is covered even though the friend is not mentioned in the policy, generally speaking. College students living away from home are covered when they are home for a visit. Some companies, however, require a small extra premium for this and list them as an occasional driver.
2. *Rental cars.* This section also spells out what coverage is available for someone who rents a car while on vacation in another city. When renting a car, individuals are usually told that the rental company has full liability coverage but with a $2,000 or $3,000 deductible on their collision coverage. The renter would have to pay up to that amount in the event of an accident. Rental car companies will attempt to persuade individuals to buy a policy to provide additional protection at a rate of $10 to $13 per day; this is an astronomical rate. Before renting a car, an individual should check with his or her insurance agent. The personal policy may apply and provide the same protection for any rental car.

This paragraph spells out what is not covered. Generally, coverage is not provided in most foreign countries, although some policies do provide coverage if the claim occurs within 25 miles of the border. If the client goes into the interior of Mexico, he or she needs to buy Mexican insurance. In Canada, on the other hand, the insured has coverage. A person should check with his or her insurance agent to ascertain whether or not protection is provided by the regular policy if going abroad.

*Exclusions*

Many policies exclude coverage if a car is used for business purposes. Even if the car is used only on a part-time basis, a special rider needs to be purchased.

This provides protection against damages for (1) inflicting bodily injuries or death in an automobile accident, (2) damaging or destroying someone's property, and (3) providing legal defense if necessary.

1.  *Bodily injuries.* If an individual becomes legally liable for bodily injuries or death, the cost could ruin him or her financially. Even if it is not the insured's fault, he or she might become involved in an expensive legal battle. Proving negligence (or the lack of it) is not always easy, and courts do award high damages.
2.  *Damage to the property of others.* Less property liability coverage is needed than for bodily injuries because even an expensive car, if totally wrecked, will not result in as high a damage claim as in the case of bodily injuries or death.
3.  *Policy limits.* There are limits to the amount a policy will pay, both for bodily injuries and property damages. In the case of bodily injuries there is a per-person limit and a per-accident limit. Bodily injury limits might be $50,000 to $100,000, or $100,000 to $200,000 and even higher. A $50,000 to $100,000 limit means the most the insurance company will pay is $50,000 to any one victim and $100,000 for all the victims in a single accident. In the case of property liability the limits are generally $10,000, $25,000, or $50,000; the limits nearly always apply to each accident, not to each car.

It is recommended that the client choose a high limit, especially for bodily injuries, because today it is common for courts to award high damages. Moreover, premiums do not rise greatly as limits are increased. For people who have acquired wealth, a $250,000 to $500,000 limit is not unreasonable. The explanation is clear: just because one carries insurance in the amount of $100,000 does not mean that this is all he or she will be liable for; an individual may obtain a judgment against the insured for $200,000 or more. In this case, if the coverage is only $100,000 the company will pay that and the insured will be personally liable for the balance.

Since additional premiums required to finance a large liability policy are not great, it is recommended that a high priority be placed on liability coverage. Coming up with a dollar figure is difficult, but some experts feel an individual should have, at least for bodily damage, protection of an amount equal to his or her net worth. Others would add somewhat more than this to take into account future earnings. Net worth is often used because that is what is in danger if a lawsuit is filed and a person doesn't have insurance protection.

Others feel that the proper amount of liability insurance should be geared to the current pattern of jury award in the geographical area where the insured lives. According to this, one would need more insurance in New York of California, where awards are typically higher than elsewhere. On the other hand, in Mississippi, Arkansas, or North Dakota, one would need less. It is also true that sometimes there is no logical pattern to court awards, and hence it is somewhat arbitrary to determine liability insurance this way. Nevertheless, a judgment could be based on both patterns of court awards and the client's net worth.

This coverage is sometimes called *personal injury protection coverage* and provides that the company will pay within specified monetary limits, generally from $500 to $5,000, "all reasonable expenses incurred within three years from the date of the accident for necessary medical, surgical, and dental services, including prosthetic devices, and necessary ambulance, hospital, professional nursing and funeral services" to persons injured "while in or upon, or entering into or alighting from the automobile . . . of the insured."

*Part B-I: medical payment insurance*

This also covers injuries as a result of "being struck, knocked down, or run over by an automobile," or injured in a collision. If persons have this insurance, they and their family are covered while riding in another auto, as a pedestrian, on a bicycle, or in any other way. People riding in the policyholder's car are also covered. Often this insurance will pay even if the other person was at fault and his or her medical payment insurance paid for some of the client's expenses. The client's policy will pay, in such a case, that portion of the expenses that the other person's policy did not pay, up to the limits of the policy. Damages may also be recovered from the other person's auto liability coverage (Part A) if he or she was at fault. Finally, the health insurance policy (discussed in Chapter 11) may pay for any residual expenses incurred but not paid by any of the above coverage.

The rates for this coverage are relatively low, and it is highly recommended. Rates do vary with the amount of coverage. The limits on this type of insurance may be $1,000, $2,000, $3,000, and on up to $10,000. The limit applies on a per-person basis, not a per-accident basis.

Some companies break medical insurance down into B-1 (discussed immediately above) and B-2. B-2 provides the same coverages as B-1 and in addition, some loss of income for the insured, if he or she is unable to earn income for a time. This then is short-term disability insurance and has relatively low limits.

*Part B-2: personal injury insurance*

Most states now require companies to offer policyholders **uninsured motorist coverage** for a slight extra premium. Uninsured motorist coverage is simple and relatively inexpensive. It states that if the policyholder is injured as the result of an accident with an uninsured and negligent motorist or by a hit-and-run driver, his or her company will in effect insure that uninsured motorist for whatever amount specified in the policy. Generally the limits for bodily injury go up to $15,000 for one individual, and $30,000 for one accident. For property damage the limit

*Part C: uninsured-underinsured motorist coverage*

may go as high as $15,000. If the policy has this coverage, the insured's own insurance company pays him or her, but generally only for bodily injuries. A few companies, however, will also pay a collision claim under this coverage if an individual has a collision policy with them.

The insurance company, after it pays the insured, has the right to sue the other motorist to recover what it paid. In practice this is often difficult because the uninsured motorist probably has no assets. Or if the driver injures someone without stopping, there is little the company can do unless the driver is subsequently apprehended.

In the case of a motorist having some insurance but less than the client's coverage under this clause, his or her company will pay that amount and the client's company will pay the difference.

*Part D: coverage for damage to the insured's own car*

This provides coverage for damages to the insured's car due to collision and causes other than collision. Each is rated separately, and each has a separate premium and a separate deductible. The causes other than collision are often referred to as **comprehensive coverage** and this coverage protects against loss caused by a number of perils.

*Collision insurance*

Collision insurance coverage pays for the damages caused by a collision with another vehicle, by skidding off the road and smashing into a fixed object, or by rolling over. The insured has this protection regardless of who was at fault. If the client was at fault, the client's insurance company will pay. If the other person was at fault, his or her company will generally pay. If it's an uninsured or hit-and-run motorist, the client's company will pay in accordance with Part C, discussed above. There are several features common to all collision policies.

1.　*Deductible.* Deductibles may be selected such as $100, $200, $500, or even a $1,000. The insurance covers the cost of repairs less the deductible, or the actual car value less the deductible if the car is totaled.

　　The higher the deductible the lower the premiums, because the risk to the company is less. If one is a careful driver, he or she can save money by selecting a higher deductible. Table 12–4 shows how premiums decline as the deductible rises.

2.　*Actual cash value.* Actual cash value is the replacement cost less depreciation; in the case of an automobile it is also usually the market value of the vehicle. On some occasions, a car can be repaired after a collision, but the cost of repairing it is greater than the value of the car before the loss. In such a case, the cost of repairs does not enter into the matter. If the car was valued at $1,000 before a loss and has a junk value of $100 after the loss, and there is a $300 deductible in the policy, the company is liable only in the amount of $700—although it might cost $1,200 to restore the car to its original condition.

Table 12–4

*Insurance premiums: collision
insurance yearly premiums*

| Deductible | Premiums |
| --- | --- |
| $200 | $257 |
| 250 | 243 |
| 500 | 161 |

These rates are for a Chevrolet Caprice. Rates will vary regionally. Rates would be somewhat higher if the driver were a male under 25 years of age.

3.  *Cars financed on the installment plan.* If a car is financed, the lending institution usually insists that the car purchaser be insured. When a bank finances the purchase of a new car, the car itself is used as the collateral for the loan. If the driver runs the car into a telephone pole and wrecks it, the collateral is thereby reduced by an amount equal to the amount of the damages. Consequently, the bank is without collateral and, if the purchaser refused to pay the bank, it would have no other recourse than to sue on a promissory note that it holds; the purchaser might then have insufficient assets with which to pay off the judgment. To protect themselves, financial institutions demand that the auto be covered by collision and comprehensive insurance.

4.  *Subrogation.* One of the concepts that should be understood in connection with collision insurance is subrogation. Under the terms of the collision policy, the insured agrees that the company shall have the legal right to proceed against a negligent third party causing the loss and to provide damages in the name of the insured. The company has the right to step into the shoes of the insured, as it were, to proceed against a person causing the loss, and the insured agrees to cooperate fully with the company. Suppose a person is parked in a legal manner and another person driving negligently hits the parked car, causing damages of $1,000. If the insured has a $200 deductible collision policy, the company will pay the insured $800 and, under the terms of the policy, may commence a lawsuit against the negligent party to recover the $800 plus the $200 deductible. The insured person may in this manner recover his or her $200 out-of-pocket costs because the total amount of the suit will be $1,000.

Comprehensive insurance covers nearly all perils other than collision. Protection is given for any direct and accidental loss or damage to the automobile covered, as well as damage to the equipment usually attached to the vehicle. In addition, the automobile is covered for fire and theft. The important clause from the point of view of the insured states

*Damages to a car by causes other than collision: comprehensive insurance*

that the company shall be liable for "breakage of glass, and other loss caused by falling objects, fire, theft, explosion, earthquake, windstorm, hail, water, flood, malicious mischief or vandalism, riot, or civil commotion." The company limits its maximum liability to the actual cash value at the time of the loss. Although it has the option of repairing or replacing the damaged property, its maximum obligation is still limited to the actual cash value. Most comprehensive policies are written with a deductible provision, generally a $50 or $100 deductible.

One coverage often put into some comprehensive policies is a clause providing for rental reimbursement for loss of use. In this case, insured persons are paid, within limitations, for a vehicle that they may rent if their car is stolen. Sometimes car rental fees are also paid by the insurance company while a car is being repaired after it has been damaged in a collision. This, however, is usually taken care of by the liability section of the other driver's insurance company if he or she was at fault.

Rates on a comprehensive policy vary with the region where one lives, based on the past experience of loss. Rates in big cities are higher than in smaller towns or in rural areas because of the greater likelihood of vandalism, accidents, and the like. In certain rural areas of Colorado and Kansas, however, the lack of vandals is more than offset by the existence of hail or a combination of wind and dust, both of which will take the paint off a car.

## OTHER IMPORTANT ASPECTS OF AUTOMOBILE INSURANCE

We will now examine a number of other things about automobile insurance with which one should be familiar.

### No-fault insurance

No-fault insurance was developed because it was felt that many accident victims were inadequately compensated for their losses. Due to high medical costs, legal fees, court costs, and lost wages, many victims sustained losses even after being compensated by an insurance company. On the other hand, many critics felt many victims were overcompensated for pain and suffering. No-fault was an attempt to strike a balance. A victim would be fully compensated for his or her losses, but would not be paid for pain and suffering. Under no-fault insurance, the victim's insurance company will pay regardless of who is at fault. The insurance company can then sue the other driver or his or her insurance company. Often much time and money are saved by avoiding going to court, particularly if it is not clear who is at fault.

At present about twenty-four states have some variation of no-fault laws on their books, but there is no agreement regarding what is meant by no-fault insurance. Purists insist that true no-fault would bar tort lawsuits for minor injuries. The injured party would be required to accept payment for injuries and not be permitted to sue for pain and suffering.

The injured party would receive payments from his or her insurance company to compensate for these three types of losses:

1. Income lost while injured
2. Medical and hospital bills
3. Expenses incurred in hiring others to perform services formerly performed by the victim.

There are presently three main types of no-fault laws on the books of the various states.

1. *Modified no-fault.* Under modified no-fault an injured person receives some benefits but is not permitted to sue the other driver unless and until the claim reaches a certain dollar amount. Above that amount the victim could sue for pain and suffering.
2. *Expanded no-fault.* These are also sometimes called add-on no-fault. Under these laws, injured parties would receive modest sums automatically. However, they would not lose the right to sue for over and above that amount, including suing for pain and suffering. The idea here is that if some benefits are paid, the injured party may be satisfied and not sue.
3. *Pure no-fault.* Under pure no-fault, an injured person could not sue under any circumstances; torts would be eliminated. A person could not collect for pain and suffering, but could collect unlimited amounts for lost wages and medical bills. No state has enacted a pure no-fault law, although Michigan has come closest. Under Michigan law torts are eliminated except in the cases of death, permanent disfigurement, or disability.

Since only about one-half of the states have no-fault insurance, there are numerous cases in which a driver from a non-no-fault (tort) state has an accident in a no-fault state with a driver covered by no-fault insurance, and vice versa. In such a case the no-fault driver is paid by his or her insurance company. Then that company and the other driver's insurance company settle the other driver's claim in the usual way. For example, if a Massachusetts driver (no-fault) has an accident in Texas (non-no-fault), the Massachusetts driver's claims are paid by his or her insurance company. This is because most no-fault policies are valid in all states. Then the Texas driver and his or her insurance company and the Massachusetts company settle the claim in the usual way, either amicably out of court or in court if necessary. If a Texas driver has an accident in Massachusetts, the same procedure is followed.

The advocates of no-fault insurance maintain that under it not only are settlements for injuries made more quickly, but they are more certain. Indeed, they are almost automatic. Under the tort (or fault) system usually lengthy legal battles must be fought. Also if the victim is partly at fault, the doctrine of contributory negligence prevents a settlement. Proponents also argue average no-fault settlements often result in the victim's getting more because there would be no court costs or attorney's fees to dilute the settlement. Under the tort system, less than one half of the liability insurance premium dollar is returned to the accident victim, according to a U.S. Department of Transportation study. Finally, proponents believe that no-fault saves time and money for the insurance companies, not only in the form of court costs and attorneys' fees, but in administrative expenses, which could reduce insurance premiums.

The opponents of no-fault say it is unfair in that it allows no settlement for pain and suffering or mental anguish. They also argue that by allowing damages automatically, many people who don't deserve them get them. (Presumably there are people who are at fault and have themselves caused or at least contributed to, their injuries.) This, opponents say, increases insurance company costs and results in higher premiums.[4]

*Financial responsibility laws*

A few states have compulsory insurance laws, and many others have laws concerning financial responsibility even though they have no compulsory insurance laws. In states that have financial responsibility laws, individuals must prove financial responsibility; they may do this by proving they are adequately insured. Moreover, they need only prove they have adequate liability insurance. What amount is adequate varies from state to state.

The purpose of financial responsibility laws is to protect the victims of automobile accidents. The law attempts to do this by encouraging people to have at least the minimum amount of insurance and in this way increase the probability of the victim's being able to collect to compensate for the damages.

While the purpose of financial responsibility laws is admirable, in some states these laws are ineffective because of either court rulings or poor enforcement. In others they work fairly well. In some states, the car registration of a motorist who fails to prove financial responsibility is withdrawn.

*Preferred risks*

Some companies issue preferred risk policies as a competitive device to increase their share of the market. They screen their policyholders carefully and then sell them a policy at a lower premium. In short, as a reward for safe driving the rate is lowered. Lowered rates are given only

---

4. Both sides maintain that their system would result in lower premiums. Neither side's case can be proven. The coming of no-fault insurance has not reduced premiums: indeed they have soared in recent years. However, much of this increase is attributable to inflation. A comparison of premiums in no-fault and tort states shows no discernible pattern.

to selected risks, those who have had a safe record for a number of years. In addition, some companies emphasize that they specifically will sell insurance only to nondrinking drivers, and that because of this they can charge lower premiums.

Rates vary from one section of the country to another, in part because juries typically grant larger awards in some areas. The cost of living is also higher in some sections of the country. Rates may also vary within any geographic region; generally they are higher in big cities than in small towns. Table 12–5 shows some of this regional variation for one national company.

*Insurance premiums' variations*

Rates also vary somewhat with the age and sex of the driver. Male drivers under age 25 pay a higher premium because they have a higher accident rate. In some states those who are under 25 and married get some reduction from the general under-25 rate. The driving record may also affect the rate. In some states if a person has had several (the number varies from state to state but two to four is most common) moving traffic violations, his or her rates may be pushed above the regular rate even if there have been no accidents. If one has had an accident and gotten a ticket, the rate could be adjusted upward even more. On the other hand, some companies reduce rates below regular rates for those drivers between ages 30 and 60 who have good driving records. The age range 30 to 60 is dependent on the theory that drivers under 30 are less cautious than those over 30, and that the reflexes of drivers over 60 have slowed down. Finally, rates on collision and comprehensive coverage vary with the type of auto as well as the factors noted above. The more expensive the auto, the more expensive the insurance.

Table 12–5   *Automobile rate comparisons*

| *Automobile coverage—limits* | *Los Angeles, California* | *Austin, Texas* | *Ames, Iowa* | *Boston, Massachusetts* |
|---|---|---|---|---|
| Bodily injury-property damage 100/300/50 | $  686 | $214 | $122 | $  537 |
| Medical $2,000 | 98 | 14 | 8 | 14 |
| Collision $100 deductible | 404 | 254 | 134 | 617 |
| Comprehensive $100 deductible | 178 | 81 | 50 | 293 |
| Uninsured motorist—financial responsibility limit | 84 | 8 | 6 | 17 |
| Total | $1,450 | $571 | $320 | $1,478 |

*Note:* In all cases the cars are used only for pleasure and no driver is under twenty-five. The rates are subject to change at any time due to inflation, larger court awards, rising auto repair prices, and other factors beyond the control of the insurance industry. Rates furnished by a large, well-known national company. The rates apply to a Chevrolet valued at $14,000 and are annual premiums. Includes bodily injury liability of $100,000/$300,000 and property liability of $50,000, medical insurance of $1,000, uninsured motorist coverage, and collision and comprehensive coverage—both of which have a $100 deductible.

**Box 12–2
How to lower your
client's auto
insurance
premiums**

1. *Shop around.* Not all companies charge the same premiums for the same coverage. In some states maximum rates are set by the state insurance commission, but companies may deviate their rates below these ceilings.

   The more efficiently run companies do provide insurance at a lower rate. This is true of both automobile and homeowner's insurance.

2. *Consider increasing the deductible.* Do this on both collision and comprehensive insurance.

   If one increases the collision deductible from $100 to $250 on a $10,000 car, the premiums will decline by as much as $50 per year. If one raises the deductible to $500, the premiums will drop by another $50 and sometimes more. Doing the same on comprehensive insurance will reduce premiums by similar amounts.

3. If one has an old car worth $1,000 or less, consider dropping collision entirely.

4. If there are teenagers in the family, be sure they go through an approved driver's education program when they first learn to drive. Most high schools have these programs. Many insurance companies reduce rates somewhat for people who have gone through a driver's education program.

5. Many communities have defensive driving courses, which anyone may take and which are approved and sponsored by the National Safety Council. Many insurance companies reduce rates for people who have had these courses.

6. If someone has more than one car, he or she is eligible for the multicar discount. Be sure to get it.

7. Individuals should be sure they are charged the correct rate for which the car is being used. Rates vary not only with the number of miles driven per year but also with such driving factors as:
   a. to and from work
   b. pleasure
   c. business and professional use
   d. carpool, or
   e. some combination of the above. For example, if a person stops driving to and from work and joins a carpool, this could save premium dollars.

## AN INSURANCE PROGRAM: HOW MUCH AUTO INSURANCE TO BUY?

How much insurance does a person need, or how much should he or she buy? That depends. It is in part a personal value judgment based on priorities. It also depends on the income and how much the budget permits. The higher the income, the higher the insurance needs, and also the higher the amount which can be afforded. Moreover, some types of insurance deserve a higher priority than others.

*Liability insurance needs*

Liability insurance should receive the highest priority. Indeed this is an absolute must. But how much coverage should one buy? The client's net worth is what is being protected, and that is the place to begin. Some weight might also be given to future earnings and future increases in net worth. If there is a pattern of court settlements in the area for seriously injured or killed automobile victims, consider that. One should have a fairly large liability policy even if net worth is not very great. Rates do not rise rapidly as the amount of liability insurance purchased increases.

1.  *Bodily injury liability.* This should receive a higher priority than property liability because this is where the court awards are the highest. As a bare minimum we would suggest $20,000 to $40,000 bodily liability protection. However, buying a $250,000 to $500,000 limit would only cost about $33 more. Table 12–6 shows how premiums rise with increased coverage.
2.  *Property liability coverage.* If an individual is on a really tight budget he or she might skimp a bit here; but as Table 12–6 shows, rates here, too, do not rise much as coverage increases.

If a person really needs a large amount of liability insurance, he or she should buy an umbrella package. Most auto insurers do not write more than $250,000/$500,000–$100,000 of bodily injury and property liability coverage, but many have a liability umbrella policy for as high as several million dollars. An umbrella policy normally has a high deductible, so one would need that same high coverage through regular insurance. The umbrella covers all liability claims in excess of that for both the home and the auto. For the coverages, premiums are relatively cheap; in most states a $1,000,000 umbrella policy can be purchased for about $125 per year, and a $2,000,000 policy for about $200.[5] An umbrella policy should have a deductible equal to the auto bodily injury policy limit, and would take over when that had been exhausted.

*An umbrella policy*

It should be noted that while an umbrella covers all members of the family for personal liability, it does not cover liability because of professional malpractice. That is considered a commercial activity and is covered by malpractice insurance discussed below.

Should one have collision insurance, and if so how large a deductible should he or she have? The answers depend upon the value of the car, how much one drives, where one drives, and the kind of driver he or she is, factors that cannot be measured mathematically.

*Collision insurance: how large a deductible should one carry?*

Once a car depreciates below a given figure, collision insurance should be dropped. The more one drives the more likely he or she is to

---

5. This is the basic policy which would apply to an insured with two cars and one home. Add $10 to $15 for each additional car or home.

Table 12–6    *Insurance premiums for auto liability insurance—yearly rates*

| Property liability coverage | Premiums | Bodily injury liability coverage | Premiums |
|---|---|---|---|
| $ 15,000 | $103 | $20,000/$40,000 | $ 85 |
| 25,000 | 106 | $25,000/$50,000 | 94 |
| 50,000 | 112 | $50,000/$100,000 | 101 |
| 100,000 | 117 | $100,000/$200,000 | 112 |
| | | $250,000/$500,000 | 118 |

These rates are for a Chevrolet Caprice. Rates will vary regionally. Also rates would be somewhat higher if the driver were a male under age 25.

have an accident. If one drives mostly in the country or small towns, the likelihood of an accident is less than if one lives in a city and drives there, especially on freeways. Only the insured knows what kind of driver he or she is; hence only that person can judge this point. But if one drives defensively, he or she does not need insurance as much (or can live with a higher deductible) as would be the case if one drives offensively. Premiums on collision insurance vary regionally as well as with the value of the car. Calculate the annual premium plus the deductible as a percentage of the car's value. Remember this percentage will go up as the deductible is increased, and this is a good way to save money. This ratio may also go up as the car becomes older and loses its value. Check with an agent to see what the saving would be if the deductible were increased.

If one can reduce premiums by as much as $100 per year by increasing the deductible by $300, the insured will save money by doing so if he or she has an accident less frequently than about every three years. If a person is an average driver and has a wreck, there is about a fifty-fifty chance it will be the other person's fault, and his or her insurance company will pay. This improves the odds; now the $100 saved per year will finance the $300 additional deductible about every year and a half. Depending upon where one lives and how expensive a car is owned, he or she can save from $100 to $200 per year in premiums by choosing a $500 deductible.

When to drop collision insurance completely is a more difficult question. Once the annual premiums plus the deductible together amount to a substantial percentage of the value of the car, one should consider dropping it. Suppose a car is worth $1,000 and one has a $100 deductible policy with an annual premium of $100. If the car were totaled, the out-of-pocket cost would be $200 (the premium plus the deductible). The insured is paying $200 to protect $800 of property (the car's value of $1,000 less $200 out-of-pocket cost). This ratio is 25 percent, and one should consider dropping the collision insurance. The car will continue to decline in value as the years pass.

**317**

Comprehensive needs should be evaluated in the same manner as collision needs were evaluated. How much money can be saved by raising the deductible? Most people will want comprehensive on a new car. As the car gets older, the person will have to decide when the cost of protecting the property is costing more than it is worth, and some thought should be given as to how often a claim is filed. However, comprehensive insurance is cheaper than collision insurance and the deductible is generally lower; hence, one may want to keep comprehensive coverage for a longer time than collision coverage.

*Comprehensive insurance: how large a deductible should one carry?*

Uninsured-underinsured motorist coverage is the cheapest insurance of all, costing only a few dollars per year, and unless one is on a very tight budget he or she should consider it. This also covers the insured in the event that he or she is the victim of a hit-and-run driver. Not only does it cover property damages, but it also reimburses one for injuries suffered at the hands of a hit-and-run driver.

*Uninsured-underinsured motorist coverage*

For most people automobile and home insurance will provide adequate protection. However, some individuals need additional coverage, which will be briefly discussed here. Some of these fall into the categories of property, liability, life, and specialty insurance.

**OTHER MISCELLANEOUS INSURANCE**

People who own boats will in some cases need to buy a special policy. In some states the homeowner's policy will cover a boat, but often only insofar as liability coverage is concerned. In such a case one would need a special policy for property protection. In other states the homeowner's liability coverage will not even cover a boat—or if it does, only to a limited extent. If one owns a boat, this should be investigated, and whatever additional coverage is needed should be purchased.

*Boat insurance*

The boat property coverage protects against such hazards as fire, theft, sinking, collision, capsizing, explosion, windstorm, hail, submerged objects, vandalism, and lightning. The policies, written in much the same manner as the automobile collision policy, are generally written as either $100, $200, or $500 deductible policies.

The liability part is written to cover personal liability such as hitting a swimmer, injuring passengers as the result of a fire aboard the boat, and ramming another boat with resulting personal injury to the persons aboard that vessel. The policies are generally written with a limit of $10,000 to $25,000, but they go higher at an extra cost.

Malpractice insurance primarily protects doctors and nurses against personal liability damage suits arising out of actual or alleged professional carelessness; in recent years lawyers, accountants, and other profession-

*Malpractice liability insurance*

als have been buying it in increasing numbers. This type of insurance is sold by some fire and casualty companies.

Malpractice insurance used to be quite cheap, but this has changed in some states recently, especially with respect to doctors. Because of a changing legal philosophy, not only are large awards now being made in malpractice suits, but in addition the courts have been more liberal in making awards. In some states even hospitals have lost their immunity from lawsuit. Consequently, in malpractice suits in those states both the doctor and the hospital are sued. California and New York are two states in which more and larger awards have recently been granted. As a result, malpractice insurance rates are very high in those states. Nevertheless, most doctors feel they must have this kind of protection. In some cases, medical societies or groups of doctors have formed their own insurance pool. Each of them puts so much into a fund each month, which is then used to aid those doctors who are sued. This is really self-insurance. In the case of nurses, engineers, and certain other low-risk professionals, the cost of malpractice insurance is still low.

*Trip and travel insurance*

Trip and travel insurance policies are a package that includes some term life insurance and some medical insurance. The life insurance could cover a person for all accidental deaths occurring while the insured is on the trip or (at a reduced premium) just accidental deaths occurring while the insured is on the airplane, in or around the airport, or in a limousine going to or coming from the airport. Some are written so that if the insured is killed while in a common carrier his or her beneficiary(ies) get a certain amount, but get somewhat less if the insured is killed while on the trip but not in a common carrier.

Most of these policies also have a medical insurance feature that pays up to 75 percent of the principal sum for medical bills due to an accident (but not due to an illness) while on a trip. There are a few exclusions regarding the medical insurance—for example, medical bills due to a skiing or hunting accident are not covered.

Generally these single trip policies can be purchased in values from $5,000 to $300,000. A person who travels frequently may want to purchase travel insurance protection—which is available and provides the same protection described above for any trips during the year—rather than purchase it separately for each trip.

*Specialty insurance: group legal insurance*

Some experts believe that before too long insurance to pay for legal fees will be available on a group basis. Even today a few people have such protection, but generally it is financed through a labor union, credit union, or other organization; insurance companies are not yet involved.

Generally, a contract is negotiated between a group and a law firm, which provides certain legal services free to the individual members of the group. The group pays the fees, and the individuals pay indirectly through higher dues or some other such method. But this uses the insurance principle by spreading actuarially over large numbers the legal fees of the few unfortunate enough to get into trouble.

Major lawsuits are not covered, but such things as divorce, drafting of wills, minor disputes with landlords or finance companies, disagreements with retail merchants, and minor traffic violations are handled. In many cases relatively small sums of money are involved, and most persons are reluctant to spend money on attorney's fees (and possible court costs). The result is they often pay any claim made or represent themselves in court and invariably lose.

## SUGGESTED READINGS

*Analysis of Automobile No-Fault Statutes.* New York: General Adjustment Bureau, Inc.

Athearn, James L. *Risk and Insurance.* St. Paul, Minn.: West Publishing Co., 1984.

*Best's Review, Property-Liability Edition.* Oldwick, N.J.: A. M. Best Company, Inc. Monthly publication.

Cockerell, Hugh. *Lloyd's of London.* Homewood, Ill.: Dow Jones-Irwin, 1984.

*CPCU Journal,* Malvern, Pa.: The Society of Chartered Property and Casualty Underwriters (CPCU). Quarterly publication.

Dorfman, Mark S. *Introduction to Insurance,* 3rd ed. Englewood Cliffs, N.J.: Prentice Hall, 1987.

"Family Guide to Property and Liability Insurance." New York: Insurance Information Institute.

Gordis, Philip. *Property and Casualty Insurance.* Indianapolis, Ind.: Rough Notes Company, 1984.

Greene, Mark R., and Trieschmann, James. "Risk and Insurance." Cincinnati: South-Western 1984.

Huebner, S. S., et al. *Property and Liability Insurance.* Englewood Cliffs, N.J.: Prentice Hall, 1982.

*Insurance Review.* New York: The Insurance Institute. Monthly publication.

Mehr, Robert I., and Cammack, Emerson, *Principles of Insurance.* Homewood, Ill.: Dow Jones-Irwin, 1985.

*National Underwriter.* Chicago: The National Underwriter Co. Weekly publication.

"Property and Casualty Fact Book," New York: Insurance Information Institute. An annual publication.

*Risk Management.* New York: The Risk and Insurance Management Society, Inc. Monthly publication.

Vaughan, Emmet J. *Fundamentals of Risk and Insurance,* 5th ed. New York: John Wiley and Sons, 1989.

# IV Managing investments

Part IV deals with investments of all kinds.

Everyone earning an income should generate some savings. These savings should then be put to work to earn an investment income.

All investors need to have some funds in a safe and liquid form for emergency purposes. These investments should be in savings institutions. There are two reasons: first; these emergency funds need to be in a very safe place; second, until the investor gains some experience with more risky investments, he or she might wish to use the savings institutions as a safe "parking lot" for funds. Because of this safety feature, generally they earn a bit less than other investments. Chapter 13 covers all of the savings institutions and also clarifies the mysteries of interest rates.

Chapter 14 introduces the reader to the fundamentals of direct investments: investing directly in corporate securities (stocks and bonds) rather than investing indirectly through savings institutions as was discussed in Chapter 13.

Chapters 15 and 16 go one step further and spell out the various types of securities. There are a number of different bonds and common and preferred stocks; all of these are discussed in Chapter 15.

Chapter 16 provides general information on securities and on the securities markets. How securities are quoted in the financial pages of the newspapers and how they are bought and sold are discussed. There is also some information on investment strategies which is intended to aid the investor in deciding *which securities* to buy and *when* to buy them.

Chapter 17, the final chapter in Part IV, covers mutual funds. Mutual funds offer professional management of funds and diversification, with a variety of portfolio objectives to match various investor needs. The chapter also covers certain other investments such as rental real estate, and closes with a few comments on highly speculative investments such as gold and diamonds. While gold and diamonds are not for everyone, they might be right for a few people.

# 13 Savings and investing through savings institutions

**HIGHLIGHTS**     This chapter should provide an understanding of the role of financial institutions in the investor's savings plans, the types of savings accounts they provide, and how savings earn interest income. The following topics will be discussed:

1 Savings invested indirectly
2 Who saves and why?
3 Savings institutions and savings
4 Types of deposits
5 What to look for before deciding on a savings account
6 Penalties for early withdrawals of certificates of deposit
7 Nondepository institutions
8 U.S. savings bonds
9 The power of compounding interest
10 Nominal, real, and after-tax interest rates
11 How most institutions calculate interest

**INTRODUCTION**

Before seriously considering investing directly in securities (discussed in Chapters 14 through 16), the investor needs adequate cash reserves and highly liquid savings deposits for living expenses, special purchases, and emergencies. Living expense funds should be kept in a checking account, either interest bearing or noninterest bearing. These were discussed in Chapter 4; here we will discuss savings and time deposits which, generally speaking, earn a higher interest than checking accounts. Some of these deposits must be pledged for a specific period of time, and there may be a penalty for early withdrawals; others, however, may be withdrawn at any time without a penalty. This is where special purchase or emergency funds should be kept. Most people invest some of their savings in a bank, savings and loan association, credit union account, or mutual savings bank. Deregulation of these financial institutions and increasing competition have created a wide range of savings deposit options. Therefore, deposits should be managed as carefully as any investment.

All the various savings options stress safety, convenience, and interest return. The most troublesome aspect of these is the variety of accounts from which to choose. So, it's well worthwhile to examine what each type has to offer as well as things to consider before deciding on the one (or ones) best suited to achieve the client's goals.

*Savings and investing indirectly*

Savings come from earned income and represent that portion of income that is not spent on consumption. It is invested indirectly when money is deposited with a financial institution that, in turn, invests the money in mortgages, loans, or securities on the investor's behalf. The individual essentially is entering into a contract with an institution in which he or she is paid a stated (fixed) interest rate on the money for a fixed period of time. Thus, financial institutions serve as a channel into which many small savers' moneys are deposited and from which a large dollar amount of money can then be invested in businesses, mortgages, and governments. This "flow of funds" is depicted in Figure 13–1.

There is an important difference between savings invested indirectly

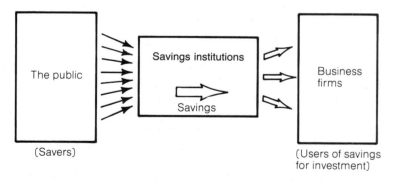

Figure 13–1          *Dollar flows through the economy*

in deposits and direct investments such as stocks, bonds, and real estate. The key feature of federally insured deposits is safety. All deposits are safe because both principal and interest are insured by the full faith and credit of the U.S. government.

Direct investments, in contrast, usually involve the risk of losing principal. While there is the potential for greater rates of return compared to a savings account, there is no guarantee that this will occur. This means that direct investments should be made only with funds the client is willing to expose to more risk—that is, after he or she has invested some funds indirectly and can now afford to assume more risk. Direct investments in securities will be discussed in Chapters 14 through 16. In this chapter we will discuss the various types of deposits offered by the depository institutions, but first we will examine "who saves and why."

Most savings are generated by those whose income is high enough and who are over forty-five years of age. While many low-income groups save some money, the dollar volume is small. High savings among those over forty-five is related to the life cycle variation in the budget, discussed in Chapter 2. Up to about age forty-five or fifty are the high consumption years. After the children have left and the house is paid for and full of furniture and other consumer-durable goods, more savings are generated out of any budget.

*Who saves and why?*

Economists generally agree that there is a positive correlation between income and savings; that is, the higher a person's income, the higher is the dollar volume of savings. There may also be a slight correlation between interest rate and savings. If interest rates are higher, there is a greater reward and greater incentive to save. But this theory is controversial and hard to prove. Studies at the University of Michigan Survey Research Center and elsewhere have suggested that there are a number of other factors influencing savings—such as past income, direction of change in income, size of family, and age—but the effects of these variables are difficult to measure. Moreover, personal savings tend to fluctuate year-to-year. For instance, since 1980 they have fluctuated from a high of 7.5 percent to a low of 3.2 percent of after-tax income. Table 13–1 shows how personal savings have fluctuated over the years.

People save for a variety of reasons—emergencies, a down payment on a home, a vacation, a child's education, or retirement. The investor's first savings are for emergencies or a "nest egg" that should be put in a safe place where they can be obtained easily and quickly, such as a thrift institution. How large nest-egg savings should be depends on the client's age, number of dependents, stability of employment, diverse sources of income, size of insurance deductibles, disability income, and so on. It becomes a personal judgment, but a rough rule-of-thumb is an amount equal to three-to-six times the person's monthly income. Other savings may be invested differently from emergency or nest egg-savings, but some of them too will be invested in savings institutions. Investments

Table 13—1 *Personal savings*

| Year | Dollar Savings in billions | Savings as % of income |
|------|---------------------------|------------------------|
| 1980 | 136.9 | 7.1 |
| 1981 | 159.4 | 7.5 |
| 1982 | 153.9 | 6.8 |
| 1983 | 130.6 | 5.4 |
| 1984 | 164.1 | 6.1 |
| 1985 | 125.4 | 4.4 |
| 1986 | 124.9 | 4.1 |
| 1987 | 101.8 | 3.2 |
| 1988 | 144.7 | 4.2 |
| 1989 | 204.4 | 5.4 |
| 1990 | 206.6 | 5.1 |
| 1991 | 202.1 | 5.3 |

*Source: Economic Indicators,* Dec., 1992, Council of Economic Advisers, p. 6.

such as stocks and bonds should be considered after an adequate nest-egg savings cushion has been established. (See Chapters 14 through 17.)

## SAVINGS INSTITUTIONS AND SAVINGS

Savings institutions are outlets for personal savings and are classified as *depository* and *nondepository institutions*. There are four major depository institutions in the United States:

Commercial banks
Savings and loan associations
Credit unions
Mutual savings banks

They are called depository institutions because they issue a "secondary" or "indirect" security for an individual's money that is called a deposit account. The two key features of deposits are, first, they are often highly liquid (can be withdrawn at any time at the depositor's option); and second, they are safe because most deposits are insured by an agency of the U.S. government (see below.)[1] The institutions may also provide greater diversity for the client's investment.

Nondepository savings institutions are more diverse in nature; the major ones are:

Life insurance companies
Private pension funds

---

1. Some deposits (called "certificates of deposits") are less liquid because they are pledged for a specific period of time, which may be several years. This is explained more fully below.

Money market mutual funds
Cash management accounts
U.S. savings bonds

Life insurance companies were discussed in Chapter 10, while private pension funds will be discussed in Chapter 18. In this chapter, we will focus on the role of depository institutions, money market mutual funds, cash management accounts, and nonmarketable U.S. savings bonds (not to be confused with marketable U.S. government bonds, which will be discussed in Chapter 15) in the overall savings plans.[2]

Besides providing liquidity and safety, all these institutions help the investor's money earn more money by providing investment expertise and "economies of scale" for many savers who lack the time or skill or who are too small to invest directly in securities.

Commercial banks, savings and loan associations (also known as thrifts), and credit unions are found in all states; mutual savings banks are found in only seventeen of the fifty states, and in Puerto Rico. They are located primarily in New England, the Middle Atlantic states, and on the West Coast. While there are some technical and legal differences between mutual savings banks and savings and loan associations, for all practical purposes they are the same.

Some of these savings institutions provide the traditional checking account (discussed in Chapter 4) that does not earn interest. In addition, they all compete with each other for the public's savings dollars on which they do pay interest. Figure 13–2 shows the growth of deposits over the last few years held by commercial banks.

All depository institutions offer a variety of interest-bearing deposits, but they can be classified into four main categories—the **passbook savings account**, the **interest-bearing checking account**,[3] **money market deposit account**; and the **certificate of deposit** (CD).[4]

If savings are invested in a savings institution, the account is simply

**THE DEPOSITORY INSTITUTION AND THE VARIOUS DEPOSITS**

---

2. While U. S. savings bonds may not appear to be "institutions," they are direct obligations of the U.S. government and provide an outlet for individual savings. Indeed, they are one of the safest and most liquid assets available and perform the same functions as institutions. Hence, logically they may be treated as such.

3. Interest-bearing checking accounts were originally called "negotiated order of withdrawal" (NOW) accounts a few years ago when only a few institutions were offering them. Now they have a number of different names, but they are actually interest-bearing checking accounts.

4. The Federal Reserve System classifies interest-bearing checking accounts and passbook accounts as savings deposits, and all of the various CDs as time deposits. The reason is that the CDs are not as liquid as the others since they cannot be withdrawn until their date of expiration without a penalty. The penalty for early withdrawal is discussed below. The Fed's terminology is unfortunate because all the various deposits earn interest and hence are savings vehicles (deposits).

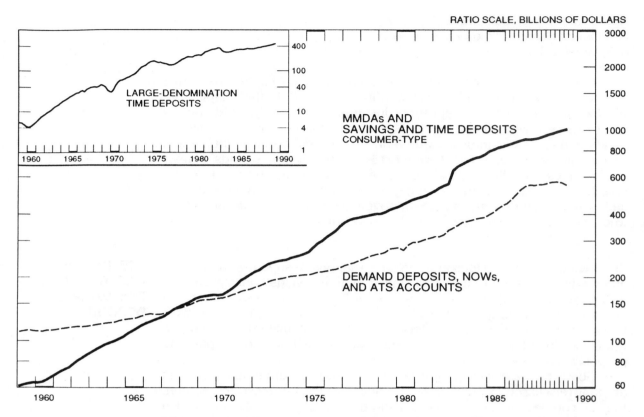

RATIO SCALE, BILLIONS OF DOLLARS

Figure 13—2 *Principal liabilities of commercial banks, seasonally adjusted, quarterly averages. (Source: 1989 Historical Chart Book, Board of Governors of the Federal Reserve System, p. 79.)*

a contract between the investor and the savings institution. In some cases, however, funds are expected to be pledged for a specific period of time and not withdrawn before then. This is true in the case of certain CDs. If they are withdrawn early, a penalty may be imposed, as will be explained below.

**Passbook savings accounts**

Passbook accounts are the oldest type of savings deposits. In the olden days a depositor was given a little book into which entries showing deposits and withdrawals were made. The passbooks have largely been replaced by plastic cards and computer printouts. Some institutions such as credit unions don't even use the term "passbook" anymore, but the term "passbook savings account" is still in use.

Passbook savings deposits are very liquid because they can be withdrawn at any time without a penalty. There are usually no service charges and, in many cases, funds can be transferred to an interest-bearing checking account by telephone. Interest rates tend to be relatively low on both of these deposits (about 5 percent).

Negotiable Orders of Withdrawal (NOW) accounts can be withdrawn without penalty and generally earn an interest rate comparable to pass-book accounts. Their key feature, though, is that they have unlimited check-writing privileges. A monthly service fee may be charged if the balance falls below a certain level, which varies from institution to institution. In some cases these monthly service charges are assessed if the average balance falls below a certain level, and in other cases if the minimum balance does.[5] But, generally the cost is only a few dollars per month. In fact, the interest earned should more than offset the service charges unless the account is quite small.

If an individual needs a checking account, this may be the one to choose. Some institutions do not return the canceled checks. In these cases, the checkbook comes with a carbon copy for record keeping purposes, plus a regular monthly statement showing all transactions will be mailed to the customer. An individual should analyze his or her personal finances to see if collapsing the passbook and noninterest-bearing checking accounts into a new interest-bearing checking account is worthwhile. One of the factors to consider in this regard is "will service charges be eliminated?"

In summary, it may be cost effective to eliminate a noninterest-bearing checking account, unless its average balance is very small because then it will be cheaper to stay with a noninterest-bearing account. Analyze both types of accounts to see what the service charges, if any, would be in each of them. (Most institutions waive their monthly service charge if a higher minimum balance is kept.) Remember—money left in a noninterest-bearing account is not working for the account-holder.

Institutions also have what is referred to as a SuperNOW account, although they often give it different names. Generally this account pays a higher interest rate than the NOW account, but a higher minimum or average balance is required. If the balance falls below the minimum, the individual earns the lower regular NOW account rate. Some institutions restrict the number of checks that may be written per month on a SuperNOW; others do not. Some institutions also charge so much for each check written, because they wish to restrict activity in the SuperNOW accounts.

*Interest-bearing checking accounts—NOW and superNOWS*

Money market deposit accounts (MMDAs) came into existence in the 1970s when money market interest rates became very high. Savers began to take money out of their low-yielding passbook accounts and put them into nondepository institutions that offered the higher money

*Money market deposit accounts*

---

5. There are significant differences between these two. When an account falls below a stated amount in a minimum balance account the individual is charged a fee. In an average balance account the balance can occasionally fall below the minimum but the accountholder won't be charged as long as the average balance remains above the required level.

market rates. (See money market funds below). To remain competitive, savings institutions began offering MMDAs whose interest rates were tied to money market rates—hence, their name. The interest rate paid on these accounts may float; that is, it is changed by the institutions periodically as money market rates change. Many institutions limit the number of checks per month that may be written on these accounts. There is a minimum balance (often as high as $5,000) on these accounts. If the balance falls below this, there may be a flat monthly fee assessed. Additional deposits may be made into an MMDA with no limit.

*Certificates of deposit*

Maturities of **certificates of deposit (CDs)** can extend up to ten years, and the rate of interest they pay is usually a little higher than on other deposits. Some institutions will provide a CD tailored to any number of days or months desired. Also most institutions have a minimum dollar amount below which they will not issue a CD. Generally this is $1,000 but some institutions will go as low as $500 or even $100. When money is put into a CD, expect to leave it there until maturity because of the high early withdrawal penalty. In an emergency, though, money can be borrowed at a relatively low rate of interest by using the CD as collateral for the loan.

*The sweep arrangement: a special account*

The sweep account is an arrangement whereby surplus funds in a lower interest-yielding account are periodically (say, weekly or monthly) automatically swept into a higher-yielding account. For example, a NOW account may serve as a depository for transactions balances, and may be balanced at, say, $2,000. Funds in excess of that amount in multiples of $100 are swept out by computer on a periodic basis into a higher-yielding account. When the NOW account falls below $2,000, multiples of $100 are swept in. The NOW account is therefore stabilized between $1,900 and $2,100.

*Selecting the depository institution—things to keep in mind*

Under deregulation, depository institutions are no longer all the same. To select one, the following factors should be considered.:

1. What is the quoted interest rate?
2. How is the rate compounded—quarterly, monthly, weekly, daily, or continuously? This will affect the interest earned.
3. How is the balance on which interest is paid calculated? Is interest paid on the average monthly balance, minimum balance, day-in, day-out balance, or some other method?
4. When is the interest earned credited to the account? If interest is calculated daily but only credited to the account quarterly or

monthly, the investor has quarterly or monthly (not daily) compounding.

5. Is the interest rate reduced if the balance falls below a certain minimum, and how much is the reduction?
6. Is there a monthly fee if the balance falls below a certain minimum, and how much is it?
7. What is the dollar amount of any such minimum described above? Different institutions have different policies regarding minimum balances.
8. What is the penalty for early withdrawals for those deposits which have been pledged for a specific period?
9. On checking accounts, are there limited or unlimited checking privileges?
10. What are the fees, if any, for telephone transfers from one account to another?
11. What are the fees, if any, for checking the dollar balance via telephone?
12. What are the fees for stopping payment on a check?

There are other important things an individual should know about deposits. For example, don't forget about deposits; they may disappear. Also, in some cases there is a penalty for early withdrawal of deposits. In addition, the safety of deposits should be a concern.

**SOME IMPORTANT NOTES ON DEPOSITS**

"Use it or lose it." Some states have five-year escheat laws. This means if the account is inactive for five years, the institution must turn it over to the state. A deposit is inactive if the depositor does not deposit into it or withdraw from it. Even if interest is paid and credited every year, the account may still be considered inactive. To protect an account, the accountholder should deposit (or withdraw) a dollar periodically. Even a CD that runs six or seven years may escheat. In some states even a one-year CD, if it is merely rolled over every year as it renews, may be considered inactive. To be sure, convert it to a CD of a different maturity periodically.

*Don't abandon savings deposits: the escheat laws*

All of the above-mentioned deposits, in most but not all depository institutions, are insured by an agency of the United States government up to $100,000. This is true of deposits in most commercial banks, savings and loan associations, mutual savings banks, and credit unions. There are, however, a few institutions that do not have deposit insurance; these should probably be avoided. Those institutions that are insured will display a metal sign indicating this in a prominent place, usually near the tellers' windows. Remember, too, that the $100,000 of insurance applies per person per institution, not per account. Hence, if an individual has

*Safety of deposits: deposit insurance*

several accounts, they are commingled, and all of them together come under the $100,000 protection if they are in the name of the same person in the same institution. However, an individual and his or her spouse may each have a separate account in the same institution, and each would be insured up to $100,000, for a total insurance coverage of $200,000. A third joint account would provide total coverage of $300,000. Other members of the family could also each have $100,000 of separate coverage. If funds are in excess of that amount, they should be split between two or more insured institutions for complete coverage and safety.

*Penalties for early withdrawal of CDs*

While passbook savings accounts—and any account on which checks may be written—may be withdrawn without penalty at any time, this is not usually true of CDs. Different penalties for early withdrawal are imposed by different institutions. The most common penalty is the loss of three-months' interest if the CD was pledged for less than one year. If pledged for more than one year, six-months' loss of interest may be assessed.

To illustrate, say a saver has a two-year, 8 percent CD for $1,000, and withdraws it all after one year. A six-month penalty of $1/2 \times (0.08 \times \$1000)$ or $40 would be deducted from the CD amount. In fact, it is possible that the penalty may eat up not only any interest earned but part of the principal too. Returning to our example above, let us now assume the $1,000 CD is withdrawn a day or two after the money is deposited. In this case the saver may get only $960 back.

Obviously, penalties are imposed to discourage early withdrawals. So, as mentioned earlier, if the money is needed before maturity, investigate the possibility of using the CD as collateral for a low-interest loan. This may be less costly than paying a penalty.

## NONDEPOSITORY SAVINGS INSTITUTIONS

There are a number of nondepository institutions, which are nevertheless considered savings institutions. One of these (life insurance companies) was discussed earlier, and one (pension funds) will be discussed in Chapter 18. Two others will be discussed here.

*Money market mutual funds*

A **money market fund** is a mutual fund that invests the client's money in an array of very short-term, relatively safe money-market securities.[6]

---

6. These underlying securities are almost exclusively treasury bills and commercial paper. Treasury bills are short-term debt obligations of the United States government and hence are the safest investment that may be purchased. Commercial paper is the same type of short-term debt obligation issued by large, well-known corporations with excellent credit ratings like IBM or GM. Hence they too are very safe. See Chapter 15 for more information on treasury bills.

It issues the investor shares against a portfolio of these securities that it buys in large denominations by pooling the funds of many investors. Many are offered by brokerage houses, one of the more well known of which is Merrill Lynch's "Ready Assets" fund.

Although not federally insured, only one money market fund has failed in their sixteen-year history, and those losses were minimal. Interest, net of operating expenses and management fees of 0.25 percent to 1.00 percent of the account's value, is passed through to the investor monthly. Either the interest can be reinvested into new shares or a check can be received for the interest amount. Check-writing privileges (usually $500 minimum) allow easy access to the funds.

Money market deposit accounts (provided by banks and other depository institutions) and money market funds are very similar. Interest rates on money market funds float with short-term market rates, while money market deposit accounts may or may not float depending on the institution.[7] However, MMDAs at depository institutions are government insured, whereas money market funds are usually not insured—although some do have private insurance. Despite this, the high-quality, short-term nature of their securities normally makes them relatively safe. Money market funds are more impersonal than dealing with a financial institution. There is no local office for depositing and withdrawing funds. All business is done through the mail or a toll-free telephone call. Finally, money market funds generally require a smaller minimum balance, and there is no charge if the balance falls below the minimum; i.e., the depositor continues to earn the same interest rate. On the other hand, the minimum amount a check can be written for is higher.

In the early 1980s, Merrill Lynch, a major brokerage firm, introduced an innovation they called the **Cash Management Account (CMA)**. The idea was to reduce the monthly paperwork for consumers by combining the monthly statement for checking, credit card, mutual fund, and brokerage statements all into one monthly statement. Now, most brokerage houses and some banks and S&L's offer these "all-in-one" accounts.[8]

*Cash management accounts*

Using Merrill Lynch as an illustration, $20,000 is needed to open a cash management account but it can be in cash, securities, or both. The account includes a conventional securities (brokerage) account, a check-

*Debit cards*

---

7. A floating rate moves up (or down) automatically with changes in the market; no decision need be made by the institution's managers.

8. The all-in-one accounts offered by banks and S&L's are precisely the same as a brokerage house cash management account. That is, they usually bundle *separate checking, savings,* and *credit accounts* into one statement rather than there being one account as with brokerage firms.

ing account, a credit card, and possibly a debit card. A **debit card**, unlike a credit card, means payments for purchases are automatically taken out of the assets in the account (see Chapter 5). There is often an annual fee for this account.

Any excess cash in a cash management account, say, from dividends or interest, is swept weekly into a money market fund. In other cases, if insufficient cash is available to cover purchases of securities, Merrill lends the depositor the money up to a certain amount.[9] This is one main advantage of using a brokerage versus a bank cash management account. On the other hand, banks and S&L's provide slight reductions in charges on certain services that brokerage firms do not offer; and as noted above, the banks' and the savings and loans' deposits are insured. The bottom line in choosing a CMA is not easy. Each one is different; and some of the features they offer may be of no value to the client, yet he or she will be paying for them. For example, some bank CMAs do not offer brokerage services but they may be more convenient to use. Bank CMAs may provide services not found in a brokerage CMA—for example safe deposits, travelers' checks, copying, and notary services. Also, annual fees can vary.

## UNITED STATES SAVINGS BONDS

United States government bonds can be classified into marketable and nonmarketable but redeemable.[10] The marketable bonds are sold by brokers and some banks and appeal primarily to larger investors and institutions. They will be discussed in greater detail in Chapter 15. The nonmarketable bonds will be discussed here because they are designed for the small investor and because they are classified as thrift institutions. These bonds are issued in two different series; they were formerly called Series E and Series H, but in January, 1980, the Treasury made a few changes and the bonds are now called Series EE and HH. The older Series E and H bonds sold prior to 1980 are, of course, still outstanding.

### Series EE

Series EE and HH bonds, being nonnegotiable, are also nonmarketable. They cannot be used as collateral for a loan nor can they be sold to a third party. However, they are redeemable, which means that they can be returned to the U. S. Treasury at the option of the bondholder. However,

---

9. The amount borrowed is called a margin loan. The amount you can borrow is limited to 50 percent of the market value of your stocks on deposit and 90 percent on treasury securities. The actual interest rate you pay is based on what is called the broker loan rate, which, technically, can change day-to-day.

10. Marketable securities are those securities which are negotiable and therefore can be easily sold to third parties. Many marketable securities are listed on the New York stock exchange. Those that are not sold "over the counter." Consequently, marketable securities may be bought or sold by making a telephone call to a broker.

they must be held for at least six months. Because of this redeemability, their price is stabilized and they do not fluctuate inversely with changes in the interest rate.[11]

Series EE bonds are discounted, whereas Series HH bonds are not. This merely means that Series EE bonds are sold below their face value and as time passes, their value rises to reflect accrued interest. These bonds come in denominations with face values of $50, $75, $100, $200, $500, and $1,000, $5,000, and $10,000. Since they are discounted, they are sold at a price below these figures.

Series EE bonds are sold at one-half of their face value and then appreciate as they approach maturity. On November 1, 1982, the U. S. Treasury changed the interest rate and hence the appreciation schedule of Series EE bonds. Bonds sold after that date have a floating interest rate that floats in accordance with the rate paid by the Treasury on five-year marketable securities. This variable rate works as follows. Every six months the Treasury Department compiles the average market interest rate on all Treasury marketable securities that are five years from their maturity during the previous half year. The rate on new Series EE savings bonds for the next six months is 85 percent of that market average. At the end of five years, the ten semiannual averages are added, averaged, and the average compounded on a semiannual basis to determine a bond's five-year yield. Series EE bonds held longer than five years have additional semiannual market averages computed in and compounded. This means, then, that since these bonds appreciate in value to accrue interest, their appreciation also varies; the appreciation is a function of the level of the interest rate. At maturity, the market value of these bonds may be at or above their face value. There is also a proviso in these Series EE bonds that guarantees a floor on the interest rate that the bondholder will receive if he or she holds these bonds for five years or more. This rate is 6 percent. If the interest rate were never to rise above 6 percent, these bonds' value would rise to their face value in twelve years. If interest rates on them are above 6 percent, the bonds will be redeemable at face value sooner. In this case, if the bonds are held after reaching face value, their value may rise further. The interest (appreciation) on these Series EE bonds is not taxed until realized when the bonds are cashed in (although the purchaser can elect annual taxation.). This tax deferral makes the yield a little more attractive than their rate suggests. Interest on these bonds is not subject to state and local taxes.

---

11. The reason Congress made these bonds nonnegotiable and redeemable was to protect the small investor from the unpleasant experience that took place regarding bonds sold during World War I. Those bonds were negotiable (and hence marketable). Many people bought bonds during the war but after the war their price fell drastically as interest rates rose. If people had to liquidate them due to an emergency, they suffered a substantial capital loss. Why the price of marketable bonds fluctuates inversely with changes in the interest rate is explained in Chapter 14.

The new Series EE bonds with a floating interest rate tied to the market rate are a more competitive investment, which, together with their tax-deferred status, has made them a fairly popular investment.

*Series HH*

The interest on Series H and HH bonds, which are sold in units of $500, $1,000, $5,000, and $10,000, is payable semiannually beginning six months after issue date; it is paid on each interest date by check and mailed to the addressee of record. These bonds are always sold at their face value. They are not coupon bonds, however. They are registered bonds and the interest is automatically sent to the bondholder. Series HH (and the old H) bonds purchased before November 1982 yield 8.5 percent per year. This 8.5 percent is fixed for ten years and cannot float up as can Series EE. To receive the full 8.5 percent interest, however, the bonds must be held five years or more. If they are redeemed sooner, they will be redeemed at less than face value, so the return drops below 8.5 percent.

The Treasury stopped selling Series HH over the counter on November 1, 1982. However, Series EE may be converted to Series HH. But since November 1986, Series HH bonds pay only 6 percent.

There is a limit to how many Series EE and Series HH a person may buy each year—$30,000 (face value) in the case of Series EE and $20,000 in the case of HH. A married couple may each purchase that amount.

An investor may obtain Series EE or HH bonds (or cash them in) at any large national bank. In addition, many employers have established a means whereby employees may buy Series EE bonds through payroll withholding.

*Liquidity and risk*

All types of United States government securities are highly liquid. (Liquidity has to do with how quickly something can be converted to money.) The marketable bonds (all but Series EE and HH) can be sold by telephoning a broker or a bank. A highly organized market exists for these bonds. The nonmarketable Series EE and HH bonds are redeemable at the option of the bondholder. Hence they, too, are very liquid. They can be redeemed at almost any commercial bank.

While there is absolutely no risk of default involved in holding any government bonds, there is a risk of possible capital loss involved in holding all government bonds except Series EE and HH. Since their market price is permitted to fluctuate freely with the forces of supply and demand, it is possible that, if a person wishes to sell bonds before they mature, he or she will have to accept a lower price than that paid. However, since Series EE and HH are redeemable by the Treasury, their price is in effect stabilized; there is no risk whatsoever attached to these bonds.

In the case of CDs where the principal does not vary greatly, if at all, the interest calculation is relatively easy to make. The interest rate paid generally varies with the dollar amount of the CD, and the length of time for which it is pledged; that is, the larger the dollar amount and the longer it is pledged, the higher the interest rate. However, the institution merely applies the interest rate to the principal balance to obtain the dollar amount of interest.

There is, however, the problem of compounding. Interest can be compounded annually, semiannually, quarterly, monthly, weekly, daily, and even continuously. The way a deposit is compounded makes a great deal of difference, as we shall see below.

In the case of the passbook account and the various checking accounts, where the principal amount in the account fluctuates, a second problem arises—that is, how to determine the balance to which the agreed upon interest rate is applied. This too makes a considerable difference, as we shall see below.

First, however, we will explore the theory of interest—why it is paid, the various methods of compounding, and the effect of compounding. Then we shall examine how interest is calculated by most institutions.

**SOME NOTES ON
INTEREST RATES**

Interest is mysterious to some people; it shouldn't be. Interest income is also sometimes viewed as somehow being less virtuous than other income, an erroneous view. There is nothing mysterious about interest and there should be no stigma attached to receiving it. Figure 13–3 shows how interest rates have changed over the years. Interest is the payment for the use of capital just as rent is the payment for the use of real property. Interest can be justified in several ways. Capital is productive and hence, like labor, it receives a return. Labor receives a wage; capital receives an interest payment. Liquid capital (money), however, must first be turned into real capital (plant and equipment) before it is productive.

*The theory of interest*

Interest is also paid because the supplier of capital (the lender) assumes a risk (large or small) that the loan will not be repaid. This is the risk of default, and lenders must be paid a fee (interest) to entice them to assume that risk. Moreover, the higher the risk of default, the higher the interest payment must be. If the risk is high enough, no one will advance the capital, and there is a fringe of unsatisfied would-be borrowers.

A third reason for the payment of interest is that most people prefer present dollars (or consumption) to future dollars. A lender gives up (it is hoped temporarily) present dollars, and hence present consumption, for future dollars, and hence future consumption. This is a personal sacrifice. For postponing consumption, the person must be given the reward of greater consumption in the future. Interest is a payment for abstinence, and is also called time preference. People prefer present consumption to future consumption; they have a positive time prefer-

PERCENT PER ANNUM

COMMERCIAL PAPER
1-MONTH

AAA CORPORATE BONDS
STANDARD & POOR'S
(DATA NOT AVAILABLE AFTER 1983)

Figure 13—3     *Long- and short-term interest rates, annually. (*Source: 1989 Historical Chart Book, *Board of Governors of the Federal Reserve System, p. 96.)*

ence, and interest must be paid as a bribe to entice them to postpone consumption. Money or goods today are more valuable than the same money or goods in the future. The old saw perhaps explains interest best: "A bird in the hand is worth two in the bush."

*Simple interest*

When a contract is made between a borrower and a lender, the borrower agrees to pay the lender a fixed percentage sum of the amount borrowed (called the principal) periodically. Usually the amount of interest to be paid is stated as so much per year. If the agreement calls for an 8 percent interest rate, then on a $1,000 loan the borrower must pay $80 per year. The contract could call for an $80 payment to be made every year, or it could stipulate a $40 payment every six months or $20 every three months. In each case, it would be 8 percent per year. If the interest payment is made each time it is due, the amount borrowed remains a constant ($1,000 in the case above), and the interest becomes a constant percentage of a constant principal sum. This is **simple interest**. However, this is not always what is done; consequently, we also have compound interest.

If the contract calls for the interest to be retained by the borrower, the principal sum grows as time passes. If a lender makes available to a borrower $1,000 to be compounded at 8 percent for a number of years, at the end of one year the $80 interest is added to the original loan of $1,000, which now becomes $1,080. The next year the interest is 8 percent of $1,080, or $86.40. The $86.40, instead of being paid to the lender, is again added to the principal sum of $1,080, now making it $1,166.40. Now interest will be calculated on $1,166.40, and so it goes year after year. This has been called paying interest on interest; i.e., **compound interest**. Figure 13–4 shows how $10,000 will build up over the years due to compounding.

*Compound interest*

   In the above case interest was compounded annually. It can also be compounded semiannually, quarterly, monthly, weekly, daily, or continuously. Compounding semiannually would call for adding $40 to the principal sum at the end of six months then figuring interest on $1,040 for the second six months and so on. Compounding results in a fixed percentage rate being calculated on an ever-increasing principal sum and becoming proportionately greater with each passing period.

If a dollar is earning compound interest, it will eventually double in value. How quickly a dollar will double is determined by the interest rate and by how frequently it is compounded (annually, semiannually, quarterly, monthly, or even daily). There are tables that show how a dollar will grow over the years at various interest rates. If tables are not available, the time needed to double can be approximated by applying **the rule of 72**. Divide the interest rate into 72 to get the approximate time needed for money to double, if earnings are compounded annually; for example, at 6 percent a dollar would double in 12 years (72 ÷ 6 = 12).

*The rule of 72*

**Yield** is similar to the interest rate, but it is not always the same. In the case where simple interest is paid, yield and interest are the same. But if interest is compounded, yield is higher than the stated interest rate. Moreover, the extent to which yield exceeds the interest rate is determined by the frequency of compounding. The more frequent the compounding, the higher the yield above the stated rate. Therefore, when choosing a savings institution it is important to know not only the interest rate but the frequency of compounding. Table 13–2 shows the yield that results from several different frequencies of compounding.

*Yield*

   While the difference between interest and yield is not great when interest rates are low, at higher rates it is significant—especially if large dollar amounts are involved over a number of years. This is

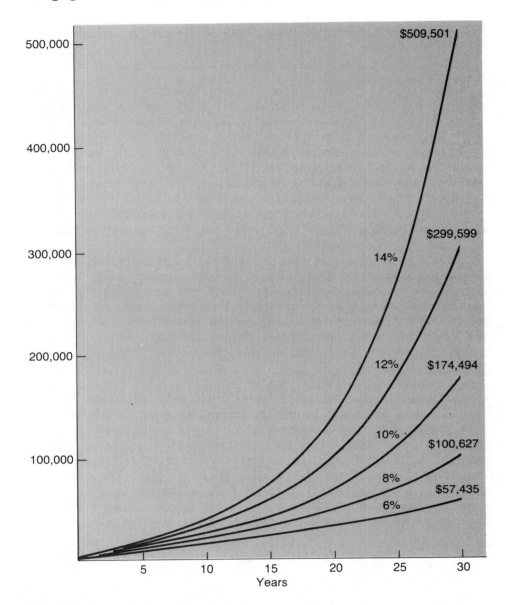

Figure 13–4    $10,000 compounded annually

illustrated by Table 13–3, which shows the different rates of growth of $5,000 invested at 10 percent, but with different frequencies of compounding. In 20 years the investor will have earned an additional $3,308 with daily rather than annual compounding. This is because with daily compounding the real interest (or yield) is 10.52 percent. The extra 1/2 percent makes quite a difference.

*Real annual yield resulting from daily and continuous compounding at various interest rates*    Table 13—2

| Stated rate (%) | Yield due to quarterly compounding | Yield due to monthly compounding | Yield due to daily compounding | Yield due to continuous compounding |
|---|---|---|---|---|
| 5.00 | 5.01 | 5.11 | 5.13 | 5.20 |
| 5.25 | 5.35 | 5.36 | 5.39 | 5.47 |
| 5.50 | 5.61 | 5.62 | 5.65 | 5.73 |
| 5.75 | 5.88 | 5.90 | 5.92 | 6.01 |
| 6.00 | 6.14 | 6.17 | 6.18 | 6.27 |
| 6.50 | 6.66 | 6.70 | 6.72 | 6.81 |
| 7.00 | 7.19 | 7.23 | 7.25 | 7.36 |
| 7.50 | 7.71 | 7.76 | 7.79 | 7.90 |
| 8.00 | 8.24 | 8.30 | 8.33 | 8.45 |
| 8.50 | 8.77 | 8.84 | 8.88 | 9.00 |
| 9.00 | 9.31 | 9.38 | 9.42 | 9.55 |
| 9.50 | 9.84 | 9.92 | 9.96 | 10.11 |
| 10.00 | 10.38 | 10.47 | 10.52 | 10.67 |
| 10.50 | 10.92 | 11.02 | 11.07 | 11.23 |
| 11.00 | 11.46 | 11.57 | 11.63 | 11.80 |
| 11.50 | 12.01 | 12.13 | 12.19 | 12.37 |
| 12.00 | 12.55 | 12.68 | 12.75 | 12.94 |
| 12.50 | 13.10 | 13.24 | 13.31 | 13.51 |
| 13.00 | 13.65 | 13.80 | 13.89 | 14.09 |
| 13.50 | 14.20 | 14.37 | 14.45 | 14.67 |
| 14.00 | 14.75 | 14.93 | 15.02 | 15.25 |
| 14.50 | 15.31 | 15.50 | 15.60 | 15.84 |
| 15.00 | 15.87 | 16.08 | 16.18 | 16.43 |

*Yield under continuous compounding*

As we have seen, compounding may be frequent or infrequent. Under daily compounding, simple interest for one year is calculated; that number is then divided by 365 and added to the principal, and so on. It is even possible to compound continuously. While the mathematics of this is complex, we have tables that will approximate the result. Under continuous compounding, the year is simply broken down into a larger number of units, sometimes as many as 1,000. This, of course, can be done with modern computers.

It should be noted that the interest must be credited to the principal as soon as it is calculated or else it is not compounding. For example, some institutions calculate the interest every day, but store it in the computer and add it to the principal at the end of the quarter. In such a case this is really quarterly compounding.

Table 13–2 shows the effective interest rate (or yield) that results from various methods of compounding.

Table 13–3    *Buildup of $5,000 at 10 percent with various frequencies of compounding*

| Time in years | Interest compounded annually (10.00%) | Interest compounded quarterly (10.00%) | Interest compounded daily (10.00%) |
|---|---|---|---|
| 1 | $ 5,500 | $ 5,519 | $ 5,526 |
| 5 | 8,053 | 8,193 | 8,243 |
| 10 | 12,969 | 13,425 | 13,590 |
| 15 | 20,886 | 21,999 | 22,404 |
| 20 | 33,637 | 36,048 | 36,935 |

## Nominal and real interest rates

The **nominal interest rate** is just another name for the stated interest rate; for example, 8 percent on $1,000 is $80 per annum. The *real interest rate* is the rate that has been adjusted for inflation by subtracting the rate of inflation from the nominal rate. For instance, if inflation were 5 percent per year, then with an 8 percent nominal rate the real rate would be 3 percent (8 percent minus 5 percent) and the return in real dollars would be $30. Table 13–4 and Figure 13–5 show how real interest rates have varied over the years.

## After-tax nominal interest rate

The **after-tax nominal interest rate** depends on the client's particular tax bracket. To obtain it, subtract the tax bracket from 1.00 and multiply this number by the nominal interest rate. Staying with our example, if the individual were in the 15 percent tax bracket, the after-tax nominal rate would be 6.8 percent.

$$(1.00 - 0.15) \times 0.08 = .85 \times 8 = 6.8\%$$

For someone in the 28 percent bracket, the after-tax nominal rate would be 5.76 percent.

$$(1.00 - 0.28) = .72 \times .08 = 5.76\%$$

## After-tax real interest rate

The after-tax nominal interest rate is adjusted for inflation in the same manner as the before-tax nominal rate. In our example above, the 6.80 percent after-tax nominal rate becomes 1.8 percent (after-tax nominal rate – inflation = 6.80 – 5.0 = 1.80 percent) if the individual is in the 15 percent tax bracket. Similarly, for a 28 percent bracket, the after-tax real rate would be 0.76 percent (5.76 percent – 5 percent = .76 percent). This clearly demonstrates how both inflation and taxes can erode the investor's return. It is even possible for inflation rates to be greater than the nominal rate, as in the 1979 to 1981 time period, which

*Real interest rates*                                                    Table 13–4

| Year Ending Dec. 31 | Inflation Rate | High Grade Corp. Bonds | Real Rate | 3–6 Month Com'l. Paper | Real Rate |
|---|---|---|---|---|---|
| 1950 | 5.8 | 2.6 | –3.2 | 1.7 | –4.1 |
| 1951 | 5.9 | 3.1 | –2.8 | 2.3 | –3.6 |
| 1952 | 0.9 | 3.0 | 2.1 | 2.3 | 1.4 |
| 1953 | 0.6 | 3.1 | 2.6 | 2.3 | 1.7 |
| 1954 | –0.5 | 2.9 | 3.4 | 1.3 | 1.8 |
| 1955 | 0.4 | 3.1 | 2.7 | 3.0 | 2.6 |
| 1956 | 2.9 | 3.4 | 0.5 | 3.6 | 0.7 |
| 1957 | 3.0 | 3.7 | 0.7 | 3.8 | 0.8 |
| 1958 | 1.8 | 4.1 | 2.3 | 3.3 | 1.5 |
| 1959 | 1.5 | 4.6 | 3.1 | 4.9 | 3.4 |
| 1960 | 1.5 | 4.4 | 2.9 | 3.2 | 1.7 |
| 1961 | 0.7 | 4.4 | 3.7 | 3.2 | 2.5 |
| 1962 | 1.2 | 4.2 | 3.0 | 3.3 | 1.1 |
| 1963 | 1.6 | 4.4 | 2.8 | 4.0 | 2.4 |
| 1964 | 1.2 | 4.4 | 3.2 | 4.2 | 3.0 |
| 1955 | 1.9 | 4.7 | 2.8 | 4.7 | 2.8 |
| 1966 | 3.4 | 5.3 | 1.9 | 6.0 | 2.6 |
| 1967 | 3.0 | 6.9 | 3.9 | 5.6 | 2.6 |
| 1968 | 4.7 | 6.5 | 1.8 | 6.1 | 1.4 |
| 1969 | 6.1 | 7.8 | 1.7 | 8.8 | 2.7 |
| 1970 | 5.5 | 7.4 | 1.9 | 5.7 | 0.2 |
| 1971 | 3.4 | 7.1 | 3.7 | 6.0 | 2.6 |
| 1972 | 3.4 | 7.2 | 3.8 | 5.5 | 2.1 |
| 1973 | 8.8 | 7.7 | –1.1 | 9.1 | 0.3 |
| 1974 | 12.2 | 8.6 | –3.6 | 9.0 | –3.2 |
| 1975 | 7.0 | 8.6 | 1.6 | 6.0 | –1.0 |
| 1976 | 4.8 | 7.8 | 3.0 | 4.7 | –0.1 |
| 1977 | 6.8 | 8.4 | 1.6 | 6.6 | –0.2 |
| 1978 | 9.0 | 9.2 | 0.2 | 10.4 | 1.4 |
| 1979 | 13.3 | 10.6 | –2.7 | 12.8 | –0.5 |
| 1980 | 12.4 | 12.4 | 0.0 | 16.5 | 4.1 |
| 1981 | 8.9 | 14.5 | 5.6 | 12.1 | 3.2 |
| 1982 | 3.9 | 11.2 | 7.3 | 8.5 | 4.6 |
| 1983 | 3.8 | 12.3 | 8.5 | 9.8 | 6.0 |
| 1984 | 4.0 | 12.0 | 8.0 | 8.2 | 4.2 |
| 1985 | 3.8 | 10.1 | 6.3 | 7.6 | 3.8 |
| 1986 | 1.1 | 9.1 | 8.0 | 5.7 | 4.6 |
| 1987 | 4.4 | 9.9 | 5.5 | 7.0 | 2.6 |
| 1988 | 4.4 | 9.9 | 5.5 | 9.0 | 4.6 |
| 1989 | 4.6 | 8.8 | 4.2 | 8.3 | 3.7 |
| 1990 | 6.1 | 9.1 | 3.0 | 7.6 | 1.5 |

Figure 13–5   *Real interest rates, 1950-1990 (market rate less inflation rate.)* (Source: Johnson's Investment Company Charts, 1989, *Hugh A. Johnson Co., Buffalo, N.Y., p. 27.)*

means individuals were actually losing money in terms of purchasing power. Table 13–5 shows how taxes and inflation erode interest income and principal. Here we are earning 8 percent, but inflation is only 4 percent.

## HOW INTEREST RATES ARE CALCULATED BY MOST INSTITUTIONS

We have seen above that how interest is compounded makes a difference in determining the true yield. In the case of accounts on which checks may be written, and which therefore fluctuate, two other factors are important in determining how much interest is earned. They are (1) how the institution determines the balance to which the interest rate is applied, and (2) when the interest is credited to the account.

There are three common methods used to determine the dollar amount to which the interest rate is applied.

*Determining the account balance*

1.   Low or minimum balance. If the investor's interest period is a month, and the beginning balance was $1,000, and a deposit was made of $600 and a check was written for $500 (as shown in the

*Nominal interest, real interest, after-tax nominal interest, and after-tax real interest with 4 percent inflation (nominal interest 8 percent)*  Table 13—5

|  | Percent | Dollars |
|---|---|---|
| 1. Amount invested | % | $1,000.00 |
| 2. Nominal interest | 8 | 80.00 |
| 3. Inflation dilution | | |
|     a. Interest—diluted by inflation ($80 × 4%) | 4 | 3.20 |
|     b. Principal—diluted by inflation ($1,000 × 4%) | 4 | 40.00 |
|     c. Total dilution (principal and interest) | 4 | 43.20 |
| 4. Real interest ($80.00 − $3.20) | 4 | 76.80 |
| 5. Tax dilution of interest | | |
|     15 percent bracket (line 2 times tax bracket) | 1.2 | 12.00 |
|     28 percent bracket (line 2 times tax bracket) | 2.24 | 22.40 |
| 6. After-tax nominal interest (line 2 minus line 5) | | |
|     15 percent bracket | 6.8 | 68.00 |
|     28 percent bracket | 5.76 | 57.60 |
| 7. After-tax real interest (line 6 adjusted for 4% inflation) | | |
|     15 percent bracket* | 2.8 | 28.00 |
|     28 percent bracket | 1.76 | 17.60 |

*If a person is in the 15 percent tax bracket, his or her investment after taxes has grown to $1,068 after one year, but after an added adjustment for inflation it is only about $1,026.87 in real terms. If, on the other hand, he or she is in the 28 percent tax bracket, the investment after one year and after taxes is $1,057.60. But after an adjustment for inflation, the investment grew to only $1,016.48. These figures do not match the figures on line 7 precisely because of rounding. With 4 percent inflation, the after-tax nominal return is not reduced by 4 percent (the inflation rate) to get the real return, but by the reciprocal of 4 percent, which is 3.85 percent. See Chapter 1 for a discussion of how the value of money (and hence bonds) declines reciprocally with inflation. (Calculated by the author.)

table below), the interest rate calculation would be applied to the minimum balance of $1,100. If the check had been written before the deposit, then only $500 (minimum balance) would have earned interest.

| | Deposits | Checks | Balance |
|---|---|---|---|
| Opening Balance | | | $1,000 |
| Deposit: 10th of month | $600 | | $1,600 |
| Check: 20th of month | | $500 | $1,100 |

**2.** Average balance. In the above case the average balance of $1,233 would have earned interest.

**3.** Actual balance. Under this method interest is calculated every day on the actual money in the account as follows:

| | Deposits | Checks | Balance |
|---|---|---|---|
| Opening Balance | | | $1,000 |
| Deposit: 10th of month | $600 | | $1,600 |
| Check: 20th of month | | $500 | $1,100 |
| Interest would be received on: | | | |
| $1,000 for 10 days | | | |
| $1,500 for 10 days | | | |
| $ 900 for 10 days | | | |

In the above three examples, if the investor were earning 6 percent, he or she would receive monthly interest of $5.00 ($1,000 × 6% ÷ 12), $6.17, and $6.17 respectively, with methods one, two, and three. In this case the average balance and the actual balance are about the same, but this is not usually the case.

This last method is the fairest and best from the depositor's viewpoint. Interest is being earned on the actual money in the account.

This latter method is sometimes called day-in day-out (DIDO) interest. The interest period is one day, and the computer calculates interest daily. Check to see what method the institution is using. The additional interest earned with a DIDO account can be substantial, especially with a fairly large account.

*When interest is credited to the account*

There is a difference, however, between daily interest calculation and daily interest compounding. In order to have daily compounding the interest must be calculated daily and also credited to the account daily. Many institutions calculate interest every day, but then the computer holds it and credits it to the account only at the end of the month, or sometimes not until the end of the quarter. Such a case constitutes monthly or quarterly compounding. If an account is earning 6 percent with daily compounding, the true interest or yield is really 6.18 percent, as shown in Table 13–2.

## SUGGESTED READINGS

"The Arithmetic of Interest Rates." New York: The Federal Reserve Bank of New York.

*The Banker's Magazine.* A banking quarterly review, published by Warren, Gorham, and Lamont, Inc., Boston, Mass.

*Barrons,* Dow Jones and Company. Weekly publication.

"Borrowers, Lenders, and Interest Rates." Richmond, Va.: The Federal Reserve Bank of Richmond.

Carrol, Frieda. *The Joys of Saving and Economizing.* Atlanta: Bibliotheca Press, 1985.

*Credit Union National Association Yearbook.* Madison, Wis.: Credit Union National Association. Annual publication.

"Depository Institutions and Their Regulators." New York: The Federal Reserve Bank of New York.

*Directors Digest.* Chicago: United States League of Savings Associations. Monthly publication.

*Federal Home Loan Bank Board Journal.* Washington, D.C.: Federal Home Loan Bank Board. Monthly publication.

*Finance Facts Yearbook.* Washington, D.C.: National Consumer Finance Association. Annual publication.

Gup, Benton E. *Financial Intermediaries,* 2nd ed. Boston: Houghton Mifflin, 1988.

*International Credit Union Yearbook.* Washington, D. C.: CUNA International, Inc. Annual publication.

*Mutual Savings Banks National Fact Book.* New York: National Association of Mutual Savings Banks. Annual publication.

*Mutual Savings Banks Annual Report.* New York: National Association of Mutual Savings Banks.

Sarnat, Marshall, and Szego, Giorgio. *Saving, Investment, and Capital Markets in an Inflationary Economy.* Cambridge, Mass.: Ballinger Publishing Co., 1982.

*Savings and Loan Fact Book.* Chicago: United States League of Savings Associations. Annual publication.

*Savings and Loan Bulletin.* Chicago: United States League of Savings Associations. Monthly publication.

*The Wall Street Journal.* Princeton, N.J.: Dow Jones and Company. Daily publication.

## APPENDIX 13: PRESENT AND FUTURE VALUES

We discussed interest rates above: what they are, how they are calculated, and why they are paid. However, you do not have to laboriously calculate interest, because you can find out the interest from the tables shown in this appendix and from other sources mentioned below. The first table, *The future worth of a present dollar,* is ordinary compound interst. The second table, *The present worth of a future dollar,* is a sort of negative interest that is called discounting. Then comes *The future worth of an annuity,* which shows how your savings deposits would grow if you deposited a uniform amount each year and it grew by compound interest. The fourth table, *The present worth of a future dollar,* is the reverse of the third. It involves interest calculations, and shows the sum of money needed today to be equal in value to a given number of future payments.

### Cases for appendix to Chapter 13

The tables in this appendix, dealing with future worth and present worth, are used in finance. If a present-value calculator is available, you can calculate these as quickly and easily as you can look them up. Also in some cases, there may be monthly payments rather than annual payments. Tables A13–1 and A13–2 are constructed for annual flows. There are also monthly tables available. In some cases, the yearly interest rate can be divided by 12 to get the monthly rate. If you have a monthly rate of less than one percent (½ of 1 percent, for example), you can approximate the answer by taking one-half of the sum under the column for 1 percent in Tables A13–3 and A13–4. To be accurate, however, you will need to use monthly tables or your present-value calculator.

The two cases illustrate two uses to which these tables can be put.

Cases

1. Cynthia Jean Reed recently signed a lease to rent a house for 12 months at $600 per month. Cynthia asked the landlady if she would give her a discount if she paid some or all of the rent in advance. Claire Baldwin, her landlady, told her she could pay the present value of any future rent discounted at 10 percent. What would Cynthia have to pay if she paid the entire twelve-months' rent in advance? What would her last six-months' rent be if she paid that in advance after having lived in the house six months?

2. Jim and Terry Chism established a college trust fund for their child at birth in the form of a deposit in a thrift institution. Terry deposits $20 per month into it, which earns 6 percent; but at the end of every year she transfers the funds into a long-term CD that earns 7 percent. How much money will be on hand at the end of 18 years when the child is ready for college?

*Future worth of a present dollar*

The present worth of $1 is, of course, $1. At 6 percent, however $1 will grow to $1.06 in one year. Consequently, the future worth of a dollar in one year is $1.06 and in two years it is $1.124, if compounded at 6 percent. This is shown by the formula:

$$(1 + i)^N$$

Where $N$ is the number of years involved, and $i$ is the going interest rate. This is the formula for calculating compound interest discussed above. Tables have been constructed taking the formula into account. One dollar compounded at 6 percent for ten years will be worth $1.791. Table A13–1 shows these values.

*Present worth of a future dollar*

There is also the opposite of the future worth of a present dollar, i.e., present worth of a future dollar. The present worth of a future dollar is less than a dollar by whatever is the going interest rate. This is called discounting, and it is taking interest away rather than adding it. This is shown by the following formula:

$$(1 + i)^{-N}$$

Table A13–2 shows these values.

*Future worth of an annuity*

The concept of the future worth of an annuity is the amount of money that would exist at some future time if one added $1 per year and it was growing at an interest rate of 6 percent. If one added $1 per year for twenty-five years and it was earning 6 percent, it would have grown to $54.865; $25 of this would have been the contribution and $29.865 would have been interest. This is shown by the formula:

$$\frac{(1 + i)^N - 1}{i}$$

Table A13–3 shows the various figures.

### Present worth of a future annuity

Finally, there is the present worth of a future annuity, that is, the lump sum of money that today has the same value as periodic future payments, the total of which would be larger than the lump sum. For example, at 6 percent, $12.783 in hand is worth twenty-five annual payments of $1 each. This is shown

by the formula: $\dfrac{1 - (1 + i)^{-N}}{i}$

Table A13–4 can be used in lieu of the formula immediately above.

Table A13 − 1    *Future worth of a present dollar* $(1 + i)^n$

| Years hence | 1% | 2% | 3% | 4% | 5% | 6% | 7% | 8% | 9% | 10% | 12% |
|---|---|---|---|---|---|---|---|---|---|---|---|
| 1 | 1.010 | 1.020 | 1.030 | 1.040 | 1.050 | 1.060 | 1.070 | 1.080 | 1.090 | 1.100 | 1.120 |
| 2 | 1.020 | 1.040 | 1.061 | 1.082 | 1.102 | 1.124 | 1.145 | 1.166 | 1.186 | 1.210 | 1.254 |
| 3 | 1.030 | 1.061 | 1.093 | 1.125 | 1.158 | 1.191 | 1.225 | 1.260 | 1.295 | 1.331 | 1.405 |
| 4 | 1.041 | 1.082 | 1.126 | 1.170 | 1.216 | 1.262 | 1.311 | 1.360 | 1.412 | 1.464 | 1.574 |
| 5 | 1.051 | 1.104 | 1.159 | 1.217 | 1.276 | 1.338 | 1.403 | 1.469 | 1.539 | 1.611 | 1.762 |
| 6 | 1.062 | 1.126 | 1.194 | 1.265 | 1.340 | 1.419 | 1.501 | 1.587 | 1.677 | 1.772 | 1.974 |
| 7 | 1.072 | 1.149 | 1.230 | 1.316 | 1.407 | 1.504 | 1.606 | 1.714 | 1.828 | 1.949 | 2.211 |
| 8 | 1.083 | 1.172 | 1.267 | 1.369 | 1.477 | 1.594 | 1.718 | 1.851 | 1.993 | 2.144 | 2.476 |
| 9 | 1.094 | 1.195 | 1.305 | 1.423 | 1.551 | 1.689 | 1.838 | 1.999 | 2.172 | 2.358 | 2.773 |
| 10 | 1.105 | 1.219 | 1.344 | 1.480 | 1.629 | 1.791 | 1.967 | 2.159 | 2.367 | 2.594 | 3.106 |
| 11 | 1.116 | 1.243 | 1.384 | 1.539 | 1.710 | 1.898 | 2.105 | 2.332 | 2.580 | 2.853 | 3.479 |
| 12 | 1.127 | 1.268 | 1.426 | 1.601 | 1.796 | 2.012 | 2.252 | 2.518 | 2.813 | 3.138 | 3.896 |
| 13 | 1.138 | 1.294 | 1.469 | 1.665 | 1.886 | 2.133 | 2.410 | 2.720 | 3.066 | 3.452 | 4.363 |
| 14 | 1.149 | 1.319 | 1.513 | 1.732 | 1.980 | 2.261 | 2.579 | 2.937 | 3.342 | 3.797 | 4.887 |
| 15 | 1.161 | 1.346 | 1.558 | 1.801 | 2.079 | 2.397 | 2.759 | 3.172 | 3.642 | 4.177 | 5.474 |
| 16 | 1.173 | 1.373 | 1.605 | 1.873 | 2.183 | 2.540 | 2.952 | 3.426 | 3.970 | 4.595 | 6.130 |
| 17 | 1.184 | 1.400 | 1.653 | 1.948 | 2.292 | 2.693 | 3.159 | 3.700 | 4.328 | 5.054 | 6.866 |
| 18 | 1.196 | 1.428 | 1.702 | 2.026 | 2.407 | 2.854 | 3.380 | 3.996 | 4.717 | 5.560 | 7.690 |
| 19 | 1.208 | 1.457 | 1.754 | 2.107 | 2.527 | 3.026 | 3.617 | 4.316 | 5.142 | 6.116 | 8.613 |
| 20 | 1.220 | 1.486 | 1.806 | 2.191 | 2.653 | 3.207 | 3.870 | 4.661 | 5.604 | 6.728 | 9.646 |
| 25 | 1.282 | 1.641 | 2.094 | 2.666 | 3.386 | 4.292 | 5.427 | 6.848 | 8.623 | 10.835 | 17.000 |
| 30 | 1.348 | 1.811 | 2.427 | 3.243 | 4.322 | 5.743 | 7.612 | 10.063 | 13.268 | 17.449 | 29.960 |

| 14% | 15% | 16% | 18% | 20% | 24% | 28% | 32% | 36% |
|---|---|---|---|---|---|---|---|---|
| 1.140 | 1.150 | 1.160 | 1.180 | 1.200 | 1.240 | 1.280 | 1.320 | 1.360 |
| 1.300 | 1.322 | 1.346 | 1.392 | 1.440 | 1.538 | 1.638 | 1.742 | 1.850 |
| 1.482 | 1.521 | 1.561 | 1.643 | 1.728 | 1.907 | 2.067 | 2.300 | 2.515 |
| 1.689 | 1.749 | 1.811 | 1.939 | 2.074 | 2.364 | 2.684 | 3.036 | 3.421 |
| 1.925 | 2.011 | 2.100 | 2.288 | 2.488 | 2.932 | 3.436 | 4.007 | 4.653 |
| 2.195 | 2.313 | 2.436 | 2.700 | 2.986 | 3.635 | 4.398 | 5.290 | 6.328 |
| 2.502 | 2.660 | 2.826 | 3.185 | 3.583 | 4.508 | 5.629 | 6.983 | 8.605 |
| 2.853 | 3.059 | 3.278 | 3.759 | 4.300 | 5.590 | 7.206 | 9.217 | 11.703 |
| 3.252 | 3.518 | 3.803 | 4.435 | 5.160 | 6.931 | 9.223 | 12.166 | 15.917 |
| 3.707 | 4.046 | 4.411 | 5.234 | 6.192 | 8.594 | 11.806 | 16.060 | 21.647 |
| 4.226 | 4.652 | 5.117 | 6.176 | 7.430 | 10.657 | 15.112 | 21.199 | 29.439 |
| 4.818 | 5.350 | 5.926 | 7.288 | 8.916 | 13.215 | 19.343 | 27.983 | 40.037 |
| 5.492 | 6.153 | 6.886 | 8.599 | 10.699 | 16.386 | 24.759 | 36.937 | 54.451 |
| 6.261 | 7.076 | 7.988 | 10.147 | 12.839 | 20.319 | 31.961 | 48.757 | 74.053 |
| 7.138 | 8.137 | 9.266 | 11.974 | 15.407 | 25.196 | 40.565 | 64.359 | 100.712 |
| 8.137 | 9.358 | 10.748 | 14.129 | 18.488 | 31.243 | 51.923 | 84.954 | 136.97 |
| 9.276 | 10.761 | 12.468 | 16.672 | 22.186 | 38.741 | 66.461 | 112.14 | 186.28 |
| 10.575 | 12.375 | 14.463 | 19.673 | 26.623 | 48.039 | 86.071 | 148.02 | 253.34 |
| 12.056 | 14.232 | 16.777 | 23.214 | 31.948 | 59.568 | 108.89 | 195.39 | 344.54 |
| 13.743 | 16.367 | 19.461 | 27.393 | 38.338 | 73.864 | 139.38 | 257.92 | 468.57 |
| 26.462 | 32.919 | 40.874 | 62.669 | 95.396 | 216.542 | 478.90 | 1033.6 | 2180.1 |
| 50.950 | 66.212 | 85.850 | 143.371 | 237.376 | 634.820 | 1645.5 | 4142.1 | 10143. |

Table A13—2    *Present value of a future $1 (1 + i)$$^{-n}$*

| Years hence | 1% | 2% | 4% | 6% | 8% | 10% | 12% | 14% | 15% | 16% | 18% |
|---|---|---|---|---|---|---|---|---|---|---|---|
| 1 | 0.990 | 0.980 | 0.962 | 0.943 | 0.926 | 0.909 | 0.893 | 0.877 | 0.870 | 0.862 | 0.847 |
| 2 | 0.980 | 0.961 | 0.925 | 0.890 | 0.857 | 0.826 | 0.797 | 0.769 | 0.756 | 0.743 | 0.718 |
| 3 | 0.971 | 0.942 | 0.889 | 0.840 | 0.794 | 0.751 | 0.712 | 0.675 | 0.658 | 0.641 | 0.609 |
| 4 | 0.961 | 0.924 | 0.855 | 0.792 | 0.735 | 0.683 | 0.636 | 0.592 | 0.572 | 0.552 | 0.516 |
| 5 | 0.951 | 0.906 | 0.822 | 0.747 | 0.681 | 0.621 | 0.567 | 0.519 | 0.497 | 0.476 | 0.437 |
| 6 | 0.942 | 0.888 | 0.790 | 0.705 | 0.630 | 0.564 | 0.507 | 0.456 | 0.432 | 0.410 | 0.370 |
| 7 | 0.933 | 0.871 | 0.760 | 0.665 | 0.583 | 0.513 | 0.452 | 0.400 | 0.376 | 0.354 | 0.314 |
| 8 | 0.923 | 0.853 | 0.731 | 0.627 | 0.540 | 0.467 | 0.404 | 0.351 | 0.327 | 0.305 | 0.266 |
| 9 | 0.914 | 0.837 | 0.703 | 0.592 | 0.500 | 0.424 | 0.361 | 0.308 | 0.284 | 0.263 | 0.225 |
| 10 | 0.905 | 0.820 | 0.676 | 0.558 | 0.463 | 0.386 | 0.322 | 0.270 | 0.247 | 0.227 | 0.191 |
| 11 | 0.896 | 0.804 | 0.650 | 0.527 | 0.429 | 0.350 | 0.287 | 0.237 | 0.215 | 0.195 | 0.162 |
| 12 | 0.887 | 0.788 | 0.625 | 0.497 | 0.397 | 0.319 | 0.257 | 0.208 | 0.187 | 0.168 | 0.137 |
| 13 | 0.879 | 0.773 | 0.601 | 0.469 | 0.368 | 0.290 | 0.229 | 0.182 | 0.163 | 0.145 | 0.116 |
| 14 | 0.870 | 0.758 | 0.577 | 0.442 | 0.340 | 0.263 | 0.205 | 0.160 | 0.141 | 0.125 | 0.099 |
| 15 | 0.861 | 0.743 | 0.555 | 0.417 | 0.315 | 0.239 | 0.183 | 0.140 | 0.123 | 0.108 | 0.084 |
| 16 | 0.853 | 0.728 | 0.534 | 0.394 | 0.292 | 0.218 | 0.163 | 0.123 | 0.107 | 0.093 | 0.071 |
| 17 | 0.844 | 0.714 | 0.513 | 0.371 | 0.270 | 0.198 | 0.146 | 0.108 | 0.093 | 0.080 | 0.060 |
| 18 | 0.836 | 0.700 | 0.494 | 0.350 | 0.250 | 0.180 | 0.130 | 0.095 | 0.081 | 0.069 | 0.051 |
| 19 | 0.828 | 0.686 | 0.475 | 0.331 | 0.232 | 0.164 | 0.116 | 0.083 | 0.070 | 0.060 | 0.043 |
| 20 | 0.820 | 0.673 | 0.456 | 0.312 | 0.215 | 0.149 | 0.104 | 0.073 | 0.061 | 0.051 | 0.037 |
| 21 | 0.811 | 0.660 | 0.439 | 0.294 | 0.199 | 0.135 | 0.093 | 0.064 | 0.053 | 0.044 | 0.031 |
| 22 | 0.803 | 0.647 | 0.422' | 0.278 | 0.184 | 0.123 | 0.083 | 0.056 | 0.046 | 0.038 | 0.026 |
| 23 | 0.795 | 0.634 | 0.406 | 0.262 | 0.170 | 0.112 | 0.074 | 0.049 | 0.040 | 0.033 | 0.022 |
| 24 | 0.788 | 0.622 | 0.390 | 0.247 | 0.158 | 0.102 | 0.066 | 0.043 | 0.035 | 0.028 | 0.019 |
| 25 | 0.780 | 0.610 | 0.375 | 0.233 | 0.146 | 0.092 | 0.059 | 0.038 | 0.030 | 0.024 | 0.016 |
| 26 | 0.772 | 0.598 | 0.361 | 0.220 | 0.135 | 0.084 | 0.053 | 0.033 | 0.026 | 0.021 | 0.014 |
| 27 | 0.764 | 0.586 | 0.347 | 0.207 | 0.125 | 0.076 | 0.047 | 0.029 | 0.023 | 0.018 | 0.011 |
| 28 | 0.757 | 0.574 | 0.333 | 0.196 | 0.116 | 0.069 | 0.042 | 0.026 | 0.020 | 0.016 | 0.010 |
| 29 | 0.749 | 0.563 | 0.321 | 0.185 | 0.107 | 0.063 | 0.037 | 0.022 | 0.017 | 0.014 | 0.008 |
| 30 | 0.742 | 0.552 | 0.308 | 0.174 | 0.099 | 0.057 | 0.033 | 0.020 | 0.015 | 0.012 | 0.007 |
| 40 | 0.672 | 0.453 | 0.208 | 0.097 | 0.046 | 0.022 | 0.011 | 0.005 | 0.004 | 0.003 | 0.001 |
| 50 | 0.608 | 0.372 | 0.141 | 0.054 | 0.021 | 0.009 | 0.003 | 0.001 | 0.001 | 0.001 | |

| 20% | 22% | 24% | 25% | 26% | 28% | 30% | 35% | 40% | 45% | 50% |
|---|---|---|---|---|---|---|---|---|---|---|
| 0.833 | 0.820 | 0.806 | 0.800 | 0.794 | 0.781 | 0.769 | 0.741 | 0.714 | 0.690 | 0.667 |
| 0.694 | 0.672 | 0.650 | 0.640 | 0.630 | 0.610 | 0.592 | 0.549 | 0.510 | 0.476 | 0.444 |
| 0.579 | 0.551 | 0.524 | 0.512 | 0.500 | 0.477 | 0.455 | 0.406 | 0.364 | 0.328 | 0.296 |
| 0.482 | 0.451 | 0.423 | 0.410 | 0.397 | 0.373 | 0.350 | 0.301 | 0.260 | 0.226 | 0.198 |
| 0.402 | 0.370 | 0.341 | 0.328 | 0.315 | 0.291 | 0.269 | 0.223 | 0.186 | 0.156 | 0.132 |
| 0.335 | 0.303 | 0.275 | 0.262 | 0.250 | 0.227 | 0.207 | 0.165 | 0.133 | 0.108 | 0.088 |
| 0.279 | 0.249 | 0.222 | 0.210 | 0.198 | 0.178 | 0.159 | 0.122 | 0.095 | 0.074 | 0.059 |
| 0.233 | 0.204 | 0.179 | 0.168 | 0.157 | 0.139 | 0.123 | 0.091 | 0.068 | 0.051 | 0.039 |
| 0.194 | 0.167 | 0.144 | 0.134 | 0.125 | 0.108 | 0.094 | 0.067 | 0.048 | 0.035 | 0.026 |
| 0.162 | 0.137 | 0.116 | 0.107 | 0.099 | 0.085 | 0.073 | 0.050 | 0.035 | 0.024 | 0.017 |
| 0.135 | 0.112 | 0.094 | 0.086 | 0.079 | 0.066 | 0.056 | 0.037 | 0.025 | 0.017 | 0.012 |
| 0.112 | 0.092 | 0.076 | 0.069 | 0.062 | 0.052 | 0.043 | 0.027 | 0.018 | 0.012 | 0.008 |
| 0.093 | 0.075 | 0.061 | 0.055 | 0.050 | 0.040 | 0.033 | 0.020 | 0.013 | 0.008 | 0.005 |
| 0.078 | 0.062 | 0.049 | 0.044 | 0.039 | 0.032 | 0.025 | 0.015 | 0.009 | 0.006 | 0.003 |
| 0.065 | 0.051 | 0.040 | 0.035 | 0.031 | 0.025 | 0.020 | 0.011 | 0.006 | 0.004 | 0.002 |
| 0.054 | 0.042 | 0.032 | 0.028 | 0.025 | 0.019 | 0.015 | 0.008 | 0.005 | 0.003 | 0.002 |
| 0.045 | 0.034 | 0.026 | 0.023 | 0.020 | 0.015 | 0.012 | 0.006 | 0.003 | 0.002 | 0.001 |
| 0.038 | 0.028 | 0.021 | 0.018 | 0.016 | 0.012 | 0.009 | 0.005 | 0.002 | 0.001 | 0.001 |
| 0.031 | 0.023 | 0.017 | 0.014 | 0.012 | 0.009 | 0.007 | 0.003 | 0.002 | 0.001 | |
| 0.026 | 0.019 | 0.014 | 0.012 | 0.010 | 0.007 | 0.005 | 0.002 | 0.001 | 0.001 | |
| 0.022 | 0.015 | 0.011 | 0.009 | 0.008 | 0.006 | 0.004 | 0.002 | 0.001 | | |
| 0.018 | 0.013 | 0.009 | 0.007 | 0.006 | 0.004 | 0.003 | 0.001 | 0.001 | | |
| 0.015 | 0.010 | 0.007 | 0.006 | 0.005 | 0.003 | 0.002 | 0.001 | | | |
| 0.013 | 0.008 | 0.006 | 0.005 | 0.004 | 0.003 | 0.002 | 0.001 | | | |
| 0.010 | 0.007 | 0.005 | 0.004 | 0.003 | 0.002 | 0.001 | 0.001 | | | |
| 0.009 | 0.006 | 0.004 | 0.003 | 0.002 | 0.002 | 0.001 | | | | |
| 0.007 | 0.005 | 0.003 | 0.002 | 0.002 | 0.001 | 0.001 | | | | |
| 0.006 | 0.004 | 0.002 | 0.002 | 0.002 | 0.001 | 0.001 | | | | |
| 0.005 | 0.003 | 0.002 | 0.002 | 0.001 | 0.001 | 0.001 | | | | |
| 0.004 | 0.003 | 0.002 | 0.001 | 0.001 | 0.001 | | | | | |
| 0.001 | | | | | | | | | | |

Table A 13–3    Future worth of an annuity $\dfrac{(1 + i)^n - 1}{i}$

| Years hence | 1% | 2% | 3% | 4% | 5% | 6% | 7% | 8% | 9% | 10% | 12% |
|---|---|---|---|---|---|---|---|---|---|---|---|
| 1 | 1.000 | 1.000 | 1.000 | 1.000 | 1.000 | 1.000 | 1.000 | 1.000 | 1.000 | 1.000 | 1.000 |
| 2 | 2.010 | 2.020 | 2.030 | 2.040 | 2.050 | 2.060 | 2.070 | 2.080 | 2.090 | 2.100 | 2.120 |
| 3 | 3.030 | 3.060 | 3.091 | 3.122 | 3.152 | 3.184 | 3.215 | 3.246 | 3.278 | 3.310 | 3.374 |
| 4 | 4.060 | 4.122 | 4.184 | 4.246 | 4.310 | 4.375 | 4.440 | 4.506 | 4.573 | 4.641 | 4.770 |
| 5 | 5.101 | 5.204 | 5.309 | 5.416 | 5.526 | 5.637 | 5.751 | 5.867 | 5.985 | 6.105 | 6.353 |
| 6 | 6.152 | 6.308 | 6.468 | 6.633 | 6.802 | 6.975 | 7.153 | 7.336 | 7.523 | 7.716 | 8.115 |
| 7 | 7.214 | 7.434 | 7.662 | 7.898 | 8.142 | 8.394 | 8.654 | 8.923 | 9.200 | 9.487 | 10.089 |
| 8 | 8.286 | 8.583 | 8.892 | 9.214 | 9.549 | 9.897 | 10.260 | 10.637 | 11.028 | 11.436 | 12.300 |
| 9 | 9.369 | 9.755 | 10.159 | 10.583 | 11.027 | 11.491 | 11.978 | 12.488 | 13.021 | 13.579 | 14.776 |
| 10 | 10.462 | 10.950 | 11.464 | 12.006 | 12.578 | 13.181 | 13.816 | 14.487 | 15.193 | 15.937 | 17.549 |
| 11 | 11.567 | 12.169 | 12.808 | 13.486 | 14.207 | 14.972 | 15.784 | 16.645 | 17.560 | 18.531 | 20.655 |
| 12 | 12.683 | 13.412 | 14.192 | 15.026 | 15.917 | 16.870 | 17.888 | 18.977 | 20.141 | 21.384 | 24.133 |
| 13 | 13.809 | 14.680 | 15.618 | 16.627 | 17.713 | 18.882 | 20.141 | 21.495 | 22.953 | 24.523 | 28.029 |
| 14 | 14.947 | 15.974 | 17.086 | 18.292 | 19.599 | 21.051 | 22.550 | 24.215 | 26.019 | 27.975 | 32.393 |
| 15 | 16.097 | 17.293 | 18.599 | 20.024 | 21.579 | 23.276 | 25.129 | 27.152 | 29.361 | 31.772 | 37.280 |
| 16 | 17.258 | 18.639 | 20.157 | 21.825 | 23.657 | 25.673 | 27.888 | 30.324 | 33.003 | 35.950 | 42.753 |
| 17 | 18.430 | 20.012 | 21.762 | 23.698 | 25.840 | 28.213 | 30.840 | 33.750 | 36.974 | 40.545 | 48.884 |
| 18 | 19.615 | 21.412 | 23.414 | 25.645 | 28.132 | 30.906 | 33.999 | 37.450 | 41.301 | 45.599 | 55.750 |
| 19 | 20.811 | 22.841 | 25.117 | 27.671 | 30.539 | 33.760 | 37.379 | 41.446 | 46.018 | 51.159 | 63.440 |
| 20 | 22.019 | 24.297 | 26.870 | 29.778 | 33.066 | 36.786 | 40.995 | 45.762 | 51.160 | 57.275 | 72.052 |
| 25 | 28.243 | 32.030 | 36.459 | 41.646 | 47.727 | 54.865 | 63.249 | 73.106 | 84.701 | 98.347 | 133.334 |
| 30 | 34.785 | 40.568 | 47.575 | 56.805 | 66.439 | 79.058 | 94.461 | 113.283 | 136.308 | 164.494 | 241.333 |

| 14% | 16% | 18% | 20% | 24% | 28% | 32% | 36% | 40% | 50% |
|---|---|---|---|---|---|---|---|---|---|
| 1.000 | 1.000 | 1.000 | 1.000 | 1.000 | 1.000 | 1.000 | 1.000 | 1.000 | 1.000 |
| 2.140 | 2.160 | 2.180 | 2.200 | 2.240 | 2.280 | 2.320 | 2.360 | 2.400 | 2.500 |
| 3.440 | 3.506 | 3.572 | 3.640 | 3.778 | 3.918 | 4.062 | 4.210 | 4.360 | 4.750 |
| 4.921 | 5.066 | 5.215 | 5.368 | 5.684 | 6.016 | 6.362 | 6.725 | 7.104 | 8.125 |
| 6.610 | 6.877 | 7.154 | 7.442 | 8.048 | 8.700 | 9.398 | 10.146 | 10.846 | 13.188 |
| 8.536 | 8.977 | 9.442 | 9.930 | 10.980 | 12.136 | 13.406 | 14.799 | 16.324 | 20.781 |
| 10.730 | 11.414 | 12.142 | 12.916 | 14.615 | 16.534 | 18.696 | 21.126 | 23.853 | 32.172 |
| 13.233 | 14.240 | 15.327 | 16.499 | 19.123 | 22.163 | 25.678 | 29.732 | 34.395 | 49.258 |
| 16.085 | 17.518 | 19.086 | 20.799 | 24.712 | 29.369 | 34.895 | 41.435 | 49.153 | 74.887 |
| 19.337 | 21.321 | 23.521 | 25.959 | 31.643 | 38.592 | 47.062 | 57.352 | 69.814 | 113.330 |
|  | 23.044 | 25.733 | 28.755 | 32.150 | 40.238 | 50.399 | 63.122 | 78.998 | 98.739 |
|  |  |  |  |  |  |  |  |  | 170.995 |
| 27.271 | 30.850 | 34.931 | 39.580 | 50.985 | 65.510 | 84.320 | 108.437 | 139.235 | 257.493 |
| 32.089 | 36.786 | 42.219 | 48.497 | 64.110 | 84.853 | 112.303 | 148.475 | 195.929 | 387.239 |
| 37.581 | 43.672 | 50.818 | 59.196 | 80.495 | 109.612 | 149.240 | 202.926 | 275.300 | 581.859 |
| 43.842 | 51.660 | 60.965 | 72.035 | 100.815 | 141.303 | 197.997 | 276.979 | 386.420 | 873.788 |
| 50.980 | 60.925 | 72.939 | 87.442 | 126.011 | 181.87 | 262.36 | 377.69 | 541.99 | 1311.7 |
| 59.118 | 71.673 | 87.068 | 105.931 | 157.253 | 233.79 | 347.31 | 514.66 | 759.78 | 1968.5 |
| 68.394 | 84.141 | 103.740 | 128.117 | 195.994 | 300.25 | 459.45 | 700.94 | 1064.7 | 2953.8 |
| 78.969 | 98.603 | 123.414 | 154.740 | 244.033 | 385.32 | 607.47 | 954.28 | 1491.6 | 4431.7 |
| 91.025 | 115.380 | 146.628 | 186.688 | 303.601 | 494.21 | 802.86 | 1298.8 | 2089.2 | 6648.5 |
| 181.871 | 249.214 | 342.603 | 471.981 | 898.092 | 1706.8 | 3226.8 | 6053.0 | 11247.0 | 50500.0 |
| 356.787 | 530.312 | 790.948 | 1181.882 | 2640.916 | 5873.2 | 12941.0 | 28172.0 | 60501.0 | 383500.0 |

Table A13—4 *Present worth of a future $1 received annually for N years* $\dfrac{1 - (1 + i)^{-n}}{i}$

| Years (n) | 1% | 2% | 4% | 6% | 8% | 10% | 12% | 14% | 15% | 16% | 18% |
|---|---|---|---|---|---|---|---|---|---|---|---|
| 1 | 0.990 | 0.980 | 0.926 | 0.943 | 0.962 | 0.909 | 0.893 | 0.877 | 0.870 | 0.862 | 0.847 |
| 2 | 1.970 | 1.942 | 1.886 | 1.833 | 1.783 | 1.736 | 1.690 | 1.647 | 1.626 | 1.605 | 1.566 |
| 3 | 2.941 | 2.884 | 2.775 | 2.673 | 2.577 | 2.487 | 2.402 | 2.322 | 2.283 | 2.246 | 2.174 |
| 4 | 3.902 | 3.808 | 3.630 | 3.465 | 3.312 | 3.170 | 3.037 | 2.914 | 2.855 | 2.798 | 2.690 |
| 5 | 4.853 | 4.713 | 4.452 | 4.212 | 3.993 | 3.791 | 3.605 | 3.433 | 3.352 | 3.274 | 3.127 |
| 6 | 5.795 | 5.601 | 5.242 | 4.917 | 4.623 | 4.355 | 4.111 | 3.889 | 3.784 | 3.685 | 3.498 |
| 7 | 6.728 | 6.472 | 6.002 | 5.582 | 5.206 | 4.868 | 4.564 | 4.288 | 4.160 | 4.039 | 3.812 |
| 8 | 7.652 | 7.325 | 6.733 | 6.210 | 5.747 | 5.335 | 4.968 | 4.639 | 4.487 | 4.344 | 4.078 |
| 9 | 8.566 | 8.162 | 7.435 | 6.802 | 6.247 | 5.759 | 5.328 | 4.946 | 4.772 | 4.607 | 4.303 |
| 10 | 9.471 | 8.983 | 8.111 | 7.360 | 6.710 | 6.145 | 5.650 | 5.216 | 5.019 | 4.833 | 4.494 |
| 11 | 10.368 | 9.787 | 8.760 | 7.887 | 7.139 | 6.495 | 5.988 | 5.453 | 5.234 | 5.029 | 4.656 |
| 12 | 11.255 | 10.575 | 9.385 | 8.384 | 7.536 | 6.814 | 6.194 | 5.660 | 5.421 | 5.197 | 4.793 |
| 13 | 12.134 | 11.343 | 9.986 | 8.853 | 7.904 | 7.103 | 6.424 | 5.842 | 5.583 | 5.342 | 4.910 |
| 14 | 13.004 | 12.106 | 10.563 | 9.295 | 8.244 | 7.367 | 6.628 | 6.002 | 5.724 | 5.468 | 5.008 |
| 15 | 13.865 | 12.849 | 11.118 | 9.712 | 8.559 | 7.606 | 6.811 | 6.142 | 5.847 | 5.575 | 5.092 |
| 16 | 14.718 | 13.578 | 11.652 | 10.106 | 8.851 | 7.824 | 6.974 | 6.265 | 5.954 | 5.669 | 5.162 |
| 17 | 15.562 | 14.292 | 12.166 | 10.477 | 9.122 | 8.022 | 7.120 | 6.373 | 6.047 | 5.749 | 5.222 |
| 18 | 16.398 | 14.992 | 12.659 | 10.828 | 9.372 | 8.201 | 7.250 | 6.467 | 6.128 | 5.818 | 5.273 |
| 19 | 17.226 | 15.678 | 13.134 | 11.158 | 9.604 | 8.365 | 7.366 | 6.550 | 6.198 | 5.877 | 5.316 |
| 20 | 18.046 | 16.351 | 13.590 | 11.470 | 9.818 | 8.514 | 7.469 | 6.623 | 6.259 | 5.929 | 5.353 |
| 21 | 18.857 | 17.001 | 14.029 | 11.764 | 10.017 | 8.649 | 7.562 | 6.687 | 6.312 | 5.973 | 5.384 |
| 22 | 19.660 | 17.658 | 14.451 | 12.042 | 10.201 | 8.772 | 7.645 | 6.743 | 6.359 | 6.011 | 5.410 |
| 23 | 20.456 | 18.292 | 14.857 | 12.303 | 10.371 | 8.883 | 7.718 | 6.792 | 6.399 | 6.044 | 5.432 |
| 24 | 21.243 | 18.914 | 15.247 | 12.550 | 10.529 | 8.985 | 7.784 | 6.835 | 6.434 | 6.073 | 5.451 |
| 25 | 22.023 | 19.523 | 15.622 | 12.783 | 10.675 | 9.077 | 7.843 | 6.873 | 6.464 | 6.097 | 5.467 |
| 26 | 22.795 | 20.121 | 15.983 | 13.003 | 10.810 | 9.161 | 7.896 | 6.906 | 6.491 | 6.118 | 5.480 |
| 27 | 23.560 | 20.707 | 16.330 | 13.211 | 10.935 | 9.237 | 7.943 | 6.935 | 6.514 | 6.136 | 5.492 |
| 28 | 24.316 | 21.281 | 16.663 | 13.406 | 11.051 | 9.307 | 7.984 | 6.961 | 6.534 | 6.152 | 5.502 |
| 29 | 25.066 | 21.844 | 16.984 | 13.591 | 11.158 | 9.370 | 8.022 | 6.983 | 6.551 | 6.166 | 5.510 |
| 30 | 25.808 | 22.396 | 17.292 | 13.765 | 11.258 | 9.427 | 8.055 | 7.003 | 6.566 | 6.177 | 5.517 |
| 40 | 32.835 | 27.355 | 19.793 | 15.046 | 11.925 | 9.779 | 8.244 | 7.105 | 6.642 | 6.234 | 5.548 |
| 50 | 39.196 | 31.424 | 21.482 | 15.762 | 12.234 | 9.915 | 8.304 | 7.133 | 6.661 | 6.246 | 5.554 |

| 20% | 22% | 24% | 25% | 26% | 28% | 30% | 35% | 40% | 45% | 50% |
|---|---|---|---|---|---|---|---|---|---|---|
| 0.833 | 0.820 | 0.806 | 0.800 | 0.794 | 0.781 | 0.769 | 0.741 | 0.714 | 0.690 | 0.667 |
| 1.528 | 1.492 | 1.457 | 1.440 | 1.424 | 1.392 | 1.361 | 1.289 | 1.224 | 1.165 | 1.111 |
| 2.106 | 2.042 | 1.981 | 1.952 | 1.923 | 1.868 | 1.816 | 1.696 | 1.589 | 1.493 | 1.407 |
| 2.589 | 2.494 | 2.404 | 2.362 | 2.320 | 2.241 | 2.166 | 1.997 | 1.849 | 1.720 | 1.605 |
| 2.991 | 2.864 | 2.745 | 2.689 | 2.635 | 2.532 | 2.436 | 2.220 | 2.035 | 1.876 | 1.737 |
| 3.326 | 3.167 | 3.020 | 2.951 | 2.885 | 2.759 | 2.643 | 2.385 | 2.168 | 1.983 | 1.824 |
| 3.605 | 3.416 | 3.242 | 3.161 | 3.083 | 2.937 | 2.802 | 2.508 | 2.263 | 2.057 | 1.883 |
| 3.837 | 3.619 | 3.421 | 3.329 | 3.241 | 3.076 | 2.925 | 2.598 | 2.331 | 2.108 | 1.922 |
| 4.031 | 3.786 | 3.566 | 3.463 | 3.366 | 3.184 | 3.019 | 2.665 | 2.379 | 2.144 | 1.948 |
| 4.192 | 3.923 | 3.682 | 3.571 | 3.465 | 3.269 | 3.092 | 2.715 | 2.414 | 2.168 | 1.965 |
| 4.327 | 4.035 | 3.776 | 3.656 | 3.544 | 3.335 | 3.147 | 2.752 | 2.438 | 2.185 | 1.977 |
| 4.439 | 4.127 | 3.851 | 3.725 | 3.606 | 3.387 | 3.190 | 2.779 | 2.456 | 2.196 | 1.985 |
| 4.533 | 4.203 | 3.912 | 3.780 | 3.656 | 3.427 | 3.223 | 2.799 | 2.468 | 2.204 | 1.990 |
| 4.611 | 4.265 | 3.962 | 3.824 | 3.695 | 3.459 | 3.249 | 2.814 | 2.477 | 2.210 | 1.993 |
| 4.675 | 4.315 | 4.001 | 3.859 | 3.726 | 3.483 | 3.268 | 2.825 | 2.484 | 2.214 | 1.995 |
| 4.730 | 4.357 | 4.033 | 3.887 | 3.751 | 3.503 | 3.283 | 2.834 | 2.489 | 2.216 | 1.997 |
| 4.775 | 4.391 | 4.059 | 3.910 | 3.771 | 3.518 | 3.295 | 2.840 | 2.492 | 2.218 | 1.998 |
| 4.812 | 4.419 | 4.080 | 3.928 | 3.786 | 3.529 | 3.304 | 2.844 | 2.494 | 2.219 | 1.999 |
| 4.844 | 4.442 | 4.097 | 3.942 | 3.799 | 3.539 | 3.311 | 2.848 | 2.496 | 2.220 | 1.999 |
| 4.870 | 4.460 | 4.110 | 3.954 | 3.808 | 3.546 | 3.316 | 2.850 | 2.497 | 2.221 | 1.999 |
| 4.891 | 4.476 | 4.121 | 3.963 | 3.816 | 3.551 | 3.320 | 2.852 | 2.498 | 2.221 | 2.000 |
| 4.909 | 4.488 | 4.130 | 3.970 | 3.822 | 3.556 | 3.323 | 2.853 | 2.498 | 2.222 | 2.000 |
| 4.925 | 4.499 | 4.137 | 3.976 | 3.827 | 3.559 | 3.325 | 2.854 | 2.499 | 2.222 | 2.000 |
| 4.937 | 4.507 | 4.143 | 3.981 | 3.831 | 3.562 | 3.327 | 2.855 | 2.499 | 2.222 | 2.000 |
| 4.948 | 4.514 | 4.147 | 3.985 | 3.834 | 3.564 | 3.329 | 2.856 | 2.499 | 2.222 | 2.000 |
| 4.956 | 4.520 | 4.151 | 3.988 | 3.837 | 3.566 | 3.330 | 2.856 | 2.500 | 2.222 | 2.000 |
| 4.964 | 4.524 | 4.154 | 3.990 | 3.839 | 3.567 | 3.331 | 2.856 | 2.500 | 2.222 | 2.000 |
| 4.970 | 4.528 | 4.157 | 3.992 | 3.840 | 3.568 | 3.331 | 2.857 | 2.500 | 2.222 | 2.000 |
| 4.975 | 4.531 | 4.159 | 3.994 | 3.841 | 3.569 | 3.332 | 2.857 | 2.500 | 2.222 | 2.000 |
| 4.979 | 4.534 | 4.160 | 3.995 | 3.842 | 3.569 | 3.332 | 2.857 | 2.500 | 2.222 | 2.000 |
| 4.997 | 4.544 | 4.166 | 3.999 | 3.846 | 3.571 | 3.333 | 2.857 | 2.500 | 2.222 | 2.000 |
| 4.999 | 4.545 | 4.167 | 4.000 | 3.846 | 3.571 | 3.333 | 2.857 | 2.500 | 2.222 | 2.000 |

# 14 The fundamentals of direct security investments

**HIGHLIGHTS**
In order to understand the fundamentals of direct investments and to set the stage for acquiring stocks and bonds, this chapter discusses the following:

1   The various forms of business organization; the investor should know about the organizational structure of the business firm in which he or she invests.
2   Alternative investment objectives a person may wish to achieve
3   Short-run versus long-run investments
4   The risks inherent in any business venture
5   Techniques used in an attempt to reduce risk
6   The sources of investment data needed to make intelligent investment decisions

In this chapter we will introduce direct investments. When we invest directly we make our savings available directly to the business that will actually use it, rather than indirectly by putting them into a depository institution. A person may invest directly by becoming part owner of a business or by directly lending it money. When investing in a business directly, securities (for example, bonds or stock) will be received to prove the investment has been made.

## FORM OF BUSINESS ORGANIZATIONS

Generally business firms are organized into single proprietorships, partnerships, or corporations. While partnerships and single proprietorships outnumber corporations in the United States, they are far less important by every other test. Noncorporate businesses have fewer employees, own fewer assets, and produce and sell much less. They are primarily small businesses owned by a few people—often by a single family. There are also some family-owned corporations, but they are nearly always small. While some corporations are small, nearly all partnerships and single proprietorships are; and all large business entities are corporations.

### The single proprietorship

The **single proprietorship** is a business owned by one person. It is the simplest form of organization, and the easiest and quickest to enter. There need be no charter application or other papers to fill out to enter business. Business assets are commingled with the personal assets of the owner, as are business debt and personal debt. While there can be numerous employees, there can be only one owner. This form of business is fine for some small firms, but it cannot grow very large.

### The partnership

The **partnership** can be comprised of two or more partners. It has some advantages over the single proprietorship. With several partners, usually more capital can be raised, and a number of varying talents may be brought together.

To form a partnership, a partnership agreement must be drawn up. All states have laws governing partnerships and the agreement spells out the duties, rights, and liabilities of each partner.

While a partnership has some advantages over the single proprietorship, it has some disadvantages as well. It is less flexible if several partners have to be consulted before a decision can be made. It is not permanent; the death of one partner dissolves the partnership. Perhaps the greatest single drawback of a partnership is that all partners are liable without limits for the debts of the business.[1] One partner can

---

[1] There are limited partnerships, but generally all partners are liable for all business debts.

commit the others by the decisions he or she makes. Nevertheless, the partnership form of organization works well in many cases. If confidence exists between partners, it may be fine for small business. But like the single proprietorship, it is virtually impossible for a partnership to grow into a truly big business firm.

A **corporation** is a legal entity. It has been defined by Chief Justice Marshall as "an artificial being, invisible, intangible, and a device only in contemplation of law." It has many of the rights, duties, and powers of an individual. It can sue and be sued; it can sign contracts, borrow money, own property, and carry out regular business affairs. A corporation raises money by selling shares in itself called **common stock**. Because a corporation is artificial, it cannot do any of these things itself, but they are done in its name by the corporation's board of directors, elected by its owners.

*The corporate form*

The various states grant corporation charters, and a corporation comes into existence when the certificate of incorporation is accepted by the proper state agency, usually the secretary of state of the state in which incorporation takes place. The people who do the incorporating are the owners and are called the **stockholders**. They invest money by buying the corporation's stock which is then used to acquire business assets (capital) to carry out the business activity for which the corporation was organized.

As noted above, corporations issue and sell shares in themselves called **stock**; they also issue **bonds**. If an individual buys either, he or she is investing in a business directly.

*Corporate bonds and stock*

Bonds are certificates of indebtedness; if an investor buys bonds he or she is lending the business money. The investor is a creditor. All of the terms of the loan are fixed; a certain percentage interest rate will be received on the money for a certain period of time after which the corporation must also repay the loan.

Corporate stocks are certificates of ownership (also called **shares**); if an investor buys stock, he or she becomes a part owner of the business (in a sense, joining the club.) However, no return is promised on the money. If the corporation is successful, it will earn a profit and, as an owner, part of that will be the investor's. It will not necessarily be received in the form of cash, because the corporation may retain it. Only if the board of directors decides to pay out all or part of the earnings in the form of dividends will stockholders receive cash. On the other hand, if the corporation is unsuccessful and suffers losses, the investor will share in those. There is no promise made that the stock will ever be redeemed. As a stockholder, the only thing the investor is promised is that he or she will be permitted to vote for the board of directors who will manage the corporation.

Stockholders, then, assume more risk than bondholders. Bondholders must receive their interest before stockholders may get anything. Stockholders are described as providing risk or venture capital.

There is also a special type of stock called **preferred stock** that stands between bonds and common stock. Preferred stockholders' claims are satisfied after bondholders' but before common stockholders.' We will discuss both bonds and stock in detail in Chapter 16.

*Advantages of the corporate form of business organization*

The advantages of the corporate form of organization include:

1.  One's liability is limited to his or her actual investment in the corporation, and one's personal assets cannot be used to pay the debts of the corporation. In a single proprietorship or partnership, personal assets are available to pay business debts. Since the corporation is a legal entity, only corporate assets may be used to satisfy claims against the corporation. The individual stockholders can lose only what they paid for their own stock. This makes many people willing to invest in a corporation, which permits raising large aggregates of capital.

2.  Shares of stock (or ownership) in a corporation are easily transferred to another person. Corporate stock is negotiable, and can be sold to any other individual, or can be inherited by survivors. This gives a corporation an indefinite life and also contributes to raising large aggregates of capital. A partnership, in contrast, is dissolved upon the death of a partner, and if a partner wishes to sell his or her share to another person, the partners must agree.

3.  The small as well as the large investor may easily invest in corporations. Extremely small amounts of capital (as little as a few dollars) can be committed to the corporation by buying a single share of stock. This permits thousands of individuals collectively to be owners of businesses, which in turn also contributes to raising large amounts of capital.

4.  The above advantages all contribute to the ability of the corporation to amass high sums of capital, to grow large, and to enjoy the benefits of greater efficiencies that often accompany greater size.

There may be other benefits that arise from the giant corporation. For example, if a firm is big it can hire better managerial and other specialized talent than can a small firm. On the other hand, some observers have expressed concern over the separation of ownership and control that a giant corporation makes inevitable. They state that the millions of stockholders who own (but are far removed from) the corporation cannot possibly influence the managers who control the corporation. The managers may or may not be stockholders, but in any event, they are not responsible to their constituents and this, it is alleged, is unhealthy in a democracy.

The first step in making an investment is to decide upon the investment objectives. Then those securities most likely to help to achieve them will need to be selected. Goals and objectives may be any of the following:

1. Liquidity
2. Income
3. Capital gains or growth
4. Security of principal
5. Hedging inflation

or perhaps several or all of these.

Liquidity has to do with how quickly and easily an asset can be turned into cash without a price concession. Money is 100 percent liquid, while other assets vary depending upon their relative "moneyness." Cash is the most liquid of all assets. The term cash equivalents is sometimes used by financial planners. These are cash or almost cash, such as savings accounts, some CDs, etc. (see Chapter 13). After cash and cash equivalents, the degree of liquidity for assets is in general followed by certain U.S. government securities, high-grade corporate bonds, preferred and common stock traded on organized exchanges, over-the-counter securities, first mortgages on real estate, and real estate holdings. Generally, securities listed on organized exchanges are very liquid because they can be sold at the market price by making a telephone call. Selling real estate, on the other hand, takes time. Some liquidity is important for all investors—the amount desired varies.

*Liquidity*

Another investment objective might be to achieve a good income. Some companies achieve higher earnings (profits) then others and they may pay out a high proportion of these earnings to the stockholder in the form of dividends. These are the income stocks. Sometimes bonds too yield a relatively high return. An investor with income as an objective would choose from among these higher-yielding securities.

*Income*

Capital gains, or capital appreciation as it is sometimes called, is an important modern investment objective. A capital gain may be defined as "the increase in value of an asset when it is sold, over what it was when purchased." This attitude toward capital gains as an objective is something that has developed within the past thirty years. Before that, the ideas of income, liquidity, and safety were the objectives that were stressed. Many people invest in securities they believe will result in capital growth rather than income. This may involve investment in the type of firm that has growth possibilities or the purchase of a security the investor has reason to believe is depressed in value. Capital gains—if one

*Capital gains*

is successful in obtaining them—often give a greater return on one's investment. This fact has made capital gains very attractive to some investors.

*Security of
principal*

Safety or security of principal means the preservation of capital values through a conservative investment policy. It is a truism, of course, that this is the prime objective of any investor. Everyone desires to preserve the original principal. This can be done by good judgment, avoidance of highly speculative risks, and attempting to preserve capital from market fluctuations. Unhappily, all this is easier said than done. Moreover, security of principal and liquidity are somewhat inconsistent with high yield. A person who wants high yield or rapid appreciation must assume more risk and accept a greater likelihood of no return or sometimes of actual loss. There are a number of different risks associated with holding securities, and they are examined in detail below.

*Hedging inflation*

Some investors may feel that prices will continue to rise. When prices rise, the real value of certain assets declines, whereas the value of others tends to rise with inflation. Historically, common stock and real estate were considered the best hedges against inflation. Bonds, on the other hand, since they are fixed investments, are generally eroded by inflation. If the price level doubles, the value of the dollar falls by half. If prices rise, the person with fixed dollar assets suffers a loss in value of his or her assets. If one is dependent upon fixed dollars for income—as, for example, are the retired—one's standard of living will necessarily decline.

"*Gracious, I don't want to bring him back. I'd just like his advice on some investments.*"
(Source: *Permission Cartoon Features Syndicate; from* The Wall Street Journal.)

Historically speaking, however, the price of common stock has at least kept up with, and in many periods surpassed, the rate of inflation.

The main reason why the prices of common stock should be a good hedge against inflation is that corporations often plow earnings back into the business. This means that new machinery, plants, and so forth are purchased on behalf of the stockholder. As a result, the value of one's stock should rise. If the corporation is also providing a good or service, the demand for which is growing rapidly, its price may be outpacing inflation. If so, this will be reflected in corporate profits and this too should contribute to rising stock prices. Figures 14–1 and 14–2 illustrate how good an inflationary hedge stocks have been over the long run. One chart shows the cost of living and the Dow Jones Industrial stock average. The other one shows the cost of living, Standard & Poor's 500 stock index, earnings, and dividends. As you can see, stocks have more than held their own in the long run.

*Common stocks and the cost of living, 1897–1990* (Source: Johnson's Investment     Figure 14–1
Company Charts, 1991, *Hugh A. Johnson Co., Buffalo, N.Y., p. 11.*)

Figure 14–2   *Cost of living, dividends, and Standard & Poor's 500 stock index 1926–1989.* (Source: Johnson's Investment Company Charts, 1991, *Hugh A. Johnson Co., Buffalo, N.Y., p. 13.)*

## SHORT-RUN VERSUS LONG-RUN INVESTMENTS

How short is the short run? Any definition is, of course, arbitrary but certainly holding a security for less than a year or two is short run. Holding a security for twenty years or even five or ten is a long-run investment. You may draw your own chronological line. It is generally conceded that the small investor should play largely in the long-run or in the intermediate-run end of the field. If an individual is a large investor, it might be worthwhile to devote the energy, time, and perhaps money needed to make a short-term gain. However, the small investor may not have the time to watch an investment constantly. Also he or she cannot hire expensive professional advice. Moreover, even if he or she does make a nice short-term gain, in absolute dollars it is likely to be small. Therefore, a small investor who gets in and out of the market frequently on a short-term basis will pay commissions that may eat heavily into any profits earned.

Therefore, most small investors probably should buy securities with an eye toward holding them for the long run. This does not mean that the investor should salt them away and forget about them. Any long-term investment can also turn sour and investors should review their portfolios periodically. Nevertheless, for most small investors the goal should be long-run investments—that is, held for at least a few years—not short-run speculation.

## INVESTMENT RISKS

Our system is not a profit system as so many people like to claim. Rather it is a profit-and-loss system. Some firms prosper and show a profit while others lag behind and have losses. No firm can have losses in the long run and survive. And indeed, some firms go out of business from time to time. When they do, the stockholder absorbs the loss. Being an investor, then, is risky business. However, the reward for successfully assuming risk is financial gain, generally as profits in one form or another.

**Risk** refers to the possibility of future loss and how likely it is that this possibility will occur. Since there are a number of different risks involved in any investment, it is important that investors recognize those to which they may be exposed. Risks can be classified into six major types.

### Risk of business failure

While some businesses prosper, others fail. In the event of business failure, a stockholder, having invested "equity" capital, may be entirely wiped out. Bondholders who have loaned money to a company may also find themselves wiped out, but not as frequently as stockholders. If the bonds are secured by certain specific corporate assets, the bondholders may sell these assets and sometimes recover all of the loan, though more often than not they recover less. If the bonds are unsecured, the holder often collects much less than the loan.

It is generally conceded that one way to lessen the likelihood of being wiped out is to diversify one's investments by types of securities and issuers and to buy only the securities of financially strong firms.

### Market risk

Market risk is the particular risk resulting from fluctuations in market prices of securities over time, which may or may not have anything to do with how well a business firm is doing. Stock prices may decline due to a lowering of earnings in a particular firm, such as decline stemming from poor management or even a change in the public's tastes. Or earnings may fluctuate due to the business cycle, which will cause the market price of securities to fluctuate.

Price fluctuations in securities may also arise as a result of investor psychology. Many persons may decide simply to stay out of the market, thus reducing demand for securities and consequently lowering prices, even though firms' profit have not declined and may even have risen.

*Price level risk*

Another type of risk is that of changes in the purchasing power of money. This risk is particularly applicable to those assets whose value is stated in terms of a fixed number of dollars. People who hold bonds and savings accounts are assuming this risk, as are people who hold idle cash. Indeed, those who hold idle cash are the most vulnerable to this risk.

For example, if a person holds money and the value of the dollar falls—which is another way of saying that prices rise—then in terms of real purchasing power the person who holds the money has lost. If the value of the dollar rises—which is another way of saying prices have declined—the real purchasing power of the dollar has risen and the person who holds the money gains. In a period of rising prices, the astute investor will try to move away from fixed assets into items such as common stock and real estate, which tend to appreciate with rising prices. In a period of falling prices (which we hardly see any more), the investor should move from real estate and common stock into fixed assets yielding a fixed return, such as bonds.

This brings us to the *nominal* rate of return and the *real* rate of return. The nominal rate of return is the money rate without an adjustment for inflation, and the real rate is the rate after the inflationary adjustment. If an investor holds a $1,000 bond paying 10 percent for one year during which prices rise by 8 percent, the nominal (money) rate of return is 10 percent and the real return is 2 percent. To convert the nominal rate to the real rate, subtract the rate of inflation from the nominal interest rate. In the above case, the real value of the $1,000 principal sum that was invested in the bond has also declined in real terms. The $1,000 investment grew to $1,100 in nominal terms. The real interest return was $20. The $1,000 original investment is now worth only $920 in real terms. Adding the $20 in real interest to the real value of the principal makes the total investment now worth only $940.

*Interest rate risk*

Interest rate risk is the risk of loss that results from changes in the price of bonds due to fluctuations in prevailing rates of interest. It is important primarily for investments in fixed obligations such as bonds and preferred stock. When interest rates rise, bond prices fall; conversely, when interest rates go down, bond prices rise. There is nothing mystical about this process; it really makes sense. We will illustrate this with an example which, while using an unrealistically low interest rate, illustrates the principle because the interest rate doubles. Suppose a corporation issues a $1,000 bond at 5 percent. This is a contractual obligation and the corporation must pay the holder $50 per year. Later, if interest rates double to 10 percent, in theory—depending upon the maturity—the old bond would drop in price to about $500. The reason is that with rates at 10 percent, any new bond issues would have to be offered with this same 10 percent yield; investors with $1,000 can now expect to get a return of $100 on their investments. Therefore, the holders of the old bonds will attempt to sell them and attain the new rate, thus forcing the price down, until its market price is such that the fixed payment of $50 becomes closer to 10 percent of the bond's market price.

Actually the price of the old bond will not go down to $500, because the company still has an obligation to repay the original $1,000 loan on the due date. If the bond becomes due the year after the new interest rate, obviously it would be foolish for the holders of the bonds to sell at $500 when all they have to do is to wait a year and then demand $1,000 from the corporation. The bonds will nevertheless decline somewhat, and if they have twenty or more years to run, they will decline considerably.

If the interest rate declines, bond prices rise. Again suppose one holds a $1,000 bond paying 10 percent or $100 per year. If the interest rate declines to 5 percent, all a new investor can now expect as a yield on an investment of $1,000 is $50. Consequently, the demand for existing bonds paying $100 will increase and *theoretically* the older bond will rise to $2,000, again depending on maturity. Competition to obtain the older bond will theoretically bid its price up to the point where the $100 interest becomes 5 percent of the price of the bond, that is, $2,000. Again for practical reasons, however, it never goes that high.

Buying long-term bonds, then, is risky during periods when interest rates are volatile. An individual might think, however, that 10 percent is a fair return and is willing to hold it until maturity. Then there may be paper losses, but no actual losses; and in 20 years the investor will get back the $1,000, but then he or she will be hurt by inflation; what will $1,000 be worth in 20 years?[2]

---

[2] The longer the time to maturity, the greater the change in the price of a bond due to a given change in the interest rate. A bond would have to run to perpetuity (never become due) for a doubling of the interest rate to cut its market price in half. For example, if the interest rate rose from 12 to 15 percent, then a $1,000 bond maturing in twenty years would decline to $850, because in twenty years the bond would be redeemed at its face value of $1,000. Hence the $150 capital appreciation over this period must be prorated over twenty years and included in the $120 per year the bond pays. The bond would appreciate $7.50 per year; hence the total yield would be $127.50, which is 15 percent of $850.

The formula for determining the market price ($P$) of a bond is

$$P = I \left| \sum_{n=1}^{M} \frac{1}{\left(1 + \frac{i}{2}\right)^n} \right| + F \left| \frac{1}{\left(1 + \frac{i}{2}\right)^M} \right|$$

where

$P$ = current market price
$I$ = coupon interest payment in dollars
$n$ = payment periods per year (2 in the case of most bonds)
$M$ = total number of payments
$i$ = market rate of interest
$F$ = face value of the bond

In the case of a bond maturing in ten years paying $130 per year ($65 every six months) at a time when the market rate of interest is 12 percent, we would have

$$P = \$65 \times 11.4699 + 1000 \times 0.3118$$

and the market value of the bond would be $1,057.34.

Whether long-term bonds are a good buy, then, is a function of future interest rates. This introduces an element of the unknown. If an investor thinks interest rates will go no higher, bonds might be an okay buy, especially if they are likely to come down; there would then be a nice capital gain. On the other hand, if it is believed interest rates will rise in the future, refrain from buying bonds. Wait until they do rise and then buy.

What causes changes in the interest rate? They are caused by changes in the demand for and in the supply of money. If money is thought of as any other commodity and interest as the price of the commodity, then when the demand is high and the supply constant, the price or interest rate will rise. When the demand is low, the price goes down, provided of course that the supply remains constant. The supply of money is to a degree regulated by the Federal Reserve System, and in this way so too is the interest rate. The basic reasons for this regulation of the interest rate are twofold. If the Federal Reserve had reason to fear deflation and recession, it would attempt to lower interest rates to make borrowing by businesspersons more attractive, with the idea that if interest rates are lowered and borrowing occurs, new capital will be created with a resulting upswing in the economy. On the other hand, if the Federal Reserve Board feared inflation, it would raise the interest rate, on the philosophy that if rates are high, businesspersons will be deterred from new capital formation to a certain degree and forces of inflation will be lessened.

*Financial risk*

Financial risk is related to the debt (bond)-equity (common stock) ratio of a company, and is related to the obligation the corporation has to bondholders, preferred stockholders, and common stockholders, respectively. A high debt-to-equity ratio means that the corporation has a large fixed obligation (interest) to pay each year. If sales and profits decline severely in any one year, this could cause a burden. It is even possible that the heavy interest payment could not be met, and there would be losses instead of profits. The higher the debt-to-equity ratio, the higher the financial risk. However, a business often has some control over this risk.

*Political risk*

Political risk has to do with changes in the legal environment in which the business must operate. If the government changes taxes, tariffs, subsidies, or imposes wage or price controls, these changes could affect profits. Political risk would also include the psychological response and possible overreaction on the part of the public and the business community to a statement by the president or other government leaders.

*Risk and expected rate of return*

There is often a trade-off between risk and rate of return. However, the future return is seldom certain; hence, we have the concept of **expected**

***rate of return***. If the client wants a high rate of return, he or she will have to accept a high risk; or conversely, only the possibility of a high return will entice the investor to assume a high risk. Some investors are more risk adverse than others and will not commit to high-risk vehicles; they will accept a lower but more certain return.

The term expected rate of return is crucial. A high-risk investor may expect (or hope for) a high return, but he or she may not get it. If an investor makes a high-risk investment, the return will be high if it materializes, but the likelihood of it materializing is less.

The higher the risk, the higher the return if it materializes, but the probability of it materializing also declines with risk. Figure 14–3 shows the trade-off between risk and expected rate of return. To be sure, some of the rankings may be a bit arbitrary. For example, some over-the-counter stock may be less risky than some listed stock. Nevertheless, the general scale is valid.

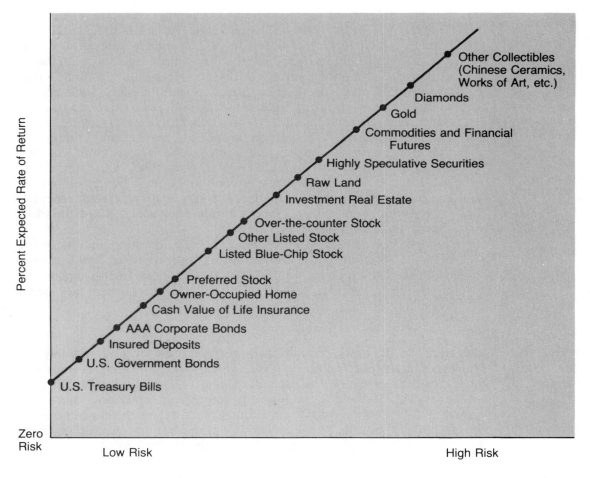

*Risk and expected rate of return*                                        Figure 14–3

## REDUCING THE RISK OF INVESTMENTS

Not much can be done about political risk and one must operate within the existing political environment. Interest rate risk is difficult to diffuse. If one can forecast changes in interest rates he or she can take advantage of this, but such forecasts are extremely difficult. When buying long-term bonds, one rule might be to buy them only if the yield is attractive enough to hold them to maturity, and then do so. Any future paper losses will not be realized. To be sure, one may possibly be prevented from taking advantage of future higher yields. If concerned about future changes in the interest rates, buy only short-term fixed obligations so the risk of capital loss is smaller. One can invest for a year or two easily and hold the securities until they mature. Then he or she will have only temporary paper losses or gains. An individual may also get a higher interest return by going short, because during periods of very high interest rates, short-term rates are often above long-term ones.

### Reducing certain specific risks

1. Financial risk (excess leverage in the firm's capital structure) can be lessened by not buying the securities of highly leveraged firms. (See Chapter 15). Study balance sheets and examine the stability of earnings. A firm that has good, stable earnings is able to service a higher debt-to-equity ratio than a firm whose earnings fluctuate.
2. In reducing the price level risk, strive to invest in firms whose sales and product prices are likely to keep up with inflation. Their profits will probably keep up with inflation too, and, if profits keep up, the prices of their securities are more likely to rise.
3. The risk of business failure can be reduced by selecting companies that are financially strong, innovative, and whose products are presently in great demand and likely to remain so. With bonds, this risk can be reduced by investing only in A-rated bonds or better.
4. For market risk, some companies are less vulnerable than others— for example, companies selling a product for which the demand is stable, such as food.
5. Interest rate risk can be lessened by not investing in long-term bonds or preferred stock. Investing in short-term fixed obligations can lessen the interest rate risk, as shown above in the section on interest rate risk. By going short term, however, there will be a lower interest rate return in many cases.

### Reducing overall risk by business trend analysis

The trend of business conditions is indicated weekly and monthly by figures on inventories, durable goods sales, price movements, employment, unemployment, industrial output, and GDP—figures that can give a clue as to whether the economy is moving up or down. There are cyclical movements up and down, but also broad overall long-run trends of economic expansion. By identifying broad upward or downward swings, and acting accordingly, risk can be reduced. If, for example, business conditions seem to be improving, one can buy securities with more confidence. If business conditions in general seem to be deteriorating, investors can reduce their risk by taking a more conservative stand regarding securities.

Industries are classified into groups for investment analysis—banks, food processing, rails, and the like—and a movement either upward or downward of the business cycle may affect them in varying degrees. Although generally if there is an upward movement in business conditions, all groups move upward, and if there is a downward movement, all groups have a tendency to move downward, some groups move to a lesser degree in either direction. Utility company earnings and sales are relatively stable, although there has been a cyclical trend upward. Auto stock tends to be more volatile, moving more rapidly upward during periods of expansion and just as rapidly downward during periods of contraction. Within each group, there are individual firms whose performance may be quite different from that of the group as a whole. Even during periods of contraction some firms earn more than others. Generally this can be attributed to good management. Within any group, one can find firms that have consistently paid good dividends to investors even during periods of severe recession, while others dealing with the same products are able to pay earnings only during relatively good times.

One can reduce risk by investing mostly in those industries that typically have done well and whose future looks more promising than that of the economy as a whole. Finally, if investors select not only industries that have done well but firms that have the best records within good industries, they can generally reduce risk even more.

Risk can be reduced by **diversification**, which is not putting all one's eggs in one basket. This is more difficult for a small investor than for a large one. But diversification is relative, and even a small investor should be able to obtain some. It can be achieved by firm, by industry, by type of security, and by investment objectives. If an investor decides to buy oil company stock, he or she should pick two or three or even four different companies, choosing the ones which seem best from the history of the industry and firm analyses. Diversity may be achieved by buying stock of firms in different industries; and by purchasing different types of securities, say, bonds and stock. The investment objective should be diversity, that is, some investments for growth, some for income, and some for stability.[3] Diversification reduces risk by broadening the investment base, and the securities will probably include some that will fare better than average.

One excellent way of diversifying is to invest in mutual funds. These will be discussed in Chapter 17.

*Reducing overall risk by diversification*

---

[3] From a functional point of view, common stock can be classified into income, growth, cyclical, speculative, and defensive stock, classifications discussed in Chapter 15.

**SOURCES OF INVESTMENT INFORMATION**

Financial information can be obtained from newspapers, magazines, books, investment services, banks, brokers, investment counselors, and other sources.

*Newspapers*

Greater amounts of information about business conditions are now in the financial pages of any large city newspaper, but certain newspapers are superior to others. Any serious investor should probably subscribe to *The Wall Street Journal,* a financial paper published daily in six regional editions as a morning paper. This journal publishes articles on general business and economic conditions in the United States and abroad. It also has stories and articles on specific industries and corporations and news on labor and government relations. It is a treasure house of business and financial statistics, of past, present, and future trends. It also has complete stock market quotations, including the Dow Jones averages and bond quotations. *The New York Times* also has a good financial section, containing news articles and in-depth analyses of business conditions in general and of specific businesses and industries.

*Magazines and other publications*

The better business and financial magazines are *Barron's Weekly, Forbes, Business Week, U. S. News and World Report,* and *Fortune Magazine.* These publications have articles on business and finance. They analyze general economic conditions, industries, and specific firms. The *Federal Reserve Bulletin* and the monthly *News Letters* published by the various district Federal Reserve Banks contain scholarly but readable articles on business and finance and many useful financial statistics. The President's Council of Economic Advisers publishes its monthly *Economics Indicators,* which contains a wealth of statistical information. All of these, and, in addition, many books and pamphlets, are available in any good library.

*Brokerage firms*

Many large brokerage houses have libraries available to the public that contain many of the above publications. They also publish special studies and analyses made by their own research departments. Many brokerage firms have their own weekly or monthly newsletter.

Additional information may be obtained from stockbrokers regarding both industries as a whole and individual corporations. Each industry is classified in relation to the general market as "relatively favorable," "average," or "relatively unfavorable." Individual securities are listed as "long-term investment," "high income," "good quality—wider price movement," or "speculative." Such listings are in accord with the various investment objectives.

*Investment services*

Although there are a number of services from which one may obtain research and advisory services on whole industries and individual companies, the most popular are Standard and Poor's, Moody's Investors Service, Fitch Investors Service, the Value Line Investment Survey, and Argus Research Corporation. These services specialize in furnishing the public with the basic facts and figures on all securities publicly marketed and on the companies issuing them. From these services one may obtain information covering a period of many years on the assets, income, earnings, dividends, and stock prices of various corporations. These services also make studies of specific firms. The first page summary on one such study on American Telephone and Telegraph is shown in Figure 14–4. The cost of these services can be hundreds of dollars, but an interested individual may examine them free in a broker's office or at most large public and university libraries. These investment services make industry studies in which they appraise the future outlook at the various firms within each industry and their common stock. Standard and Poor's publishes their listed stock report, a one- or two-page summary of every company listed on the New York Stock Exchange that provides some vital statistics and analyzes recent developments and future prospects of the firm. This summary comes out periodically with a separate sheet for each listed firm. It is called the "Yellow Sheet" in brokerage offices because it is printed on yellow paper. A reproduction of Standard and Poor's Yellow Sheet on International Business Machines is shown in Figure 14–5. Standard and Poor's also publishes a "Blue Sheet," an identical analysis for companies listed on the American Stock Exchange, and a "Green Sheet" for many over-the-counter securities, but only the better known ones.

*The stock exchanges*

The New York Stock Exchange has its own research department and makes available a number of publications free of charge, among them *The New York Stock Exchange Market* and the *New York Stock Exchange Fact Book*. The American Stock Exchange makes available similar booklets called *Understanding the American Stock Exchange* and *AMEX Databook*.

Some of the smaller regional securities exchanges also have free publications. Some exchanges have libraries that contain extensive information and are open to the public. While many of the publications of the organized exchanges will not provide specific investment information, they provide good background information in the areas of business, finance, and economics.

*Investment counselors or advisors*

Investment counselors will tailor an investment program for the individual investor according to the person's investment objectives. Investment counselors are professional investors and have their own skilled research departments. They, too, publish many studies, but these are available only to their customers.

Investment counselors will first determine the investment objectives of their clients. If they are older retired persons, they may need income. If they are younger persons, the objective may be growth. Once the

September 10, 1990
Vol. 15, No. 85

# ATLANTIC RICHFIELD COMPANY

**BUY**

## HIGHLIGHTS

Atlantic Richfield is in the unique position of producing more crude oil than its refineries consume, thus insulating it somewhat from potential crude oil shortages should fighting break out in the Middle East. The company's integrated West Coast operations stretch from substantial production facilities on Alaska's North Slope to gasoline distribution outlets in Southern California, and an expanded international exploration program is exposing the company to potentially large discoveries. But Alaska is the key to Arco's profits. The Exxon Valdez incident is taking its toll on the company in the form of higher future costs to prevent a recurrence of the disaster. On the production side, despite the hostile environment in which it operates, the company rates among the lowest in production costs. In refining and marketing, Arco is able to provide the consuming public with high volumes of "clean" gasoline because of its position as the largest producer of MTBE, a blending compound that reduces exhaust emissions. Moreover, because its two refineries use its relatively low-cost Alaskan crude, Arco is able to hold the line on gasoline prices.

| | | | |
|---|---|---|---|
| Price: 139 | | 12-Mo. Rge: 140 - 96 | |
| Symbol: ARC | | Options Exch.: CBOE | |
| DJIA: 2596.29 | | S&P 500: 320.46 | |

| Earnings | 1989 | 1990E | 1991E |
|---|---|---|---|
| (FY 12/31) | $11.26 | $10.00 | $10.70 |
| P/E Ratio: | | 13.9 | 13.0 |
| (vs S&P 500) | | 0.97 | 1.00 |
| 1985-89 Range: 0.67-1.11 | | | |

| Earnings Growth Rates: | 1985-89 | 1989-93 |
|---|---|---|
| ARC | 64% | 11% |
| S&P 500 | 7% | 6% |

Div.: $5.00          Yield: 3.6%
Financial Strength: High

Expected 12-18 Month Price Behavior
  Relative to the S&P 500: Above Average
Common Shares Outstanding: 173.4 Mil.

*Closing Price as of 9/6/90*

## RECOMMENDATION

We recommend purchasing the shares of Atlantic Richfield for above-average capital gains and secure income. At a price of $140 per share, the shares trade at a 31% discount to appraised net asset value of $204.05. Although the share price has recently exceeded the cash flow multiple of 5.7 — the highest it has been in the past 10 years — surging crude prices are expected to cause cash flow to accelerate. Furthermore, an active share repurchase program is likely to bolster per share data. The dividend, long stagnant at $1.00 per share, was boosted in the first quarter of 1989 to $1.125 and again in the first quarter of 1990 to the current $1.25. What's more, the company is unique among its peers in its ability to produce more crude than its refineries consume, placing it at a distinct advantage.

Figure 14—4   *A sample investment research analysis.* (Source: Argus Research Report. This report was reprinted courtesy of Argus Research Corporation, 17 Battery Place, N.Y.C., 10004.)

# Int'l Business Machines                    1210

NYSE Symbol IBM Options on CBOE (Jan-Apr-Jul-Oct) In S&P 500

| Price | Range | P–E Ratio | Dividend | Yield | S&P Ranking | Beta |
|-------|-------|-----------|----------|-------|-------------|------|
| Aug. 3'90 | 1990 | | | | | |
| 108⅛ | 123⅛-94½ | 16 | 4.84 | 4.5% | A | 0.76 |

## Summary

IBM is the world's dominant manufacturer of mainframe computers and is also a major supplier of minicomputers, computer peripheral equipment, personal computers, networking products, and system software. An earnings recovery is foreseen for 1990, reflecting the absence of restructuring costs and translation gains from a weaker dollar. In August, the company announced it would put its domestic typewriter and small printer products businesses into a new unit to be majority owned by Clayton & Dubilier.

## Current Outlook

Earnings for 1990 are expected to increase to $10.00 a share from $6.47 in 1989, which included a $2.58 restructuring charge. Earnings for 1991 are projected at $11.20.

The $1.21 quarterly dividend is the minimum expectation.

Gross income should rise almost 8% in 1990 and slightly less in 1991, benefiting from healthy demand overseas and a modest resurgence in domestic demand for IBM's main hardware products, plus translation gains from a weaker dollar. Profit margins should improve, with gains from the domestic cost containment program more than offsetting pricing pressures in the mainframe and minicomputer markets.

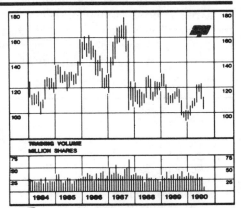

## Revenues (Billion $)

| Quarter: | 1991 | 1990 | 1989 | 1988 |
|----------|------|------|------|------|
| Mar. | --- | 14.19 | 12.73 | 12.06 |
| Jun. | --- | 16.50 | 15.21 | 13.91 |
| Sep. | --- | --- | 14.31 | 13.71 |
| Dec. | --- | --- | 20.46 | 20.00 |
| | --- | --- | 62.71 | 59.68 |

Revenues for the first half of 1990 advanced 10%, year to year, reflecting increased overall hardware sales and significantly higher software and leasing revenues. Profit margins benefited from the higher volume and initial benefits from the cost reduction program. After sharply higher interest expense, net income increased 6.8%, to $4.26 a share (on 1.9% fewer shares) from $3.92.

## Capital Share Earnings ($)

| Quarter: | 1991 | 1990 | 1989 | 1988 |
|----------|------|------|------|------|
| Mar. | E1.85 | 1.81 | 1.61 | 1.57 |
| Jun. | E2.55 | 2.45 | 2.31 | 1.63 |
| Sep. | E1.80 | E1.70 | 1.51 | 2.10 |
| Dec. | E5.00 | E4.04 | 1.04 | 3.97 |
| | E11.20 | E10.00 | 6.47 | 9.27 |

## Important Developments

**Aug. '90—** IBM announced that it will consolidate its domestic typewriter, keyboard, intermediate and personal printers and supplies business into a new subsidiary to be majority owned by Clayton & Dubilier, Inc. IBM may also place the rest of its worldwide information products business in the subsidiary.

**Feb. '90—** A new line of high performance technical workstations was introduced.

**Jan. '90—** The company restructured its domestic operations, resulting in a $2.4 billion pretax charge in the fourth quarter of 1989, equal to $2.58 a share after taxes. Savings from expected capacity reductions and technology investment writedowns could add $1.00 to share earnings by 1991.

**Nov. '89—** Directors approved the repurchase of and additional $4 billion of IBM stock.

**Next earnings report expected in mid-October.**

## Per Share Data ($)

| Yr. End Dec. 31 | 1989 | ¹1988 | 1987 | 1986 | 1985 | 1984 | 1983 | 1982 | 1981 | 1980 |
|-----------------|------|-------|------|------|------|------|------|------|------|------|
| Tangible Bk. Val. | 66.33 | 65.78 | 62.81 | 55.40 | 50.60 | 41.79 | 38.02 | 33.13 | 30.66 | 28.18 |
| Earnings² | 6.47 | 9.27 | 8.72 | 7.81 | 10.67 | 10.77 | 9.04 | 7.39 | 5.63 | 6.10 |
| Dividends | 4.73 | 4.40 | 4.40 | 4.40 | 4.40 | 4.10 | 3.71 | 3.44 | 3.44 | 3.44 |
| Payout Ratio | 72% | 47% | 50% | 56% | 41% | 38% | 41% | 47% | 62% | 56% |
| Prices—High | 130⅞ | 129½ | 175⅞ | 161⅞ | 158¾ | 128½ | 134¼ | 98 | 71½ | 72¾ |
| Low | 93⅜ | 104¼ | 102 | 119¼ | 117⅜ | 99 | 92¼ | 55⅝ | 48⅜ | 50⅜ |
| P/E Ratio— | 20-14 | 14-11 | 20-12 | 21-15 | 15-11 | 12-9 | 15-10 | 13-8 | 13-9 | 12-8 |

Data as orig. reptd. 1. Reflects acctg. change. 2. Bef. spec. item(s) of +0.53 in 1988. E-Estimated.

Standard NYSE Stock Reports
Vol. 57/No. 156/Sec. 11

**August 13, 1990**
Copyright © 1990 Standard & Poor's Corp. All Rights Reserved

Standard & Poor's Corp.
25 Broadway, NY, NY 10004

Standard & Poor's NYSE Stock Report, 'Yellow Sheet.' (Source: Standard & Poor's Equity Services. This report was up-to-date at the time of publication; subsequent changes are reflected in current Standard & Poor's reports.) Reprinted by permission of Standard & Poor's, a division of McGraw-Hill, Inc.                    Figure 14–5 objectives have been determined, different portfolio questions are indicated. The counselors give their clients constant surveillance of their securities. Clients may give counselors authority to buy or sell on their behalf and instruct their brokers to execute their counselor's orders. Or they may wish to retain veto power over their counselor's advice and execute their orders themselves.

*Corporation reports*     Before an investor buys any security, he or she may want to examine that corporation's financial reports—its balance sheet and income statement. Such reports give assets, liabilities, sales, expenses, earnings, dividends, and many more statistics, as well as top management's view concerning the future outlook of the business. Most corporations will send their balance sheet and income statement on request; brokerage houses also have many on file in their offices. (A sample balance sheet is shown in Figure 14–6).

| | |
|---|---|
| *I. Assets* | |
| **Current Assets** | |
| Cash | $    200,000 |
| Accounts receivable | 14,600,000 |
| Inventory | 10,200,000 |
|   Raw materials | |
|   Goods in process | |
|   Finished goods | |
| **Fixed Assets** | |
| Land | $ 5,000,000 |
| Building and equipment | 20,000,000 |
|   Total assets | $50,000,000 |
| | |
| *II. Liabilities* | |
| **Current Liabilities** | |
| Accounts payable | $13,500,000 |
| Short-term bank loan | 15,500,000 |
| **Fixed Liabilities** | |
| Bonds outstanding (9%) | $10,000,000 |
|   Total Liabilities | $39,000,000 |
| | |
| *III. Owner's Equity* | |
| Preferred Stock: 200,000 shares @ $10 per share | $ 2,000,000 |
| Common Stock Outstanding: 1,000,000 of par value $1 | 1,000,000 |
| Amounts in Excess of Par Value Received for Stock (paid in surplus) | 7,000,000 |
| Retained Earnings (Earned Surplus) | 1,000,000 |
|   Total Owner's Equity | $11,000,000 |
|   Total Liabilities and Owner's Equity | $50,000,000 |

*XYZ Corporation—year end income sheet, December 31, 199X.*     Figure 14–6

Many laypersons are overwhelmed by these reports and feel that since they cannot understand them, there is no need to read them. However, there is nothing difficult about either the balance sheet or the income statement. The personal balance sheet and cash flow statement were studied in Chapter 3. The corporate balance sheet and income statement are similar, except that different items and larger dollar amounts are involved. We shall work through both statements below.

A balance sheet contains three major parts: assets, liabilities, and owner's equity—sometimes called **net worth**. Total assets are always equal to total liabilities plus net worth. Net worth, the difference between assets and liabilities, is the stockholder's equity.

*The balance sheet*

Let us examine assets first. They are split into short-term assets (current assets) and long-term assets. Short-term assets include cash, which is self-explanatory; since it is a nonearning asset, firms try to keep cash amounts low. Accounts receivable is the money owed the corporation because of sales that have been made and presumably will be collected within thirty days. Inventories, too, are self-explanatory. Fixed assets are valued at their cost less depreciation—the degree to which they are worn out. The company has total assets, with which it earns income. Assets permit the company to conduct its business.

To acquire these assets, however, the corporation has to assume some liabilities. Current liabilities are those due to be paid within a short time. Accounts payable come about because the firm buys, say, raw materials, which it will pay for within thirty days. They also include such things as accrued wages and taxes due but not yet paid. The short-term bank loans are money the company borrowed from a bank on a short-term basis. Fixed liabilities came about because when the present plant was built, the corporation sold $10,000,000 of bonds to finance it. Total liabilities represent the total amount the corporation owes, but some of these debts need not be paid for many years, although the interest on them must be paid annually.

The final item is owner's equity, and it belongs to the stockholders. It is the residual amount—the assets with which the company operates less the liabilities the company eventually will have to pay. Net worth (or owner's equity) is split into preferred stock, common stock at par (or face) value, amount of capital paid in excess of par value, and retained earnings. Preferred stock is generally listed first because it is closer to bonds. It must be first netted out before getting the book value of the common stock. The par (or face) value of the common stock is shown and, immediately below it, the amount in excess of par received for it.[4]

---

[4] Par value is the face value of stock. It is not as important today as it was a number of years ago. In addition, some stock is issued as no-par stock. Par value is discussed in greater detail in the next chapter.

This third item is often referred to as paid-in surplus. The final item under net worth is retained earnings. It is also referred to as earned surplus, and it means profit the company earned in previous years but retained rather than paid out in dividends. Everything under net worth except the preferred stock belongs to the common stockholders. If that is divided by the number of shares of common stock outstanding, we obtain the book value per share of common stock (to be explained in Chapter 15).

The balance sheet shows how much capital the company has to work with as well as how much of it is represented by bonded indebtedness and how much by stock. By comparing assets and earnings (found in the income statement), the reader can ascertain the return on invested capital. By comparing earnings with net worth, the percentage return on stockholder's equity and the earnings per share of common stock can be obtained.

*The income statement*

While the balance sheet is a presentation of the company's affairs at a given moment in time, like a photograph, the **income statement** is a presentation of what happened to the company over a period of time, usually a year, like the flow of water during a year. A hypothetical income statement is shown in Figure 14-7.

The income statement, also called a profit and loss statement or an operating statement, shows the expenses of the company during the year and also the company's earnings or profits. These flows or sales increase the company's (and the stockholder's) well-being; outflows decrease it. Inflows or gross receipts are the same as sales, which were $11,700,000 for our company last year. Total costs are shown at $9,400,000 and are broken down into various components. For most manufacturing firms, labor costs are by far the largest item. The other costs are self-explanatory, with the exception of depreciation. Depreciation charges are made because fixed assets such as plant and equipment eventually wear out. When they do, the company must have the money on hand to replace them. In our case, the building and equipment is valued at

| | |
|---|---|
| Sales | $11,700,000 |
| Selling costs (advertising, etc.) | 350,000 |
| Cost of raw materials | 3,300,000 |
| Labor costs | 3,750,000 |
| Interest cost (on bonds) | 900,000 |
| Other costs (utilities, telephone, etc.) | 100,000 |
| Depreciation | 1,000,000 |
| Total Cost | 9,400,000 |
| Income (before taxes) | 2,300,000 |
| Taxes | 1,104,000 |
| After-tax profits | 1,196,000 |

*XYZ Corporation—year end balance sheet, December 31, 199X.*      Figure 14—7

$20,000,000. If we assume it has a useful life of twenty years with no scrap or salvage value, we must set aside one-twentieth of its value or $1,000,000 every year so that when it wears out we will be able to replace it. Depreciation is an expense and reduces profits by $1,000,000 per year. However, it is a unique kind of cost, one that does not cause a cash outflow from the company. While the $1,000,000 depreciation expense reduces profits by that amount, the company still has the money and will keep it invested somewhere and add to it every year until the time comes to replace the building and equipment.

After taxes, profits are $1.196 million, which is just over 10.8 percent return on total net worth. This sum of $1.196 million can be paid to the stockholders in the form of a cash dividend or it can be retained by the company, in which case it will go into the earned surplus account in the balance sheet for next year. Most companies split their after-tax profits, paying some to the stockholders and retaining some. However, in the above case there are 200,000 shares of preferred stock outstanding, and they must be paid a dividend before the common stock shareholders may receive anything. If we assume that they receive a 10 percent dividend on their par value of $2,000,000, this reduces profits by $200,000, which leaves a profit for the common stockholders of $996,000. This is a return of 11.07 percent on the common stockholders' equity of $9,000,000.

When analyzing balance sheets and income statements, it is often wise to read past reports to discover trends. Are sales rising and if so, how much? How have profits behaved over a number of years? Are the ratios of costs to sales rising or declining? These and many other important questions should be kept in mind when analyzing corporation reports. For example, we should also examine earnings per share. This is obtained by dividing earnings, after taxes and after making an allowance for a payment to the preferred stockholders, by the total number of shares of common stock outstanding. In our case we had after-tax earnings of $1.196 million. After the allowance shown above for preferred stockholders of 10 percent, there remains $996,000, which accrues to the common stockholder and amounts to 99.6 cents per share ($996,000 ÷ 1,000,000 shares).

Our company may or may not declare a dividend. If it does, we have a concept called ***dividends per share***. By examining this over the years, we can determine if dividends per share are rising, falling, or remaining relatively constant. This may influence whether or not we wish to buy the stock.

We may also wish to compare earnings per share (99.6 cents in our case above) with the market price of the common stock. If we divide the market price of the common stock by the earnings, $.996, we get a concept called the ***price-earnings ratio***. This ratio may be ten or twenty; it varies from stock to stock. But it is an indicator of whether the stock might be priced too high or whether it is a genuine bargain. Finally, we may want to determine the yield of the common stock. This is simply

**382**

Managing investments

the annual dividends per share divided by the market price of the stock and expressed in percentage terms.

Security analysts do not agree whether earnings per share or dividends (yield) per share are the best indicator of a stock's value, but all of these should be taken into account in making investment decisions.

## SUGGESTED READINGS

*American Stock Exchange Annual Report.* New York: American Stock Exchange.

*Barron's Educational Edition.* Princeton, N.J.: Dow Jones and Company.

*Barron's Weekly.* Princeton, N.J.: Dow Jones and Company.

"Before You Say Yes; Fifteen Questions to Ask About Investments." Pueblo, Colo.: Consumer Information Center.

Engel, Louis. *How to Buy Stocks.* New York: Bantam Books, 1983.

*The Exchange.* Magazine published monthly by the New York Stock Exchange, New York.

Farrell, James L., Jr., and Fuller, Russell J. *Modern Investments and Security Analysis.* New York: McGraw-Hill, 1987.

*Financial Analysts Journal.* New York: The Financial Analyst Federation. A bimonthly publication.

"Financial World, the Investment Magazine." New York: Financial World Partners. Monthly publication.

Fisher, Lawrence, and Lorie, James H. *Rates of Return on Investments in Common Stocks.* New York: Merrill Lynch, Pierce, Fenner, and Smith.

*Fortune.* A monthly magazine containing a great deal of information on business, economics, and finance.

Freund, William C., and Lee, Murray G. *Investment Fundamentals.* New York: American Bankers Association.

*How to Invest in Stocks and Bonds.* New York: Merrill Lynch, Pierce, Fenner, and Smith.

*How Professors Use The Wall Street Journal.* Princeton, N.J.: Dow Jones and Company.

*How to Read a Financial Report.* New York: Merrill Lynch, Pierce, Fenner, and Smith.

*How to Understand Financial Statements.* New York: New York Stock Exchange.

*How You Get More Out of Financial News.* Princeton, N.J.: Dow Jones and Company.

*The Insider's Guide to the Wall Street Journal.* Princeton, N.J.: Dow Jones and Company.

*The Market Place.* Chicago: Chicago Board of Trade.

"50 of the Most Common Financial Planning Mistakes and How to Avoid Them." New York: Dean Witter Reynolds. You may obtain this from a Dean Witter broker.

Spiro, Herbert T. *Finance for the Non-Financial Manager.* New York: John Wiley and Sons, 1982.

*Time.* A weekly magazine that contains a good deal of information on business and finance.

*Understanding Financial Data in The Wall Street Journal.* Princeton, N.J.: Dow Jones and Company.

*Understanding the New York Stock Exchange.* New York: New York Stock Exchange.

*U. S. News & World Report.* A weekly magazine that contains a good deal of information on business and finance.

*The Wall Street Journal.* Princeton, N.J.: Dow Jones and Company. Daily publication.

*The Wall Street Journal Educational Edition.* Princeton, N.J.: Dow Jones and Company.

"What Every Investor Should Know." Pueblo; Colo.: Consumer Information Center.

# 15 Investing in securities: stocks and bonds

**HIGHLIGHTS**     Bonds and stocks should be considered for acquisition by most investors, and in order to permit the investor to make more intelligent decisions when purchasing them this chapter covers the following:

1   The various corporate bonds
2   U.S. government securities
3   State and local bonds
4   Bond ratings and bond yields
5   Common stock and some of its value concepts
6   Earnings, yield, and capital gain on common stock
7   Stock classifications in accordance with various investment objectives
8   The various types of preferred stock

In this chapter we will examine the wide variety of securities (obligations of issuers) available to the investor. The issuers of securities are, generally, business firms and government, and they represent the demand for savings or, in other words, the supply of securities.

The buyers of securities represent the supply of savings, or the demand for securities. The demand for securities can be further broken down into institutional demand and individual demand. Institutional demands stem from life insurance companies, corporate pension funds, mutual funds, and commercial banks. We will discuss securities pertinent to the individual investor.

The securities we will be discussing are **bonds** and **stocks**. While bonds will probably not be the first investment most people will make, they are among the safest, if selected carefully. By safe here we mean safe from the risk of default. Stocks, on the other hand, are more risky. We will discuss bonds first.

## THE ARRAY OF BONDS

Corporate bonds are certificates of indebtedness to the issuing corporation; they are credit instruments used in raising long-term funds. They are legal liabilities of the corporation. Bonds are long-term obligations, and the corporation is obligated to pay a fixed interest rate for so many years, then to redeem the bond at face value. This interest must be paid even if it is not earned. The interest on bonds must be paid before a payment can be made even to preferred stockholders (discussed below). In the event the corporation is liquidated, bondholders are repaid their capital before preferred stockholders. Bonds are considered senior securities: their needs must be taken care of first.

### Corporate bonds in general

Corporate bonds are nearly always issued in denominations of $1,000 face value, also referred to as **par value**. When the word "bond" is used, it is assumed to be of that denomination. The interest rate shown thereon is called the coupon rate which, if 9 percent, obligates the corporation to pay $90 per year until the bond matures. Often, this would be paid as $45 every six months, or $22.50 quarterly.

Bonds may be sold at their face value, above it, or below it. If a bond is sold below par, it is said to be at a discount; if above par, it is at a premium. If a bond sells at a premium and has a coupon rate of 10 percent, the yield is less than 10 percent. A bond sold at a discount has a yield greater than its coupon rate. Yields and the coupon rate, then, are not the same. Bond prices fluctuate in the market inversely with changes in the going market interest rate, as noted in the previous chapter. Generally, when corporations offer new issues of bonds, they are issued at par or close to it.

Most corporation bonds are coupon bonds, that is, they have interest coupons attached, and generally a coupon is due and payable every six months. The bondholder clips the coupon and mails it to the trustee for the interest. Often the coupons can be redeemed at banks. These bondholders are the people Thorstein Veblen had in mind when he referred to "the coupon clippers." Noncoupon bonds do exist, the interest on which is automatically mailed to the bondholder by the trustee.

Most bonds in the United States are **registered.** They have the name of the owner on the face of the instrument, and they cannot be transferred without endorsement. The corporation issuing the bond must have a trustee (usually a bank) who keeps the records and mails interest payments.

Some bonds, however, are bearer bonds, which means that they are not registered. These are rare in the United States. Bearer bonds are always coupon bonds, whereas registered bonds can be either coupon or noncoupon bonds.

In addition to corporate bonds, there are United States government bonds and state and local bonds, called municipal bonds. Each of these can be classified into subgroups. Figure 15–1 is a picture of a corporate bond.

*Debentures*

A debenture bond is issued by a corporation and no specific assets are pledged. The general credit rating of the corporation is at stake, and any and all assets not otherwise pledged can be seized if these bonds are in default. For example, if certain other bonds (described below) are also outstanding for which specific assets have been pledged, then these specific assets cannot be used to satisfy the claims of debenture bondholders until the other bondholders' claims have been met. Where the debentures were issued first, they usually have a clause in them that requires they have equal rights with any future mortgage bonds. There are, however, also subordinated debentures, which are like second mortgages and stand further back. They may be subordinated to regular debentures, to mortgage bonds, or to any other kind. Since they are riskier, they usually yield a higher return.

*Convertible bonds*

Convertible bonds can be exchanged for a predetermined number of common stocks at the option of the bondholder. Convertible bonds are also usually debentures, but they need not be. The principle of convertible bonds is similar to that of convertible preferred stock. If the corporation does well, the convertibles take on the features of common stock, whereas if the corporation does poorly, the convertibles have the features of bonds. Convertible bonds pay a fixed interest rate like any bond and must be redeemed at maturity. However, they include a clause that permits the bondholder to convert them to common stock in the future at a rate determined when the bond is issued. If, for example, the common stock of the corporation were selling at $100 per share when the convertibles came out, the convertibility feature would permit one

Figure 15—1    *A corporate bond. (Source: Courtesy Sprague Electric Company and the First National Bank of Boston.)*

$1,000 bond to be converted to approximately ten shares of common stock at the option of the bondholder. If two or three years later the common stock were selling at $150 per share, the $1,000 bond could be converted into securities worth about $1,500. Thus, the market price of the bond would be bid up to about $1,500. Convertible securities, then, both preferred stock and bonds, may permit the holders to have their cake and eat it too. Corporations issue them for two reasons: (1) The corporation may be weak, or it may be issuing bonds at a time when savings are in short supply, and hence it must add the convertibility feature as a sweetener to sell them; (2) It may issue convertible bonds because this reduces the interest rate, say, from 8 to 7 percent.

*Callable bonds*

**Callable bonds** might be debentures, mortgage bonds, or another kind, but in addition they can be called in and the principal repaid at the option of the corporation. The corporation will insert the call feature if it believes it can refinance later at a lower rate of interest or if it believes that it will be able in the future to operate with less bonded capital. Often they cannot be called in until a specific future time, but after that they may be redeemed at any time. The call provision usually states that if the bond is called, it will be at a premium above par. Generally, the call premium is one year's interest if the call is made a year or two from issue, and lesser amounts on later calls. There is no certainty of locking oneself in on a long-term basis at a high rate if these are purchased.

There are a number of other bonds with which you should be familiar. For example, there are **corporate mortgage bonds**, which are secured by a mortgage on a specific piece of corporate real estate. Title to the property may be transferred to a third party who acts as a trustee and can sell the property and pay the bondholders if the bonds are in default.

*Other corporate bonds*

There are **collateral trust bonds** secured by specific corporate assets other than real estate, such as securities of other companies.

**Equipment trust bonds** are secured by equipment owned by the corporation, such as machinery or rolling stock in the case of railroads. The assets behind these bonds may also be sold if necessary to satisfy bondholders' claims.

There are also **serial bonds**. These can be debentures or any other kind. Serial bonds are numbered with the different numbers maturing at different times. The corporation redeems a few each year according to a predetermined schedule.

Discount bonds are outstanding bonds that were issued some time ago.

*Discount bonds*

Discount bonds have a market price below their face value. Since at maturity they must be redeemed at face value, the buyer will enjoy a capital gain.

There are two reasons why some bonds are sold at a discount. First, the corporation's credit rating may have worsened since the bonds were issued. Second, all bonds decline in value when the going market interest rate rises above the fixed stated interest (coupon) rate of any bond. The extent of the discount will be determined by the amount the market interest rate moves above the coupon rate and the length of time remaining until the bond matures. High discount, high quality bonds are a good buy when interest rates are at a peak and are expected to decline drastically.

These bonds, which pay no interest but are deeply discounted when sold, have become popular recently. They are much like the Series EE U.S. government savings bonds, permitting investors to lock in at a yield that can be calculated for the entire period until maturity. Ordinary positive coupon bonds yield interest, usually semiannually, and it must be rein-

*Zero coupon bonds*

vested at whatever the going rate may be at that time. This may be beneficial or harmful depending on what happens to interest rates after buying the bonds. With zero coupon bonds, one does not have the reinvestment bother or investment cost. These bonds can be either corporate or U. S. Treasury bonds.

Unlike the other discount bonds described above, however, the annual market appreciation of these bonds is taxed as it occurs and as ordinary income, even though not yet received. For this reason, the discount bonds discussed first (Series EE) may be the better buys.

The major problem with long-term zero coupon bonds is the same as that with any long-term bond: interest rates could go even higher. There is also a second reason why an individual should think hard before buying any long-term zero coupon bonds: in 20 or 30 years the issuing corporation may not even exist. With positive coupon bonds the investor would at least have received some interest along the way.

## Junk bonds

A few years ago **junk bonds** became somewhat popular. While they are still available they are less popular now. Junk bonds are high-risk instruments issued by some corporations. Because the risk of default is higher, they yield a higher interest rate. Sometimes they are issued by corporations to raise funds with which to take over (buy) other corporations. They are considered high risk and recently some have been in default. Nevertheless some investors buy them because of their high yield.

The term "junk bonds" is a generic term relatively new and is used by the press and some laypersons. Professionals and others in the finance community refer to certain bonds as speculative and even highly risky (see below under bonds and credit ratings). Anything B and below under Moody's rating and B or below under Standard and Poor's is a speculative bond. A new term is currently being used by some people— "trash bonds." These are presumably even riskier than "junk bonds."

## Mortgage-backed and agency bonds

Recently, **residential mortgage-backed bonds** have been developed. These are not regular corporate bonds, but rather are issued by private financial institutions and government agencies like the Government National Mortgage Association (GNMA). When an investor buys these bonds, the funds are used to finance residential housing: mortgages are the underlying securities. The home-owner's monthly mortgage payments are usually passed through, and the investor receives a monthly cash flow that represents both interest and return of principal. There are a few non-pass-through mortgage-backed bonds, however; in this case the investor receives interest every six months and then the principal in one lump sum a number of years later, just like a regular bond.

Since these bonds' yield comes from mortgages, their yield is often quite high. Those that are issued by GNMA (called agency bonds) are also riskless insofar as default is concerned, because they are guaranteed by the full faith and credit of the U.S. government; they are as safe as any U.S. government securities. Unfortunately for many small investors, the minimum purchase of such riskless bonds is $25,000. However, the small investor may buy them via a mutual fund, as we shall see in Chapter 18.

Receiving the principal back in installments over the years may present a reinvestment problem. The investor must also, of course, separate the interest received from the principal in order to calculate the yield, but there are formulas to do this. These bonds have become a popular investment outlet recently.

Three varieties of marketable securities will be discussed here. (Non-marketable Series EE and HH savings bonds were presented in Chapter 13.)

*U.S. government marketable securities*

Marketable U.S. Treasury Bonds are long-term obligations generally running up to 30 years. Since they are marketable, they fluctuate in the market inversely with fluctuations in the interest rates. Financial institutions are important buyers of long-term government bonds. Insurance companies, investment companies, and private pension funds commit millions of long-term dollars in government bonds each year.

U.S. government bonds

For those bonds issued before 1986, they could be bearer bonds or registered bonds. The bearer bonds have a coupon and interest is paid every six months. To collect the interest, it is merely necessary to detach the coupon when the interest is due, take it to a bank, and deposit it. The bank will collect the interest. In the case of registered bonds, the interest, when due, is automatically deposited into the investor's bank account. Since 1986 all bonds are now sold on what is called a "book entry" basis, and the interest is automatically deposited in the investor's account when due.

**Treasury notes** are similar to Treasury bonds but generally have shorter maturities: they run from two to as high as ten years. They have a coupon (are not discounted), which provides for an interest payment every six months; they are negotiable and marketable, so they fluctuate in the market inversely with fluctuations in their interest rate. These securities are like government bonds, except their maturities are shorter. These notes are now sold only on a "book entry" basis, and the interest is automatically deposited in the investor's account.

Treasury notes

These bills are short-term bearer obligations of the United States government. Because they are discounted when issued, the interest is the difference between the price at which the Treasury sells them and their face value. The minimum amount that may be purchased is $10,000, and after the first $10,000 they can be obtained in multiples of $5000. They

Treasury bills

have a maturity of ninety days, six months, and sometimes one year. While some individuals buy them if they have funds temporarily idle while seeking long-term investments, **_Treasury bills_** are primarily purchased by financial institutions in order to put their funds to work immediately while they are seeking permanent long-term outlets for them. Sometimes, however, industrial corporations buy them with funds set aside for future tax or dividend payments.

Relatively small investors might buy these securities during periods when interest rates are very high. This is especially true if their rates are higher than those of depository institutions.

Treasury bills can be purchased through a bank, which makes arrangements to buy them in a block and parcel them out to customers. Banks used to provide this service free, but in recent years they have begun to assess a fee. The cost varies from bank to bank, but is generally from $25 to $30 per transaction.

*State and local securities*

State and local government securities appeal to high-income investors because their interest income may be exempt from federal taxation. Usually bonds of a state or a political subdivision of a state are exempt from state income taxes as well. Because of this exemption, municipal bonds often yield a lower return than United States government securities. Competition on the part of wealthy investors for these securities reduces the yield below that indicated by the risk and often below that of United States Treasury obligations. The justification given for tax exemption is that it reduces the cost of financing schools and other public purposes at the local level. The opponents of tax exemption argue that it is merely a loop-hole that enables high-income groups to avoid the payment of taxes. An investor in the highest tax bracket should investigate them. A person in the 28 percent bracket would have to get an 8.3 percent return on alternative investments to be as well-off after taxes as one is with a 6 percent tax-exempt return. Table 15–1 shows the

Table 15–1    *Taxable equivalent yield table*

| Federal Tax Bracket | Tax-Exempt Yield | | | | | | |
|---|---|---|---|---|---|---|---|
| | 5.00% | 5.50% | 6.00% | 6.50% | 7.00% | 7.50% | 8.00% |
| | | | Taxable Equivalent Yield | | | | |
| 15% | 5.88 | 6.47 | 7.05 | 7.64 | 8.23 | 8.82 | 9.41 |
| 28% | 6.94 | 7.63 | 8.33 | 9.02 | 9.72 | 10.41 | 11.11 |
| 31%* | 7.25 | 7.97 | 8.70 | 9.42 | 10.14 | 10.87 | 11.59 |

* If 5% surcharge applies

tax-equivalent yield which would have to be obtained on corporate securities to match various tax-free rates.[1]

Not only do state and local governments issue these tax exempts, but so do their political subdivisions, such as schools, sewer and water districts, toll road commissions, and others. There are different kinds of such tax-exempt securities, some of which are long-term securities (bonds) and some short-term notes. They may be classified as follows:

1. Short-term tax-exempt municipal notes
2. General obligation bonds
3. Special tax bonds
4. Revenue bonds

Many municipal bonds are general obligation bonds. They are secured by the full faith and credit of the taxing entity issuing them, that is, the full and unlimited taxing powers of the issuing government are pledged to back them up. These presumably are the least risky municipal bonds. The risk, of course, varies from one government to another.

General obligation bonds

Special tax bonds are secured not by the full faith and credit of the issuing government, but only by part of it. They are payable only from a specific and listed tax source. In some cases, a new specific tax is imposed to support a new bond issue when it comes out. For example, a new sewer system may be financed by such bonds which are then to be repaid by a special tax levied on the citizens. These are riskier than full faith and credit bonds of the same entity, and hence their yield is higher.

Special tax bonds

Revenue bonds are not full faith and credit bonds. These are frequently issued by certain political subdivisions such as a toll road commission or a state university, that have no taxing powers. However, the interest and principal is to be repaid by the revenue (tolls from turnpikes or rent from college dormitories) to be raised by whatever the bonds finance. Sometimes municipal water and electric departments sell such bonds, which are to be repaid solely from the water and electricity rates that are charged. Since no government's faith and credit are pledged, these revenue bonds are generally considered riskier; and their yield is higher than bonds of the same entity that have taxing power behind them.

Revenue bonds

Short-term tax-exempt municipal notes are also short-term notes generally running from six months to two years which would appeal to those investors who are uncertain about long-term interest rates and do not want

Short-term tax-exempt municipal notes

---

1. Prior to August 1986, all securities issued by state and local governments were tax exempt; since then some of them are not. Primarily those that are not are the industrial development bonds issued by communities to attract new businesses. Be sure to check this before purchasing them.

to become locked in at a fixed rate for a number of years. By purchasing these, the investor will be able to reappraise the situation a year hence.

These notes may be full faith and credit or revenue obligations. The full faith and credit are sometimes tax anticipation notes, that is, taxes due in six months or a year are pledged to pay off these notes. The revenue notes are backed by revenue expected some time in the near future.

Some of these short-term notes are construction notes, sometimes called bond anticipation notes. They are used to finance the construction of something that will take a year or two. When the construction is complete, long-term bonds are sold to pay off the short-term notes.

**State and local bond trusts**

Recently, a number of open-end investment companies (or mutual funds)[2] have been established through which tax-exempt bonds can be purchased indirectly. They can be purchased in multiples as low as $1,000. Most of the bonds in these trusts are A-rated or better. However, some of the trusts are spiced with some lower-rated bonds in order to increase the yield. These are discussed at greater length in Chapter 17.

*Bonds and credit ratings*

The amount of interest paid on corporate bonds is determined by the credit rating of the company, length of maturity of bonds, and demand for and supply of money at the time of the issuance of the bond. With U.S. government bonds, credit rating is not a factor; however, both length of maturity of bonds and demand and supply of money at the time of the issuance will determine the rate paid by the federal government. For example, if the supply of money is short, the rates of the "governments" will be forced up just as is the interest rate with any other borrower. However, because of the relatively riskless character of the government issues, the amount paid by the government in interest will be lower than that paid by corporations. The rate on state and local bonds, too, varies with the same factors, although, as noted above, the tax-free interest generally keeps the rate on these securities low.

Interest rates on all fixed obligations vary with the length of time the securities run to maturity. Generally when rates are relatively low, long-term bonds yield more than short-term debt obligation. However, when interest rates are relatively high, often short-term obligations yield a higher return than long-term.

With respect to credit rating, the higher the rating, the lower the interest rate on corporation bonds as well as on state and local bonds. There are services that assign a credit rating to bonds, these ratings being an attempt to measure the quality of bonds or their degree of "gilt-edgedness." Moody's, which is one of the most widely used bond rating services, has nine classifications of risk. Triple A bonds are the highest quality and C bonds the lowest. A triple A bond carries little risk

---

2. Open-end investment companies, which are also called mutual funds, are discussed in greater detail in Chapter 17.

of default, whereas a C bond is in default and has very little prospect of ever being paid off. If the investor buys a C bond, he or she might be buying a lawsuit.

The accompanying list gives the nine ratings assigned by Moody's. A broker can tell an investor which rating any corporate bond has. Remember any bond below Baa (which is medium grade) is a speculative bond investment.

*Moody bond ratings*

Aaa
Aa
A
Baa
Ba
B          Speculative Bonds
Caa
Ca
C          In Default

Standard and Poor's, another service similar to Moody's, has slightly different symbols, and more classifications. Standard and Poor's ratings are shown below.

*Standard and Poor's bond ratings*

AAA
AA
A
BBB
BB
B
CCC
CC          Speculative
C
DDD          In Default The different D bonds indicate that the bondholders
DD                  would get different amounts back upon liquidation, with the
D                   D rating being the lowest.

We have already learned that a bond has a coupon rate of interest and a market rate of interest, the latter also called the **yield**. For example, if a $1,000 bond has a coupon rate of 9 percent, this indicates that the corporation will pay a fixed dollar amount ($90) per year. But if a person purchased such a bond that matures in one year at a discount (he or she paid, say, $990.90) the actual yield is equal to the $90 interest received plus the $9.10 capital appreciation. The actual percentage yield is $99.10 ÷ $990.90 or 10 percent.

We should also recognize the following yield concepts:

*Bond yields*

1. Nominal yield and real yield
2. Average yield to maturity
3. Annual yield to maturity
4. Tax-equivalent yield of a municipal security
5. Tax-free equivalent yield of a taxable yield

**Nominal yield and real yield**

The nominal yield is stated in money terms and not adjusted for inflation. To convert the nominal yield to the real yield, we must subtract the rate of inflation from the money (nominal) yield. If, in the case discussed above, the price level had risen by 5 percent during the year, the real yield would, of course, be 5 percent.

**Average yield to maturity**

In a few cases (primarily U. S. Series EE bonds), the actual yield is not the same each year. U. S. Series EE bonds, you will recall, are discounted. In addition, the interest rate which they receive floats; it is tied to the rate of five-year U.S. government marketable securities, and varies with that market rate. Consequently, the average rate to maturity cannot be calculated until the bonds are actually cashed in. Nevertheless, it is a valid concept.

**Annual yield to maturity**

There is also the similar but slightly different concept of annual yield to maturity, which is important if the bond is sold at below (or above) par and has a number of years to run. This comes about because, in calculating yield to maturity, the investor must consider not only the dollar amount of interest received each year but also the annual capital gain (or loss) as the bond matures and its market price moves toward its face value. The following formula approximates the yield to maturity:

$$\frac{\left(\begin{array}{c}\text{annual interest}\\\text{payment}\end{array}\right) + \dfrac{\text{maturity value less market price}}{\text{years to maturity}}}{\dfrac{\text{maturity value + market price}}{2}}$$

For example, a bond with a face value of $1,000 paying a coupon interest rate of 8 percent running over 10 more years, and purchased at $800, will give us:

$$\frac{\$80 + \dfrac{(\$1,000 - \$800)}{(10)}}{\dfrac{\$1,000 + \$800}{2}} = \frac{\$80 + \dfrac{200}{10}}{\$900}$$

$$\frac{80 + 20}{900} = \frac{100}{900} = 11.1 \text{ percent}$$

The tax-equivalent yield is the term used when discussing municipal bonds. Since interest on municipal bonds is not taxed, a 5 percent return there is also the after-tax yield. The tax-equivalent yield is that yield you would have to get on a corporate bond so that, after personal income tax on it, you would have the same amount left that you could have earned on a municipal bond. Consequently, the tax-equivalent yield will vary depending on the individual income tax bracket. For a person in the 28 percent tax bracket, the tax-equivalent yield to a 5 percent municipal bond is 6.944 percent; for a person in the 15 percent tax bracket, it is 5.88 percent. The tax-equivalent yield, then, is that level to which the yield must be adjusted up to provide a sufficiently higher return so as to enable the investor to pay taxes and still be as well-off as with a tax-exempt yield.

To obtain the tax-equivalent yield, divide the tax-free yield by 1 minus the investor's tax bracket; use the following formula:

$$\frac{\text{tax-free yield}}{1 - \text{tax bracket}} = \frac{.05}{1 - .28} = \frac{.05}{.72} = .06944$$

The tax-equivalent yield of a 5 percent tax-free yield for a person in the 28 percent tax bracket is 6.944 percent.

A table showing the various tax-equivalent yields is shown in Table 15–1.

We can also go in reverse and find the tax-free equivalent of a taxable yield. We multiply the taxable yield by 1 minus the tax bracket. Or use the formula (taxable yield) × (1 – tax bracket). In the above case:

$$.06944 \times 1 - .28 = .06944 \times .72 = .049999$$

Bonds, as you have seen, can be classified into several categories. Stocks have only two categories—common and preferred. Common stock represents the ultimate of risk capital; preferred stock is less so. Figure 15–2 is a picture of a common stock certificate.

## THE ARRAY OF STOCKS

For all practical purposes, there is only one kind of common stock. Common stockholders are the residual recipients of a corporation's income. Because they receive what is left after all others get their prior claim, common stockholders' futures are closely tied to that of the corporation. If the corporation does well, the common stockholders do well. If the corporation does poorly, the common stockholders suffer. Common stockholders are also the last to be paid off in the event the corporation must be liquidated and sell its assets. Owning common stock then is riskier than owning other securities, and thus the market value of common stock fluctuates more than that of other securities.

Common stock ownership conveys no rights except the right to vote

*Common stock certificate. (Source: Courtesy General Motors Corporation.)* Figure 15—2

at stockholders meetings, where the corporation's board of directors is elected and certain other corporate decisions are made.[3]

*Some value concepts of common stock*

There are four general methods of valuing common stock: (1) par value, (2) book value, (3) market value, and (4) liquidation value. In most states it is now possible to issue a no-par-value common stock and often this is done, although historically stock always had a par value. These terms can sometimes be confusing and need to be explained.

1.  **Par value** is the face value of the stock printed on the certificate. A fixed and arbitrary value is assigned when the stock is issued; it has little financial significance. Even when the stock is issued, it may be at or above par. Today stock is usually sold substantially above

---

3. In recent years some corporations have issued non-voting common stock. If an investor buys these, he or she has no voice in corporate affairs but does share in corporate profits.

par. Historically, par value was higher and a more meaningful indicator of what the stock was worth. If a stock was sold at below par, the stockholder was often held liable for the difference between the price paid for it and par value. Today this is no longer true because stock cannot legally be sold below par when it is first issued. Stock that has no printed face value is called no-par stock. Par value has some meaning insofar as preferred stock is concerned because the dividend is often based on par value. Preferred stock is explained in greater detail below, where the importance of par value on preferred stock will become clear.

2.   **The book value** of common stock is an accounting concept. It is what the stock is worth today from an accounting point of view. When you examined the corporate balance sheet you were introduced to the concept of net worth (assets minus liabilities). The net worth, less a possible allowance for preferred stock belongs to the common stockholder. It is also called the stockholder's equity. Net worth (minus preferred stock outstanding, if any) divided by the total number of shares of common stock outstanding is the book value per share.

3.   **Market value** is what you have to pay for the stock if you wish to buy it—or what you will get if you sell it. It is often above book value, and, if so, it is because the expected future income has been taken into account by investors, and their demand has bid up the market price. This process is sometimes referred to as "discounting the future." Market value may also be lower than book value, if investors feel pessimistic toward that particular stock.

4.   **Liquidation value** is meaningful only if the corporation is unsuccessful and goes out of business. In such a case, if there is anything left after all bills have been paid (including paying off bondholders and preferred stockholders), it is prorated to holders of the common stock. Liquidation value may be zero or even negative. All corporate assets would have to be sold, and if they were specialized assets, no ready market for them would exist. Only some other corporation might be willing to buy them, or they might have scrap value only.

The earnings and yield on common stock vary greatly from firm to firm and from time to time. **Earnings** are simply the total earnings after taxes per share. The yield is less than earnings because an adjustment must be made to net out the corporation's retained earnings. **Yield** then is the actual dividends paid as a percentage of the price of the stock. An example of earnings and yield will clarify this.

*Earnings, yield, and capital gain on common stock*

$$\frac{\text{total after tax earnings}}{\text{total number of shares outstanding}} = \frac{\$7,500,000}{1,000,000 \text{ shares}} = \$7.50/\text{share}$$

In most cases part of this $7.50 is paid out in the form of dividends and part is retained and plowed back into the corporation for expansion.

However, the entire $7.50 belongs to the stockholder, and that portion retained will increase the book value and hopefully the market value of the stock. Earnings per share is an important criterion in determining whether an individual might want to buy a given stock. A comparison of earnings with the market price of a given share gives us its price earnings ratio which is an important analytical tool, when comparing stock within an industry. Let's assume our stock above, earning $7.50 per share, is selling at $75. We now may calculate its price earnings ratio (PER). It is

$$\frac{\text{market price}}{\text{earnings per share}} = \frac{\$75}{\$7.50} = 10$$

Yield as noted above is simply the annual dividend payment per share divided by the market price. In our example above, assume that there is a 50 percent dividend payout rate. Then

$$\frac{\text{dividends per share}}{\text{market price per share}} = \frac{\$3.75}{\$75.00} = 5\% \text{ yield}$$

In the above case where, in addition to a $3.75 dividend, $3.75 is retained by the corporation, the market price (as well as the book value) of the stock will tend to rise. However, this is true only if the retained profits are successfully reinvested in expanding the business and its profits. In such a case the stockholders get part of their reward in the form of capital appreciation rather than in cash dividends.

Traditionally it has been felt by most investors that the total earnings on a common stock should be higher than the yield on bonds—to compensate the investor for the greater risk associated with common stock. Generally, the dividend yield alone on common stock is lower than the yield on bonds, but the total earnings (dividends plus retained earnings) on common stock should be superior to bond yield. In many cases they are, but the retained earnings are not always reflected in common stock price appreciation, and in such a case, the yields and capital appreciation on stock combined might be below the yield on bonds. This has sometimes been the case in some years.

However, investing in common stock has traditionally been one of the better ways to participate in the future economic growth of the country because profits rise with growth, and this often shows up in the form of capital gains on stock. Economic growth is a function of population growth and of technological change. Technological change will enhance profits either by reducing costs or by bringing forth new or improved products, or by some combination of the two. New and improved products enhance profits by increasing sales.

Figure 15–3 illustrates how dividends have risen over the past eighty-six years in relation to the cost of living. If we considered the total earnings on common stock (dividends plus retained earnings), the record of common stock would look even better.

Perhaps the best measure of how good an investment a common stock has been is to take into account the total economic increment it

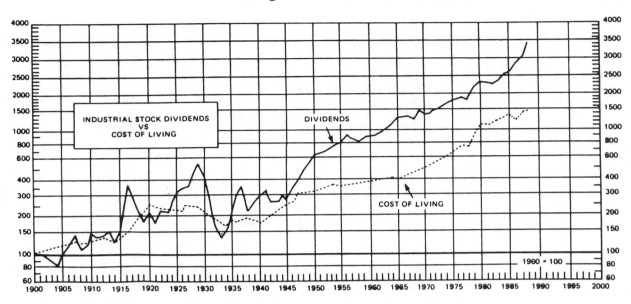

*Industrial stock dividends versus cost of living.* (Source: Investment Companies, Mutual Funds and Other Types, 1989, **CDA/Wiesenberger, a division of CDA Investment Technologies** Inc. p. 54.)

Figure 15–3

has provided its owner. This includes cash dividends as well as capital gains, which are influenced by retained earnings but may very well be higher or lower than retained earnings indicate they should be. Suppose an investor had purchased a common stock for $50 per share. Suppose too that its after-tax earnings were $5 per share and that it retained $2.50 and paid a cash dividend of $2.50. Clearly its dividend yield would be 5 percent and its total earnings 10 percent, but if the market price of the stock had increased over the year to $60 per share, the total economic increment it has provided is $12.50 (the $2.50 of retained earnings is included in the $10 capital gain, but the $2.50 dividend is not). A return of $12.50 on a $50 investment is 25 percent. To be sure, in order to realize this capital gain in the form of cash, the stockholder would have to sell the stock. Nevertheless, the capital gain cannot be ignored. The next year it may be more or less. Table 15–2 illustrates these ratios; Figure 15–4 shows how corporate dividends, profits, and taxes have fluctuated in recent years.

Some firms have raised more capital via the sale of bonds both absolutely and relative to their total capital than other firms. This variation can be explained in part by management philosophy. However, it is also in part due to different kinds of business operation. Certain types of firms can safely raise a larger proportion of their capital by selling bonds than can others because their earnings are more stable from year to year.

*The capital structure of a firm: one reason why earnings vary (leverage)*

Table 15—2  *Possible returns on stock*

| ABC stock | | | Percent return on investment |
|---|---|---|---|
| Purchase price | | $50.00 | |
| Earnings (per year) | | 5.00 | 10% |
|    Dividend | $2.50 | | 5% |
|    Retained earnings | | | |
| Capital gains | | 10.00 | 20% |
|    Due to retained earnings | 2.50 | | |
|    Due to other factors | 7.50 | | |
| Economic increment | | 12.50 | 25% |

Such a firm may use more borrowed capital in the hope of increasing the earning (and yield) on its common stock. Raising capital via bonds imposes a fixed cost upon the corporation and introduces *leverage* into its earnings. Leverage can be positive or negative. Positive leverage comes about if a business can borrow capital at, say, 8 percent by selling bonds, and then earn 10 percent with it. The 2 percent differential accrues to the common stockholder. However, negative leverage will be generated if next year the firm earns only 6 or 7 percent on the capital it borrowed at 8 percent. Firms that have high and stable earnings can safely build more leverage into their capital structure than can low- and fluctuating-income firms. An illustration will make leverage clear.

Two hypothetical firms (see Tables 15–3 and 15–4) are identical to begin with and each earns a 10 percent return. Then they both expand, firm A by selling another million dollars of common stock and firm B by selling a million dollars of bonds. Both firms doubled in size and in sales and in profits before any interest was paid. However, the earnings return to common stock rose to 12 percent for firm B and remained unchanged for firm A. This is an illustration of positive leverage.

If, next year, both firms' incomes before interest were to fall to $120,000, then firm A would be earning 6 percent for its stockholders while firm B would earn only 4 percent. This is an illustration of negative leverage. Certain firms whose incomes are more stable, like utilities, often are able to take greater advantage of leverage. This also explains why their incomes are often higher.

While the amount of leverage a firm has built into its capital structure may influence earnings, it is by no means the only factor. The quality of management, the type of product it sells, and how effectively it innovates and creates new and better products are equally important. Nevertheless, the investor should look at a firm's capital structure before buying securities, especially if he or she is concerned that business conditions may worsen in the future and with them corporate profits. It

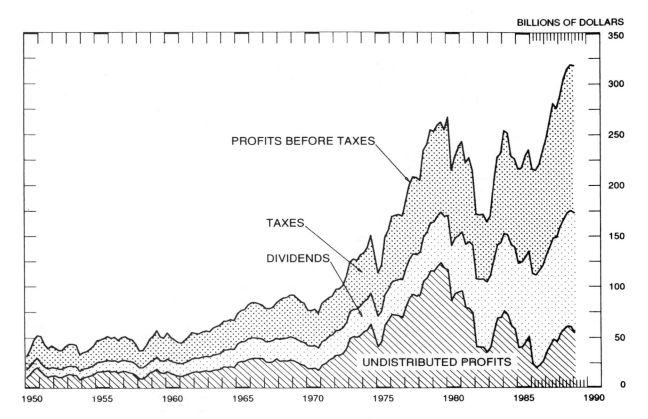

BILLIONS OF DOLLARS

PROFITS BEFORE TAXES

TAXES

DIVIDENDS

UNDISTRIBUTED PROFITS

1950   1955   1960   1965   1970   1975   1980   1985   1990

*Corporate profits, taxes, and dividends, seasonally adjusted annual rates, quarterly.*   Figure 15–4
*(Source: 1989 Historical Chart Book, Board of Governors of the Federal Reserve System, p. 60.)*

may be a method of rejecting certain stocks if the investor is taking a defensive position.

A stock's **beta** is an indicator of its volatility relative to the market. The   *Beta*
overall market has a beta of one. A stock's beta is the total return of that stock (both price appreciation and dividends received) relative to the return of the market—as measured by some index such as Standard and Poor's and some average of dividends for the market.

   If a stock has the average beta of one, its return is proportionate to the market's return. If, on the other hand, a given stock generates a 20 percent return versus the market's 10 percent, its beta is 2. A 5 percent return versus a 10 percent return for the market indicates a beta of 0.5.

   Beta also measures declines. Beta is considered an indicator of risk. The higher the beta above one, the more it swings with market changes;

Table 15–3    *Capital structure of a firm*

| Before expansion | | | |
|---|---|---|---|
| **Firm A** | | **Firm B** | |
| Capital stock (20,000 shares at $50 per share) | $1,000,000 | Capital stock (20,000 shares at $50 per share) | $1,000,000 |
| After tax earnings | 100,000 | After tax earnings | 100,000 |
| Percentage return | 10% | Percentage net | 10% |

Table 15–4    *Capital structure of a firm*

| After expansion | | | |
|---|---|---|---|
| **Firm A** | | **Firm B** | |
| Capital stock (40,000 shares at $50 per share) | $2,000,000 | Capital stock | $1,000,000 |
| | | Bonds at 8% | 1,000,000 |
| | | After tax but before interest earings | 200,000 |
| After tax earnings | 200,000 | Interest | 80,000 |
| Percentage return | 10% | Earnings for shareholders | 120,000 |
| | | Percentage return | 12% |

the lower the beta is below one, the greater the stability of that stock relative to the market. To be sure, a stock's beta can change; any beta is only a reflection of what has happened in the past. Nevertheless, the past can be an indicator of what might happen in the future.

## Rankings of common stock

Bonds have long been rated according to their credit-worthiness, with AAA being the highest quality, as explained above. Stock ratings, or rankings, have been developed in recent years. The best known of these is Standard and Poor's. Stocks are ranked somewhat differently than bonds, however. Stocks are not ranked in degree of protection for principal and dividends. Standard and Poor's considers such things as the product produced, managerial capabilities, financial structure, and past earnings and dividends, with great emphasis placed on financial strength. An A+ rank would be a firm that is extremely strong financially, like IBM. In addition, growth and stability of earnings are assessed, and the long-run record of performance. Then a ranking is assigned, with A+ being the highest. The following eight rankings are currently used:

A+    Highest
A      High
A –    Good
B+    Median
B      Speculative
B–    Highly speculative
C      Marginal
D      In reorganization

Common stock can be classified into a number of categories. It is possible to identify growth stock, income stock, cyclical stock, defensive stock, blue-chip stock, speculative stock and others. Stocks change; so a stock that at one time may be considered a growth stock may at another time be regarded as an income stock. Also, some stock may have the characteristics of several classifications; defensive and income stocks, for instance, may in some cases be the same. Obviously some stock may have some of the attributes of all four. Income and growth stocks—indeed all stocks—have some cyclical aspects. Nevertheless, many stocks fall into patterns. You should select stock in accordance with your investment objectives, discussed in the previous chapter.

*Classification of common stock*

When stocks are classified as speculative or blue-chip, they are classified according to risk. These are relative terms, as there is an element of speculation in all stock and an element of investment in all. The least speculative (most blue-chip) stock over the years has probably been American Telephone and Telegraph. The most speculative (least blue-chip) stock is probably Dry Gulch Gold and Uranium, or some other stock like it. We shall examine all of these classifications.

**Growth stocks** are generally considered to be those that have good growth stock earnings but a very low dividend yield because the company is reinvesting the bulk of its earnings in expansion. This investment increases both the book value and the market value of the stock, and the stockholder's goal in such a case presumably is to achieve capital gains through the appreciation of the stock. A growth company should also be doing better each year than the year before. It is not only using its earnings to expand capacity, but it is producing a product for which the demand is expected to increase in the future.

Growth stock

To buy a growth stock one may have to pay a high price, as many of them have excessively high price-earnings ratios, because the stock market is said to discount the future. If the company is earning a high rate of return per dollar invested and the rate is expected to increase further because the demand for the product is going to increase in the future, the market price of the stock will be bid up. Since the future profits of the company look good, up goes the market price of its stock. This process is called *discounting future profits.* In some cases it may be too late to buy such a stock; but, if the company continues expansion at its present rate, the stock will often continue to climb.

Let us assume that a given growth stock has discounted profits five years into the future and is selling for $100 per share. Its price-earnings ratio is out of line from an investment point of view; but if it is really a growth company, then five years from now it will still have discounted profits five years into the future (or perhaps seven) and may be selling for $200 per share. The opposite possibility is that its growth may be over or slowing down and that it may not rise much above $100. The secret to success in growth stocks is to find them first. This often means buying a speculative security. The investor wants the stock of a firm that will become the IBM of the space industry. If a person buys a proven growth stock, he or she pays for it, since it has already discounted the future. Some stocks that are typically looked upon as being growth stock include those of IBM, Coca-Cola, and some of the newer, smaller minicomputer companies. Growth stocks generally appeal to people who do not need income at the present time but who want capital gains they will take later.

Income stock

***Income stocks*** are those in companies whose earnings are good but that either are not growing much or are growing with external funds.[4] They may be mature companies producing a product for which the demand has stabilized. They are companies, moreover, that pay out a large proportion of their earnings each year in the form of dividends. Utilities, tobacco, and food are considered such income areas. Not only are dividends fairly high but they are steady because the earnings of the companies are steady. AT&T for many years has been considered an income stock par excellence; it had for a long time yielded a good, steady return. But because of divestiture of the operating companies a few years ago, this is no longer true. Now many of the utilities would be considered the best income stock. Income stocks in general appeal to people who may need income and who would benefit less from long-term growth. However, a good yield is one criterion that should be used by everyone in selecting stock for a well-balanced portfolio.

Cyclical stock

***Cyclical stocks*** fluctuate widely over swings in the business cycle and have high betas. They are the stocks of those companies whose sales and earnings vary greatly. The steel, nonferrous metals, and machine tool industries are examples. Because earnings fluctuate, so too do dividends and the market price of the stock. Nearly all stock fluctuates somewhat with swings in the business cycle, but cyclical stocks do so more than others.

Investors who buy a cyclical stock are betting that economic and

---

4. External funds are funds obtained by selling new issues of bonds or common stock.

business conditions will improve. In this connection, a word of warning is in order. The buyer should beware of selecting a cyclical stock after there has been an unusual jump in either sales or earnings unless the outlook is relatively certain that the up-trend will continue. Once sales, earnings, or both have risen substantially, it is often already too late to buy cyclicals; now is the time to sell.

The Wall Street maxim in relation to cyclical stock is "Buy on bad news, sell on good." Investors in cyclical stock should buy when sales and earnings are down and sell when these figures are favorable. To do so one must, of course, be flexible and in a position to hold on to the stock for a considerable period of time, frequently for several years. However, this is true for any stock. No one but a professional speculator, and certainly no small investor, should go into the stock market on a short-term basis.

*Defensive stock* is often income stock. It would probably be more accurate to say that most defensive stock is income stock but not as many income stocks could be classified as defensive. A defensive stock is one that declines less than most on a general downturn. By the same token, it may not rise as much in a general upturn. These stocks have low betas, because the company's sales and hence its income are more stable over the business cycle since the demand for its product is more stable. Such companies include some of the food and cigarette makers, but usually utilities are considered the best defensive stocks. Some utilities have been considered growth stock recently, especially if they are in an area that is growing rapidly. Most utilities, however, pay out a considerable portion of their earnings as dividends and hence are more income and defensive than growth and defensive. Some analysts look upon defensive stock as the opposite of cyclical stock. If an individual expected the economy in general to be heading into a recession, he or she might well sell cyclical stocks and buy either bonds or defensive stock. This is known as taking a defensive position.

When classifying stock according to risk, **blue-chip stock** is the least risky—least risky both as to missing a dividend and declining in price, although the price does decline when the market in general declines. Generally, however, the price of blue-chip stocks will decline less in a general downturn than the average. They are the stocks of the old well-established companies that have proved they can earn profits. They cannot be classified by industries at all, because some industries have both blue-chip companies and firms that either are not tested or that for other reasons are considered highly speculative.

A list of blue-chip stock would include General Electric, American Telephone and Telegraph, Exxon, Standard Oil of California (now called Chevron), and other firms of similar financial strength.

Defensive stock

Blue-chip stock

**Speculative stock**

***Speculative stocks*** are untried securities, often stocks of new, small firms whose chances for success are not great or firms that at least are untested. Some of the small mining and uranium stocks are examples, as are the small electronics companies. Investors should not put any money in these stocks unless they can afford to lose it if the worst comes. The probability of gain is small, but the amount of gain would be great if it should come. One assumes a great risk in buying them. A small investor with few funds should probably never buy highly speculative securities. A person of means may want to invest in them occasionally.

Speculation is a relative term, as pointed out before, and some people take a chance on a mildly speculative stock. Of course, all stock has at least a slight element of speculation attached to it.

*Preferred stock*

Many investors consider ***preferred stock*** somewhere between bonds and stock, more risky than bonds but less so than common stock. As such, it appeals to certain moderately conservative investors.

Preferred stock is a special kind of stock issued by a corporation that gives a preference to the purchaser. Generally, the preference takes the form of a fixed return or dividend and a preference as to assets. For example, a preferred stockholder may be given a 9 percent return. This 9 percent is figured on the face or par value of the stock. Thus if a stock share were issued at $100 par and it were a 9 percent preferred, the stockholder would be entitled to $9.00 per annum on each share of stock he or she holds, provided there are enough profits to pay the $9. This $9 per share, moreover, is due and payable before any distribution can be made to the common stockholders.

In addition to the preference in the form of earnings, preferred stockholders are generally entitled to share in the assets of the corporation at dissolution before the common stockholders may receive any of the money. That is, if the corporation goes out of business either voluntarily or involuntarily, preferred stockholders will divide the assets and pay themselves off at par value before the common stockholders may receive any part of the assets. Some variations of preferred stock are examined below. Figure 15–5 shows a preferred stock certificate.

**Cumulative and noncumulative preferred stock**

A corporation issuing 9 percent ***cumulative preferred stock*** is liable to the preferred stockholders for past dividends that have not been paid. Suppose a company fails to pay dividends for three years, and the stock (with a $100 par value) calls for a payment of 9 percent and is cumulative; then the company must pay the cumulative preferred stockholders $27 at the end of the three years before any money is payable to the common stockholders.

Notice that corporations do not have to pay dividends to preferred stockholders even if they have the profits. They must merely pay the preferred before they may pay the common; and if the preferred is cumulative, they must pay all back dividends before common can be

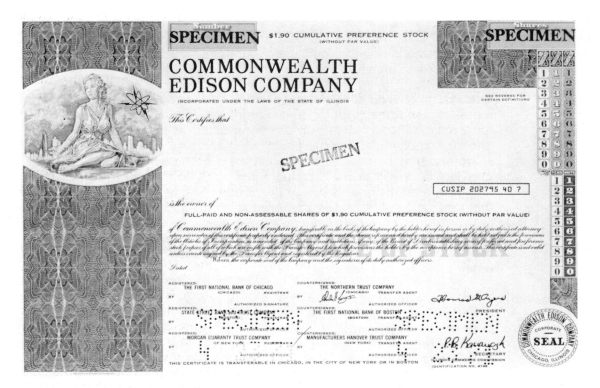

*A preferred stock certificate. (Source: Courtesy of Commonwealth Edison Company and   Figure 15—5
the First National Bank of Boston.)*

paid. Sometimes there are limits to how far back dividends have to be paid, such as three-year or five-year cumulative. Other preferred cumulative stocks have no limits, and all back dividends have to be paid before common stockholders can receive anything. On noncumulative preferred stock the corporation need only pay the current year's dividends before it may pay dividends on the common stock.

With this type of preferred stock, if the earnings are sufficient, preferred stockholders not only are given their agreed dividends but are entitled to share equally in the dividends paid to the common stockholders. Generally where there is a ***participating preferred stock,*** the preferred stockholders are paid their agreed-upon rate, say $9 per share, then the common stockholders are paid an equal dividend, and after that the remainder of the money is distributed equally among the preferred and the common stockholders.[5]

Participating
preferred

---

5. In this case the dividend to the common stockholder would not necessarily be $9, because the price of the common and preferred stock is not usually the same. The

**Cumulative participating preferred**

Obviously these two features can be combined, and we have then a preferred stock that must be paid past dividends before common is paid any preferred dividends, and then will share equally with the common anything that remains.

**Callable or redeemable preferred**

*Callable preferred stock* is preferred stock issued by a corporation with a provision that the corporation has an option to buy the stock back from the preferred stockholders on terms specified at the time the stock is issued. For example, callable preferred stock may be issued at $100 per share and may be callable at $110. That is, if the corporation desires to exercise its option, it may buy back the stock at the call price of $110.

Corporations issue stock of this nature so that if the market is such that they could issue a new preferred at, say, 7 or 8 percent rather than at the old rate of 9, they can convert. Or they may wish to clean up their capital structure and eliminate the preferred. In the market seldom will the market price exceed the call price because of the possibility of redemption by the issuer.

**Convertible preferred**

This is preferred stock that can be exchanged for common stock by the stockholders at their option. The exchange ratio is determined at the time the stock is issued. Therefore, if the common stock of the corporation appreciates in the market, it will pull the preferred up with it. *Convertible preferred stock* has all the advantages of preferred, as well as of the common, just as in the case of convertible bonds, which were discussed above.

**A final note on preferred stock**

Preferred stock may have the features of a bond or the features of common stock, or some of each. If it is participating preferred, it is a bit closer to common because it shares the good fortune of the common. However, it may not share as much of the bad. If it is noncallable and nonparticipating, it is closer to a bond. Its rate of return is fixed, and it will fluctuate in the market like a bond with variations in the interest rate. If it is convertible into common, it again shares in the good fortune of common but not necessarily in the bad because it will rise in price with the common but will not necessarily fall if the market price of the common declines.

---

common stock may be selling for $50 per share, whereas the preferred in this example has a face value of $100. Moreover, the price of the common stock often fluctuates widely over time. Therefore a participating agreement must be spelled out at the time the preferred stock is issued; generally it will give the common the same percentage return that the preferred has received, after which they share equally. But this means that the common must be evaluated at the time the preferred is issued, because its price fluctuates in the market. Usually the market price (or some price near it) of the common at the time the preferred is issued is taken; the common would get 9 percent of that, and then sharing would begin.

## SUGGESTED READINGS

*The ABC's of Market Forecasting.* Princeton, N.J.: Dow Jones and Company.

*American Stock Exchange Annual Report.* New York: American Stock Exchange.

*Barron's Weekly.* Princeton, N.J.: Dow Jones and Company.

"Before You Say Yes: Fifteen Questions to Ask About Investments." Pueblo, Colo.: Consumer Information Center.

Blodgett, Richard. *The Merrill Lynch Guide to Financial Planning.* New York: Simon and Schuster, 1983.

"The Dow Jones Averages; A Non-professional's Guide." Princeton, N.J.: Dow Jones and Company.

*The Exchange.* Magazine published monthly by the New York Stock Exchange, New York.

Farrell, James L., Jr., and Fuller, Russell J. *Modern Investments and Security Analysis.* New York: McGraw-Hill, 1987.

*Financial Analysts Journal.* New York: The Financial Analyst Federation. Bimonthly publication.

"Financial World, the Investment Magazine." New York: Financial World Partners.

Fischer, Donald, and Jordan, Ronald. *Security Analysis and Portfolio Management,* 4th ed. Englewood Cliffs, N.J.: Prentice Hall, 1987.

"For Tax-Free Income, Ask About Municipal Bonds." New York: Dean Witter Reynolds. You may obtain this from your Dean Witter broker.

*Hedging Highlights.* Chicago: Chicago Board of Trade.

*How to Invest in Stocks and Bonds.* New York: Merrill, Lynch, Pierce, Fenner, and Smith.

"How to Read Stock Market Quotations." Princeton, N.J.: Dow Jones and Company.

*How You Get More Out of Financial News.* Princeton, N.J.: Dow Jones and Company.

*The Insider's Guide to the* Wall Street Journal. Princeton, N.J.: Dow Jones and Company.

*Instruments of the Money Market.* Richmond, Va.: Federal Reserve Bank of Richmond, 1986.

*The Kiplinger Washington Letter.* A weekly newsletter with a good deal of material on business and finance.

"Moody's Handbook of Common Stock." New York: Moody's Investors Services. Quarterly publication.

*New York Stock Exchange Fact Book.* New York: The New York Stock Exchange. Annual publication.

"Quarterly Review of the Bond Market." New York: The Federal Reserve Bank of New York.

*Questions and Answers About the Stock Market.* New York: Merrill, Lynch, Pierce, Fenner, and Smith.

Reilly, Frank K. *Investment Analysis and Portfolio Management.* Chicago: The Dryden Press, 1985.

*Tax-Exempt Bonds and the Investor.* Washington, D.C.: Investment Bankers Association of America.

*Understanding Financial Data in the Wall Street Journal.* Princeton, N.J.: Dow Jones and Company.

*U. S. News & World Report.* A weekly magazine that contains a good deal of information on business and finance.

*United States Government Securities: Basic Information.* Dallas: Federal Reserve Bank of Dallas.

*The Wall Street Journal.* Princeton, N.J.: Dow Jones and Company. Daily publication.

*Well Beyond the Average: The Story of Dow Jones.* Princeton, N.J.: Dow Jones and Company.

*What Every Woman Investor Should Know.* Washington, D.C.: Investment Bankers Association of America.

"What Every Investor Should Know." Pueblo, Col.: Consumer Information Center.

# 16 The investor and the securities market

**HIGHLIGHTS**    This chapter examines the securities market. In order to help the reader understand the market and to develop investment strategies, this chapter examines the following:

1    The securities exchanges, brokers, and dealers
2    The quoting of securities
3    How securities may be bought and sold
4    Dividends on common stock
5    Other things one should know about securities
6    The options market

## INTRODUCTION

An investor who wishes to buy or sell securities does so in the open market. The open market for securities is "the works." It consists of all the organized exchanges on which securities are listed and also the over-the-counter market. Broadly defined, it also includes the brokers and dealers who operate in the open market and make it go. In this chapter we shall examine the open market and the buying and selling of securities therein. We will also examine earnings on stock and some supplemental material on securities.

## SECURITIES EXCHANGES: BROKERS AND DEALERS

In the United States there are two major organized exchanges (the New York Stock Exchange and the American Stock Exchange) whose major function is to facilitate the trading of securities. In addition, there are a number of smaller regional exchanges. While the greatest volume of business on the organized exchanges takes place in the area of common and preferred stock, they also handle the sale of some bonds and warrants. To deal directly on an exchange, one must be a member or own a seat. Many of the members are security dealers as well as brokers; they are broker-dealers. Brokers are individuals who execute orders for third parties for a commission. Dealers, on the other hand, act as principals and buy for their own accounts and also sell from them, hoping for a profit margin between the buy and sell prices. That is, they keep an inventory in securities, and in doing this they are said to make a market in the securities they buy and sell.

### The New York Stock Exchange (NYSE)

The New York Stock Exchange is by far the largest of the various exchanges in the United States. About 1,500 corporations have their common stock listed thereon. In addition, about 3,000 bonds and 800 preferred stocks are also listed, which makes the total listing on the "big board" almost 5,200 securities.

In order to be listed on the New York Stock Exchange a corporation must meet certain minimum requirements. These requirements have to do with the number of shares outstanding, number of stockholders, and size of the corporation as measured by assets and earnings. In addition, listed corporations must publish their financial reports and reveal certain financial facts. The American Stock Exchange and the various regional exchanges discussed below also have minimum listing requirements, but they are less stringent than those on the NYSE.

To trade on the NYSE, one must own a seat, and obtaining a seat is not easy. The only way to do so is to buy one from a member willing to relinquish it. The exchange is a very exclusive club. Brokers who are not members must trade (buy and sell) through someone who is a member.

The members of the exchange are classified into a number of categories. About half the members are commission brokers; the rest are divided among floor brokers, specialists, registered traders, bond dealers, or a combination of the above capacities at different times.

1. *Commission brokers.* Some members act solely as commission brokers. These are the ones who are partners or officers of firms doing business with the public. They have offices where they contact the public (in the case of a large firm like Merrill Lynch they have many members and many offices throughout the country). They buy and sell securities for their customers in return for which they are paid a commission.

2. *Floor brokers.* These are the members of the exchange who assist commission brokers who are unable to handle all of the volume when trade is heavy. They ensure that orders are executed quickly. They used to be called contract brokers a few years ago, and before that "two-dollar" brokers because that was the fee they charged. Their fee is now higher and comes out of the regular fee paid to the commission broker.

3. *Specialists.* The physical area of the New York Stock Exchange being large, it is frequently impossible for a member to get around fast enough to execute customers' orders. Certain brokers therefore specialize in buying and selling certain stocks at certain posts on the exchange floor. Each security is sold at a given location, and the specialists stay at that post and execute orders for a few securities at the order of their fellow brokers. In addition, some specialists will use their inventories to fill odd lot orders (discussed below).

4. *Registered traders or floor traders.* These are members who buy and sell on their own accounts; they deal in stocks themselves with the idea of making a profit on their purchases. They are able to do so because as members of the stock exchange they do not pay a regular commission, but a greatly reduced member commission. In addition, they are also professional traders, and they get in and out of the market on a short-run basis and take advantage of short-run price movements of common stock. Sometimes they also serve either as commission brokers for a few customers or as floor brokers for other commission brokers.

People have been buying and selling securities for many years, and the market has had many ups and downs, because the market is one of the most, if not the most, sensitive of all institutions in our society. It reacts to any and all news, good or bad. Bad news will nearly always send it down; what is considered good news may send it up or down. These are the short-run fluctuations. The long-run trend has been up more often than down.

*The historical record of the NYSE*

While the deepest and most severe stock market decline took place with the crash in 1929, there have been other sharp declines as well. After the 1929 crash the market generally stayed depressed until the big bull market shortly after World War II. Since that time there have been a number of ups and downs, but generally the trend was up until the crash on October 19, 1987, which rivaled the crash of 1929.

At various times, different stocks have been popular. For a number of years after World War I, railroad stocks were the "in thing." While they made somewhat of a comeback after the Great Depression, they never regained their former popularity. More recently, electronics, computers, and other "hi-tech" firms have been the glamour items in the stock market. Much of the historical record of the stock market can be seen graphically in Standard and Poor's chart in Figure 16–1.

*The American Stock Exchange (AMEX)*

The second major stock exchange is the American Stock Exchange, called AMEX for short. This market was originally outside in the street, but has been inside since 1921. There are fewer securities listed on the American Stock Exchange than on the New York Exchange, and the requirements for listing are less rigorous, but the same criteria are used. About 900 securities are listed on the American Exchange. As for commission brokers, specialists, and so forth, the operation of the American Exchange is much like that of the New York Stock Exchange.

*The regional exchanges*

The New York and the American Stock Exchanges are national institutions. There are also a number of smaller stock exchanges that serve only the region in which they are located. The three major regional exchanges are the Midwest Stock Exchange, the Philadelphia-Baltimore-Washington Stock Exchange, and the Pacific Coast Stock Exchange. Many of the stocks listed for the regional exchanges are also listed on either the New York or the American Stock Exchange. The existence of the Pacific Coast Exchange permits trading in those dually listed stocks three additional hours after the close of the NYSE and AMEX. In addition, the regional exchanges list some securities of regional companies that are listed nowhere else.

*Brokerage commissions*

There are brokerage commissions which the investor must pay when buying or selling securities. On large orders the broker will negotiate commissions in advance with the buyer or seller. On most regular orders, however, brokers have a schedule they follow, and these schedules vary somewhat from broker to broker.

The calculation of the commissions by the regular brokerage houses is complex and a table showing them is not possible. However, three variables are taken into account in setting them.

1. The dollar amount of money committed. Commissions, as a percent of the money committed, decline as the latter rises.
2. The number of shares purchased. Commissions per share decline as the number of shares purchased increases.
3. The price of shares. Commissions per share rise as the per share price of the shares selected declines. This one can offset the first two factors.

If, for example, a person buys 100 shares priced at $50 (commits $5,000), one (typical) broker will charge $101. If the person purchases 200 shares priced at $25 per share (again, commits $5,000), the same broker will charge $130; and on 500 shares at $10 the person would pay $161.

*Discount brokers*

In recent years discount brokers (also called security discount houses) have sprung up. They charge commissions that are often substantially below those charged by regular brokerage houses. They can do this because they offer no investment advisory services and provide no research reports. They merely execute orders. On the purchases discussed above, the commissions charged by a discount broker would often be as low as one-half of those charged by regular brokers. Many of these discount brokers are affiliated with banks that have moved into the securities business; to obtain the services of one a person need merely call the bank.

*Buying odd lots*

On the organized exchange, transactions are usually carried out in round lots that consist of 100 shares. However, small investors would want lesser amounts. There used to be dealers who specialized in odd lots and who would maintain an inventory in stock and buy and sell in any amounts from 1 to 99, but these have passed from the scene. Odd-lot transactions are now carried out directly by some brokers who maintain an inventory of stock and stand willing to trade in any odd-lot amounts. Those (usually smaller) brokers who do not themselves maintain an inventory will fill their customer's odd-lot orders by going to members of the New York Stock Exchange (usually specialists or registered traders) who do carry an inventory and who do deal in odd lots, although this is a minor part of their business.

Buying odd lots is a little more expensive (per share) than buying round lots. At one time there was a special "odd lot" fee of $.125 per share but this has pretty much gone by the boards. Currently commissions are set by most brokers based on the number of shares traded, the price per share, and the total number of dollars committed (see above for a more complete discussion of this point).

*Securities dealers*

Securities dealers make a market in a security and buy and sell on their own account. They are not paid a commission but earn their living on the difference between what they pay for a security and what they sell it for.

For example, a share of stock may be quoted as having an asked price of $11 and a bid price of $10. This means that the dealer will pay the seller $10 for the stock share; on the other hand, the buyer must pay $11. This leaves a spread of $1, out of which the dealers pay their expenses and receive their profits. Because dealers stand ready to buy

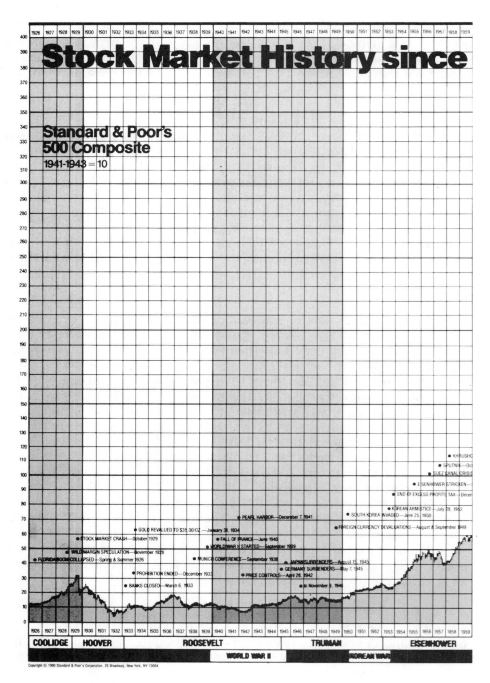

Figure 16—1    *Stock market and business history since 1926.* (Source: *Courtesy of Standard &*
                *Poor's Index Services.   This report was up-to-date at the time of publication;*
                *subsequent changes are reflected in current Standard & Poor's reports.)*
                *Reprinted by permission of Standard & Poor's, a division of McGraw-Hill, Inc.*

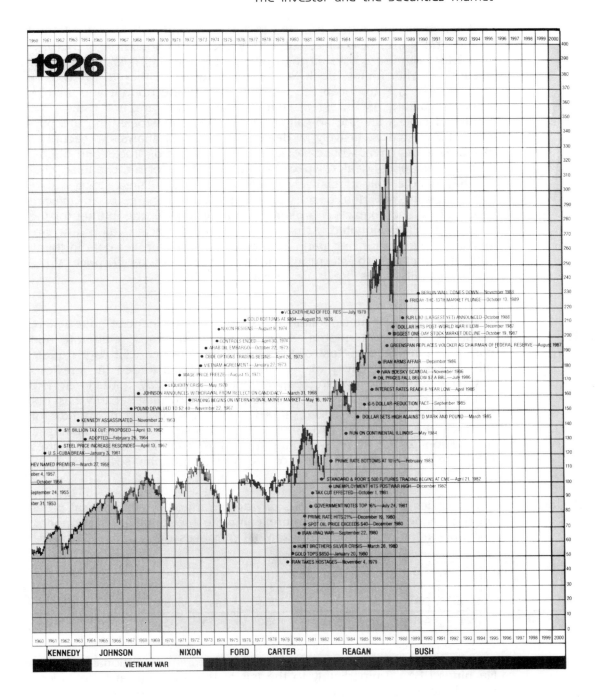

and sell at all times, they are said to "make a market." Dealers' bid and asked prices are, of course, subject to change without notice.

Stocks that are sold through dealers are usually "over-the-counter" securities. While many stock issues are listed on either the New York Exchange or the American Stock Exchange and are bought and sold by a broker acting as an agent, many other issues are not listed. The nonlisted stocks are the so-called over-the-counter stocks and are purchased and sold exclusively by dealers. In the final analysis, a securities dealer is a merchant whose stock in trade consists of stocks and bonds. In most instances, dealers specialize in a few lines of merchandise, that is, they handle only a relatively small number of unlisted stocks.

When an individual desires to purchase some shares of an unlisted stock, he or she contacts a broker. The broker checks the market for the unlisted stock designated. Actually, the broker contacts dealers who are making a market for that particular issue. Then the broker gets in touch with the purchaser to inform him or her of the lowest asked price. If the purchaser still wants the issue, a sale is made.

## QUOTING SECURITIES

Almost every daily metropolitan newspaper has a financial page where securities prices are quoted, some of which are more elaborate and complete than others. Most of the more complete financial pages quote the price and the activity of the stocks and bonds traded the previous day, but some late evening papers have current day quotations. The emphasis here is on the word "traded." If a particular security has not been traded, it is not listed. If ABC, Inc. has not been traded, for instance, the price is not given, obviously because no price has been set. In addition to the listed securities, the more complete financial pages carry the bid and asked prices of the over-the-counter securities.

### The listed stock

Those issues traded the previous day are arranged in alphabetical order on the financial page of the more complete metropolitan newspapers, and appear as shown below. (example purposes only)

| 52 weeks | | | | | | | | | | | |
|---|---|---|---|---|---|---|---|---|---|---|---|
| High | Low | Stock | Sym. | Div. | Yield % | P/E ratio | vol 100s | Hi | Low | Close | Net Change |
| 114¾ | 83⅛ | IBM | IBM | 4.84 | 5.8 | 12 | 13505 | 83⅞ | 83⅛ | 83⅜ | +⅛ |

The third column shows that the stock here is International Business Machines (IBM). Immediately to the left of that the high and low prices of that stock over the past 52 weeks are indicated. Moving now to the right, we will note all the other information the quotation conveys. Under "Div." we see 4.84 indicating that dividends of $4.84 per share were paid over the past year. The "yield %" column shows 5.8, the dividend yield as a percent of the market price of the stock. However, some earnings were retained by the company and hence the price-earnings ratio of 12 is shown in the next column. Then we see that sales for the day were 1,350,500 shares; that during the day's trade the stock of IBM fluctuated and reached a high of $83⅞ per share, a low of $83⅛; and that it closed at $83⅜. On the basis of these figures, why was there a net change of +⅛ of a point? The net change figure is the difference between the closing price for that day and the closing price of the previous day, not the difference between the high and the low on the day in question. Obviously, yesterday's closing price can be either higher or lower than today's closing price. The preceding day's closing price in our example was 83¼. Note that stocks advance or decline in steps of one-eighth of one dollar.

Frequently there is a footnote in the quotations, a lower case letter. Footnotes that appear are explained at the bottom of the list of quotations under the heading of explanatory notes. A footnote under the explanatory notes may point out that the corporation is in bankruptcy or in receivership or one of a number of other valuable bits of information.

Shown (in Table 16–1) is a list of the most active stocks, a market diary indicating the number of stocks that advanced or declined, and new highs and lows on the NYSE.

*The Dow Jones averages*

In addition to prices of individual stocks, most financial pages also publish the Dow Jones averages, which are supposed to indicate which way the market is going in general. The Dow Jones average is really four different averages: one for industrials, one for transportation, one for utilities, and one a composite of the other three. These averages date back to 1896.

The industrial average, based on the stock of thirty industrial companies, is calculated by adding the prices of these thirty stocks and then dividing to obtain an average.[1] The transportation average with twenty transportation company stocks in it (this formerly included just rails, but now it has some airlines and trucking lines as well) is calculated in the same way, as is also the utility average, which contains the stock of fifteen utilities.

There are a number of criticisms of the Dow Jones averages, especially of the industrial average. First, it is argued that thirty stocks are not a large enough sample. Second, all of the stocks in the Dow Jones averages are blue chips such as General Motors, General Electric, Exxon, and DuPont; such stocks as these, it is argued, are not representative of the market as a whole. Finally, the Dow Jones averages are

---

1. The divisor is not thirty, however. Rather, adjustments have been made to take into account stock splits (see the appendix for this chapter). This adjustment involves changing the divisor to account for splits.

Table 16–1 *Most active stocks and market diary on NYSE*

*Most active stocks week ended March 30, 1992 on NYSE*

| MOST ACTIVE ISSUES | | | | | DIARIES | | | |
|---|---|---|---|---|---|---|---|---|
| NYSE | VOLUME | CLOSE | CHANGE | | NYSE | MON | FRI | WK AGO |
| Oak Industries | 3,567,600 | 2 | + | $\frac{1}{4}$ | Issues traded | 2,236 | 2,225 | 2,227 |
| AT&T | 2,242,800 | 41 | + | $\frac{5}{8}$ | Advances | 712 | 449 | 699 |
| Waste Mgmt | 1,699,400 | $37\frac{7}{8}$ | − | $1\frac{1}{8}$ | Declines | 922 | 1,244 | 996 |
| RJR Nab Hldg | 1,682,200 | $9\frac{1}{4}$ | − | $\frac{1}{8}$ | Unchanged | 602 | 532 | 532 |
| Adv Micro Dvc | 1,506,900 | $17\frac{3}{8}$ | − | $\frac{1}{8}$ | New highs | 20 | 19 | 58 |
| IBM | 1,350,500 | $83\frac{3}{8}$ | + | $\frac{1}{8}$ | New lows | 34 | 28 | 26 |
| Glaxo Hldgs | 1,343,100 | 28 | + | $\frac{5}{8}$ | zAdv vol (000) | 49,539 | 23,405 | 53,341 |
| Chemical Bk | 1,308,100 | $33\frac{3}{8}$ | − | $1\frac{1}{4}$ | zDecl vol (000) | 64,124 | 1234,299 | 77,851 |
| Amer Express | 1,209,100 | x23 | ..... | | zTotal vol (000) | 133,980 | 166,020 | 156,620 |
| Chrysler Corp | 1,154,300 | $17\frac{5}{8}$ | + | $\frac{1}{2}$ | Closing tick[1] | −307 | −189 | +167 |
| PepsiCo | 1,117,200 | $34\frac{1}{8}$ | − | $\frac{1}{4}$ | Closing Arms[2] (trin) | 1.00 | 1.92 | 1.02 |
| Citicorp | 1,102,800 | 17 | − | $\frac{3}{8}$ | zBlock trades | 2,903 | 3,597 | 3,380 |
| Telefonos Mex | 925,800 | 57 | − | $\frac{1}{2}$ | **NASDAQ NMS** | | | |
| Intl Game Tech | 924,500 | $31\frac{1}{4}$ | − | $2\frac{1}{8}$ | Issues traded | 4,235 | 4,234 | 4,222 |
| Amoco Corp | 916,000 | $42\frac{3}{4}$ | − | $\frac{7}{8}$ | Advances | 948 | 731 | 911 |
| **NASDAQ NMS** | | | | | Declines | 1,159 | 1,442 | 1,188 |
| Intlgt Electro | 6,593,100 | $13\frac{1}{2}$ | − | 7 | Unchanged | 2,128 | 2,061 | 2,123 |
| Intel Corp | 5,756,500 | $53\frac{1}{4}$ | − | 2 | New highs | 52 | 52 | 92 |
| Apple Cmptr | 3,027,100 | $58\frac{1}{8}$ | − | $2\frac{7}{8}$ | New lows | 31 | 36 | 15 |
| Seagate Tech | 1,581,400 | $12\frac{3}{8}$ | − | $\frac{1}{2}$ | Adv vol (000) | 45,305 | 29,093 | 52,439 |
| Amgen | 1,440,100 | $62\frac{3}{8}$ | + | $\frac{7}{8}$ | Decl vol (000) | 80,058 | 140,748 | 65,387 |
| Borland Intl | 1,272,500 | $53\frac{5}{8}$ | − | $\frac{3}{8}$ | Total vol (000) | 154,207 | 203,963 | 148,858 |

only crudely adjusted for splits. Over the years many of the stocks have been split a number of times; moreover, not all of the thirty have been split the same amounts. Those companies that have never split their stock or have split it less have a greater weight in the averages than the others. The adjustment to correct for stock splits noted in the footnote earlier has only partially done so.

The Dow Jones industrial stock price averages are shown in Table 16–2.

**Other stock market indicators**

There are a number of other indicators that attempt to show which way the market is going. These indicators, however, use index number devices (see Chapter 1). These index numbers measure movements in stock prices much as the cost of living was measured in Chapter 1. The best-known such stock indices are the Standard and Poor's and the New York Stock Exchange composite index of all common stocks that are traded on the New York Stock Exchange each day. About 2,200 stocks are listed, but a few are not traded each day. Therefore the number of stocks in the index varies from day to day but usually is close to 2,200. The New York Stock Exchange index was started in 1966, which is the

Table 16–2

## DOW-JONES INDUSTRIAL AVERAGE
## 65 YEAR PERFORMANCE
## 1926-1990

| Year | Market High | Market Low | Market Close | Market Annual Change | Earnings | Dividends | Annual Total Return | Year-end Yield | Year-end P/E Multiple | Book Value | Consumer Price Index 1982-84 = 100 |
|---|---|---|---|---|---|---|---|---|---|---|---|
| 1925 | – | – | 156.66 | – | – | – | – | – | – | – | 17.9 |
| 1926 | 166.64 | 135.20 | 157.20 | 0.3 | 11.39 | 5.54 | 3.9 | 3.51 | 13.8 | 75 2 | 17.7 |
| 1927 | 202.40 | 152.73 | 202.40 | 28.8 | 8 72 | 6.04 | 32.6 | 2.98 | 23.2 | 77 9 | 17.3 |
| 1928 | 300.00 | 191.33 | 300.00 | 48.2 | 15.97 | 9.76 | 53.0 | 3.25 | 18.8 | 84 1 | 17.1 |
| 1929 | 381.17 | 198.69 | 248.48 | -17.2 | 19.94 | 12.75 | -12.9 | 5.13 | 12.5 | 91 3 | 17.2 |
| 1930 | 294.04 | 157.51 | 164.58 | -33.8 | 11.02 | 11.13 | -29.3 | 6.76 | 14.9 | 91 2 | 16.1 |
| 1931 | 194.36 | 73.79 | 77.90 | -52.7 | 4 09 | 8.40 | -47.6 | 10.78 | 19.1 | 86 9 | 14.6 |
| 1932 | 88.78 | 41.22 | 59.93 | -23.1 | (.51) | 4.62 | -17.1 | 7.71 | * | 81 8 | 13.1 |
| 1933 | 108.67 | 50.16 | 99.90 | 66.7 | 2.11 | 3.40 | 72.4 | 3.40 | 47.4 | 80 5 | 13.1 |
| 1934 | 110.74 | 85.51 | 104.04 | 4.1 | 3.91 | 3.66 | 7.8 | 3.52 | 26.6 | 80 7 | 13.4 |
| 1935 | 148.44 | 96.71 | 144.13 | 38.5 | 6.34 | 4.55 | 42.9 | 3.16 | 22.7 | 82 50 | 13.8 |
| 1936 | 184.90 | 143.11 | 179.90 | 24.8 | 10.07 | 7.05 | 29.7 | 3.92 | 17.9 | 85 55 | 14.0 |
| 1937 | 194.40 | 113.64 | 120.85 | -32.8 | 11.49 | 8.78 | -27.9 | 7.27 | 10.5 | 88 30 | 14.4 |
| 1938 | 158.41 | 98.95 | 154.76 | 28.1 | 6.01 | 4.98 | 32.2 | 3.22 | 25.8 | 87 13 | 14.0 |
| 1939 | 155.92 | 121.44 | 150.25 | - 2.9 | 9.11 | 6.11 | 1.0 | 4.07 | 16.5 | 95 58 | 13.9 |
| 1940 | 152.80 | 111.84 | 131.13 | -12.7 | 10.92 | 7.06 | - 8.0 | 5.38 | 12.0 | 98 75 | 14.1 |
| 1941 | 133.59 | 106.34 | 110.96 | -15.4 | 11.64 | 7.59 | - 9.6 | 6.84 | 9.5 | 102 33 | 15.5 |
| 1942 | 119.71 | 92.92 | 119.40 | 7.6 | 9.22 | 6.40 | 13.4 | 5.36 | 13.0 | 107 50 | 16.9 |
| 1943 | 145.82 | 119.26 | 135.89 | 13.8 | 9.74 | 6.30 | 19.1 | 4.64 | 14.0 | 113 03 | 17.4 |
| 1944 | 152.53 | 134.22 | 152.32 | 12.1 | 10.07 | 6.57 | 16.9 | 4.31 | 15.1 | 118 33 | 17.8 |
| 1945 | 195.82 | 151.35 | 192.91 | 26.6 | 10.56 | 5.69 | 31.0 | 3.47 | 18.3 | 122 74 | 18.2 |
| 1946 | 212.50 | 163.12 | 177.20 | - 8.1 | 13.63 | 7.50 | - 4.3 | 4.23 | 13.0 | 131 40 | 21.5 |
| 1947 | 186.85 | 163.21 | 181.16 | 2.2 | 18.80 | 9.21 | 7.4 | 5.08 | 9.6 | 149 08 | 23.4 |
| 1948 | 193.16 | 165.39 | 177.30 | - 2.1 | 23.07 | 11.50 | 4.2 | 6.49 | 7.7 | 159 67 | 24.1 |
| 1949 | 200.52 | 161.60 | 200.13 | 12.9 | 23.54 | 12.79 | 20.1 | 6.39 | 8.5 | 170 12 | 23.6 |
| 1950 | 235.47 | 196.81 | 235.41 | 17.6 | 30.70 | 16.13 | 25.7 | 6.85 | 7.7 | 194 19 | 25.0 |
| 1951 | 276.37 | 238.99 | 269.23 | 14.4 | 26.59 | 16.34 | 21.3 | 6.07 | 10.1 | 202 60 | 26.5 |
| 1952 | 292.00 | 256.35 | 291.90 | 8.4 | 24.78 | 15.48 | 14.2 | 5.30 | 11.8 | 213 39 | 26.7 |
| 1953 | 293.79 | 255.49 | 289.90 | - 3.8 | 27.23 | 16.11 | 4.8 | 5.56 | 10.7 | 244 26 | 26.9 |
| 1954 | 404.39 | 279.87 | 404.39 | 39.5 | 28.18 | 17.47 | 45.5 | 4.32 | 14.4 | 248 96 | 26.7 |
| 1955 | 488.40 | 388.20 | 488.40 | 20.8 | 35.78 | 21.58 | 26.1 | 4.41 | 13.7 | 271 77 | 26.8 |
| 1956 | 521.05 | 462.35 | 499.47 | 2.3 | 33.34 | 22.99 | 7.0 | 4.60 | 15.0 | 284 78 | 27.6 |
| 1957 | 520.77 | 419.79 | 435.69 | -12.8 | 36.08 | 21.61 | - 8.4 | 4.96 | 12.1 | 298 69 | 28.4 |
| 1958 | 583.65 | 436.89 | 583.65 | 34.0 | 27.95 | 20.00 | 38.6 | 3.43 | 20.9 | 310 97 | 28.9 |
| 1959 | 679.36 | 574.46 | 679.36 | 16.4 | 34.31 | 19.38 | 19.7 | 2.85 | 19.8 | 339 02 | 29.4 |
| 1960 | 685.47 | 566.05 | 615.89 | - 9.3 | 32.21 | 20.46 | - 6.3 | 3.32 | 19.1 | 369 87 | 29.8 |
| 1961 | 734.91 | 610.25 | 731.14 | 18.7 | 31.91 | 21.28 | 21.1 | 2.91 | 22.9 | 385 82 | 30.0 |
| 1962 | 726.01 | 535.76 | 652.10 | -10.8 | 36.43 | 22.09 | - 7.8 | 3.39 | 17.9 | 400 97 | 30.4 |
| 1963 | 767.21 | 646.79 | 762.95 | 17.0 | 41.21 | 23.20 | 20.6 | 3.04 | 18.5 | 425 90 | 30.9 |
| 1964 | 891.71 | 766.08 | 874.13 | 14.6 | 46.43 | 25.38 | 17.9 | 2.09 | 16.5 | 417 39 | 31.2 |
| 1965 | 969.26 | 840.59 | 969.26 | 10.9 | 53.67 | 28.61 | 14.1 | 2.95 | 18.1 | 453 27 | 31.8 |
| 1966 | 995.15 | 744.32 | 785.69 | -18.9 | 57.68 | 31.89 | -15.7 | 4.06 | 13.6 | 475 92 | 32.9 |
| 1967 | 943.08 | 786.41 | 905.11 | 15.2 | 53.87 | 30.19 | 19.0 | 3.34 | 16.8 | 476 50 | 33.9 |
| 1968 | 985.21 | 825.13 | 943.75 | 4.3 | 57.89 | 31.34 | 7.7 | 3.32 | 16.3 | 521 08 | 35.5 |
| 1969 | 968.85 | 769.93 | 800.35 | -15.2 | 57 02 | 33.90 | -11.6 | 4.24 | 14.0 | 542 25 | 37.7 |
| 1970 | 842.00 | 631.16 | 838.92 | 4.8 | 51.02 | 31.53 | 8.8 | 3.76 | 16.4 | 573.15 | 39.7 |
| 1971 | 950.82 | 797.97 | 890.20 | 6.1 | 55.09 | 30.86 | 9.8 | 3.47 | 16.2 | 607 61 | 41.1 |
| 1972 | 1,036.27 | 889.15 | 1,020.02 | 14.6 | 67.11 | 32.27 | 18.2 | 3.16 | 15.2 | 642 87 | 42.5 |
| 1973 | 1,051.70 | 788.31 | 850.86 | -16.6 | 86.17 | 35.33 | -13.1 | 4.15 | 9.9 | 690 23 | 46.2 |
| 1974 | 891.66 | 577.60 | 616.24 | -27.6 | 99.04 | 37.72 | -23.1 | 6.12 | 6.2 | 746 95 | 51.9 |
| 1975 | 881.81 | 632.00 | 852.41 | 38.3 | 75.66 | 37.46 | 44.4 | 4.39 | 11.3 | 783 61 | 55.5 |
| 1976 | 1,014.79 | 858.70 | 1,004.65 | 17.9 | 96.72 | 41.40 | 22.7 | 4.12 | 10.4 | 798 20 | 58.2 |
| 1977 | 999.80 | 800.85 | 831.17 | -17.3 | 89.10 | 45.84 | -12.7 | 5.52 | 9.3 | 841 76 | 62.1 |
| 1978 | 906.44 | 742.72 | 805.01 | - 3.1 | 112.79 | 48.52 | 2.7 | 6.03 | 7.1 | 890 69 | 67.7 |
| 1979 | 897.61 | 796.67 | 838.74 | 4.2 | 124 46 | 50.98 | 10.5 | 6.08 | 6.7 | 859 41 | 76.7 |
| 1980 | 1,000.20 | 759.98 | 963.99 | 14.9 | 121 86 | 54.36 | 21.3 | 5.64 | 7.9 | 928 50 | 86.2 |
| 1981 | 1,024.05 | 824.01 | 875.00 | - 9.2 | 113.71 | 56.22 | - 3.4 | 6.43 | 7.7 | 975 59 | 93.9 |
| 1982 | 1,070.55 | 776.92 | 1,046.54 | 19.6 | 9.15 | 54.14 | 25.8 | 5.17 | * | 881 51 | 97.6 |
| 1983 | 1,287.20 | 1,027.00 | 1,258.64 | 20.3 | 72.45 | 56.33 | 25.7 | 4.48 | 17.4 | 888 21 | 101.3 |
| 1984 | 1,286.60 | 1,086.60 | 1,211.57 | - 3.7 | 113.58 | 60.63 | 1.1 | 5.00 | 10.7 | 916 70 | 105.3 |
| 1985 | 1,553.10 | 1,176.79 | 1,546.67 | 27.7 | 96.11 | 62.03 | 32.8 | 4.01 | 16.1 | 944 97 | 109.3 |
| 1986 | 1,955.57 | 1,502.29 | 1,895.95 | 22.6 | 115.59 | 67.04 | 26.9 | 3.54 | 16.4 | 986 48 | 110.5 |
| 1987 | 2,722.42 | 1,738.74 | 1,938.83 | 2.3 | 133.05 | 71.20 | 6.0 | 3.67 | 14.6 | 1.008 95 | 115.4 |
| 1988 | 2,183.50 | 1,879.14 | 2,168.57 | 11.8 | 215.46 | 79.53 | 16.0 | 3.67 | 10.1 | 1.075 47 | 120.6 |
| 1989 | 2,791.41 | 2,144.64 | 2,753.20 | 27.0 | 221.48 | 103.00 | 31.7 | 3.74 | 12.4 | 1.276 14 | 126.1 |
| 1990 | 2,999.75 | 2,365.10 | 2,633.66 | - 4.3 | 172.05 | 103.70 | - 0.6 | 3.94 | 15.3 | 1.340 00E | 133.8 |
| Increase 1926-1990 | +1.700% | +1.649% | +1.581% | – | +1.411% | +1.772% | – | – | – | - 1.682% | +647% |

*Source:* Johnson's Investment Company Charts, 1991, *Hugh A. Johnson Co., Buffalo, N.Y., p. 10.*

## STOCK MARKET
### STANDARD & POOR'S PRICE INDEX

STANDARD & POOR'S 500 STOCK INDEX
65 Years — 1926-1990

Figure 16–2    *Source:* Johnson's Investment Company Charts, 1991, *Hugh A. Johnson Co., Buffalo, N.Y.,*
p. 13.

base year; the prices of all stocks traded on a given day are added up
on a computer, and then the figure is compared to the base year figure.
The New York Stock Exchange also has an index for industrials, consisting of 1,000 stocks; one for utilities, which includes 136 stocks; one
for transportation, made up of 76 stocks, and one for the stocks of 75
financial institutions of various kinds. Table 16–3 shows a number of
other stock market indicators.

The Standard and Poor's index uses the average stock prices from
1941 to 1943 as the base year and that figure has been set to 10. The
current figure, then, shows the increase since then. The Standard and
Poor's index includes four hundred stocks in the industrial index, twenty

Table 16–3

## STOCK MARKET DATA BANK — 3/30/92

### MAJOR INDEXES

| HIGH | LOW (†365 DAY) | | CLOSE | NET CHG | | % CHG | †365 DAY CHG | | % CHG | FROM 12/31 | | % CHG |
|---|---|---|---|---|---|---|---|---|---|---|---|---|
| **DOW JONES AVERAGES** | | | | | | | | | | | | |
| 3290.25 | 2863.82 | 30 Industrials | 3235.24 | + | 3.80 | + 0.12 | + | 354.05 | + 12.29 | + | 66.41 | + 2.10 |
| 1467.68 | 1101.55 | 20 Transportation | 1372.38 | − | 7.29 | − 0.53 | + | 270.83 | + 24.59 | + | 14.38 | + 1.06 |
| 226.15 | 195.17 | 15 Utilities | x203.87 | + | 0.63 | + 0.31 | − | 10.04 | − 4.69 | − | 22.28 | − 9.85 |
| 1192.83 | 1023.95 | 65 Composite | 1157.65 | − | 0.55 | − 0.05 | + | 133.70 | + 13.06 | + | 0.83 | + 0.07 |
| 396.64 | 343.91 | Equity Mkt. Index | 380.27 | − | 0.50 | − 0.13 | + | 33.35 | + 9.61 | − | 11.63 | − 2.97 |
| **NEW YORK STOCK EXCHANGE** | | | | | | | | | | | | |
| 231.84 | 202.10 | Composite | 222.99 | − | 0.32 | − 0.14 | + | 19.58 | + 9.63 | − | 6.45 | − 2.81 |
| 290.02 | 253.72 | Industrials | 279.37 | − | 0.57 | − 0.20 | + | 25.02 | + 9.84 | − | 6.45 | − 2.26 |
| 102.27 | 87.76 | Utilities | 93.44 | + | 0.17 | + 0.18 | + | 0.67 | + 0.72 | − | 8.69 | − 8.51 |
| 212.02 | 162.80 | Transportation | 199.48 | − | 0.90 | − 0.45 | + | 36.68 | + 22.53 | − | 2.39 | − 1.18 |
| 177.72 | 147.12 | Finance | 172.42 | − | 0.17 | − 0.10 | + | 24.63 | + 16.67 | − | 0.26 | − 0.15 |
| **STANDARD & POOR'S INDEXES** | | | | | | | | | | | | |
| 420.77 | 368.57 | 500 Index | 403.00 | − | 0.50 | − 0.12 | + | 31.70 | + 8.54 | − | 14.09 | − 3.38 |
| 499.27 | 438.51 | Industrials | 479.41 | − | 0.92 | − 0.19 | + | 39.77 | + 9.05 | − | 13.31 | − 2.70 |
| 362.50 | 263.44 | Transportation | 339.29 | − | 1.83 | − 0.54 | + | 75.85 | + 28.79 | − | 2.17 | − 0.64 |
| 155.70 | 133.52 | Utilities | 138.20 | + | 0.48 | + 0.35 | − | 5.17 | − 3.61 | − | 16.96 | − 10.93 |
| 35.14 | 28.77 | Financials | 34.09 | + | 0.01 | + 0.03 | + | 5.02 | + 17.27 | − | 0.01 | − 0.03 |
| 154.74 | 119.18 | 400 MidCap | 144.89 | − | 0.69 | − 0.47 | + | 23.04 | + 18.91 | − | 1.70 | − 1.16 |
| **NASDAQ** | | | | | | | | | | | | |
| 644.92 | 473.08 | Composite | 602.07 | − | 2.60 | − 0.43 | + | 121.21 | + 25.21 | + | 15.73 | + 2.68 |
| 741.92 | 523.54 | Industrials | 674.28 | − | 4.83 | − 0.71 | + | 131.08 | + 24.13 | + | 5.33 | + 0.80 |
| 632.09 | 522.07 | Insurance | 611.44 | + | 0.11 | + 0.02 | + | 63.82 | + 11.65 | + | 10.35 | + 1.72 |
| 396.93 | 309.34 | Banks | 395.14 | + | 1.24 | + 0.31 | + | 85.80 | + 27.74 | + | 44.58 | + 12.72 |
| 285.08 | 208.31 | Nat. Mkt. Comp. | 265.66 | − | 1.15 | − 0.43 | + | 53.08 | + 24.97 | + | 5.92 | + 2.28 |
| 296.32 | 207.84 | Nat. Mkt. Indus. | 268.82 | − | 1.95 | − 0.72 | + | 51.64 | + 23.78 | + | 1.03 | + 0.38 |
| **OTHERS** | | | | | | | | | | | | |
| 418.99 | 356.79 | Amex | 393.61 | − | 0.75 | − 0.19 | + | 35.67 | + 9.97 | − | 1.44 | − 0.36 |
| 266.85 | 228.21 | Value-Line (geom.) | 256.73 | − | 0.66 | − 0.26 | + | 20.31 | + 8.59 | + | 7.39 | + 2.96 |
| 212.61 | 167.00 | Russell 2000 | 202.95 | − | 0.89 | − 0.44 | + | 32.64 | + 19.17 | + | 13.02 | + 6.86 |
| 4121.28 | 3529.97 | Wilshire 5000 | 3956.85 | − | 7.09 | − 0.18 | + | 404.67 | + 11.39 | − | 84.25 | − 2.08 |

stocks in the transportation industry, forty in the utility index, forty in the financial index, and a composite of all five hundred of these stocks. Both the Standard and Poor's and the New York Stock Exchange indices are considered more reliable indicators of which way the market in general is moving than the Dow Jones averages because they include more stocks. Figure 16–2 shows the movement of the Standard & Poor's indicators over the years.

*Bull and bear markets*

**Bull and bear markets** are technical terms to indicate which way the market in general is going. If the market rises far enough and long enough, it is referred to as a bull market. If it falls far enough and long enough, it is referred to as a bear market. The stock averages discussed above are the tests used to determine whether the market is bullish or bearish. If the market just bounces around and moves up and down a bit from day to day, it is neither bearish nor bullish. To have a bull or bear market there must be a trend. The investors who buy heavily because they believe the market will rise in the future are called bulls. Those who are selling because they believe a decline is coming are called bears. And if the bulls outnumber the bears, the market will rise. If the reverse is the case, it will fall. Figure 16–3 is a diagram of a bull and bear market.

*Over-the-counter stocks*

Some people have the idea that if a stock is not listed and consequently is traded over the counter, there must be something wrong with it. This is just not true. Many over-the-counter stocks are as good as and frequently better than some of the securities listed on the organized

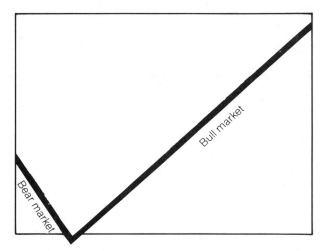

Figure 16–3  *Ups and downs of the market.*

exchanges. There are, however, some securities that do not qualify for listing, and these over-the-counter stocks are riskier.[2]

There are really three **over-the-counter** markets. There is the national over-the-counter market, which is quoted in greater detail than just a few years ago. The national market is linked by the National Association of Security Dealers Automated Quotation System (NASDAQ). It is a nationwide computer system and all trades are recorded. This market has evolved to the point where it is almost like the New York Stock Exchange. A quotation would appear as follows:

| 52 weeks | | | | | Yield | P/E | vol | | | | Net |
| High | Low | Stock | Sym | Div | % | ratio | 100s | Hi | Low | Close | Change |
| --- | --- | --- | --- | --- | --- | --- | --- | --- | --- | --- | --- |
| 31¼ | 11¼ | Justin Ind | JSTN | .40 | 1.4 | 13 | 418 | 29½ | 28⅜ | 29¼ | — |

In this case the stock is Justin Industries, a manufacturer of building materials. The high and the low for the past 52 weeks are shown at the left. Then, as we move to the right we see that 41,800 shares changed hands; the high and the low for the day were 29½ and 28⅜ respectively, and the last sale changed hands at 29¼, which was the same as the last sale yesterday.

There are some regional over-the-counter securities that are reported less fully because they are traded less frequently. Nevertheless some dealers hold an inventory in these stocks and make a market in them; that is, they stand ready to buy and sell at all times. Their asked price is always higher than their bid price, and the difference between the two is their profit margin. These stock quotations would appear in *The Wall Street Journal* as follows:

| Stock | Sales | Bid | Asked | Net Change |
| --- | --- | --- | --- | --- |
| Aphton | 54 | 20¾ | 21¾ | — |

The stock is Aphton Pharmaceuticals. A total of 5,400 shares changed hands on that day, and dealers stood ready to buy it at 20¾ and sell it at 21¾. There was no change in the price of the stock from the last bid price of the previous day.

The third over-the-counter market is for even smaller firms than the second market described above. It works just like the second (regional) market, but even less information is reported. A quotation appears below for Amertech, a small manufacturer of electrical instruments.

---

2. In order to be listed, the firm must be of a certain size as measured by assets. It must also have a minimum number of common stocks outstanding and a minimum number of stockholders. And it must be willing to publish certain basic financial facts about itself. Some firms that qualify for listing prefer to remain unlisted.

| Amertech | Bid | Asked |
|----------|-----|-------|
| Amertech | 1½ | 1⅝ |

It conveys only what the investor may buy (or sell) the stock for. This market is so small that not all stocks are traded every day, and the listings are published only weekly, usually on Monday.

*Corporate bond quotations*

Corporate bonds are frequently listed on both the New York and the American exchanges. Those that are not so listed are traded over the counter. Bond quotations are not printed on the financial pages of all daily newspapers but may be found in financial papers such as *The Wall Street Journal*.

The quotations for bonds traded on the exchange are listed in alphabetical order. After the name of the company there appears the coupon rate of interest paid per $1,000, which is the face value of the corporate bonds, and the maturity date. We will use as an example AT&T (American Telephone and Telegraph). They have a number of different issues outstanding but one reads as follows:

| Bonds | Cur. yield | Vol. | Close | Net change |
|-------|------------|------|-------|------------|
| AT&T 7⅛ 03 | 7.6 | 13.6 | 94¼ | +⅛ |

The coupon rate of 7⅛ percent ($70.125 per $1,000 bond) will be paid until the year 2003 when the bond matures. The current yield of 7.6 percent is shown next, then the sales volume, in thousands of dollars, followed by the closing price for the day, and finally the net change in the closing price from the previous day (note that the coupon rate of 7⅛ provides a yield of 7.6 percent because the bond is selling at $942.50).

Corporate bonds always have a face value of $1,000, but the newspaper quotations drop the last digit. A quotation of under 100 means that the bond is selling at a discount, while over 100 indicates it is at a premium.

The closing price of the bond quoted above was 94¼. This indicates that it was selling at $942.50, and since this is at a discount of $57.50 the actual yield is 7.6 as shown, and is above the 7⅛ coupon rate. The easy way to get the market price of a bond is to convert the stock market page quote to decimals and then multiply by 10. For example, a quote of 94¼ would become $94.25 × 10 = $942.50.

The person buying corporate bonds must also pay brokerage commissions. These commissions also vary from broker to broker, but generally they are a certain percentage of the money committed together with a fixed fee. This percentage declines as the amount of money involved rises. In addition to the percentage fee, there is a flat per-bond fee which is about $15. Where the fee is fixed is determined by the number of bonds purchased and the length of time to maturity, declining with the number of bonds bought and rising with the length of time to maturity. Figure 16–4 shows the growth in bond trading over the past few years.

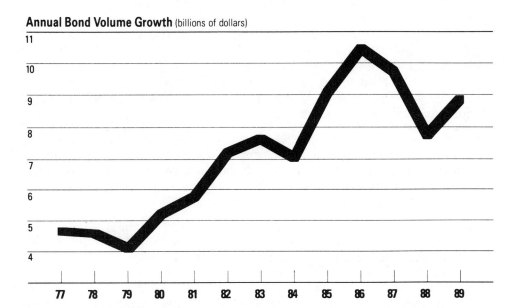

**Annual Bond Volume Growth** (billions of dollars)

*Annual bond volume growth (billions of dollars). (Source:* New York Stock Exchange Fact Book, *1990, p. 44.)*    Figure 16–4

Marketable United States Treasury bonds are quoted differently from corporate bonds. First, they are priced in thirty-seconds of a dollar. Second, there are bid and asked prices because they are all sold over the counter.    *Treasury bond quotations*

Thus the following quotation means that this is a United States bond issue carrying a 9-1/2 percent coupon interest rate; it will mature in November, 1995. At the close of the trading day, the bid price was 109:03. Actually 109:03 means 109 and 3/32, or 109.09375. Since Treasury bonds are sold in units of $1,000, 109.09375 × 10 = 1090.94, the bid price. The asked price of 109.1562 means 109 and 5/32, or 109.15625 × 10 = $1091.562. The change of +5 means the price has gone up by 5/32 or about $1.56 since the previous day. At the current price the yield or return is 6.62 percent interest.

| Rate | Mo. | Yr. | Bid | Asked | Chg. | Yield |
|------|-----|-----|--------|--------|------|-------|
| 9½ | Nov. | 95 | 109:03 | 109:05 | +5 | 6.62 |

A quote of 109:03 is 1090 plus 3/32 because the last digit before the decimal point is always zero (0) and it is also always dropped in the financial page quotations. That is, there is always an invisible "0" just before the decimal point. When converting thirty seconds (32s) to actual dollars, it must be remembered that since bonds come in denominations of $1000s, 32/32s equal $10, not $1.00, hence in a rising market when 32/32 is reached the last quoted digit rises by one (1). In the above case 109 becomes 110, and the bond price is $1,100.

It should be noted that in the government bond market, transactions take place in the millions and even hundreds of millions of dollars. This explains the narrow spread between the bid and asked price. This market is dominated by institutions, and is not appropriate for individuals unless they are extremely wealthy. If the small investor wishes to trade in this market he or she should do so through mutual funds. (See Chapter 17.)

## BUYING AND SELLING SECURITIES

Securities can be purchased for cash or they can be purchased with borrowed funds, that is, on margin.

### Cash sales

In a cash sale, when the transaction is completed, a bill is sent to the purchaser, who has five business days in which to pay for the stock. When selling, the seller also has five days in which to deliver the securities. The purchaser may actually take physical possession of the stock or he or she may instruct the broker to hold the stock for him or her in the purchaser's account. This is referred to as keeping in the street name and is discussed below.

### Margin purchases

Margin purchases are made with funds that are partly borrowed. The word "margin" refers to the percentage of the buyer's own funds needed to buy stock: the remainder may be borrowed from a broker. For example, if a share of stock is priced at $100 and the margin requirement is 75 percent, the purchaser must have that in cash, and may borrow no more than $25. Currently margin requirements are 50 percent; consequently, one half of the money for stock purchases may be borrowed. The Federal Reserve System sets margin requirements, and they have been as high as 100 percent in the past (no borrowed money may be used). The Federal Reserve raises margin requirements if it is believed there is excessive speculation in securities. If the market (and the economy in general) is in the doldrums, the Federal Reserve may lower margin requirements, thus making it easier for investors to enter the market with borrowed funds. This in turn, it is hoped, would increase the demand for stock and also create an environment more favorable to overall economic activity.

An investor has an incentive to buy on margin only if he or she feels the price of securities will rise by more than the interest cost of the loan.

A problem could arise if the investor on margin is wrong and the market declines. Then the margin could be wiped out and the investor would have to cover. This works as follows: the rules require that the market price of the stock must be at least equal to the borrowed funds. In the case of a stock selling at $100 purchased with a 50 percent margin requirement, there would be no problem until and if the market price declined below $50. But if the price declined to $45, the borrowed funds ($50) would be $5 more than the market value of the stock. The investor would be called by the broker to "cover"; that is, come up with $5 more of his or her own funds (then the market price of $45 is again equal to the loan). Today, with relatively high margin, the market would have to come down a good deal before an investor would have to cover. However, in former days when margins were often much lower (sometimes only 10 percent) this was sometimes a problem. For example, a $100 stock would only have to decline below $90 before a 10 percent margin was wiped out and the broker would call for the investor to cover. If he or she could not, the stock would be sold. In those days during a declining market the inability of many margin investors to cover resulted in their stock being sold. This contributed further to the decline. This is another reason why relatively high margins are required today.

*Short sales*

Short sales are the opposite of margin purchases. The investor has an incentive to sell short only if he or she believes the price of a stock will decline. When selling short, the stock is borrowed from a broker (stock can be borrowed just like money) and sold at its current price in the market. For example, if a stock is selling at $100 per share, an investor may borrow it from his or her broker and sell it. Then if, sometime later, its price declines to $80, it can be purchased in the open market (from the same broker it was borrowed from), and repaid, with a realized profit of $20 less brokerage fees. The short seller is also required to make up any dividend which was missed while he or she held a short position in the broker's stock. Selling short, then, is a speculative technique that enables persons to make a profit if they correctly forecast that the price of the security they purchased will decline. If those who have taken a short position are wrong and the security rises in price, they lose money.

Since both buying on margin and selling short are engaging in speculation, it is not recommended for the small investor, especially one who is a relative newcomer to security investments.

*Types of orders*

There are a number of types of orders either to buy or sell that an individual might place with a broker. These are the following:

1. Limit order. An order to buy or sell a certain number of shares under certain specific conditions. For example, one might order the broker to buy one hundred shares of ABC if the price declines from

its present level of $50 to $45, or to sell a number of shares if the stock rises to a certain level.

2. Market order. Either a buy or a sell order of a specific number of shares of a specific security at the current market price. It is left to the broker to obtain the best price possible for the client if it is an over-the-counter security and hence subject to haggling pricewise.

3. Good-till-canceled order. A type of order continuing in force until it is either executed or canceled. This applies to conditional orders. A new order at a different price cancels the former order if made by the same customer.

4. Stop order. An order to buy or sell conditioned upon a specific price. Frequently it is used as a selling device in order to prevent losses or as an attempt to ensure a profit. For example, a person may have purchased a stock at $10 and it may have risen to $20. The purchaser may have reason to believe that it will advance even higher, but for protection in the event of a downward movement, he or she may place a stop order at $15. Thus if the stock does go down to $15 per share, the order will be executed immediately. This is sometimes called a stop loss order because it prevents the stock from falling below a certain price.

## DISTRIBUTION OF EARNINGS FROM STOCKS

There are a number of reasons why people own common stock: capital gains, hedging inflation, and dividend income. Figure 16–5 illustrates how dividends, the cost of living, earnings, and stock prices have risen over the years. There are both cash dividends and stock dividends.

*Cash dividends*

Dividends must be paid out of corporate earnings. The percentage of earnings distributed varies from company to company, but generally runs from 40 to 80 percent. However, in some cases cash dividends are zero; the corporation retains its entire earnings. Dividends do not have to be paid; rather they are declared at the discretion of the board of directors of the company. Most states have laws providing that dividends may be paid only out of current or past earnings. They may not be given out of paid-in capital.

1. *The declaration date and the announcement date.* The day the board of directors meets and declares a dividend is the declaration date. The day this declaration is announced to the press is the announcement date. Often these two dates may be the same, but sometimes the public announcement may be delayed a few days. Firms listed in the NYSE are required to send prompt notices of dividend declarations to the Exchange.

2. *The ex-dividend date.* The ex-dividend date is the first day that the purchaser of a stock does not receive the dividend that has been declared on it. Thus when it is said that a stock is ex-dividend, it

**STANDARD & POOR'S 500 STOCK INDEX**
**1970-1989**

COST OF
LIVING

EARNINGS

DIVIDENDS

PRICE
INDEX

PRICE
EARNINGS
RATIO

+320%
+284%
+250%
+224%
−9%

1970 1971 1972 1973 1974 1975 1976 1977 1978 1979 1980 1981 1982 1983 1984 1985 1986 1987 1988 1989

*Performance of the Standard & Poor's stock index 1970–1989.* (Source: Johnson's    Figure 16–5
Investment Company Charts 1990, *Hugh A. Johnson Co., Buffalo, N.Y., p. 17.*)

is being sold without the dividend. This is five business days before the record date, because the rules of the New York Stock exchange allow five days in which to deliver stock one has sold or five days to pay for stock one has bought. The price of a stock often drops by the amount of the dividend when it goes ex-dividend.

**3.** *The record date.* This is the date when the corporation counts heads to determine who owns how much stock. The NYSE rules require that the record date be at least ten days later than the announcement date. Owners as of this date, according to the corporation's records, will receive the dividends.

**4.** *The payment date.* This is the date the dividends are actually paid. Established corporations with a good record of earning and a pattern of dividend payments usually pay dividends quarterly. The dividend checks are mailed to the stockholders of record by the trustee (usually a trust department of a bank) who keeps the stockholder records for the corporation. Figure 16–6 calendars these important dates.

*Stock dividends*    Directors may avoid a cash distribution by using a stock dividend. For example, a 10 percent stock dividend would result in each stockholder receiving from the company one additional share for every ten shares currently held. If fractional shares are issued because the stockholder's holdings are not evenly divisible by ten, provisions are usually made for stockholders to buy (or sell) fractional shares from the corporation so they can come out even. While increasing the number of ownership shares, this policy leaves the owner with the same equity as formerly held in the corporation. Although theoretically such a device should cause a decline in the value of shares because it has increased the supply of the stock, occasionally the reverse is true because it may cause more interest in that particular stock and thus create more demand for it.

| SUNDAY | MONDAY | TUESDAY | WEDNESDAY | THURSDAY | FRIDAY | SATURDAY |
|---|---|---|---|---|---|---|
| | | | 1 | 2 | 3 <br> ABC Corp. met and declared dividend | 4 |
| 5 | 6 | ABC Corp. 7 <br> announced a dividend to be paid Sept. 30 to stockholders of record Sept. 23 | 8 | 9 | 10 | 11 |
| 12 | 13 | 14 | 15 | 16 | 17 <br> Ex-dividend Date | 18 |
| 19 | 20 | 21 | 22 | 23 <br> Record Date | 24 | 25 |
| 26 | 27 | 28 | 29 | 30 <br> Payment Date | | |

Figure 16–6    *Dividend dates calendar.*

## SUGGESTED READINGS

*Amex Databook*. Fact book published annually by the American Stock Exchange, New York.

*American Stock Exchange Annual Report*. New York: American Stock Exchange.

*Barron's Educational Edition*. Princeton, N.J.: Dow Jones and Company.

Christy, George A., and Roden, Foster P. *Finance: Environment and Decisions*. New York: Harper & Row, 1986.

*"The Dow Jones Averages; A Non-Professional's Guide."* Princeton, N.J.: Dow Jones and Company.

Engel, Louis. *How to Buy Stocks*. New York: Bantam Books, 1983.

*"The Exchange Market and the Public Interest."* The New York Stock Exchange Annual Report. New York: New York Stock Exchange.

Farrell, James L., Jr., and Fuller, Russell J. *Modern Investments and Security Analysis*. New York: McGraw-Hill, 1987.

*Financial Analysts Journal*. New York: The Financial Analyst Federation. A bimonthly publication.

Fischer, Donald, and Jordan, Ronald. *Security Analysis and Portfolio Management*. 4th ed. Englewood Cliffs, N.J.: Prentice Hall, 1987.

*Forbes Magazine*. A weekly magazine with a great deal of material about business and finance.

Francis, Jack Clark. *Investments Analysis and Management*. New York: McGraw-Hill, 1986.

Hardy, C. Colburn. *Dun and Bradstreet's Guide to Your Investments*. New York: Harper and Row, 1986.

*How Over-the-Counter Securities Are Traded*. New York: Merrill Lynch, Pierce, Fenner, and Smith.

*How Professors Use The Wall Street Journal*. Princeton, N.J.: Dow Jones and Company.

*How to Read a Financial Report*. New York: Merrill Lynch, Pierce, Fenner, and Smith.

*"How to Read Stock Market Quotations."* Princeton, N.J.: Dow Jones and Company.

*"Market Statistics."* Chicago: The Chicago Board of Options Exchange.

*The Merrill Lynch Guide to Writing Options*. New York: Merrill Lynch, Pierce, Fenner, and Smith.

*"Moody's Handbook of Common Stock."* This is published quarterly by Moody's Investors Services.

*New York Stock Exchange Fact Book*. New York: New York Stock Exchange. Annual publication.

*The New York Stock Exchange Market*. Princeton, N.J.: Dow Jones and Company.

*"OTC Profiles."* New York: Standard and Poor's. Monthly publication.

Radcliffe, Robert C. *Investments: Concepts, Analysis and Strategy*. Glenview, Ill.: Scott, Foresman, 1987.

*Rates of Return on Investments in Common Stock*. New York: Merrill Lynch, Pierce, Fenner, and Smith.

Reilly, Frank K. *Investment Analysis and Portfolio Management*. Chicago: The Dryden Press, 1985.

*Standard & Poor's Stock Guide*. New York: Standard & Poor's Corporation. Quarterly publication.

*Understanding Financial Data in The Wall Street Journal*. Princeton, N.J.: Dow Jones and Company.

*Understanding the New York Stock Exchange*. New York: New York Stock Exchange.

*Well Beyond the Average: The Story of Dow Jones*. Princeton, N.J.: Dow Jones and Company.

*What Every Woman Investor Should Know*. Washington, D. C.: Investment Bankers Association of America.

# APPENDIX 16: SUPPLEMENTARY MATERIAL ON COMMON STOCK

There are a number of other points on common stock with which the investor should be familiar. Among them are: what to do if one loses securities, keeping securities in the street name, stock splits, preemptive rights, stock warrants, and the options market for common stock.

## What to do if a person loses securities

If a person takes physical possession of securities, they should be kept in a safe place such as a safety deposit box at a bank. Since most securities are registered, they can be replaced, but this is neither easy nor cheap. If securities are lost, notify the transfer agent immediately. If the investor does not know the name of the agent, the broker may know, although sometimes a person may have to write to the company issuing the stock. The transfer agent will want the certificate numbers of the missing shares. Consequently, the investor should have a list of these numbers available.

Upon notification, the transfer agent puts a stop on the stock to prevent its sale. The next step is to get the company to issue new replacement shares. This costs money. Nearly all companies require an indemnity bond as protection against any possible future loss. While the corporation would not suffer a loss if the old securities reappeared and were successfully sold, a brokerage house would, and the bond is used to indemnify them. Generally a bond of 100 percent of the value of the securities is required. The bond can be put up in cash or a bonding company can do it. If a bonding company is used, premiums that generally amount to about 4 percent of the stock's value will have to be paid.

## Keeping securities in the street name

To eliminate the possibility of loss, some investors keep their securities in the street name. This merely means that the purchaser does not take physical possession, but rather leaves the securities with the broker, who stores them in a safe. This makes it easier to sell the securities. All that is required is a phone call; the owner need not sign them and deliver them to the broker. This also protects the individual from loss of the securities due to fire, theft, or misplacement. The reason securities held in the street name can be sold by making a phone call is that they are in the broker's name. The securities of hundreds of customers are all lumped together this way. While in theory there is some danger here, they are as safe as money in the bank. The brokers are subject to the regulations of the New York Stock Exchange and the Security and Exchange Commission. They cannot sell these securities without permission, nor may they borrow money on them. The brokers must carry a fidelity bond to cover losses due to fraud and insurance to cover theft.

## Security insurance

There is some slight danger if the broker goes bankrupt, but there is protection even here. In 1970, Congress passed, and the president signed, a bill establishing the Securities Investor Protection Corporation (SIPC). It is to security buyers what the Federal Deposit Insurance Corporation (FDIC) is to bank depositors. It protects investors up to $500,000 per account against the loss of securities due to failure of broker-dealers. Many brokers have an additional $500,000 per account with private insurance companies. This does not, of course, protect the investor from losses suffered by corporations that have issued the stock. Rather, it protects investors who keep their securities in the street name and have their broker keep physical possession of them. This protection was a result of the stock market crash in 1970 that caused some broker-dealers to fail.

All broker-dealers engaged in interstate security operations must join the SIPC. They are assessed an annual fee, which varies with the size of their operations. These fees go into a fund used to reimburse security owners who suffer losses when their broker goes into bankruptcy.

### Stock gifts to minors: uniform gifts to minors act

Most states have passed the Uniform Gifts to Minors Act, which makes it easier for a person to buy securities for his or her children. The security will be made out to "Jane Doe, Trustee for John Doe, Junior" under the Texas Uniform Gifts to Minors Act, or of whatever state the investor is a resident. The income is taxable only if the minor child has a high enough income to pay taxes. The gift is, and must be by law, irrevocable. However, the trustee can sell the security as long as he or she retains the principal on behalf of the child. The interest (or dividends) too must be retained for the child. The trustee may only manage the securities. No one, not even the child, can touch the fund until the child becomes twenty-one (now eighteen in many states), at which time he or she gains full control. Many people buy small amounts of high-quality securities for their children and build a portfolio to be used later to finance specific projects such as a college education.

### Stock splits and stock dividends

A stock split occurs when a corporation increases the number of shares of stock outstanding by sending additional shares of stock to existing stockholders without demanding additional payment. In so doing, the total net worth of the corporation is unaffected, and yet the book value of each individual share is reduced. Theoretically, the existing stockholders have received nothing that increases their share of the corporate assets. For purposes of illustration, assume a corporation with a net worth of $15,000,000 and one million shares, which would make the book value $15 per share. If the stock is split two for one—meaning that each shareholder is to receive two shares in exchange for each share now held—a shareholder who had one hundred shares before would now have a total of two hundred.[3] But the company, since it received no additional capital, would still have a net worth of $15,000,000. Since now twice as many shares have a claim on it, the book value of each share would drop from $15 to $7.50. If the market value had been $30 per share before the split, theoretically it would fall to $15. Often, however, the market value does not fall quite this much. The point is that the shareholders' positions would not be changed. The question then is, why do corporations split the stock?

The main reason is that lower-priced stock sometimes has a psychological attraction to investors. Then, too, lower-priced stocks are more accessible to more people. When the stock is split, more investors are attracted to the stock and consequently there may be a tendency for market prices to be forced upward more rapidly from the lower price. Also many people, not knowing that theoretically they are no better off, think that somehow the stockholders have magically got something for nothing. Because this makes this corporation's stock more attractive to them, they buy it and bid up its price.

---

3. The stock must be exchanged because par value is cut in half. If the stock is no-par stock, a two-for-one split could be accomplished without an exchange. The company would simply mail the stockholder one additional share for each share owned.

From a financial point of view, a stock split and a stock dividend are the same. A two-for-one split or a 100 percent stock dividend would double the number of shares a person had and would cut the book value in half. Theoretically, the market price would be cut in half, too. The two-for-one split discussed above and a 100 percent stock dividend would accomplish the same dilution per share. Generally stock dividends are used when smaller dilution is desired. (Many stock dividends are 10 to 20 percent.) Sometimes, however, stock dividends are used when a corporation cannot or does not want to pay a cash dividend but feels it must declare something to satisfy the stockholders. A stock dividend is not taxable as income. Table A16-1 and Figure A16-1 show the stock splits and dividends over the past few years.

### Preemptive rights

The capital of a firm may be reduced or increased. A capital reduction is rare, and it would necessitate returning to the stockholder part of the stockholder's capital. This could happen in a government antimonopoly action against a company which was then required to divest itself of certain assets. It is common, however, for a corporation to increase its capital; then the question is, what

are the rights of the stockholders under such a situation? It can readily be seen that the relative strength of an individual stockholder could be affected if the capital of the corporation is increased. Suppose again that there are ten stockholders, each with one share, and the total assets of the corporation consist of $1,000. Thus each of the stockholders may be said to own 10 percent of the corporation and also 10 percent of the voting rights. Suppose further that the corporation desires to issue $1,000 in additional stock so that its total assets will be $2,000. To accomplish this, it sells ten additional shares at $100 each. If an outsider buys all these shares, then his or her interest in the corporation will be 50 percent, and all old stockholders will have their interest reduced from 10 percent per share to 5 percent. Thus the old stockholders will be adversely affected by such a transaction.

To prevent this sort of imposition on the existing stockholders, "preemptive rights" have been developed. A preemptive right is the right of the existing stockholders to purchase a proportionate share in the increase of the capital stock of the corporation. This right does not always exist. In some cases it exists because the corporate charter grants it and in some cases because the state law of the state of incorporation requires it. If nei-

Table A16—1 **Stock dividends and splits, 1980-1989**

|  | Less than 25% | 25% to 49% | 50% to 99% | 2-for-1 to 2½-for-1 | 3-for-1 to 3½-for-1 | 4-for-1 | Over 4-for-1 | Total |
|---|---|---|---|---|---|---|---|---|
| 1989 | 28 | 9 | 34 | 66 | 2 | 2 | 1 | 142 |
| 1988 | 34 | 11 | 29 | 25 | 4 | 1 | — | 104 |
| 1987 | 36 | 18 | 59 | 118 | 10 | 1 | 2 | 244 |
| 1986 | 43 | 22 | 78 | 118 | 9 | 1 | 1 | 272 |
| 1985 | 40 | 17 | 43 | 60 | 6 | — | — | 166 |
| 1984 | 57 | 12 | 50 | 51 | 6 | 1 | 1 | 178 |
| 1983 | 54 | 21 | 80 | 131 | 12 | — | 2 | 300 |
| 1982 | 61 | 21 | 36 | 28 | — | — | — | 146 |
| 1981 | 63 | 23 | 67 | 98 | 6 | 2 | 1 | 260 |
| 1980 | 65 | 25 | 55 | 98 | 5 | 1 | — | 249 |

Note: Includes common and preferred issues. Data based on effective dates.

(Source: *New York Stock Exchange Fact Book*, 1990, p. 41)

**Annual number of stock splits***

*Stock distributions of 3 for 2 or more.

*Annual number of stock splits. (Stock distribution of 3 for 2 or more.) (Source: New York Stock Exchange Fact Book, 1990, p. 41.)*          Figure A16–1

ther state law nor corporate charter grants preemptive rights or if they are waived, then the corporation may go to the public or outside investors if it wants to expand its capital. A **stock right**, therefore, is defined as a privilege possessed by a stockholder to purchase a **pro rata share** of a new stock issue offered by the corporation at a specific price and for a specific time period.

Suppose a corporation desires to raise about $7,500,000. It has outstanding one hundred thousand shares of common stock valued in the market at $100 per share. If it sells one hundred thousand new shares at $75 per share, it will have its $7,500,000. In accordance with preemptive rights it will give all existing stockholders the right to buy one new share for each share they already have. In this case, the company is increasing its capital by 75 percent. I have put the example this way to simplify calculations. Usually a firm will increase its capital by only 10 to 20 percent, and a person in such a case will have the right to buy a new issue for every ten or five shares he or she owns, respectively.

The firm usually sells the new stock at a price below the market price of the outstanding shares in order to expedite the sale. Since there cannot be two prices, when the new issue comes out, the market price of the old will fall and the new will rise; and the price, in the example above, will be approximately $87.50. Mr. A who before had one share valued at $100, purchased a new one for $75. His total investment is $175 or $87.50 per share. If Mr. A had ignored his rights, he would now have only one share valued at $87.50. His equity would have been diluted by $12.50. The example also illustrates the value of these rights; it is, in this case, $12.50.

If Mr. A could not afford to pay $75 for his new share, he could have sold his rights for $12.50 in cash and prevented a dilution of his equity in this way. That is to say, rights are valuable and if one does not have the money to exercise them, sell them. If one neither exercises nor sells them, they will expire after a time. Usually the company will offer to buy an investor's rights if he or she does not wish to exercise them. Sometimes if a large issue is coming out, an organized market develops in rights and one can both buy and sell them from a broker.

When rights are granted, the person who buys that stock in the market automatically gets the right, until the stock goes "ex-right." This is logically the same as a stock going "ex-dividend." For example, the company issuing the rights announces that stockholders of record on Monday, Oct. 18, will receive the rights. The stock goes "ex-rights" in the market five days before this date because of the five day delivery rule.

When a stock goes "ex-rights" its price in the market generally declines by the amount of the value of the right.

Companies issue rights because it is an easy way to raise capital, and it is also cheaper than to come out with a general public issue. It saves the corporation investment bankers' fees; the stockholders also receive their stock more cheaply because they don't have to pay commissions.

Since persons usually get a right for every ten or twenty shares they already have, there arises the problem of fractional rights. Suppose you had fifteen shares of stock and were given rights to buy one share of new stock for every ten of the old. Obviously you cannot buy 1-1/2 new shares. Usually the company will either buy back fractional rights or offer to sell the investor enough fractions for an even number of shares.

A formula can be used to calculate the value of a right, although ordinary logic and arithmetic are all that is needed in a simple case such as the one discussed above. However, if eight or ten shares of stock are required to obtain the right to buy one new share, the formula may be helpful. It is the market price less the subscription price divided by the number of old shares plus one, which are needed to get one of the new.

Or,

$$\frac{M - S}{N + 1} = V$$

Where

$M$ = market value of old shares
$S$ = subscription price
$N$ = number of shares needed to buy one of the new
$V$ = value of the right

In the case above we had,

$$M = \$100$$
$$S = 75$$

and hence our formula tells us

$$\frac{\$100 - \$75}{2} = \$12.50$$

A second reason for preemptive rights—very important in most cases—is to prevent dilution of control. For example, if an investor owned 10 percent of the stock in a given corporation, he or she would have 10 percent of the votes at the stockholders' meetings. If the person were not permitted to continue to buy the same 10 percent of any new issues, his or her relative voting strength would decline. This is not important for most stockholders because they have so few shares that they don't really have any influence at corporate elections. However, for a few large stockholders it might be a factor.

### Stock warrants

A warrant is a certificate evidencing an option to purchase new securities, usually common stock, at a stated price for a stated time period. Sometimes, however, the time period is for perpetuity. The distinction between the right and the warrant is that the right is generally issued under the preemptive right privilege to existing stockholders, while a warrant may be issued aside from the preemptive rights to nonstockholders. Warrants are originally attached to other securities when they are issued and generally are attached to either bonds or preferred stock. Some warrants are not detachable, and hence they cannot be sold separately; but others are detachable, and a market exists for them.

When a corporation feels that it may have difficulty in selling a particular preferred stock or bond issue, it may offer warrants along with each security that will enable the purchaser to buy additional shares of common stock. These warrants, called "purchase warrants," are generally extended for relatively long periods of time or even perpetually. Thus preemptive stock rights are different from warrants. The rights have a relatively short life (days or weeks). When a corporation attaches warrants to bonds or preferred stocks, it is able to sell them more easily. Since warrants permit the holder to purchase common stock at a predetermined price, they are a speculative device. They make the mother security more attractive, a fact best illustrated with an example.

Suppose the Adjax Corporation issues 9 percent bonds maturing in twenty years with detachable warrants on the bonds. Anyone who buys a bond also gets a warrant. The warrant permits the owner to purchase one share of common stock at, say, $30 per share at any time during the next three years. The common stock is presently selling for $20 per share, however, and hence the warrant has speculative value only. If it is detachable, it may sell for a dollar or $.50 or even less. But the $30 and the three-year period are fixed. If common stock of the Adjax Corporation rises say, $40 before the three years have elapsed, the warrant will be worth $10; its price will have moved from $1 to $10. This is a tremendous percentage increase, but it is in the nature of warrants. They have great leverage. Once the stock rises above the warrant price, warrants have positive value and will appreciate by some multiple of the further appreciation of the common stock. Warrants also move downward with common stock but by greater magnitudes.

If you buy bonds with warrants attached, the warrant may have value in the future. If it does not, you simply remain a bond investor.

Corporations attach warrants to bonds (or preferred stock) as "sweeteners"; it may reduce the interest that they have to pay. While not many corporations have issued warrants in recent years, there are still many detached ones outstanding, and they are traded almost daily. Don't take the plunge into warrants, because they are highly speculative, and are only for the brave and those who can assume great risk.

### What to do with rights and warrants
Many investors have no idea what to do with either rights or warrants, some of which are destroyed physically and many of which are permitted to lapse. Three choices are open to the investor. One is to permit them to lapse; many people do just this. Another alternative is to exercise the right and the warrant if and when it has value; however, it may be that investors holding the warrants or rights are unable to do this because they lack available cash or are unwilling to because they lack any further interest in the particular stocks issued. The third alternative is to sell the rights, and the warrant if it is detachable, which can be done through any broker.

### The options markets: Puts and calls
Although there are a number of other stock options[4] the major ones are puts and calls, both of which are speculative devices.

---

4. The various stock options one can buy in the options market should not be confused with the stock-option plans many corporations make available to their key employees. In the case of corporate stock option plans, certain key executives are granted the privilege (option) of buying a certain number of shares of common stock from the corporation, usually at the market price of the stock at the time the option is granted. The

## Calls

A call option is a contractual and legal privilege for buying a given number (usually one hundred) of shares of a given common stock for a given period of time at a price determined at the time the call is purchased. For example, if you buy, say for $200, a thirty-day call on United States Steel (now USX) at $25 this means that at any time during the next thirty days the seller is required to sell you one hundred shares of U. S. Steel for $25 per share if you request it. If U. S. Steel rises to $45 during this period, your $200 will have grown to $2,000. Your net return is $1,800 ($2,000 minus the $200 option price). This again is a tremendous percentage return on your money. If U. S. Steel does not move, on the other hand, you have lost $200. Options permit one to speculate in one-hundred-lot shares with only a relatively few dollars; they also hold out the possibility of a high rate of return on one's money; and the maximum amount that can be lost is the price of the option.

## Puts

A put option is exactly the reverse of a call option. It is the privilege of selling 100 shares of a given stock for a given period of time at a price determined at the time the put is purchased. A person buying a put is speculating that the market price of that stock is going down.

Options may run up to nine months before they expire. A market in options is now being made on the Chicago Board of Options Exchange, the American Stock Exchange, the Philadelphia Stock Exchange, the Pacific Stock Exchange, and the New York Stock Exchange. The Chicago exchange is by far the largest. It is to the options market what the New York Stock Exchange is to the stock market.

If you wish to buy (or sell) an option, your broker can make the arrangement through one of the organized options markets mentioned above. There are brokerage commissions for this that are similar to (but generally a little lower than) the stock commissions discussed above.

Option quotations on the Chicago Board of Options Exchange, might appear as follows:

| Option and N.Y. close | Strike price | Calls—last | | | Puts—last | | |
|---|---|---|---|---|---|---|---|
| | | Apr | May | July | Apr | May | July |
| IBM 83¼ | 85 | 1³⁄₁₆ | 2⅜ | 4 | 2¹¹⁄₁₆ | 4⅜ | 5⅝ |

It identifies first the corporation (IBM) on which there is an option and below it the price (83¼) at which IBM stock closed on the New York Stock Exchange that day. Moving to the right we see the strike price at which the shares may be purchased by the option owner. Next comes the "April, May, and July Calls—last," which means it is a call option and the price of the last trade is quoted just below the months shown. The months refer to when the options on IBM will expire; buyers have some choice as to how long they want their option to run. The prices 1³⁄₁₆, 2⅜, and 4 are the prices per share of the last option traded for each of the three expiration dates and are called the premium. However, since options are always for 100 shares, the prices are really $118.75, $237.50, and $400.00 respectively. The options will expire on the third Saturday of the month shown (options always expire on the third Saturday

---

option price is then, however, frozen for the executives for a period of time, usually several years or more. Then if the market price rises substantially, the option holders can execute and make a nice gain. The main justification for providing key executives stock options is to give them a vested interest in the corporation and hence a greater incentive to perform well.

of the month shown).[5] If an investor wants a call option for 100 shares that runs to the third Saturday of July, it will cost $400, but will permit one to buy 100 shares of IBM at $85 per share even though its current price was 83¼ that day. Obviously, the buyers of this option believe the price of IBM will rise.

The next three quotations convey the same information on puts. The first quotation is for April and it is 2¹¹/₁₆. This means the premium is $2.6875 per share. This translates into $268.75 for 100 shares. The quotations also show that for $437.50 the buyer of that option has the right to sell 100 shares of IBM at $85 per share until the third Saturday (Friday) of May. Obviously, the buyers of such an option believe that the price of IBM will decline. If you examine the options quotations in *The Wall Street Journal,* you will note that sometimes an "r" or an "s" appears. An "r" means that no option for that stock was traded that day; an "s" means no option going out that far exists.

### Straddles and combinations

There are also options involving straddles and combinations. A "straddle" consists of both a put and a call option on the same stock, with the same strike price, and the same expiration date. A "combination" is the same as a straddle except that the put and the call have a different strike price, expiration date, or both. Straddles and combinations can become complex. However, if the investor operates in this market and the stock does not move in either direction, he or she will have earned a double premium if they are sold rather than bought.

---

5. Since the market is closed on Saturday, the options really expire on the third Friday of the month, but this is a technicality. The option will state that it will expire on the first Saturday after the third Friday of the month in question.

### Writing options

Instead of thinking about buying options, sophisticated investors are thinking in terms of selling them (called "writing options"). There are two ways of writing call options: covered and uncovered. If an investor writes a covered call option, this means he or she already has the stock; an uncovered call is on a stock the individual does not own and is a little riskier. Many financial advisers feel that writing covered options is a good strategy for conservative investors because it can increase their yield, as we shall see below.

Many option writers adhere to the following two rules of thumb. Never write a call on a stock not already owned (write only covered options). Write calls only on stock a person is thinking about selling anyway—or at least would not mind selling if the price went much higher, that is, on a stock that has risen about as much as he or she thinks it will and on which one is willing to take a capital gain or on a stock that has not done well and one is ready to sell for that reason. Some option writers, however, select what they think will be a good income stock and one that does not fluctuate much in price and then sell options on it. It is not unusual for option writers to double their yield on a stock by writing options. For example, if a person owns a stock providing a 6 percent dividend yield, writing several options per year on it could very well yield an additional 6 percent or even more. There are three ways in which an investor can benefit from owning a stock. There is, first, the dividend; second, possible capital appreciation (there is also the possibility of capital losses); and third, option income. All three should be netted to obtain the true economic improvement.

## SUGGESTED READINGS

*The ABC's of Option Trading.* Princeton, N.J.: Dow Jones and Company.

*Barron's Weekly.* A weekly financial newspaper published by Dow Jones and Company.

"*Characteristics and Risks of Standardized Options.*" Chicago: The Options Clearing Corporation.

Fischer, Donald, and Jordan, Ronald. *Security Analysis and Portfolio Management,* 4th ed. Englewood Cliffs, N.J.: Prentice Hall, 1987.

"*How Security Investor Protection Corporation Protects You.*"

Washington. D.C.: Security Investor Protection Corporation (SIPC).

"*Interest Rate Options.*" Dean Witter Reynolds. You may obtain this from your Dean Witter broker.

"*The Merrill Lynch Guide to Writing Options.*" New York: Merrill Lynch, Pierce, Fenner, and Smith.

"*The Versatile Option.*" Chicago: The Chicago Options Exchange.

*Understanding Options.* Chicago: The Chicago Options Exchange.

*The Wall Street Journal.* A financial newspaper published daily by Dow Jones & Company.

"*What Every Investor Should Know.*" Washington, D.C.: The Securities and Exchange Commission.

# 17 Investment companies (mutual funds) and other investment vehicles

**HIGHLIGHTS**

In order to provide the reader with an understanding of investment companies, real estate, and certain other investment vehicles and how they work, this chapter examines the following:

1 The two major types of investment companies
2 The various objectives of investment companies
3 The advantages and disadvantages of investment companies
4 Where you can obtain information on investment companies
5 The highly specialized and technical commodities market
6 The futures market in securities
7 A number of different possible real estate investments
8 A special investment company: real estate investment trusts
9 Investments in collectibles

## INTRODUCTION

Some people would like to invest in corporate stocks but do not care to buy them directly, either because they feel stocks are too risky or because they lack the time needed to review their portfolio frequently—and portfolio review is required. If a client is in this category, he or she may wish to investigate investment companies, also sometimes called "mutual funds." An investment company is a financial intermediary (or financial institution) that collects, usually in small dollar amounts, the savings of many individuals. It then invests these funds in the securities of other corporations. The savings of many small savers are pooled to become one large fund to be managed collectively for the benefit of all of the participants. An investment company, therefore, is a specialized one-layer financial holding company. The persons who buy the securities of these investment companies are said to be investing indirectly. They own part of the investment company, and the investment company owns the securities of other companies. The securities the investment company owns, on behalf of its owners, are referred to as the underlying securities, and it is the value of the underlyings that gives value to the shares of the investment companies. The relationship of the investment company, its owners, and the underlying securities is shown in Figure 17–1.

## CLASSIFICATION OF INVESTMENT COMPANIES, AND NET ASSET VALUE

As noted above, certain types of investment companies are also called mutual funds. The terms **mutual fund**, **investment company**, and **investment trust** are used to designate a variety of financial institutions that provide investors with the opportunity of investing indirectly in various corporations. In reality, however, only the open-end investment company (the open-end as opposed to the closed-end company will be explained below) is referred to as a mutual fund by the financial community. Generally, investment companies invest most funds they receive in common stock, but some companies buy substantial amounts of bonds and preferred stock. Any profits are shared among the shareholders of the mutual fund.

Figure 17–1 *Investment company relationships*

Investment companies can be classified as open-end and closed-end, and further classified according to their investment policies and objectives.

Closed-end investment companies have a relatively fixed amount of capital. To issue securities they need permission from the Securities and Exchange Commission (SEC), just like any corporation. They then have an authorized common stock issue, and when that is sold, they can sell no more unless another issue is approved. Once that issue is sold, therefore, an investor can no longer purchase it directly from the company but only from a broker in the open market. Moreover, closed-end investment companies do not stand ready to redeem their securities as do open-end companies. Some shares of closed-end companies are listed on the stock exchanges; some are sold over the counter. When buying and selling them, one pays the brokerage fees described in Chapter 16. The price of closed-end shares is, therefore, determined not only by the price of the underlying securities, but by all the psychological factors that affect the supply and demand of closed-end shares in the market. There have been times when the market price of closed-end shares has been below the market price of the underlying securities. This is referred to as selling at a discount. In other years some closed-end shares have been at a premium or above the value of their underlying securities.

*Closed-end investment companies*

Closed-end investment companies sometimes also acquire capital by selling bonds to the public, a practice that introduces the element of leverage into their capital structure. (See Chapter 15.) Building a lot of leverage into a firm's capital structure can in some cases result in a sudden and rapid increase in earnings and hence in the price of the common stock, but the reverse can also happen. Closed-end investment companies have various amounts of leverage built into their capital structure, the amount varying from time to time, depending on their management's appraisal of what the future holds in store.

There is no legally set limit to the number of shares an open-end investment company (mutual fund) may sell. The number of shares is limited only by what investors will buy. Such a company issues its shares continuously as it sells them; it is called open-end because its capitalization is not fixed.

*Open-end investment companies (mutual funds)*

Open-end funds also stand ready to buy back their shares from investors at any time at a price determined by the price of the underlying securities. Their price is calculated daily by dividing the total number of shares outstanding into the market values of the portfolio of the underlying securities.

Since open-end funds raise no capital by selling bonds, their entire capital is equity capital. No leverage is built into capital structure, although it might be in their underlying securities. Many open-end companies charge what is known as a loading fee when they sell their shares. These fees vary substantially from fund to fund, and some are paid when the funds are purchased and some when redeemed. Some charge both and some do not charge any loading fees at all. Loading fees are discussed in greater detail below.

It should be noted that open-end companies are much more popular than closed-end companies. Figure 17–2 shows the growth of both closed-end and open-end companies over the years.

*Net asset value*

The term **net asset value** is used to indicate the price of mutual funds. It is calculated as follows: First, the market value of all the underlying securities in the fund's portfolio are added up. Then the liabilities are totaled and subtracted from the aggregate assets. Third, the result is divided by the number of mutual fund shares outstanding. This is done daily on a computer; mutual fund shares fluctuate daily with fluctuations in the price of their underlyings. Since the price of mutual fund shares is determined directly by the price of the underlying securities, they are never sold at a premium or discount as may be the case when closed-end company shares are involved. Moreover, the funds stand ready to buy back (redeem) their shares at the net asset value whereas closed-end companies do not.

## OBJECTIVES OF INVESTMENT COMPANIES

The buyer of investment company shares faces the same problem as does the direct buyer of common stock: which one to buy? There are hundreds of investment companies. Moreover, their records are not the same, and their objectives are not the same. Even among those with the same objectives, records vary. When an individual buys investment company (mutual funds) shares, he or she must first of all examine the ones with the same objectives as he or she has, and then choose what appears to be the best fund within that group.

All mutual funds state their objectives—for example, growth or income. These objectives are spelled out in the fund's prospectus. A prospectus is a document that all funds are required to make available to investors by the Securities and Exchange Commission (SEC). The SEC is a government agency that regulates the securities industry. The prospectus discloses certain information, as required by the SEC, and is useful in evaluating whether a given fund is appropriate for a given investor. To be sure, some funds may have several objectives. Nevertheless, funds may be classified as follows:

1. Growth funds
2. Income funds
3. Growth and income funds
4. Balanced funds
5. Tax-exempt funds

*Growth of investment companies.* (Source: Investment Companies, 1989, **CDA/Wiesenberger,**       Figure 17–2
**a division of CDA Investment Technologies** Inc., p. 12.)

**6.** Money market funds
**7.** Other funds

*Growth funds*

The objective of a growth fund's managers is to achieve long-term growth (or price appreciation) in the value of the securities in their portfolio. Certain growth industries would be selected for their portfolio and firms within those industries with a proven record of growth in sales and earnings and firms that typically plow a high percentage of their earnings back into the business are the target.

*Income funds*

Funds with the objective of earning income would purchase more bonds and blue-chip stocks. They would select stocks in companies with a good record of earnings and a history of a high dividend payout. There are many income funds, and they generally appeal to investors needing income, such as retired individuals.

You may wish to review growth stock and income stock (discussed in Chapter 15) because those are precisely the stocks that these funds would seek.

*Growth and income funds (equity income)*

Those funds striving for both income and growth could be the balanced funds mentioned below or widely diversified common stock funds with an emphasis on blue-chip stocks. These funds' portfolios would also probably include some utilities, which have a good record of earnings and some of them a good record of growth, especially if they are located in an area with heavy population growth.

*Balanced funds*

A fund that has balanced objectives is one that usually emphasizes growth, income, and stability or maintenance of principal. However, these three objectives are given various weights or priorities at different times. The fund has bonds, common stock, and often preferred stock in its portfolio. The relative amounts of bonds and stock vary from time to time, depending on the fund's managers' appraisal of future conditions. If the future looks gloomy, they may take a more defensive position by increasing the proportion of bonds. These balanced funds are also sometimes called diversified funds.

*Tax-exempt funds*

In recent years mutual funds have been established that buy only state and local bonds on which the interest is exempt from personal income tax. These appeal to investors in a high tax bracket.

In many cases, the minimum amount of state and local bonds that may be purchased directly is $5,000. Owning them indirectly through a fund makes it possible to own them in lesser amounts.

In the 1970s a number of money market funds were developed when interest rates, especially the rate for short-term notes, were very high. Money market funds specialize in buying very short-term securities in the money market. Such things as Treasury bills, commercial paper, and bankers' acceptances are selected. These are highly technical areas, and few individuals are able to buy these securities directly; it takes thousands of dollars to buy commercial paper, for example. These funds always become popular when short-term rates are high; later when rates come down, moneys are withdrawn. Money market funds feature stability of principal due to the nature of underlying securities. *Money market funds*

Money market funds were developed to enable the small investor to get into this high interest area. Most of them were established and are managed by the various brokerage houses. Generally, they do not charge a commission when the small investor buys or sells. Rather they take a fraction "off the top." For example, if they earn, say, 8 percent interest, they will keep about .4 or .5 percent, leaving 7.6 for the investor. The interest on these funds fluctuates daily. Until recently thrift institutions and banks could not compete with these funds when interest rates were high, because the maximum interest they could pay was set by federal law. Today, with interest rate ceilings eliminated, the thrifts can and do compete. Indeed the thrifts have an advantage; their accounts are insured up to $100,000, whereas money market funds are not. However, money market funds still tend to pay a higher rate of interest than thrift accounts.

Some funds purchase mortgage-backed securities, such as those issued by the Government National Mortgage Association (GNMA). These are the so-called "Ginnie Maes" and have become quite popular. These government agencies invest in residential mortgages. They are, however, very safe because the bonds are guaranteed by the U.S. government. They also often yield a bit more than most other bonds of equal risk. They appeal to the more conservative investor, who prefers income to capital appreciation. Other mortgage-backed securities are issued by the Federal National Mortgage Association (FNMA or "Fannie Mae") or the Federal Home Loan Mortgage Corporation (FHLMC or "Freddie Mac"). These securities are considered very safe but are not directly guaranteed by the U. S. government. *Government agencies; Mortgage-backed securities funds*

There are a number of other funds. One of these is the **specialty** or **sector fund**, which invests only in a single industry, say, electronics. Needless to say, a sector fund may also be a growth or income fund. Figure 17–3 shows some of the mutual funds classified by objectives. *Other funds*

At one time the so-called hedge funds were popular, but recently they have fallen from favor. They would take a very aggressive position

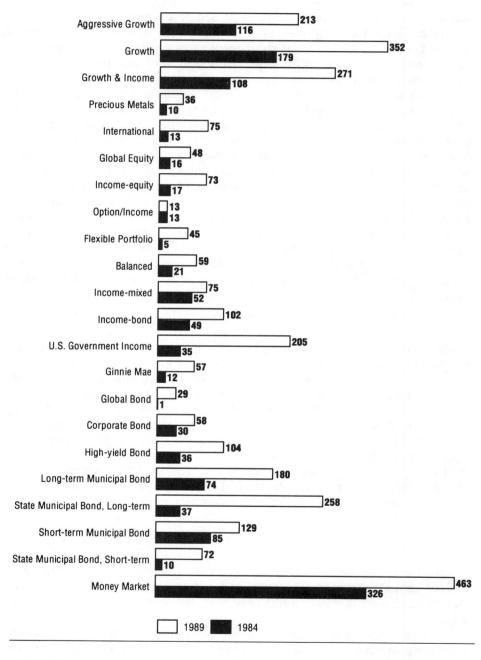

**Number of Mutual Funds Classified by Investment Objective**

| Objective | 1989 | 1984 |
|---|---|---|
| Aggressive Growth | 213 | 116 |
| Growth | 352 | 179 |
| Growth & Income | 271 | 108 |
| Precious Metals | 36 | 10 |
| International | 75 | 13 |
| Global Equity | 48 | 16 |
| Income-equity | 73 | 17 |
| Option/Income | 13 | 13 |
| Flexible Portfolio | 45 | 5 |
| Balanced | 59 | 21 |
| Income-mixed | 75 | 52 |
| Income-bond | 102 | 49 |
| U.S. Government Income | 205 | 35 |
| Ginnie Mae | 57 | 12 |
| Global Bond | 29 | 1 |
| Corporate Bond | 58 | 30 |
| High-yield Bond | 104 | 36 |
| Long-term Municipal Bond | 180 | 74 |
| State Municipal Bond, Long-term | 258 | 37 |
| Short-term Municipal Bond | 129 | 85 |
| State Municipal Bond, Short-term | 72 | 10 |
| Money Market | 463 | 326 |

☐ 1989   ■ 1984

Figure 17–3   *Number of mutual funds classified by investment objective. (*Source: 1990 Mutual Fund Fact Book, *Investment Company Institute, Washington, D.C., p. 29.)*

because their goal was short-term capital gains. They were highly leveraged and often purchased securities on margin.

There are also index funds, which invest only in securities that are included in the Standard and Poor's 500 industrial index or which attempt to duplicate index performance. This will ensure that they do as well as the market but no better. If a fund is willing to settle for performance equal only to the market averages, one may wonder about its "professional" management. Any investor can easily do this, if he or she has enough capital. Some funds invest only in bonds and preferred stock. These appeal to the more conservative investor.

The real estate investment trust (REIT) is another special fund that was very popular a few years ago. Technically, the real estate investment company is a trust. Nevertheless, the result is the same as that of an investment company; a number of individuals provide the capital, which is then invested in real estate. The real estate company is subjected to certain legal restrictions to prevent speculation in land. Real estate investments in general are discussed below, as well as the real estate investment company.

Finally, there is the small business investment company (SBIC) very much like the investment companies described above except that, as the name implies, it invests solely in small business. These companies have received favorable tax treatment by Congress to encourage the flow of equity capital to small firms. These investment companies work closely with the Small Business Administration, which has some federal funds available to small business.

Many mutual funds, especially the larger and more well-established ones, are set up in what are referred to as "groups" or "family of funds." One management team will handle a growth fund or income fund and perhaps several more. This amounts to several funds with different investment objectives being brought under the same roof. This union broadens the appeal of the group and, for individual investors, provides greater flexibility since they can switch from one fund to another within the group, as their investment objectives change. Making such a change may require paying a small transfer fee.

*Grouping of funds*

The investor should know about the advantages and disadvantages of investing in investment companies. It will also be necessary to learn where information on investment companies can be obtained to help select what will be the better ones or, more specifically, the ones most appropriate for the needs of the client. Finally, the individual should be aware of the cost of buying mutual shares. These are primarily commissions for the salespersons and are called **loading fees.** They are not uniform, and there are some no-load funds, which will be discussed below.

**OTHER THINGS YOU SHOULD KNOW ABOUT INVESTMENT COMPANIES**

*Advantages and disadvantages of mutual funds*

Three advantages may accrue to the buyer of mutual funds, as opposed to the purchaser of common stock directly, especially to a small investor. They are diversification, professional management, and constant surveillance. A disadvantage of some funds is the high acquisition cost. In addition, funds charge management fees, and sometimes 12b-1 fees, which cover promotional expenses.

Diversification

The small investor, to be sure, finds it more difficult to diversify than the large investor. Diversification, as noted before, consists of investing in a number of different industries or types of investments. Small investors with only a few thousand dollars cannot buy common stock of many different industries. They either have to assume the higher risk of "putting all of their eggs in one basket," or at most a few baskets, or have to reduce the risk (and possibly the return) by investing conservatively. Mutual funds make a real contribution in aiding small investors to diversify.

Professional management

The management qualities of mutual funds vary greatly. If an investor selects a good mutual fund, the added fees paid for management are probably well worth it. On the other hand, the person might get management that is professional only in the sense that they charge a fee.

Constant surveillance

This is probably a plus. Many small investors make excellent choices regarding the common stock they buy, but then forget about them. A given stock that is a good buy today may not be so six months or a year from now. Not only should an investor try to buy good stocks at the right time, but he or she should sell them at the right time, or at least before it is too late. Small investors may not have the time (even if they have the ability) constantly to watch and analyze their portfolio.

Cost

A potential disadvantage of investing in some mutual funds is the acquisition cost. These loading fees, as they are called, vary from fund to fund, and there are some no-load funds (examined below). In addition to the loading fees that may be necessary to acquire mutual funds, management charges fees to manage the funds, generally financed out of the income that the underlying securities provide. Nevertheless, it is another cost that comes out of income the mutual fundholder otherwise would receive. However, the load may be worthwhile if the fund performs well. Although the load should be a factor in evaluating funds, it should not be the only consideration.

Management costs are a fraction of 1 percent or more of the total assets in the fund. Often this is .5 or .6 percent of the first $500,000 in the fund and is then scaled down in several steps as the size of the fund increases. It should be noted however that these management fees are assessed annually for as long as the investor owns the shares. The acquisition cost (load) is shown in the mutual fund quotation on the financial pages of newspapers like *The Wall Street Journal*. It is the difference between the net asset value (NAV) and the offer price. It goes to the broker or other middleman from whom the investor buys the funds. Mutual fund shares are redeemable at the option of the holder and often without a redemption fee.

Some mutual funds will scale the loading fees down in a series of steps on large purchases. However, the first reduction does not usually apply until the amount purchased is about $10,000 or $15,000, depending on the fund.

*Hidden costs*

In recent years some mutual funds have imposed two additional hidden costs. There is, first, the so-called 12b-1 fee to cover the fund's advertising, mailing, and printing costs.[1] It can be assessed every year; it is over and above the management fees, and it can go as high as 1.25 percent of net asset value. Second, a low-load reinvestment fee has been added by a few funds. It may be as high as 3 to 4 percent of the dividends and capital gains that the fund reinvests on the client's behalf. It too can be an annual fee. The investor should investigate these hidden fees before selecting a fund. Even some of the no-load funds (discussed below) have these hidden fees.

*No-load funds*

A number of open-end investment companies (mutual funds) sell their shares directly to the public at the asset value and do not have a loading charge. These companies, however, do not solicit business as actively as others; if an individual wants to buy their shares, he or she has to take the initiative. They do not have brokers actively selling their shares; hence there are no commissions and no loading fees. Investors have been becoming more interested in these funds recently.

Because they have no sales staff, it is a little more difficult for the potential investor to obtain pertinent information on no-load funds. However, a person may write the company and get its literature and prospectuses. In addition, many of these companies have toll-free phone numbers for potential investors. Also, there is the Mutual Fund Education Alliance (MFEA)[2] located at 1900 Erie, Suite 120, Kansas City, Mo, 64116 (telephone 816-471-1454), which is a new and additional source of information.

If one writes the MFEA, it will send a list of its members. This will include the size of each of the funds, when it was organized, its investment objectives, and its address. Individuals can then select those that have the same investment objectives they are seeking and contact

---

1. The term 12b-1 refers to the section of the Investment Company Act that allows this fee.

2. This alliance's members are virtually all "NO LOAD" funds, although there are a few "LOW LOAD" members. The alliance defines a low load fund as one which charges 3.5 per cent or less.

them. Since there are no salespersons, individuals will have to contact the company itself to buy the shares.

An investor can identify the no-load funds in the financial pages easily. There is a NL in the column, "offer price." When no-load funds are purchased, they are purchased at the net asset value. Table 17–1 shows how some mutual fund listings would appear on the financial pages. "NAV" is the net asset value; the offer price is what one would have to pay. The difference between the two represents the loading fee, except where an NL appears under the offer price. "NAV chg." indicates the change in the net asset value from the previous day. Most of the early no-load funds developed out of the operations of investment counselors; they developed their mutual fund operations to service smaller clients. Recently some no-load funds have been developed by some investment services, the incentive being the management fees they would get. The no-load funds generally charge the same management fees as the other mutual funds, and some have the hidden fees discussed above.

*Liquidation or withdrawal of mutual funds*

Some people invest in mutual funds for a specific purpose such as retirement income or financing a child's college education. When an investor wishes to withdraw, he or she may do so at the net asset value, and often no fees are charged. An investor may withdraw in a lump sum or in any one of a number of different installment plans, either monthly, quarterly, semiannually or annually. Further, one may withdraw only the income earned by the fund and leave the principal intact, or one may dip into the principal. If an individual withdraws from the fund for retirement purposes, he or she should consider converting the fund into an income

Table 17–1   *Sample of a mutual fund listing*

|  | NAV | Offer price | NAV Chg. |
|---|---|---|---|
| AAL Mutual: | | | |
| CaGr | 13.59 | 14.27 | – .01 |
| Inco | 10.01 | 10.51 | +.03 |
| MuBd | 10.31 | 10.82 | +.01 |
| AARP Investment Program: | | | |
| CaGr | 31.22 | NL | – .04 |
| GiniM | 15.68 | NL | +.01 |
| GthInc | 28.15 | NL | – .04 |

NAV stands for net asset value per share. The offering price includes net asset value plus maximum sales charge, if any. NAV Chg. indicates the change in the net asset value from the previous day.

fund if this has not already been done. If the fund is with a family system, an investor may switch from, say, a growth fund to an income fund for only a nominal transfer fee of $5 or $10. Most of the larger funds are grouped, and have an income fund, growth fund, balanced fund, and so on. This is another reason why the mutual fund purchased must be selected with care; selecting a good group (or "family") provides greater flexibility.

If an investor switches from one fund to another within a group, in setting up a withdrawal program (or at any time), he or she may be realizing a substantial capital gain and have a tax problem. Hence taxes must be given some consideration when deciding whether to switch or not.

General information on investment companies can be obtained from the same sources that are available for any other type of investment information. The financial pages of most metropolitan newspapers carry price information and sometimes articles on certain companies. Papers like *The Wall Street Journal* and magazines like *Forbes, Business Week,* and *Barron's* are other good sources. *Forbes, Barron's,* and *Business Week* especially should be noted because they make special studies from time to time wherein they analyze and compare the past record of various investment companies. *Forbes* magazine has a special annual study of mutual funds every fall, with articles and analyses of mutual funds and statistical data on each of the major funds. There are statistics on assets, sales charges (loading fees), expenses per $100 of fund assets, dividend returns, and average annual growth rates over a number of years, as well as the performance over the most recent twelve months. Various investment services, such as Moody's, Value Line Investment Services, and Standard and Poor's, publish information on investment companies. In addition, a broker may have a wealth of useful information.

*Information on investment companies*

Three investment company services specialize in analyzing and publishing information on investment companies. Two of these services publish their major reports annually: *Investment Companies, Mutual Funds, and Other Types,* by Wiesenberger Financial Services, Inc., One Pennsylvania Plaza, New York 10119; and *Johnson's Investment Company Charts,* published by Hugh A. Johnson and Company, 246 Homewood Avenue, Buffalo, New York. These studies analyze most of the leading investment companies, appraise their various performances, and compare them with the performance of the stock market in general. The Wiesenberger Study and the Johnson Study can be purchased or can be perused at many brokerage houses and at any good library.

Lipper Services of New York is the third major investment company service. It publishes a wide variety of data. In addition, Lipper makes a thorough study of mutual funds quarterly, in which it analyzes past performances and presents statistics indicating the various funds' relative performance.

*Which funds have done well?*

When choosing what fund to buy, the investor should do so in light of the investment objectives. Even after choosing a growth fund or a balanced fund or an income fund, many choices are available. Not all funds perform the same, and differences in performance can be attributed primarily to the differences in management.

Just as stock price averages have been constructed to show how stock prices are moving, averages or indexes can also be constructed of the price of mutual funds to show how mutual funds in general are performing. There are the Lipper index, the Johnson's Charts average, and the Wiesenberger index. Figure 17–4 shows several mutual fund indexes. One is for a number of growth funds, one for growth-income funds, one for income funds, and one for a number of balanced funds.

Figure 17–4     *Wiesenberger mutual fund indexes. These indexes are based on the price movements of a representative group of large mutual funds and reflect the "total return" on a presumed investment with income dividends reinvested and capital gains accepted in shares. The indexes do not, however, reflect average management performance for the various groups and should not be considered as such. Five funds are used in the indexes for the balanced funds, 10 each make up the income and growth-income categories, and 13 funds are included in the growth group. (Source:* Investment Companies, 1989, **CDA/Wiesenberger, a division of CDA Investment Technologies** *Inc., p. 172.)*

These records can be compared with that of Standard and Poor's industrial average, or with the Dow Jones averages.

We can also analyze the performance of the mutual funds with Johnson's statistics. Johnson has five mutual fund averages: (1) a growth fund average, (2) an aggressive growth fund average, (3) a growth and income fund average, (4) an income fund average, and (5) a balanced fund average. Table 17–2 shows these averages over the last few years and also the annualized rate of return. In addition, the table shows the Dow Jones Industrial Averages, the Standard and Poor's composite stock index, and other financial indicators to compare with the mutual fund average.

Lipper Services also publishes overall mutual fund performance indicators. Lipper has an index for growth funds, for growth and income funds, and for balanced funds. It is published in *The Wall Street Journal* and in *Barron's Weekly*.

## SECURITIES MARKETS OF THE PAST 30 YEARS
### 1960 - 1989

Table 17–2

| | RESULTS OF A $10,000 INVESTMENT WITH ALL INCOME REINVESTED | | | | | | | | | |
|---|---|---|---|---|---|---|---|---|---|---|
| | 5 Years 1985-1989 | | 10 Years 1980-1989 | | 15 Years 1975-1989 | | 20 Years 1970-1989 | | 30 Years 1960-1989 | |
| | Total | % Rate of Return | Total | % Rate of Return | Total | % Rate of Return | Total | % Rate of Return | Total | % Rate of Return |
| Cost of Living | 11,975 | 3.7 | 16,441 | 5.1 | 24,297 | 6.1 | 33,448 | 6.2 | 42,891 | 5.0 |
| Value of the Dollar | 8,351 | — | 6,082 | — | 4,116 | — | 2,990 | — | 2,331 | — |
| Dow-Jones Industrial Average | 27,291 | 22.2 | 51,078 | 17.7 | 89,738 | 15.8 | 84,607 | 11.3 | 137,147 | 9.1 |
| Standard & Poor's 500 Stock Index | 25,055 | 20.2 | 48,907 | 17.2 | 96,584 | 16.3 | 85,661 | 11.3 | 179,682 | 10.1 |
| Municipal Bonds | 19,935 | 14.8 | 23,872 | 9.1 | 31,752 | 8.0 | 41,563 | 7.4 | 42,269 | 4.9 |
| Long Term Corporate Bonds | 20,129 | 15.0 | 33,919 | 13.0 | 44,870 | 10.5 | 62,054 | 9.6 | 73,375 | 6.9 |
| Long Term Government Bonds | 21,229 | 16.2 | 35,659 | 13.6 | 45,385 | 10.6 | 63,510 | 9.6 | 73,254 | 6.9 |
| U.S. Treasury Bills | 13,,931 | 6.9 | 23,453 | 8.9 | 32,321 | 8.1 | 43,190 | 7.6 | 63,457 | 6.4 |
| Johnson Growth Fund Average | 20,652 | 15.6 | 42,491 | 15.6 | 126,063 | 18.4 | 82,667 | 11.1 | 216,082 | 10.8 |
| Johnson Growth & Income Fund Average | 20,952 | 15.9 | 44,365 | 16.1 | 98,822 | 16.5 | 91,359 | 11.7 | 187,411 | 10.3 |
| Johnson Balanced & Income Fund Average | 17,828 | 12.3 | 35,045 | 13.4 | 67,297 | 13.6 | 69,948 | 10.2 | 140,437 | 9.2 |
| Johnson Corporate Bond Fund Average | 15,763 | 9.5 | 27,466 | 10.6 | 40,359 | 9.7 | 47,957 | 8.2 | 75,322 | 7.0 |
| Johnson Gov't Securities Fund Average | 15,751 | 9.5 | 26,945 | 10.4 | 32,259 | 8.1 | 47,599 | 8.1 | — | — |
| Johnson Municipal Bond Fund Average | 16,529 | 10.6 | 22,498 | 8.4 | — | — | — | — | — | — |

NOTE: Rate of Return is Compounded Annual Percentage Rate.

*Source: Johnson's Charts, 1989,* Hugh A. Johnson, Inc., Buffalo, New York. p. 18.

While mutual fund averages and indices are useful, the prospective buyer must also look at the record of individual companies. Some performed even better than the fund averages shown and some, not so well. Individuals can get literature from the fund they are interested in buying and compare its past record with both the overall fund indicators, the Standard and Poor's index, and the Dow Jones averages. This gives a clue to how well the fund is managed. A good past performance is no assurance of success in the future; however, it's probably better to bet on a past winner. In addition, the fund manager should be evaluated to ascertain past experience and to predict possible future performance.

Investors can also compare the growth of many individual funds with both the Standard and Poor's stock index and the Dow Jones averages by using Johnson's Charts, which can be found at many brokerage houses. Johnson has plotted the performance of individual funds and has included a transparent overlay of both the Dow Jones and the Standard and Poor's market indicators. By using these charts, an investor can see at a glance how funds compare with the stock market indicators.

## INTRODUCTION TO OTHER OUTLETS FOR SURPLUS FUNDS

In addition to mutual funds, a person may invest in commodities, real estate, and a number of unusual (sometimes called exotic) investments. Each of these will now be examined. We hasten to add; however, that with the exception of real estate, these are not for the typical small investor because there is a larger element of speculation involved. Nevertheless, they may be right for some people.

### Traditional commodities[3]

Traditionally when one speaks of commodities, one has in mind such things as wheat, corn, sugar, sow bellies (bacon), and so on. In 1980 and early 1981 certain exotic items such as gold, diamonds, antiques, Chinese ceramics, and the like (which, with the possible exception of gold, aren't really commodities at all) gained some popularity. Then, in 1982 and 1983, they lost some of that luster, but in the future—who knows?

The price of certain commodities fluctuates widely over short periods of time for a variety of reasons. The supply can change sharply due to crop failure caused by adverse weather or loss of production due to a strike. Demand for certain commodities, too, can fluctuate due to changed public tastes or governmental policies. These sharp changes in supply and demand can create sharp price changes. Because of these fluctuations, speculators have entered the market.

There are futures prices and spot or cash prices. The spot price is the price paid for delivery today, but the futures price is the price paid

---

3. I wish to acknowledge the help I have received in developing the section on commodities from Professor Edna Villar of The American University.

today for commodities to be delivered at a specified time in the future. There is a one-month, two-month, three-month futures price, and so on.

If you believe the price of corn will rise and you buy corn futures, you are referred to as being "long." If you expect the price to decline and you sell, you are referred to as being "short." If your expectations come true, you make a profit. If prices turn against you, you suffer losses.

Since there are futures markets in commodities, and professional speculators that operate in them, business firms that use these commodities can hedge their operations and protect themselves from sharp price fluctuations. In the process the speculator may make a lot of money. There is also the so-called "short hedge" and the "long hedge."

The short hedge works as follows: Suppose a candy manufacturer has signed a contract to supply some candy. The price has been set, and it will take a month or more to make and deliver the candy. In the meantime, the manufacturer does not want to carry a large inventory of sugar but wants to protect itself against sharp price increases. He will buy sugar futures. This will freeze the price of sugar for, say, thirty days. While the future price may be slightly higher than the present or spot prices, it is known, and presumably the candy manufacturer negotiates the contract with future prices in mind. For the small price differential, he can avoid carrying a large inventory in sugar and also protect himself (hedge) against sharp price increases in sugar, his major input cost.

*The short hedge*

The long hedge involves holding an inventory and selling a contract for future delivery to hedge (protect) the inventory from a sharp drop in prices. For example, a miller, storage company, or exporter may have a large inventory of wheat that he would like to hedge against a price change. If he sells a contract for future delivery and the price falls, he will suffer a loss on his inventory, but it will be offset by a profit from his futures contract. If the price rises, exactly the reverse happens.

*The long hedge*

There are speculators, hence a futures market, in certain foods, grains, fats and oils, textiles, and metals. Futures quotations may be found in the financial pages of large metropolitan newspapers. The Chicago Board of Trade is the largest commodities market in the nation. There are a number of others, including the Kansas City Board of Trade, the Minneapolis Board of Trade, the Chicago Mercantile Exchange, the New York Coffee, Cocoa, and Sugar Exchange, the New York Cotton Exchange, and the New York Commodity Exchange. Table 17–3 shows the futures market prices for coffee and cotton as reported in *The Wall Street Journal*.

*Commodity market*

There is also a futures market in Treasury bills, certain other short-term, intermediate-term, and long-term U.S. government securities, and common stock. If a person believes interest rates are coming down in the

*The futures market in securities*

Table 17–3   *Futures prices as published in* The Wall Street Journal

| | | | | —Food & Fiber— | | | | |
|---|---|---|---|---|---|---|---|---|

**Cocoa (CSCE)—10 metric tons; $ per ton.**

| | | | | | | | | |
|---|---|---|---|---|---|---|---|---|
| July | 1,585 | 1,598 | 1,576 | 1,583 − | 2 | 2,160 | 1,534 | 8,155 |
| Sept | 1,612 | 1,618 | 1,602 | 1,609 | . . . | 2,204 | 1,555 | 12,780 |
| Dec | 1,642 | 1,646 | 1,631 | 1,641 + | 2 | 2,197 | 1,587 | 8,092 |
| Mr89 | 1,672 | 1,675 | 1,669 | 1,675 + | 5 | 2,088 | 1,625 | 3,728 |
| May | 1,700 | 1,700 | 1,700 | 1,698 | . . . | 2,088 | 1,652 | 592 |
| July | 1,725 | 1,725 | 1,715 | 1,715 − | 4 | 1,985 | 1,680 | 1,597 |
| Sept | 1,743 | 1,743 | 1,743 | 1,738 − | 6 | 1,850 | 1,709 | 429 |

Est vol 3,303; vol Fri 3,955; open int 35,373, − 14.

**Coffee (CSCE)—37,500 lbs.; cents per lb.**

| | | | | | | | | |
|---|---|---|---|---|---|---|---|---|
| July | 138.00 | 138.10 | 136.15 | 137.47 + | 2.19 | 146.25 | 110.00 | 9,684 |
| Sept | 138.75 | 138.90 | 137.30 | 138.47 + | 2.30 | 147.75 | 111.01 | 7,986 |
| Dec | 139.50 | 140.00 | 138.40 | 139.90 + | 2.57 | 150.25 | 114.00 | 3,683 |
| Mr89 | 139.50 | 140.20 | 138.50 | 139.96 + | 2.47 | 150.50 | 131.50 | 1,377 |
| May | 140.00 | 140.00 | 139.75 | 139.95 + | 1.32 | 150.75 | 133.35 | 456 |

Est vol 5,775; vol Fri 6,140; open int 23,282, − 324.

**Cotton (CTN)—50,000 lbs.; cents per lb.**

| | | | | | | | | |
|---|---|---|---|---|---|---|---|---|
| July | 67.25 | 68.37 | 67.20 | 68.34 + | 1.96 | 81.40 | 53.90 | 8,974 |
| Oct | 64.65 | 64.65 | 64.40 | 64.65 + | 2.00 | 73.00 | 54.45 | 4,684 |
| Dec | 63.44 | 63.44 | 63.24 | 63.44 + | 2.00 | 70.20 | 53.85 | 17,127 |
| Mr89 | 63.00 | 63.89 | 63.00 | 63.89 + | 2.00 | 67.90 | 54.70 | 2,047 |
| May | 63.50 | 63.98 | 63.13 | 63.98 + | 2.00 | 65.15 | 56.40 | 456 |
| July | 63.60 | 64.08 | 63.60 | 64.08 + | 2.00 | 64.08 | 56.50 | 147 |

Est vol 6,000; vol Fri 6,356; open int 33,435, − 50.

*Source: The Wall Street Journal,* June 7, 1988. Reprinted by permission of *The Wall Street Journal,* © Dow Jones & Company, Inc., 1988. All Rights Reserved Worldwide.

future (government security prices are going to rise), he or she may buy security futures. If the investor is right, he or she will make money. If one's view is that interest rates will rise (security prices will fall) and the investor is right, he or she could make money by selling futures.

The trading unit for Treasury bill futures is one million dollars and for longer-term securities $100,000. However, margins are very low and only a few thousand dollars are required to take a position. It is also possible to hedge with government securities, but only very large investors or institutions such as insurance companies are in a position to do so.

With stock market futures, trading is carried out in one of the stock indexes, such as Standard and Poor's 500, the Value Line Index, or the New York Stock Exchange Composite Index. For example, if an investor buys (or sells) the Standard and Poor's index futures, he or she is speculating on the future prices of 500 different stocks. If the Standard and Poor's index is 213, but one expects it to rise to 230 and buys, he or she would make money if correct and lose if wrong. If an investor expects it to decline, he or she should do the reverse.

An individual may also buy common stock indexes on margin, generally at about 50 percent.

It is also possible to hedge via common stock indexes—just as in the case of commodities or government securities. However, this would be of interest primarily to institutional investors and wealthy individuals. While these futures markets are in securities, the actual operations are carried out not in the security exchange, but on the commodities exchange.

There are now also stock index options—that is, an investor may buy puts and calls on the indexes and not buy the index itself. (Puts and calls on stock were discussed in Chapter 16.) Several exchanges are offering options on the index futures.

It should be noted that futures are highly speculative and are not appropriate for a small investor.

There are two major ways of investing in real estate, first, investing in mortgages, and second, owning real property outright. If an individual invests in mortgages, he or she is lending money to a home owner to help finance a home; on this loan he or she receives interest.

**REAL ESTATE INVESTMENTS**

A mortgage is a legal document given by the prospective home owner (borrower) to the lender. The borrower who gives the mortgage is called the mortgagor and the lender who receives the mortgage is called the mortgagee. The mortgage stipulates the terms of the loan such as the interest rate, the monthly payments, and the length of time over which the loan is to be repaid. In addition, the borrower agrees to pay all taxes, assessments, and other charges levied against the property, also to keep it in good repair and fully insured against fire and other hazards.

*Mortgages*

The mortgage also provides for foreclosure and repossession of the home by the mortgage lender in the event that the home owner defaults. In some states a deed of trust is used in place of a mortgage but it provides for the same arrangements.

Most mortgage loans are made by financial institutions such as savings and loan associations and mutual savings banks, but there is no reason why an individual with surplus funds cannot make such a loan to a home owner. When a person makes a mortgage loan, he or she in effect pays off the seller of the home (sometimes the builder if it is a new home) and the purchaser gives the lender a mortgage as described above.

Mortgages are negotiable just like corporate bonds, and can be sold just like corporate bonds. The interest rate on a mortgage is usually fixed for the duration of the loan, and hence if interest rates rise after a given mortgage has been agreed upon, the market price of the mortgage declines. The market price of mortgages, then, fluctuates inversely with changes in the going interest rate, and consequently mortgages may be sold at a premium or at a discount from their face value, just as in the case of corporate bonds. (See Chapter 14.)

*Determination of mortgage yields*

Since the price of mortgages, purchased from another mortgagee, fluctuates, the yield is not necessarily the same as the fixed interest rate specified in the mortgage itself. Also, mortgages are not as liquid as corporate bonds; it takes time to sell them to someone else. For this reason, the yield on mortgages is generally higher than that on corporate bonds. The true yield on a mortgage, of course, is determined by how much above or below face value it is sold. To determine the approximate yields, the following formula is used.[4]

$$Y = \frac{R(P) + \left(\dfrac{P - C}{N}\right)}{\left(\dfrac{P + C}{2}\right)} \times 100$$

$Y$ = approximate yield
$P$ = principal balance of the mortgage
$C$ = the cost to the investor of the mortgage
$N$ = number of years the mortgage runs until paid
$R$ = coupon rate of interest the mortgage carries

Assume, for example, a ten-year-old mortgage with an unamortized face value of $50,000 running over ten years, bearing a fixed interest rate of 10 percent which an individual can purchase for $35,000.

$$(1) \quad Y = \frac{10(\$50,000) + \left(\dfrac{\$50,000 - \$35,000}{10}\right)}{\left(\dfrac{\$50,000 + \$35,000}{2}\right)} \times 100$$

$$(2) \quad Y = \frac{5,000 + \left(\dfrac{\$15,000}{10}\right)}{\dfrac{85,000}{2}} \times 100$$

---

4. Note the word "approximate." The reason for approximation is that the components of the problem are themselves only averages. The figures used are generally average interest earned per year. This is true where monthly payments are made (this is not the case, however, in this oversimplified problem). To be strictly accurate, yields must be figured using compound interest functions.

(3) $\quad Y = \dfrac{\$5,000 + \$1,500}{\dfrac{85,000}{2}} \times 100$

(4) $\quad Y = \dfrac{\$6,500}{\$42,500} \times 100 =$

(5) $\quad Y = 15.29$ percent approximate yield

We noted above that a mortgage is less liquid than corporate bonds, and hence the yield should be higher. Mortgages also generally are riskier than corporate bonds, which also will increase their yield above bonds. However, the degree of risk varies with the credit rating of the mortgagor. When making a mortgage loan, one must appraise the credibility of the mortgagor. A person must also consider the age and the condition of the house, and what portion of its total value he or she is financing. The general rule is that the individual should not make a mortgage loan in excess of 75 percent of the value of the house. It should also be remembered that some costs are involved if one has to foreclose and repossess the home. All this will have a bearing on the yield on mortgage loans. A person must also decide whether the yield on a given mortgage is sufficiently higher than alternative investment opportunities. If it is not, one can bargain to increase it by asking for a larger discount. Whether the above 15.29 percent yield is adequate depends on the investor's alternative investment opportunities.

*Second mortgages*

In the above discussion we had in mind first mortgages. There are also second mortgages, which are riskier. In the event of a foreclosure and sale of a house on which the mortgagor has defaulted, the second mortgage is not paid off until after the first mortgagee has been completely repaid. Assume a home valued at $100,000 with a $60,000 mortgage. If the home is sold, the buyer would need a $40,000 down payment to take over the existing mortgage. If he had only $25,000, he could offer a second mortgage for $15,000, and he would now have two mortgages to pay. Second mortgages are for smaller dollar amounts and run over fewer years than first, generally from five to twelve years. While riskier, second mortgages provide a higher yield; and if the mortgagor has a sufficiently high income and good enough credit rating, many mortgage lenders will assume the higher risk in order to obtain the higher yield. Second mortgages generally have a maximum amortization period of twelve years and yield as high as 20 percent. The yield on discounted second mortgages is calculated by using the above formula just as in the case of the first mortgages.

*A final word of caution*

When accepting a mortgage be sure that the mortgagor has a strong credit rating. This is especially true in an innovative mortgage (see Chapter 8). If a lender escalates interest on the mortgagor and it creates a hardship for him or her, it may also be unpleasant for the lender. If a mortgagor's income rises substantially over the years, the investment is probably safe; otherwise it might not be. If the mortgages in the portfolio have balloon payments, one may have to refinance them in order to avoid a default. To be sure an individual can foreclose on the loan if necessary, but that is a lengthy and expensive process.

*Real estate investment trusts*

Another possible outlet for surplus funds is the real estate investment trust (REIT), which generally resembles a closed-end investment company. It is a specialized holding company that sells stock in itself to the public. However, instead of investing in stocks as a mutual fund generally does, the REIT invests in real estate mortgages, actually owning the property, or both. The main inducement for the real estate investment is that it is exempt from paying the corporate income tax provided it distributes at least 95 percent of its income to the holders of the trust certificate of ownership.

For the trust to be exempt from the corporate income tax, it must strictly follow the law, which requires:

1.  That there be more than one hundred shareholders
2.  That no five persons directly or indirectly own 50 percent or more of the shares
3.  That 95 percent of its taxable income must be distributed to the shareholders
4.  That it derive at least 75 percent of its gain from rents, capital gains, or mortgage income
5.  That it derive no more than 25 percent of its income from dividends and interest in other concerns (provided that only 75 percent of its income results from investments outlined in point 4; for example, if 85 percent of the income were from rents, then only 15 percent would have to come from dividends and interest in other concerns)
6.  That it hold property for a minimum of four years
7.  That it be separate from the management of the real estate it holds

The trust provides more liquidity than most real estate investments. A trust certificate may be sold like stock. If the investor wishes to become part of a trust, he or she may purchase a certificate.

Real estate investment trusts are specialized closed-end investment companies. In addition, some of them borrow money and have leverage built into their capital structure just as do some closed-end investment companies. In recent years, they have become an additional source of substantial mortgage capital, and this capital does not seem to dry up as much during periods of extremely tight credit as is the case with more traditional sources.

Real estate investment trusts (REIT) have also begun to specialize to some extent. There are now about five types: (1) equity, (2) short-term mortgage construction, (3) long-term mortgage, (4) hybrid, and (5) specialized. Most of them can be classified as those that buy securities representing real estate investments (mortgages) and receive a fixed-interest income and those that buy the real estate directly and receive a rental (and perhaps a capital gain) income.

Many individuals who invest in real estate shy away from the real estate investment trust because of the lack of individual control and the fact that the investment must be in income-producing property. For example, the trust cannot purchase a piece of raw land for development purposes or for capital gains. These two facts have prevented the trust from becoming as successful as it might have.

So far we have discussed primarily buying securities that represent real estate investments. It is also possible to own and manage real estate directly, primarily for income purposes, but also for capital gains, as a hedge against inflation, or for tax reasons.

*Owning real estate directly*

Income properties are generally divided into categories: residential income properties, including individual homes, duplexes, and apartment houses, and nonresidential, including commercial space, office space, and industrial or warehouse space.

When an investor buys rental property, he or she must choose whether to buy a single family dwelling, a duplex, a triplex, or an apartment. How much money one is able to invest will be a constraint that may rule out everything but a single family unit. If an individual is able to invest more and has a choice, he or she must come to grips with the following questions:

Residential

1. What type of residential unit is in the greatest demand? Indeed, what is the demand for all of the various types of units?
2. What is the supply of currently available rental units of the various types which would be in competition in providing housing? It is possible that the demand for apartments is greater than for single family units, but nevertheless apartments may be overbuilt while single family rentals are very scarce.
3. What size of family unit (small or large house) is in greatest demand relative to the available supply?
4. What part of the community is the best location for various types of residential units?
5. What is the cost of acquiring a residential unit? (Generally, the cost per square foot is less on a multifamily than on single units.)
6. What are maintenance costs and rental incomes?

All this will require an analysis of population growth in the area, residential values, monthly rents, construction rates, rental unit vacancy rates, yield on capital invested, whether the population is in large part transient or permanent, and personal income.

Until a few years ago, residential rental property had been an excellent investment. It provided an inflationary hedge, a tax shelter, capital gains in excess of the rate of inflation, and fairly good investment return. This is less true today. However, real estate may still be a good investment in some cases, especially in certain parts of the country. In some geographical areas real estate prices have declined but then so too have rents; in those areas where rental income has remained firm, residential prices have not declined, or at least not as much. The major optimistic point in residential investing is that interest rates have declined.

Not too many years ago, investing in rental property usually resulted in at least a small positive cash flow. If a person buys rental property today, he or she will quite likely have to accept a negative cash flow, at least temporarily.[5] Nevertheless, purchasing rental property may still be a good long-run investment in certain areas, if one is very selective.

**Calculating the yield on direct real estate investments**

To analyze rental property as an investment, one must look at the cash flow, the tax consequences, expected future cash flow, and expected price appreciation of the property. Table 17–4 provides a starting point.

An investor purchases a duplex for $150,000, makes a down payment of $40,000, and finances the remainder at 10 percent over 30 years. The net rental income amounts to $15,800, which after taxes, insurance, and mortgage payments generates a modest cash flow of $216. In earlier days, an investor could expect a larger positive yield, but this is much more difficult today.

The 1986 tax law changed the depreciation schedule on residential rental property, which must now be depreciated over 27.5 years on a straight-line basis. This means the owner may take only 3.636 percent depreciation per year (100/27.5 = 3.636). In our example, depreciation comes to $4,727 per year and provides that much of a tax shelter—it can offset that much of other income and shield it from taxes. Is this duplex, then, a good investment? It depends on one's tax bracket, among other things. In the 28 percent tax bracket, the depreciation on this investment will save $1,324 in taxes. In the 15 percent bracket, the tax savings will be only $709. The cost of this tax shelter is the cash-flow yield. Is it worth it? The investor should also remember that insurance, interest payments, maintenance, and property taxes (totaling $16,434) are also tax deductible. If the owner is in the 28 percent bracket, $4,602 of these payments are shifted to the government. Adding in depreciation, a total of $5,925 is shifted; at the 15 percent bracket a total of $3,174 is shifted. Table 17–5 shows this.

Also, in the future, rents will probably rise, and the cash flow may become larger. Finally, the owner may have a good inflationary hedge.

---

5. A negative cash flow merely means that the mortgage payments, taxes, and insurance are in excess of rental income.

*Rental property as a tax shelter*                                          Table 17—4

| | | | |
|---|---|---|---|
| Duplex: | | | $150,000 |
| Down payment | | | 40,000 |
| Mortgage at 10 percent interest—thirty years | | | 110,000 |
| Rental income: | | | |
| Two units at $700 per month each | $16,800 | | |
| Maintenance, repairs, and vacancy | 1,000 | | |
| Net rental income | | $15,800 | |
| Taxes and insurance | | 4,000 | |
| Mortgage payment ($965.84 per month) | | 11,584 | |
| Cash flow | | $ 216 | |
| Equity buildup first year (about $12.50 per month) | $150 | $ 150 | |
| Cash flow plus equity buildup | | $ 366 | |
| Depreciation over 27.5 years | | | |
| straight line ($130,000 × .03636) per year | | | 4,727 |
| Interest first year (mortgage payment less equity buildup) | | | 11,434 |
| Taxes and insurance | | | 4,000 |

*Source:* Calculated by author.

*Potential yield and tax shelter of rental property*                        Table 17—5

| | | |
|---|---|---|
| Rental income | | $16,800 |
| Expenditures: | | |
| Interest on mortgage | $11,434 | |
| Insurance | 1,000 | |
| Taxes | 3,000 | |
| Maintenance and repairs | 1,000 | |
| Depreciation | 4,727 | |
| Total | | 21,161 |
| Loss | | 4,361 |
| Cash flow | | 366 |

Since depreciation is a noncash outflow, there is a modest $366 cash inflow.

$21,161 × 28% = $5,925 = taxes shifted to the government.
$21,161 × 15% = $3,174 = taxes shifted to the government.

Whether the above duplex is a good investment, then, depends on personal circumstances, and what the future rent increases and price appreciation will be. With respect to these latter two points, *where* the rental property is located may be crucial. If it is in a fast-growth area, the risk would be less than in a low-growth or declining area.

**Real estate and leverage**

We learned in Chapter 15 that borrowing money introduces leverage into the capital structure of a corporation. Leverage comes about when an individual pays less interest for borrowed money than he or she can earn with it. This is also sometimes true with real estate investments. If there is positive leverage, it is advantageous to minimize the down payment on a real estate investment, and borrow as much as possible. Keep in mind, however, that leverage can be negative as well as positive, in which case the person is paying a higher rate of interest than he or she is able to earn with the borrowed funds. Table 17–6 illustrates how leverage comes about via real estate investments.

**Nonresidential real estate**

Logically, investing in nonresidential property is similar to investing in residential—there is a rental cash inflow, as well as maintenance, taxes, insurance, mortgage payments, and depreciation. More money is usually needed to invest in nonresidentials.

Nonresidential property may be classified as commercial and business, office and professional, and industrial and warehouse. When investing in any of these, a person must, among other things, analyze population and business growth and their patterns, vacancy rates, parking facilities, transportation arteries, and zoning ordinances.

**Older buildings**

Sometimes if an individual invests in older real estate, he or she may also be able to take an investment tax credit.[6] Generally, when investing in real estate, individuals may not take this credit; but if they buy and rehabilitate older buildings, in addition to the depreciation (cost recovery) allowance described above, they may be eligible for the investment tax credit as well.

The investment tax credit applies only to buildings built before 1936. Expenditures incurred in rehabilitating buildings built before 1936 will qualify for a 10 percent investment tax credit. In the case of a building certified by the IRS as being a historical structure, the investment tax credit may be as much as 20 percent. The investment tax credit applies only to the rehabilitation cost, not the acquisition cost. If a person buys a building certified as a historical structure for $60,000 and spends $40,000 rehabilitating it, the rehabilitation investment tax credit could be as much as $8,000.

**Undeveloped (raw) land**

Some people feel undeveloped land is a superior investment to rental property. Sometimes it is, and sometimes it is not. To be sure, the owner does not have to worry about leaky roofs, broken furnaces, or poor tenants who pay the rent late and are complainers. On the other hand, it yields no income, and there are taxes to pay plus interest on the loan,

---

6. See Chapter 7 for a discussion of the investment tax credit. The 1986 tax change eliminated the ITC for most items, but retained it in a few cases, including a few real estate investments.

*Leverage provided by real estate*  Table 17—6

| Total Investment—Duplex | | $150,000 |
|---|---|---|
| | With Leverage | Cash Transaction |
| Borrow | $135,000 | $ 0 |
| Owner's funds | 15,000 | 150,000 |
| Rental income | 15,800 | 15,800 |
| Interest | 13,500 | 0 |
| Before-tax earnings | 2,300 | 15,800 |

$$\text{Before-tax return on owner's investment} = \frac{2,300}{15,000} = 15.3\% \qquad \frac{15,800}{150,000} = 10.5\%$$

To be sure, these figures are gross, or before income taxes. In addition, property taxes and insurance have been deducted, but they are deductible from the owner's income taxes.

The leverage after federal income (assuming a 28 percent bracket) is as follows:

$$\frac{\$1,656}{\$15,000} = 11.04\% \qquad \frac{\$11,376}{\$150,000} = 7.5\%$$

which can use up money quickly. There is also no depreciation to provide a tax shelter. The land would have to appreciate in value by substantially more than enough to offset these factors to make the investment worthwhile. If one buys land in a fast-growing area, this may happen, but such land has already been discounted into the future for a number of years, and hence is very expensive. If an investor buys land that is not in a growth area that becomes a growth area, he or she has made a shrewd investment, or was lucky and will probably have a nice capital gain.

An investor should be wary of raw land in general. It should be checked out carefully with respect to taxes, interest on the loan, expected future growth in the area, and present and possible future zoning restrictions.

**COLLECTIBLES: GOLD, DIAMONDS, AND OTHERS**

For a brief period during the late 1970s and early 1980s, when inflation was at the double-digit level, gold, diamonds, and certain other items became popular as investment outlets. People thought they were inflationary hedges, but this did not prove to be the case. Speculative fever drove their prices up rapidly; then came just as rapid a price collapse.

People invested in such things as:

Works of art
Chinese ceramics
Antique furniture
Antique cars
Rugs

Stamps, coins, and rare books
Gold and silver
Precious gems

It is very difficult to profit from investments in collectibles; as with other investments, the investor must maintain current and extensive knowledge of the item in order to do well. However, information on collectibles is not as readily available as for other investments. In addition, trends on collectibles are difficult to forecast.

*Gold and silver*

Gold and silver reached their peaks of $884 and $56 per ounce, respectively, during the speculative fever in 1980.

Gold and silver earn no interest or dividend return, and there are storage costs involved. While they are generally not inflation hedges, for psychological and historical reasons sometimes gold and silver have become a panic haven as they did in 1979 and 1980 when inflation exceeded double-digit levels.

Gold may be purchased in the form of coins—the Krugerrand, the Canadian Mapleleaf, or the Austrian Corona—rather than bullion. Each of these coins contains about one ounce of gold and fluctuates in value with the market price of bullion. Coins are easier to store than bullion, and they need not be assayed when sold.

*Diamonds and other precious stones*

The price of diamonds and other precious stones rose drastically in 1980, and then collapsed. Diamonds are even riskier than gold, because they are not homogeneous. It is difficult to judge the quality of the various gems or compare one with another. Gold is homogeneous; coins are stamped and bullion need only be assayed to determine its purity.

## SUGGESTED READINGS

*The Appraisal Journal.* Chicago: American Institute of Real Estate Appraisers. Quarterly publication.

*Appraisal Review Journal.* This journal is published three times per year by the National Association of Review Appraisers, St. Paul, Minn.

*Areuea; Journal of the American Real Estate and Urban Economics Association.* This journal is published quarterly.

Arnold, Alvin, Wurtzebach, Charles, and Miles, Mike. *Modern Real Estate.* New York: John Wiley and Sons, 1987.

*Barrons.* A weekly financial newspaper. Princeton, N.J.: Dow Jones and Company.

"Before You Speculate." Chicago: The Chicago Mercantile Exchange.

Donoghue, William E., and Tilling, Thomas. *William E. Donoghue's No-Load Mutual Fund Guide: How to Take Advantage of the Investment Opportunity of the '80s.* New York: Harper and Row, 1984.

"Forbes Mutual Fund Survey." Forbes Magazine. This is an annual survey that comes out every fall.

"For High Yields in Short-Term Investments Ask About Money Market Instruments." New York: Dean Witter Reynolds. You may obtain this from a Dean Witter broker.

Green, Fred T. *Thrift and Home Ownership.* Chicago: United States League of Savings Associations.

"Guide to Financial Futures." Chicago: Chicago Board of Trade, Market Planning and Support Division.

*Hedging Highlights.* Chicago: Chicago Board of Trade.

*How to Buy and Sell Commodities.* New York: Merrill Lynch, Pierce, Fenner, and Smith.

"Introduction to Hedging." Chicago: Chicago Board of Trade, Educational Services.

*Investment Companies, Mutual Funds, and Other Types.* Latest edition of this annual publication by Wiesenberger Financial Services, New York.

*Johnson's Investment Company Charts.* Latest edition of this annual publication by Hugh A. Johnson Company, Buffalo, N.Y.

*Mutual Fund Fact Book.* Washington, D. C.: Investment Company Institute. Annual publication.

"Profit Opportunities in a Managed Futures Account." New York: Dean Witter Reynolds. You may obtain this from any Dean Witter broker.

*The Real Estate Appraiser and Analyst.* This is a bimonthly publication of the Society of Real Estate Appraisers, Chicago, Ill.

*Real Estate Center Journal.* College Station, TX.: Texas A & M University. Quarterly publication.

*Real Estate Review.* Boston: Warren, Gorham & Lamont. Quarterly publication.

Rugg, Donald D., and Hale, Norman B. *The Dow Jones-Irwin Guide to Mutual Funds,* revised ed. Homewood, Ill.: Dow Jones-Irwin, 1986.

SBA, *What It Is, What It Does, SBIC Financing for Small Business, SBIC Industry Review, SBIC Industry Trends.* Washington, D.C.: Small Business Administration. The Small Business Administration (SBA) is a government agency and it publishes numerous pamphlets on small business management. It also publishes a *Handbook of Small Business Finance.*

Smith, Halbert, and Corgel, John. *Real Estate Prospectives.* Homewood, Ill.: Dow Jones-Irwin, 1987.

"Speculating in Futures." Chicago: Chicago Board of Trade, Educational Services.

*U.S. News and World Report.* A weekly magazine that contains a good deal of information on business and finance.

*Well Beyond the Average: The Story of Dow Jones.* Princeton, N.J.: Dow Jones and Company.

Wiedemer, John P. *Real Estate Investments.* Englewood Cliffs, N.J.: Prentice Hall, 1987.

Wofford, Larry E. *Real Estate,* 2nd ed. New York: John Wiley and Sons, 1987.

# V Retirement and estate planning

The first chapter of this section, on retirement planning, discusses three means of providing for retirement that are available for most people. There is, first of all, Social Security that most people have to build on. Second, there are the client's personal investments that will yield an investment income.

The client's personal investments may, of course, be in the form of life insurance annuities, securities, rental property, and even some others.

Most people who earn a wage or salary will have a pension plan with their employer; this is the third source of retirement income.

For the self-employed there are Keogh accounts, and in some cases people may have individual retirement accounts (IRAs). All of these are discussed.

The other, and last, chapter is designed to introduce the planner to techniques that may help his or her client to save estate taxes upon death and to allocate assets as desired. Wills, trusts, and gifts are discussed.

Change is very rapid in the area of retirement and estate planning. This is because of court decisions, congressional action, and innovations on the part of the finance industry. Therefore, it is suggested that the planner make a conscientious effort to maintain current knowledge on an ongoing basis.

# 18 Retirement planning, Social Security, annuities, and other pension plans

**HIGHLIGHTS**

In order to acquaint the reader with the various techniques for achieving a decent life during the retirement years, this chapter discusses the following:

1 Social Security and what it provides
2 The Social Security tax structure, which finances Social Security benefits
3 Annuities and how they work
4 Fixed and variable annuities
5 Regular corporate pension plans and how they work
6 Two special corporate pension plans
7 Individual retirement programs available
8 The various options when funds are withdrawn

## INTRODUCTION

This chapter deals with retirement income. Social Security, savings and annuities, and certain pension plans are the trinity of retirement programming. Pension plans may, in turn, be broken down into corporate pension plans (or government plans for government employees) and individual pension plans. In addition, some people have other assets (for example, bonds, stocks, and rental real estate), which will also yield income during retirement. Stocks, bonds, real estate, and the like, were discussed in previous chapters; in this chapter we will discuss formal retirement plans—Social Security, annuities, and corporate and individual pension plans.

## SOCIAL SECURITY

Social Security will provide the retiree with some tax-free retirement income.[1] That tax-free income is also indexed—at least currently—to protect the recipient from inflation. Social Security benefits will vary depending in part upon earned income while the person was working; but even if the individual is drawing the maximum benefits, it by itself may not provide a decent retirement standard of living, and he or she will need to supplement it. Indeed Social Security never was—and is not now—intended to provide an adequate retirement income. Rather it was intended to provide a minimum base or starting point on which to build and which, if supplemented, could provide for an adequate retirement. It was believed that with Social Security as a base most people could provide for their retirement years.

Social Security provides a total of four different benefits.

1.  Old-age retirement
2.  Survivors' benefits
3.  Disability benefits, and
4.  Medicare. (Medicare was discussed in Chapter 11; the other three will be discussed here.)

### Who is covered?

Almost everyone in the labor force, including self-employed persons, is included under Social Security; this also includes members of the armed forces. Today the only exceptions are certain federal employees, some state and local employees, and ministers and other members of religious orders who file a form stating they are conscientiously opposed to receiving Social Security benefits because of religious convictions.

Prior to January 1, 1984, federal employees were not covered by Social Security. They had their own alternative pension system. In 1983,

---

1. Up to one-half of the benefits received by taxpayers whose income exceeds certain base amounts is subject to income taxation. See section entitled "Social Security and Income Taxes."

however, Congress provided for coverage for federal workers effective in 1984 and later years, but applying only to workers hired after that time. For state and local workers, coverage was voluntary prior to 1984; now it is mandatory. Moreover state and local employees could drop out before 1984. Now they may no longer terminate their participation in the Social Security system.

Everyone under Social Security must pay Social Security taxes (also called payroll taxes). In 1992 this was 7.65 percent on the first $55,500 of earnings. This is matched by the employer, and the sum is paid to the Social Security Administration. The taxes are increased periodically by Congress, but the wage base to which the taxes apply is increased nearly every year. This is adjusted to reflect changes in wage levels. Of the 7.65 percent tax, 1.45 percent goes to finance Medicare. In 1992, the taxable wage to which this 1.45 percent applies was raised to $130,200.

*Social Security taxes*

  The self-employed pay a higher tax because there is no matching contribution. In 1992 the self-employment tax was 15.30 percent on the same base of $55,500. In 1983, Congress amended the Social Security tax and raised sharply the tax that the self-employed pay. They now pay exactly double what people who work for others pay. Part of the Social Security tax is earmarked to finance Medicare, and the remainder finances retirement benefits, disability benefits, and survivors' benefits.

  As noted above, the income base (taxable wage) will be adjusted upward annually to take into account average wage level increases throughout the U.S. Table 18–1 shows how both the taxable wage and the tax rate have increased over the years. Since Social Security taxes are withheld through payroll deductions, they are automatically stopped when the maximum base income is reached. However, if a worker has two or more employers, he or she may have a tax withheld in excess of the maximum because each employer is required to withhold the maximum amount. If so, the taxpayer can get it back by taking it as a credit against personal income tax when he or she files the annual return.

To build up Social Security benefits, individuals must earn what are called **quarters of coverage**. In 1992, a person receives one quarter of coverage for every $520 of earned income on which he or she pays Social Security taxes. Therefore, four quarters of coverage—the maximum that may be earned for the year—are obtained in any year during which the person paid Social Security taxes on $2,280 of earned income. (Income from dividends, interest, rent, or capital gains is not subject to Social Security taxes and hence does not count.) It does not matter when during the year a person earns this $2,280; even if earned all in one day, he or she will receive four quarters of coverage. This quarters-of-

*Building protection: quarters of coverage*

Table 18–1          *Social Security taxes*

| Year | Taxable wage | Employed | | Self-employed | |
| | | Tax rate | Maximum tax | Tax rate | Maximum tax |
|------|--------------|----------|-------------|----------|-------------|
| 1978 | $17,700 | 6.05% | $1,070.85 | 8.10% | $1,433.70 |
| 1979 | $22,900 | 6.13% | $1,403.77 | 8.10% | $1,854.90 |
| 1980 | $25,900 | 6.13% | $1,587.67 | 8.10% | $2,097.90 |
| 1981 | $29,700 | 6.65% | $1,975.05 | 9.30% | $2,762.10 |
| 1982 | $32,400 | 6.70% | $2,170.80 | 9.35% | $3,029.40 |
| 1983 | $35,700 | 6.70% | $2,391.90 | 9.35% | $3,337.95 |
| 1984 | $37,800 | 7.00% | $2,646.00 | 14.00% | $5,292.00 |
| 1985 | $39,600 | 7.05% | $2,791.80 | 14.10% | $5,583.60 |
| 1986 | $42,000 | 7.15% | $3,003.00 | 14.30% | $6,006.00 |
| 1987 | $43,800 | 7.15% | $3,131.70 | 14.30% | $6,263.40 |
| 1988 | $45,000 | 7.51% | $3,379.50 | 14.02% | $6,759.00 |
| 1989 | $48,000 | 7.51% | $3,604.80 | 15.02% | $7,209.60 |
| 1990 | $51,300 | 7.65% | $3,924.45 | 15.30% | $7,848.90 |
| 1991 | $53,400 | 7.65% | $4,085.10 | 15.30% | $8,170.20 |
| 1992 | $55,500 | 7.65% | $4,245.75 | 15.30% | $8,491.50 |

*Note:* By law, the taxable wage will be increased automatically every year to take into account average wage-rate increases in the U.S. The tax rate, too, is increased frequently. Call the local Social Security Field Office for the latest figures.

*Source: U.S. Department of Health, Education & Welfare, Social Security Administration*

coverage base will be adjusted upward to take into account average wage-level increases in future years.

Quarters of coverage are important because they determine whether a person is eligible to receive benefits. The amount of benefits is determined by the person's income while employed. That is, there is a loose and indirect connection between what a person earns (and pays in the form of Social Security taxes) and benefits received.

The number of quarters of coverage needed to qualify for Social Security benefits varies with the year in which the retiree becomes 62, in the case of retirement benefits, and with the age when a person dies or becomes disabled in the case of those benefits. These variations range from a minimum of 30 quarters to a maximum of 40 for retirement benefits, and 6 to 40 quarters in case of survivors' or disability benefits.

To calculate the quarters of coverage needed to qualify permanently for Social Security retirement benefits, work through the following three steps.

**1.** Take the year in which the person was born
**2.** Add 62 to it
**3.** Subtract 1951 from the result

For example

$$
\begin{array}{r}
1923 \\
+62 \\
\hline
1985 \\
1951 \\
\hline
34
\end{array}
\quad = \text{quarters of coverage needed.}
$$

Social Security taxes go into a special Social Security trust fund. The moneys are then invested in a special issue of U.S. government securities from which the money earns interest. Since Social Security taxes flow into the fund and Social Security benefits flow out of the trust fund, in any one year the fund may be built up or depleted.

*Social Security trust funds; what happens to money collected?*

A few years ago Congress created several new trust funds; there is now a separate one for retirement benefits, disability payments, hospital benefits, and medical benefits (see Figure 18–1). Until the early 1980s much more money was flowing out in the form of benefits than was flowing in in the form of taxes, and the trust funds were dangerously depleted. Because of this in late 1983 Congress raised Social Security taxes substantially. Currently, with the exception of hospital and medical funds, far more funds are flowing in in the form of taxes than are flowing out in the form of benefits. Consequently, the nonmedical funds today have large surpluses.

It should be noted that the Social Security taxes individuals pay are

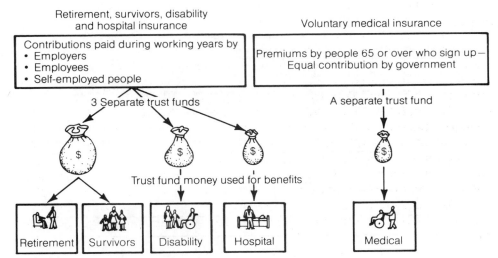

*Trust fund money can be used only for benefits and for the costs of administering the corresponding programs. (Source: U.S. Department of Health, Education and Welfare.)*  Figure 18–1

not earmarked to pay their benefits when they retire. Rather they are commingled and used to pay benefits to those presently retired. Later when a person retires, the members of the labor force at that time will be paying Social Security taxes that will be used to provide for his or her benefits. In this way an intergenerational transfer takes place.

*The wage statement request*

Once a year, anyone may check his or her records by filling out a wage statement request—as illustrated in Figure 18–2—and sending it to any district office of the Social Security Administration. This should be done

FOLD HERE

**REQUEST FOR STATEMENT OF EARNINGS**
(PLEASE PRINT IN INK OR USE TYPEWRITER)

| | FOR SSA USE ONLY |
|---|---|
| **AX** | |
| **SP** | |

**I REQUEST A SUMMARY STATEMENT OF EARNINGS FROM MY SOCIAL SECURITY RECORD**

Full name you use in work or business

**NH** | First | Middle Initial | Last

**SN** | Social Security number shown on your card | | Your date of birth | **DB** Month | Day | Year | **A**

**MA** | Other Social Security number(s) you have used | **SX** Your Sex ☐ Male ☐ Female

**AK** | Other name(s) you have used (Include your maiden name)

FOLD HERE

**PRIVACY STATEMENT**

The Social Security Administration (SSA) is authorized to collect information asked on this form under section 205 of the Social Security Act. It is needed so SSA can quickly identify your record and prepare the earnings statement you requested. While you are not required to furnish the information, failure to do so may prevent your request from being processed. The information will be used primarily for issuing your earnings statement.

I am the individual to whom the record pertains. I understand that if I knowingly and willingly request or receive a record about an individual under false pretenses I would be guilty of a Federal crime and could be fined up to $5000.

| Sign your name here: (Do not print) | TELEPHONE NO. (Area Code) | DATE |
|---|---|---|

SEND THE STATEMENT TO:    (to be completed in ALL cases.)

**PN** | Name

**AD** | Address (Number and Street, Apt. No., P.O. Box, or Rural Route)

City and state | **ZP** | Zip Code

Form **SSA-7004-PC-OP1** (9/85)
Destroy prior editions

Figure 18–2    *Request for statement of earnings. (Source: U.S. Department of Health, Education and Welfare.)*

at least every three years because that is the limit for correcting errors. A wage statement request card can be obtained from any Social Security district office, and there is one in all large cities. Look in the telephone directory under United States government for the address and phone number of the nearest field office.

When someone hears from Social Security headquarters, he or she can check his or her figures with the amount the employer claims to have reported, shown on the W2 income tax forms. The Social Security Administration's records will not show what the tax deductions have been, but rather whether the income has been reported and its dollar amount. That is the only important item to verify because future Social Security payments will not be based directly on the taxes but rather on the income reported to the Social Security Administration. If the figures are not in agreement, the individual should contact the Social Security field office right away.

When individuals reach age 65 they may receive full benefits (and remember full benefits vary with earned income) if they have the proper quarters of coverage. One may retire any time; but if retirement occurs before age 65, he or she will receive permanently reduced benefits, as explained below.

*Retirement benefits*

Benefits are determined, among other things, by the income earned during the working years, but the actual dollar level is calculated by applying a complex formula. When a person is near retirement age, he or she should visit a local Social Security Field Office. While they cannot calculate the benefits precisely until retirement, they can, and will, give an approximation. When one does retire and receives benefits, they are adjusted every January to offset cost-of-living increases.

The benefits will vary with the number of dependents. A husband and wife will receive more than a single person; if there are children under 18, even larger monthly payments are made.

A married couple, both of whom work, will have a choice. Since they both pay taxes, they both earn benefits. Moreover, each will earn benefits for his or her spouse. When they retire, each may take his or her benefits as an individual, or one member may take his or her benefits as a worker with a spouse. They have the choice of taking the higher.

The law does, however, discriminate against some two-income married couples. In some cases there is a Social Security benefit payment reduction for any public pension (federal, state, or local) received. Affected are benefits based on a spouse's Social Security. Moreover, for the reduction to be made, a retiree must have a non-Social Security type public pension in his or her own right. This discriminates against couples in which both work but only one has Social Security, and the one who does not has a public pension plan other than Social Security. An example will clarify this. A and B are a married couple both of whom work. A has Social Security, and B has a pension plan under a state or local government but not Social Security. When they retire, the Social Security benefits to be paid because B is a dependent of A will be reduced because B has a pension from a state or local government. The payment due B may be reduced by as much as two-thirds, depending on the size of the state benefit.

*Early or late retirement*

An individual may receive benefits as early as age 62, but if he or she does, those benefits are reduced. Benefits are calculated in the regular way and are then reduced by five-ninths of 1 percent for each month the retiree is under age 65 at the time of retirement. If a person retires at age 62, he or she is 36 months under age 65; hence retirement benefits are 80 percent of what they would be at age 65 ($36 \times 5/9 = 180/9 = 20$).[2] No retirement benefits are available before age 62.

Delaying retirement beyond age 65 will increase the regular benefits by 3 percent for each year up to age 70, the maximum increase being 15 percent.

*Limits to earnings*

The law requires that if a person is drawing Social Security benefits and is under age 70, he or she loses some benefits for any earned income above a certain level. ("Earned income" consists of wages and salaries; "unearned income" consists of interest and dividends). Unearned income is not included in the calculation. There are two different possible losses; one for people between age 65 and 70, and one for those between 62 and 65.

In 1991 the maximum amount a person 65 or over (but under 70) may earn without losing benefits is $10,200 per year. The Social Security benefits are cut by **one** dollar for every **three** dollars of earned income above this $10,200 exempt amount.

A person between the ages of 62 and 65 is subject to a different rule. He or she has an exemption of only $7,440 per year. A person in this age category loses **one** dollar of benefits for every **two** dollars of earned income above the exempt amount. The exempt amount is increased yearly to offset increases in the cost of living. This provision of the law no longer applies when the recipient reaches age 70; he or she can then earn as much as desired and still receive full benefits.

*Disability payments*

Disability payments dollarwise are calculated exactly the same way as retirement benefits, and dollarwise they are the same amount as retire-

---

2. Beginning in the year 2000, early retirement benefits will be reduced by 15/18 of 1 percent for each month that a retiree is under 65. At 62, then, retirement benefits would be 70 percent of what they would be at age 65 ($36 \times 15/18 = 540/18 = 30$).

ment at age 65 benefits. To qualify a person must be unable to engage in any substantial gainful activity. If the disabled person is merely unable to perform his or her regular work, that is not enough to qualify the person if other work can be performed. Moreover, the disability must be expected to last at least twelve months. Disability payments start after a five-month waiting period.

The amount of work credit (quarters of coverage) needed to qualify for disability benefits varies with the age of the person when he or she becomes disabled. Before age 24, only one and a half years (six quarters) are needed during the three-year period just before the disability started. During ages 24 through 31, the person needs credit for one-half the time between age 31 and the time the disability occurred. After age 31, the amount of credit needed varies with the age of the person from a low of five years (20 quarters) between the ages of 31 to 42, to a high of ten years' coverage for a person becoming disabled at age 62 and older.

*Survivors' benefits: family benefits*

In the case of death, the survivors receive a lump-sum settlement as well as a monthly payment. The lump-sum settlement is $255.00. The monthly benefit varies with the income of the deceased as well as with the number of dependents.

Normally these dependents are unmarried children under the age of 18—up to 19 if still in high school—and a spouse. The payments are made to the mother on behalf of the children if they are under 16. From ages 16 to 18 the payments are made to the children, but they must be unmarried. If the children are in high school, the payment may continue until age 19.

A surviving spouse under 60 without dependent children does not qualify as a dependent and does not receive benefits until reaching age 60.

*Social Security and income taxes*

The 1983 changes in the law increased Social Security taxes for everyone, but the increase was particularly severe for the self-employed. To soothe the pain of this, Congress authorized a Social Security tax credit—but only for the self-employed—which could be used to reduce personal income taxes a bit. This tax credit was 2.3 percent in 1985, and 2 percent in 1986 through 1989. Beginning in 1990, this credit was eliminated, but it was replaced by a tax deduction equal to 50 percent of the self-employment tax.

The 1983 law also made a portion of Social Security benefits taxable, in some cases, for the first time. The law defines a base amount of income, which is $25,000 ($32,000 on a joint return). If one-half of Social Security benefits, together with adjusted gross income and interest income on tax-exempt bonds, exceeds the base amount, a tax is due. The tax would be due on the lower of the following two items:

**1.**    One-half of Social Security benefits
**2.**    One-half of the excess of the combined income over the base amount.

## ANNUITIES

An annuity is a contract with a life insurance company in which the company agrees to pay the annuitant an income stream for a specific period of time. The income stream may be fixed in dollar amounts per month or per year, or it may be variable. The specific period of time for which the payment is to be made may be for a given number of years, or it may be for life. If it is for life, the annuitant cannot outlive his or her principal. An annuity then is a device to enable a person to retire. Annuities are sold by life insurance companies because life contingencies are involved. Life insurance protects the insured's beneficiaries from having the income stream cut off due to a premature death. An annuity can protect an annuitant from outliving his or her accumulated assets due to a lengthy retirement period.

### The annuity principle

To be sure, if the assets are large enough a person can live on his or her investment income and never dip into the principal. But an annuity will enable a retiree to dip into the principal and still not outlive it. This is because, as with life insurance, the insurance company applies the law of averages to large numbers of individuals. If each individual from among a large group of people of the same age were to rely on his or her individual accumulated assets, some would outlive their principal; others would not. Insurance companies, however, can guarantee that none will outlive their principal. While the company does not know which individuals in a large group will die at what age, the company does know how many will die at each age. The insurance company can scientifically liquidate the principal sum of all the individuals. Those who live to a ripe age will be drawing on the funds of those who die earlier.

Annuities are the opposite of life insurance, but life contingencies are involved. As with life insurance, the law of averages is applied to large numbers. Annuity tables are used, which indicate how many individuals out of a large group will still be alive at the end of each year. Annuity tables go up to 110 years and are different from mortality tables.

### Uses of annuities

Generally annuities are used to provide retirement income. However, they can also be used to free capital and hence increase the retirement income and sometimes to save taxes. For example, if a person had accumulated assets of $200,000 over the years, he or she could invest this conservatively at, say, 8 percent and have an annual income of $16,000 to supplement other retirement income that might be received. An annuity could increase this. A man age 65 can buy a single-premium straight-life annuity paying $10,741 per year for about $100,000. The other $100,000 could be invested to yield $8,000 or $9,000. The total income on the $200,000 is enlarged because the annuitant is scientifically liquidating part of the principal. To be sure, there may be less left for one's heirs, and hence it might not be appealing. However, in the above case, 64.7 percent of the $10,741 would not be taxable because it is a return of principal rather than interest income.

Annuity premiums can be paid monthly, quarterly, semiannually, or annually, just like life insurance. Premiums are paid over the years, and a principal sum is accumulated on behalf of the individual. Over the years the annuity builds up a cash surrender value just like permanent life insurance. In the case of annuities this is called account value. Again, as in the case of life insurance, a person can turn in an annuity at any time and take the account value. If the individual dies prior to when the payments are to begin, the beneficiaries generally receive the principal sum. However, some insurance companies pay either the account value or the sum of all premiums paid in, whichever is the greater. This method of buying an annuity is a planned savings program.

*Annuity premiums*

It is also possible to buy an annuity in one lump-sum payment. People of some means may do this. Also people may use the cash surrender value of their paid-up life insurance policy to buy a single premium annuity when they wish to retire. This is generally one of the settlement options of life insurance policies.

The annuitant selects when he or she wants the annuity payments to begin—monthly, quarterly, semiannually, or annually. The dollar amount of the payment an annuitant will receive is determined by several factors: first, the principal sum built up on his or her behalf. This sum is dependent on the total dollars in premiums paid, plus the interest earned over the years. Then an allowance must be made for expenses by the insurance company. Finally, the amount of the annuity is determined by the life expectancy of the annuitant, and the type of annuity selected.

*Annuity benefit payments*

The older the person is when he or she starts receiving payments, the higher the payment for any principal sum. Women, since they live longer than men, on the average, receive a slightly lower payment than men of the same age with the same principal sum, because a woman will generally receive the payment for a longer period of time.

Most annuities are deferred annuities; that is, premiums are paid over the years and benefits are deferred until later in life. But there are also immediate annuities, where one lump-sum premium is paid and benefits begin immediately. Whenever payments begin, there are a number of options from which to choose.

*Annuity settlement options*

An annuitant may select a lump-sum settlement or a number of installments. There are three major installment annuities:

1.  *Straight life.* This annuity provides for a periodic payment until the annuitant dies. This could be for one month or for thirty years or more, depending on how long the individual lives. If the annuitant dies after even only one monthly payment has been made, the insurance company keeps the remainder of the principal sum built up on the annuitant's behalf. There is nothing left for his or her heirs. For this reason such an annuity guarantees the annuitant the largest possible payment. For this same reason this type of annuity is not very popular.

2.  *Life annuity with period certain.* This annuity pays an income to the annuitant for life, with a minimum number of payments guaranteed. If the annuitant dies before the guaranteed number of payments have been made, they continue to be made to the beneficiary until the guaranteed minimum has been made. Quite often a 10- to 20-year (120-240 months) period is selected. The insurance company must make payments until the annuitant dies or until ten (or twenty) years have passed, whichever occurs last.

    An individual of a given age with a given principal sum built up, will receive a smaller yearly payment with this guarantee than without it.

3.  *Guaranteed premium refund annuity.* This annuity is also called the "installment refund annuity." It will pay an income for life with a guarantee that the total amount to be paid will be at least equal to the total premiums paid. If the person dies before collecting all the premiums he or she has paid over the years, the beneficiaries receive the difference. This difference can be taken in installments or in one lump sum.

**The joint and survivorship annuity**

The joint and survivorship annuity guarantees a payment for the entire life of two individuals. Since two individuals are involved, the risk to the insurance company is greater, and hence a given principal sum will provide a smaller benefit payment than will an annuity on one individual. The premiums needed to guarantee a given income are higher on a joint and survivorship annuity than on a single annuity. Often, but not always, the joint annuity is written so that when one member dies the payments, while they continue, decrease in amount. Generally this reduction is to 75 percent, 66.6 percent, or even to 50 percent of what the two individuals were receiving, which lowers the cost somewhat.

Most annuity contracts (as well as life insurance contracts with a cash surrender value) permit the option of converting to a joint annuity at the time payments are to begin.

**The fixed annuity**

Traditionally, annuities were nearly always fixed annuities, contracts in which everything was determined and agreed to in advance. The only thing the insurance company did not know was the dollar amount of interest the annuity would earn over the years on future premiums, but a conservative assumption was made. The premiums were invested in bonds or mortgages that yielded a known return for a known period of time. The insurance company then could calculate accurately how large a principal sum would be generated for any annuitant. When the annuitant retired, the insurance company would be able to guarantee a fixed dollar payment per month or per year for life. Actuaries have constructed tables that deplete the principal sum actuarily but also make an allowance for interest to be earned on the declining principal.

The major problem with fixed annuities is that inflation erodes the principal sum both while it is being built up and also while it is being paid out. Consequently, fixed annuities have become somewhat less popular in recent years and interest has shifted toward the variable annuity.

The variable annuity was developed in an attempt to protect the annuitant against inflation both during the premium-paying years and during retirement. Premiums on variable annuities are invested in common stocks. This is very much like investing in mutual funds which was described in Chapter 17. Some insurance companies manage their own portfolio through a subsidiary broker-dealer and some place it with an established mutual fund. A portfolio may be designed specifically for the life insurance company involved or an existing mutual fund may be used.

*The variable annuity*

The investor will usually have several choices with respect to the type of portfolio into which his or her premiums are to go. For example, a growth fund, an equity income fund, a bond fund, a money market fund, or a somewhat higher risk, capital appreciation equity portfolio may be selected.

Under a variable annuity contract the premiums paid are used to buy a block of stock called an accumulation unit. For example, if premiums are $300 per month, this $300 may buy ten units in one month and fifteen units in another as the price of the unit fluctuates. The principal sum being built up on the annuitant's behalf would accumulate more and more units as time passed. These units, and hence the principal sum, would fluctuate in value. Hopefully, however, each unit would rise in the long run and this, together with the new units being purchased, would provide protection against inflation.

When the person retires, the retirement income is calculated as follows: First, the value of the accumulation units is calculated at their market value to obtain the principal sum. The first annual payment is then calculated in the same way as a fixed annuity would be. If, for example, the principal sum is $200,000, and the actuarial tables indicate that for a person of his or her age a $10,000 annual payment could be made on a fixed annuity of the type chosen, then the first payment from the variable annuity would also be $10,000. The initial payment ($10,000) is then divided by the present market value of one accumulation unit.

This indicates how many accumulation units are currently required to meet the $10,000. Suppose the market value of one accumulation unit is $50; then two hundred units are needed to make the first payment, and future payments will always be equal to the fluctuating value of two hundred units. It is expected that the value of the units will rise in the long run, increasing the $10,000 annual retirement income.

Most variable annuity contracts will give an annuitant the option to convert a variable annuity into a fixed annuity at retirement. In such a case the $10,000 initial payment described above would become fixed and guaranteed. The insurance company would simply convert the $200,000 principal sum in the accumulation units into fixed obligations in order to finance this. In such a case the annuitant would have hedged against inflation during the accumulation period but not after retirement.

*The cost of annuities*

Several factors determine the cost of an annuity:

1. The age of the person receiving the annuity figured at the time the annuity is to begin
2. The age of the person when he or she begins paying premiums
3. The type of annuity selected
4. The monthly annuity payment desired
5. The sex of the annuitant

Since annuities are the opposite of life insurance, the older a person is when payments are to begin, the lower the cost of a given payment. This is obvious, for the older a person is, the fewer the payments will be, on the average.

Insofar as annuity premium payments are concerned, they also vary with the age of the person when he or she buys the annuity, if it is a deferred annuity. A younger person will pay premiums for more years than an older person, and hence the yearly premium will be lower.

The cost also varies with the type of annuity. The straight life annuity, where the payments continue until the death of the annuitant with no guaranteed number of payments, is the least costly.

The larger the monthly payments desired, the higher the cost.

Since women live longer than men, a fixed monthly payment for a woman will generally be made longer than it will for a man of the same age. Or a fixed sum of money will buy a smaller annuity income for a woman.

*The taxation of annuities*

Annuity premiums are after-tax dollars, but the investment incomes they earn are not taxed during the accumulation period. Rather they are deferred until the annuitant starts drawing benefits. Then the principal sum comes out tax free, but the investment income earned is taxed.

Consequently, the two must be separated. There is also the problem of which comes out first. The IRS assumes they come out simultaneously, but since the dollar amounts are not necessarily the same, a calculation must be made, and this calculation also takes into account that the principal sum is earning more interest as it is being depleted. The result is that part of the benefit is taxed and part is not. The total principal sum (premiums paid plus interest and dividends earned) is annuitized to obtain the expected lifetime return. Then the following formula is used to obtain the taxable proportion:

$$\frac{\text{total premium contributions}}{\text{expected lifetime return}}$$

An example will make this clear. Suppose a person pays premiums of $2,000 per year for 20 years. At 8 percent return it would have grown to $98,845.84 in 20 years. This will buy a 65-year-old male a monthly annuity of $912.50; and a smaller amount for a younger person. The IRS has life expectancy tables; but assume for this example that the life expectancy for a 65-year-old male is 20 years. The monthly income annualized, and then annuitized ($912.50 x 12 x 20 = $219,000) is $219,000. That is the expected lifetime return. The formula mentioned above gives us the following result:

$$\frac{\text{premium contributions}}{\text{expected lifetime return}} = \frac{40,000}{219,000} = 18.26 \text{ percent.}$$

Hence 18.26 percent of the $912.50 monthly annuity payment is not taxable; the remainder is. Once the total of the nontaxable portion equals the total premium paid in (in this case $40,000), all future payments from the annuity are totally taxable.

The Internal Revenue Service imposes a penalty tax on early withdrawals (before age 59.5 years of age) from an annuity contract. A 10 percent tax is imposed on premature payments (full or partial surrender, loans or dividend payments), except under the following circumstances: (1) the contract-holder is age 59 and one-half or older; (2) the contract-holder is disabled; (3) the payment is from a qualified retirement plan; (4) the payment is made because of the death of the annuitant; or (5) the payments are made under an immediate annuity over the life of the annuitant. The life insurance company issuing the annuity contract may also impose certain back-end fees, called surrender charges, for contracts surrendered before a certain time period has elapsed, usually five to ten years after initial purchase.

**PRIVATE (AND GOVERNMENT) PENSION PLANS**

Most corporations of any size have developed pension plans for their employees to provide a retirement income when they retire from the labor force, usually at age 65. Such plans are designed to supplement

Social Security retirement benefits. Regular money contributions are paid into the fund and are invested to earn interest. The fund then is available upon retirement. In some cases, deductions are withheld from the employee's wages, matched by the employer, and paid into the fund. In other cases, the employer makes the entire contribution.

How good a plan an individual has is determined by the retirement benefits it promises, its vesting provisions, and the extent to which it is funded. One should investigate his or her plan to determine these things. How much the plan promises in the way of retirement benefits may be obvious, but an employee should also consider what happens to the funds built up in his or her behalf if he or she terminates employment prior to retirement, and how sound the plan is—that is, how likely it will be able to deliver what it promises.

*Vesting and portability*

Vesting concerns what happens to the funds built up on behalf of the employee if employment should terminate prior to retirement. If an employee is vested, employees may take the funds with them; if he or she is not vested, the funds will be lost. A few plans provide immediate and full vesting, but most plans provide for partial delayed vesting; that is, a portion of the funds are vested every so many years until eventually full vesting is achieved.

Since there is bound to be some turnover, lack of immediate vesting permits higher benefits to those who do retire, with a given cost, or reduces the cost of a pension plan with a given retirement program. Some employers also feel that delayed vesting reduces labor turnover. It is debatable whether this in itself is desirable, because it reduces the mobility of labor; mobility of both labor and resources is required, many argue, to keep our economy dynamic. In any event, those workers who leave the firm before vesting occurs subsidize those who stay and finally retire. Federal regulations that now require certain vesting provisions as well as other matters are spelled out below.

Some vested plans are also portable; if so, the funds are combined with the funds of any new employer's plan. If they are vested but not portable, the employee usually gets his or her funds in one lump sum when he or she moves. In such a case, he or she can roll them over into an IRA (see below). If this applies to your client, he or she should consider such a rollover; otherwise there can be complex tax problems.

*Funding*

Funding is another technical term with which a person should be familiar. A pension plan can be 100 percent funded, partially funded, or zero percent funded. If a plan is not at all funded (zero percent), it is referred to as a pay-as-you-go plan. In such a case, an employer takes whatever money is needed out of operating revenue and pays retired employees a pension; the employee contributes nothing. This, of course, reduces profits. A pay-as-you-go plan is considered actuarially unsound and there are very few of them.

At the other extreme are the fully funded plans (100 percent funded). A fully funded pension plan is one where assets are accumulated each year in an amount equal to the future pension benefits earned that year.[3] Actuarially the future cost of a pension plan can be predicted with a high degree of accuracy. If the pension plan is then designed so that the annual buildup of future benefits (discounted to present value) is always equal to the annual buildup of assets, there is 100 percent funding. In such a case, every employee could be paid his or her pension at any and all times. One hundred percent funding can be achieved by keeping the benefits lower than in a partially funded plan, or the contributions (cost of the pension fund) higher. Most pension plans provide for substantial tax benefits (see below). To receive these tax benefits they must be approved (qualified) by the I.R.S., and to be approved they must meet certain minimum funding requirements. See below for a further discussion of this.

Funding and vesting are somewhat related. If a plan has delayed vesting, then many of the contributions made for personnel who leave the company will be left in the fund. They can be used to pay benefits to employees who actually do retire.

Prior to the passage of the Employee Retirement Income Security Act (ERISA) of 1974, there were very few federal controls over private pension funds and only loose, haphazard regulations at the state level. The act was passed in response to complaints that many workers were not obtaining their benefits upon retirement. Generally this was because either their pension funds were not adequately funded and moneys for retirement payments were not available or the plan did not provide vesting when the employee left prior to retirement.

*Employee Retirement Income Security Act (ERISA)*

The federal act's main purpose was to establish minimum requirements regarding vesting and funding, but it contained some other provisions as well. For example, the act provides that each fund make an annual report to the Secretary of Labor and provide all employees covered with full information regarding their benefits, including access to financial records.

The act also established the Pension Benefit Guarantee Corporation

---

3. More precisely, 100 percent funding may be defined as existing when the present value of all current assets is equal to (1) the present value of all current liabilities (benefits) together with (2) the present value of all future expected liabilities (benefits). The actuaries take into account only current assets (and not expected future assets); in the case of liabilities, however, both current and expected future liabilities (benefits) are taken into account.

(PBGC). This is a government corporation and operates much like the FDIC. It guarantees pension rights, and if a pension fund collapses and cannot pay pension benefits the PBGC could pay eligible retirees up to $2,352.27 per month (1992). The PBGC is financed with premiums collected from the employer amounting to $19.00 per worker per year, with additional premiums due for underfunded plans. The penalty premiums for underfunded plans amounted to $9.00 per year for every $1,000 by which a plan is underfunded.

The act established minimum vesting procedures which were altered later with The Tax Reform Act of 1986. Now employers may choose one of two alternative methods of allowing workers to obtain vesting. First, they may decide to grant full vesting after five years and provide nothing until then. Second, the employer may grant 20 percent vesting after three years, 40 percent after four years, 60 percent after five years, 80 percent after six years, and full (100 percent) after seven years.

*Pension plans and benefits*

When a person retires he or she will receive pension benefit payments in accordance with the provisions of the plan. These vary. In some cases, the fund will simply buy the retiree an annuity from a life insurance company. In such a case, he or she will have to consider all the types of annuities discussed above.

Some pension funds will allow a person to withdraw benefits upon retirement in one lump sum rather than in installments. Others do not give this option. If a retiree withdraws in one lump sum there could be a complex tax problem. The same is true if he or she withdraws this entire sum over, say, ten years, rather than over a longer period.

Some pension plans provide that the contributions made on the employee's behalf are invested on his or her behalf, and then when one retires, the money built up is his or hers. If a fixed percentage of compensation is contributed by the employer each year, this is called a **money purchase plan**. If the employer can vary the **annual** contribution (and even not contribute in a given year), then the plan is known as **a profit sharing plan**. Both of these plans are known as **defined contribution plans**. The amount of benefit is determined by how much was paid in and how successful the fund managers are in investing the funds. Nothing is guaranteed while the fund is being built up. At retirement, one can usually take the benefits in one lump sum or in installments. A money purchase plan is subject to minimum funding requirements.

There are other so-called **fixed benefit plans** (sometimes called **defined benefit plans**). Under these plans, the funds contributed on one's behalf are commingled with those of fellow employees. While each employee has a claim, there are no specific dollars designated to each person. Instead of an individual fund for each employee, there is a collectively owned group fund.

At retirement, the benefits are calculated by a formula that usually takes into account the salary range over the last five or so years, and the length of time with the company. For example, a retiree might receive 1 percent of his or her average salary over the last five years for every year with the company. If the average salary over the last five years was $50,000 and one was with the company thirty years, the pension would be $15,000 per year.

Under these plans the benefits then are not as directly tied to the contributions as is the case in the money purchase or profit sharing plans. Under this plan, the group fund could be used to provide a monthly payment or the fund could buy an annuity with a life insurance company; the practice varies.

While most defined benefit plans are not fully (100 percent) funded, they must meet the IRS minimum funding requirements. The law requires some funding, enough to make it actuarially sound. Also only the defined benefit plan must pay premiums to the Pension Benefit Guarantee Corporation discussed above.

ERISA defines the minimum and maximum contributions and/or benefits to which qualified plans must adhere. If these limits are not met each year, the employer could lose the tax deduction for the plan contributions or possibly have tax penalties assessed.

*Tax benefits of most private pension plans: the qualified plans*

Most plans are qualified and therefore they receive certain tax benefits. For a plan to be qualified it must be in compliance with federal law and the rules and regulations of ERISA and subsequent tax law. For example, the plan must not be discriminatory (all employees must be treated equally), and it must be in compliance with vesting and funding requirements as determined by ERISA. Most pension plans are funded with dollars that are not taxed, and hence substantial benefits are obtained. Most plans are what is called qualified, that is, they must be approved by the Internal Revenue Service. If the plan is nondiscriminatory in that all employees participate in it on the same basis and it is in compliance with the Employee Retirement Income Security Act discussed above, it will be approved.

Employer funds going into an approved (qualified) plan are tax sheltered; that is, an income tax is not paid on them by the employee. In addition, the interest and dividends that they earn are not taxable, nor is any capital gain that may accrue. In reality they are merely tax deferred. They are taxed as income upon retirement as an individual withdraws funds. It should also be noted that any contributions made by employers are fully deductible for them on their tax return during the year in which they are made.

*Employee after-tax contributions*

There are some pension plans (known as thrift plans) into which the employee pays after-tax dollars that are then matched by the employer. The employer's contributions are not taxed to the employee until received at retirement, and neither are the fund's earnings. But since the employee's contributions were taxed before they went in, there is a special problem. When the retiree receives the benefits, his or her contributions are not taxed but the employer's contribution and the investment income it has earned are. Each benefit payment received then is partly tax free and partly taxed from the beginning. The calculation to determine what proportion is taxed is made just as in the case of an annuity discussed above.

The total principal sum is annuitized to obtain the expected lifetime income payments just as in the case of an annuity as explained above in the section entitled "The Taxation of Annuities." Then the same formula is applied:

$$\frac{\text{employee's total contribution}}{\text{expected lifetime return}}$$

For example,

$$\frac{100,000}{500,000} = 20 \text{ percent.}$$

Therefore, 20 percent of each retirement check received is tax free and 80 percent is taxed. However, after the retiree in this example has received $100,000 tax free, the entire amount of the additional payments is taxed.

## OTHER RETIREMENT PLANS

*Two special corporate pension plans: the simplified employee pension plan (SEP), and the 401(K) plan*

There are two special corporate pension plans. They are the Simplified Employee Pension Plan and the 401K Salary Reduction Plan.

Corporations, partnerships, and sole proprietorships may establish a Simplified Employee Pension plan (SEP) for their employees. There is less red tape involved in establishing an SEP; therefore they appeal to smaller businesses. The employer must sponsor the plan but need not be involved in most of the administration; the employee may choose the custodian. Moreover, the employee may utilize a custodial IRA in which the employee directs the IRA custodian concerning the investment decisions. The employer can be the only contributor to the SEP or it can be set up as a salary reduction arrangement with only the employee or a combination of the employee and employer contributing. If the employer contributes to the SEP, 25 percent up to a maximum of $30,000 per year may be contributed to the SEP or, if both an SEP and another defined contribution plan are funded, to both plans combined. (If the employer funds both an SEP and a defined-benefit plan, combined contribution limits also apply; these are beyond the scope of this textbook.) If the SEP is offered on a cash or deferred arrangement basis, the employee's annual contribution may be no greater than $7,000 indexed for inflation. (In 1992, the maximum amount is $8,728.) The earnings and capital gains that accrue are also tax free until the person retires and begins drawing benefits. The funds cannot be withdrawn until the year in which the individual becomes 59-1/2 years of age, and the person must start withdrawing funds when he or she reaches age 70-1/2. There is normally a special 10 percent penalty tax (which is over and above the regular income tax) for early withdrawal of funds. SEP contributions are fully and immediately vested.

These plans are defined in the section of the Internal Revenue Code known as 401(k) that permits tax-deferred salary reductions. Under this plan, a plan participant may reduce his or her salary up to an annual maximum of 25 percent or $7,000 (indexed annually for inflation) whichever is less, annually and set the reduction aside for retirement purposes. (In 1992, the indexed amount is $8,728.) Neither the contribution to the plan nor the investment income or capital gain on it is taxed until it is withdrawn upon retirement; that is, taxes are deferred.

*Deferred compensation plans; 401(K)s*

As with an SEP, a person may not set up this type of a plan on his or her own. An employer must establish and sponsor a plan; employees may then tie into it. New plans may be set up or existing corporate profit-sharing plans may be amended to include 401(k) provisions. This type of plan is very complex and certain other limitations apply; but if your client's employer has one, your client should investigate it.

Employee contributions are fully and immediately vested. The penalty for early withdrawals applies to this type of plan. It should be noted that the $8,728 (as indexed) annual tax-deferred limit applies only to the employee's contribution. The employer may add more, both in the case of an SEP and a 401(k).

All government-sponsored (administered) pension plans are exempt from the 1974 Federal Employee Retirement Income Security Act. This includes all local government plans as well as state plans. There are hundreds of government pension plans, some of which are very good and some of which are rather poor. Consequently, only certain generalizations can be made. Even though government plans are exempt from the 1974 act, they can be approved by the IRS, and if they are, the tax benefits discussed above apply.

*Government pension plans*

Some government plans are managed by life insurance companies. Those are actuarially and financially very sound. Other government funds are managed by trust departments of commercial banks and are generally fairly high quality plans.

Still other government plans are managed by the governing unit itself or an agency established by the government for that purpose. In such a case, funding varies from plan to plan; it ranges from fairly high to virtually zero. Vesting provisions vary from relatively early and complete vesting to no vesting whatsoever until the employee retires. If a client is a government employee and has a pension plan, it is suggested that the plan be investigated very closely to determine just what benefits are provided.

*The individual retirement account (IRA)*

In addition to the retirement plans discussed above, there are individual retirement accounts. The 1986 change in the tax law eliminated the deductible IRA for some people. However, many are still eligible. If a person is eligible and establishes an IRA, up to $2,000 per year of earned income may be placed into it on a tax-deferred basis. That is, the $2,000 contribution is not taxed, nor are the earnings or capital gains on it until withdrawn at retirement. The contribution must be based on earned income (wages and salary); interest, dividends, rent, or other property income do not count.

An individual is eligible for a full IRA deduction if he or she is:

**(1)** employed but the employer does not have a pension plan.
**(2)** self-employed, and does not have a Keogh Plan (see the discussion of the Keogh plan below).
**(3)** employed and has a pension plan at work, but his or her adjusted gross income (AGI) is less than $40,000 if married, and $25,000 if single. The $40,000 ($25,000) AGI test must be met before the IRA deduction.[4]
**(4)** self-employed and has a Keogh plan but the adjusted gross income is less than $40,000 if married and $25,000 if single.

A married individual is eligible for a reduced IRA deduction if he or she is employed, has a retirement plan at work and has an AGI of $40,000 or more (but not above $50,000). In such a case, the individual must reduce his or her deduction by 20 percent for every dollar of AGI above $40,000. For example, if AGI is $41,000, the deductible contribution may be $1,800. If AGI is $45,000, the maximum deductible contribution is $1,000. At $50,000, the deduction is completely phased out. For single taxpayers the above limits become $25,000 and $35,000, respectively.

If both spouses have earned income and are eligible as described above, each may establish a separate IRA, and hence $4,000 per year may go tax deferred into a retirement account.

There is also a spousal IRA. It is applicable to a married couple of

---

4. In calculating AGI an individual must also take into account interest and dividend Income. That is, while dividend and interest income cannot be used to determine contributions to an IRA, it does count in determining eligibility.

which only one has earned income—wages and salary—and if they qualify for an IRA as described above. Then an extra $250 per year may be set aside on behalf of the non-income-earning member. The spousal IRA must also be set up as two separate accounts; they may not be commingled. Spousal accounts need not be split into $2,000 and $250, however. Varying amounts of dollars may go into them; the only rule is that the nonworking person's account must receive at least $250. But they could be split into $1,125 each.

If an individual is self-employed and the spouse has no earned income, he or she might want to consider employing the nonworking spouse at least until $2,000 is earned, so that each may establish a $2,000 IRA. In addition, the wages paid to the spouse may be deducted as a business expense. If this is done, however, be sure the spouse does bona fide work, contributes to the business, and is paid at reasonable rates.

An IRA may then accumulate earnings and capital gains tax deferred. Regular income taxes will be due upon retirement when the money is drawn out. The individual may not touch the funds in the account until age 59-1/2 without a penalty, and withdrawals must begin at age 70-1/2. The penalty for early withdrawals is also the same (10 percent extra tax). When funds are withdrawn, he or she may take them all in one lump-sum payment, convert them to an annuity, or choose an income stream spread over the number of years equal to the life expectancy. (If married, an individual may even spread them over the joint life expectancy of both. See the section "When Funds Are Withdrawn" below for a more detailed discussion of this.)

It should be noted that if a person has both a corporate pension plan and an IRA, and if he or she retires and takes the corporate pension

The following table will work for most people in permitting them to calculate their deductible and nondeductible IRA.

| Single income | Married filing jointly | Allowable deductible contribution | Allowable nondeductible contribution |
|---|---|---|---|
| $25,000 | $40,000 | $2,000 | $ 0 |
| 26,000 | 41,000 | 1,800 | 200 |
| 27,000 | 42,000 | 1,600 | 400 |
| 28,000 | 43,000 | 1,400 | 600 |
| 29,000 | 44,000 | 1,200 | 800 |
| 30,000 | 45,000 | 1,000 | 1,000 |
| 31,000 | 46,000 | 800 | 1,200 |
| 32,000 | 47,000 | 600 | 1,400 |
| 33,000 | 48,000 | 400 | 1,600 |
| 34,000 | 49,000 | 200 | 1,800 |
| 35,000 | 50,000 | 0 | 2,000 |

**Box 18—1
The partially deductible IRA and the nondeductible IRA at a glance**

in one lump sum but is not yet 70-1/2 years of age, he or she may roll the pension payment over into an IRA tax free and let it accumulate tax deferred until age 70-1/2. This should be studied very carefully, however, because if pension funds are withdrawn in one lump sum, they can, under certain circumstances, be subject to special five-year forward averaging tax provisions. On the other hand, if a retiree rolls the funds over into an IRA, he or she can postpone taxes until age 70-1/2 when they are withdrawn, but the privilege of using the five-year forward averaging for one lump-sum withdrawal will be lost.

*The nondeductible IRA*

If one (or both) spouse does not qualify for a deductible IRA, he or she may still establish nondeductible IRAs. That is, the $2,000 annual contribution is made with after-tax dollars, but it can accumulate interest, dividends, and capital gains that are tax deferred until withdrawn at retirement. Accumulating tax-deferred earnings is still very advantageous. Tables 18-2 and 18-3 and Figures 18-3 and 18-4 show the buildup of a deductible IRA, a nondeductible IRA, and a regular savings account at various interest rates and tax brackets.

*Keogh plans*

If an individual is self-employed, he or she may establish his or her own retirement fund. These are called Keogh plans, and the only requirement for establishing one is to be self-employed. This includes people who work for a corporation and have a corporate pension plan, but they are self-employed on the side (moonlighting), if they otherwise qualify.

The ERISA requirements for corporate plans apply equally to Keogh plans. The types of retirement plans are also the same—profit-sharing, money purchase, or defined benefit plans. An unincorporated business must also include all employees who meet the minimum eligibility requirements. Benefits for these employees—known as common law employees—must also be comparable to the benefits provided for the owner(s).

*The S corporation*

In recent years many self-employed, especially service professionals—such as doctors and lawyers—have chosen the corporation rather than remaining unincorporated. If a doctor (or a group of them) incorporates, his or her fees flow into the corporation, which now pays him or her a salary. The corporation may now establish a pension fund for him or her.

A businessperson may incorporate as a traditional corporation or he or she may incorporate as what is known as an "S" corporation, which is what many professionals have done. In an S corporation all corporate income or losses are taxed as personal income or losses even if not passed through.

Table 18–2 Buildup of an individual retirement account—$2,000 deposited at beginning of each year—28 percent tax bracket

| | Interest at 6% | | | Interest at 8% | | | Interest at 10% | | | Interest at 12% | | |
| | With IRA | | Without IRA | With IRA | | Without IRA | With IRA | | Without IRA | With IRA | | Without IRA |
| End of Year | Deductible | Nondeductible | IRA | Deductible | Nondeductible | IRA | Deductible | Nondeductible | IRA | Deductible | Nondeductible | IRA |
| | 1 | 2 | 3 | 1 | 2 | 3 | 1 | 2 | 3 | 1 | 2 | 3 |
|---|---|---|---|---|---|---|---|---|---|---|---|---|
| 5 | 11,951 | 8,604 | 8,189 | 12,672 | 9,124 | 8,544 | 13,431 | 9,670 | 8,913 | 14,230 | 10,246 | 9,296 |
| 10 | 27,943 | 20,119 | 18,306 | 31,291 | 22,530 | 19,849 | 35,062 | 25,245 | 21,531 | 39,309 | 28,303 | 23,364 |
| 15 | 49,345 | 35,528 | 30,805 | 58,649 | 42,227 | 34,807 | 69,899 | 50,328 | 39,394 | 83,507 | 60,125 | 44,654 |
| 20 | 77,985 | 56,150 | 46,248 | 98,845 | 71,169 | 54,598 | 125,005 | 90,724 | 64,684 | 161,397 | 116,206 | 76,874 |
| 25 | 116,313 | 83,745 | 65,327 | 157,709 | 113,694 | 80,785 | 216,364 | 135,782 | 100,485 | 298,668 | 215,041 | 125,625 |
| 30 | 167,603 | 120,674 | 88,899 | 244,692 | 176,178 | 115,435 | 361,887 | 260,559 | 151,171 | 540,585 | 389,221 | 199,429 |
| 35 | 236,242 | 170,094 | 118,023 | 372,204 | 267,787 | 161,281 | 596,254 | 429,303 | 222,927 | 966,926 | 696,187 | 311,109 |
| 40 | 328,095 | 236,229 | 154,004 | 559,562 | 402,885 | 221,941 | 973,704 | 701,067 | 324,512 | 1,718,285 | 1,237,165 | 480,122 |

Note:

Column 1 ASSUMES $2,000 ANNUAL INVESTMENT COMPOUNDED at 6%, 8%, 10% AND 12%.

Column 2 ASSUMES $1,440 ($2,000 LESS 28% TAX) ANNUAL INVESTMENT COMPOUNDED AT 6%, 8%, 10% AND 12%).

Column 3 ASSUMES $1,440 ($2,000 LESS 28% TAX) ANNUAL INVESTMENT COMPOUNDED AT 4.32% (6% LESS 28% TAX); 5.76% (8% LESS 28% TAX); 7.2% (10% LESS 28% TAX) AND 8.64% (12% LESS 28% TAX)

Value calculated as of the end of the year.

Table 18–3   Buildup of an individual retirement account—$2,000 deposited at beginning of each year—15 percent tax bracket

| End of year | Interest at 6.00 percent | | | Interest at 8.00 percent | | | Interest at 10.00 percent | | | Interest at 12.00 percent | | |
|---|---|---|---|---|---|---|---|---|---|---|---|---|
| | With IRA | | Without IRA | With IRA | | Without IRA | With IRA | | Without IRA | With IRA | | Without IRA |
| | Deductible | Nondeductible | IRA | Deductible | Nondeductible | IRA | Deductible | Nondeductible | IRA | Deductible | Nondeductible | IRA |
| | 1 | 2 | 3 | 1 | 2 | 3 | 1 | 2 | 3 | 1 | 2 | 3 |
| 5 | 11,951 | 10,158 | 9,892 | 12,672 | 10,771 | 10,399 | 13,431 | 11,417 | 10,929 | 14,230 | 12,096 | 11,483 |
| 10 | 27,943 | 23,752 | 22,578 | 31,291 | 26,597 | 24,849 | 35,062 | 29,803 | 27,363 | 39,309 | 33,413 | 30,145 |
| 15 | 49,345 | 41,943 | 38,846 | 58,649 | 49,851 | 44,928 | 69,899 | 59,415 | 52,074 | 83,507 | 70,981 | 60,475 |
| 20 | 77,985 | 66,288 | 59,707 | 98,846 | 84,019 | 72,826 | 126,005 | 107,104 | 89,251 | 161,397 | 137,188 | 109,767 |
| 25 | 116,313 | 98,866 | 86,459 | 157,909 | 134,223 | 111,591 | 216,364 | 183,909 | 145,103 | 298,668 | 253,868 | 189,876 |
| 30 | 167,603 | 142,463 | 120,765 | 244,692 | 207,988 | 165,454 | 361,887 | 307,604 | 229,114 | 540,585 | 459,497 | 320,071 |
| 35 | 236,242 | 200,805 | 164,758 | 372,204 | 316,374 | 240,296 | 596,254 | 506,816 | 355,438 | 966,926 | 821,887 | 531,663 |
| 40 | 328,095 | 278,881 | 221,173 | 559,562 | 475,628 | 344,289 | 973,704 | 827,648 | 545,386 | 1,718,285 | 1,460,542 | 875,544 |

Value calculated as of the end of the year.

Column 1: $2,000 invested and compounded at 6, 8, 10, and 12 percent.

Column 2: $1,700 invested and compounded at 6, 8, 10, and 12 percent.

Column 3: $1,700 invested and compounded at 5.10, 6.80, 8.50, and 10.20 percent.

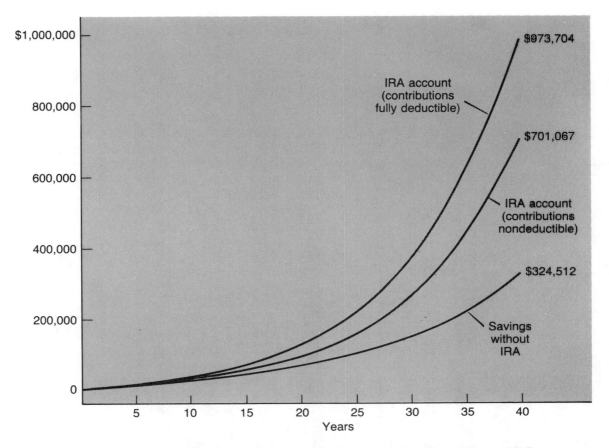

*Growth of IRA account ($2,000 per year) compared to unsheltered savings, 10 percent    Figure 18–3*
*compounded annually, 28 percent tax bracket.*

If one incorporates as an S corporation, the funds which may be set aside tax-deferred are identical to those permitted under a corporate plan. An S corporation pension plan may be set up as a profit-sharing, money purchase, or defined-benefit plan.

If a client is self-employed and establishes a Keogh account or an S corporation pension plan, the plan must be nondiscriminatory. That is, it must provide for all employees as soon as they qualify on the same basis as the client. "As soon as they qualify" are the crucial words, because the law permits the employer to require that they be employed for two years before they become eligible to participate. Once they are eligible, however, the employer must make the contribution on their behalf, and it must be the same percentage of their salary as is the contribution for the employer.

*What about employees?*

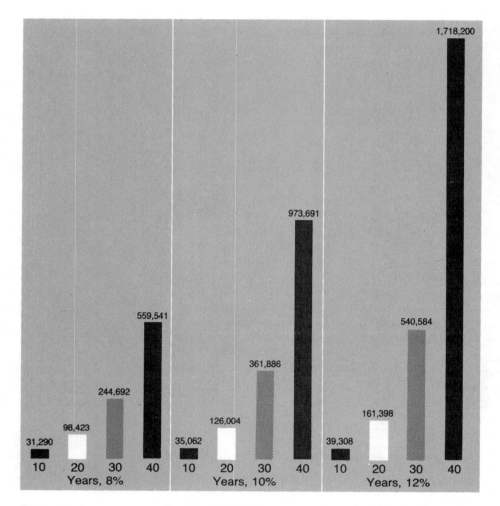

Figure 18–4                    *Growth of $2,000 per year in an individual retirement account for 10, 20, 30, and 40 years at 8, 10, and 12 percent (compounded annually)*

*Tax-sheltered annuities (TSA)—403(b) plans*

Certain people are permitted under Section 403(b) of the Internal Revenue Code to purchase tax-sheltered annuities. These are also sometimes referred to as tax-deferred annuities (TDA) and supplemental retirement annuities (SRA). People who work for tax-exempt organizations, including schools and colleges, are eligible; people who work for profit-making corporations are not. Congress authorized these tax-sheltered annuities some years ago because tax-exempt institutions have less of an incentive to establish a pension plan for their employees, since there are no tax benefits available to institutions that are already exempt. Even if these institutions have since established pension plans for their employees (and most have), their employees may still purchase tax-

When a nondeductible IRA is withdrawn, only the income and capital gains (not the contributions) it has earned are taxable. Hence, good records are needed to separate these two items. It is advised that the nondeductible IRA be kept in a separate account to simplify this task. The retiree must prove to the satisfaction of the IRS what the total nondeductible contributions have been.

There is a new form that must be attached to the 1040. It is Form 8606 which shows the annual nondeductible contribution. When funds are withdrawn, the IRS may require the proof. Hence, all past 8606 forms must be kept. Mandatory lifetime record keeping may be upon us. However, some experts believe the IRS will eventually allow a separation of contributions and earnings to be made upon the first year of retirement, and ease the record keeping burden a bit after that. Nevertheless, this does add to the paperwork burden.

**Box 18—2 Keeping tabs on a nondeductible IRA**

sheltered annuities because the pensions that tax-exempt institutions provide are less generous than those of profit-making corporations.

The 1986 tax changes added a cap on the total dollars that may go into a 403(b) plan. It is a percentage of salary up to a maximum of $9,500 per year. This figure will be indexed in the future when the SEP and 401(k) limit reaches $9,500; then all three will continue to track inflation. If the person has sheltered less than that maximum in previous years, part of it may be recaptured. For example, if clients cannot afford to shelter all of the income the law allows during their thirties and forties, they may wish to recapture all or part of that during their fifties when their income does permit. There is also a recapture cap, and it is $3,000 per year, making the total sum that may be put into a 403(b) $12,500 per year.[5]

There is a very complex formula which must be worked through to determine eligibility for the catch up. The formula takes into account past salary, past contributions, and length of time with the employer.

If such an annuity is purchased, neither the premium paid nor the annuity's earnings are taxed until the person retires and receives the benefits. As in the case of other plans discussed above, there is a 10 percent penalty for early withdrawal of funds prior to age 59-1/2. The penalty is waived in some circumstances.

*Deferred compensation plans—457 plans*

Deferred compensation plans are similar to tax-sheltered annuities, but there is a technical difference. Many college and universities, municipal and state governments and other nontaxable entities have set up these plans in addition to tax-sheltered annuities. But one or the other must be chosen; a person may not have both.

Under these plans, a person may defer annually up to 25 percent of his or her salary or $7,500, whichever is less. If an individual has

---

5. The recapture is permitted only if the person has been with the present employer continuously for 15 years or more.

another tax-sheltered plan with his or her employer, both the individual's and the employer's contribution to it are counted within the 25 percent. Any Keogh contribution is not. This deferred income and the earnings or capital gains on it are not taxed until received. Just as in the case of a TSA, if a person has not deferred all income permitted in past years, he or she may now go back and pick it up, if eligible.

The employer withholds this deferred income and invests it on the employee's behalf. Currently these funds may be invested in life insurance policies, annuities, mutual funds, or savings institutions. The contribution which may be made to a 457 plan is fixed and is not indexed to offset inflation, nor according to present law will it be (unlike the 403(b) plans) when the SEP and the 401(k) reach $9,500, as noted above.

## WHEN FUNDS ARE WITHDRAWN

When an individual decides to retire, there are several options available. A corporate or Keogh plan document will define what "normal retirement age" is, usually as age 65 and/or a certain number of years with the company. The plans may also define policies on early retirement, for instance, age 55 and 15 years of service, and on retirement after normal retirement age, for instance, retirement after age 65. Keep in mind, however, that withdrawing these funds before age 59-1/2 will result in a 10 percent penalty tax in many cases.

Keep in mind too that there is now a penalty for excessive withdrawals even after becoming eligible for withdrawals at age 59-1/2. It comes about in the form of an additional 15 percent excise tax on all annual withdrawals in excess of a certain amount, which is indexed for inflation. In addition, this 15 percent tax applies to lump sum withdrawals exceeding a certain amount.

Finally, there is a floor specifying the minimum withdrawal that must be made annually after April 1 of the year following attainment of age 70-1/2. There is a 50 percent penalty tax on the deficiency between actual withdrawals and the required floor.

The method of distribution of the retirement benefits will also be defined by the plan document. Sometimes a lump-sum payment is permitted; or, the company will distribute monthly or annual payments based on the retirement formula; or, the company will purchase an annuity on behalf of the retiree.

Under no circumstances can the commencement of retirement benefits from any source (corporate, IRA, TSA, etc.) be delayed later than age 70-1/2 or else the retiree faces a severe penalty (see above). The rule is that the person must begin withdrawing funds by April 1 of the year following the year in which he or she reaches age 70-1/2. If the person's birthday falls in the last half of any year (say, 1992) he or she does not reach age 70-1/2 until 1993. Hence, one can postpone distributions until April of the year after that—in the above case, 1994, even though he or she reached age 70-1/2 on January 1, 1993. This same rule

Table 18—4     *Table of joint life expectancy*

| Beneficiary's age in year the retiree became 70½ | Years of withdrawals |
| --- | --- |
| 53 | 31.5 |
| 54 | 30.7 |
| 55 | 29.9 |
| 56 | 29.1 |
| 57 | 28.3 |
| 58 | 27.6 |
| 59 | 26.8 |
| 60 | 26.2 |
| 61 | 25.5 |
| 62 | 24.9 |
| 63 | 24.2 |
| 64 | 23.6 |
| 65 | 23.1 |
| 66 | 22.6 |
| 67 | 22.0 |
| 68 | 21.5 |
| → 69 ← | → 21.0 ← |
| 70 | 20.5 |
| 71 | 20.1 |
| 72 | 19.8 |
| 73 | 19.4 |
| 74 | 19.1 |
| 75 | 18.7 |
| 76 | 18.5 |
| 77 | 18.2 |
| 78 | 17.9 |
| 79 | 17.7 |
| 80 | 17.6 |
| 81 | 17.4 |
| 82 | 17.2 |

It is important to assure that these minimum distribution requirements are met because insufficient distributions after age 70½ may result in a 50% federal tax penalty on the amount by which the distribution fell short of the required minimum.

*Source:* Internal Revenue Service

If a person withdraws a retirement account in one lump sum, invests it in a withdrawable interest-earning account, and withdraws sums periodically for retirement benefits, the question arises: how long will the money last? It depends on

**Box 18—3**
**How long will money last**

1. the payout rate and
2. the earnings.

The following table illustrates this. For example, if the payout rate is 14 percent and the earnings are 9 percent, the funds will last 11.5 years.

| Payout rate (Percent) | 1 | 2 | 3 | 4 | 5 | 6 | 7 | 8 | 9 | 10 | 11 | 12 | 13 | 14 | 15 |
|---|---|---|---|---|---|---|---|---|---|---|---|---|---|---|---|
| 1 | | | | | | | | | | | | | | | |
| 2 | 69.4 | | | | | | | | | | | | | | |
| 3 | 40.6 | 55.0 | | | | | | | | | | | | | |
| 4 | 28.8 | 34.7 | 46.3 | | | | | | | | | | | | |
| 5 | 22.3 | 25.6 | 30.6 | 40.3 | | | | | | | | | | | |
| 6 | 18.2 | 20.3 | 23.2 | 27.6 | 35.9 | | | | | | | | | | |
| 7 | 15.5 | 16.9 | 18.7 | 21.2 | 25.2 | 32.6 | | | | | | | | | |
| 8 | 13.4 | 14.4 | 15.7 | 17.4 | 19.7 | 23.2 | 29.8 | | | | | | | | |
| 9 | 11.8 | 12.6 | 13.6 | 14.7 | 16.3 | 18.4 | 21.6 | 27.6 | | | | | | | |
| 10 | 10.6 | 11.2 | 11.9 | 12.8 | 13.9 | 15.3 | 17.2 | 20.2 | 25.7 | | | | | | |
| 11 | 9.6 | 10.1 | 10.7 | 11.3 | 12.2 | 13.2 | 14.5 | 16.3 | 19.1 | 24.1 | | | | | |
| 12 | 8.7 | 9.2 | 9.7 | 10.2 | 10.8 | 11.6 | 12.6 | 13.8 | 15.5 | 18.0 | 22.7 | | | | |
| 13 | 8.1 | 8.4 | 8.8 | 9.2 | 9.7 | 10.4 | 11.1 | 12.0 | 13.2 | 14.7 | 17.2 | 21.5 | | | |
| 14 | 7.4 | 7.8 | 8.1 | 8.5 | 8.9 | 9.4 | 10.0 | 10.7 | (11.5) | 12.6 | 14.1 | 16.3 | 20.4 | | |
| 15 | 6.9 | 7.2 | 7.5 | 7.8 | 8.2 | 8.6 | 9.1 | 9.6 | 10.2 | 11.1 | 12.1 | 13.5 | 15.6 | 19.5 | |
| 16 | 6.5 | 6.7 | 7.0 | 7.2 | 7.6 | 7.9 | 8.2 | 8.7 | 9.2 | 9.9 | 10.7 | 11.7 | 13.2 | 15.0 | 18.7 |
| 17 | 6.1 | 6.3 | 6.5 | 6.8 | 7.0 | 7.3 | 7.7 | 8.0 | 8.4 | 8.9 | 9.6 | 10.2 | 11.2 | 12.5 | 14.4 |
| 18 | 5.7 | 5.9 | 6.2 | 6.3 | 6.6 | 6.8 | 7.1 | 7.4 | 7.7 | 8.2 | 8.7 | 9.2 | 9.9 | 10.8 | 12.1 |
| 19 | 5.4 | 5.6 | 5.7 | 6.0 | 6.2 | 6.4 | 6.7 | 6.9 | 7.2 | 7.6 | 7.9 | 8.4 | 8.9 | 9.7 | 10.5 |
| 20 | 5.2 | 5.3 | 5.5 | 5.7 | 5.8 | 6.0 | 6.2 | 6.4 | 6.7 | 7.0 | 7.3 | 7.7 | 8.2 | 8.7 | 9.3 |

*If earnings rate is equal to or greater than payout rate money can last indefinitely*

**Percent earnings on investment**

on age 70-1/2 applies to retirement distributions from IRAs, SEPs or TSAs. "Normal retirement age" for these plans is defined as any age after 59-1/2.

When receiving retirement benefits, the retiree may elect a lump-sum withdrawal which may be eligible for five-year forward averaging, a favorable one-time tax benefit. The retiree may not use this special tax on funds distributed from an IRA. There is a formula which permits the taxpayer to compute the special tax and hence the tax is paid all at once during the year of the distribution. However, if a retiree was age 50 or older on January 1, 1986, the tax law permits him or her to choose ten-year forward averaging as defined under the pre-1986 Internal Revenue Code.

If the retiree receives an annuity, income tax is paid on payments as received. We described that process earlier in the chapter. If the retiree receives a life expectancy distribution the IRS has special life expectancy tables which define the minimum annual payment based on age and sex. If this method is used, each year's payment is recalculated based on the fund balance and the new year's life expectancy. For example, at age 65, John Smith's life expectancy is 17 years. He must receive 1/17 of his retirement fund as a minimum payment during this first year. The second year, John's life expectancy is 16.5 years; his minimum annual distribution must be 1/16.5 of the remaining fund balance. Until age 70-1/2, a retiree may stop withdrawals if he or she wishes; after age 70.5, this may not be done.

If the retiree withdraws funds over the life expectancy years and he or she has a spouse, the funds may be withdrawn over the joint life expectancy.[6] This will increase the number of pull-out years, and will postpone and almost certainly reduce taxes. As a retiree pulls funds out over a single life or joint life expectancy, the balance remaining will continue to grow, tax deferred. The IRS has joint life expectancy tables that must be used. Table 18-4 is one such joint life expectancy table. It shows that a person, age 70-1/2, and his or her spouse, age 69, have a joint life expectancy of 21 years, and hence 1/21 of the sum in the retirement fund must be withdrawn that year. The next year and the one after that, the withdrawal requirements drop to 1/20.5 and 1/20.1, respectively.

If the retiree is over 70-1/2, he or she may not skip a year and then make it up by withdrawing a larger amount the following year. If the person fails to take out at least the minimum required each year, the IRS will assess a 50 percent excise tax penalty on the difference between what was taken out and what the withdrawal should have been.

As noted above, if funds are withdrawn before age 59-1/2, there is a penalty in the form of a 10 percent surtax on funds withdrawn in most cases.

---

6. For actuarial reasons, and because the figures are based on averages, the joint life expectancy is somewhat longer than the longest single life expectancy of the couple. It is not, of course, the sum of the two.

## SUGGESTED READINGS

Allen, Everett T., et al. *Pension Planning: Pensions, Profit Sharing and Other Deferred Compensation Plans,* 6th ed. Homewood, Ill.: Dow Jones-Irwin, 1988.

"And One Day You Retire," Hartford, Conn.: Aetna Life Insurance Co.

Brosterman, Robert, and Brosterman, Thomas. *The Complete Estate Planning Guide.* New York: A Mentor Book, 1988.

"Choosing a Retirement Plan." Dean Witter Reynolds, Inc. You may obtain this from your Dean Witter broker.

"Company Retirement Plans Eight Years After ERISA." St. Louis: Center for the Study of American Business, Washington University.

"The Economics of Retirement." St. Louis: Center for the Study of American Business, Washington University.

Esperiti, Robert A., and Peterson, Renno L. *The Handbook of Estate Planning,* 2nd edition. New York: McGraw-Hill Book Company, 1988.

"Federal Estate and Gift Taxes." Pueblo, Col: Consumer Information Center.

"Financing Your Social Security Benefits; If You Become Disabled." Washington, D.C.: U.S. Department of Health, Education and Welfare. (SSA)-79-10029. Annual Publication.

"A Guide to Individual Retirement Accounts (IRA's)." Pueblo, Col.: Consumer Information Center.

"If You Work While You Get Social Security Payments." Washington, D.C.: U.S. Department of Health, Education and Welfare, Social Security Administration. Annual Publication.

"IRA Investment Strategies." Dean Witter Reynolds, Inc. You may obtain this from a Dean Witter broker.

"IRA Rollover." Dean Witter Reynolds, Inc. You may obtain this from a Dean Witter broker.

Krass, Stephen J., and Keschner, Richard L. *The Pension Answer Book.* Greenvale, N.Y.: Panel Publishers, 1987.

*Life Insurance Fact book.* New York: Institute of Life Insurance. Annual publication.

"On the Way Up: A Description of Life Insurance and Annuities." Hartford, Conn.: Aetna Life Insurance Co.

"Pension Facts." Washington, D.C.: American Council of Life Insurance. Annual publication.

*Questions and Answers on Retirement Plans for the Self-Employed, Retirement Plans for Self-Employed Individuals.* Washington, D.C.: Internal Revenue Service.

"*Social Security,*" and *Supplement to Social Security Handbook,* Washington, D.C.: U.S. Department of Health, Education and Welfare. You can get it free by writing or calling your local Social Security field office. Offices are located in all big cities. Annual publication.

"Social Security Information for Young Families." (SSA 10033). Washington, D.C.: U.S. Department of Health, Education and Welfare.

"Social Security in Your Financial Planning." Washington, D.C.: U.S. Department of Health, Education and Welfare. Annual publication.

Swanson, Robert E., and Swanson, Barbara M. *Tax Shelters: A Guide for Investors and Their Advisors.* Homewood Ill.: Dow Jones-Irwin, 1985.

"A Woman's Guide to Social Security." Washington, D.C.: U.S. Department of Health, Education and Welfare. Publication No. (55A) 79-10127.

"Your Medicare Handbook." Washington, D.C.: U.S. Government Printing Office.

"Your Social Security." Washington, D.C.: U.S. Department of Health, Education and Welfare. Publication No. (55A) 05-10035.

"Your Social Security Earnings Record." U.S. Department of Health, Education and Welfare. Annual publication.

"Your Social Security Rights and Responsibilities." Washington, D.C.: U.S. Department of Health, Education and Welfare. Publication No. 05-10077.

# 19 Estate planning: wills, gifts, and trusts

**HIGHLIGHTS**      In order for a person to protect acquired assets from estate taxes and to distribute them as he or she sees fit, this chapter discusses the following:

1   Information needed to be assembled in order to engage in estate planning
2   The document known as a will and what it can do
3   What happens to property upon death in the absence of a will
4   Trusts and how they are of value in estate planning
5   Gift taxes and how gifts may reduce taxes
6   Estate taxes and how these taxes may be minimized

*"No one is asked when he wishes to enter life; no one is asked when he wishes to leave."*

—Kierkegaard

## INTRODUCTION

No one cares to discuss his or her own death. However, it is inevitable. Consequently, everyone should think about the disposition of acquired property with some deliberate plan.

There are several reasons for this. First, if a person wishes to control the disposition of property, that person must state in writing who is to receive it. An individual may also wish to reduce taxes that would otherwise deplete the estate; there are gift and estate taxes that can be minimized by planning. Without a plan it might be necessary to dispose of a farm or business to pay estate taxes. Additionally, if there are minor children, one would want to designate the person who would act as guardian for them.

The major tools of estate planning that will be discussed in this chapter are wills, gifts, and trusts. The financial planner does not take the place of the attorney in estate planning. Nevertheless, he or she needs to be familiar with the tools of estate planning. The planner needs to appreciate the importance of a will, estate taxation, expenses involved, and the distribution of property.

## WILLS

Nearly everyone should have a will for the reasons noted above; they are not just for the rich or the elderly. Moreover, as the years pass, assets do accumulate, and any individual may be worth more than he or she realizes.

### Gathering the facts

Since every individual and every family is unique, each estate plan will be unique. There is, however, some basic information that is important to every estate plan, and the financial planner and the client's attorney must have the information to plan the best estate for the testator's or testatrix's needs.[1]

### Residence and domicile

The residence and domicile are important to any plan. **Domicile** is the name given to a person's permanent home, and **residence** is the place where one lives without the intention of making a permanent home. (They may be the same place, but if not, the site of the domicile determines where the person's will is to be probated.) As a general rule, marital rights that may attach to the property, such as dower or community-property rights, are determined by the domicile, as are state inheritance taxes.

---

1. These terms are used to describe respectively a male and a female who has a will.

The person's family status is very important. A prior marriage or a separation can have an effect on one's legal ability to make gifts of property in a will. A prior spouse may have a claim against the estate. The financial planner and the attorney will want to know whether there are plans to have more children and whether any present children are dependents.

      The planner and the attorney will also want to know whether there are other living relatives from whom the person may expect an inheritance. This is important in developing an estate plan that will best conserve assets, since inheritances often constitute a large portion of the assets of an estate.

*Family status*

If a person has a safety deposit box, where are the box and the key? Upon a death it may be necessary for the attorney to obtain a court order to open the box, and it is simpler if the location of the box is immediately known.

*Safety deposit box*

The financial planner or attorney will want to know about the person's beneficiaries, their names, addresses, relationship, financial needs, and character traits. The reason for wanting to know financial needs is that the testator may wish to provide financial means to enable them to live at the same standard as at present or even better. The character traits of the proposed beneficiaries are also important. Perhaps one of the proposed beneficiaries gambles or indulges in some vice; in this case the establishment of a trust that would provide funds over time may be more appropriate rather than funds in a lump sum that might be gambled away or spent in loose living.

*Beneficiaries*

The first step in estate planning and in making a will is to take a financial inventory. The reader was first introduced to a balance sheet in Chapter 3. At this point the balance sheet needs to be used again. All assets and liabilities are listed at their fair market value, and then the net worth is determined. The following personal balance sheet (Table 19–1) is a beginning. We have added hypothetical figures for some of the entries, and there are some blanks to fill in (also a blank to show the yield on all earning assets).

*Taking a financial inventory*

There are a number of things that wills can accomplish. There are also, of course, many legal technicalities one should know about wills. While this book will not make the reader an expert able to draw up wills, it should provide an appreciation for the problems involved and the importance of having the client work with an experienced and competent attorney.

*Modern wills*[2]

---

2. If a person dies intestate (without a will) that person will be subject to the will the state of domicile has drawn up for him or her. This will be discussed further on.

Table 19—1  *Personal (or family) balance sheet*

| Assets | Example | Personal entry | Percent return | Liabilities | Example | Personal entry |
|---|---|---|---|---|---|---|
| Cash (inc. checking accounts) | $    750 | _____ | _____ | Mortgage on owner-occupied home | $30,000 | _____ |
| Savings deposits (inc. certificates of dep.) | 5,000 | _____ | _____ | Other mortgages | — | _____ |
| Life insurance (estimated cash surrender value) | 15,000 | _____ | _____ | Notes & loans payable (inc. installments) | 2,000 | _____ |
| Annuities (est. cash surrender value) | 5,000 | _____ | _____ | Other unpaid bills | 300 | _____ |
| Gov. sec. of all kinds | — | _____ | _____ | Long-term business debts | — | _____ |
| Tax-exempt state and local securities | — | _____ | _____ | Short-term business liabilities (inc. accounts payable) | — | _____ |
| Corporation bonds | — | _____ | _____ | | — | _____ |
| Common stock | — | _____ | _____ | Loans against life insurance | — | _____ |
| Mutual funds | 5,000 | _____ | _____ | Other liabilities | — | _____ |
| Vested corp. pension benefits (exclude Soc. Sec.) | 10,000 | _____ | _____ | Total Liabilities | $32,300 | _____ |
| Individual pension benefits (inc. Personal Service Corp., Keogh, and IRA) | — | _____ | _____ | Net Worth | $118,450 | |
| Stock options and profit sharing benefits | — | _____ | _____ | | | |
| Real estate (owner occupied) | 100,000 | _____ | _____ | | | |
| Rental property | — | _____ | _____ | | | |
| Other long-term business assets | — | _____ | _____ | | | |
| Short-term business assets (e.g., accts. receivable) | — | _____ | _____ | | | |
| Personal assets (furniture, car, jewelry, etc.) | 10,000 | _____ | _____ | | | |
| Other assets | — | _____ | _____ | | | |
| Total Assets | 150,750 | _____ | _____ | | | |

A *will* is ordinarily a writing that provides for the distribution of property on the death of the writer but confers no rights prior to that time. In short, the will is ineffective prior to the death of the writer of the will.

Moreover, the writer may destroy or cancel the will at any time. The person making the will is known as the *testator*, if a man, or the *testatrix*, if a woman. If a person dies leaving a will, he or she is said to have died testate. One who dies without a will is said to have died intestate. A gift of land by way of a will is known as a devise, and the person receiving the gift, a devisee. A bequest, or legacy as it is sometimes called, is a gift of personal property, and the person to whom the personal property has been given is called a legatee. To be valid, a will must satisfy the requirements as to both the *intention* of the testator and the *formality* of expression of the intention.

There can be no will unless the testator manifests an intention in writing and in the will to make a provision that the will be effective on his or her death. This is called a *testamentary intent*. There likewise can be no will unless the testator has testamentary capacity (generally the requirement that the testator be of sound mind). He or she need not possess superior or even average intelligence. He or she is only required (1) to plan conceptually the distribution of his property, (2) not to execute the will as a fraud, and (3) not to be under the undue control of some other person in the execution of the will.

Wills must be witnessed. The act of witnessing the will, known as attestation, generally includes the signing of the will by the witnesses after a clause that states that the witnesses have observed the testator sign the will. Publication is the act of the testator's informing the attesting witnesses that the document he is signing before them is his will. The person making the will need not inform the witnesses of its contents. He merely announces that the document is his will and that he requests the witnesses to attest to his signature. This constitutes the publication. In a few states, witnesses are not required but in general two or three witnesses are necessary. In those states where witnesses are required, it is generally specified that they are credible or competent and that they have no interest in the will.

Upon the death of the testator or testatrix, the will must be probated. "Probate" means to prove. It is the job of the executor named in the will to go to court, prove that the will is valid, and carry out its terms. When specific pieces of property are to go to named persons, the executor transfers the property to those persons. Where specific property is not designated to go to named persons, it is the function of the executor to obtain a court order, sell the property, and distribute the proceeds. The first thing that the executor is bound to do is to pay off the debts of the estate and settle taxes.

Executors are paid a fee for their services. If the testator or testatrix appoints an executor, the fee is generally agreed on in advance. Since probating a will is a complex and technical operation, probably an experienced attorney should be appointed. If no executor has been designated, the court will appoint one, and his or her fees will be determined in accordance with state law. Fees vary from state to state and with the size of the estate. Generally, however, executor's fees range from 4 to 5 percent of the first $5,000 or $10,000 of the estate and are then scaled down in a series of steps to about 1 to 2 percent of that portion of an estate in excess of $200,000 or $250,000.

The probating of the will is not always simple. Some states require the witnesses who attested the execution of the will to testify regarding the execution. Frequently, the witnesses are dead or for some other reason unable to testify. To forestall the possibility of preventing the probating of many wills, most states permit a will to include a self-proving clause. The will is signed and attested in the usual manner. The writer and witnesses then execute an affidavit before a notary public acknowledging their acts. The affidavit is appended to the will, which may then be admitted to probate without the testimony of these witnesses.

*How to reduce assets requiring probate*

Probate is time consuming and costly. Therefore, many people plan ahead to lessen the assets requiring probate. There are several methods of doing this.

1. Gifts. Obviously if a person gives away part of the estate prior to death, it will reduce the assets requiring probate. It may also reduce estate taxes, as will be explained later. To be sure, there are gift taxes, but they too can be legally avoided, as will also be explained later.
2. Joint tenancy with right of survivorship. If property is held jointly, it passes automatically to the survivor without going through probate.
3. Tenancy by the entirety. This is very similar to joint tenancy and such property also passes without going through probate. These two types of joint ownership are explained in greater detail below.
4. Trusts. If a person places property into a trust, it too passes without going through probate. The use of trusts is explained below.
5. Life insurance proceeds. The death benefits go directly to the beneficiary(ies) without going through probate.

*The general contents of a will*

In general, wills contain the following items:

1. A statement of the domicile of the testator or testatrix.
2. A statement revoking prior wills: "I hereby revoke all wills and codicils by me at any time heretofore made."
3. A provision for payment of debts and funeral expenses. This may read, "I direct that all my just debts and funeral expenses be paid

as soon after my death as may be practicable or as they come due." The testator should communicate in the will his or her idea of the just debts that he or she intends the executor to pay or add the clause "as they become due." A simpler "just debts" clause may be interpreted as "all debts." Consider the plight of the widow who learns that the residence she expects to live in for the rest of her life must be sold for its equity value to pay off a mortgage on it—a just debt.

4. Funeral and burial directions may sometimes be included but need not be; they may read for instance, "I direct that my body be cremated."

5. A provision for the disposition of property. This may read, "I give and bequeath to my beloved wife Jane DeFoe all property which I shall own or be entitled to at my death." More than one person may, of course, be named as beneficiaries.

6. A secondary provision for the disposition of property to a secondary heir in the event the first-named person predeceases the testator or testatrix.

7. A statement about legacies. These are usually of two types: the general legacy and the specific legacy. The general legacy is a gift of money to an individual, paid out of the general assets of the estate. It is not a bequest of a particular thing or a particular fund designated from all others of the same kind.[3] The general legacy may read, "I give and bequeath to my dear friend Howard G. Jensen the sum of $1,000." The specific legacy is a bequest of a particular thing, which is a specified part of the estate, distinguished from all other property of the same kind.[4] If there were inadequate assets to pay all the bequests, the general legacy would be scaled down, but a specific legacy may read, "I give and bequeath to my dear friend James G. Richardson my entire stamp collection."

8. Charitable or religious bequests. Such a statement may read, "I give and bequeath the sum of $1,000 to the Lord Nelson Home for Wayward Boys."

9. A statement concerning the residual estate. This includes all of the remaining items that have not yet been disposed of by the will and is dealt with by means of a so-called residuary clause giving away or disposing of all that remains in the testator's estate. This may read, "All the rest, residue, and remainder of my estate, of whatsoever kind and nature, and wheresoever situated, of which I may be seized or possessed or to which I may be entitled at the time of my death, not hereby otherwise effectually disposed of (including any property over which I have the power of appointment), I devise and bequeath to my beloved wife, Jane DeFoe."

3. *Armstead v. Union Trust Co.*, 61 F2d 677.
4. *Byme v. Hume*, 86 Mich. 546.

10. A statement naming the executor who will probate the will. Generally anyone not specifically disqualified by law will be permitted to be the executor. Often this is the surviving spouse, an adult child, or some other blood relative or close friend of the family. However, if there is a large estate and probate may be technically complex, an experienced attorney or the trust department of a bank may be named executor. Many states require that an executor furnish a bond to assure that he or she will faithfully carry out his or her duties. A will may, however, contain a statement requesting that no bond need be furnished.
11. Frequently a will appoints a guardian if there are minor children.
12. Normally if there is a surviving spouse, no other guardian is needed; hence this provision appoints a guardian only if the spouse predeceases the testator or testatrix.
13. A statement about the witnesses and a place for them to sign their names.
14. A statement regarding the notary public who must see that the witnesses sign the will in the presence of the testator or testatrix and then notarize and sign the document. Sometimes a self-proving affidavit is added, to ease probate by vouching for the validity of the signatures.

*The joint will*

A joint will is defined as a single testamentary instrument that contains the wills of two or more persons. Typically, it is executed by husband and wife, and typically each leaves his or her property to the other, and only when they are both gone will the children inherit anything. These are the so-called Ma and Pa wills. Many authorities feel that the joint will should not be used because it can lay the groundwork for future litigation.

Essentially the joint will contains the same general type of clauses with regard to burial instructions and appointments of executors as does the will made by an individual. However, the residuary clause in a joint will gives the residue of the estate to each other. Another important clause in this joint or mutual will is the following:

> "We do hereby declare that the mutual and reciprocal dispositive provisions [this is the clause in a will providing for the disposition of the property] herein for the benefit of the other have been made pursuant to an understanding and agreement that each has made the provisions herein in consideration of the other similarly providing, and upon condition that neither of us will during our lives alter, amend, or revoke such provisions without the written consent of the other, nor will the survivor alter, amend, or revoke the same, after the death of the first of us to die."

Such a statement is important because it expresses the intent of the parties that neither will revoke or alter the will without the consent of the other. In the absence of this clearly expressed intent, it may be held that the execution of the joint will without reference to the terms of the instrument is not sufficient evidence of an enforceable contract to devise between the testator and testatrix. In short, either of the parties may subsequently make another will that is likely to take precedence over the joint will.

*The common disaster clause*

All wills should have a common disaster clause. Otherwise if a husband and wife have an automobile accident and both are killed, there might be litigation to determine who died first. If the wife died first and the wife had a will leaving the property to her husband, her property, together with what he owned, would pass according to the terms of his will. However, with his wife dead, the property cannot pass to her. If there were children, the will would probably provide for them. But if there were no children and the husband's will did not specifically state who was next in line, all of the property might go to the husband's relatives and the wife's kin would receive nothing. To provide against this, a common catastrophe clause is frequently inserted in a will. This clause may read as follows:

> "Any person who shall have died at the same time as I, or in a common disaster with me, or under such circumstances that it is difficult or impossible to determine which died first, shall be deemed to have predeceased me."

Both the husband's and wife's will would then pass property as if each had died last. Each person's property would then pass according to his or her will, and if there were no children, each side's relatives would get something.

*The codicil*

A codicil to a will is defined as an addition or change executed with the same formalities as required in the will itself. Generally it is better to draw a new will than to have a codicil. The codicil may, for instance, eliminate a person already designated as a beneficiary under the terms of the will; if so the door is left open for that beneficiary to contest the will, which is extremely costly to the estate and may end up with property not being disposed of in accordance with the intention of the testator or testatrix.

The codicil refers to the will and is dated. It contains a dispositive provision and is attested to by the number of witnesses required in accordance with the state statute. Above the signatures of the witnesses is the following clause:

> "The foregoing instrument consists of one page and was made on the third day of April 1993, signed and sealed at the end thereof, and at the same time published and declared by James J. Defoe, the above named Testator, as and for a codicil to his Last Will and Testament dated the third day of April 1993, in the presence of each of us, who, this attestation clause having been read to us, did at the request of said testator, in his presence and in the presence of each other sign our names as witnesses thereto."

*Holographic wills*        Holographic wills are instruments that are wholly handwritten by the testator as a will and meet only some of the formal requirements of a will. They must always be signed and dated, but witnesses are not necessary. Not all states recognize holographic wills, and those that do may recognize them to pass property only up to a given amount of value. Typically, a holographic will is written at the time when the testator becomes aware of impending death and decides to alter completely his or her will or suddenly realizes there is none. Holographic wills written on envelopes, napkins, and even clothing have been admitted to probate in many states.

A holographic will supersedes an existing will and often is the only will a testator has written. Why isn't every note a person would write concerning the distribution of property designated to be a holographic will? This type of will, like any other, must meet certain minimal formal requirements. More importantly, the writing must express a testamentary intention by its author.

*Where a will*        If a will cannot be found after the death of the testator or testatrix it is
*should be kept*        presumed that he or she destroyed it with the intent of revoking it. This presumption can be overcome only by proving fraudulent destruction or by showing that the person was mentally incapable of possessing the intention to revoke.

There are generally four things that can be done with the will once it has been written.

1.    In the majority of cases, the will is left with the attorney who drew it or a financial planner, who either puts it in an office safe or places it in a safety deposit box in a financial institution. A copy is also usually given to the testator or testatrix.
2.    Where a financial institution has been named as one of the executors, the will is generally placed with that institution for safekeeping.
3.    The will can be placed in the person's own safety deposit box. This is sometimes objected to on the grounds that often it takes a court order for the box to be opened after death. However, the box must be opened in any case, and the state tax department officials who are present when the box is opened will have no objection to the removal of the will after an inventory has been taken of the contents of the box.
4.    The will may be kept in the home in a strongbox. This is the least recommended place, because it is too easily accessible to destruction by persons other than the testator and it may easily be lost or mislaid.

It is best to make several copies of the will and keep them in all of the above places.

A sample of a modern will is shown in Figure 19–1. Figure 19–2 is

## KNOW ALL MEN BY THESE PRESENTS:

That I, _____ of Travis County, Texas, being of sound and disposing mind and memory, and above the age of eighteen years, do make and publish this my last will and testament, hereby revoking all wills heretofore made by me.

### I.

I direct that all my just debts shall be paid.

### II.

Should my beloved wife, _____, survive me, I give to her all property which I shall own or be entitled to at my death.

### III.

Should my said wife not survive me, I give all property which I shall own or be entitled to at my death to my son, _____.

I hereby appoint my wife, _____, independent executrix of this my last will and testament, and I direct that no bond shall be required of her as such executrix, and I further direct that no action shall be had in the County Court or any other court in relation to the administration and settlement of my estate other than the probating and recording of this my last will and testament and filing of an inventory and list of claims in the manner provided by law.

If my said wife does not survive me, I appoint my son _____, independent executor of my will without bond under the same terms and conditions which would have obtained had my wife served as independent executrix.

IN TESTIMONY WHEREOF, I have hereunto set my hand, this the _____ day of _____, in the presence of _____ _____ and _____, who witness my signature and attest this my last will and testament at my request as attesting witnesses.

(name) _____

The above instrument was now here on the date hereinabove set forth, subscribed by _____, the testator, in our presence and in the presence of each other, and we, as attesting witnesses at his request and in his presence and in the presence of each other, sign our names hereto as attesting witnesses.

_____

_____

Before me, the undersigned authority, on this day personally appeared

_____,

_____, and

_____ known to me to be the testator and the witnesses, respectively, whose names are subscribed to the annexed or foregoing instrument in their respective capacities, and, all of said persons being by me duly sworn, the said

_____, testator, declared to me and to the said witnesses in my presence that said instrument is his last will and testament, and that he had willingly made and executed it as his free act and deed for the purposes therein expressed; and the said witnesses, each on his oath stated to me, in the presence and hearing of the said testator, that the said testator had declared to them that

*Sample of a modern will.*                                      Figure 19—1

said instrument is his last will and testament, and that he executed same as such and wanted each of them to sign it as a witness; and upon their oaths each witness stated further that they did sign the same as witnesses in the presence of the said testator and at his request; that he was at that time nineteen years of age or over and was of sound mind; and that each of said witnesses was then at least fourteen years of age.

Testator             

Witness             

Witness             

Subscribed and acknowledged before me by the said
_____, testator, and subscribed and sworn to before me by said
_____ and _____, witnesses, this the _____ day of _____, 1984.

_____
Notary Public, Travis County, Texas

Figure 19–1     *(continued)*

a sample of the oldest known will in existence today. It was written by the Egyptian Pharaoh, Uah, and was executed in 2548 B.C. We have also found what is believed to be the shortest will ever probated. It contained just ten words: "Being of sound mind and body, I spent it all."

*The last letter of instructions*

Every person should write a letter of last instructions and leave it in an easily accessible place as well as with every member of the family. A copy should also be given to the family lawyer, if there is one, and another copy should be placed in a safety deposit box. This letter should probably be rewritten and updated every year or two as the individual's assets and other conditions change.

It should be noted that a letter of last instructions is not a will or a substitute for a will; both are needed. A letter of last instructions is a supplementary document to a will. This letter should, among other things, include a list of all the individual's assets and liabilities and indicate where the documents are located.

As a minimum, it should include the following:

1. A statement of where the will, if any, may be found.
2. Funeral instructions, if necessary. Some people wish to be cremated, others, buried. Some wish to donate certain organs (e.g., eyes) to others after death. In any case all members of the family should have general knowledge in advance of future funeral arrangements.
3. A statement regarding a safety deposit box—where it and the key are located.

### AMENEMHAT IV,

#### Year 2, Month Paophi, Day 18

I, Uah, am giving a title to property to my wife SHEFTU, the woman of Gesab who is called Teta, the daughter of Sat Sepdu, of all things given to me by my brother Ankh-ren. She shall give it to any she desires of her children she bears me.

I am giving to her the Eastern slaves, 4 persons, that my brother Ankh-ren gave me. She shall give them to whomsoever she will of her children.

As to my tomb, let me be buried in it with my wife alone.

Moreover as to the house built for me by my brother Ankh-ren, my wife shall dwell therein without allowing her to be put forth on the ground by any person.

It is the deputy Gebu who shall act as guardian of my son.

Done in the presence of these witnesses:

KEMEN, Decorator of Columns.

APU, Doorkeeper of the Temple.

SENB, son of Senb, Doorkeeper of the Temple.

*Will from 2548 B.C., translated by the American University at Cairo.*                    Figure 19—2

4. A list of all life insurance policies and their location.
5. An inventory of all stocks and bonds, and where they are kept.
6. A list of all other property such as real estate, mutual funds, and business property, and their location.
7. The person's Social Security number should be recorded.
8. A statement indicating what benefits the deceased may have from his or her employer. There may be pension benefits, death benefits, profit-sharing plans, and other benefits to which the deceased's estate or survivors may have a claim.
9. A list of all deposits in banks, savings and loan associations, mutual savings banks, or credit unions.
10. A list of memberships in all unions, professional associations, lodges and fraternal organizations, and veterans groups. There may be financial benefits because of memberships in some of these organizations.
11. A list of all just debts owed to the person and accounts receivable, the interest rate they bear, the terms of payment, and where to locate the documents to prove their validity.
12. A list of all the just debts owed by the individual, the interest rate they bear, the terms of their repayment, and the location of the pertinent documents.

*Living wills*

In recent years, there has been some litigation over life-support systems being used to continue the life of terminally ill people who are often in great pain or in a vegetative state. Recently California passed a right-to-die-in-dignity law, and other states are likely to follow. This permits life-support systems to be withdrawn in such cases. Also some people have written living wills in which a person authorizes, permits, and requests that the life-support system be withdrawn if he or she is in a situation such as that described above. Sometimes the deceased wishes to become a donor of certain transplantable organs. If so, this should be spelled out in the living will, because eyes and certain other organs must be removed immediately upon death.

*If a person dies intestate (without a will)*

Everyone already has one will because the state in which the person is domiciled has drawn one up for him or her. The property of a person dying intestate will pass according to the intestacy laws of the state of domicile. This may not be in accordance with the wishes of the deceased. It is particularly important that individuals whose needs are not met through state intestacy laws have wills drawn to ensure appropriate distribution of property.

Intestacy laws vary from state to state. Generally, however, they distribute property in the following order of priority of claims.

1. *Spouses and children.* Surviving spouses and children are first in line and they generally receive the main share of the estate and

If a person dies intestate, it is unlikely that property will be distributed according to his or her wishes. For example, state laws make no provision for favorite charities or special relationships to receive any funds. In the absence of a will, there may be cumbersome procedures and high legal expenses. If a person dies intestate (without a will) much higher estate taxes may be due (see the section called "Gift and estate taxes").

A problem may also arise if there are minor children. If both parents are dead they have no control over who will rear minor children. They may be sent across the country to live with a relative, while the deceased may have preferred that their children be raised by friends in the community.

If a large share of an estate passes to minor children, it may be placed in trust until they are 18. This may make the family financially strapped while the children are growing up; then at 18 they get a large sum of money.

It is even possible in some states where the deceased was divorced and remarried that his share would go to his second wife or her children, rather than to his first wife or her children.

**Box 19–1**
**Make a will**

perhaps all of it. In some states the surviving spouse will receive the bulk of the estate, but in others the children will receive a substantial amount. It is possible, then, that without a will a spouse might have insufficient assets.

2. *Lineals.* Lineals are blood relatives of the deceased. The major portion of an estate not distributed to the surviving spouse and children is generally distributed to lineals (brothers and sisters) although sometimes parents also have a claim to part of it.

3. *Parents.* If the estate has not been exhausted by this time, the remainder is commonly distributed to the decedent's parents.

4. *Collateral heirs.* Other more distant relatives with a common ancestry are considered. Cousins, uncles, and the like are next in line. Usually there is not much left by now.

Distant relatives will exhaust any estate if it gets that far, but one more step is provided by law in most states. It takes effect in the very rare case when a person dies intestate and has no heirs—no surviving spouse, children, or parents, also no cousins or other blood relatives, and no one with a common ancestry. Where does his or her property go? It goes to his or her state tax collector.

Administration of estates is the means of distributing property of a decedent who died intestate. When no will is left, the court or an officer designated by law appoints one or more persons who are then entitled to administer the estate of the decedent. More often than not, close

*Administration of estates*

relatives of the deceased make application to the court for the so-called letter of administration. Such a letter gives the administrator the obligation of gathering the assets of the deceased, paying the debts and taxes of the estate, and then distributing the assets in accordance with the statute pertaining to distribution of the estate. Generally, the letter of administration is granted to the first relative or person who applies. In some cases where there are creditors of the deceased and no previous application for letter of administration has been made, the letter may be granted to a creditor. In the absence of a creditor, applications, or known relatives, the letter may be issued by the court to a public administrator. In any event, once the letter has been granted to the administrator, the job becomes much the same as that of the executor of an estate.

## HOW CERTAIN PROPERTY IS HELD: NONPROBATE PROPERTY

The question immediately arises: "How should major assets be held?" This is important for married couples with respect to such assets as checking accounts, savings deposits, real estate, securities, and perhaps some others. There are four legal forms of joint ownership.

1. Tenancy by the entirety
2. Joint tenancy with right of survivorship
3. Tenancy in common
4. Community property

How property is held will vary from state to state depending on the laws of that state.

### Tenancy by the entirety

Only two people married to each other are able to hold real property in the form of tenancy by the entirety, and personal property cannot be held in this form. They are both equal owners. This is the one way in which a person could own his or her home in most cases in many common law states. The deed is made out to both parties, and when one dies the deed passes cleanly to the other. Both signatures must be obtained when selling the property. Some community property states do not permit property ownership in the form of tenancy by the entirety.[5]

### Joint tenancy with right of survivorship

Joint tenancy can involve more than two owners. If it is between a husband and wife, it should spell out, "with rights of survivorship," under which the surviving spouse takes full title to the property on the death of the other. This type of ownership is not possible in some community

---

5. The community property states are Arizona, California, Idaho, Louisiana, Nevada, New Mexico, Texas, and Washington. Recently Wisconsin passed legislation which provides for a similar type of arrangement.

property states. Hence, in states like Texas or California a husband and wife can enter into such an ownership agreement with their separate property only but not with their community property unless they first partition their community into separate property. The one exception to this is U.S. Government securities. They can be community property and still be held in the form of a joint tenancy with right of survivorship because they are governed by federal law, which takes precedence.

This can also involve more than two owners. The ownership interest of the survivors of property held in common is not changed by the death of one owner. In community property states, only separate property of either spouse can be held in the form of tenancy in common.

*Tenancy in common*

Community property is a legal concept valid only in community property states. Under the law, most property acquired during a marriage is owned 50 percent by each spouse. However, each member of a married couple can have separate property. This would include property acquired prior to marriage, that acquired after marriage through a gift or inheritance, and possibly previous community property that was partitioned earlier. In a community property state, on the death of one spouse one-half of all community property passes to the deceased's estate. If there is no will spelling out who is to receive it, the property passes in accordance with the law of inheritance, and the surviving spouse and the children usually are the heirs. However, the surviving spouse may not get it all or even the main share; the children may get as much as one-half. This is true of personal as well as real property.

*Community property*

Real estate, securities, and bank accounts typically should be held jointly with rights of survivorship in most common law (based on English law) states insofar as married couples are concerned. Then, on the death of one, the survivor acquires it automatically and directly without the necessity of probating a will. In community property states, this cannot be done, and a will may be the only way to assure that the survivor will get all of the estate. In the absence of a will, the children might get some of it in certain community property states.

Gifts and trusts are useful in estate planning because both of them can reduce taxes, i.e., gift and estate taxes—not income taxes. Gift taxes are paid by the giver, not the recipient; estate taxes are taxes on the assets left by the deceased.

**TRUSTS**

Equally important, the use of the trust allows the creators some control over their assets even after they die. The trust can also provide financial security to those who are inexperienced or incapable of managing their financial affairs, such as minor children.

*Creation of the trust*

The trust is an arrangement whereby title to property is transferred by the creator or settlor to another person (trustee) for the benefit of a third party (beneficiary or *cestui que* trust). The property placed in trust is called the corpus, the trust *res*, the trust fund, or the trust property. The title to the corpus is split, with the trustee holding the property for an ascertainable length of time, and all benefits from the corpus go to the beneficiaries. The beneficiaries who receive the income from the trust during their lifetime are known as **life tenants** (income beneficiaries); those beneficiaries who receive the corpus (principal) of the trust upon the death of the last of the life tenants are known as the **remaindermen** (principal beneficiaries).

Generally, a trust may be created for any purpose that is not against public policy. For instance, a trust created from funds obtained from the commission of a felony is void, as is a trust created to encourage divorce. There are other prerequisites that each state imposes for the creation of a valid trust. Two of the most important are intention and capacity.

There must be an intention on the part of the settlor, declared in writing, to convey property to a trust for the benefit of beneficiaries. Secret, unexpressed intentions will not effectively create a trust. There must also be a manifest intent to impose enforceable duties on the trustee to manage the property for the benefit of another.

In addition to intent, there must be capacity among all the parties involved to create a trust. The settlor must have the capacity to convey property. Thus insane persons and minors, who cannot validly convey property, lack the capacity to create a trust. The trustee must be capable of owning property and meeting the requirements of being a fiduciary. For example, no person convicted of a felony is capable of being a fiduciary. While settlors can name themselves as beneficiaries, they cannot be their own trustee. (There are exceptions to this in some states.) Finally, a definite beneficiary who is capable of owning property is required. The beneficiary must be named or, as will be discussed later, capable of being determined under a definite standard.

*The* inter vivos *and testamentary trust*

The *inter vivos* trust, or so-called living trust, is one created by the grantor during his or her lifetime. The grantor also may be the beneficiary. In general, the *inter vivos* trust may be either irrevocable or revocable. The testamentary trust is one set up through a will, and it becomes effective upon the death of the grantor.

*The revocable trust*

The revocable trust can be terminated by the creator at any time. It can also be set up to terminate automatically at a specific time in the future.

If the beneficiary is someone other than the creator (for example, a minor child), gift taxes do not apply. It is not a gift; the creator still has full control over it. The creator can even tell the trustee how to invest the funds, and he or she can change these managerial instructions from time to time. Generally the creator will give only broad general investment instruction and leave wide discretion with the trustee. The major reason some people set up such trusts is to turn day-to-day management decisions over to someone else because they do not want to be bothered, they feel they can increase the return on their assets through a trust, or the beneficiary may be a minor or otherwise inexperienced in finance. The income earned by such a trust may be disbursed to the beneficiary or left to accumulate in the trust. In either case, it is taxable income. The trustee will report it to the creator or grantor, and he or she must then declare it on the tax return.

The creator can never terminate (revoke) an irrevocable trust. He or she also usually gives up all income earned by it, but this need not be so. The creator gives up the right not only to revoke but also to alter or amend the trust. The creator can put some loose control into the trust agreement—such as, for example, it will be invested only in bonds, or at least 50 percent in bonds—or the trustee can be given complete discretion.

*Irrevocable trusts*

The creator may set up an irrevocable (living) trust and name himself or herself as the beneficiary with the right to receive the income from it. The creator would probably name someone else to become the beneficiary after his or her death, or stipulate that the trust then be dissolved and someone receive the corpus. A reason for making the creator the beneficiary would be to achieve the peace of mind of having someone competent manage his or her financial affairs, and also to protect his or her assets from being dissipated due to possible loss of financial sophistication in the future from illness or the like. Such a trust, however, would not be protected from claims of creditors; an irrevocable trust which made someone else the beneficiary would be protected from the creator's creditors. The property of a trust in which the grantor is also the beneficiary would also be includible in the grantor's estate upon his death. Estate taxes would have to be paid at that time. Whoever received the corpus of the trust when it was dissolved (called vesting) would also be subject to estate taxes upon his or her death.

An irrevocable trust may, however, name someone other than the grantor as the beneficiary. This is looked on as a gift, and gift taxes might be due (see below) rather than estate taxes on the death of the grantor.

There are several ways in which an irrevocable trust may reduce income taxes. A person might create an irrevocable trust for the benefit of a child with the idea of creating an educational fund. In such a case the income from the corpus might not be passed through to the beneficiary until he or she had enrolled in a university. The income earned by the trust fund would be taxable to the trust, at a relatively low rate, and not to the father or mother, who might be at a high tax bracket. Thereby the grantor could accomplish two things: (1) reduce the total amount of tax paid, and (2) provide a fund for the education of his or her child. If the trust passes its earnings through to the beneficiary, he or she would pay the taxes, presumably again at a lower rate. How a trust can reduce future estate taxes is explained further on.

## The testamentary trust

A testamentary trust is one that is created by a provision in a will. The trust agreement would have to be written in advance, and on the death of the grantor, it would become effective. Such a trust would be subject to estate taxes, but, as we shall see later, it could reduce estate taxes of the beneficiaries. A testamentary trust is irrevocable, and much of what was said just previously applies. In addition to tax reduction, a reason for the creation of such a trust is to protect the beneficiary who is inexperienced. It may be undesirable, for instance, to leave a large estate consisting of investments in securities to a person lacking experience in investments. Or it may be desirable to leave property to a trustee in order to provide income for a wife for life, and at her death to provide that the corpus of the trust pass on to the children or their heirs. Often, too, property is left to the trustee to hold and to invest and to pay the income to minor children, with the corpus passing to them when they become of age.

## Simple and complex trusts

A trust may be simple or complex. A simple trust is one in which all of the income from the trust is given to the beneficiary; a complex trust is one that retains the income at least until some predetermined time in the future, which must be spelled out in the trust agreement, if it is an irrevocable trust. The beneficiary is liable for the taxes on the income he or she receives from a simple trust. With a complex trust, the trustee pays the taxes, using some of the income for this purpose, in accordance with whatever tax bracket the income of the trust indicates.

A complex trust may also be set up so that part of the income is passed through to the beneficiary and part is retained. In such a case, that portion passed through is taxed as described above under the simple trust, and that part retained is taxed as described under a complex trust.

## A college trust fund and gifts to a child

If parents wish to save for their children's (or grandchildren's) college education they could establish a trust for them. This can save taxes, if they are in a higher percent bracket, by transferring income from the parent's bracket to the child's lower (usually 15 percent) rate. This must be done very carefully, however; and it must be done differently if the child is under 14 years of age than when he or she is 14 or over, as will be explained further on.

Parents may set up a formal trust administered by a third party (trust department of a bank) or a custodial trust under the Uniform Gifts

If a trust earns income, that income is taxed. If it is a simple trust, the beneficiary who receives the income pays that tax at his or her rate. If, however, the trust retains the income (as it does in a complex trust), then the trust must pay income tax on it. Trusts compute their income tax under a separate rate schedule that applies only to them. The table below illustrates these taxes.

*For tax year 1991*

| Taxable income | | | Tax | On excess |
| Over | Not over | Pay + | rate percent | over |
| --- | --- | --- | --- | --- |
| $      0 | $ 3,450 | $      0 | 15 | $      0 |
| 3,450 | 10,350 | 517.50 | 28 | 3,450 |
| 10,350 | . . . . | 2,449.50 | 31 | 10,350 |

to Minors Act, which they themselves may administer.[6] The custodial trust may include savings deposits, stock, bonds, and so forth but all must be in the child's name.

Parents may now make gifts to the trust on the child's behalf. To avoid gift taxes, the gift must be limited to $10,000 per year ($20,000 if married); see below in the section "How Gifts Can Save Taxes" for an explanation of how the gift tax works. Parents may make periodic contributions to the trust so that when the child is ready for college the funds will be available.

If the child is 14 years of age or older, this is all that must be done; the income from the trust is taxed at the child's presumably 15 percent rate.[7]

If the child is under 14, however, it is more difficult to shift income, but it can be done. The law provides that unearned income, such as income from a trust, of a child under 14 is taxed at the parents' rate. However, this is not true of the first $1,100 of unearned income. As noted before, earned income consists of wages and salaries, and most people under age 14 have little of that. Unearned income is defined by the IRS as investment (interest and dividend) income. In the case of a child under 14, the first $550 of unearned income is not taxed, and the second $550 is taxed at the child's rate; not until income rises above

---

6. A custodial trust is automatically established if a parent sets up a deposit (or purchases bonds or stock) in the child's name.

7. A dependent child does not get the personal exemption and also does not get the standard deduction on unearned income. Hence, the entire trust income is taxed at 15 percent. Unearned income is interest or dividend income, which is what the trust income is. If the child has earned income (wages or salary), the standard deduction does apply to that income.

Table 19—2   *Tax on the first $1,000.*
*of a child's trust income*

| | |
|---|---|
| Unearned income | $1,100 |
| Standard deduction | 550 |
| Net unearned income | 550 |
| Taxed at child's rate | 15% |
| Tax | $82.50 |

$1,100 is it taxed at the parent's higher rate. As Table 19–2 shows, the tax on the first $1,100 is only $82.50. Hence, a person may still set up a college trust fund (or for any other purpose) and set aside a fairly substantial sum before its income is taxed at the parents' rate. A trust could be set up at birth and provide modest tax benefits.

*The power of invasion*

Unfortunately, one cannot predict the future, even in economic terms. A person may believe that he or she has provided sufficient cash assets to maintain his or her spouse and child; he or she has established a testamentary trust and provided that the income therefrom shall go to the support of the spouse and child. However, as the years pass, the cost of living may rise by far more than was anticipated. It may be then that the income from the trust fund will be insufficient to support the spouse and child. In practice, therefore, a statement is frequently inserted to provide that the trust fund itself may be used to support the beneficiaries if the need arises. This dipping into the principal is called the **power of invasion**. It may be unlimited, with the amount to be taken from the fund left to the best judgment and discretion of either the beneficiary or the trustee; or it is sometimes limited to a certain percentage of the trust fund over the annual income per year.

Needless to say, the importance of the clause cannot be stressed too strongly if the purpose of the trust is for the support and maintenance of the beneficiaries. Although the courts can authorize the reformation of the trust agreement to allow dispersal of a portion of the corpus as long as no one beneficiary is deprived of his or her rightful share, this is undesirable for the beneficiaries since litigation is a costly and time-consuming process. If the principal is dipped into, the trust's future earnings are likely to decline, which may necessitate dipping into the principal even further. In such a case, it is possible that the beneficiary could outlive his or her principal sum.

*The rule against perpetuities*

This rule prevents even irrevocable trusts from going on and on. That is, while an irrevocable trust cannot be revoked by its grantor, it must eventually be liquidated. Or in legal terms, it must *vest,* that is, it must be liquidated and pass to someone. Of course, the person or persons receiving the property can immediately set up another trust. However, when a trust vests, the people receiving it may pay an estate tax when they die.

*When* a trust must finally be liquidated varies from state to state. Generally it must vest 21 years after the death of the "lives in being" at the time the creator dies and those who are mentioned in the trust. Unborn heirs who might be referred to in the trust do not count. A parent may set up a trust that can continue during the lives of all children, grandchildren, and great-grandchildren, if any, that were mentioned in the will and were alive on the day of his or her death, plus 21 years. Only 21 years after the death of the last survivor of the above group would the trust have to be liquidated.

In some states, this "lives in being" has been modified, and the trust must vest after the death of not more than two lives mentioned in the trust and who are living at the testator's death—the plus 21 years being removed. This is the so-called "measured lives" doctrine.

A well-drawn trust, then, must provide for a method of determining who gets what, when it is finally liquidated. If a trust spans two or more generations before liquidation, there may be grandchildren and even great-grandchildren of the creator who will finally share in the distribution of the property. A simple equal per capita distribution for all claimants would be unfair because some grandchildren might be alive and others dead, and also some grandchildren would have produced more heirs than others. Because of this, most trusts provide *per stirpes* distribution.

A *per stirpes* distribution dilutes the principal along ancestral lines. In the above case, for example, the great-grandchildren whose parents are dead should get all of their parents' share. The great-grandchildren of living parents should get nothing, or at least no more than a portion of their parents' share. (They may get their parents' share later.) Also, an only great-grandchild of one of the creator's grandchildren should get more than each of the two great-grandchildren of another one of the creator's grandchildren. Figure 19–3 illustrates a *per stirpes* distribution.

Assume those nine without crosses are alive and have a claim. In some cases the law (or proviso in the trust) would provide for nothing for the children of C and D (that is, nothing to I, J, and K, the great-grand-children of the creator); they may get their share later through their parents when the parents die. However, the only child of D would eventually get twice what each of the two children of C would eventually get. (This assumes D has no children in the future and that both C and D neither add to nor deplete the principal.) The four offspring of A and B have claim to exactly 50 percent of the trust; if the trust were $1,000,000, they would each get $125,000. C and his offspring together would have a claim to $250,000 but the offspring might have to wait. The same is true of D and his offspring. If D were dead, his child (K, the great-grandchild of the creator) would get $250,000.

A trust that continues through two or more generations before it vests, with the heirs along the way receiving only the income, is often

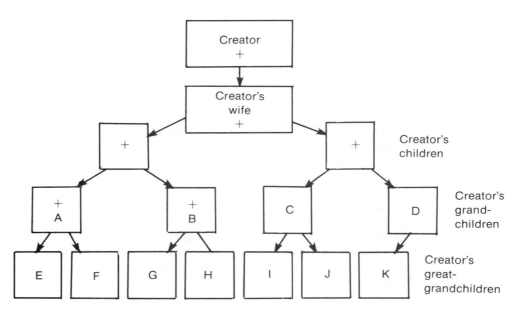

Figure 19—3    Per stirpes *distribution of property.*

called a "generation-skipping" trust, and at one time it postponed taxes. There were no further estate taxes due until the death of the people in whom the trust finally vested. This has now been changed to some extent. For example, if a trust is established in a way so that it vests, not in the children but rather in the grandchildren or even the great-grandchildren—a generation-skipping trust—estate taxes are due when the children die, in whom the trust would normally have vested.

The above, however, applies only to relatively large trusts. Taxes may still be postponed if the "generation-skipping" trust is not in excess of $1,000,000.

*The power of appointment*

A power of appointment is defined as a device by which the owner of property grants to another person or persons the power to designate, within whatever limits he or she wishes, how the property shall be distributed after the original beneficiary dies.

In other words, it is a device giving the beneficiary of a trust the right to alter the disposition of the trust *res* or trust fund on his or her death through his or her will. For example, A, by will, leaves property to his son, in trust, the income from the trust fund to be paid to the son for life, and the property upon the death of the son to pass to his son's children. If the son dies before his wife, it may be that his widow will have no means of support; consequently there may be included in A's will a provision giving his son the power of appointment. This would mean that the son through his will could change the distribution of the property by providing that on his death the income should go to his widow for life and on her death to his children. What this does is to enable A to look into the future through the eyes of his son; what may be considered wise today may be considered absurd tomorrow. The main reason for including the power of appointment in a trust agreement, then, is to protect the fund for the several life beneficiaries.

It is the prerogative of the settlor to name the trustee for the trust. Since this person is to be responsible for the corpus of the trust for a number of years, the selection of the trustee is critical. Although a private individual can be named as trustee if he or she is willing to take on the responsibilities and duties of a fiduciary for the nominal fee involved in managing the trust, the settlor generally finds it more satisfactory to name an organized trust corporation or trust department of a bank as the trustee. The settlor could expect trust companies and banks to have a larger and more experienced staff to administer the trust and a greater willingness to take on the strict liabilities of being fiduciary than could generally be found in an individual.

*The trustee—the role of the fiduciary*

Gift taxes are imposed on the giver (the recipient need not pay), and estate taxes are imposed on the estate (property) of the deceased before the heirs may receive the residual. These used to be separate taxes with separate rate schedules. Recently, however, Congress combined the gift and estate tax rate into one common schedule—the unified gift and estate tax. This tax is applicable to all taxable transfers, either through gifts while living or through an estate after death. Indeed, dying and leaving an estate are now considered as making one final gift. However, there are exclusions and exemptions before either gift or estate taxes need be paid.

**GIFT AND ESTATE TAXES**

Many states also have gift and estate taxes. Some even have inheritance tax, a tax on the recipient of an estate. Practices vary so much from state to state that little can be said about them except for two general comments. First, most states taxes of this sort are less severe than the federal taxes, and even the federal estate and gift taxes do not bring in vast sums. For example, in 1991, total gift and estate tax receipts at the federal level were just over $11.1 billion.[8] Second, the severity of the state taxes and exemptions varies with the closeness of the kin. Spouses are taxed less severely than children, and children less severely than other relatives. Moreover, the Federal Tax Code allows a tax credit for a *large proportion of all state inheritance and estate taxes.*

*State death taxes credit*

---

8. *The Federal Reserve Bulletin*, March, 1992, p. 27.

*Foreign death taxes credit*

If a person owns property in other countries, he or she may be subject to foreign death taxes. However, just like state death taxes, the U.S. tax code allows a credit against federal taxes for any foreign death taxes paid.

*Annual gift tax exclusions*

Every individual has an annual gift tax exclusion and a lifetime gift tax exemption. The annual exclusion is $10,000 per year per recipient. A person could give away $1 billion without paying a gift tax if he or she gave $10,000 to 100,000 people. More realistically, if a person has four children, he or she could give each $10,000 tax free annually, for a total of $40,000 per year. In addition, the law allows gifts to pay for qualified medical expenses or school tuition tax free, over and above this $10,000.

*Split gifts*

The split gift is sometimes referred to as a joint gift made by the husband and wife. It, too, can result in tax savings. The law provides, among other things, that a gift made by one person to any person other than his or her spouse can be considered as having been made one-half by him and one-half by her, if so elected. This is true even if only one of them has an income.

The net effect is that the annual exclusion may be doubled, and a husband and wife may make an annual gift of $20,000 times the number of donees without paying any gift tax whatsoever.

*Lifetime gift or estate tax exemption*

There is also an overall lifetime gift or estate tax exemption. This exemption is $600,000. Everyone has this lifetime exemption; hence a married couple together may give away (or leave an estate of) $1,200,000 tax free. This is above the $10,000 per year ($20,000 in the case of a joint gift) exclusion per recipient. It should be noted, however, that while the $10,000 exclusion applies only to gifts, the $600,000 exemption is unified and applies to the combination of the gifts and the estate.

*Converting the exemption to a credit*

In reality, however, the exemption is converted to a tax credit. The tax is calculated as if there were no exemption, and then the tax credit is subtracted from the tax so calculated. The tax credit on a $600,000 estate is $192,800, the same as the tax; hence no tax is due on transfers up to that amount. Table 19–3 shows how the lifetime tax exemption has risen over the years through 1987 with the tax credit equivalent, which is still in effect today.

*The marital deduction*

The marital deduction refers to transfers between spouses. The marital deduction applies to both gifts and estates, and it is 100 percent. All gifts to spouses and all estates left to spouses are now completely tax free.

*Lifetime unified gift and estate tax exemption*                                          Table 19—3

| Year | Amount of credit | Exemption equivalent | Lowest tax bracket rate (percent) |
|------|------------------|---------------------|-----------------------------------|
| 1984 | $ 96,300 | $325,000 | 34 |
| 1985 | 121,800 | 400,000 | 34 |
| 1986 | 155,800 | 500,000 | 37 |
| 1987 and later | 192,800 | 600,000 | 37 |

The unified gift and estate tax is progressive and varies from 18 to 55 percent. Table 19–4 shows how the tax rates have declined during the last few years. Since it often takes a few years to settle an estate, the rates in effect a few years ago are still used. Table 19–5 shows the unified federal gift and estate tax rates in effect currently; they really range from 37 to 55 percent, however, not from 18 to 55 percent as the table suggests.[9] The tax is also cumulative, and because of this, each future taxable gift is taxed at a higher and higher rate. For example, if a person makes a $100,000 taxable gift, the proper tax rate is applied; if then the next year another $100,000 taxable gift is made, the tax on it is calculated as if it were a $200,000 gift. The actual tax so obtained is then reduced by the amount of the tax paid on the previous $100,000 gift.

  The estate tax is calculated just like the gift tax, by applying the proper tax rate to the sum of all previous cumulative lifetime taxable transfers plus the deceased's estate. That is, all previous taxable gifts are added to the estate before calculating the tax on it. You will recall the government now looks on leaving an estate as one final gift—and gift and estate taxes are the same. By including all previous transfers, the estate is pushed into a higher tax bracket. To be sure, a credit is given for previous gift taxes paid.

*How gift and estate taxes are calculated*

There are eight steps in calculating the estate tax.

1.  *Step 1.* Calculate the *gross estate,* which includes:
    **a.** Cash
    **b.** Real estate
    **c.** Stock and bonds

*The actual estate tax calculation*

---

  9. Technically speaking, rates will still range from 18 to 55 percent but the unified gift and estate tax exemption provides everyone with some relief at the lower end of the scale. That is, the exemption (which is converted to a credit) exempts enough dollars so the minimum rate becomes 37 percent. The maximum estate and gift tax rate was scheduled to decline to 50 percent in 1988, but in the 1986 tax changes, congress postponed this decline until 1993.

**542**

Retirement and estate planning

Table 19—4    *Reduction in top-bracket rates*

| Transfers made and decedents dying in | Top-bracket rate | Top-bracket amount in excess of |
|---|---|---|
| 1983 | 60% | $3,500,000 |
| 1984–1992 | 55 | 3,000,000 |
| 1993 and later | 50 | 2,500,000 |

Thus when fully implemented in 1993 transfers will be taxable at progressive marginal rates ranging between 37 percent and 50 percent.

Table 19—5    *Unified federal estate and gift tax rates*

| Taxable estate of gift Over (1) | But not over (2) | Tax on (1) | Rate on excess (1) |
|---|---|---|---|
| *1987 and thereafter until 1993 when the maximum rate drops to 50 percent* | | | |
| 0 | $ 10,000 | $ 0 | 18 |
| $ 10,000 | 20,000 | 1,800 | 20 |
| 20,000 | 40,000 | 3,800 | 22 |
| 40,000 | 60,000 | 8,200 | 24 |
| 60,000 | 80,000 | 13,000 | 26 |
| 80,000 | 100,000 | 18,200 | 28 |
| 100,000 | 150,000 | 23,800 | 30 |
| 150,000 | 250,000 | 38,800 | 32 |
| 250,000 | 500,000 | 70,800 | 34 |
| 500,000 | 750,000 | 155,800 | 37 |
| 750,000 | 1,000,000 | 248,300 | 39 |
| 1,000,000 | 1,250,000 | 345,800 | 41 |
| 1,250,000 | 1,500,000 | 448,300 | 43 |
| 1,500,000 | 2,000,000 | 555,800 | 45 |
| 2,000,000 | $2,500,000 | 780,800 | 49 |
| 2,500,000 | $3,000,000 | 1,025,800 | 53 |
| 3,000,000 | — | 1,290,800 | 55 |

   d. Life insurance (if the ownership of the policy has been transferred to the beneficiary; generally this is not included)
   e. The home (one-half if owned jointly with spouse or if in a community property state)
   f. Any other assets of value
2. *Step 2.* Subtract the deductions to obtain the *taxable estate.* The deductions include:
   a. The marital deduction
   b. Funeral expenses

   c. Administrative expenses in settling the estate
   d. Debts including mortgage debt on the home
   e. Charitable contributions—that portion of the estate, if any, which will pass to a qualified charity
   f. Taxes, if debts or administrative expenses
3. *Step 5.* Add all prior taxable gifts made since 1976.
4. *Step 4.* Calculate the tax on the amount in Step 3. This is the tentative *estate tax.*
5. *Step 5.*Subtract all taxes paid on all prior taxable gifts made since 1976.
6. *Step 6.* Subtract the unified federal gift and estate tax credit.
7. *Step 7.* Next, subtract the state death tax credit.
8. *Step 8.* Then, subtract the foreign death tax credit, if any.

The remainder is the tax due.

   Table 19–6 shows the actual estate tax calculation. It should be noted that the marital deduction was not taken. This would be true in the case of a single person. However, if the deceased were married, the marital deduction could be taken where shown. This would eliminate taxes completely, because transfers between spouses (lifetime gifts or through an estate) are tax free. However, as shown below, the marital deduction does not reduce taxes; it only defers them. Setting up a trust and taking the marital deduction on a lesser amount will actually reduce taxes, as will also be shown later.

*Federal estate tax calculation*                                            Table 19—6

| | | |
|---|---:|---:|
| Gross estate | | $2,000,000 |
| Deductions: | | |
|   a. Funeral expenses | $ 5,000 | |
|   b. Administrative expenses | 20,000 | |
|   c. Debts, including mortgage debts | 45,000 | |
|   d. Taxes | 5,000 | |
|   e. Charitable contribution | 20,000 | |
|   f. Marital deduction | 0 | |
|   Total deductions | $95,000 | 95,000 |
| Taxable estate | | $1,905,000 |
| Taxable gifts made after 1976 | | 800,000 |
| Tax base (taxable gifts and estate) | | $2,705,000 |
| Tentative estate tax | | 1,134,450 |
|   Credit for federal gift taxes paid earlier | $ 75,000 | |
|   Unified gift and estate tax credit | 192,800 | |
|   Credit for state death taxes | 60,000 | |
|   Credit for foreign death taxes | 0 | |
| Total credits | $327,800 | 327,800 |
| Estate tax due | | $ 806,650 |

*How gifts can save taxes*

Gifts can save taxes for three reasons. First, the $10,000 ($20,000 on joint gifts) annual exclusion for a recipient, as noted above, is over and above the $600,000 unified gift and estate tax exemption.

Second, gifts prevent appreciable assets from being evaluated at a higher level later when an estate is probated, and hence reduce taxes.

Third, the $192,800 unified credit can be used earlier by making a gift. In a sense the credit is borrowed interest-free from the IRS. Table 19–7 shows how gifts are taxed. The tax on the first $700,000 taxable gift is $229,800, but the unified credit of $192,800 reduces it to $37,000. Essentially $600,000 was transferred tax free. The tax on the second taxable gift is $38,800 because the tax is progressive and cumulative, which means that previous taxable gifts must be added in when making the calculation on the second gift. Consequently, the second taxable gift of $100,000 is taxed as if it were an $800,000 gift; the tax on it of $267,800 is offset by the tax ($229,800) on the first gift, for a tax liability of $38,000. There is no unified credit for this second gift because the first gift used it all up. However, this unified credit reappears later on when the estate tax is due.

Both gifts in our example in Table 19–7 go into the estate tax base when the person dies, and hence the $600,000 exemption (converted to a credit of $192,800) reappears and can be taken again in making the final estate tax calculation. This is shown in Table 19–6. However, adding all gifts ($800,000 in our example) increases the final estate tax because the rates are progressive, but is partially offset by the unified credit.

As we shall later see, a person should also not waste that $600,000 exemption ($192,800 unified credit) when calculating the final estate tax by making excessive use of the marital deduction.

*How a trust can save taxes*

An irrevocable trust can also be used to reduce estate taxes, because the surviving spouse will not inherit the deceased's property. Rather the property goes into an irrevocable trust and by-passes the survivor who receives

Table 19–7     *How gift taxes are calculated*

|  | Gift | Tax | Unified credit | Actual tax paid |
|---|---|---|---|---|
| First gift | $710,000 | | | |
| Annual exclusion | 10,000 | | | |
| Taxable gift | 700,000 | $229,800 | $192,800 | $37,000 |
| Second gift | $110,000 | | | |
| Annual exclusion | 10,000 | | | |
| Taxable gift | 100,000* | $267,800 | 0 | $38,000 |

*The second gift is taxed as if it were an $800,000 gift, which makes the tax $267,800. It is then offset by $229,800, which is the tax on the previous $700,000 gift even though it was mostly nullified by the unified credit.

only the income from it. While the surviving spouse could inherit the entire estate tax free, there would be more taxes to pay when he or she died; the marital deduction could become a trap. To achieve the tax savings, $600,000 of the couple's assets (equal to the unified credit of $192,800) must bypass the surviving spouse. Then, the surviving spouse's taxable estate would be smaller, thus saving taxes. Consider the following example of a couple who jointly own $1,200,000 of taxable assets.

1. The first spouse dies, and his or her share of the estate passes tax free—due to the marital deduction there is no tax on transfers between spouses.

*Without a bypass trust*

2. The survivor dies and leaves an estate of $1,200,000, which is taxed.
3. The tax on a $1,200,000 estate is $427,800; but after the unified credit of $192,800 is applied, the tax is $235,000.

1. The first spouse dies and $600,000 goes into an irrevocable trust, for example, established by the deceased's will, and the survivor gets the income from it.[10]

*With a bypass trust*

2. There is a $192,800 tax on this $600,000 going into the trust, but after the unified credit of $192,800, it becomes zero. The tax is on the property of the deceased for the privilege of passing property to, in this case, the trust.
3. The survivor dies and leaves an estate of $600,000, not $1,200,000—the $600,000 in trust on her behalf is not hers.
4. The second partner's estate tax after the unified credit is also zero.
5. The total tax with trust is zero.
6. The tax savings are $235,000.

If a trust is used in the manner described above, the marital deduction will be lost. Assets placed into a regular trust—and hence not subject to the estate tax upon the death of the surviving spouse—do not qualify for the marital deduction. However, in the case above, the marital deduction is not needed; the $192,800 unified credit knocks out taxes. It should be remembered that the husband and wife each have an exemption of $600,000 (credit of $192,800), and each should use it. The deduction

*The exemption (unified credit) or the marital deduction?*

---

10. If we are assuming a community property state, each member already owns one-half of the property and the deceased cannot put his or her spouse's property into a trust. In a noncommunity property state, the entire $1,200,000 could be put into trust, but then the tax would be on $1,200,000 just as in the case of not having a trust. The community property states are Arizona, California, Idaho, Louisiana, Nevada, New Mexico, Texas, and Washington. Property rights in these states are based on Spanish law that assumes that a man and wife are one person. In the remainder of the states—called common law states—property rights are based on English common law. Wisconsin now has a system patterned after community property.

should not be wasted by not taking it, and relying on the marital deduction instead. For estates larger than our example, a trust of $600,000 should also be established to reduce taxes and then the marital deduction used to postpone tax on the remainder of the estate until the spouse dies.

*The Q-tip trust: an alternative approach*

It is possible to establish a qualified terminable interest property trust— called a Q-tip trust. This is a special trust that is subject to the estate tax when the surviving spouse dies. Because of this, the marital deduction may be taken on behalf of the deceased when the Q-tip is used. Under the Q-tip the surviving spouse would receive the income for life, and the trust's assets would then pass to the children. The advantage of the Q-tip over passing assets directly via the marital deduction is that the first partner to die does not lose control over the distribution of his or her assets after the death of the surviving spouse. This is important in the event that the surviving spouse remarries and decides to leave the assets to the new spouse, thereby freezing out the children. The Q-tip prevents this. In some cases it would be wise to set up a regular trust for $600,000 and a Q-tip trust for the remainder.

Trusts are very complex, and if one is used, it must be tailor-made to the particular situation. However, if properly used, both gifts and trusts may reduce taxes.

## SUGGESTED READINGS

Ashley, Pritcher B. *You and Your Will; The Planning and Management of Your Estate.* New York: New American Library, 1985.

Brosterman, Robert, and Brosterman, Thomas. *The Complete Estate Planning Guide.* New York: A Mentor Book, 1988.

Crumbley, D. L., and Milam, Edward E. *Estate Planning in the '80s; A Guide for Advisors and Their Clients.* Homewood, Ill.: Dow Jones-Irwin, 1986.

Englebrecht, John, and Fowler, Leslie. *Federal Taxation of Estates, Gifts, and Trusts,* 2nd ed. Englewood Cliffs, N.J.: Prentice Hall, 1987.

Esperiti, Robert A., and Peterson, Renno L., *The Handbook of Estate Planning;* 2nd edition. New York: McGraw-Hill Book Co., 1988.

*Estate Planners Quarterly.* New York: Farnsworth Publishing Co.

"Estate Tax Planning." Hartford, Conn.: Aetna Life Insurance Co.

Farr, James A., and Wright, Jackson. *Estate Planners Handbook.* Boston: Little, Brown, 1986.

*Federal Estate and Gift Taxes.* Chicago: Commerce Clearing House.

*Fundamental Concepts of Estate Planning.* New York: Practicing Law Institute, 1984.

Guilfoyle, A. P., Fossett, Alice W., Thomas, William W., and Scoville, Samuel S. *Tax Facts on Life Insurance.* Cincinnati, Ohio: The National Underwriter Company. Annual Publication.

"Highlights of the Tax Reform Act of 1986." Chicago: Arthur Andersen & Co.

Holzman, Robert S. *Encyclopedia of Estate Planning,* revised ed. New York: Boardroom Books, 1985.

Internal Revenue Service. *A Guide to Federal Estate and Gift Taxation.* U.S. Treasury Department, Internal Revenue Service. This pamphlet can be obtained from the local IRS office.

*Journal of the American Society of Chartered Life Underwriters.* Bryn Mawr, Pa.: American Society of Chartered Life Underwriters. Quarterly publication.

Kahn, Arnold D. *Family Security Through Estate Planning,* 2nd ed. New York; McGraw-Hill, 1984.

"Planning for Life and Death; Real Property, Probate and Trust Law." Chicago: American Bar Association Information Services.

"The Price Waterhouse Guide to the New Tax Law." New York: Bantam Books, 1986.

Sommerfield, Ray M., Anderson, Herschel M., and Brock, Horace R. *An Introduction to Taxation,* 4th ed. New York: Harcourt, Brace and World, 1988.

"Tax Reform 1986, Analysis and Planning." Chicago: Arthur Andersen & Co.

*Trusts and Estates, The Journal of Estate Planning and Administration.* New York: Communication Channels. Monthly publication.

*Use of Trusts in Estate Planning, 1986.* New York: Practicing Law Institute, 1986.

"Wills: Why You Should Have One and the Lawyer's Role in Its Preparation." Chicago: American Bar Association Information Services.

"Year End Strategy for Individuals Planning for 1986 and Beyond." Chicago: Arthur Andersen & Co.

## APPENDIX 19: TECHNICAL APPENDIX

*(Glossary of Terms)*

**Administrator:** One who administers a decedent's estate during probate. He or she differs from the executor in that the administrator is appointed by the judge of the probate court when no executor is named by a will or when the appointed executor is unable to perform the duties.

**Attestation:** The witnessing of a paper's execution and a signed statement to that effect.

**Beneficiary:** The person or persons who are (is) to receive certain benefits spelled out in a trust, insurance policy, or other documents.

**Bequest:** A gift of personal property or money under a will.

**Cestui que** *trust* The beneficiaries of a trust. (Called cetty for short.)

**Codicils** Writings executed subsequent to a will and forming a part thereof.

**Collateral heirs** Persons who are not descendants of the decedent but who are related through a common ancestor. Generally they include cousins and aunts and uncles of the decedent.

**Corpus; trust** res The body of the trust; the assets.

**Decedent** A deceased person.

**Devise** A gift of real property by the last will and testament of the donor. In contrast, a bequest or legacy is a gift of personal property or money.

**Devisee** Person receiving a gift of land by way of will.

**Domicile** The place of the permanent home of a person. The place of domicile is largely a matter of intention, though declarations of intention contrary to the actions of a person do not always control. A person has only one domicile at one time. It is not necessarily the same place as one's residence because domicile is the home, the fixed place of habitation, whereas residence is a transient place of dwelling. The domicile determines where wills are probated.

**Donor**      One who makes a gift. Also the person who creates a trust (or money).

**Escrow**      An agreement under which certain executed documents, e.g., deeds, are delivered into the hands of a third person to be held until specified conditions are fulfilled and then delivered to the person so performing or, in the case of default, returned to the person executing the document.

**Estate**      The interest that anyone has in property, being used particularly in connection with the interests owned by a person in real property. Also the total property of whatever kind owned by a decedent before the property is distributed according to the terms of a will, or by the laws of inheritance if the owner died intestate.

**Estate in severalty**      An estate that is held by a person in his or her own right only, without any other person being joined or connected.

**Executor**      The personal representative of a testator, appointed by the testator and approved by the judge of a probate court to take charge of the testator's estate, pay the debts, and distribute the balance of the property to the beneficiaries of the will pursuant to the order of the probate court.

**Fee simple**      The highest in dignity and the greatest in extent of the estates in real property.

**Fiduciary**      The person or institution who manages the financial affairs of a trust.

**Gift causa mortis**      An unrevoked gift of personal property made in expectation of death.

**Grantee**      One to whom a conveyance is made by deed.

**Grantor**      The person who creates a trust.

**Holographic will**      A will written entirely by the testator with his own hand.

**Inter vivos gift**      A gift among the living, in contrast to a gift by will or in anticipation of death.

**Inter vivos trust**      A trust created during the lifetime of the grantor.

**Intestate**      Having no will. An intestate is a decedent who left no will or a defective will. Property not included in a will is often called intestate property.

**Joint tenancy**      Two or more persons owning the same land and having the same unity of interest, time, title, and possession together with the right of survivorship.

**Legacy**      Specific legacy: a gift of personal property, generally a specific item of value, under a will. General legacy: a gift of a certain sum, but no specific asset cited.

**Legatee**      Person receiving a legacy or bequest.

**Lineals**      Blood relatives of a decedent.

**Per stirpes**      The method of distribution of the assets of a grant after the death of the original beneficiary. The children (grandchildren) share in the same proportions that their parents did (or would have).

**Probate**      The procedure of proving a will before a court having jurisdiction over the administration of the estate of a deceased person.

**Settlor**      The creator of a trust; also called grantor, trustor, and donor.

**Spendthrift trust**      A trust created to provide a fund for the maintenance of a beneficiary and at the same time to secure it against his or her improvidence or incapacity. Generally, the trust principal is beyond the reach of creditors.

| | |
|---|---|
| ***Tenancy by the entirety*** | Title in real property held by husband and wife together; based on the common-law concept that provides rights of survivorship. Property held by the entirety can only be disposed of by the joint action of the husband and wife. |
| ***Tenancy in common*** | A type of co-ownership of property by which the owners have undivided interests in the property. The interests may be unequal in quantity, may have been created at different times, and may have been derived from different sources. The co-owners are also known as cotenants. A cotenant may sell or otherwise dispose of his or her interest without consent of the other cotenants, and the new owner takes the right of the cotenant from whom he or she took interest. There is no survivorship right between cotenants, and the undivided interest may be disposed of by will or, in the absence of a will, descends to the heirs of the deceased cotenant, as would other property of the same kind. All of the tenants, in the absence of agreement between them to the contrary, have equal rights of possession regardless of inequality in their undivided interests. |
| ***Testamentary instrument*** | A legal document such as a will or trust bestowing certain rights to certain individuals after the death of the person making the instrument. |
| ***Testamentary trustee*** | A trustee appointed by or acting under a will in order to carry out a trust created by a will. |
| ***Testate*** | A testate is a decedent who left a will. Property included in the will is often called testate property. |
| ***Testator*** | The term may be used to describe either a man who has made a will or a decedent who left a will. |
| ***Testatrix*** | A female testator. |
| ***Trustee*** | The person who holds the legal title to trust property for the purposes as stated by the terms of the trust. The person for whose benefit the trust was created is called the beneficiary or *cestui que* trust. |